WHAT THE
BIBLE
IS ALL ABOUT

The Living Bible Edition

HENRIETTA C. MEARS

Tyndale House Publishers, Inc.
Wheaton, Illinois

© 1953, 1954, 1960, 1966, 1983
by Gospel Light Publications

Living Bible edition © 1987
by Tyndale House Publishers, Inc.

Library of Congress Catalog Card Number 87-50007
ISBN 0-8423-7902-9
All rights reserved
Printed in the United States of America

5   6   7   93

CONTENTS

PART TWO: THE NEW TESTAMENT

FOREWORD

Dr. Billy Graham

Millions of people today are searching for a reliable voice of authority. The Word of God is the only real authority we have. His Word sheds light on human nature, world problems, and human suffering. And beyond that, it clearly reveals the way to God.

The message of the Bible is the message of Jesus Christ, who said, *I am the Way—yes, and the Truth, and the Life* (John 14:6). It is the story of salvation; the story of your redemption and mine through Christ; the story of life, of peace, of eternity.

Our faith is not dependent upon human knowledge and scientific advance, but upon the unmistakable message of the Word of God.

The Bible has a great tradition and a magnificent heritage. It contains sixty-six books written over a period of several hundred years by many different men. Yet the message, divinely inspired by the Holy Spirit, is clear throughout. The sixty-six books become one.

The Bible is old, yet it is ever new. It is the most modern book in the world today. There is a false notion that a book as ancient as the Bible cannot speak to the needs of modern man. Men somehow think that in an age of scientific achievement, when knowledge has increased more in the past twenty-five years than in all preceding centuries put together, this ancient Book is out of date. But all who read and love the Bible know that it is relevant for our generation.

It is in the Holy Scriptures that we find the answers to life's ultimate questions: Where did I come from? Why am I here? Where am I going? What is the purpose of my existence?

One of the greatest needs in the church today is to come back to the Scriptures as the basis of authority, and to study them prayerfully in dependence on the Holy Spirit. When we read God's Word, we fill our hearts with his words, and God is speaking to us.

William Lyon Phelps, called the most beloved professor in America, and one-time president of Yale University, made the oft-quoted statement, "I thoroughly believe in a university education for both men and women, but I believe a knowledge of the Bible without a college course is more valuable than a college course without the Bible."

One of the greatest tragedies today is that, although the Bible is an available, open book, it is a closed book to millions—either because they leave it unread or because they read it without applying its teachings to themselves. No greater tragedy can befall a person or a nation than that of paying lip service to a Bible left unread or to a way of life not followed. The Bible, the greatest document available for the human race, needs to be opened, read, and believed.

This book, *What the Bible Is All About*, will help make the reading and study of God's Word interesting, challenging, and useful. I commend it to you.

CHAPTER 1

UNDERSTANDING THE BIBLE

The Bible Portrays Jesus Christ, the Savior of the World

"Behind and beneath the Bible, above and beyond the Bible, is the God of the Bible."

The Bible is God's written revelation of his will to men.

Its central theme is salvation through Jesus Christ.

The word *Bible* comes from the Greek word *biblos*, which means "book."

The Bible contains sixty-six books, written by forty authors, covering a period of approximately sixteen hundred years. The authors were kings and princes, poets and philosophers, prophets and statesmen. Some were learned in all the arts of the times and others were unschooled fishermen. Other books soon are out of date, but this Book spans the centuries.

The Old Testament was written mostly in Hebrew (a few short passages in Aramaic). About a hundred years (or more) before the Christian Era the entire Old Testament was translated into the Greek language. The New Testament was written in Greek.

The word *testament* means "covenant" or "agreement." The Old Testament is the covenant God made with man about his salvation before Christ came. The New Testament is the agreement God made with man about his salvation after Christ came.

In the Old Testament we find the covenant of law. In the New Testament we find the covenant of grace, which came through Jesus Christ. One led into the other (Galatians 3:17-25).

The Old commences what the New completes.

The Old gathers around Sinai—the New around Calvary.

The Old is associated with Moses—the New with Christ (John 1:17).

The Old Testament begins with God (Genesis 1:1). The New Testament begins with Christ (Matthew 1:1).

From Adam to Abraham we have the history of the human race. From Abraham to Christ we have the history of the chosen race. From Christ on we have the history of the church.

"Most people's knowledge of history is like a string of graduated pearls without the string," said a historian. This statement seems to be especially true of Bible history. Many people know the Bible characters and the principal events, but they are hopelessly lost when they are called upon to connect the stories in order. Anyone who has experienced the thrill of learning to place the individual characters in their right settings of place and time can realize the difference it makes in the enjoyment of God's Word.

Pick up the "pearls" in the Scriptures and string them into order from Genesis to Revelation so that you can "think through" the Bible story.

INTERESTING FACTS

Old Testament Books
Law—five
History—twelve
Poetry—six
Prophecy—sixteen (Major, four; Minor, twelve)

New Testament Books
The New Testament was written to reveal to us the character and teaching of Jesus Christ, the mediator of the New Covenant, by at least eight men, four of whom—Matthew, John, Peter, and Paul—were apostles; two—Mark and Luke—were companions of the apostles; and two—James and Jude—were brothers of Jesus. The books were written at various times during the second half of the first century.

The books in the New Testament may be grouped this way:

Gospels—four
History—one

Prophecy—one
Letters—twenty-one (Pauline, thirteen; General, eight)

The major themes of the New Testament are God, man, sin, redemption, justification, sanctification, glorification. In two words—*grace, glory.* In one word—*Jesus.*

Christ quotes from twenty-two Old Testament books: in Matthew, nineteen times; in Mark, fifteen; in Luke, twenty-five; in John, eleven.

The book of Hebrews quotes from or alludes to the Old Testament eighty-five times.

Revelation quotes the Old Testament 245 times.

Number of verses—31, 102
Longest chapter—Psalm 119
Shortest chapter—Psalm 117
Longest book in the Old Testament—Psalms
Longest book in the New Testament—Luke

Old Testament—Principal Places

The twelve principal places around which the history of the Old Testament is written are:

1. Eden
2. Ararat
3. Babel
4. Ur of the Chaldeans
5. Canaan (with Abraham)
6. Egypt (with Joseph)
7. Sinai
8. Wilderness
9. Canaan (with Joshua)
10. Assyria (captivity of Israel)
11. Babylon (captivity of Judah)
12. Canaan (Palestine—return of the exiles)

As you build the story of the Bible around these places you see the whole history in chronological order.

Still another way to think through the Bible is by following the great facts in order.

Old Testament—Principal Facts
1. Creation (Genesis 1:1–2:3)
2. Fall of man (Genesis 3)
3. Flood (Genesis 6–9)
4. Babel (Genesis 11:1-9)
5. Call of Abraham (Genesis 11:10–12:3)
6. Descent into Egypt (Genesis 46–47)
7. Plagues (Exodus 7–12)
8. Passover and Exodus (Exodus 12)
9. Giving of the Law (Exodus 19–24)
10. Wilderness wanderings (Numbers 13–14)
11. Conquest of the Promised Land (Joshua 11)
12. Dark ages of the chosen people (Judges)
13. Anointing of Saul as king (1 Samuel 9:27–10:1)
14. Golden age of Israelis under David and Solomon, united kingdom (2 Samuel 5:4-5; 1 Kings 10:6-8)
15. The divided kingdom — Israel and Judah (1 Kings 12:26-33)
16. The Captivity (2 Kings 17; 25)
17. The Return (Ezra)

New Testament—Principal Facts
1. Early life of Christ
2. Ministry of Christ
3. Church in Jerusalem
4. Church extending to the Gentiles
5. Church in all the world

Period of the Patriarchs to Moses (Genesis)
1. Creation
2. Fall
3. Flood
4. Dispersion
5. Call of Abraham
6. Descent into Egypt, bondage

Period of Great Leaders: Moses to Saul (Exodus to Samuel)
1. Exodus from Egypt
2. Wandering in wilderness
3. Conquest of Canaan
4. Rule of the judges

Period of the Kings: Saul to the Captivities
(Samuel, Kings, Chronicles, the prophetical books)
1. The united kingdom—Saul, David, Solomon
2. The divided kingdom—Judah, Israel

Period of Foreign Rulers: Captivities to Christ
(Ezra, Nehemiah, Esther, prophecies of Daniel and Ezekiel)
1. Captivity of Israel
2. Captivity of Judah

Period of the New Testament: Christ and the Church
(Gospels, Acts, Letters)
1. The life of Christ
2. The church in Jerusalem
3. The church extending to the Gentiles
4. The church in all the world

HOW TO STUDY THE BIBLE

Remember that in God's Word the foundation of Christianity is laid in the revelation of the one and only true God. God chose a people (the Israelis) to show forth this truth and to preserve a record of himself.

The Bible tells us of the origin of sin and how this curse separates man from God. We discover how utterly impossible it is for the law to bring to man the salvation that he needs, for *no one can ever be made right in God's sight by doing what the law commands* (Romans 3:20). Then we find the promise of a Savior, One who was to come *to search for and to save* souls that were lost and give his life *a ransom for many* (Luke 19:20; Matthew 20:28). We see all through the ages that one purpose is evident: preparing a way for the coming of the Redeemer of the world.

There is no royal road to learning, and certainly there is no royal road to knowledge of the Bible. The Spirit of God will lead us into all truth, to be sure, but God's command is that we do our best to be approved, workmen who do not need to be ashamed (2 Timothy 2:15).

You must give to the Bible attention with intention, and it is intention that will necessitate attention. Perhaps there is so little attention to Bible reading today because there is so little intention.

We must come to it with a purpose, with a clearly defined object; we must know what we are about.

Many say, "The Bible is so great. I don't know where to begin and don't know how to go on." This is often said quite earnestly and sincerely. And it is true that, unless we have some method, we will surely lose the very best results, even though we may spend much time with the Book.

G. Campbell Morgan once stated, "The Bible can be read from Genesis 1 to Revelation 22 at pulpit rate in seventy-eight hours." A lawyer challenged him on that. Morgan told him to go on and try it before he challenged. The lawyer went home and read the Bible in less than eighty hours.

Do you want to read the Bible through? Leave eighty hours for it. Plot out that time. How much time can you give each day? How many days a week? This is a highly practical proposition and should be seized by the very busiest. We are all busy and must take time for it. If we are going to know the Bible, we must give time to it and arrange for it. We must adjust our lives so that time is made. Unless we do, we will never come into any worthy knowledge of the Word, for it is impossible from pulpit ministry to get that knowledge of the Word that is possible and is indeed needful. The Bible reveals the will of God so as to lead man into it. Each book has a direct teaching. Find out what it is and shape your life by it.

Now the Bible, although it is a library, is also "the Book." It is a story, a grand story that moves on from beginning to end. Here surely is something that is phenomenal in literature. Suppose, for instance, you were to cover the great fields of knowledge, such as law, history, philosophy, ethics, and prophecy, and you were to bring these different subjects all together and bind them up into one book. What, to begin with, would you call the book? Then what unity could one possibly expect to find in such a jumble of subjects? Such an infinite number and variety of themes and styles as are found in the Bible, brought together across not a few generations but across centuries, make the likelihood of any unity being present amazingly small. No publisher would risk publishing such a book, and if he did, nobody would buy it or read it. That is, however, what is done in the Bible.

Remember, the books of the Bible were given to us by forty different men over a period of about sixteen hundred years. All these are brought together and are called "the Book." We can begin at Genesis and read on through to the end. There is no jar. We can pass from one style of literature to another as easily as though we were reading a story written by one hand and produced by one life, and indeed we have here a story produced by one Mind (2 Peter 1:21), though not written by one hand.

While divine, the Bible is human. The thought is divine and the revelation is divine, but the expression of the communication is human. *It was the Holy Spirit* [divine element] *within these godly men* [human element] *who gave them true messages from God* (2 Peter 1:21).

So we have here a book unlike all others. The Book—a divine revelation, a progressive revelation, a revelation of God to man communicated through men—moves on smoothly from its beginning to its great end. In Genesis we have beginnings, in Revelation we have endings, and from Exodus to Jude we see how God carried out his purpose. We can't dispense with any part of it.

Bible history takes us back into the unknown past of eternity, and its prophecies take us into the otherwise unknown future.

The Old Testament is the foundation; the New Testament is the superstructure. A foundation is of no value unless a building is built upon it. A building is impossible unless there is a foundation. So the Old Testament and New Testament are essential to one another. As Augustine said:

The New is in the Old contained,
The Old is in the New explained.

ONE BOOK, ONE HISTORY, ONE STORY

The Bible is one book, one history, one story, his story. Behind ten thousand events stands God, the builder of history, the maker of the ages. Eternity bounds one side, eternity bounds the other side, and time is in between: Genesis—origins, Revelation—endings, and all the way between, God is working things out. You can go down into the minutest detail everywhere and see that there is one great purpose moving through the ages: the eternal design of the Almighty God to redeem a wrecked and ruined world.

The Bible is one book, and you cannot take it in pieces and expect to comprehend the magnificence of divine revelation. Don't suppose reading little scraps can ever be enough—we would scorn reading any other book, even the lightest novel, in this fashion. God has taken pains to give a progressive revelation, and we should take pains to read it from beginning to end. We must see it in its completeness, doing deep and consecutive work on the Bible itself. We must get back to the Book.

Another way we can study the Bible is by groups—law, history, poetry, major and minor prophets, Gospels, Acts, Letters, and Revelation. Here again we find great unity, for *I have come to do your will, to lay down my life, just as the Scriptures said that I would,* says Christ. Everything points to the King.

Each book has a message, and we should endeavor to discover what that message is. Read until you discover the message of the book. For instance, in John it is easy to discover the purpose, for it is stated in John 20:31. It is not always stated this clearly, but the truth can be found.

In one sense we should treat the Bible as we treat any other book. When we get a book from the library we would never treat it as we do the Bible. We would never think of reading just a paragraph, taking some ten minutes, reading a little at night and then reading a little in the morning, and so spending weeks, perhaps months, in reading the book through. No interest could be maintained in any story by such a procedure. Take a love story, for instance. We would naturally begin at the beginning and read right through to the end, unless we turned back to the finish to see how the story ended.

Do you come to the Bible with such eagerness? Do you read with that purpose and persistence? The Bible is not a book of texts—it is a story, a revelation, to be begun and pursued and ended as we start and continue other books. Don't trifle with the Bible. Don't divide it into short devotional paragraphs and think you have understood its messages. It may be excusable for someone who can hardly read to open the Bible and take whatever his eyes light upon as the message of God. Many people do that, but the Bible shouldn't be misused in that manner. We must come to it in a commonsense fashion. Believe that every book is about something, and read and reread until you find out what that something is.

First read the Book, not books about the Book, nor turn to the commentaries. They will come in good time, perhaps, but give the Book a chance to speak for itself and to make its own impression, to bear its own testimony.

Don't wish to put on colored glasses of man's opinions and then read through the interpretation put on it by other minds. Let the Spirit of God himself teach you. Each person has a right to read it for himself. Read it seeking for illumination. It is a revelation, and God will flash light upon the page as you come humbly.

The Word of God is alive, and every part is necessary to the perfection of the whole. We don't say that every part is equally important. If you were to ask me whether I would give up my finger or my eye, of course I would part with my finger. So with the Word of God. All is necessary to make a perfect whole, but some portions are more precious than others. You can't take away the Song of Solomon and have a perfect revelation. No one says the Song of Solomon is comparable with John's Gospel, but both are parts of an organism, and that organism is not complete if any part is missing.

The Bible is a whole and can't be tampered with. For example, to add anything to the book of Revelation or to take anything from it would mar its absolute perfection (see Revelation 22:18-19). The canon of Scripture is closed. Other works throw valuable light upon it, but Scripture stands unique, alone, and complete, and the parts all partake of the perfection of the whole.

Read a Book a Week

So we come to the books as complete in themselves, yet bearing in mind their vital relation to what precedes and what succeeds. We should read them one at a time. Read a book in a week.

Now don't suppose that this is impossible. It is not. How much time do you spend reading in twenty-four hours? How much time on newspapers? Magazines? How much time do you give to fiction? To other reading? And how much time do you give to television? Now the longest of these books doesn't take longer than some people devote to reading in one day.

There are some of the larger books in the Old Testament, such as Genesis, Exodus, Deuteronomy, Isaiah, that might take several hours to read with care. If that is too much, divide them into seven equal parts, but put your reading into strict limits. Don't give yourself time to lose the impression made by the first reading before you get to the second, and don't suppose that you can grasp the content and intent of any book at a single reading.

You don't suppose that as you walk down the corridors of an art gallery and look at the pictures you see the gallery. You see some pictures on the wall, but you don't know what they are about. You must sit in front of a picture and study it.

CHRIST, THE LIVING WORD

The Old Testament is an account of a nation (the Jewish nation). The New Testament is an account of a Man (the Son of man). The nation was founded and nurtured by God in order to bring this man into the world (see Genesis 12:1-3).

God himself became a man so that we might know what to think of when we think of God (John 1:14; 14:9). His appearance on the earth is the central event of all history. The Old Testament sets the stage for it. The New Testament describes it.

As a man, Christ lived the most perfect life ever known. He was kind, tender, gentle, patient, and sympathetic. He loved people. He worked marvelous miracles to feed the hungry. Crowds—weary, pain-ridden, and heartsick—came to him, and he gave them rest (Matthew 11:28-30). It is said that if all the deeds of kindness that he did were written, the world could not contain the books (John 21:25).

Then he died—to take away the sin of the world and to become the Savior of mankind.

Then he rose from the dead. He is alive today. He is not merely a historical character but a living Person—the most important fact of history and the most vital force in the world today. And he promises eternal life to all who come to him.

The whole Bible is built around the story of Christ and his promise of everlasting life. It was written only so that we would believe and understand, know and love, and follow *him*.

Apart from any theory of inspiration or any theory of how the Bible books came to their present form or how much the text may have suffered in passing through the hands of editors and copyists or what is historical and what may be poetical—assume that the Bible is just what it appears to be. Accept the books as we have them in our Bible as units. Study them to know their contents. You will find there is a unity of thought that indicates that one Mind inspired the writing of the whole series of books, that it bears on its face the stamp of its Author, that it is in every sense the *Word of God*.

SELECTED BIBLE READING

Sunday: God-Given (2 Timothy 3:14-17)
Monday: Should Be Treasured (Deuteronomy 11:1-9; Joshua 1:8-9)
Tuesday: Should Be Kept (Psalm 119:9-18)
Wednesday: A Light (Psalm 119:105-117)
Thursday: Food (Isaiah 55:1-11; Matthew 4:4)
Friday: Fulfilled (Luke 24:36-45)
Saturday: Complete (Revelation 22:8-21)

PART ONE
THE OLD TESTAMENT

CHAPTER 2

UNDERSTANDING GENESIS

Genesis Portrays Jesus Christ, Our Creator God

Genesis is the seed plot of the Word of God. The title *Genesis*, which is Greek, means "origin," and the first word in the Hebrew of Genesis is translated "in the beginning"—words that indicate both the scope and the limits of the book. It tells us the beginning of everything except God. Another thing to notice is that it tells only of beginnings. There is no finality here. Upon its truths all the future revelation of God to man is built.

Satan appears to have special hostility toward the book of Genesis. No wonder the Adversary has bent his attacks upon it. It exposes him as the enemy of God and the deceiver of the human race, it foretells his destruction, and it depicts his doom (ch. 3).

Without Genesis our knowledge of a creating God would be pitifully limited; we would be woefully ignorant of the beginnings of our universe. Genesis is the book of beginnings:

1. The beginning of the world (1:1-25)
2. The beginning of the human race (1:26–2:25)
3. The beginning of sin in the world (3:1-7)
4. The beginning of the promise of redemption (3:8-24)
5. The beginning of family life (4:1-15)
6. The beginning of a man-made civilization (4:16–9:29)
7. The beginning of the nations of the world (ch. 10–11)
8. The beginning of the Hebrew race (ch. 12–50)

Adam began with God and fell through disobedience (3:1-24). Abel began with God by the blood of sacrifice (4:4).

Noah began with God by way of the ark (6:8, 14, 22).
Abraham began with God when he built altars (12:8).
These all made new beginnings for the race.

Genesis is the record of the beginnings of all these things. No wonder that when people, because of spiritual blindness (Ephesians 4:18), reject God's revelation in this peerless record of beginnings, they worship chance as the creator, beasts as their ancestors, and fallen humanity as the flower of natural evolution!

Genesis begins with "God" but ends "in a coffin." This book is a history of man's failure. But we find that God meets every failure of man. He is a glorious Savior. We find that *the more we see our sinfulness, the more we see God's abounding grace forgiving us* (Romans 5:20).

Genesis gives us at least two thousand years of record. It is not entirely history; it is a spiritual interpretation of history. In two chapters God flashes on the wall an account of the creation of the world and of man. From there on we see the story of redemption. God is bringing lost man back to himself.

We have noted Satan's reasons for attacking this majestic book. Its authorship by Moses, its scientific accuracy, and its literal testimony to human sin as deliberate disobedience to God have all been bitterly assailed. The Word of God, however, definitely declares Genesis to be one of the living oracles delivered to Moses. To its infallible truth and its testimony to the Messiah, our Lord Jesus set his seal (John 5:46-47).

When Genesis goes, a divine Creator, a divine creation, a divinely promised Redeemer, and a divinely inspired Bible must also go. Around its sacred pages is the protection of the Holy Spirit of God, who inspired its words. If there were more study of Genesis instead of so much argument about it, its truth would be clearer.

Many origins are recorded in the first eleven chapters: the natural universe, human life, sin, death, redemption, civilization, nations, and languages.

The remainder of the book from Genesis 12 on deals with the beginnings of the Hebrew race, first in its founding through Abraham, then in its subsequent development and history through the great figures of Isaac, Jacob, and Joseph. This great Hebrew nation was founded with a definite purpose, that through it the whole world should be blessed.

INTERESTING OUTLINES OF GENESIS

In Genesis 12:1-3, God promised Abraham, a believer in him, that he and his descendants would:

1. Be blessed
2. Become a great nation
3. Be used to bless all nations

God repeated these promises twice more to Abraham (18:18; 22:15-18), and also to Isaac and Jacob (26:1-5; 28:13-15).

Seven great names and messages are:

1. Bow with Abel at the cross of the slain lamb.
2. Get in step with Enoch and walk with God.
3. Believe God and launch out with Noah on God's waters.
4. Go forth with Abraham in faith.
5. Dig wells with Isaac and get down to divine resources.
6. Climb ladders with Jacob and see God.
7. Be true like Joseph and live with God.

Won't you make a genesis (beginning) of new love to your Lord in your own life?

Genesis answers the great questions of the soul:

1. The eternity of God
2. Where did man come from?
3. Where did sin come from?
4. How can sinful man get back to God (Abel's sacrifice)?
5. How can man please God (Abraham's faith)?
6. How can we have power with God and man (Jacob's surrender)?

Three words give us an outline of Genesis:

1. Generation (1:1)
2. Degeneration (3:1)
3. Regeneration (12:1)

Genesis is the record of human failure, first in an ideal environment (Eden), then under the rule of conscience (from the Fall to the flood), and finally under patriarchal rule (Noah to Joseph). In every case of human failure, however, God met man's need with marvelous promises of sovereign grace. It is therefore fitting that the Bible's first book shows us the failure of man under every condition met by the salvation of God.

Hints of the Messiah in Genesis:

1. Woman's offspring (3:15)
2. Jacob's ladder (28:12)
3. Judah's scepter (49:10)
4. The entrance into the ark for safety (7:1, 7)
5. The offering up of Isaac (22:1-24)
6. Joseph lifted from pit to throne (37:28; 41:41-44)

Remember, Jesus Christ is the center of the Bible. He is somewhere on every page.

The Patriarchal Period

The period of the patriarchs is the groundwork and basis of all history. It covers the time from Adam to Moses. In consequence of people's failures during this early period, God called out an individual, Abraham, who was to become the father of the Hebrew nation. We enter into this period in Genesis 12.

God called out Abraham and made a covenant with him— known as the Abrahamic Covenant—promising to bless Abraham, to make him the father of a great nation, and to bless all peoples on earth through him (12:1-3). You should be familiar with this covenant. If you are not, the whole study of the chosen people in the Old Testament and the church in the New Testament will have little meaning. God repeated this covenant to Abraham's son, Isaac, and again to his grandson, Jacob (26:1-5; 28:13-15). He repeated it to no one else, although the covenant is reaffirmed repeatedly throughout the Bible (Psalm 72:17; Acts 3:25-26; Galatians 3:6-9; Hebrews 6:13-18; etc.).

These three patriarchs, therefore, are the covenant fathers, and that is why you read in Scripture, *I am the God of your ancestors—of Abraham, Isaac, and Jacob* (Acts 7:32). He never adds anyone else. God gave his covenant to these three, and it was for them to communicate it to others.

From Family to Nation

A very large portion of the story of Genesis is devoted to Joseph (ch. 37–48). Why? Because Joseph is the link between the family and the nation. Up to the time of Joseph, Genesis deals with a family, the family of Abraham, Isaac, and Jacob. At the end of Genesis, some seventy people constitute the family of Jacob, but God is still dealing with a family. Read about this family and the blessings that Jacob gave to each of his sons in Genesis 49.

The moment we turn the page and step into Exodus, we find God dealing with a nation, not a family. During the long period from the end of Genesis to the opening of Exodus this nation has developed. Joseph is the link between the family and the nation.

Joseph is a character presented without fault—not that he had no faults, but his faults are not recorded. He was a man of flesh and blood like us. God honored him, for there are at least 130 parallels between the life of Joseph and the life of Jesus. He is therefore the messianic patriarch, the patriarch who reflected Christ himself.

THE AUTHOR OF GENESIS

The age-long Hebrew and Christian position is that Moses, guided by the Spirit of God, wrote Genesis. The book closes about three hundred years before Moses was born. Moses could have received his information only by direct revelation from God or from historical records to which he had access that had been handed down from his forefathers. See what Jesus said about Moses (Luke 24:27; John 7:19).

Every year there are being dug up in Egypt and Israel evidences of writing in Moses' day and of the historical truth of what is recorded in the Pentateuch. Moses was educated in the palace of Pharaoh and *was taught all the wisdom of the Egyptians* (Acts 7:22), which included the literary profession. Moses did make use of writing (Exodus 34:27; Numbers 17:2; Deuteronomy 6:9; 24:1, 3; Joshua 8:32).

No doubt the creation story was written long before, maybe by Abraham or Noah or Enoch. Who knows? Writing was in common use before the days of Abraham. In Ur, as in every important city in Babylonia, there were libraries with thousands of books, dictionaries, grammars, reference works, encyclopedias, works on mathematics, astronomy, geography, religion, and politics. No doubt Abraham had received traditions or records from Shem about the story of Creation and the Fall of man, and of the flood. Abraham lived in a society of culture, books, and libraries. He no doubt made careful and accurate copies of all that happened to him and of the promises God had made to him. He put it all down on clay tablets in the cuneiform writing to be handed down in the annals of the nation he was founding.

CREATION
GENESIS 1–2

As the book begins we see these words untarnished by the ages. We have the Bible's declaration of the origin of this material universe. God called all things into being *by the mighty power of his command* (Hebrews 11:3). He spoke and worlds were formed. Interpretations of the method of God may vary, but the truth of the fact remains.

God's creative work was progressive:

1. The world of matter (1:3-19)
2. The system of life (1:20-25)
3. Man, the crown of creation (1:26-27)

Who was the God mentioned so many times in the first thirty-one verses of Genesis? Read John 1:1 and Hebrews 1:1. Here we see that the One who redeemed us by his precious blood, our Savior, was the Creator of this universe. Someone has said that God the Father is the architect, God the Son is the builder, and God the Holy Spirit is the beautifier of the universe. We find the Holy Spirit in Genesis 1:2.

In chapter 1 we have the account of creation in outline. In chapter 2 we have part of the same in detail. The detail concerns the creation of man, for the Bible is the history of the redemption of man.

Know this: God created man in his own image to have fellowship with himself. Man cut himself off from God by sin. It is only when sin is removed that we can have fellowship again. This is why Jesus Christ came to this earth, that he might carry *the load of our sins in his own body when he died on the cross* (1 Peter 2:24). Read in 1 John 1 how sin keeps us not only from fellowship with God but with one another. First John 1:9 tells us what we can do to have a restored fellowship.

THE FALL
GENESIS 3-4

Adam and Eve were created in a state of innocence but with the power of choice. They were tested under the most favorable circumstances. They were endowed with clear minds and pure hearts, with the ability to do right. God gave them his own presence and fellowship (3:8).

Satan, the author of sin, acting through a serpent, tempted Adam and Eve to doubt God's Word. They yielded to the temptation and failed in the test. Here sin entered the world. Satan still influences men to disobey God. The results of Adam and Eve's sin are described in Genesis 3. They were separated from God, the ground was cursed, and sorrow filled their hearts.

In mercy God promised One who would redeem mankind from sin (3:15). The offspring of the woman (the virgin-born Jesus) would come to destroy the works of the devil (1 John 3:8).

Immediately after the Fall people began to offer sacrifices to the Lord. No doubt these sacrifices were ordered of God. They were for the purpose of keeping before man the fact of his fall and of the coming Sacrifice. It would be by the shedding of Jesus' blood that man was to be redeemed from sin and death (Hebrews 9:22).

Two of Adam's sons, Cain and Abel, brought their sacrifices to the Lord. *Cain brought the Lord a gift of his farm produce and Abel brought the fatty cuts of meat from his best lambs* (4:3-4). Abel's offering was accepted while Cain's was rejected. From our knowledge of the Word it is quite evident that it was not accepted because any sacrifice had to be brought to the Lord with proper motivation and through faith and obedience. Cain became angry with his brother, Abel, and in his anger killed him.

The first writing began when God put a "mark" or "sign" on Cain (4:15). That mark stood for an idea and the people knew what it stood for. Thus "marks," "signs," and "pictures" came to be used to record ideas, words, or combinations of words. These pictures were made on pottery or hard clay tablets, painted or engraved. This is the kind of writing found in the lowest levels of the prehistoric cities of Babylonia. The oldest known writings are pictures on clay tablets.

Long before God gave the law to Moses (Exodus 20) we find several very definite ordinances given in the book of Genesis. At the very beginning God instituted the Sabbath (2:1-3) and marriage (2:24).

The law of the tithe was evidently observed. Read about Abraham's tithe in Genesis 14:20, and read Jacob's words in Genesis 28:22. God had evidently made people realize from the very beginning that they were only stewards of all they had.

This civilization before the flood is called the antediluvian civilization. It perished in the judgment of the flood. It was the civilization started by Cain. It ended in destruction.

The Bible teaches and archaeology confirms that the people of the world before the flood were not mere savages. They attained a considerable degree of civilization. Everything in material civilization is touched on in Genesis 4:16-22. While not much is known about the antediluvian people, some places have been discovered that could possibly be from this period. Some relics of their handwork that have been uncovered give evidence of a civilization such as the Bible seems to describe.

In three cities, Ur, Kish, and Fara, the layer of silt possibly left by the flood has been found. Underneath the flood deposit in Ur, layers of rubbish full of stone and flint instruments, colored pottery, seals, and burnt brick were found. The same is true of the other two cities.

Turn to Genesis 4:16-22 and see what is mentioned of early civilization:

1. Herdsmen: *To Adah was born a baby named Jabal. He became the first of the cattlemen and those living in tents* (4:20)
2. Musicians: *His brother's name was Jubal, the first musician—the inventor of the harp and flute* (4:21)
3. Craftsmen and manufacturers: *Tubal-cain . . . opened the first foundry forging instruments of bronze and iron* (4:22)
4. Builders: *When Cain founded a city, he named it Enoch, after his son* (4:17)

The civilization founded by Cain may have been equal to that of Greece or Rome, but God's judgment was upon it because of man's wickedness (6:5-7).

THE FLOOD
GENESIS 5–9

The account of the flood in the Bible is very plain and straightforward. The story is not told because it is startling or interesting but because it is an incident in the history of redemption that the Bible relates. Evil had grown rampant. It threatened to destroy everything that was good. God sent the flood to restore good upon the earth.

Adam and Eve had yielded to an outward temptation, but from then on people were yielding to temptation within. After the Fall, God gave the world a new beginning, but soon the wickedness of man increased until there remained only one righteous man, Noah. *When God saw the extent of human wickedness, and that the trend and direction of men's lives were only towards evil, he was sorry he had made them. It broke his heart* (6:5-6). God was going to separate the righteous from the wicked. He was taking the first step toward a chosen nation.

God had been long-suffering in his patience with people, and his Holy Spirit had striven with them. Noah had warned them for 120 years while he was building the ark. Even after Noah and his wife and his three sons and their wives—taking with them two of every unclean animal and fourteen of every clean animal—had entered into the ark of safety, there was a respite of seven days before the flood came. But God's mercies were refused and so people had to perish (ch. 6–7). Noah was saved from the flood by the ark (a perfect symbol of Christ, our Ark of safety). When Noah came out of the ark, the first thing he did was to erect an altar and worship God (8:20).

Out of the fearful judgment of the earth by the flood, God saved eight persons. He gave the purified earth to these people with ample power to govern it (9:1-6). He gave them control of every living thing on earth and sea. For the first time God gave man human government. Man was responsible to govern the world for God.

BABEL
GENESIS 10–11

After the flood the world was given a new start. But instead of spreading out and repopulating the earth as God had commanded, they built the great tower of Babel in defiance of God. The great Jewish historian, Josephus, declares that the tower of Babel was built because the people did not want to submit to God. They thought they could establish a worldwide empire that would be independent of God. Man tried to glorify himself, but God's purpose is that man will glorify only him. So God sent a confusion of languages and scattered the people all over the earth. A difference in language tends to separate people and to slow progress in commerce, arts, and civilization.

THE CALL OF ABRAHAM
GENESIS 12–38

In spite of the wickedness of the human heart, God wanted to show his grace, his "unmerited favor." He wanted a chosen people:

1. To whom he might entrust the Holy Scriptures
2. To be his witness to other nations
3. Through whom the promised Messiah could come

He called a man named Abram to leave his home in idolatrous Ur of the Chaldeans to go to an unknown land where God would make him the father of a mighty nation (12:1-3; Hebrews 11:8-19). This begins the history of God's chosen people, Israel.

Wherever Abraham went he erected an altar to God. God highly honored him by revealing himself to him. He was called "a friend of God." God made a covenant with him that he would be the father of a great nation and that through him *the entire world would be blessed* (12:1-3). His family became God's special charge so that they could be a blessing to others. God dealt with them as with no other people. The Jews are always spoken of as God's chosen people.

Through Isaac, Abraham's son, the promises of God were passed down to Jacob, who, despite his many faults, valued God's covenant blessing. He was enthusiastic about God's plan of founding a nation by which the whole world would be blessed. Jacob in his wanderings suffered for his sin but through chastening came out a great man. His name was changed to *Israel—one who has power with God* (32:28). This is the name by which God's chosen people were called—Israelis. Jacob's twelve sons became the heads of the twelve tribes of Israel.

DESCENT INTO EGYPT
GENESIS 39–50

Isaac and Rebekah made the mistake of playing favorites with their two sons. Isaac favored the hunter Esau. Rebekah favored the quiet Jacob. Jacob did the same thing in the treatment of his son Joseph, which aroused jealousy in the other sons. Joseph is one of the outstanding noble characters of the Old Testament. It was through Joseph that Jacob's family was transplanted into Egypt. Joseph's life is one of the most perfect illustrations in the Bible of God's overruling providence. He was sold as a slave at seventeen. At thirty he became ruler in Egypt. Ten years later his father, Jacob, entered Egypt.

After Isaac's death and after Joseph had been sold into Egypt, Jacob and his sons and their children, numbering seventy in all, went down into that land because of a famine. Here they were exalted by the pharaoh who was reigning at that time. When he learned that they were shepherds, he permitted them to settle in the land of Goshen where they grew in number, wealth, and influence.

God knew that it was necessary for the Israelis to leave Canaan until they had developed national strength so that they could take possession of the land of Canaan. God wanted to safeguard them against mingling and intermarrying with the idolatrous races then in the land.

In Jacob's dying words to his twelve sons (ch. 49), we see again the promise to Judah of a descendant who would be the coming ruler. Remember, Christ is called the *Lion of the tribe of Judah* (Revelation 5:5).

The book of Genesis ends in failure. The last words are *in a coffin in Egypt.* Only death marks the pathway of sin, *for the wages of sin is death* (Romans 6:23). The people needed a Savior!

There are eight names mentioned in Genesis that we should remember in order: God, Adam, Satan, Noah, Abraham, Isaac, Jacob, Joseph.

There are six places of supreme importance in connection with the history of Genesis—Eden, Ararat, Babel, Ur of the Chaldeans, Canaan (the Promised Land), Egypt.

SELECTED BIBLE READING

Sunday: Creation (Genesis 1:1-5, 26-31; 2:7-22)
Monday: Fall (Genesis 3)
Tuesday: Flood (Genesis 6:1-7; 7:7-24; 8:6-11, 18-22; 9:1-16)
Wednesday: Beginning of Languages (Genesis 11:1-9)
Thursday: Abrahamic Call and Covenant (Genesis 12:1-9; 13:14-18; 15:1-21; 17:4-8; 22:15-20; 26:1-5; 28:10-15)
Friday: Story of Joseph (Genesis 37; 42)
Saturday: Jacob's Final Blessing (Genesis 49)

CHAPTER 3

UNDERSTANDING EXODUS

Exodus Portrays Jesus Christ, Our Passover Lamb

Exodus follows Genesis in much the same relation as the New Testament follows the Old Testament. Genesis tells of man's failure under every test and in every condition. Exodus is the thrilling epic of God hurrying to man's rescue. It tells of the redeeming work of a sovereign God.

Exodus is preeminently the book of redemption in the Old Testament. It begins in darkness and gloom yet ends in glory. It commences by telling how God came down in grace to deliver an enslaved people, and it ends by declaring how God came down in glory to dwell among a redeemed people.

Exodus, which is Greek, means "the way out." Without Genesis the book of Exodus has no meaning. In the original Hebrew, it begins with the word *and* (as do many other books of the Old Testament). The story is continuing. This seems to point out that each author was not just recording his own story but only his part of a great drama that began in the events of the past and looked forward to what would come. Take the five books of Moses—Genesis, Exodus, Leviticus, Numbers, Deuteronomy. Each book is about something, and those five things are vitally related to one another.

The Great Hero, Moses
Exodus gives us the story of Moses, the great hero of God. (See Hebrews 11:23-29.) Dwight L. Moody, a great evangelist of the late nineteenth century, said that Moses spent

Forty years thinking he was somebody
Forty years learning he was nobody
Forty years discovering what God can do with a nobody.

The Law

The last half of Exodus (ch. 19–40) teaches us that the redeemed must do the will of their Redeemer, consecrating themselves to his service and submitting to his control. Therefore, the moral law is given, followed by the ceremonial law, which was provision for the violator of the moral law.

The Tabernacle

God gave the tabernacle as a detailed picture of the Redeemer to come, in his many offices, and as a dwelling place for his visible glory on earth. Its wonderful symbolism is rich in Christian truth.

THE BONDAGE
EXODUS 1–2

As this book opens, three-and-a-half centuries have passed since the closing scene of Genesis. The book of Genesis is a family history. The book of Exodus is a national history. We have no account of what happened during this long period of silence. The patriarch Abraham died when Jacob, his grandson, was fifteen years old. Jacob's favorite son, Joseph, had been sold as a slave into Egypt and had risen to great power and influence. The sons of Jacob had gained great favor because of their brother Joseph. There were only seventy Hebrews that went to Egypt, but before they left Egypt the people had grown into a nation of three million.

When Joseph died and a new dynasty came to the throne in Egypt, the wealth and great numbers of the Hebrews made them objects of suspicion in the eyes of the Egyptians. The pharaohs, wishing to break them, reduced them to slavery of the worst sort. This was hard for a people who had lived as free men with every favor upon them. They remembered the promises God had given to Abraham and his descendants, and it made this bondage doubly hard to understand.

The story told in the books of Exodus, Leviticus, Numbers, and Deuteronomy shows that God did not forget the promise he made to Abraham—*I will cause you to become the father of a great nation* (Genesis 12:2).

The family records of Abraham, Isaac, and Jacob no doubt had been carried into Egypt, and there they became part of Israel's national annals. Through the long years of bondage the Hebrews clung to the promise that one day Canaan would be their home.

We will see God coming down to deliver the people from Egypt (3:7-8). Now the individuals and families had been organized into a nation. God was going to give them laws with which to govern themselves. He was going to take them back to the land he had promised them.

THE EXODUS
EXODUS 3-4

Think of the preparation that had to be made for moving so great a host: *six hundred thousand of them, besides all the women and children, going on foot. People of various sorts went with them; and there were flocks and herds—a vast exodus of cattle* (12:37-38).

No doubt it was a well-organized expedition. Moses had appealed to Pharaoh again and again to let the Israelis go (5:1; 7:16). The plagues and the negotiations that Moses had to make with Pharaoh must have lasted nearly a year. This gave the Israelis more time to gather their things together. The plagues taught the Israelis some great things, besides forcing Pharaoh to let them go.

In the construction of any great building a blueprint has to be drawn and a pattern made. Our salvation was designed by God *before he made the world* (Ephesians 1:4). We find the pattern in the book of Exodus. Exodus is the historical picture of divine grace in God's redemption of man to himself by Jesus Christ, who is both our great Messenger (Moses) and High Priest (Aaron) (Hebrews 3:1).

The story of Exodus is repeated in every soul that seeks deliverance from the enmeshing and enervating influence of the world. From this point of view, the book is human, from the first verse to the last. The things that happened are an example to us, and they were written for our instruction. We study Exodus in order to see God's way of delivering sinful man and his gracious purposes in rescuing him.

THE PASSOVER
EXODUS 12-19

Exodus 12 gives us the thrilling story of the Passover, the clearest Old Testament picture of our individual salvation through faith in the shed blood of our Lord Jesus Christ. In this chapter is the basis for calling Christ *the Lamb of God* and for the many tender references to his crucifixion as the death of our own Passover Lamb. *Christ, God's Lamb, has been slain for us* (1 Corinthians 5:7). As the Passover (ch. 12) is the heart of the book, so the whole book is a pattern of our salvation. Perhaps the Israelis did not know the significance of this feast the night before they left Egypt, but they believed God and obeyed.

God had sent nine plagues on Egypt in order to make Pharaoh willing to let the people go. With each plague there was a hardening of Pharaoh's heart. Finally God said that the firstborn in all Egypt would die. This tenth plague would have fallen on the Hebrews too if they hadn't killed the Passover lamb and been protected by its blood of redemption (12:12-13).

Every person should study the divine order of the Passover as it is given in Exodus 12:

First, *Take a lamb* (Hebrews 9:28; Isaiah 53:6; John 19:14; 1 Corinthians 5:7). It was not the spotlessness of the living lamb that saved them, but its death (Hebrews 9:22; 1 John 1:7; Revelation 1:5). It is not Christ's sinless life that saves us, but his death on the cross.

Second, *Sprinkle the blood.* It is not enough for the lamb to be slain. The blood was sufficient but was not effective unless applied. Every Israeli individually had to apply it to his own household—over the doorway, not under. What have you done with the blood of your Passover Lamb who died on Calvary (Exodus 12:22; John 1:12)?

The blood was applied with hyssop—a common weed obtainable by everyone—typical of faith. The blood above the door was what saved them. Not what they thought about it but what they did with it counted. *When I see the blood, I will pass over you* (12:13).

Not blood in the basin but blood applied saves a soul. Not all the blood shed on Calvary's cross can save a soul from death unless it is applied, then—*When I see the blood, I will pass over you.* Not feelings, not personal worthiness, but one thing saved them—the blood (Hebrews 9:22).

Third, *Eat the lamb.* After the blood was shed and sprinkled, there was direction for nourishment. So with us: salvation first, then feeding—fellowship, worship, life, and service. *My flesh is the true food* (John 6:54-58).

Fourth, *Remove the yeast.* Yeast is often a symbol of sin—for example, *the yeast of the Pharisees* (Matthew 16:6). The yeast of unrighteousness must be removed from our lives if we are to eat with God. *Search me. . . . Point out anything you find in me that makes you sad* (Psalm 139:23-24).

Fifth, *Eat bitter herbs.* Christ tasted the bitter cup for us, and we, too, must suffer some bitterness. *Since Christ suffered and underwent pain, you must have the same attitude he did; you must be ready to suffer, too* (Hebrews 12:11).

The lamb was to be feasted upon not raw, not unbaked, but a suffering lamb who passed through fire. All was to be eaten in a hurry, and nothing was to be left over. Not a bone was to be broken! Christ's body was broken but not his bones (Psalm 34:20; John 19:36).

Sixth, *Be ready to leave.* They ate the food fully dressed, standing, and ready to go. All provision was made for the journey. What a contrast that night—peaceful feasting in the houses of Israel, awful mourning in the houses of Egypt!

We have read here of the Passover. Now comes the Passage. The Passover sealed them. The Passage through the Red Sea steeled them. They left Egypt under the blood, a marked people. They passed through the Red Sea directed, a determined people. God led them out and shut the door behind them!

THE GIVING OF THE LAW
EXODUS 20-24

In this part of Exodus we see the law given, broken, and restored. Up to this time in Israel's history all had been grace and mercy. God heard the cry of their bondage and answered them. God selected a leader and trained him. God defeated their enemies. God fed them, yet they rebelled. Now a new order of things is brought about at Sinai.

The law demands nothing short of perfection. The psalmist says, *God's laws are perfect* (Psalm 19:7, read also verses 8-11). Ever since the law was given only one Man has been able to keep it perfectly. Christ not only kept the law, but he paid the complete penalty for the broken law. Christ suffered so that we could be spared (see Hebrews 9:13-15; 10:1-22; 1 Peter 1:18-20).

If no one could keep the law, why was it given? That we might know our great sinfulness. The law did not make us sin, but it showed us that we are sinners. A physician comes and looks at a child, and the symptoms reveal that he has measles. He gives the child some medicine that makes him break out. The doctor did not make the child have measles, but he proved that measles was there. (Read Genesis 4:4-5; Romans 8:1-4; 3:19-28.)

The law is God's mirror to show us our sinfulness. *The law itself was wholly right and good* (Romans 7:12).

There are two mountain peaks that confront each other in God's Word:

1. Mount Sinai, with all of its horror, thundered forth the law (ch. 19).
2. Opposite this God placed Calvary. Calvary took away all the fire and thunder and made possible a meeting place between God and the sinner.

Each of us has a choice as to how we will approach God, either by law or by blood (Hebrews 12:18-29).

No provision was made in the law for failure. It is all or nothing—keep the whole law or all of it is broken. One hole in a bowl, one crack in a pitcher, makes it unfit for its purpose. One flaw in a character mars the perfection God requires under the law.

Laws may be divided into two parts:

1. Laws regarding man's attitude toward God
2. Laws regarding man's attitude toward other people

We are told that God gave all these words. God gave the whole testimony (20:1), and man assumed the whole responsibility for keeping it (19:8). Why did Israel accept the law rather than cry for mercy? Human pride always makes us think that we can please God by ourselves. Before the Israelis even received the law or started to keep it they were dancing around the golden calf, worshiping a god they had made (32:1-10, 18).

THE BUILDING OF THE TABERNACLE
EXODUS 25–40

This part of Exodus is one of the richest veins in the Bible's inexhaustible mines. We must use our imagination and reason as we enter the holy precincts and gaze upon the significant furniture. The sanctuary or holy dwelling place that God told Moses to build would point to Christ and tell of his person and work.

The Outer Court
Here we see the bronze altar on which the burnt offerings were sacrificed (27:1-8). Remember, Christ is our sin offering. The basin was there for the cleansing of the priests before they could enter into the Holy Place to render their service (30:18).

The Holy Place
Herein was the golden lampstand (25:31-40), typifying Christ, the Light of the World; the bread of the Presence (25:23-30), for Christ is the Bread of Life; and the golden altar of incense (30:1-10), symbolizing Christ's intercession for us.

The Most Holy Place
If we draw back the beautiful veil (which typifies the body of Christ), we will see the Ark of the Covenant, the symbol of God's presence. The High Priest came into the Most Holy Place only once a year to sprinkle the blood of atonement. The book of Hebrews tells us that Christ is not only our High Priest but also our atonement, and so we can go into the Most Holy Place (the presence of God) at any time with boldness.

The Tabernacle Itself
The Tabernacle, with the cloud of glory over it, taught the people that God was dwelling among them (25:8). The Tabernacle was the common center and rallying point that could be moved from time to time. Its colors and structure are symbols of the person and work of Jesus Christ. (Some critics have said that the account of the Tabernacle and its wonderful structure could not be true because the times were too primitive, but research has given abundant evidence of great skill in such matters long before the Exodus. Fine linen was used in many ways. Fine work in gold

has been discovered in the tombs dating back as early as the twelfth Egyptian dynasty, and Moses lived in the eighteenth dynasty.)

Thus we see that redemption was not an afterthought with God (Ephesians 1:4).

The Law was broken in the people's hearts before it was broken by Moses' hand.

Over against Sinai is Calvary!

God's mirror reveals but never cleanses.

The blood of the Lamb makes us safe; our trust in God's Word makes us sure.

God's plan will never be frustrated.

SELECTED BIBLE READING

Sunday: Bondage (Exodus 1)
Monday: The Call of Moses (Exodus 3–4)
Tuesday: The Plagues (Exodus 7–11)
Wednesday: The Passover (Exodus 12)
Thursday: The Law (Exodus 20)
Friday: The Worship (Exodus 25:1-9; 28:1-14, 30-43)
Saturday: Moses' Commission Renewed (Exodus 33:12–34:17)

CHAPTER 4

UNDERSTANDING
LEVITICUS

Leviticus Portrays Jesus Christ, Our Sacrifice for Sin

"Get right," say the offerings. There are five of them: burnt offering, grain offering, thank offering, sin offering, guilt offering.

"Keep right," say the feasts. There are eight of them: Sabbath, Passover, Pentecost, Trumpets, Atonement, Shelters, the Sabbatical Year, and the Year of Jubilee.

Leviticus is called the Book of Atonement (16:30-34).

God says, *Be holy as I am holy* (11:44-45; 19:2; 20:7, 26).

The book of Leviticus was God's picture book for the Israelis to help them in their religious training. Every picture pointed forward to the work of Jesus Christ.

The title *Leviticus* suggests the subject matter of the book—the Levites and the priests and their service in the Tabernacle. It is also called the Book of Laws. We remember that in the book of Exodus God gave Moses exact instructions about how to build the Tabernacle and about the institution of the priesthood to carry on the service in this Holy Place.

As Leviticus opens, the Israelis were still at Mount Sinai. God was continuing to give his instructions for orderly worship in the Tabernacle.

Leviticus is a timely book for it insists on keeping the body holy as well as the soul. It teaches that redeemed people must be holy because their Redeemer is holy. It gives us not only the key for our spiritual life and its holy walk, but it surprises us with real lessons in hygiene and sanitation. The Jews, with their long and vigorous lives, are wonderful evidence of the result of these lessons.

Leviticus is a divine book. The opening verse gives us the clue to the whole: *The Lord now spoke to Moses from the Tabernacle, and commanded him to give the following instructions to the people of Israel. . . .* Leviticus is God speaking to us through the Tabernacle and its meaning.

Leviticus is a personal book. The fourth verse intimates this: *The person bringing [his gift] is to lay his hand upon its head.* Notice that God expects each person to bring his own gift. The way is often as important as the gift. Have you an offering for the Lord? Then this book will appeal to you.

SACRIFICE AND SEPARATION
LEVITICUS 1:1–6:7

One of the most important questions in life is "How can an unholy people approach a holy God?"

At the very beginning of Leviticus we see God making provision for his people to approach him in worship. This book shows redeemed Israel that the way to God is by sacrifice, and the walk with God is by separation.

Isn't it strange that deep down in every heart there is a sense of guilt and the feeling of a need of doing something to secure pardon or gain the favor of the one wronged? The pagan brings his sacrifice to the altar of his gods, for he realizes that he cannot do anything about his sin himself. He must make an atonement for it.

The pagan cannot see beyond his sacrifice. When we look at the sacrifices in this book, we find that they are only symbols. They point to the Perfect Sacrifice for sin that was to be made on Calvary. All the sacrifices in this book point to *the Lamb of God who takes away the world's sin* (John 1:29).

Sin may be forgiven, but it must receive its penalty. *The wages of sin is death* (Romans 6:23). Sin keeps us from drawing near to God. He is too pure to behold evil. There can be no fellowship between God and the sinner until sin has been dealt with. The only way is sacrifice. *Without the shedding of blood there is no forgiveness of sins* (Hebrews 9:22).

Five offerings are described in Leviticus. God wants us to understand the awful reality of sin, so he asks for a sacrifice each day.

Here is a list of the offerings, with key words to identify them. Learn this simple outline to fix in mind the first six chapters of Leviticus:

1. Burnt offering: surrender of Christ for the world (ch. 1)
2. Grain offering: service of Christ in life (ch. 2)
3. Thank offering: serenity of Christ in life (ch. 3)
4. Sin offering: substitute of Christ for sin (4:1–5:13)
5. Guilt offering: satisfaction by Christ for demands of God ·(5:14–6:7)

The Burnt Offering (ch. 1)
The burnt offering is a symbol of Christ offering himself without spot to God. Christ offered himself in the sinner's place (1:4).

This offering of dedication came first because sacrifice comes first. No one begins with God until he has yielded all to God (1:3). This was the most common sacrifice in the ancient Temple. There were daily burnt offerings.

Dedication is man's part; consecration is God's part. We dedicate ourselves to God; he consecrates us—to his service.

Consecrate me now to thy service, Lord,
By the power of grace divine;
Let my soul look up with a steadfast hope,
And my will be lost in thine.

We sing, "Take my life and let it be consecrated, Lord, to thee." This is a burnt offering.

The Grain Offering (ch. 2)
This is the sacrifice of daily devotion.

As the burnt offering typifies Christ in death, so the grain offering typifies Christ in life.

The fine flour speaks of the character of Christ—his perfection in thought, in word, in action. Let us feed on the perfect grain offering.

We must come to him first with our whole burnt offering. Then we keep coming with our continual grain offering. It is our very best, our gift of life. But remember that the slain offering must come first.

The Thank Offering (ch. 3)

This offering represents fellowship and communion with God. It is an offering of thanksgiving and peace. *Christ is our peace* (Ephesians 2:14). *For Christ's death on the cross has made peace with God for all by his blood* (Colossians 1:20).

The Sin Offering (4:1–5:13)

This shows us Christ on the cross in the sinner's place.

In this offering we see an acknowledgment of sin. In the other offerings the offerer comes as a worshiper, but here as a convicted sinner. God holds us accountable for our sin. We are like criminals who have been tried, found guilty, and sentenced to death.

Though placed last, the sin and guilt offerings are included in all that goes before. The only reason burnt offerings, grain offerings, or thank offerings can be made is that the blood of pardon has been shed. God has accepted the one offering of his Son, which every lesser offering typified.

The pagan brings a sacrifice to his god; the Christian accepts the sacrifice from his God.

The Guilt Offering (5:14–6:7)

Christ has even taken care of our sin against others.

The blood of the guilt offering cleanses the conscience and sends the guilty back to the one he has wronged, not only with the principal but with a fifth added (6:5). The injurer is forgiven and the injured becomes an actual gainer.

It is a grave error to suppose that you are safe and right if you live up to your own conscience. God has standards. We can never comprehend his holiness.

None of these sacrifices forgave sin. They only pointed forward to the true Sacrifice, God's very own Son (Hebrews 10).

You will notice that young bulls, oxen, goats, sheep, turtledoves, and pigeons were mentioned for sacrifice. The offering was determined by the ability of the one who brought it.

What we bring is our sin; what Christ brings is the offering and the atonement for sin.

THE PRIEST
LEVITICUS 8–10

We have been studying the great subject of sacrifice, but no person could bring his own sacrifice to God. He had to bring it to the priest, who in turn would offer it to God.

God chose one tribe out of the twelve to care for the Tabernacle. This was the tribe of Levi. One family of Levites, Aaron's, was to be the priests. The priests had charge of the sacrifices and were supported by the tithes of the people.

The priest went from man to God with the prayers and praises of the people. He stood for them and pleaded their cause.

The burdened Israeli who desired to approach God brought his animal to the court of the Tabernacle. At the altar of burnt offerings he laid his hand on the animal's head to express his penitence and consecration. The animal was killed and its blood sprinkled on the altar.

The priest representing the worshiper then came to the basin and washed his hands in it, thus indicating the clean life that should follow the forgiveness of sins. He entered the Holy Place, passed by the sacred furnishings, the lampstand, the table of bread, and came to the altar of incense, where prayer was offered.

One day in the year the High Priest passed beyond the veil that separated the Holy Place and the Most Holy Place and stood before the mercy seat, with the blood of the atonement, to intercede for the people.

The priest could not consecrate himself. Moses acted for God in this service. Each priest presented his body a living sacrifice for service just as Paul instructed (Romans 12:1-2).

The priests had charge of the sacrifices. The Levites were their assistants. They took care of the Tabernacle, formed choirs, were guides and instructors in the later Temple.

Notice the opening of Leviticus 10. At the very beginning of the history of the work of the priesthood there were evidences of failure. Nadab and Abihu, two sons of Aaron, offered unholy fire before the Lord, *contrary to what the Lord had just commanded them! So fire blazed forth from the presence of the Lord and destroyed them.*

We read in Leviticus 10:3 that Aaron held his peace. He was their father, but he dared not question God. We talk too much before God. We must learn to walk softly in the divine Presence. The other priests were solemnly charged to show no signs of mourning and to abide at their posts.

The priests were the ministers of the sacrifices that we have just been studying. Each was a picture of the great sacrifice of Christ for the sin of the world.

Animal sacrifices are no longer necessary because all sacrifices were fulfilled in Christ. Therefore priests are no longer necessary. Christ himself is the great High Priest for man (Hebrews 2:17; 4:15). He is the only mediator between God and man. There is no one else who can put himself between God and man.

Christ is our High Priest and he is at the right hand of the Father today making intercession for us. We approach God by him and him alone (Hebrews 10:12; 7:25; John 14:6).

When we see Christ as Sacrifice, we see beauty and completeness. When we see Christ as Priest, we see his divine perfection, *yet he is able to understand our weaknesses* (Hebrews 4:15).

As Sacrifice he establishes the relationship of his people with God. As Priest he maintains that position.

We read of this perfect and eternal priesthood in the book of Hebrews. Heaven, not earth, is the sphere of Christ's priestly ministry. He never appeared in the Temple on earth to offer sacrifice. He went there to preach and teach but not to sacrifice.

THE EIGHT FEASTS
LEVITICUS 23

As the first part of the book has to do with offerings and the offerers, so the last part of the book deals with feasts and feasters. Five great festivals are mentioned in Leviticus 23.

The sacrifices spoke of the blood that saved. The feasts spoke of the food that sustains. Both are of God.

The sacrifices correspond to the cup of the Lord's Supper that reminds us of Christ's death on the cross whereby we are redeemed. The bread of Communion witnesses to his life of which we are partakers.

The Festival of the Sabbath (23:1-3)
The Sabbath was given the foremost place. It was a perpetually recurring feast to be obeyed through the whole year on every seventh day. It was a day of worship and rest, celebrating the finished work of God in creation (Genesis 2:2-3). Christians celebrate the first day of the week, the day our Lord arose from the grave (Luke 24:1; Acts 20:7; 1 Corinthians 16:2). Thus we celebrate the finished work of redemption.

The Festival of the Passover (23:4-5)
The Passover spoke of redemption and was celebrated every spring at our Easter time. It was Independence Day for the Is-

raelis. They did not celebrate it by fireworks and parades but by a great service of worship to God. Every Jew who was able made his way to Jerusalem.

Passover lasted one day, but the Festival of Unleavened Bread, which immediately followed, lasted seven days. With these the year began.

The Jews were still celebrating this festival when our Lord was on this earth. Read in the Word the times that he went to the Passover festival (Luke 2:41-52; Matthew 26:19; John 13). The Jews today celebrate this same festival. They are still looking for their Messiah.

The Festival of Pentecost (23:15-22)

This festival was observed fifty days after the Festival of the First Fruits, which symbolized Christ's resurrection and ours (1 Corinthians 15:20). It was fifty days after Christ's resurrection that the Holy Spirit descended upon the disciples and the church was born. Pentecost was the birthday of the church. The death and resurrection of Christ had to be accomplished before the descent of the Holy Spirit.

The Festival of Trumpets (23:23-25)

This was the New Year's Day of the Israelis—*Rosh Hashanah*. It was celebrated in the fall about mid-September, with horns and trumpets blown throughout the day.

The Day of Atonement (23:26-32)

This was the greatest day in the history of God's chosen people. On this day the sins of the nation were confessed. Confession is always the first step toward righteousness. It reveals a right attitude toward sin. It leads to a desire for forgiveness. God says, *If we confess our sins to him, he can be depended on to forgive us and to cleanse us from every wrong* (1 John 1:9).

On this day God's relationship to his people was established— all the sins, failures, and weaknesses of the people were atoned for. The blood was shed and the sins of the people were covered so that God could live among his people in spite of their uncleanness.

We learn in Leviticus 16 that God was hidden behind a veil in the Tabernacle and man was at a distance. *The penalty for intrusion is death* (16:2). The way was not yet made open for man to approach God. But now we *can come fearlessly* (Ephesians 3:12). We can run into God's presence at any time, for Christ has made the way possible for us. In the book of Leviticus, God was shut in from man and man was shut out from God.

The Day of Atonement was the only day in the year when the High Priest was permitted to enter the Most Holy Place. He went in with an offering for the atonement of the sin of the people. *Atonement* means "cover." This offering "covered" the sins of the people until the great sacrifice on Calvary was made. None of these offerings "took away" those sins.

The Festival of Shelters (23:33-36)

This was the last festival of the year. It commemorated the time when the Israelis lived in tents during their wilderness journey. It was celebrated in the fall of the year and lasted an entire week. The people lived in outdoor shelters and heard the reading of the Law.

The Festival of the Passover and the Festival of Shelters kept before the Israelis the marvelous way in which they were delivered from Egypt and were sustained in the wilderness. God did not want them to forget the way in which the gods of Egypt were utterly discredited and the great nation of Egypt was humbled.

The Festival of Shelters recalled to their minds that by their own disobedience they were compelled to wander forty years in the wilderness. But in spite of their unbelief, God was faithful in caring for them and in bringing them to their inheritance. These days reminded them of their dependence on God and the blessings that would come if they would be obedient to his will.

The Sabbatical Year (25:1-7)

This was the year of meditation and devotion. It was a year-long Sabbath, held once every seven years. The purpose and character of the Sabbath was magnified. God impressed it upon the minds of the people.

God wanted to impress upon them that the land was holy unto him. There was quietness over the whole land during these days. All breathed the spirit of rest and meditation. Every day was like the Sabbath, and the minds of the people were kept on the things of the Lord. The Law was read. This time exerted a tremendous influence upon the lives of the people.

The Year of Jubilee (25:8-24)
This was celebrated every fiftieth year. It was inaugurated on the Day of Atonement with the blowing of trumpets. As in the Sabbatical Year, the land was not cultivated. The blowing of the trumpets that ushered in the year released every slave. Jewish writers tell us that the Year of Jubilee was observed at the time of the fall of Judah in 586 B.C. References are made to it in Isaiah 61:1-2 and Ezekiel 7:12-13.

Another outstanding event was the restoration to the original owner of all land that had in any way been taken away. That is, it was returned to the family to whom it had been assigned in the original distribution. What a wise provision this was from an economic standpoint. But God no doubt had a more far-reaching plan bearing upon the coming of the Messiah. Every tribal and family register needed to be carefully kept so that the rights of all would be protected. This would apply to Judah, the tribe from which the Messiah was to come. From these registers our Lord's genealogy could be exactly traced.

Seven is a significant number in Leviticus. Like Revelation, Leviticus is built around a series of sevens: Every seventh day was a Sabbath. Every seventh year was a Sabbatical Year. Every seven times seven years was followed by a Year of Jubilee. Pentecost was seven weeks after Passover. In the seventh month were the festivals of Trumpets, Shelters, and Atonement. Pentecost and Passover each lasted seven days.

This book is for a redeemed people, showing how God is to be approached and worshiped. The book of Exodus is the book of redemption, but the book of Leviticus tells how the redeemed ones can worship God.

SELECTED BIBLE READING

Sunday: Burnt Offering (Leviticus 1)
Monday: The Priests (Leviticus 8)
Tuesday: Pure Food Laws (Leviticus 11)
Wednesday: The Day of Atonement (Leviticus 16)
Thursday: The Festivals of the Lord (Leviticus 23)
Friday: God's Pledge (Leviticus 26)
Saturday: Dedication (Leviticus 27)

CHAPTER 5

UNDERSTANDING NUMBERS

Numbers Portrays Jesus Christ, Our "Lifted-Up One"

The Israelis were saved to serve. So is every child of God today.

Beware of unbelief! The Apostle Paul says to us: *You were getting along so well. Who has interfered with you to hold you back from following the truth?* (Galatians 5:7). God tells us that unbelief hinders blessing (Hebrews 3:19).

Numbers might be called the Wilderness Wandering. This wandering extended from Sinai to the border of Canaan, the land of promise, and covered about forty years.

It might also be called the Book of Murmurings, because from beginning to end it is filled with the spirit of rebellion against God. *"For forty years I watched them in disgust,"* the Lord God says. *"They were a nation whose thoughts and heart were far away from me. They refused to accept my laws"* (Psalm 95:10).

Numbers is indeed the book of the wilderness, recording the pitiable failure of Israel at Kadesh-barnea and the consequent wanderings and experiences of the people in the wilderness. It records the pilgrimage, warfare, service, and failure of the second generation of the nation after the Exodus from Egypt. This, however, is not all the message of Numbers. Chapters 1–10 give us the divine legislation, chapters 11–20 tell the story of the nation's failure, but the closing chapters of the book record Israel's return to God's favor and final victory, even in the wilderness.

While the annals of many powerful nations of that same time are lost to the world, these of a comparative handful of people are preserved. The reason for this is because the Messiah who would redeem the world was to come from this people. This is the reason God was so patient with them. He wanted to preserve them for himself. In 1 Corinthians 10 we learn that the things that happened to them are examples to us. In other words, their whole history is an object lesson, illustrating God's dealing with us today.

The key thought is discipline. Numbers is the fourth book of Moses. Someone has said that the order of the books is as follows:

In Genesis we see man ruined.
In Exodus, man redeemed.
In Leviticus, man worshiping.
In Numbers, man serving.

This is the order the Law lays down. Only a saved man can serve and worship God. Remember, we are saved to serve. We are not saved by good works, but we are saved to do good works (Ephesians 2:10). The law can bring us to the land of promise, but only our divine Joshua (Christ) can bring us in. Paul says that the law is the teacher and guide to bring us to Christ (Galatians 3:24). The law cannot save us, for *salvation is not a reward for the good we have done, so none of us can take any credit for it* (Ephesians 2:9).

Leviticus deals with the believer's worship. Numbers deals with the believer's life.

In Leviticus we see the believer's privileges. In Numbers the wilderness is the drill field.

If you know five names, you will master the story of the book of Numbers:

Moses, the great leader.
Aaron, the High Priest, Moses' brother.
Miriam, who was Moses' and Aaron's sister.
Joshua and Caleb, the two spies who dared to believe God, the only men of their generation who lived to enter Canaan.

The geography of the book takes us:

1. From Sinai to Kadesh
2. From Kadesh around back to Kadesh
3. From Kadesh straight to the border of Canaan.

The Israelis learned that:

1. They must trust God and not man in the day of crisis (Psalm 37:5). Read Numbers 13:26–14:25.
2. God would supply all their needs (Philippians 4:19).
   He gave them food (11:6-9)
   He gave them meat (11:31-33)
   He gave them water (20:8)
   He gave them leaders (1:1, 3)
   He gave them a promised land (14:7-8)
3. They must worship God according to his instructions.

It was God's plan that the Israelis go straight into the land that he had promised them, the land of Canaan, but the people would not. Because of the people's rebellion, God said that all those at Kadesh over twenty years old, except Joshua and Caleb, would die without entering the land. A new generation grew up during the forty years of wandering, so at the end the nation was about as strong in numbers as the day they left Egypt (ch. 26).

PREPARATION FOR THE JOURNEY
NUMBERS 1–12

As the book opens we see the Israelis in the wilderness of Sinai. The Law had been given, the Tabernacle had been built, and the priests had been assigned to their service. Now God was going to prepare the nation for its work. The teachings of this book are very applicable to the Christian life.

Order is heaven's first law. We see God numbering and arranging the tribes (ch. 1–2), choosing and assigning duties to the priests and Levites (ch. 3–4). God is the author of order.

The thought of God numbering his people and gathering them around himself is most precious to our hearts. He lived in the camp. The twelve tribes guarded the Tabernacle of the Lord. The Levites camped directly around the court, and Moses and Aaron and the priests guarded the entrance whereby God was approached.

The circumference of the camp arranged in this way and facing the Tabernacle is supposed to have been twelve miles. What an imposing sight the camp must have been from the outside, in the midst of the desert, with God stretching over them in a cloud by day and fire by night (9:15-23). He was their night light and their day shade. Their shoes did not wear out and their garments did not get old. Think of 600,000 men twenty or older and about three million men, women, and children in this great camp! But the most glorious thing was that God was in their midst.

In the first chapter Moses was commanded to take a census. The Lord knows all by name that are his (2 Timothy 2:19; Philippians 4:3). Even the hairs of our head are numbered. How wonderful to know that God cares for each of his children!

For Christians too there is a census, for Christ numbers his jewels and knows those who are his. God has a *Book of Remembrance drawn up in which he recorded the names of those who feared him and loved to think about him* (Malachi 3:16).

In this chapter we find the declaration of genealogy of the tribes of Israel. Can you trace your genealogy to the risen Lord (John 1:12)?

Here were about three million people on a sterile desert, not a blade of grass, not a drop of water, no visible means of support. How were they to be fed? God was there! How were they to trace their way through a howling wilderness where there was no path? God was there!

God's presence provides everything! What? Are all these three million to be fed on air? Who has charge of the commisary? Where is the baggage? Who is to attend to the clothing? God was there! In faith's arithmetic God is the only figure that counts.

No one had gone before to blaze a trail for the Israelis. There was not a footprint, not a landmark. It is much like our life as Christians today. We are passing through a trackless desert—a moral wilderness. There is no trail. We would not know where to walk except for one little sentence from the lips of the Lord: *I am the Way* (John 14:6). He will guide us step by step. There is no uncertainty, for he said, *If you follow me, you won't be stumbling in the darkness* (John 8:12).

God gave his children a cloud to guide them by day and a pillar of fire by night. It is interesting to see how they were guided one step at a time. They did not know when they were to go and when to stop, but the Ark of the Covenant (signifying God's presence) went ahead of them, the cloud always leading (10:33).

Sin crept into this well-ordered camp life. The people began to murmur against God. God sent judgment of fire (11:1-3). Then they complained about their food (11:4). It seemed monotonous. They longed for the garlic and onions of Egypt, and they wanted fish. As a result of their complaining, God sent them quails for thirty days. They made gluttons of themselves and *as everyone began eating the meat, the anger of the Lord rose against the people and he killed large numbers of them with a plague* (11:33).

Then we read of the sin of Aaron, the High Priest, and Miriam, Moses' sister. God had chosen Moses to be the leader of this great nation, and Aaron and Miriam were only his assistants. Jealousy crept into their hearts. They wanted more honor. Miriam's terrible punishment was to be smitten with leprosy for seven days (12:1-16).

We find the invitation of God's marching nation to the people around them: *Come with us and we will do you good; for the Lord has given wonderful promises to Israel* (10:29). Can we say this? Do we say it to those around us?

The Ark of the Covenant is the Word of God in the midst of the people.

The sound of the silver trumpet is the witness of a faithful prophet.

The pillar of fire and of cloud is the comfort and guidance of the Holy Spirit.

The Tabernacle and its ordinances make the worship of the sanctuary.

Christ "the High Priest" of our profession gives significance to it all.

We are just humans making many mistakes and capable of wandering far. God has given us these heavenly attendants and guides. Who does not need them? Who can make progress without them? Invite others to join our band and go with us. We should always be taking others by the hand and inviting them to go with us.

WILDERNESS WANDERINGS
NUMBERS 13–20

After one year at Mount Sinai the Israelis journeyed to Kadesh, located at the southern border of the Promised Land. Afraid to enter, they turned back and wandered in the wilderness to the south and east until that generation died. They did not travel all the time but remained in some places with their flocks and herds grazing on the surrounding hills. When the cloud lifted, they marched. They finally approached Canaan from east of the Dead Sea.

Think of the lost years of wandering from Kadesh and back to Kadesh because they would not believe God. After two years in the wilderness, the Israelis could have gone into the land of promise immediately had it not been for the sin of unbelief. They listened to the discouraging words of most of the spies.

When the spies came back and told them about the giants in the land and the high-walled cities, their hearts failed them. They would not listen to Joshua and Caleb who agreed with all that was told, but added, *Let us go up at once and possess it . . . for we are well able to conquer it* (13:30). But the people would not trust God. They said, *Let's elect a leader to take us back to Egypt* (14:4).

When they refused to enter Canaan, the door was closed to them. It meant wandering in the wilderness for forty years. God said that he would not allow any of those who were over twenty years old to enter Canaan, except Joshua and Caleb.

At the beginning, the journey from Sinai to Kadesh was a swift and jubilant one! Then came sad doubt and delay. Hesitant Israel was plunged down into the waiting years of wilderness wanderings. Sadly Moses reminded them of it: *It took us thirty-eight years to finally get across Zered Brook from Kadesh! For the Lord had decreed that this could not happen until all the men, who thirty-eight years earlier were old enough to bear arms, had died* (Deuteronomy 2:14).

They were eleven days from the land of promise, but they turned back! They could have made eleven days of progress, but they chose forty years of wandering.

God took the Israelis out of Egypt so that he could take them into Canaan, the land of promise. God did not want the Israelis just to come out of Egypt. He wanted to have them come into the Promised Land. This they could have done in comparatively few days, not more than two or three weeks. You remember the spies made the trip and returned within forty days. As we have already seen, their fear disqualified them to take over the land of promise.

Often our fear keeps us from enjoying all that God wants to give us. We fear what others will say. We fear what might happen if we put our trust completely in Christ.

One of the reports of the spies was that there were giants in the land and that the Israelis *felt like grasshoppers before them* (13:33).

This account tells part of the story of every life, even of many

Christians. Giants of selfishness and greed, far outranking the Anakim, oppose our advance! But when the returns are all in, the fact remains that there is One with us stronger than they!

Like the ten spies, we can be pessimists, or like the two, optimists. Like the ten, we can put difficulties between us and God and say we are not able, or like the two, we can put God between the difficulties and ourselves and say we are able!

We start out with high hopes in the enthusiasm of our first love. Ahead lies the land of possibilities and achievement. Then the giants appear—giants of opposition from without, giants of fear from within. Our faith fails. We forget God. We compare our difficulties with our own strength rather than committing them to the great arm of God. Then we turn back into the wilderness of half trust, half victory, and whole despair.

Numbers 33 is the pitiful logbook of this journey: They went

From Kibroth-Hattaavah to Hazeroth;
From Hazeroth to Rithmah;
From Rithmah to Rimmon-parez;
From Rimmon-parez to Libnah;
From Libnah to Rissah;

etc., to the end of this dismal chapter! Going and going, camping and leaving, but never arriving anywhere. An endless circle of aimless wandering with no success. When we doubt God we find this to be our experience, too. We feel defeated and discouraged. We wander around but never accomplish anything. It is like a swinging door—lots of motion but getting no place.

Before this scene ends we find Israel murmuring again, this time because of the shortage of water. They complained bitterly to Moses and Aaron and said they wished they had never been brought out of Egypt. The land was dry and parched, and there was no water to drink. Moses and Aaron again went to God. God told Moses to take his rod and speak to the rock before the people, and the rock would give forth water.

Moses' patience was at an end. The people had complained about everything. In a fit of anger he called the people rebels, and instead of speaking to the rock he struck it. Water gushed out. Even though Moses disobeyed, God was faithful and kept his promise.

Is it not sad that even children of God fail under testing? Moses' error was great, yet it showed him to be just like us.

Moses put himself up as God: *Listen, you rebels! Must we bring you water from this rock?* (20:10). This dishonored God. Because Moses struck the rock a second time (see first time, Exodus 17:5-6) instead of speaking to it, he was not permitted to enter the Promised Land. Christ, like the rock, was to be struck down once for our sins (1 Corinthians 10:4). He need not be struck down again.

One of the important things that we have not covered is an incident in Numbers 17. Aaron's priesthood had been questioned, so God himself was to confirm it. The leader of each tribe selected a dead rod, and the twelve rods were put in the Tabernacle overnight. God put life into Aaron's. So we find that all the authors of the religions of the world have died—even Christ died—but only Christ was raised from the dead and exalted to be our High Priest (Hebrews 4:14; 5:4-10).

ON TO CANAAN
NUMBERS 21-36

As this scene opens we discover that all the Israelis who left Egypt had died except Moses, Aaron, Joshua, Caleb, Miriam, and the children who were under twenty years of age when the spies entered the land. Why was this?

Finally, while they were still in Kadesh, Miriam, Moses' sister, and Aaron, his brother, now over one hundred years old, died.

Israel was to move on again. They started from Kadesh, this time with faces set resolutely toward the land of promise. The way was difficult, much harder than before, but faith had been renewed, discipline had done its work, and the arm of God went forth conquering and to conquer.

Learn here the lesson of God's second best. God offers the perfect way. If we refuse it, it is gone forever. Every male over twenty years of age who refused to go into the land of promise the first time (except Joshua and Caleb, who believed God) died in the wilderness. Not one of them entered the land.

But God is kind, and he sets before us another way, a second best. He may even offer a third, for his mercy is wonderful. He forgives us seventy times seven times. He brings us through, provides for us, never failing in his grace; but, oh, how much we miss and how many burdens we have to bear by not taking the first and the best! How costly this is!

Israel was complaining again, although over and over again God had proven to them that his way was best. Discontent and murmuring seem to have been ingrained habits of the Israelis. Grumbling is the easiest thing in the world to learn. "No talent, no self-denial, no brains, no character is required to set up the grumbling business" are the words written in a large business office. What's the use of grumbling? It never makes a heavy burden light. It never subtracts from ills. Instead it always adds to them.

Israel battled with the Canaanites and became discouraged. Then they grumbled because they had to march around the land of Edom instead of through it. They growled again against God and against Moses because they loathed the manna (21:5). They never were content.

This time God sent poisonous snakes among the people that caused suffering and death. After they confessed their sin, Moses prayed for their deliverance. God did not take away the snakes but told Moses to make a bronze snake and fasten it to a pole so that all could see it. As soon as they looked, they would live (21:6-9).

The Bible reveals that the whole human family has felt the serpent's sting of sin—death. The only way man can live is by looking to the One who took upon himself the likeness of men and was lifted up on the cross to take the sting of death upon himself. If we look on him, our Savior, we will live (John 3:14-15).

SELECTED BIBLE READING

Sunday: The Guiding Cloud (Numbers 9:15-23)
Monday: The Report of the Spies (Numbers 13:16-33)
Tuesday: Israel's Unbelief (Numbers 14:1-14)
Wednesday: Water from the Rock (Numbers 20:1-13)
Thursday: The Bronze Snake (Numbers 21:1-9)
Friday: Balaam's Beast (Numbers 22)
Saturday: The Cities of Refuge (Numbers 35:6-34)

CHAPTER 6

UNDERSTANDING DEUTERONOMY

Deuteronomy Portrays Jesus Christ, Our True Prophet

This book shows the blessings of obedience and the curse of disobedience.

Everything depends on obedience—life itself, possession of the Promised Land, victory over foes, prosperity and happiness. We find this book teaching the inflexibility of the law. "You must" and "You must not" occur over and over again—"A blessing if you obey" and "A curse if you will not obey."

The book of Deuteronomy is a collection of the orations and songs of Moses that he gave as his farewell to the Israelis. These noble orations were given as he stood on the great divide between his earthly and heavenly life. He was looking from the top of Pisgah Peak over a century of the past crammed full of epoch-creating events. Then he turned his gaze upon the future of the people he was about to leave.

The book contains a most interesting and instructive summary of the wilderness history of Israel, and in the last chapter we find an account of Moses himself. Carefully compare Moses' review of the events with the account itself given in Exodus and Numbers. It will be found that Deuteronomy gives the divine rather than the human view. Compare Deuteronomy 1 with Numbers 13–14.

Deuteronomy is a book of remembrance. The name *Deuteronomy* means "second law," which indicates that the law is re-

63

peated. This Moses did to remind the people of what God had done for them and what they were to do to serve him when they reached the Promised Land. It omits the things that relate to the priests and Levites and includes the things that the people should know.

The book is the last of the five books of Moses. You often hear these books called the Pentateuch, meaning "five books."

Genesis tells of the beginnings of the chosen nation Israel. Exodus relates the organization of the people into a nation and the giving of the law. Leviticus tells the way this people were to worship God. Numbers gives a story of the wanderings of this people. Deuteronomy relates the final preparation for entering the Promised Land.

Deuteronomy covers only about two months, including the thirty days of mourning for Moses. Moses delivered his counsels probably within a period of seven days and about a month before the people crossed the Jordan (1:1-3).

Moses was the writer but not the author of the Pentateuch. Over five hundred times in these first five books we find expressions like these: *The Lord spoke . . . God said*, etc. Who is the divine Author of the Bible? (See 2 Peter 1:21.)

The Christian heart always quickens its beat when it comes to Deuteronomy, for this book was a favorite with our Savior. From this book he quoted in his conflict with the adversary in Matthew 4:1-11 and Luke 4:1-13. These passages were his weapons with which he repelled the tempter: Deuteronomy 8:3; 6:16; 6:13; and 10:20. He took Deuteronomy as his code of conduct. Deuteronomy, Moses' last charge to his people, is God's book on obedience.

You will come to appreciate the full force of Deuteronomy only as you read its pages. Read it through in a single sitting.

Nothing in the Old Testament has any more powerful appeal for the spiritual life. No book in all the Word of God pictures better the life that is lived according to God's will and the blessings showered upon the soul who comes into the richness and fullness of spiritual living along the rugged pathway of simple obedience.

If you want a taste of heaven on earth, become familiar with Deuteronomy. Get in step with Moses and march ahead by way of the Honey Land—Canaan, *a land "flowing with milk and honey"* (Exodus 3:8).

MOSES' FIRST ADDRESS: "LOOKING BACK"
DEUTERONOMY 1-4

As the book opens we see the Israelis on the border of the land of Canaan, a place where eleven days' journey, some forty years before, could have brought them. Yet it had taken forty years. How slowly they had covered the ground! What windings and turnings! We marvel at Israel's slowness. We can rather marvel at our own! We, like they, are kept back by unbelief. How often we have to go over the same ground again and again. We should be shamed at the time it takes us to learn our lessons! God is such a faithful teacher. He never lets us pass on to another grade until we are ready.

How deplorable is unbelief! God never fails us when we put our trust in him, but he cannot do many great miracles because of our unbelief (Matthew 13:58).

Several hundred years before, God had promised to Abraham and his posterity a rich and wondrous land upon whose borders they were standing (Genesis 17:8). Now they were ready to enter after all the years of anticipation and hope. The closing chapters of Numbers finds them camped by the Jordan, waiting to go over into the good land itself.

As we shall see, in Deuteronomy God is putting before the Israelis the conditions of their entering and holding the land. We see all these conditions summed up in one great word: *obedience.*

The Israelis entered the Promised Land under the conditions of the law.

The book of Deuteronomy is one long plea for hearty obedience to God based on two grand motives of love and fear. *And now, Israel, what does the Lord your God require of you except to listen carefully to all he says to you, and to obey for your own good the commandments I am giving you today, and to love him, and to worship him with all your hearts and souls?* (10:12-13).

In the first four books of the Pentateuch God was choosing Israel. Here he was letting Israel choose him.

Only Caleb and Joshua were left from that generation that had come out of Egypt. All the others were dead. The younger men now alive had suffered hardships in the wilderness wanderings and were ready and anxious for conquest! But Moses had to rehearse the law to them. He knew his work was finished, for

God had told him that another would lead them into Canaan (Numbers 20:12).

Moses, the grand old man, was now 120 years old. We see him giving his farewell address to the people whom he had led for forty years.

Moses gave the Israelis a look back. He recalled the history of Israel and reviewed their wanderings. He reminded them of God's faithfulness and urged them to be grateful and obedient. He likened God's care of them to a loving father who cares for his little ones lest they get lost in the wilderness or be injured by the heat of the sun. He supplied all their needs and they lacked nothing (2:7).

Moses spoke to his beloved people in the most earnest and eloquent way and appealed to them to serve and obey God. His words still echo down the corridors of time!

Moses' work was done. He had spent the last forty years of his life in delivering his people from the bondage of Egypt, in guiding them through the many dangers that confronted them. He had trained them and given them forms of government, laws, and religious institutions. He had molded them into a nation.

The Israelis were now at the end of their journey, in the plain east of the Jordan, overlooking the land they had come so far to possess. It lay before them in the glories of springtime. But the impassable Jordan River rolled between, and walled cities rose up in seemingly impregnable strength.

MOSES' SECOND ADDRESS: "LOOKING UP"
DEUTERONOMY 5-26

In Deuteronomy 12:1 we see the key to this section: *These are the laws you must obey when you arrive in the land.* Israel was going into a new land, and everything would depend on their constant and intelligent obedience to God who was giving them the land. God wanted to teach Israel the love that is the real fulfillment of the law (Romans 13:8-10; Matthew 27:37-40).

Moses here set forth the law simply and clearly so that it would take living hold of the people. God says, "You are my people. I love you. I have chosen you. I am with you. I will protect you. I am only asking you to obey me for your good." He says, *Be holy, for I am holy.* Since God's people are his, he wants them to walk in the world in the way that befits them, separating themselves from evil (ch. 14). They should show love toward their fellows (ch. 15). They must gather together to worship (ch. 16).

Today people are careless about going to church to worship. This speaks of spiritual decay. God demands discipline. (See Deuteronomy 17 and Hebrew 10:25.)

In Deuteronomy 18, God tells of the great Prophet, the Lord Jesus Christ. He alone knows the future. In this day, many are turning to fortune-tellers, mediums, people who call back the dead, and the black art of sorcery. If you want to know what God thinks about the modern seance, look up Isaiah 8:19-20; Leviticus 19:31; 20:6; and study the dark story in 1 Samuel 28 in the light of 1 Chronicles 10:13.

God showed the Israelis that their highest duty was to exhibit the spirit of loving obedience. They were to be thankful, yes, really thankful. They were to be full of joy and gladness. Why shouldn't they be joyful in the best land on earth and with such a loving God? Surely they ought to be glad and love their God with all their heart. But Moses' heart was burdened because he knew that Israel had a hard heart and the people were self-willed (31:24-29).

If we compare Deuteronomy 21:22-23 with John 19:31, we see why Christ was cursed as he hung between heaven and earth on the cross. In Galatians 3:10-13 we read that he was cursed because he was bearing our sin (see also 2 Corinthians 5:21). Notice the effect this had on Paul (2 Corinthians 5:14-15).

MOSES' THIRD ADDRESS: "LOOKING OUT"
DEUTERONOMY 27–33

We see Moses giving the people some solemn warnings. He first spoke of the blessings that the Israelis could enjoy if they would be obedient. He then told them the results of disobedience. Misfortune would follow them in everything they would under-take—in business, in farming, and in health. They would suffer for their disobedience to God (28:15-68).

Deuteronomy 28 is a most remarkable chapter! It traces what Israel might have been through obedience (ch. 1–14) and is yet to be in the millennial age to come. (See Isaiah 60–62; Zechariah 14:8-21; Jeremiah 31:1-9; Deuteronomy 30:1-10; Romans 11:25-31.)

God spoke this more than three thousand years ago, yet

Deuteronomy 28:63-67 describes Israel and the Jews as they are today:

1. "Scattered"—they will be scattered from one end of the earth to the other. Today the Jews are everywhere—there are German Jews, Russian Jews, Italian Jews, American Jews, etc. (v. 64).
2. "Restless"—no rest for the Jews in these countries (v. 65).
3. "Sorrowful"—think of the way the Jews have been treated in many countries (vv. 65-67). God foretold all this!

Moses spoke to Joshua, his personal attendant through the wilderness. Joshua was now eighty years old, and Moses committed to him the leadership of this great people! Read his words in Deuteronomy 31:7-8.

The charge that Moses gave to the people and to Joshua was built on one great fact: "The Lord is with you; be strong." If God is present, fear is baseless!

This grand old man, 120 years of age, stood as a witness to the grace of God. He sang a song for Israel (ch. 32). Moses had celebrated the deliverance of Israel from Egypt with a song (Exodus 15), and now he closed his life's work with another. He wrote a third, which we know as Psalm 90. Christians have always had a song! And in heaven throughout the ages everyone will sing!

After the song and final words of blessing, Moses climbed Pisgah Peak in Mount Nebo, and there God showed him the Promised Land toward which his face had so long been set. Moses never came back. He died there, and God buried his servant, though no one knows exactly where the grave is. God buries the workman but carries on the work. Why was Moses' grave hidden? No doubt it would have become the object of superstitious idolatry.

The horde of slaves made into a nation by Moses wept for him thirty days. Had it not been for their perversity they might still have had him with them.

We read of Moses again in the Gospels. One day Jesus took Peter, James, and John and climbed up Mount Hermon in the northern part of Palestine. Then Moses and Elijah appeared and talked with Jesus about his coming death (Matthew 17:1-3).

SELECTED BIBLE READING

Sunday: Forward March (Deuteronomy 1)
Monday: Instructions (Deuteronomy 5–6)
Tuesday: The Messiah-Prophet (Deuteronomy 18:15-22)
Wednesday: God's Covenant (Deuteronomy 30)
Thursday: The Song of Moses (Deuteronomy 32)
Friday: God's Blessings (Deuteronomy 33)
Saturday: The Death of Moses (Deuteronomy 34)

CHAPTER 7

UNDERSTANDING JOSHUA

Joshua Portrays Jesus Christ, Captain of Our Salvation

When we open the book of Joshua, we are beginning the second division of the Old Testament, the books of history. No book has more encouragement and wisdom for the soldier of the cross than Joshua. It is full of spiritual truth.

Joshua could be called the Book of Conquest or the Battlefield of the Canaan Heritage. This book relates the settlement of the Israelis in Canaan, proving God's faithfulness in keeping his promise with Abraham. What was the promise (Genesis 17:8)?

This book bears the name of Joshua, the hero of this great conquest. The name *Joshua* was originally *Hoshea*, meaning "salvation." Moses later changed it to *Jehoshua*, which means "The Lord's Salvation." Joshua is called the servant of Jehovah, one by whom God issued his orders and by whom he accomplished his purposes—God's prime minister.

This book goes on where Deuteronomy leaves off. It is a continuation of the history of the chosen people. The chosen people were led out of bondage by Moses and led into the Promised Land by Joshua. In this book, Israel not only overcame the enemy but occupied the land that God had promised them.

We see an anticipation in Deuteronomy:

Moses passed through the Red Sea.
Moses led Israel from bondage.
Moses gave a vision of faith.
Moses told of an inheritance.

We see realization in Joshua:

Joshua passed over Jordan.
Joshua led Israel into blessing.
Joshua led them into a life of faith.
Joshua led them into possession.

Joshua completed what Moses began! God never leaves his work unfinished. Remember, the great Craftsman always has another tool sharpened and ready for use. Service awaits everyone. You can always honor God best by taking up your task with a strong and resolute heart that trusts God.

"Moses is dead!" But the march must continue! God's voice was still speaking to Joshua. Yes, God's voice is still speaking today, and if we listen we will hear him speak to us.

"Moses is dead!" But no man is indispensable to the God of heaven. The greatest that ever lived is only a servant, and when he completes his task God has another to follow in his train.

To destroy slavery was the great motive that nerved Livingstone to his heroic life in Africa. For thirty years he toiled, pushing his way through the jungles, over thirty thousand miles, to give Christ to the people there and attempting to discover the source of the Nile. He thought this would give him greater influence when he would plead at home for the cause of the African slaves. But others discovered the source of the Nile; others freed the slaves. He died alone with God in the wild African forests. But his heroic Christian death touched the hearts of his countrymen as not even his life had done, and Christian Britain determined to finish his work and free the African slaves.

So it is in all our work in the world, especially in our Christian service. We are just a part in a mighty whole. Do your little part and do not care if it is not singled out in the completed whole. The waters of the brook are lost in the river.

God had been getting Joshua ready for years. He was born in slavery in Egypt, but God led him out and made him a co-laborer with Moses. He was always a valiant captain. He was the one that was almost stoned to death because he urged the Israelis to advance to Canaan forty years before (Numbers 14:6-10).

For all you know, God may have set his heart to appoint you a captain of his army or to make you a standard-bearer in the legion of his cross. Are you getting ready?

Remember as we study Joshua that God gives—man takes

(Deuteronomy 1:11). This book deals with overcoming the enemy and occupying the land. God says, "Take it all."

This book seems to fall into two great parts. If you can only remember this much of an outline, you will remember the most important things:

1. Conquest of the Promised Land (ch. 1–12)
2. Occupation of the Promised Land (ch. 13–24)

MOBILIZATION OF THE ARMY
JOSHUA 1–2

Open your Bible to the text. We find the Israelis right on the border of the land, as given in Joshua 1:4—wilderness on the south, Lebanon mountains on the north, Euphrates River on the east, Mediterranean on the west.

Joshua was the leader of the Israelis now, for Moses had died! Joshua stood with a bowed head and a lonely heart, for his wise counselor and friend was gone. But God said to him, *I will not abandon you or fail to help you. . . . Be bold and strong! Banish fear and doubt! For remember, the Lord your God is with you wherever you go. Now that my disciple is dead . . . lead my people across the Jordan River and into the Promised Land* (1:5, 9, 2).

Moses had to die before the Israelis could go into Canaan. Moses could not even enter Canaan himself, to say nothing of bringing anyone else in. Israel had to wait until Moses was out of the way. To the Christian, Moses represents the law. Joshua represents Christ. Christ alone can lead us into the inheritance that is ours. Paul says, *Salvation is not a reward for the good we have done, so none of us can take any credit for it* (Ephesians 2:9). Oh, that all Christians would simply lean on their faithful Joshua and follow him only! Christ wants to lead us into what he has purchased on the cross for us. It takes Moses and Joshua together to symbolically present to us the finished work of Christ.

We see an anxious crowd of people all waiting to enter the land they had so long been promised. Can you picture the row on row of tents and all the people wondering when Joshua would say, "Go"? Joshua sent men through the camp to tell them that in three days they would cross the Jordan and to be prepared for the journey (1:10-11).

God called Joshua to lead the Israelis into the Promised Land.

We have the words that must have come to him in answer to a prayer for help in his great undertaking. *I will not abandon you or fail to help you* (1:5). These words are just as true for us.

God says some very important things in this passage:

1. Set your foot down. *I say to you what I said to Moses: "Wherever you go will be part of the land of Israel"* (1:3).
2. Take it all. *All the way from Negeb desert in the south to the Lebanon mountains in the north, and from the Mediterranean Sea in the west to the Euphrates River in the east, including all the land of the Hittites* (1:4). Not until Solomon's day, some five hundred years later, was this fully realized (2 Chronicles 9:26), but it was coming all the time.
3. Be on the move. *Now that my disciple is dead . . . lead my people across the Jordan* (1:2).
4. Take the sword. *Constantly remind the people about these laws* (1:8). (See Ephesians 6:17.)

The law was Joshua's Bible. Our Bible is far more complete, and we know more about God's will because Christ has interpreted it for us. Do we meditate upon the Word? Read God's words to Joshua (1:7).

Joshua called the officers together and gave them detailed directions. *To this they fully agreed, and pledged themselves to obey Joshua as their commander in chief* (1:16). They were ready for any service.

We see both Joshua and the people prepared for the journey. Remember, Joshua had been one of the twelve spies who had been sent to Canaan forty years before. Now he sends two scouts to bring a report of the land. Read the story of Rahab and the spies in Joshua 2.

Joshua asked them especially to find out the strength of Jericho, for this was the first stronghold they would attack after crossing the river. The spies aroused suspicion but were saved from death by Rahab, who hid them under flax that was spread on the roof of her house. The spies learned from Rahab that all the city was in terror of the Israelis and they promised that they would spare her and her household when the city was taken. Rahab let them down over the city wall in which her house was built, and they returned to tell Joshua the good news that *all the people over there are scared to death of us* (2:24).

Rahab hung a scarlet cord out of her window so that her house would be marked and spared when the city was destroyed. We find this woman's name in the genealogy of Jesus (Matthew 1:5).

The Canaanites, the people of the land, were the descendants of Canaan, the son of Ham. They were wicked and idolatrous. God had warned them in the destruction of Sodom and Gomorrah, but they had not changed a bit. Now God was going to destroy their power and give their land to the Israelis.

FORWARD MARCH
JOSHUA 3–5

Read through these chapters. Encouraged by the report the spies had brought, the Israelis moved from their camp at Shittim, six miles from the Jordan, to a spot near the swollen stream. At dawn the officers passed through the camp and ordered all to watch the Ark and follow it at a distance of about a half mile, *for you have never before been where we are going now* (3:4). The great leader, Joshua, instructed the people to sanctify themselves, for the next day the Lord would do a great miracle among them (3:5).

The Israelis had followed the cloud in the wilderness. Now they would follow the Ark of the Covenant, which represented the presence of God.

The long journey in the desert was over, and the mystery of an unknown country and an unknown life lay before them. The people grew serious with the impressiveness of a new experience. Life is always opening new and unexpected things to us. There is no monotony in the life of a Christian.

At the beginning of the exodus from Egypt there was a crossing of the Red Sea. Now at the close of Exodus there is a crossing of the Jordan River. Both were most memorable events in the history of the Israelis.

It was the time of the overflow of the Jordan, and the people of Jericho must have thought it impossible for the Israelis to cross or they would have been there to oppose them. There were no bridges and only a few fords, and these were not passable at this season of the year. The spies had crossed and recrossed by swimming, no doubt. But how could a great host cross with women and children and baggage?

God had a way. He gave the directions for the people to follow. Martin Luther said, "I know not the way he [Christ] leads me, but well do I know my Guide."

Remember how Christ told the man with the withered arm to do what he could not do—yes, to stretch it forth? The man made an attempt to do the impossible, and Christ made it possible. The way to stretch forth the palsied arm was to stretch it forth. The way to cross the Jordan was to cross it. Joshua told the priests to take up the Ark and step into the Jordan, when the river was overflowing all its banks. When the soles of their feet touched the waters of the Jordan, they stood on dry ground. And all Israel passed over on dry ground (3:9-17). With man this is impossible, but with God all things are possible. God is always doing the impossible. God's biddings are his enablings.

A man once said, "If God tells me to jump through a stone wall, it would be my duty to jump; it would be God's duty to remove the wall!"

What was the Ark? It was the symbol of God's presence. And Christ is the reality of God's presence. He says, *I am with you always* (Matthew 28:20).

He goes before us and says, "Follow me," and he sends his Holy Spirit to whisper in our ear and say, "This is the way, walk in it." The living Ark of the Covenant, Jesus, is still our guide. He will guide us in the little as well as the great things of life. Yes, *the steps of good men are directed by the Lord* (Psalm 37:23).

The Bible tells us of the crossing of the river. From the river-bed, *the place where the priests are standing,* the stones were taken and piled up on the other shore as a lasting memorial of the miracle God did for them (4:3). No formal prayer was recorded, but memorial stones were set up. The people wanted to perpetuate the memory of their great Deliverer.

THE FALL OF JERICHO
JOSHUA 6

Jericho was not far from the Jordan and was about a short twenty-minute walk from the camp at Gilgal. The author has stood on the site of the city of Joshua's conquest whose massive walls have been unearthed. The modern Jericho, or Ericha, as the village is called, is a mile away from the ancient stronghold, which was destroyed and rebuilt in the reign of Ahab.

A man, passing by a building that was being torn down, stopped to look at the laborer who was pulling away on a rope fastened to the top of the wall.

"Do you think that you are going to pull that thick wall down that way?" he finally asked in amazement.

Between his tugs the man answered, "It doesn't look that way to me, but I guess the boss knows what he's about."

And the boss did know, for the wall had been undermined, and after an hour of tug after tug the great wall vibrated, swayed, and fell down flat.

The walls of Jericho had to come down so that the Israelis could proceed to conquer the Promised Land, for Jericho was the key to southern Canaan. How could this be brought about? To the Israelis, God's directions seemed strange, but like that laborer they kept steadily at the part assigned them. They were confident that their Leader knew what they did not, and that they would soon enter the city. What was their task? Read Joshua 6.

The procession of priests, Ark, men, and trumpets that marched around the city daily were the only visible means for its capture. How futile must such a march have seemed to the people of Jericho, yes, and to the Israelis themselves. But God knew what he would do.

Some have tried to explain a scientific basis of the fall of the walls of Jericho to show that this event was not a miracle: a certain vibration would destroy the wall. When it was struck by the sound of the trumpet and shout, the wall fell before the Israelis.

Whether this is the case or not, the miracle remains that the wall fell as God had said it would (6:2-5). God accomplished the destruction with or without "scientific" means. The glory was the Lord's, not Joshua's. When the people obeyed the command of the Lord given by Joshua, they saw God's power.

The fall of Jericho before the blast of Joshua's rams' horns was a miracle so stupendous that the rationalist cannot discredit it. The Israelis believed that they were following God's plan. The seven trumpets, leading a procession seven days, and seven times on the seventh day, showed the Israelis that this was Jehovah's plan of conquest as directly as a country's flag informs people today that the property over which it waves is under the protection of that country. God put an invisible band around the foundation of that city wall and tightened it, and when God does that to the foundation of any structure, national or per-sonal—beware!

It is not hard work that is needed; it is the lack of vision that makes us fail. It is easy to blow a trumpet, a little thing to walk around a wall. The hard thing is to see the good in it. Say, "Lord, one step is enough for me."

No one wants long delays. We love to see things happen. If there must be six days of weary traveling around the walls, the seventh day will come when the walls will fall. God gives us victories through ways that seem utterly foolish to us. (See 1 Corinthians 1:17-29.)

CAMPAIGN AT AI
JOSHUA 7-8

The capture of Jericho gave the Israelis a chance to enter central Canaan. The next place strategically important was Ai, which commanded the entrance into the valley leading into western Canaan.

As he had done in the case of Jericho, Joshua sent spies to Ai to learn the situation. Made overconfident by their recent success, they gave poor counsel on their return, saying, *It's a small city and it won't take more than two or three thousand of us to destroy it; there's no point in all of us going there* (7:3). The small force was sent up the steep ascent, but when the garrison at Ai sallied forth and attacked them, the Israelis fled without striking a blow. In the disaster they all saw the withdrawal of God's guiding hand. They soon learned that they could not trust in their own strength alone. *Not by might, nor by power, but by my Spirit, says the Lord Almighty* (Zechariah 4:6).

One man's sin caused Israel's defeat. (Israel had become a nation and no one could act alone.) Achan had hidden a bar of gold and other forbidden loot. Read the story in Joshua 7. Beware of the bar of gold (7:13)! Achan alone was guilty, yet we read: *Israel has sinned and disobeyed my commandment and has taken loot when I said it was not to be taken; and they have not only taken it, they have lied about it and have hidden it among their belongings* (7:11).

No one's sins affect himself alone. None of us lives to himself. One stricken with chicken pox can infect an entire schoolroom. A few influenza germs can infect a whole nation. The sin of one becomes the sin of the community.

Every sin you commit will hunt you down, find you out, and make you pay. Know this: There has never been one sin committed on this earth for which the man who committed it did not suffer. You may escape the law of man. You cannot escape the law of God.

CENTRAL CAMPAIGN
JOSHUA 10

The Israelis went out a second time to Ai. This time they were victors. The taking of Ai shows real military strategy. In working for the Lord there must always be a recognition of the value of the best in human reason, but strategy without obedience is worth nothing. Dwight L. Moody said, "Work as if everything depended upon you, and pray as if everything depended upon God."

The fame of Israel began to spread far and wide. The kings of Canaan formed a league against the oncoming army. But we read of the treaty with the Gibeonites who played a trick on the Israelis. As a result Joshua condemned the Gibeonites to become *servants . . . chopping their wood and carrying their water* (9:21).

Then Joshua routed the allied army. Read about the hailstorm and the prolonged daylight that God sent to help his warrior (10:7-14). *Let the sun stand still over Gibeon* (10:12). Ordinary things come to a standstill when God's work is on.

NORTHERN CAMPAIGN
JOSHUA 11

After all of central and southern Canaan was in Israel's possession, a new confederacy had to be faced and conquered. The northern kings had joined together and tried to break the power of the conquering Israelis. But in divine strength Joshua routed them all. This did not all happen at once. The Bible says that it took a long time, but at last the land rested from war (11:23).

Jerusalem is so named here for the first time in the Bible. To think that since then it has become possibly the most famous place in the world! It is a city with a great past history and a bright future history. Here Christ will reign when he comes again in power and great glory (Luke 21:27).

We see God judging these wicked people, the Canaanites. Until recently it was supposed that Canaan was at this time a country of semi-barbarians. Now we know that as early as 2500 B.C. Canaan was subject to Mesopotamian rulers, whose language and civilization had been adopted there. Next came Egyptian domination, and we know the high culture of Egypt. Many of the Tell-el-Amarna tablets, dating 1350 B.C.—just after the conquest of Canaan by the Israelis—are letters to the Pharaoh of Egypt, written in the Babylonian language by tributary princes in Canaan. "At that period Canaan had already behind it a long civilized past. The country was filled with schools and libraries, with richly furnished palaces, and workshops of artisans. The cities in the coast had their fleets, partly of merchantmen, partly of warships, and an active trade was carried on with all parts of the known world."

DIVISION OF THE LAND
JOSHUA 13-24

Joshua was an old man now, about ninety years of age, and he realized that the conquest of the land was by no means complete. There yet remained many nations to be conquered. In order that the Israelis might occupy the area, he divided it among them.

"This is Judah's, this is Asher's, this is Simeon's, and this is Benjamin's," we hear the people saying as the scene opens. They said this even while the Amorites, the Jebusites, and the Hittites were in open possession of the Promised Land (ch. 13). The division made of the land was the announcement on faith of certain things that under God's guidance they proposed to realize by the long struggle that would follow.

Alas for the dull-eyed persons whose aspirations never get a foot in advance of their present achievements! Unless we keep a vision before us and dream dreams, we will never win either materially or spiritually. This is just what the Israelis did. They reached out into a hoped-for but unknown future when they divided up great stretches of country that were still in the hands of their enemies!

Though all this land was allotted to the various tribes, it was not all conquered until the time of David. All that was subdued at this time was the mountainous land; the cities and the plains were hardly touched.

The strong did not take the best part of the land because they were strong, leaving the fragments for the weak. Neither did the rich purchase the choicest spots, leaving the poor with more undesirable sites. They tried to determine God's will in the matter. God cares about distribution of goods.

Do you see any application of this principle today? God cares about the inequalities of condition of his children. He cares that the weak are thrust aside by the shrewd and strong. There is a will of God concerning all the questions of hours and wages, capital and labor. God is concerned about a more equal division of his blessings in this world. When he rules, *everyone will live quietly in his own home in peace and prosperity* (Micah 4:4).

When the assignment was made by lot, no one could be jealous. They met before the Ark of Jehovah, the symbol of his presence.

The Levites were given no land at all (14:3). You remember that this tribe was set apart for the sacred service of the priesthood.

CALEB'S PORTION
JOSHUA 14

Caleb now was eighty-five years old! Joshua and he were alone among the spies because they had dared to trust God! How many spies did Moses send into Canaan? How many of their names do you remember? No doubt these two are the only ones. Two trusted God, and these are the only names we know. As a reward for obedience, these were the only ones in their generation who were permitted to enter Canaan.

Caleb asked his friend Joshua for the high and walled cities! He added, *If the Lord is with me I shall drive them out of the land* (14:12). He valued his inheritance because of the hard work it offered and the opportunity it gave him for conquering it! Joshua's recognition of his friend and of his right to a choice possession was quick and generous. He granted him the mountain and blessed his aged friend.

Caleb was old, but he gloried in the hardness of the task. One of Helen Keller's teachers said she was the happiest person she had ever met even though she was deaf and blind. Her teacher attributed it to her having overcome so much. Caleb was the happiest man in the camp because he had overcome so much and yet had fields to conquer! Horace Mann said, "Difficulties are things which show what men are."

The Lord has never promised his children that they will have an easy time serving him. In fact, Christ said, *Here on earth you will have many trials and sorrows* (John 16:33). The promise is not for ease; the promise is for victory. Christ says, *I have overcome the world.* We grow in adversity, for we learn to trust the Lord more. Paul said to Timothy, *Take your share of suffering as a good soldier of Jesus Christ* (2 Timothy 2:3).

"General Booth, tell me what has been the secret of your success all the way through," begged a friend of the head of the Salvation Army. Slowly General Booth replied, "I will tell you the secret. God has had all there was of me."

Caleb said, *I followed the Lord* (14:8).

We might call attention to the fact that the cities of refuge that God planned, spoken of in Numbers 35 and Deuteronomy 19, were now set apart.

JOSHUA'S FAREWELL
JOSHUA 24

Joshua had become an old man. He knew that he could not live much longer. He wanted to give the people some last words of admonition.

He called first the leaders and then all the people together and urged them to remember the power and faithfulness of God and admonished them to be faithful to him. *So revere Jehovah and serve him* (24:14). He warned them against apostasy. He said, *Decide today whom you will obey. Will it be the gods of your ancestors beyond the Euphrates or the gods of the Amorites here in this land?* Then he added, *But as for me and my family, we will serve the Lord* (24:15).

It is a good thing to have people make an open confession and commit themselves to a solemn promise. These older men who had made an open confession were true to their promises. The people said that day, *We choose the Lord!*

At 110 years of age the grand old man, Joshua, died. The book closes with death. We see three graves, those of Joshua, the great leader of Israel; Eleazer, the priest; and Joseph, whose bones the Israelis had carried with them from Egypt and which were now buried in the land of promise.

Here is a great tribute to a great leader. *Israel obeyed the Lord throughout the lifetimes of Joshua and the other old men who had personally witnessed the amazing deeds the Lord had done for Israel* (24:31).

Canaan, or the promised land, was one hundred eighty miles long and approximately forty miles wide. It was in the center of mighty civilizations that made ancient history:

Egypt—300 miles south
Nineveh—700 miles northeast
Babylon—700 miles east
Persia—1,000 miles east
Greece—800 miles northwest
Rome—1,500 miles northwest

Do not pray for an easy task. Pray to be stronger!
The greatness of a man's power is the measure of his surrender. It is not a question of who you are or of what you are, but whether God controls you. "I followed the Lord," said Caleb. Are you following the Lord?
Be sure—be sure—be sure your sin will find you out.
Facts do not change; feelings do.
It is not enough to light a fire; you must put fuel on it.

SELECTED BIBLE READING

Sunday: Joshua's Commission (Joshua 1–2)
Monday: Crossing the Jordan (Joshua 3)
Tuesday: The Fall of Jericho (Joshua 6)
Wednesday: The Sin of Achan (Joshua 7)
Thursday: Occupation of the Land (Joshua 11)
Friday: Caleb's Possession (Joshua 14)
Saturday: Joshua's Farewell (Joshua 24)

UNDERSTANDING JUDGES AND RUTH

Judges Portrays Jesus Christ, Our Deliverer-Judge
Ruth Portrays Jesus Christ, Our Kinsman-Redeemer

Someone has called the book of Judges the account of the Dark Ages of the Israeli people. The people abandoned God (2:13), but God did not abandon the people (2:16).

Judges covers the period after the death of their great leader, Joshua, to the ascension of Saul to the throne of Israel. The oppressed people were ruled by judges whom God raised up to deliver them. We read, *For in those days Israel had no king* (17:6).

It was a new hour in the history of Israel. Remember, the Israelis had come from a long era of bondage in Egypt to a period of forty years when they lived in tents and wandered in the wilderness. Now the march was over. The nomads were to become settlers in a land of their own. The change was not as easy for them as they expected it to be. The book of Judges is in a way another book of beginnings where we see a new nation adjusting her national life. It is filled with struggle and disasters, but the moral courage of the people grew.

There is a decided monotony in the description of each successive stage of sin in Israel, but there is an equally remarkable variety in the instruments and methods of deliverance that God used. There is something different in the story of each judge.

There are fourteen judges—Othniel, Ehud, Shamgar, Deborah, Gideon, Tola, Jair, Jephthah, Ibzan, Elon, Abdon, Samson, Eli, and Samuel. (Abimelech, a petty ruler, was not called of God to judge.)

There were three types of judges:

1. The warrior-judge, such as Gideon and Samson
2. The priest-judge, such as Eli
3. The prophet-judge, such as Samuel

The chief judges were Deborah, Gideon, Samson, and Samuel.

Just how long these judges ruled we do not know, but it is believed about three hundred fifty years. No doubt the judges were not just one governor after another. They were probably raised up as deliverers on different occasions in different parts of the land, and the times of their rule could have been overlapped.

There is a phrase that sums up the last five chapters of the book: *Everyone did whatever seemed right in his own eyes* (17:6). We find the people falling away from God and worshiping the gods of the nations around them (2:13). They forgot that God had chosen them for a purpose—to tell the world the truth that there is but one true God. In punishment for their sins God would deliver them into the hand of another nation. Then under the oppression of these new enemies they would cry to God for mercy and he would hear them and send a judge to deliver them. And so the book is full of rebellion, punishment, misery, and deliverance. It has a minor key throughout.

The book begins with compromise and ends with confusion. This is what happens in every unsurrendered life!

One thing we learn in the book of Judges is that people who spend much of their time in disobedience to God make little progress during their lifetime. The book of Numbers recounts the forty years of wandering in the wilderness, but this book repeats again and again a record of departure from God.

The book of Judges is in sharpest contrast to Joshua.

In Joshua	In Judges
Joy	Sobs
Heavenly vision	Earthly emphasis
Victory	Defeat
Progress	Declension
Faith	Unbelief
Freedom	Servitude

Read the book of Judges through this week. It can be done in an hour or two. But learning just the great facts of the Bible, as necessary as this is, will never satisfy the Christian and make him a real blessing to others. We must know what God is teaching us.

Study carefully the following:

1. The wickedness of the human heart (2:11-13, 17, 19; 8:33-35; 10:6; 13:1).
2. God's delight in using the weak things (1 Corinthians 1:26-29). Note the stories of Ehud, an assassin with a home-made dagger (3:7-11); Deborah, a woman (ch. 4–5; see also 9:53); Gideon, from an obscure family in the smallest tribe (ch. 6) and his little pitcher-armed band (ch. 7); Shamgar, a rustic with an ox goad (3:31); Samson and his jawbone (15:14-19).
3. The Holy Spirit in Judges. Othniel—*The Spirit of the Lord took control of him* (3:10). Gideon—*The Spirit of the Lord came upon Gideon* (6:34). Jephthah—*The Spirit of the Lord came upon Jephthah* (11:29). Samson—*The Spirit of the Lord began to excite him* (13:25; see also 14:6; 15:14, etc.).

Over the book of Judges as a guide to its spiritual interpretation might be written Zechariah's great words, *Not by might, nor by power, but by my Spirit, says the Lord Almighty* (Zechariah 4:6).

Some critics of the Bible would have the history of God's chosen people start here in these dark days of the judges as a wild, lawless, nomadic people, developing finally into a higher civilization. Just because Israel failed to keep God's law does not mean there was no law. Just as today, because the people of this world disregard the Ten Commandments and put aside the teachings of Christ, it does not prove that these words were never spoken. People would love to believe that man's trend is upward. But God's Word shows us that the natural course is downward.

ISRAEL'S FAILURE
JUDGES 1:1–3:4

Joshua had died (1:1). Much of the Promised Land remained to be conquered. The first act of the Israelis was to seek God's will as to how they should commence the final conquest. They began well. They consulted God.

God appointed Judah, the kingly tribe (1:2). The work began in earnest but it ended in weakness. The people did not obey God.

The Israelis' troubles were due directly to their disobedience to God. They did not exterminate the enemies in the land but rather worshiped the idols of the people and became corrupted in their morals.

The Israelis went into the land and settled where they wanted and began to raise enough for their living. Soon an enemy would come along, catch the tribe off guard, and take the people captive. Their enemies were "fifth columnists" within. God had told his people to do away with them.

Chapter 1 is a failure chapter. They did not drive out the enemy as God had commanded. It is a record of a series of disobediences. So of course chapter 2 is a chapter of defeat and failure. God gave them up to their own will. God said, *Make no peace treaties with the people living in this land; I told you to destroy their heathen altars. Why have you not obeyed? . . . Rather, they shall be thorns in your sides* (2:2-3). The Israelis brought on their own judgment and became their own executioners. Several times Israel was on the verge of being exterminated, but thankfully God intervened.

Sometimes we wonder why God didn't remove all the enemies from the Promised Land before he let the Israelis go in. But God had a definite reason (3:1-4).

God uses the results of our lack of faith in him to prove to us our sin and weakness. He does not forget his covenant (no merit of ours), and he allows our very weakness, our guilty weakness, to drive us back to him.

God wanted the chosen people to realize that they were a holy people. They were not to mix with the wicked nations about them. They were to continually separate themselves. God knew that separation makes men strong. Christians today must remember that they cannot mix with the world. They must keep close to God and war against sin and unrighteousness. God wants us to be good warriors. Read Ephesians 6:10-18 and see the armor he provides.

And so we see that a false toleration toward a people so utterly corrupt resulted in the undoing of God's chosen people. See the result of this disobedience (2:20-22).

THE JUDGES
JUDGES 3:5–16:31

Here we have a picture of seven failures, seven servitudes, and seven deliverances. The Israelis intermarried with the heathen, worshiped at their shrines, and practiced their vices.

First Oppression (3:7-11)
SIN—Idolatry
PUNISHMENT—Eight years
DELIVERER-JUDGE—Othniel

Second Oppression (3:12-31)
SIN—Immorality and idolatry
PUNISHMENT—Eighteen years
DELIVERER-JUDGES—Ehud and Shamgar

Third Oppression (ch. 4–5)
SIN—Departed from God
PUNISHMENT—Twenty years
DELIVERER-JUDGES—Deborah and Barak

Fourth Oppression (6:1–8:32)
SIN—Departed from God
PUNISHMENT—Midianites, seven years
DELIVERER-JUDGE—Gideon

Fifth Oppression (8:33–10:5)
SIN—Departed from God
PUNISHMENT—Civil war, etc.
DELIVERER-JUDGES—Tola and Jair

Sixth Oppression (10:6–12:15)
SIN—Idolatry increased
PUNISHMENT—Philistines and Ammonites, eighteen years
DELIVERER-JUDGES—Jephthah and successors

Seventh Oppression (ch. 13–16)
SIN—Departed from God
PUNISHMENT—Philistines, forty years
DELIVERER-JUDGE—Samson

Joshua had no successor. After his death, each tribe acted independently. There was no capital and no fixed government.

There was no unity of action, except in the time of danger when the tribes combined for their own good. When the people sinned against God, their enemies defeated them and ruled them. When in their distress they sought the Lord, he sent great leaders called judges who delivered them.

But this scene is not only filled with servitude, it also records deliverances, for God was always near his people, and when they cried, he answered. God is always brooding over his disobedient children. He promises us that he will never leave us nor forsake us. We see defeat on man's part but deliverance on God's part. *The more we see our sinfulness, the more we see God's abounding grace forgiving us* (Romans 5:20).

We see his dealings with his own rebellious people whom he has crowned with his best blessings and on whom he has lavished his tender love. We find the patience of God and his constant readiness to respond to the least sign of penitence in his people (3:9, 15; 4:3-7; 6:6-12; 10:15-16).

He repeated his mercy again and again, although it was never appreciated. If you think on these things it will draw you nearer to this God of mercy and love and grace. Look up, repent, and trust God.

We have found that God fulfilled his purpose for Israel by leaving around them in Canaan a circle of strong tribes unlike each other. One of the best known nations was the Philistines who settled on the coastal plain. They were a maritime people, sea rovers and pirates, ready for any fray that promised land and gain. In wealth and civilization they no doubt presented a real contrast to the Israelis, and their equipment gave them great advantage in war. Even in the period of the judges there were imposing temples in the Philistines cities. The Hebrews feared the Philistines and did not mix freely with them. They only met in war.

FIRST APOSTASY
JUDGES 3:7-11

We find the Israelis settling among the Syrian nations. They seemed too ready to live at peace with these other nations and to yield whatever was necessary for the sake of peace. (Read the few verses 3:5-8 to see what they did.) They intermarried to make their position safer. They traded with the Amorites, Hivites, and

Perizzites. They determined on boundary lines to make things run smoothly. Next they accepted their neighbors' religion (3:7) and then their bad customs.

But soon the Mesopotamians began to oppress them (3:8). The Israelis then realized that they had a God from whom they had departed. Israel was a prodigal people. They had left the God whose presence before had assured them victory. For eight years they were under the oppression of these northern nations. Year by year conditions grew worse.

It was from the far south that God sent help in answer to their pitiful cry (3:9). The deliverer was Othniel, Caleb's nephew. No doubt he had had frequent skirmishes with the Arab marauders from the wilderness. *The Spirit of the Lord took control of him and he . . . led the forces of Israel* (3:10). First he prayed, then he went out to battle. When we see an army bow in prayer, we can have faith in their spirit and courage, for they are feeling their dependence on God!

Of first concern to Othniel was to get rid of the idolatry of Israel, teach them the law of the Lord, and remind them of their calling as a nation. Soon success and victory were theirs (3:10-11).

Othniel, the first of the judges, was one of the best. He pointed Israel to a higher level of reverence for God and his plans. Forty years of rest followed.

No man can do real service for his country who does not fear God and love righteousness more than country.

SECOND APOSTASY
JUDGES 3:12-31

God used different kinds of men to deliver his people. Israel's second judge, Ehud, was in marked contrast to Othniel, the judge without reproach.

The long peace that the country enjoyed after the Mesopotamian army had been driven out let the people fall into prosperity and to lapse again into spiritual weakness (3:12). This time the Moabites led the attack. The punishment lasted for eighteen years. Again the people cried to God, and Ehud, with whom Shamgar's name is associated, was the deliverer (3:15). This Benjamite chose his own method of action and assassinated the Moabite king. His crime is one that stinks in our nostrils. But eighty years of rest for Israel followed (3:30).

Shamgar, the man of the ox goad, follows in line (3:31).

THIRD APOSTASY
JUDGES 4-5

Next a prophetess arose in Israel (4:4). She was a rare woman whose heart burned with enthusiasm when men's hearts were despondent. Many a queen has reigned with honor and wisdom, and many a woman's voice has struck a deep note that has roused nations.

Israel had been oppressed for twenty years (4:3). The oppression was terrible under Sisera. Again they cried and God heard. This time the story of deliverance is filled with romance and song. Deborah, the daughter of the people, had gained the confidence of the people to such a degree that they had appointed her as judge.

Deborah called Barak to help her. Together they delivered Israel from oppression. The land had been so filled with Canaanite spoilers that the highways could not be used. War was everywhere, and the Israelis were defenseless and crushed, but God delivered them.

After Jabin, king of Canaan, was defeated and his nine hundred chariots turned into plowshares, we might expect that Israel would at last make a real start to accomplish her true career. The tribes had learned their third lesson and should have known by now the danger of leaving God. Without God they were as weak as babies. Would they not now bend themselves to him? Not yet. Not for more than forty years. The true reformer had not yet come. Deborah's work was not in vain. She was destroying the heathen altars and improving the land. Everywhere they were plowing new ground, building houses, repairing roads. But they were falling into the old habit of friendly association with the Canaanites.

Following deliverance from this servitude the land rested for forty years.

FOURTH APOSTASY
JUDGES 6:1-8:32

But a fourth apostasy came (6:1). This time the deliverer was Gideon, a humble farmer. The Midianites had held the Israelis under bondage for seven years. So terrible was it that the people hid themselves in caves and dens and were hunted in the mountains (6:2). Again they cried to the Lord. Gideon was called to act as deliverer. He broke down the altar of Baal and restored the worship of God. The story of the conflict is one of the most fascinating in history. Refresh yourself with the story of Gideon and his band of 300 with their pitchers and horns (7:7-24).

After the great victory over the Midianites, the Israelis sought to make Gideon king. He refused. Gideon was not perfect. We find in the record some things that he should not have done, but he did have faith that God could honor, and God gave his name a place in the Hall of Faith in Hebrews 11.

FIFTH APOSTASY
JUDGES 8:33–10:5

A fifth time we see the people falling into the sin of idolatry by worshiping the Baalim almost immediately after the death of Gideon. The record is: *As soon as Gideon was dead . . . they no longer considered the Lord as their God* (8:33). How often the personal influence of the hero is everything while he is alive but confusion follows on his death.

Gideon was one of the most successful judges to maintain order, and *the land was at peace for forty years.* But no sooner was Gideon's funeral over than discord began. There was no rightful ruler to follow. Gideon left many sons, but not one of them could take his place. Abimelech, a son of Gideon, unprincipled and brutal, secured the allegiance of the men at Shechem and usurped the position of king. He ruled three years in tyranny. He was slain by a woman, and a period of forty-five years of peace followed under the judgeships of Tola and Jair.

SIXTH APOSTASY
JUDGES 10:6–12:15

In the sixth apostasy we find the people almost entirely given over to idolatry. Their condition was appalling. God sent judgment this time from the Philistines for eighteen years. At last, sorely distressed, they cried to God. For the first time it is recorded that God refused to hear them and reminded them of how repeatedly he had delivered them (10:13). The true attitude of God toward them is found in this statement—*And he was grieved by their misery* (10:16).

Deliverance came through Jephthah. The Hebrews have always produced men of passionate religious fervor. The Arabs of the present day are much the same. Forgetting fear, they can be excited to a "holy war" in which thousands perish. Jephthah was both fierce and generous. He rose to great faith, then sank to earthly passions. We have the type in Deborah, David, Elijah, and Jephthah. Jephthah's history is full of interest. He was a man of heroic daring. Read the story of his vows and victories, especially the vow he made concerning his only child (11:30-40). After his great victory Jephthah judged Israel only six years.

SEVENTH APOSTASY
JUDGES 13–16

The seventh apostasy opens with the words, *Once again Israel sinned by worshiping other gods* (13:1). This time they were disciplined by the Philistines under whose awful oppression they lived for forty years. Here we read the story of Samson. It is a story filled with opportunity and failure. This man was appointed of God before birth to deliver Israel from the Philistines (13:5).

In those days everything was dependent upon physical strength. That was what made a leader great. In this case God used it to begin the deliverance from the Philistines. Everything should have been in Samson's favor, but he entered into an unholy alliance, which meant his downfall. The final fall occurred at Gaza (ch. 16). Nothing is more pathetic than Samson, blind and bound, grinding in the house of the Philistines, when he ought to have been delivering his nation from them (16:20-21).

The story ends with Samson and is taken up in 1 Samuel. The remaining chapters, and the book of Ruth, have their chronological place in this period.

THE APPENDIX
JUDGES 17–21

These last chapters give us a picture of anarchy and confusion. Israel had forsaken God, and now we see the depths into which they have sunk. Read Judges 17:6 and you will find the reason for it all:

1. Confusion in the religious life of the nation (17:18)
2. Confusion in the moral life of the nation (ch. 19)
3. Confusion in the political life of the nation (ch. 21)

The last chapter proves that the Israelis had lost the way to God's house, so low had they sunk. We find faithlessness, failure, and forfeiture! But God loves his own.

The biography of many a Christian in just the common run of life is like this. God opens doors and gives us grace for great tasks. Then we forget him and begin to have our interests in the world about us. This brings loss and defeat. But God hears our cry of repentance and restores us to favor again.

UNDERSTANDING RUTH

This delightful story should be read in connection with the first chapters of Judges as no doubt it gives us an idea of the domestic life of Israel during that period of anarchy. Samuel may have been the author of this book, but no one knows where or when it was written. This book, written on a separate scroll, was read at Pentecost, the harvest festival.

Ruth was the great-grandmother of David. This book establishes the lineage of David, the ancestor of Christ. It tells of the beginning of the messianic family within the messianic nation into which, over a thousand years later, the Messiah was to be born.

There are some interesting things to notice in this book. Ruth was a Moabitess. These heathen people were descendants of Lot. God, in establishing the family that was to produce the world's Savior, chose a beautiful heathen girl, led her to Bethlehem, and made her the bride of Boaz. This is God's grace. He adopts the Gentiles into Christ's family. Of course we know that although Ruth was born a heathen, through her first husband, or Naomi, she learned of the true God.

Boaz was the son of Rahab, the harlot found in Jericho (see Matthew 1:5). So we see that David's great-grandmother was a Moabitess and his great-grandfather was half Canaanite. This is found in the bloodline of the Messiah.

SELECTED BIBLE READING

Sunday: Only Partial Victories (Judges 1–2)
Monday: Institution of the Judges (Judges 3)
Tuesday: Deborah and Barak (Judges 4–5)
Wednesday: Gideon, the Farmer (Judges 6–7)
Thursday: Jephthah's Terrible Vow (Judges 11)
Friday: Samson, the Strong Man (Judges 15–16)
Saturday: The Story of Ruth (Book of Ruth)

CHAPTER 9

UNDERSTANDING FIRST SAMUEL

First Samuel Portrays Jesus Christ, Our King

We enter now our study of the king books. Let us look at the six before us:

First Samuel—Man's choice: Saul
Second Samuel—God's choice: David
First Kings—Solomon and Israel
Second Kings—Israel's kings
First Chronicles—Solomon and the Temple
Second Chronicles—The kings and the Temple

Royal history begins with the book of Samuel. The long period of the rule of the judges ends with Samuel. When Samuel came into power the people were in an awful state. They had practically rejected God, and we hear them clamoring for an earthly king (8:4-7). This book begins the five-hundred-year period of the kings of Israel (approximately 1050–586 B.C.).

The events recorded in 1 Samuel cover a period of about 115 years from the childhood of Samuel through the turbulent times of Saul to the beginning of the reign of the king whom God chose, David. In the personal lives of these three men this book gives us a graphic picture of these times. Samuel was the last of the judges; Saul was the first of the kings. The record brings us up to the time when David is ready permanently to establish the monarchy, and God is ready permanently to establish David's throne (Psalm 89).

The book may be divided under the names of three of its chief characters—Samuel (ch. 1–7), Saul (ch. 8–15), and David (ch. 16–31). The history of this book is presented to us in the attractive cloak of biography. Everyone likes a true story.

This book, of course, is named for its most prominent figure, Samuel. Probably he wrote the greater part of it through chapter 24. Nathan and Gad finished it (1 Chronicles 29:29; 1 Samuel 10:25).

SAMUEL, THE KING MAKER
1 SAMUEL 1–7

Samuel—"Name of God" is the meaning of his name. This book opens with the record of Hannah, Samuel's mother, praying for a son whom God could use. Samuel, the last of the judges, was God's answer to this prayer. *Samuel, though only a child, was the Lord's helper* (2:18).

Throughout Samuel's long and useful life he was God's man. He was preeminently a man of prayer. This first book that bears his name is a marvelous study in the place and power of prayer, illustrated from life. He was a child of prayer (3:1-19); he brought victory to his people through prayer (7:5-10); when the nation wanted a king, Samuel prayed to the Lord (8:6). Intercessory prayer was the keynote of his life (12:19-23).

It was in the dark and turbulent times of Israel that we hear the prayer of faith from the lips of a simple, trusting woman, Hannah. She asked God for a son whom she could dedicate to him for service (1:9-19).

When Samuel was born, Hannah brought him to the Tabernacle at Shiloh. Although the corruption of the priesthood was appalling, Samuel was protected and grew as a boy in the fear of the Lord (1:24-28; 2:12-26; 3:1-21).

Eli was both judge and priest at this time. He had ruled for forty years. He was an indulgent father, allowing his two sons, Hophni and Phinehas, also priests, to act in a most disgraceful manner. As a result there was moral corruption, and God warned Eli of the downfall of his house.

Fungus growth in a tree usually is not detected for a long time. Everything seems right outwardly, but when the crash suddenly comes, the state of the tree is seen. Israel had been sinning for a long time. At length the catastrophe came in the disaster recorded at this time (ch. 4).

During the next invasion of their enemies, the Philistines, Israel was defeated, the Ark was taken, and Eli's sons were killed. When Eli heard all this, the old man, now ninety-eight years of age, died of the shock.

Read the history of the Philistines' possession of the Ark. This mention of the Philistines is the first since Judges 13–16. The bondage lasted forty years (Judges 13:1), and seems to have come to a close in the days of Samuel (7:13-14), about his twentieth year as judge (7:2). The battle with this enemy probably was fought about four miles northwest of Jerusalem.

Perhaps this renewed action on the Philistines' part was due to the death of Samson. The battle soon went against Israel. They wondered why God had deserted them. While warring against God they asked God to war for them. Read the account of the revival at Mizpah (ch. 7).

We cannot win while we war against God! Apart from the immediate causes, rebellion against God is the root reason for tragic wars today. Civilization in general has not been seeking first and always the glory and will of God. The United States, as well as all other nations, has failed to meet this test. Civilized nations have failed, as they were bound to do, and they always will fail as long as God is left out.

Though this life is bound to be a fight, it may always be a winning fight if we enlist under the banner of the Captain of Our Salvation and make his will our will. *Overwhelming victory is ours through Christ* (Romans 8:37).

After Israel's first defeat by the Philistines, did they do right by looking to the Ark of God for protection (4:3-7, 10)?

The Ark of God was a very poor substitute for the God of the Ark. Many people think that when they wear religious symbols or perform religious rituals or give money to charitable causes that they will be safe. They think that these things are a charm, or talisman, to bring them victory. Only God himself brings victory.

"Man's extremity is God's opportunity!" Although at the time the loss was terrible, yet God overruled for good. Through Samuel God would provide (1) deliverance from the Philistines, (2) preparation for the kingdom, (3) a better priesthood.

As Samuel grew, the Lord was with him. . . . Then the Lord began to give messages to him there at the Tabernacle in Shiloh (3:19, 21). Shiloh was the location of the house of God from the days of Joshua to Samuel. David moved it to Jerusalem. The Ark was removed by the Philistines in Samuel's childhood and from then on Shiloh ceased to be of great importance (4:3, 11).

Under the Philistine rule Israel had no definite center of worship. Samuel grew into manhood and assumed the leadership for which he had been born. The first hopeful sign after Israel's long rebellion and defeat was that they had a sense of need. They began to want God. They *were in sorrow because the Lord had seemingly abandoned them.* God cannot do much for people who do not feel that they need anything. God pities them.

"Well," said Samuel, "if you really mean business, you've got to show me. Do something. Prove it." How? "Get rid of your strange gods." (See 7:3.) If you mean business, God will mean business. Religion is not just a matter of emotion but also of the will.

It is often easy for us to talk big, but it is another thing to live up to what we say. We often make promises to God that we never keep. How sad that sometimes our lives shout "Lie!" to what our lips say.

The people began to sorrow, and Samuel took advantage of this and called on them to return to their God and put away their idols. Samuel erected an altar and called it Ebenezer (7:12). *Ebenezer* means "stone of help." Christ our victory is called "the stone" in both the Old Testament and the New (Daniel 2:35; Matthew 21:42).

In just a brief paragraph we find the actual story of Samuel's judgeship. His home was at Ramah. From here he was a circuit rider covering his territory once a year to Bethel, Gilgal, and Mizpah, and overseeing and administering the affairs of the people (7:15-17).

Samuel established a school for the prophets, a kind of seminary, at his home in Ramah. This was the beginning of the "order" of the prophets, or seers. When the Ark was taken, the priests were scattered. This is when Samuel retired to his home in Ramah. Through Samuel, God introduced a new way of dealing with Israel. He called prophets through whom he would speak. It was with Samuel that prophecy became a definite part of the life of Israel. Samuel gathered groups about him called *sons of the prophets.* They were found in Shiloh, Gilgal, Bethel, Samaria, and Ramah.

Samuel's greatest ministry was the organization of the kingdom. The independent tribes were now going to be formed into a nation. In order to survive among other strong nations, Israel must become powerful. They had refused to take God seriously and obey him as he had commanded them, so he permitted Samuel to find a king for them. The people wanted to be "like all the other nations." God wanted them to be unlike the other nations. In Deuteronomy 17:14-20 God had prophesied that Israel would have a king, but he did not want them to become independent of him.

SAUL, THE KING CHOSEN
1 SAMUEL 8-15

God never intended Israel to have any king but himself. He would send them great leaders, and these in turn would receive their orders directly from him. But the Israelis in falling away had become restless. They wanted a king like the other surrounding nations. We find God granting their request. Here is a great lesson. We either can have God's best or his second best, his directive will or his permissive will.

Saul, their first king, was a failure. He was handsome to look at; he was tall and of a noble mien. He started out splendidly. He proved to be an able military leader. He defeated the enemies around him—the Philistines, the Amalekites, and the Ammonites.

Saul was humble at first, but we find him becoming proud and disobedient to God. No man had a greater opportunity than Saul, and no man ever was a greater failure. His jealousy of David bordered on insanity.

Inasmuch as Saul was granted to Israel as king in response to Israel's sinful demand for a king, contrary to God's will, did Saul ever really have a chance to "make good" in God's sight? Could he possibly have succeeded under such circumstances? Was he not condemned by God to failure even before he started as king?

We find the answer clearly in God's Word. In 1 Samuel 12:12-15 the prophet of God told Israel that, although they had demanded their king in defiance of God (v. 12), if both they and their king would fear Jehovah and worship him, all would be well. Note what follows this word of Samuel (vv. 16-18). Then we see the fact that Israel confessed her sin in asking for a king (v. 19), and Samuel reassured Israel, promising blessing if they would serve God.

The only reason that any soul is ever rejected by God is because that soul has first rejected God. God takes the initiative in love. *Our love for him comes as a result of his loving us first* (1 John 4:19). Man takes the initiative in sin (15:23).

Note that Saul's ordination was a:

1. Divine ordination (9:3-20). Saul went out with a bridle and came back with a scepter.
2. Prophetic ordination (10:1). Samuel was his tutor and friend. What an advantage, but it was thrown away!
3. Spiritual ordination. *The Spirit of God came upon him* (10:10). He *caused the Holy Spirit sorrow;* then he smothered him. If the Holy Spirit is to remain, he must be loved and obeyed.
4. Popular ordination. *And all the people shouted, "Long live the king!"* (10:24).

Saul failed God in several ways:

1. Presumption at God's altar (13:11-13)
2. Cruelty to his son Jonathan (14:44)
3. Disobedience in the matter of Amalek (15:23)
4. Jealousy and hatred of David (18:29)
5. Sinful appeal to the witch of Endor (28:7)

Saul waged six campaigns:

1. Against the Ammonites: Beginning of reign; against insurmountable obstacles; army mobilized with great haste; Ammonites completely ruined; Saul's prestige as king strengthened.
2. Against the Philistines: Saul's sin in assuming function of priest; God's rejection of Saul; bravery of Jonathan and single companion created panic among Philistines; enemy routed.
3. Against the Amalekites: Saul drove enemy into desert; marred success by disobedience; seized valuable property; lied to Samuel; prophet repeated that God had rejected him.
4. Against the Philistines: Saul in constant warfare with Philistines; boy David appeared after his anointing; David killed Goliath, the Philistine giant, and caused panic among the Philistines; David won distinction.
5. Against David: Blind jealousy drove Saul to seek David's life; David became an outcast; David repeatedly delivered; Saul,

David's enemy till his death; David's immortal friendship with Saul's son Jonathan.

6. Against the Philistines: Battlefield plains of Esdraelon; Saul's nighttime visit to the witch of Endor; Samuel called up; defeat and death announced; Israel completely defeated; Saul and three sons slain.

All through the years Samuel mourned for Saul. When Saul failed, Samuel was faithful in warning him, then in loneliness he mourned over him. Many verses tell the story (see 15:35).

In a battle with the Philistines, Saul and his three sons met death. Here a life so full of promise ended in defeat and failure. Saul had not obeyed God absolutely. For instance, if I were to sell one thousand acres of land but reserve one acre in the center, I would make sure I had the right to go over those one thousand acres to get to mine. One trouble with us is that we reserve a room for Satan in our hearts and he knows he has his right-of-way. This was the trouble with Saul.

Think of the difference between the end of Saul of Tarsus (Paul) and Saul the king! One put God first, the other himself!

God is showing in this book that he must be all in all, that his children have no blessing apart from him.

The morning of Saul's life was bright, but soon the sky became overcast. Then his sun set in the blackest storm clouds. Follow carefully his rise, his reign, and his ruin.

DAVID, THE KING PROVEN
1 SAMUEL 16–31

As the third division of the book opens we see Samuel mourning for Saul. God rebuked him and told him to get up and anoint the new king (16:1).

David, "the apple of God's eye," was one of the greatest characters of all times. He made great contributions to the history of Israel both spiritually and nationally.

In this book we see David as a shepherd boy, a minstrel, an armorbearer, a captain, the king's son-in-law, a writer of psalms, and a fugitive. He was anointed three times and was to be the founder of the royal line of which the King of kings would come.

David, Jesse's son and the great-grandson of Ruth and Boaz,

was born in Bethlehem. He was the youngest of eight sons. When David was only eighteen, God told Samuel to anoint him king to succeed Saul. As a boy he tended his father's sheep, and we read of his brave deeds in defending them from wild beasts.

As a harpist, David's fame reached the king. Saul's melancholy caused David to be called into the court to play. One of the most charming stories of real love in friendship is found between David and Jonathan, Saul's son.

When David was promoted to a high command in the army, his great success roused the jealousy of Saul, who determined to kill him. He made five attacks on David's life (19:10, 15, 20-21, 23-24), but God preserved David. *If God is on our side, who can ever be against us?* (Romans 8:31). David was delivered from all these dangers. Read David's words in Psalms 59 and 37.

These were trying days for the young man David who had been appointed to the kingly office. It was natural that he would go to Samuel for protection. All this was training for the one whom God was preparing for the throne. He not only learned how to handle men but how to handle himself. He became independent and courageous. He also learned, in those trying days, to trust God, not men He always awaited God's time.

He was an outcast for no wrong that he had done but because of the insane jealousy of Saul. David grew under his trials and afflictions. Instead of letting Saul's hatred harden his heart, he returned love for hate.

He learned to be a warrior during those days, too. He was to become the head of a great nation, and God was training him for active service.

Finally David took refuge in flight. During this time Samuel died. Twice was Saul's life in David's hand, but both times he spared Saul. Fearing that *Saul would kill him someday*, he took refuge among the Philistines. Psalm 56 was written then. After Saul and his sons were killed by the Philistines, David's exile ended.

The closing chapter of our book is draped in black. It gives the closing picture of one of the most disastrous failures. Saul died on the field of battle by his own hand. Advantages and opportunities in youth never guarantee success in manhood. One must keep true to God. Saul's undoing was not so much disobedience as halfhearted obedience (ch. 15). He was a victim of human pride and jealousy.

SELECTED BIBLE READING

Sunday: Samuel, "Name of God" (1 Samuel 1–3)
Monday: Samuel, the Prophet (1 Samuel 4–7)
Tuesday: Saul, the King (1 Samuel 8–12)
Wednesday: Saul, the Self-Willed (1 Samuel 13–15)
Thursday: David Anointed (1 Samuel 16–18)
Friday: David's Adventures (1 Samuel 19–20; 22; 24)
Saturday: Death of Samuel and Saul (1 Samuel 25–26; 31)

CHAPTER 10

UNDERSTANDING
SECOND SAMUEL

Second Samuel Portrays Jesus Christ, Our King

We must not only crown Christ as King of our life, but we must set him on his rightful throne.

First Samuel records the failure of man's king, Saul. Second Samuel describes the enthronement of God's king, David, and the establishment of the "House of David" through which the Messiah, Jesus Christ, would later come. When Christ comes again, he will sit upon the throne of David (Isaiah 9:7; Luke 1:32).

Second Samuel is occupied with the story of David as king (5:3). It does not tell the whole story, for that begins with 1 Samuel and runs into 1 Kings. First Chronicles deals with it from another standpoint.

The contents of this book will be easier to remember if we study it as a biography. David now occupies the field of view. He comes into his own. Let us begin with 1 Samuel 16, David's preparation and discipline. These were the testing days. David was:

1. Called from the sheepfold (1 Samuel 16:11-13)
2. Given victory over Goliath (1 Samuel 17)
3. Persecuted by Saul (1 Samuel 18 to the end)

The Israelis had clamored for a king. God first gave them one after their own heart, Saul. Then he gave them one after his own heart, David.

This is the substance of 2 Samuel:

1. David was made king over Judah (ch. 1–4)
2. David was made king over all Israel (ch. 5–24)

If we read 2 Samuel 7:18-22 and 8:14-15 we find David at his very best, at the height of his prosperity. It shows what he had become and what he might have continued to be if only he had remained faithful to God.

David was a man after God's own heart—not because of boasted perfection but because of confessed imperfections. He hid himself in God. Read what God tells us to do when we sin (1 John 1:9).

There is no one found anywhere in God's Word who was as versatile as David. He was the shepherd boy, the court musician, the soldier, the true friend, the outcast captain, the king, the great general, the loving father, the poet, the sinner, the brokenhearted old man, but always the lover of God. We find him as a sort of Robin Hood of the Bible. We love the stories of his daring courage, his encounter with lions and bears and the giant.

He was a man of wonderful personal power and charm. Can you find, as you read this book, the record that portrays the following qualities that stand out so clearly?

1. Faithfulness
2. Modesty
3. Patience
4. Courage
5. Big-heartedness
6. Trustfulness
7. Penitence

It would be good to compare Saul and David and roughly measure their stature one against the other. Both were kings of Israel. Both reigned about the same length of time, forty years. Both had the loyal support of the people, and both had the promise of God's power to back them. Yet Saul was a failure and David was a success. Saul's name is a blot on Israel's history, and David's name is honored today both by Jews and Gentiles.

What is the reason for the differences? It is important for us to find out, for these same factors may work in your life and mine, and we can deliberately choose the forces that will carry us on either course.

Saul had a brilliant start and for a while made good. But with success came pride (read Proverbs 16:18.) Thirty-five years of his reign were spent in insecurity and failure. He had lost his hold on God. He finally died a suicide in a lost battle. He left his kingdom at war with its neighbors and divided in its loyalty (1 Samuel 31).

The immediate link between the book of 1 Samuel and the book of 2 Samuel should be reviewed. After David had spared Saul (1 Samuel 26), he realized that his life was in danger, but he made the great mistake of associating himself with the Philistines instead of quietly trusting God (1 Samuel 27). Meanwhile, the closing scenes and final tragedy of Saul's life took place (1 Samuel 28–31). David's lament over Saul's death showed his attitude. Everything was clear now for David to fulfill the divine purpose and become king of Israel.

Now 2 Samuel draws our attention. Really there is no division between the first and second books. Originally the two books were one, covering the period from the beginning of Samuel's life to the end of David's. But 2 Samuel is occupied wholly with David.

After the results of Gilboa when both Saul the king and Jonathan his beloved friend lay dead, David naturally desired to know what was to be the next step. So David sought guidance of God (2:1). David did not ask about being a king but only about where he should go. The nation of Israel needed a leader, and the divine answer was that he should go up to the city of Hebron (2:3).

Hebron was one of the most ancient cities (Numbers 13:22). It was in existence in Abraham's day. When Canaan was conquered it became the possession of Caleb and was one of the cities of refuge (Joshua 14:13-15; 21:11-13). This was David's capital for the first seven years of his reign. This made it still more important. It was fifteen miles south of Jerusalem, in the center of Judah, and a strong place. It was especially suitable as a capital of the new kingdom, with the Philistines on one side and the followers of Saul on the other.

David seemed every inch a king when he spared the life of Saul. He was willing to wait for God to tell him that he would surely prevail (1 Samuel 26). He was on the heights. David's training seemed complete.

The devil would rather throw a man when he is on the heights; he falls farther and harder. He threw David. For David now passed into one of the worst periods of his life and stayed there for almost a year and a half (1 Samuel 27). David fell from a mountain peak of spiritual victory and privilege to a black valley of defeat, and he deliberately chose to stay there, weak and discouraged, for a long time. David's faith had collapsed. Without God's counsel he left the country of God's people to live in the land of the enemy, hopelessly certain of dying at Saul's hand unless he would escape. He joined Achish, king of Gath, who gave him Ziklag in which to live (1 Samuel 27:1-7).

David lied to Achish to win his favor, saying that he had raided the people of Judah when he hadn't. David met calamity. At last he flung himself on God. *But David took strength from the Lord* (1 Samuel 30:6). He asked God what to do. God answered, and under his guidance David had a real victory (1 Samuel 30).

Notice what happened at almost exactly the same time in the lives of Saul and David. Saul, an unrepentant sinner, went down to death, dragging his family and his country with him (1 Samuel 31:3-7). David, a repentant sinner, was given a glorious victory over the enemy and many were saved with him (1 Samuel 30:17-20). We are all sinners of one kind or another. Which ending do we want for our lives?

How did Saul meet his death (1 Samuel 31:4)? Why is suicide wrong? Can it ever be justified? What motive prompts suicide? Who died in the same battle with Saul (1 Samuel 31:2)? What was David's attitude when he heard of their deaths? Might one not expect him to have been glad for Saul's death? Read David's sorrowful lament over Saul and Jonathan (1:17-27).

Still in Ziklag in the enemy's country, David asked God just what he should do, but not whether he was to be king (2:1). He obeyed God and returned to Hebron where the men of Judah made him their king.

Why are we assured of David's success when he was made king? Saul chose the way of self; David chose God's way. Because of this, God called him *a man after his own heart* (see Acts 13:22). Notice that after Saul's death David made no effort to seize the kingdom by force. After Judah claimed him as king, it was seven and a half years before Israel crowned him. David knew that it was God's plan for him to be king of Israel, but he was willing to wait.

Some people grow under responsibility; others swell. We learn from Saul's failure that the surrendered life is the only secure and truly successful life.

DAVID'S RISE—SUPREMACY AND RULE
2 SAMUEL 1-10

As this book opens we find David just returning to Ziklag after his great victory over the Amalekites. He had come back weary in body but refreshed in spirit because of his great success. No doubt he was wondering what had been the outcome of that great battle at Mount Gilboa. His dearest friend, Jonathan, and King Saul were in that battle.

David was not kept in suspense long. An Amalekite from the camp of Israel came running that great distance, Bedouin style, to tell David of the disaster. No doubt the story the messenger told him was fabricated, and David dealt severely with him (1:1-16).

David's age was now thirty (5:4), and never did a man at that age, or any age, act in a nobler way. His generous heart not only forgot all that Saul had done to him but remembered all that was favorable in Saul's character.

How beautiful is the spirit of forgiveness! See that spirit when Christ was nailed to the cross (Luke 23:34) and a martyr was stoned to death (Acts 7:60). David wrote a song for this occasion called "The Song of the Bow." It is filled with extreme tenderness when it speaks of his beloved friend (1:19-27).

David inquired of God where he should set up his kingdom, and God told him in Hebron. No sooner had David gone up to the city than the men of Judah came and anointed him king over the house of Judah.

The men of Judah who came to meet David were probably the elders of his own tribe. They came to elect him as king, and although he had been anointed privately by Samuel to indicate that God had chosen him, it was natural and necessary to repeat the anointing in public as the outward and visible inauguration of his reign.

You remember that Saul was also anointed privately (1 Samuel

10:1). Anointing with oil meant a divine appointment. Saul was set apart for the service of king. He was given the right to rule the people.

However, David's kingship was not acknowledged by all of the people. Abner, the captain of Saul's army, at once took steps to appoint Saul's son to take his place.

The earnest efforts of David to ward off strife and bring the people together in recognizing him as king were all in vain. The spirit of Saul, which was so antagonistic to David, was perpetuated in Abner, who was determined to center the kingdom of Israel around the house of Saul, not of David (2:8-10).

That was the beginning of a long war between the followers of Saul and of David. David's position now became stronger and stronger, while Saul's dynasty became weaker and weaker (3:1). The cause of its weakness was that God was against it.

After seven and a half years of opposition David finally won the heart of all Israel by his justice and great spirit. He was left now without a rival. Representatives of all the tribes came to Hebron to anoint him king of the whole nation (ch. 5).

One of the great results of David's kingship was the unity of the whole nation under him as leader. He brought the various conflicting elements into one group. We find a united people under a young leader united to God. The Israelis needed only to have kept on following David's leading down the years to have gone from greatness to greatness. They had only to follow David's greater Son to have gone on from glory to glory!

David trusted God completely and did not lean on his own understanding. He put God first in everything, and God did direct him (see Proverbs 3:5-6). How did David obtain guidance? By asking for it. Just how God gave the answer we are not told. God has assured us that if we ask he will answer (1 John 5:14-15; Jeremiah 33:3). God never breaks his word. We have to make decisions almost every hour of our life. Shall I continue this course in my life? Shall my vacation be spent at home, traveling, at rest? Would we take false steps if he made the decisions for us? Could we fail?

From the anointing of David as king at Hebron, we go with him to the field of battle. The first thing that engaged David was the capture of Jerusalem, the stronghold of Zion. Since the days of Joshua, Jerusalem alone had defied the attack of Israel. It was an impregnable fortress. David thought it was best suited to be his nation's capital. The record of how it came for the first time completely into the possession of God's people is given in 2 Samuel 5:6-9 and 1 Chronicles 11:4-8.

After David had established the capital at Jerusalem, he wished to bring the Ark of God into the new ruling center. He realized the people's need for God. But we are not told that he consulted God. A tragedy followed. What was it? (See 6:1-19.) What do you know of God's directions for carrying the Ark?

It is not what we think but what God says that is important. Uzzah's human opinion was that it was all right to take hold of the Ark to keep it from falling. He was sincere, but it was directly contrary to what God said. He died. We can always know what God has said if we are willing to pay the price of knowing by studying his Word and trusting what he says (John 7:17).

What was the greatest thing David did for his people? He captured Jerusalem, built it bigger and stronger, conquered the Philistines, and unified the people. But all this would be of little use without putting God at the center. This is really what gave the nation unity and power. Neither a nation nor an individual can be great without Christ in its heart.

All the events in David's reign that followed the capture of Jerusalem may be summed up in these words: *And David became more and more famous and powerful, for the Lord of the heavens was with him* (1 Chronicles 11:9). God had been getting David ready for this reign. Training is difficult. It is good to bear the yoke in youth. Many a great man can testify to this.

David was an active man. He was fond of work. His wars with outside nations had ceased. Now he sought to find what he could do to improve and beautify his kingdom. He compared the elegance of his own palace with the Tabernacle where God lived. He thought this difference ought not to be. He called Nathan the prophet and consulted him about building a temple for God. At first it seemed as though God would let him do this, but God had a different purpose for David. Read what God told Nathan to tell to David (7:4-17).

David's spirit is again revealed in his submission to God's plan for him. God allowed him to gather materials for his son to use to build the Temple.

God's servants do not take it ill that the Lord thwarts their plans and desires. A real servant learns what God's will is and yields his will to his Master's!

Don't pass over the sweet story of David's treatment of crippled young Mephibosheth when he found Mephibosheth was his best friend's son (ch. 9).

David was powerful in every art of war, although his heart was inclined to peace. Chapter 10 recounts some perilous undertakings. This story gives the closing account of David's rise to power and prepares for the terrible story of his fall.

Under David's rule Israel reached its peak of greatness. It has been called Israel's golden age. There was no idol worship, no worldly functions when "the sweet singer of Israel," the "shepherd boy of Bethlehem," commanded the ship of state. His merchant caravans crossed the deserts, and his routes went from the Nile to the Tigris and Euphrates. Israel prospered in those days. When Israel was right with God, she was invincible against all odds.

DAVID'S FALL
2 SAMUEL 11-20

We wish the life of David could have ended before chapter 11 was written. But the golden era passed away, and what was left was a checkered tale of sin and punishment. In all of God's Word there is no chapter more tragic or more full of warning for the child of God. It tells the story of David's fall. It is like an eclipse of the sun. His sins of adultery and virtual murder were a terrible blot on David's life. He became a broken man. God forgave him, but the Word says, "Therefore murder shall be a constant threat in your family." He reaped just what he had sown. We see the harvest in his own house and in the nation.

Look over the steps in David's fall. You will find the steps downward in rapid succession.

First, he was idle (11:1-2). It was the time for a king to go to war, but he was not there. He remained in Jerusalem in the place of temptation. At evening time he got up from his bed and walked on the roof of his house. He was in that idle, listless mood that opens one to temptation. He saw the beautiful Bathsheba and he wanted her. His first sin was in the fact that he saw. Don't look on evil. Ask God to guard your eyes. Refuse the admission of sin into your mind. If David had nipped the temptation in the bud he would have saved himself a world of agony and awful sin. Instead of driving it out of his mind, he cherished it.

Next, *he sent to find out* (11:3). He found out about this woman and then brought her to his house. He forgot what was due to the faithful soldier whose wife she was.

But the next step was far worse—his sin against Uriah, one of the bravest of his soldiers. He had to get rid of him. He made Joab his confidant in sin, his partner in murder.

This sin was more terrible because it was committed by the head of the nation. This man had been signally favored by God. He was no longer a young man. He had passed through many experiences. Then, too, the excellent service of Uriah entitled him to rewards, not death.

Why do you suppose this tragic story is given in the Bible? It bears the character of a beacon, warning the mariner against some of the most perilous rocks that are to be found in the sea of life. Never neglect watching and praying. An hour's sleep left Samson at the mercy of Delilah. Don't fool with one sin even in thought. The door may be opened to a dangerous brood. It doesn't take a whole box of matches to start a fire. One will do it!

A year later the prophet Nathan visited David and charged him with his sin. We can imagine the anguish of David's heart that year. We read in Psalm 51 of David's sincere repentance. God told David that his child would die because of his sin. See how David accepted this punishment (12:13-32). When the child died, David got up and worshiped God.

"A living sorrow is worse than a dead one," says a proverb. The death of his child was a grievous sorrow to David, but the living sorrow that he endured through his beloved son Absalom we cannot imagine. The rebellion of this young man was full of tragedy. Absalom was a handsome young man, but he weaned away his father's subjects by treachery. He sat at the city gate and told the farmers what he would do if he were their ruler. When men bowed in honor, he kissed their hands. He drove a beautiful chariot drawn by prancing horses. He became a favorite.

Through a spy system he stole the kingdom from his father. When David left Jerusalem, Absalom gathered his army in Hebron and marched triumphantly into the city. Finally David prepared for battle with Absalom. During the fray Absalom was caught by his long hair in the trees of the forest.

Absalom was heartless and cruel. David suffered both in the

day of Absalom's victory and in the dark hour of his defeat and slaying. Read David's lament over Absalom when he heard the news of his death (18:19–19:4).

DAVID'S LAST DAYS
2 SAMUEL 20–24

After the rebellion was crushed, King David returned to his kingdom. New officers were installed and reconstruction began on every hand. We see David's sin in numbering the people, because God had not told him to. The land was punished with a three-day pestilence.

David gathered great provisions for the building of the Temple and directed his son Solomon to build it. David was only seventy years old when he died.

David was a mighty king and warrior. But David had faith in God. He was patient and was willing to wait for God to lead. He was humble before God and man. He was humble in his success, and when he sinned he genuinely repented. David's was a great career. He used every talent God gave him for the glory of his Creator and built up the people of God's choice. He brought Israel to the height of her glory, extending her boundaries from the Mediterranean to the Euphrates by conquest of battle. He left a rich heritage to his race—a heritage that included power, wealth, honor, and songs and psalms. But above all he left an example of loyalty to God.

Will we not all adopt David's plan of life? He started right! He began with God. He committed every plan into his keeping (Psalm 37:5). David never forgot that God was supreme. When he sinned, he bowed in penitence and sorrow, and God forgave him.

This is the *man after God's heart*. We need to understand David's life in order to understand and use the Psalms. We must know, too, why Christ was called the Son of David (Acts 13:22-23). David stands halfway between Abraham and Christ.

David had his faults. He did much that was very wrong, but he kept his nation from going into idolatry. Although his private sins were grievous, he stood like a rock for God. He sinned, but he repented and gave God a chance to forgive and cleanse him. He illustrates the conflict that Paul describes in Romans 7. He was a great saint even though he was a great sinner.

David took a chaotic nation and established a dynasty that was to last to the time of the captivity, a period of over four hundred fifty years. There never was a greater warrior or statesman than David. He made Israel the dominant power of western Asia.

The last verses of the book, 2 Samuel 24:18-25, tell of King David's buying Araunah's threshing floor. He erected an altar there. This has special significance, for on this site the great Temple of Solomon was later built.

Do not pray for an easy task. Pray to be stronger! The greatness of a man's power is the measure of his surrender. It is not a question of who you are, or of what you are, but whether God controls you.

Consider, what constitutes a missionary call? How does God call men today? The angel of God generally comes when you are busy (Judges 6:11-12):

Saul was out hunting livestock
David was tending sheep
The disciples were fishing
Luther was a busy pastor
Washington was a farmer-surveyor
Lincoln was a country lawyer
Moody was a shoe salesman
Carey was a cobbler

You say, "Those men outside the Bible never saw an angel!" How do you know they didn't? God speaks to people in many different ways and surprises them as much as he surprised the young Hebrew farmer, Gideon.

SELECTED BIBLE READING

Sunday: David Mourns for Jonathan and Saul (2 Samuel 1)
Monday: David, King of Judah (2 Samuel 2)
Tuesday: David, King of All Israel (2 Samuel 5)
Wednesday: David's House Established (2 Samuel 7)
Thursday: David's Sin (2 Samuel 11)
Friday: David's Repentance (2 Samuel 12; Psalm 51)
Saturday: David Numbers the People (2 Samuel 24)

CHAPTER 11

UNDERSTANDING KINGS AND CHRONICLES

Kings and Chronicles Portray Jesus Christ as King

UNDERSTANDING KINGS

If we reject God, he will reject us. If we obey God, he will bless us. *At about that time the Lord began to whittle down the size of Israel* (2 Kings 10:32).

In the original Hebrew in which these books were written 1 and 2 Kings formed one book, 1 and 2 Samuel another, and 1 and 2 Chronicles a third. When they were translated into the Greek language, they were divided by the translators because the Greek required one third more space than the Hebrew, and the scrolls on which they were written were limited in length.

The book of Kings (1 and 2 Kings) was written while the first Temple was standing. The book is just a continuation of the books of Samuel. As its name suggests, it records the events of the reign of Solomon and then of the succeeding kings of Judah and Israel. It covers a period of approximately three hundred fifty years and tells the story of the growth and then decay of the kingdom. We see the kingdom divided. The southern kingdom (Judah) had twenty kings, and the northern kingdom (Israel) had nineteen kings.

During Solomon's reign the kingdom reached the height of its grandeur. With the death of Solomon, the kingship really ceased to be the medium through which God governed his people. The period of the prophets was introduced at this time by the great

Elijah. First Kings ends with the story of this prophet. Second Kings centers around Elisha. The decline of the kingdoms is given until we see both Israel and Judah led into captivity.

These are the two most important books of history in the world. At first they may seem dry to you, but the lives of the kings and the stories in these books prove that:

1. When our all is on the altar, God never keeps us waiting for the fire (1 Kings 18:38). What is the spiritual meaning of this?
2. The final captivity was because of disobedience to God. It was prophesied in Deuteronomy 28:49.

Kings begins with King David and ends with the king of Babylon.

Kings opens with the building of the Temple and ends with the burning of the Temple.

Kings opens with David's first successor to the throne of his kingdom, Solomon, and ends with David's last successor, Jehoiachin, released from captivity by the king of Babylon.

THE SPLENDID REIGN OF SOLOMON
1 KINGS 1–10

As the scene opens we find King David now prematurely aged, for he was only seventy. His son Solomon was but nineteen. Because of David's feebleness we find a rebellion started against him. Adonijah's attempt to get his father's throne was natural because he was the oldest surviving son (2 Samuel 3:4). This rebellion called for prompt action, which Nathan the prophet took. David saw that Solomon was the most fit to succeed him. Solomon was God's choice (1 Chronicles 22:9; 1 Kings 2:15). It was clear that the choice of Solomon was popular (1 Kings 1:39-40). Adonijah soon saw that opposition was useless. Because of this rebellion, Solomon was crowned before David's death (1 Kings 1:30, 39, 53).

Solomon's reign began in a blaze of glory. But it was splendor without surrender. And as with Saul, Solomon's life ended in an anticlimax.

Yet Solomon was a magnificent king! His throne was the grandest the world had ever seen, and his life was filled with happenings of marvelous significance. His kingdom of sixty thousand square miles was ten times as great as what his father had inherited.

Solomon Was a Great and Good Man
1. His rearing was under the religious and wise Nathan.
2. His kingship was clear. All the city rang with the glad cry, *Solomon is sitting on the throne* (1 Kings 1:46).
3. His charge from his father was full of promise (1 Kings 2:1-9).
4. His choice of wisdom from God was a divine choice (1 Kings 3).
5. His cabinet was greater than any king of Israel ever had (1 Kings 4).
6. His lifework was the building of the Temple. Several million dollars was expended in erecting it. Its service of dedication has gone down on record because of its sublimity.
7. The kingdom he established realized at last, after four hundred years, the broad dimensions outlined to Joshua (Joshua 1:4).
8. The wealth and glory of Solomon's reign fairly took the breath of the Queen of Sheba. *There was no more spirit [breath] in her* (1 Kings 10:5).
9. His beauty of person is hinted at in Psalm 45.
10. His ardent affection is seen in the song that bears his name (Song of Solomon).

Solomon was a great and glorious king, but we soon find the note of decline.

Solomon, the Weak and Erring One
1. Unlike his father, David, Solomon dealt cruelly with his brother Adonijah (1 Kings 2:24-25).
2. Like Saul, his heart was lifted up in pride (1 Kings 10:18-29).
3. Led by his pagan wives, he fell into idolatry (1 Kings 11). *Don't be teamed with those who do not love the Lord* (2 Corinthians 6:14).

Solomon did not display spiritual wisdom. The book of Ecclesiastes, with its note of despair, is a confession of it. He did not have a heart at peace with God.

After David's final words of admonition to his son to be absolutely loyal to God, the king died, having reigned for forty years.

The Glory of Solomon's Reign

God appeared to Solomon in a dream early in his reign and told him to ask for anything he wanted. The young king's wise choice revealed his feeling of inability to do all that was put upon him. What was his request of the Lord? God gave him the wisdom for which he asked. What is God's promise to us (James 1:5)?

The youth had not been swept off his feet by his father's praise when David twice called him a wise man (1 Kings 2:6-9). Solomon had asked for an "understanding mind."

Solomon was the wisest man the world ever saw until the coming of him who could say of himself, *A greater than Solomon is here* (Matthew 12:42). All the earth acknowledged Solomon, but when the One greater than Solomon came, his own did not receive him (John 1:11). That is tragedy. But have you received him?

Solomon first organized his leaders. He gathered around him a wise company of officers of state, each having a department for which he was responsible. This led to days of tremendous prosperity in the kingdom.

The greatest undertaking of Solomon's reign was the building of the Temple. This was what his father, David, had longed to do. The immense foundation of great hewn stones on which Solomon's Temple was built remains to this day. One stone alone is thirty-eight feet, nine inches long. The huge stones, the fragrant cedar wood, and copper-covered dome gave it unusual splendor.

The Temple site was a historic spot. On Mount Moriah Abraham offered up Isaac (Genesis 22:2). We saw how David secured Araunah's threshing floor, and here today stands the Dome of the Rock, the sacred spot of the Muslims.

Men used to have to make pilgrimages to the Temple to meet God. But now we know a wonderful truth, that our bodies are the temples of God (1 Corinthians 3:16; 6:19). Your body is a real temple. God wishes to live in you, but he cannot if you are defiled with sin.

There are three earthly temples mentioned in Scripture. The first is Solomon's, which was destroyed by the Babylonians about 587 B.C. (2 Kings 25:8-9). The second was Zerubbabel's (Ezra 5:2; 6:15-18). This was not comparable in elegance to Solomon's. The third was Herod's temple, an expansion of Zerubbabel's, erected on a grander scale in 20 B.C. and completed in A.D. 64. This temple was destroyed by Titus in A.D. 70.

Read 1 Kings 9:1-28 and 10:14-29 to find the possible, not to say the probable, dangers to Solomon in all this wonderful glory. Note his high position, his great wisdom, his countless riches. It is hard not to forget God in the hour of such prosperity. One thinks only of his possessions. It was this very glory that led to Solomon's downfall.

Because of Solomon's backsliding, God raised up enemies to vex him. In the book of Ecclesiastes, Solomon describes the futility of his life at this time.

The Queen of Sheba witnessed Solomon's reign at its zenith and saw the fulfillment of David's prayer for his son, offered about a year before his death.

Solomon's reputation probably had spread through the voyages of his navy (1 Kings 9:21-28). The fame of Solomon was associated with God. His fame concerning the name of the Lord was the thing that interested her majesty, the Queen of Sheba. She was impressed by (1) Solomon himself, with his wisdom and wealth (1 Kings 10:1, 7); (2) his servants (10:8); and (3) his God (10:9).

THE KINGDOM TORN ASUNDER
1 KINGS 11–16

Solomon reigned forty years, the second great period of the complete kingdom (1 Kings 11). At first all went well, but later there was serious trouble. You note that Saul, David, and Solomon each reigned forty years (Acts 13:21; 2 Samuel 5:4; 1 Kings 11:42).

Taxes under Solomon's reign had weighed the people down. Luxury and idolatry had broken down their morale. The kingdom now was to be divided. A rise to such prosperity and power as Solomon enjoyed had its dangers. It cost money and meant increased taxation that grew into unbearable burdens and that bred the seeds of unrest and revolution.

Solomon set up a great establishment in Jerusalem. He built his famous Temple, bringing in foreign workmen and materials to do it, and then he built himself a palace that dazzled his own subjects and his foreign visitors. During this time there was corruption and graft, and under all these burdens the people grew restless and rebellious.

Consider the events leading up to the division. For years there had been jealousy between the northern kingdom (Israel) and the southern kingdom (Judah). The cause for the jealousy went back three hundred years and was due mainly to the jealousy between the tribes of Ephraim and Judah. Note the blessings that Jacob gave to Ephraim (Genesis 48:17-22; 49:22-26). And from the time of Joshua, who was of that tribe, Ephraim took a leading place. The transfer of authority to Judah came under David, who was of the tribe of Judah. All this tribal jealousy was intensified by the hardships felt by the people through Solomon's high-handed actions. His demands created oppression, and his unfaithfulness to God demanded judgment (1 Kings 11:26-43; 12:4). When Solomon's son, Rehoboam, threatened to levy heavier burdens on the people, his unwise, headstrong action added fuel to this fire.

The revolt of the ten tribes immediately followed (1 Kings 12:16), though the two tribes of Judah and Benjamin remained loyal (12:17). This tension led to the appointment of Jeroboam as king of the northern section (12:20).

The Secret of Decline

A new name of great importance appears in the pages of this story: Jeroboam. This young man of low origin had risen to notice because of faithful service and deeds done. The prophet Ahijah made a startling revelation to Jeroboam. Using Oriental imagery, he took off his new coat and tore it into twelve strips and then said to Jeroboam, *Take ten of these pieces, for the Lord God of Israel says, "I will tear the kingdom from the hand of Solomon and give ten of the tribes to you"* (1 Kings 11:31).

The kingdom was divided. The judgment was upon Solomon for his long years of luxury and pride and idolatry. Every ruler should look ahead and see toward what rocks he may be steering his kingdom, and whether or not he is heading toward the day when his power will be taken out of his hand.

Have we not seen men in our day, rising to great wealth and power in which they had piled up millions, stripped to nothing and fleeing from outraged justice?

Things do not happen by accident. There is a cause at the root of every revolution. The event may come as suddenly as an explosion, or as the eruption of a volcano, but somewhere secret causes were at work undermining the structure.

Religious apostasy had been gnawing like a deadly worm at

the root of Israel's life. One day the tree fell. Nothing destroys a nation like religious decline.

Sin Brings Division

Though they didn't know it, the people were carrying out the divine purpose (1 Kings 12:15; 11:29-33). God could not overlook the disobedience of Solomon to his clearest commands.

The kingdom of God's chosen people was divided. It has been divided for almost three thousand years. It was divided through sin. We see this kingdom go to pieces and finally into captivity (2 Kings 17; 25). It is part of the gospel, the Good News, that those two great sections of divided Israel are going to be united again on earth at Christ's return in glory. (Read the wonderful passages in Isaiah 11:10-13; Ezekiel 37:15-28.)

THE MINISTRY OF ELIJAH
1 KINGS 17-22; 2 KINGS 1

Elijah was a bolt of fire that God let loose upon wicked Ahab and idolatrous Israel. He flashed across the page of history as suddenly and terribly as a flash of lightning. *Elijah, the prophet from Tishbe in Gilead* is the brief biography by which he was introduced. His name *Elijah* means "Jehovah is my God." It fit him perfectly. He was the most outstanding of the prophets. Follow his sudden appearance, his undaunted courage, his zeal, the heights of his triumph on Mount Carmel, the depths of his despondence, the glorious rapture into heaven in the whirlwind, and his reappearance on the Mount of Transfiguration.

He was a striking character from the highlands of Gilead. His long, thick hair hung over a cloak of sheepskin. God sent him to do away with the awful worship of Baal during the reign of Ahab, who had married the wicked pagan princess Jezebel. Suddenly emerging from the desert and standing before the corrupt king in the splendor of his court, the stern prophet boldly said, *As surely as the Lord God of Israel lives—the God whom I worship and serve—there won't be any dew or rain for several years until I say the word!* (1 Kings 17:1). He was given power to shut up the heavens so there would be no rain for three and a half years. He called down fire from heaven before the prophets of Baal at Mount Carmel. He was the evangelist of his day thundering out warnings to this idolatrous people. As you read, the events in this great career will intrigue you.

THE MINISTRY OF ELISHA
2 KINGS 2–9

Elisha succeeded Elijah. He was beneficent in contrast to the fiery Elijah. Elijah trained Elisha as his successor. Elisha's ministry lasted fifty years. Most of his miracles were deeds of kindness and mercy. Elisha had a great influence on the kings of the day, and although he did not approve of what they did, he was always coming to their rescue.

Elijah and Elisha are in marked contrast to each other:

Elijah—the prophet of judgment, law, severity
Elisha—the prophet of grace, love, tenderness

Baal worship was introduced by the wicked Jezebel and after thirty years was exterminated by Elijah, Elisha, and Jehu.

THE CORRUPTION OF ISRAEL
2 KINGS 1–17

Jeroboam, the ruler of the northern kingdom (Israel), made Shechem his capital. It seemed the natural place because it was in the center of the land.

It was the custom, according to the law, to go up to Jerusalem regularly to worship (Deuteronomy 12:11, 14; 16:6, 15-16). Jeroboam was afraid to have his ten tribes journey to Jerusalem, the capital of Rehoboam's kingdom, to worship God, so he made two golden calves and placed them in convenient spots—Bethel (Genesis 28:11-19) in the south and Dan (Judges 18:29-30) in the north—so the people would not have to go to Jerusalem.

Over twenty times he is described as *Jeroboam, the son of Nebat, who made all of Israel sin.* Beware of man-made religion. We must worship where and how God tells us!

After two hundred years the people were carried into captivity by the king of Assyria (2 Kings 17). Many of God's prophets had warned Israel of captivity, but they would not turn from their idolatry to God.

The Assyrians were great and cruel warriors. They built their kingdom on their pillage from other countries. Their practices were horrible. They skinned men alive, cut out their tongues, put out their eyes, dismembered their bodies, and then made mounds of the skulls of men to instill fear! For three hundred years Assyria was a world empire.

THE CAPTIVITY OF JUDAH
2 KINGS 13–25

The southern kingdom tried for eighty years to conquer the northern kingdom, but they failed. Then there was a period of eighty years of peace between these two kingdoms following the marriage of the son of Jehoshaphat (southern king) to the daughter of Ahab (northern king). Finally there was a period of fifty years when the kingdoms intermittently warred with each other until the captivity.

In the southern kingdom there was only one dynasty (Davidic) from King Rehoboam to King Zedekiah. The great prophets of that day were Nathan, Isaiah, Micah, Jeremiah, Joel, and Zephaniah.

About 136 years after the northern kingdom had been taken into captivity by Assyria, the southern kingdom was taken captive by Nebuchadnezzar, king of Babylon. Jerusalem was destroyed, the Temple burned, and the princes led away. The people had forgotten God and refused to listen to the warnings of the prophets. God wanted his people to learn the lesson of obedience and dependence upon him.

In 1 Kings we see the kingdom of Israel, filled with pride and arrogance, falling apart. In 2 Kings, sinning yet more, Israel goes into captivity. The history of the Jews is a record of God's dealings with disobedient children. In all his punishment he is kind and merciful for he loves them still.

The moving figures and powerful factors of those days were the prophets Elijah and Elisha. Elijah was the strength of Israel. We ask today, *Where is the Lord God of Elijah?* (2 Kings 2:14). Would that we might see some of this old-time power. Elijah was the champion of the Most High. He brought God to the people. He was the pastor-evangelist of Israel's day.

There is a great difference between the fall of Israel and the fall of Judah. Israel was scattered throughout the nations for an indefinite period, but God specified the length of Judah's captivity to seventy years. Judah was to return to Jerusalem, which she did later. The Messiah was to come out of Judah, and God was preparing the way for him to come to Palestine and not to Babylon or Assyria.

God was using even the rulers of foreign nations to work out his plan. Cyrus, king of Persia, for example, was going to issue a decree that would allow the Jews to return to their homeland, Palestine.

Find answers to the following questions:

1. What was Solomon's greatest work? Describe it.
2. What books of the Bible did Solomon write?
3. Why was the kingdom divided after Solomon's death?
4. Describe the kings of Israel. How did this kingdom end? Who were her conquerors? (Know this.) Who were Israel's prophets?
5. Describe the kings of Judah. Who took Judah captive, and where was she taken?

UNDERSTANDING 1 CHRONICLES

The History of Judah
It is through such books as the Chronicles that we get the history of the Jewish nation. Through this nation our Lord came to earth. God chose this people for the fulfillment of his great promises and purposes. He is still their God (Romans 11:1) and he has his purposes yet to be fulfilled in them. In the light of this truth, books such as the Chronicles take on new meaning and power.

UNDERSTANDING 2 CHRONICLES

A Book of Revivals!
Great revivals under:

1. Asa (2 Chronicles 15)
2. Jehoshaphat (2 Chronicles 20)
3. Joash (2 Chronicles 23–24)
4. Hezekiah (2 Chronicles 29–31)
5. Josiah (2 Chronicles 35)

SELECTED BIBLE READING

Sunday: Building and Dedicating the Temple (1 Kings 6; 8)
Monday: Solomon's Glorious Reign (1 Kings 10)
Tuesday: The Kingdom Divided (1 Kings 12)
Wednesday: The Prophet Elijah (1 Kings 17–18)
Thursday: Elijah and Elisha (2 Kings 2)
Friday: The Captivity of Israel—The Northern Kingdom (2 Kings 17:7-23)
Saturday: The Captivity of Judah—The Southern Kingdom (2 Kings 25:1-21)

CHAPTER 12

UNDERSTANDING
EZRA AND NEHEMIAH

Ezra and Nehemiah Portray Jesus Christ, Our Restorer

UNDERSTANDING EZRA

Ezra and Nehemiah were one book in the Hebrew Bible, as were the two books of Samuel and Kings. These books tell the story of the return of God's chosen people after the exile. They give the record of one of the most important events in Jewish history—the return from exile in Babylon.

The time covered by these two books is about one hundred years. Both books begin at Persia and end at Jerusalem. Both center around the man who wrote them. Both stories begin with a Persian king's decree. Both tell of building as their chief theme. Both books contain a long prayer of humiliation and confession in the ninth chapter. Both end with the purification of the people.

Ezra 7:10—Ezra's keynote

Nehemiah 6:3—Nehemiah's keynote

The purposes of God may sometimes seem delayed, but they are never abandoned. *Remember what you told Moses*, prayed Nehemiah (Nehemiah 1:8). The books of Ezra and Nehemiah tell the story of how God remembered and how he brought back his people from exile. Jeremiah 29:10-13 tells us of this remembrance.

During the captivity, the prophets Jeremiah and Ezekiel told the Jews of their restoration and predicted that they would return to their own land and rebuild Jerusalem. Jeremiah, the prophet, told them this would happen at the end of seventy years. *You will be in Babylon for seventy years. But then I will come and do for you all the good things I have promised, and bring you home again* (Jeremiah 29:10). You remember that the books of Kings ended with the story of the captivity of first the northern kingdom of Israel and then the southern kingdom of Judah.

Daniel was carried away captive to Babylon at the time of the captivity of Judah. The last incident in the history was the story of Daniel in the lions' den (Daniel 6:16-24). This happened about ten years before Cyrus became king of Babylon. Daniel was an old man when these events took place.

The rebuilding of the national life of the Jews covered one hundred years.

There are two periods of time that are very important:

1. Twenty years (537–517 B.C.) from the first year of Cyrus to the sixth year of Darius, when the people under Zerubbabel, the governor, and Joshua, the priest, rebuilt the Temple. For this period read Ezra 1–6, Zechariah, Haggai, the first chapters of 1 Chronicles, the last two verses of 2 Chronicles, Psalm 126, Psalm 136, and the reference to Cyrus in Isaiah 44:23–45:8.
2. Twenty-five years (458–433 B.C.) when Nehemiah, the governor, and Ezra, the priest, rebuilt the wall of Jerusalem and restored the city. Malachi was the prophet of this day.

Ezra gives the record of both of these periods. Nehemiah tells of the second period, the building of the walls.

The book of Ezra has both a backward and a forward look. The backward look: We find a second exodus for captive Israel. The first exodus was out of Egypt. This second exodus was from Babylon. This time Ezra is leader in the place of Moses. He, like Moses, is an inspired writer and leader. Both men were great organizers, lawgivers, and teachers, raised up to fulfill God's gracious purpose and bring captive Israel out of bondage. Both of these great leaders dealt with Israel in a strong and merciful way.

The forward look: They came in timid, struggling relays back to Jerusalem. But God gave them a foothold. It was his city and it is his city still. He will again bring back his own. He will raise up Zion out of ruins.

The Jews were taken captive first by Assyria (2 Kings 17), then by Babylon (2 Kings 25). They were restored to their own land under the Persian Empire. The Babylonians had been conquered by the Medes and Persians. The ten northern tribes who were carried away to Assyria never returned.

In 537 B.C. the first Jews returned to Jerusalem from Babylon. In 516 B.C. the Temple was restored. In 479 B.C. Esther became the queen of Persia (as the wife of Xerxes). In 458 B.C. Ezra led a second expedition from Babylon. In 445 B.C. Nehemiah rebuilt the walls of Jerusalem.

RETURN AND REBUILDING OF THE TEMPLE
EZRA 1-6

As the book of Ezra opens we find Cyrus, king of Persia, making a proclamation throughout his kingdom permitting the Jews who were captives in his kingdom to return to Jerusalem.

Two hundred years before, God had prophesied that he would do this. He named Cyrus as the one he would use. The record of this remarkable prophecy, which calls a king by his name two hundred years before his time, is found in Isaiah 44:28 and 45:1-4.

Daniel's influence in the court was very powerful. He was one of the princes carried away by Nebuchadnezzar to his court. Now he was an old man.

At Cyrus's first call (537 B.C., Ezra 1:1-4), no more than fifty thousand Jews availed themselves of the opportunity of returning to Jerusalem under Zerubbabel. Notice that from this time the Israelis are called Jews because most of them were of the tribe of Judah, and the name *Jews* comes from *Judah*.

Cyrus gave back to Zerubbabel the golden vessels that Nebuchadnezzar had taken from the Temple in Jerusalem (Ezra 1:5-11). They started back on the seven-hundred-mile trek from Babylon to Jerusalem.

At the time of the captivity seventy years before, only the better classes were taken into Babylon. The rest were left in their own land to suffer (Jeremiah 24:5-8; 44:15). Now everyone did not return; only the earnest and pious Jews went back. It was a time of real sifting among the people. Most of them after seventy years had built homes and established themselves and were content to remain in Babylon. They did not care to face the dangers and hardships of returning across the desert and arriving in a city that had been destroyed.

Although the leaders were from the tribe of Judah, no doubt there were representatives from the whole of Israel. Only those who loved God were ready to make the attempt. Many of the Jews had been born in Babylon during the seventy years. These were not considered captives but exiles.

Everything is taken care of when God is in charge. Not only money for rebuilding the Temple in Jerusalem, but traveling expenses and all other needs were provided by God at Cyrus's direction (Ezra 1:4, 6). Someone has said that God used Babylon as the safety deposit vault for the silver and gold vessels of the Temple.

The names of those who returned are given in Ezra 2. The people built the altar the first thing upon returning (Ezra 3:2). They laid the foundation of the Temple. It was a time of great rejoicing. It is interesting to notice that before they built homes for themselves they first thought of a house for the Lord.

The place where sin must be dealt with must come first in every life. The heart must be right if God is to bless. The altar was the center of the Jew's religion; the cross is the center of the Christian faith.

Read about the hindrances to the work (Ezra 4). Hindrances to all real work for God are to be expected. The church will not have the help of the world.

The opposition disheartened them. They needed Haggai's message. Refer to the book of Haggai. Haggai and Zechariah, the prophets, encouraged the people from within the ranks (Ezra 4:23–5:17), and within four years the Temple was complete and dedicated (ch. 6).

Zerubbabel's Temple was very plain and simple. It was not the sumptuous edifice that Solomon's had been. In fact, it was in such contrast to the elegance of the first Temple that the old men who had seen Solomon's Temple wept aloud. But it was God's house, and so the people thanked God and took courage.

RETURN AND REFORMATION UNDER EZRA
EZRA 7-10

Ezra appears in person in the seventh chapter (458 B.C.). At least sixty years after the Jews had first returned to Jerusalem he led a second expedition from Babylon to reinforce the struggling colonists in Palestine. Ezra received a commission from King Artaxerxes (Ezra 7:11–8:14), who half-blindly aided in accomplishing God's plans for his people. Read Ezra 7:25 and find how impressed the king was with Ezra's love of God's Word. Oh, that we might live in such a way that others would learn to have respect for God's Book!

This contingent under Ezra consisted of seventeen hundred Jews. It took them four months to make the journey, and it was financed by King Artaxerxes (Ezra 7:12-26). Thirteen years later this same king authorized Nehemiah to build the walls of Jerusalem (Nehemiah 2). Cyrus, Darius, and Artaxerxes, the three Persian kings, were very friendly to the Jews.

Tradition tells us that Ezra was the founder of the synagogue worship that arose in the days of the captivity. Because the Temple had been destroyed and the people were scattered, they needed some place to worship God. Each Jewish community had its place of worship and instruction. After the Jews returned to their homeland, the synagogues were started at home as well as in other lands where they were scattered.

Old Testament history closes about one hundred years after the Jews returned from captivity. Alexander the Great (336–325 B.C.) broke the Persian hold, and world power passed from Persia to Greece. Alexander showed consideration to the Jews, as we find in history.

Ezra the Scribe

Of Ezra it is said, *He determined to study and obey the laws of the Lord . . . , teaching those laws to the people of Israel* (Ezra 7:10). His name means "Help." He belongs to the great triumvirate of the Old Testament law (Moses, Samuel, Ezra). He wrote and worked to keep the record intact and to hold Israel, God's chosen people, to her divinely appointed mission. We are indebted to Ezra for the literary and ecclesiastical renaissance of that day.

In addition to Ezra's outstanding ministry of the Word, he probably wrote portions of 1 and 2 Chronicles, and Psalm 119, which is a wonderful poem on the Word of God. As we have said, he probably instituted synagogue worship, which is the parent of our own form of worship, and assisted by the great synagogue of which he was president, he settled the canon of Old Testament Scripture. It was under Ezra that we see the great revival of Bible study.

When Ezra returned to Jerusalem he found things even worse than he had expected. Although the people had not returned to idolatry, they had intermarried with the people of the land and had done everything that the pagans had taught them (Ezra

9:1-4). The princes and rulers were the worst offenders. Ezra tore his garments and literally pulled out his hair in grief! Read Ezra's touching prayer and confession (Ezra 9:5-15).

As Ezra was praying and weeping before God, a great congregation assembled. What happened? (See Ezra 10.) The people who had gathered around him through the long hours of the day came to a consciousness of the greatness of their sin as they saw how it affected Ezra. Finally one of them spoke and acknowledged the sin. At once Ezra led them into a sacred covenant with God. Read what God says about confession of sin (1 John 1:9).

Nehemiah's Prayer

Now turn to Nehemiah 9 and you will find the prayer of Nehemiah. Prayer is the most important privilege of a Christian. Nehemiah's prayer began where Ezra's ended—with utter surrender to God. (Compare Nehemiah 9:1-2 with Ezra 9:15; 10:1.)

God had definitely promised to bring the Jews back after seventy years in Babylon (Jeremiah 25:11-12; 29:10). We read in the very first verse of Ezra that it was to fulfill this word that *the Lord gave King Cyrus the desire* to proclaim the restoration. But it is through prayer that God wishes to have his will brought to pass. The restoration was wholly undeserved by Israel but purposed in "God's heart of mercy."

See the results of this restoration of God's people to their land:

First, through the rebuilding of the Temple, God opened the door of fellowship with himself. Through the seventy years of suffering they were ready to return and build and wait until the true Servant would come.

Second, God renewed his promise of a coming Redeemer. It was prophesied that the Redeemer would be associated with Palestine.

Third, God made ready *the right time* for Christ to come, as spoken of by Paul in Galatians 4:4.

UNDERSTANDING NEHEMIAH

Repairing the City Wall (Nehemiah 1–7)

Nehemiah was the cupbearer in the court of King Artaxerxes. This was a position of high honor. But in this position of familiarity with the king he had not forgotten his people. The news that was brought to him about Jerusalem made him very sad. This sadness could not be wholly hidden, and the king detected it. The Jews had been back home for almost a hundred years but had made no attempt to build Jerusalem beyond the restoration of the Temple because their enemies made it almost impossible.

Artaxerxes' stepmother was Esther, the Jewess, who no doubt was still alive. It may have been that Nehemiah received his appointment through her influence. He was loyal enough to his people to leave the luxury of a king's court and go back to rebuild Jerusalem, the capital of his homeland. The king gave consent.

When Nehemiah reached Jerusalem in 445 B.C., Ezra had been there for thirteen years. Ezra was a priest and had been teaching the people the Word of God. But Nehemiah was a civil governor. He had come with the authority of the king of Persia to build the walls of Jerusalem. After he had been there only three days he went up and viewed the walls at night. When he saw their dilapidated condition he encouraged the people to begin building immediately. The work was accomplished in fifty-two days by assigning a portion of the wall to each family. Their attitude was expressed in the phrase, *the workers worked hard* (Nehemiah 4:6). Nehemiah was a real engineer!

First the Samaritans, the enemies of the Jews, derided them. They hindered their work so that the Jews had to keep watch night and day. Their derision turned to anger, and Nehemiah divided the men into two groups, one keeping watch while the other worked.

Then opposition rose within the ranks. Some of the Jews became tired and complained that there was so much rubbish that the walls could not be built. All this rubble had to be removed in a thick canvas pad on the carrier's back. (There were, of course, no wheelbarrows or cars to convey the material.) Then the complaint arose that the rich were demanding usury that the poor were unable to pay.

Again the enemies tried by craft to bring Nehemiah away from his building, but Nehemiah only prayed and again he foiled his enemies.

Nehemiah gave the city of Jerusalem into the charge of his brother Hanani (Nehemiah 7:1-4). When he took a census (7:5-73) the population was 42,360, besides 7,337 servants and 245 singing men and women.

Repairing the People's Morals (Nehemiah 8–13)

All the people gathered together in the street before the Water Gate in the city of Jerusalem and requested Ezra the scribe to bring out the book of the law of Moses. He stood on a pulpit of wood and read and explained the law to the people (Nehemiah 8:1-13). This public reading brought true repentance to the people and a great revival broke out. When Josiah found the book of the Law, a great reformation started. When Martin Luther read the Bible, the Protestant Reformation began. We need to have the Word read today!

Their captivity in Babylon cured the Jews of idolatry. You remember up to that time, in spite of all the warnings of the prophets, the people would worship the idols of the peoples around them. But from the days of the captivity to the present (about twenty-five hundred years) the Jews have never been guilty of this sin. The Jews had intermarried with the idolatrous neighbors, and this was the reason for their sin. Intermarriage of Christians with those who do not believe is a dangerous thing today. Paul says, *Don't be teamed with those who do not love the Lord* (2 Corinthians 6:14).

Remember, Nehemiah left a life of ease and luxury and security for a life of toil and danger and heartbreaks. He was a reformer! And no one appreciates a man who tries to reform him.

Nehemiah was a man of prayer. We do not find a blot on his character. He was fearless and courageous.

SELECTED BIBLE READING

Sunday: Jews Return to Jerusalem (Ezra 1–3)
Monday: Discouragement and Joy (Ezra 4–6)
Tuesday: Ezra's Expedition (Ezra 7–10)
Wednesday: Nehemiah Rebuilds the Wall (Nehemiah 1–3)
Thursday: Overcoming Opposition (Nehemiah 4–6)
Friday: Nehemiah Rebuilds the Morals (Nehemiah 7–9)
Saturday: Reforming through Religion (Nehemiah 11–13)

CHAPTER 13

A QUICK LOOK AT GENESIS—NEHEMIAH

TIME LINE—GENESIS TO NEHEMIAH

to 2000 B.C. (Genesis 1–11)
Period: The world before Abram—creation, sin, flood, Babel
People: Adam, Eve, Cain, Seth, Noah, Shem, Ham, Japheth

2000–1700 B.C. (Genesis 12–50)
Period: Age of the patriarchs—call of Abraham, migration to Egypt, growth of Israel
People: Abraham, Isaac, Jacob, Joseph

1700–1450 B.C. (Exodus–Deuteronomy)
Period: Oppression in Egypt—the exodus, the law, worship, wilderness
People: Moses, Miriam, Aaron, Joshua

1450–1100 B.C. (Joshua–1 Samuel 7)
Period: Conquest of Canaan and time of the Judges—invasion of Canaan, bondage and deliverance
People: Joshua, Caleb, Othniel, Ehud, Shamgar, Deborah, Barak, Gideon, Jephthah, Samson, Eli, Samuel

1100–600 B.C. (1 Samuel 8–2 Chronicles)
Period: Monarchy—kingdom established, Temple built, kingdom divided, destruction of Samaria, discovery of the law, destruction of Jerusalem

People: Saul, David, Solomon, Jeroboam, Rehoboam, Ahab, Asa, Jehu, Elijah, Elisha, Jehoshaphat, Joab, Amaziah, Jeroboam II, Hoshea, Uzziah, Jotham, Ahaz, Hezekiah, Manasseh, Josiah, Jehoiakin, Zedekiah

500–400 B.C. (Ezra–Nehemiah)
Period: Return from the exile—decree of Cyrus, close of Old Testament history
People: Zerubbabel, Ezra, Nehemiah

OUTLINE OF OLD TESTAMENT HISTORY

I. Period of Patriarchs: Adam to Moses (Genesis)
II. Period of Great Leaders: Moses to Saul (Exodus to 1 Samuel)
III. Period of Kings: Saul to the Babylonian Captivity (Samuel, Kings, Chronicles, prophetical books)
IV. Period of foreign kings: captivity to coming of Christ (Ezra, Nehemiah, Esther, Ezekiel, Daniel)

I. Period of Patriarchs: Adam to Moses (Genesis)
We find in this period: (1) God's chosen men; (2) God's chosen family; (3) God's chosen people—the tribes of Israel.

1. *God's chosen men:* In the beginning we find no nations. God chose men who made him known, but the earth became more and more wicked (Genesis 6:5).
   The chosen men were:

   Adam, created in God's image
   Seth, his godly son
   Enoch, who walked with God
   Noah, who built the ark
   Shem (Noah's son) and his descendants

   The important events during this time were:

   Creation (Genesis 1–2)
   Fall (Genesis 3)
   Flood (Genesis 6–8)
   Babel and the dispersion (Genesis 11)

Four great nations were established as a result:

Egypt in North Africa
Canaan on the Mediterranean
Babylonia between the Tigris and Euphrates rivers
Assyria, north of Babylonia

2. *God's chosen family:* The human race had failed (Genesis 6:5), so God limited his promises to a single family. He called Abraham to become the father of this nation.
   The important events are:

Abraham called (Genesis 12:1–25:11)
Jacob chosen (Genesis 25:19–36:43)
Joseph cherished (Genesis 45–46)

3. *God's chosen people:* Twelve tribes become a nation.

II. Period of Great Leaders: Moses to Saul (Exodus to 1 Samuel)
We find in this period:

1. The exodus from Egypt (Exodus)
2. The wilderness wandering (Exodus, Leviticus, Numbers, Deuteronomy)
3. The conquest of Canaan (Joshua)
4. The rule of the judges (Judges)

III. Period of Kings: Saul to the Babylonian Captivity (Samuel, Kings, Chronicles, and the Prophets)
Tribal life developed into national life. We find in this period:

1. The united kingdom — Saul, David, Solomon
2. The divided kingdom
   Kings of Israel—northern kingdom
   Kings of Judah—southern kingdom
3. The fall of the northern kingdom
4. The fall of the southern kingdom

IV. Period of Foreign Kings: Captivity to Christ (Ezra, Nehemiah, Esther, Ezekiel, and Daniel)
God was preparing the land, the people, and the world for the

coming Christ. We find in this period restoration under Persian kings.

Review the books of the Bible by stating how Christ is portrayed in each one.

SURVEY QUIZ

Who Are the Following?

1. This man (a) was never born; (b) never had a birthday; (c) owned a great estate; (d) was physically perfect; (e) was a great zoologist, giving every animal a name.
2. This man (a) was father of the oldest man in the world; (b) lived a godly life in one of the most wicked generations in the world; (c) was the only man in three thousand years who did not die; (d) walked into heaven.
3. This man (a) was radiant with righteousness in the midst of moral darkness and saved his family of seven by his faith in God; (b) was a great ship builder, but built a huge ship on a desert, miles from the sea; (c) never had to launch his ship into the sea—the sea came to it and lifted it to the top of a mountain; (d) gathered the greatest collection of animals the world has ever known; (e) had sons who were the fathers of the nations of the world.
4. This man was akin to a covered wagon pioneer: (a) he left a great city of culture at God's request and traveled across a trackless desert; (b) he left a beautiful home and lived in a tent for one hundred years; (c) he was called "a friend of God"; (d) he was the father of a great nation; (e) his son was born after he was a hundred years old; (f) angels visited him.
5. This man (a) and his young friend believed God when no one else would; (b) was a great general; (c) did not have to build a bridge to transport his army into the land that he wanted to conquer; (d) used trumpets instead of bombers and priests instead of trained soldiers to destroy a city.
6. This man (a) was an adopted child; (b) lived amidst the wealth of the day; (c) enjoyed unlimited education; (d) in spite of this, chose to identify himself with the poor people from whom he came rather than with the rulers with whom he lived; (e) was forced to live in a desert for forty years; (f) was chosen as the leader of three million people and led

them out from under the bondage of the strongest ruler of his day without firing a shot; (g) made slaves become rich overnight; (h) was the meekest man on earth and yet lost his temper; (i) talked with God; (j) died an unknown death; (k) was buried by no man.

Answers: 1. Adam 2. Enoch 3. Noah 4. Abraham 5. Joshua 6. Moses

Did You Know This?

1. Between chapters 6 and 7 of Ezra:

   ☐ Three great world battles were fought (Salamis, Thermopylae, and Marathon)
   ☐ Two great world leaders died (Confucius and Buddha)
   ☐ The events in the book of Esther took place
   ☐ Time elapsed: fifty-eight years (516–458 B.C.)!

2. In the Old Testament, Esther follows Nehemiah; in history, the events in Esther occur thirty years before Nehemiah.

The purposes of God are sometimes delayed but never abandoned.

UNDERSTANDING ESTHER

Esther Portrays Jesus Christ, Our Advocate

You have heard of the great Xerxes, king of Persia, of his famous expedition against Greece, and how the Greeks defeated his tremendous fleet at the battle of Salamis in 480 B.C. Historians tell us that this was one of the world's most important battles. Xerxes was the Ahasuerus of the book of Esther.

In the midst of this famous chapter in world history occurs the beautiful and charming story of Esther. Although God's name is not mentioned in the book of Esther, every page is full of God, who hides himself behind every word. Matthew Henry, the great Bible commentator, said, "If the name of God is not here, his finger is." God has a part in all the events of human life.

The world today cannot get rid of God; neither could Israel. He has never let his people go in the past and he will never let them go in the future. He followed them in their captivity into Babylon. When the prophets were silent and the Temple closed, God was still standing guard. When the kings of earth feasted and forgot, God remembered, and with his hand he wrote their doom or moved their hands to work his glory.

This book opens with a feast of the world's prince—Ahasuerus; it closes with the feast of God's prince—Mordecai. For a while Haman is exalted; at last, Mordecai. As you read this story, note the upsets in human history and the final triumph of God's chosen people.

Esther is like Joseph and David. God had each one hidden away for his purpose. When the day came, he brought them to the front to work out his plan. God hid Joseph away in a dungeon in Egypt, but when he was ready God placed him in the position of prime minister of that country. God always has someone in reserve to fulfill his purposes. Sometimes it is a man like Joseph, or Moses. Sometimes it is a woman like Hannah, or Esther, or Mary.

Esther stands out as God's chosen one. She is a sweet and winsome person. She had come to the kingdom for just such a time as this (4:14). We see her taking her life in her hands. As she went in for her people's sake to the king, she said, *If I perish, I perish* (4:16).

Two beautiful women join hands in behalf of God's people. They are Ruth and Esther. The books about them are the only ones in the Bible that bear the names of women. Ruth became the ancestress of the Deliverer of Israel (Jesus), and Esther saved the people so that the Deliverer could come. God carefully protected this nation through the centuries for the purpose of blessing the whole world. They could not be wiped out before they brought the Savior into the world. Their destruction was not according to God's plans. God kept this nation according to his promise to Abraham.

In what period this story was written and who was its author are unknown. In point of time, it is placed between chapters 6 and 7 of the book of Ezra. Comparatively few—not more than fifty thousand—of the captive Jews had returned from Babylon under the edict of Cyrus. Many were born in Babylon, had established themselves in business there, and were not inclined to cross the desert and begin all over again in the land of their fathers. If they had all returned to Jerusalem, the book of Esther would not have been written.

Someone has said that all the events of this book center around three feasts:

1. Feast of King Ahasuerus (ch. 1–2)
2. Feast of Esther (ch. 7)
3. Feast of Purim (ch. 9)

REJECTION OF VASHTI
ESTHER 1

The great feast to which Vashti refused to come—as has been learned from inscriptions and parallel passages in Herodotus—

was held to consider the expedition against Greece, for which Xerxes spent four years in preparation.

As this book opens the king was entertaining all the nobles and princes of his kingdom in the royal palace at Shushan. The banquet was on a colossal scale. It lasted 180 days (1:4). The men were feasting in the gorgeous palace gardens and the women were entertained by the beautiful Queen Vashti in her private apartment.

Shushan was the winter residence of the Persian kings. Remember, Nehemiah was in the palace in Shushan (Nehemiah 1:1). In 1852 its site was identified. Later the places mentioned in the book of Esther were definitely located — the "inner court," the "outer court," the "king's gate," the "palace garden." Also discovered was a die, or pur, which they used to cast lots.

When the king and princes were in the midst of their drunken revelry, the king called for Vashti so that he could show off her beauty. Of course, no Persian woman would permit this. It was an affront to her womanhood. Drunkenness had outraged the most sacred rules of Oriental etiquette. The seclusion of the harem was to be violated for the amusement of the dissolute king and his companions. Vashti refused. This made the king a laughingstock. To defend himself, he deposed the queen (1:12-22).

CROWNING OF ESTHER
ESTHER 2

The minute Ahasuerus saw Esther he made her his queen. The Jewish orphan girl, brought up by her cousin Mordecai, was lifted to the Persian throne. At this time the Persian Empire comprised over half the then-known world.

Between chapters 1 and 2, Ahasuerus made his historic attack on Greece with an army of five million men, suffering a terrible defeat.

Two years after Ahasuerus was defeated in the famous battles of Thermopylae and Salamis, he married Esther. She was his queen for thirteen years. Esther, no doubt, lived for many years into the reign of her stepson, Artaxerxes. Under this king, Nehemiah rebuilt Jerusalem. It was probably Esther's marriage to Xerxes that gave the Jews prestige at this court and made it possible for Nehemiah to rebuild Jerusalem. (See Nehemiah 2:1-8.)

The great palace of Xerxes at Persepolis, where Esther no doubt spent much of her time, has been excavated. The description of it, even in its ruin, is magnificent. The city itself was destroyed by fire by Alexander the Great in 331 B.C. It has been buried in the sands of the desert ever since. In 1930 the palace was excavated and restored as completely as possible.

To make the story of Esther more real and interesting, let us give you a little description of this palace. The foundation of the palace was a platform fifty feet high, covering an area of two and a half acres. Underneath was a vast sewer system miles in length. The walls of the palace were covered with the most magnificent carvings and reliefs and sculptures. Two large rooms in the Louvre display these treasures. When the rubbish was finally cleared away, they found these carvings preserved, as fresh and beautiful as they were when Queen Esther walked through the corridors and looked upon them.

The second chapter describes the scene in this palace. Richly colored awnings were stretched across from marble pillars to silver rods, shading the exalted guests as they reclined on gold and silver seats while they feasted gluttonously and drank heavily day after day (1:5-8).

There was a grand audience hall where men came from the four corners of the earth to pay their honor to the great king, Esther's husband. The giant columns still rise in their grandeur, speaking of the former glory of the palace. This was the place to which Esther was brought as queen.

Note: At the end of chapter 2, parenthetically, occurs the story of Mordecai's saving the king's life. This account figures prominently later in the book.

PLOTTING OF HAMAN
ESTHER 3-4

We see a form casting a shadow across the picture. This scene is one of sorrow and mourning. In Esther 3–5 we read of the ascendance of a man by the name of Haman. He was a wicked man whose day of triumph was short and whose joy endured but for a moment. (See Job 20:4-5.) We see him becoming the chief minister of the king.

Haman was a wicked monster in the life of God's chosen people. To this day during the reading of the book of Esther in a Jewish synagogue at the Feast of Purim, the congregation may be found taking part in a chorus at every mention of the name of Haman—"May his name be blotted out"—while boys pound stones and bits of wood on which his hated name is written.

When Haman appears in Esther 3:1 he had just been exalted to the highest position under the king of Persia. The high honor turned his head. He swelled with vanity and was bitterly humiliated when a porter at the gate did not do homage to him as to the king (3:2).

Inflated with pride, he could not endure the indifference of even one of his subjects. The little fault of Mordecai was magnified into a capital offense. Mordecai, a Jew, could not give divine honor to a man! Haman became so enraged that he wanted to have a wholesale massacre of all the Jews in the kingdom (3:6). To determine the day his enemies should be destroyed, he cast lots, which fell on February 28, just ten months away (3:7). Haman tried to prove to the king that all the Jews were disloyal subjects. He offered to pay the king a bribe of millions of dollars (3:9). The king signed a royal decree that meant that every Jewish man, woman, and child would be killed and all their property should be taken. Compare this treatment with that used by the Nazi regime.

Imagine the fasting and praying and the weeping in sackcloth that took place among the Jews (4:1-3). Queen Esther saw it all and inquired of Mordecai what it meant. He gave her a copy of the king's decree that told the sad story. Then he added, *Who can say but that God has brought you into the palace for just such a time as this?* (4:14).

It would do well for each one of us to pause and ask this same question. Why has God allowed me to live at this particular time? To do what is right may mean that we must jeopardize our lives. Then we must face the issue and answer with this young queen, *And if I perish, I perish.*

VENTURE OF ESTHER
ESTHER 5

Queen Esther answered the challenge of Mordecai. She who had been placed in the palace "on flowery beds of ease" had not succumbed to the luxury of her surroundings. She chose a course at terrible danger to herself for the sake of her oppressed people, the Jews.

There is one thing to do always. Do what is right and leave the rest to God. God prepares people for emergencies. Failure is not sin; faithlessness is. There is a time to act. "There is a tide in the affairs of men which taken at the flood leads on to fortune." Act when God speaks.

The beauty of Esther was that she was not spoiled by her great elevation. Though she became the queen of a great king, she did not forget the kind official who brought her up from childhood. When she once accepted her dreaded task, she proceeded to carry it out with courage. It was a daring act for her to enter unsummoned into the presence of the king. Who could tell what this fickle monarch would do? Think what he had done to Vashti!

When Esther had been received by the king, she used her resources. She knew the king's weakness for good living so she invited him to a banquet. Read what happened that night when the king could not sleep (6:1-11). How was Haman trapped (6:6)? At the second banquet Esther pleaded for her own life. She had Haman on the spot.

The king granted Esther's wish. Haman was hung on the very scaffold that he had prepared for Mordecai, and Mordecai was elevated to the place of honor next to the king.

As you study God's Word you will find that through the ages Satan has ever tried to destroy God's people, the Jews, then the church, and even Christ himself. But God has thwarted his plans. Even *the powers of hell shall not prevail against* his church. God will triumph! Christ has won the victory!

DELIVERANCE OF THE JEWS
ESTHER 6–10

The book of Esther closes with the account of the establishment of the Feast of Purim and the lifting of Mordecai to the place made vacant by Haman (10:3). Mordecai became the second man, just under the king of Persia. The Feast of Purim was to be celebrated annually. It is always inspired by the dramatic story of Esther.

The Feast of Purim, celebrated even today, sets the seal upon the accuracy of the story. The feast does not celebrate the downfall of Haman so much as the deliverance of the Jewish people.

This feast celebrates a deliverance of the Jews from a fearful danger. It was a Thanksgiving Day for the chosen people. Although they had forsaken God, he had spared them. Deliverance seems to be the keynote of Jewish history. God has always delivered this nation from danger and servitude. Even yet, God will deliver his people in the hour of their trouble.

This book of Esther is an important link in a chain of events that tells of the reestablishment of the Hebrew nation in their own land in preparation of the coming of the Messiah into the world. The Jews had escaped extermination. It was God's purpose for them to be preserved to bring forth the Savior of the world.

CHARACTER STUDY OF ESTHER

Esther is a sweet and attractive character:

Beautiful and modest (2:15)
Winsome (2:9-17; 5:1-3)
Obedient (2:10)
Humble (4:16)
Courageous (7:6)
Loyal and constant (2:22; 8:1-2; 7:3-4)

There is always one thing to do—do what is right and leave the rest with God.

God meets emergencies with human lives which he has redeemed and prepared.

Prayer moves the hand that moves the world. A devoted woman moved a determined monarch.

Those who walk in holy sincerity with Christ may walk in holy security among men.

God's pioneers leave all—to gain all.

SELECTED BIBLE READING

Sunday: Rejection of Vashti (Esther 1)
Monday: Crowning of Esther (Esther 2)
Tuesday: Plotting of Haman (Esther 3–4)

Wednesday: Venture of Esther (Esther 5)
Thursday: Mordecai Exalted (Esther 6)
Friday: Esther's Feast (Esther 7–8)
Saturday: Deliverance of the Jews (Esther 9–10)

CHAPTER 15

UNDERSTANDING
JOB

Job Portrays Jesus Christ, Our Redeemer

We have finished reading the historical books of the Old Testament—Joshua through Esther. Now we open the books of poetry—Job, Psalms, Proverbs, Ecclesiastes and Song of Solomon. These books tell of the experiences of the heart.

Job is no doubt one of the most wonderful poems ever written. Tennyson called it "the greatest poem, whether of ancient or modern literature." The scene in this amazing book is laid in the patriarchal days. For all we know, this book may be one of the most ancient pieces of finished literature in existence. It is one of the oldest books in the Bible, if not the oldest. The Word of God settles the fact that Job was a real person. God speaks through the prophet Ezekiel and says, *If Noah, Daniel, and Job were here today, they alone would be saved by their righteousness* (Ezekiel 14:14; see also 14:20). If you doubt Job's existence, you will have to refute Noah and Daniel.

It is fitting that the oldest book deals with the oldest problems. Among these is "Why do godly people suffer?" This is the theme of the book. People have always asked why God permits good people to suffer. Haven't you wondered yourself why some good person has to die of an awful disease or has to be confined to a bed of pain? The drama of Job offers a solution to these problems. We believe it gives God's answer.

It is easy to become confused about this problem of suffering. Remember that the disciples of Christ thought suffering was the result of sin in a life (John 9:2). The book of Job gives an entirely different reason for the suffering of Job. In this case, Job was being honored by God. The truth was that God could trust Job to remain faithful to him in spite of everything. How wonderful it would be if you and I learned to thank God in all that happens to us.

This book should first be read as a narrative. The story of Job is a simple one. It opens with a scene in heaven and then tells of Job's fall from prosperity to poverty. This is followed by the great discussion between Job and his four friends: Eliphaz, the religious dogmatist, much like an ancient Pharisee; Bildad, who sought to comfort Job with worn-out platitudes; and Zophar, who thought he had a corner on all religious wisdom. Then comes Elihu, the impetuous youth. Finally, the climax is reached when God speaks. Job answers, at last in a humble spirit, and the problem is solved. This is the story of the book.

Next, we should study the problem of the book. It may be stated, "Why do the righteous suffer?" We find:

First, Satan's shallow viewpoint—that the children of God love and serve him because it pays in riches and honor (1:1–2:8). Satan said that Job's godliness was selfishness, that he served God for profit, that when prosperity ended he would be godly no more. He received permission to test Job (2:6). Satan added, "Who wouldn't serve God for a handsome income of so many thousand a year? Watch him when his prosperity ends."

Second, the scarcely less false viewpoint of Eliphaz, Bildad, and Zophar (who agreed for the most part)—that the unrighteous suffer because of their sins, and the righteous are rewarded. Hence they reasoned that Job must have sinned, and this suffering was his punishment. Job was a great sufferer; therefore he must have been a great sinner. They said, *Have you ever known a truly good and innocent person who was punished?* (4:7).

Third, Elihu had a far more just answer to the problem, but his eloquent discourse was marred by conceit. He defended God and saw in affliction the chastisement of a loving Father. But this did not explain to Job the reason for suffering. Elihu argued that suffering was God's discipline to bring his sons back into fellowship with himself. He believed that suffering was sent to keep us from from sinning.

Fourth, God explained to Job (by revealing himself to him) that when men see God something always happens. The godly are allowed to suffer so that they can see themselves first. Read Isaiah 6:1-5; Genesis 17:1-3; Daniel 10:4-8. When we come to the end of ourselves, God can lift us up. Job was a good man, but

self-righteous. Read Job 29 and you will find the personal pro-
nouns "I," "my," and "me" thirty-nine times. It reminds one of
Romans 7.

God has a wise purpose in all of our suffering. God wants to
show his perfect wisdom (Ephesians 3:10). He wants the trial of
our faith to work patience. He wants to bring out the gold as by
fire. He wants to reveal real character. Furthermore, we have *a
crowd of witnesses* gathered in the great stadium of heaven to
watch us in the conflict (Hebrews 12:1-2).

How little did Job realize that so much hung on his steadfastness and trust in God. I wonder if we realize today the issues
that hang upon our faithfulness to God. If God could only find
more of us who would trust him, how much we might encourage
others to trust!

The problem of suffering has had much light thrown upon it
from the New Testament—especially from the cross of Christ.
Here we see the world's most righteous Man, the world's greatest
Sufferer. We know now that the righteous suffer with the wicked
today because of sin that fills the world with misery. We know
there are natural consequences of sin, for the godly as well as
the sinner. We have already noted that chastening is sometimes
for training and correction. There is a suffering that Christians
must endure for Christ's sake and the gospel's.

The book of Job is a commentary on 1 Corinthians 11:31-32;
Hebrews 12:7-11; Luke 22:31-32; 1 Corinthians 5:5. And it deals
with a wide scope of knowledge—the power of Satan, telling of
his might and the limit of his authority; the fact of the Resurrection; and why a person should serve God.

The book of Job tells us much about human suffering. Job's
friends, as thousands do today, made the mistake of thinking
that all suffering was God's way of punishing sin.

Do you know of any good person today who is suffering? Of
course you do. One of the greatest saints I ever knew was blind;
another was so poor that we, as children, carried him things to
eat and saved our money to buy him clothes. We gave material
things to him, but he gave spiritual blessings to us.

God allowed Stephen to be stoned (Acts 7) and Paul to have
a thorn in his flesh to hurt and bother him (2 Corinthians 12).
Even Jesus knew suffering.

What was Job's attitude toward God? He first had access to
God through the blood of the sacrifice (1:5). Then he walked
with God in integrity of heart and life.

Job had a conscience that was right toward God. He knew his heart was true and so he could accept the accusations of his friends. He finally could show them that their conclusion was wrong and that the wicked often prosper in this world (24:6).

God trusted Job; therefore he assigned to him this great problem of suffering. When Job was in the midst of his anguish he realized that it is only the gold that is worth putting into the fire. Anything else would be consumed. James said, *Is your life full of difficulties and temptations? Then be happy, for when the way is rough, your patience has a chance to grow* (James 1:2-3).

When Job was prosperous and upright and benevolent, he was in danger of becoming self-confident and could easily forget that he only held his power and place in this world as a steward of God. God does not give us great gifts just to please ourselves. The Westminster Confession tells us that the chief end of man is to glorify God. *Christ didn't please himself* (Romans 15:3). He came to glorify the Father.

God dealt with Job:

1. He was broken (16:12; 17:11)
2. He was melted (23:10)

Do you ever sing, "Spirit of the living God, fall afresh on me; melt me; mold me; fill me; use me"? Do you know what it might mean for you? This is what happened to Job.

Job never really saw himself until he saw God. This is true of every life. See how it affected Isaiah when he, as a young man, saw God (Isaiah 6:1-9).

Job was all ready to reason with God, as many do today, about his dealings with him. He could not understand him. It was a vision of God himself that completed the work in Job and brought him to the dust.

Listen to God speak of Job, *Do you still want to argue with the Almighty? . . . Do you . . . have the answers?* (40:2). Think of trying to teach the God of this universe! The wisdom of man is only foolishness with God. Hear Job's answer: *I am nothing. . . . I lay my hand upon my mouth in silence* (40:4).

God kept dealing with Job till he came to the very end of himself! Hear him speak again: *I was talking about things I knew nothing about and did not understand, things far too wonderful for me. . . . I had heard about you before, but now I have seen you, and I loathe myself and repent in dust and ashes* (42:3-6).

We find Job a chastened servant. God turned the tide and his prosperity was given back to him doubled—twice as many sheep and oxen, donkeys and camels! He rejoiced again in his sons and daughters, just the same number as before.

Job no longer asked a question but made a statement: *I know that my Redeemer lives, and that he will stand upon the earth at last. And I know that after this body has decayed, this body shall see God!* (19:25-26).

Job's vision of a future life, which had been uncertain before, was clear now. We had heard him asking a question that multitudes have asked: *If a man dies, shall he live again?* (14:14). Paul answered this question in the great resurrection chapter of the Bible, 1 Corinthians 15. Jesus answered it in his statement, *Anyone who believes in me, even though he dies like anyone else, shall live again* (John 11:25).

What a wonderful vision of the future life we have in these words! What a prophecy of the coming of the Savior!

Job was *a good man who fears God and will have nothing to do with evil* (1:8).

Job was right with man and with God, and remember, it was God who said this. God added, *He is the finest man in all the earth* (1:8). What an honor God gave to Job to use these words to describe him!

As the book opens we see Job surrounded by wealth, family, position, and friends. Let us watch this man whom God said was perfect! We see this man visited by Satan. A swift succession of calamities followed. Remember, these things did not come because of anything wrong in this man, Job. All of Job's friends thought that the reason for his trouble lay in himself. But God made it very plain in the opening of the book that this was not true.

Watch this man stripped of his wealth and reduced to poverty! His children are taken! Health is gone! Then he loses the confidence of his wife! Finally his friends go!

SATAN AND THE SAINT
JOB 1:6-2:10

In Job 1:6 the angels presented themselves before the Lord. The mystery is that Satan was among them. He was angelic, but he had fallen. There was no hint that he was out of place or that he had forced himself into the audience chamber.

In contrast to the Almighty we have the figure of the adversary, Satan. Let us stop and study this person for a while. Satan, as the accuser, is depicted with great clearness—a real being, not an imaginary one. We cannot help but contrast the Satan of the book of Job with the grotesque, gigantic, awful figure depicted by the poets. The Bible tells us that Satan comes as *an angel of light* to deceive and to tempt (2 Corinthians 11:14).

Our strange idea of the Devil is derived from Dante's *Inferno*, where he attempted to describe this monster of hell. His enormous size depicted by Dante is matched by his hideousness. We find, too, a picture of Satan given by Milton in *Paradise Lost*. His description is magnificent, but it has little justification from Scripture. This regal archfiend has no kinships with the Satan of the book of Job. Neither is Mephistopheles of *Faust* the true picture, although, no doubt, Goethe's picture of a cynical devil, gaily damning a mind, is based on the book of Job.

Satan could bring up the hosts of Sabeans and Chaldeans and have them carry away the oxen and donkeys and camels of Job (1:13-17). He could slay the sheep by lightning, cause the wind to kill Job's children, and even strike Job himself with boils. Remember, he is *the prince of the power of the air* (Ephesians 2:2).

Know this besides! Satan has great power, but there are limits to his might. Satan is mighty, but God is Almighty! Satan can break through only where God allows (1:10). What a comfort it is to know that no calamity can come to us that the Father does not allow. He *who decreed the boundaries of the seas . . . and said, "Thus far and no farther shall you come, and here shall your proud waves stop"* (38:8, 11) will never let us be tempted more than we are able to stand up against it (1 Corinthians 10:13).

Remember, Satan is so held by the Almighty that he can strike only where he is given permission (1:12).

Job tore his clothes (1:20). It is worthwhile for us to learn that we are meant to feel grief. Sorrow has its use in our life (Hebrews 13:5, 11). Jesus wept! Christ does not destroy our natural emotions. Jesus told the women of Jerusalem to weep for themselves and for their children.

Job recognized that loss and sorrow are the laws of life. We have to learn that all possessions are transient. We are losing something every moment. We cannot stop and weep over everything that is taken from us. We have to learn a hard lesson—that we can live on in spite of all our losses. We must learn, and the earlier the better, that nothing is necessary but Christ.

Only pure gold can stand the fire. All dross is burned up. God, the great metallurgist of heaven, puts us in the fire, but he watches and tries us himself. He trusts no other. When the fire has burned long enough to destroy the impurities, he pulls us out.

God spoke to Satan, *Where have you come from?* What a tragedy in the answer! *From Earth, where I've been watching everything that's going on* (1:7).

God spoke again, *Have you noticed my servant Job?* (1:8).

What do you think God meant by "noticed" Job? It is a strong word in the Hebrew language, as if he had been watching his every act. "Have you been trying to find a flaw?"

Satan said, *Why shouldn't he [fear you], when you pay him so well?* (1:9). He seemed to imply, "I'm trying to find out why this fellow is so perfect." There was a reason. *You have always protected him and his home and his property from all harm.* That was the truth, of course. Then he added, *You have prospered everything he does.* This was true also. *Look how rich he is!* (1:10). Yes, all this was correct.

But Satan went on, *Just take away his wealth, and you'll see him curse you to your face!* (1:11). Satan's charge against Job was that a man only serves God for what he can get out of it. Really Job was not so much on trial here as God. It was not a question of Job's loyalty so much as it was one of God's power. Is God able to *safely guard all that I have given to him* (2 Timothy 1:12)?

So God said, "All right, try it out! Take everything away from Job and see what happens!"

Do you see that the real conflict here was between God and Satan? God was proving the truth about his statement of Job's integrity in following him.

When the trials came, Job did not understand the meaning of all his suffering. He knew it was not because he had sinned, as his friends said. He wondered what God was doing. We will not always understand what God is working out on the battleground of our hearts. But know this: There is a reason and value to everything that God allows and *all that happens to us is working for our good if we love God and are fitting into his plans* (Romans 8:28).

Job proved that Satan's statement concerning God's children— that they only serve him for what they can get out of it—was a lie.

Don't always try to find the reason for our trials and experiences. Sometimes we will have to wait for the answer. We wonder why God allows a Borden of Yale to die when he is only a young man at the threshold of a life of service and allows an old, drunken, apparently good-for-nothing man to live.

We will never find the answer to all of God's dealings. We may be honest and sincere, as were Job's friends, but *how impossible it is for us to understand his decisions and his methods!*(Romans 11:33).

Do not be surprised to find hypocrites in every congregation of God's children. Satan comes to do mischief to saints. He distracts our attention. He sets us to criticizing. He sows dissension in the congregation. He excites the pride of preachers and singers, of givers and those who publicly pray. He chills our spirit and freezes our prayers. Yes, when the Word is being sown, the birds of the air come to pluck it away (Matthew 13:3-23).

Remember, we can never walk before God and try to lead godly lives without Satan coming in to walk with us—accusing us, finding fault with us, and vexing us.

What Kind of a Man Was Job?
He was a perfect man (1:1)
He was a prosperous man (1:2-4)
He was a praying man (1:5)
He was a popular man (29:21, 25)
He was a proven man (42:10, 12)

JOB AND HIS FRIENDS
JOB 2:11-37:24

Get acquainted with Job's friends. Let us introduce you to them. First there is courtly Eliphaz, then argumentative Bildad, and blunt Zophar, and the youthful Elihu.

This is a familiar scene. Everyone has a reason to offer as an explanation for his experiences and problems. Job's four friends came. Do you know Job was rich in friends? Generally when a man loses his wealth and position and health, he has no friends left.

There are things we can say in favor)f these men although their words of "comfort" were anything ¹ ut that. The first is that they came at all. They were friends who stuck through adversity. When all the multitude of acquaintance⸱ had forgotten Job, they came.

You notice they kept quiet for seven days. This is good! They seemed to be trying to find out the reason for all of Job's troubles before they spoke. Someone has said that instead of talking about Job, they came and talked with him.

They all had a reason; they wished to tell Job why they thought he was suffering as he did. They all agreed that he must have sinned miserably to have caused this suffering.

Eliphaz backed his argument by a dream (4:1–5:27); Bildad, by some old proverbs (ch. 8); Zophar, by experience and reason (ch. 11). Elihu came nearest the truth when he argued that suffering was God's discipline to bring the soul back into fellowship with God, but it was not the whole truth.

God called Job "a good man." His friends were wrong in charging him with sin as the only possible cause of his calamities.

Wretched Comforters

The chief question returns: "Why does God permit the righteous to suffer?" Job cried out from the ashes, "I cannot understand it. It doesn't seem right."

Job's wife, looking on discouraged, said, "Something is wrong. Your religion is a failure. Curse God and die." This literally meant, "Say good-bye to God." It was the voice of despair.

Eliphaz added, shaking his head, "God never makes a mistake. What have you done to bring this on yourself?"

Zophar spoke next, "God is all-wise. He knows man."

Elihu, God's man, said the wisest thing, "God is good; look up and trust him, for he is God."

The Righteous Comforter

The Lord now was heard from the whirlwind: *Let me ask you a question, and give me the answer* (40:7).

Then Job himself spoke: *I know that you can do anything and that nothing can stop you* (42:2). Then came the great confession: *I had heard about you before, but now I have seen you, and I loathe myself [count myself out] and repent in dust and ashes* (42:5-6).

This is the victory of submissive faith. When we bow to God's will, we find God's way. Stoop to conquer. Bend to obey. This is the lesson of Job.

The philosophy of Job's friends was wrong. Job was glad to see them, and he could pour out his troubles to them, but they did not understand him.

Job even lost his friends! He had tried to explain, but he was misunderstood. Only God understands!

THE LORD AND JOB
JOB 38–42

The scene began with God gloriously revealing himself. In a series of approximately sixty questions, God was saying, in effect, "Who can do all these things but myself?" God was thus revealed to Job, and Job to himself.

As so often is true with us, when Job came into the presence of God he forgot the speech he thought he would make (40:4-5)! There was no arguing with God. Finally, Job went flat down on his face, repenting "in dust and ashes" (42:6). This is the only place to learn God's lessons—on your face, with your mouth shut!

The Lord explained to Job (by revealing himself to him) that when men see God something always happens. The godly are allowed to suffer so that they can see themselves. Read Isaiah 6:1-5. When Isaiah saw himself as he really was, he fell on his face undone and cried out, *I am a foul-mouthed sinner.*

Did you ever think that you looked all right until some friend dropped in to invite you to go someplace with him? When you saw how immaculate your friend looked, you immediately realized how you needed a good grooming. So often this is true in the presence of Christ. The very immaculateness of his Person makes us feel sinful. Measure your life by his life and you will feel as Job did.

In Job 42 we find:

1. A consciousness of God (v. 5)
2. A collapse of Job (v. 6)
3. A commission to serve (v. 7)

As you read the chapter, you see that Job enjoyed a double portion of prosperity from the hand of God. God allows his children to suffer in order to reveal character, to set forth an object lesson, and to bring to light some hidden sin. In Job's case, that hidden sin was self-righteousness.

This book well illustrates the text of Romans 8:28. How wonderful to hear of the patience of Job and to have seen in the end that the Lord is merciful. A morning of joy always follows the night of sorrow.

Job found God in his trouble. Many know God as a Creator and believe in his greatness, but they do not really know God.

The more we understand his ways the more we will love him and put our trust in him.

Job is rich in philosophy. Ancient as the book is, it is filled with a divine record of human philosophy, the blind gropings of human wisdom. Human reason has never been able to go beyond Job's friends in explaining the great mysteries of human experience on natural grounds. (See 1 Corinthians 2:14 and Colossians 2:8.)

Job is rich in gems of spiritual truth. Be sure to read the following references: Job 1:21; 5:17; 13:15; 14:14; 16:21; 19:23-27; 23:10; 26:7-14; 28:12-28; 42:1-6. These are some of the most frequently quoted and best loved passages in the Bible.

SELECTED BIBLE READING

Sunday: Satan and Saint (Job 1–2)
Monday: Bildad Thinks Job Is a Hypocrite (Job 8)
Tuesday: Job Answers His Friends (Job 12)
Wednesday: Job's Faith (Job 19)
Thursday: Job and Elihu (Job 32–37)
Friday: God Speaks to Job (Job 38–41)
Saturday: Job Vindicated and Honored (Job 42)

CHAPTER 16

UNDERSTANDING
PSALMS

Psalms Portrays Jesus Christ, Our All in All

Oh, come let us sing to the Lord! Give a joyous shout in honor of the Rock of our salvation! (95:1). Here we take this view of the Psalms in panorama. The sights that catch and hold our attention are so numerous as to defy exhaustive treatment in one short chapter.

No doubt Psalms is the best loved book in the Old Testament. Someone has called it the solid gold of Christian experience. Slip in wherever you want and you will find a treasure. Every psalm is a direct expression of the soul's consciousness of God. With which psalms are you familiar? Pause a moment to think.

The Hebrew title of this book is *Praise*, or the *Book of Praises*, which indicates that the main contents of the book are praise, prayer, and worship. The name *Psalms* comes from Greek. We find that the early Christian fathers called it the *Psalter*.

The Psalms is the national hymnbook of Israel. It contains 150 poems to be set to music for worship. Worship is the central idea. The Psalms magnify and praise the Lord, exalt his attributes, his names, his Word, and his goodness. Every human experience is related to him.

We see the life of the believer pictured in all of its experiences of joy and sorrow, victory and failure.

There are numerous quotations from this book found in the New Testament. At least twenty of these are in direct reference to Christ and his life and death.

The Psalms are full of Christ. They describe the whole program of his suffering and death. We have Christ's own warrant for looking for him in the Psalms. He said, *Everything written about me . . . in the Psalms must all come true* (Luke 24:44). Let us look and see!

His prophetic office (22:22)
His priestly office (40:6, 8; 22; 49; 110)
His kingly office (2; 21; 45; 72)
His sufferings (22; 69)
His resurrection (16)

Another extremely useful classification of the Psalms may be made according to the subjects of the individual psalms:

Instruction (1; 19; 39)
Praise (8; 29; 93; 100)
Thanksgiving (30; 65; 103; 107; 116)
Penitence (6; 32; 38; 51; 102; 130; 143)
Trust (3; 27; 31; 46; 56; 62; 86)
Distress (4; 13; 55; 64; 88)
Aspiration (42; 63; 80; 84; 137)
History (78; 105; 106)
Prophecy of the Messiah (2; 16; 22; 24; 40; 45; 68; 69; 72; 97; 110; 118)

We speak of the Psalms as the Psalms of David. He has been considered the principal writer. He gives the keynote, and his voice rises highest in the sacred choir. But there were other authors besides him. Seventy-three of the 150 Psalms are assigned to him; fifty are anonymous. Psalm 90 is by Moses. Two are by Solomon—Psalms 22 and 127. Besides these, Asaph, David's choir leader; the sons of Korah, a family of official musicians; and Jeduthun wrote some. But let us not be too engrossed in finding who penned them. Let us rather read and enjoy these grand expressions of praise. They are of God for you. Sing them and make them your own. Catch David's note and spirit. He had marching songs, prayer songs, rally songs, hilltop songs, confession songs. Sing as you march. Keep step with David and David's Lord all the way.

MAN
PSALMS 1–41

1. Man blessed (Psalm 1)
2. Man fallen from his high position and at enmity with God (Psalms 2; 14)
3. Man restored by his blessed Redeemer, the Man Christ Jesus (Psalms 16–41)

In this section we have a collection by David of the psalms that tell of the state of man—his blessedness, fall, and recovery. Psalm 1 tells us of the road to success. Everyone wants to prosper. No one wishes to fail. The psalmist says that everyone can prosper. Think of it! It will be well for every person to master the rules for success laid down here.

Things Not to Do
1. Do not follow the advice of the ungodly
2. Do not keep company with sinners
3. Do not scoff at the things of God

Things to Do
1. Read the Bible
2. Delight in it
3. Meditate upon it

The more you read the Word the more you want to. As one great Christian leader has said, "The gospel feeds you, then it makes you hungry." It never grows stale. You cannot read it too often or too much.

Things That Result
When the Christian has followed the don'ts and dos of Psalm 1, what results? Three characteristics:

1. Planted—*like trees planted along a river bank*—the settled and steadfast life in a luxuriant soil
2. Purposive—*bearing luscious fruit each season*—the productive life
3. Prosperous—*their leaves shall never wither*—the abiding, happy life

Other psalms in this group that show the final blessings of man because of the glorious work of the Man Christ Jesus are Psalms 22, 23, and 24.

Psalm 22 tells of the Good Shepherd giving his life for his sheep. We see the cross and hear the cries of our dying Savior. As you read this psalm, you will recognize the facts.

Psalm 23 tells of the great Shepherd keeping his sheep. We read, *Because the Lord is my Shepherd, I have everything I need!* He promises to guide and keep me and to provide for me.

Psalm 24 tells of the chief Shepherd in his glory rewarding his sheep. He is my King and he is coming to reign in power and great glory.

Psalm 22 gives a picture of Calvary. We see the crucifixion portrayed here more clearly than in any other part of the Old Testament. The psalm opens with the cry of our Lord in the darkest hour of his life: *My God, my God, why have you forsaken me?* It closes with a phrase that in the original Hebrew means *It is finished*—the last cry of the Savior.

Psalm 22:6: *I am a worm, not a man, scorned and despised by my own people and by all mankind.* This tells us of the offense of the cross!

Read and compare these verses:

Psalm 22:1   Matthew 27:46
Psalm 22:6-7   Luke 23:35-36
Psalm 22:6-8   Matthew 27:39, 41, 43
Psalm 22:12-13   Matthew 27:36, 44
Psalm 22:28   1 Corinthians 15:23-24

My strength has drained away like water. . . . My heart melts like wax (22:14). This depicts excessive perspiration due to physical torture. It also means the breaking of Jesus' heart.

He tells us why his heart was broken. *Their contempt has broken my heart* (69:20). In John 19:34-35 we read that *one of the soldiers pierced his side with a spear, and blood and water flowed out. I saw all this myself and have given an accurate report so that you also can believe.*

Jesus died of a broken heart. He bore the reproach and shame for others. The bearing of our sins, which hid him from his Father's face, broke his heart. Death by a broken heart is very rare. It is caused by intense agony of suffering.

My tongue sticks to my mouth (22:15). This verse describes intense thirst. The account in the New Testament said, *Jesus . . . to fulfill the Scriptures said, "I'm thirsty."* Yes, Psalm 69:21 says, *For my awful thirst they offered vinegar.* Read John 19:28-29.

They have pierced my hands and my feet (22:16). Crucifixion! The Roman method of death by crucifixion is described here. The Jewish law did not know of this method. These words give the description of death by crucifixion—hands and feet nailed to the cross—bones of hands, arms, shoulders out of joint due to hanging from the cross, straining bone and muscle.

They divide my clothes among themselves by a toss of the dice (22:18). Even the act of the soldiers is described here. See Matthew 27:35.

ISRAEL
PSALMS 42-72

1. Her ruin (42–49)
2. Her Redeemer (50–60)
3. Her redemption (61–72)

In this section we find additional psalms compiled for use in the Temple. It opens with "a cry" from the depth of oppression— Psalms 42–49. It ends with the King reigning over the redeemed nation. *Let him reign from sea to sea, and from the Euphrates River to the ends of the earth* (72:8). Read this glorious psalm.

There are several psalms of penitence, but the chief is Psalm 51. It is a psalm of David. If you turn to 2 Samuel 11–12, you will find the story of David's sin. As you read this, notice three things that David said. When Nathan the prophet was telling David the story of the despicable rich man who took the only lamb belonging to the poor man, we hear him say to David: *You are that rich man!* David did not try to dodge the issue but said, *I have sinned against the Lord.* Then Nathan reassured him, saying, *Yes, but the Lord has forgiven you* (2 Samuel 12:13).

We think it strange when we read that David was *a man after his [God's] own heart.* When we compare what other kings would have done under the same circumstances, we are not surprised. But David confessed and said, *I have sinned against the Lord.* That is what sin is—breaking God's law.

You notice in Psalm 51 these words: *It is against you and you alone I sinned, and did this terrible thing* (51:4). This psalm is a prayer of contrition and confession. David cries for mercy from a God whom he knows is merciful and full of loving kindness.

We learn from this psalm that we must confess our sin to God (1 John 1:9) and that God can be depended on to forgive. Whenever a man is sincere in his confession to God, God will cleanse his sin.

THE SANCTUARY
PSALMS 73–89

In the psalms of this third section we see the sanctuary mentioned or referred to in almost every one. This section is concerned almost entirely with material used in worship service, and needs little comment.

We see God's counsels in relation to the sanctuary. The sanctuary is seen from its ruin to its restoration in the fullness of blessing.

THE EARTH
PSALMS 90–106

1. Blessing needed (90–94)
2. Blessing anticipated (95–100)
3. Blessing enjoyed (101–106)

The first of this group of psalms was written during the wanderings in the wilderness. The psalms are not arranged in chronological order.

Read the opening verses of Psalms 90 and 91 together: *Lord, through all the generations you have been our home! We live within the shadow of the Almighty, sheltered by the God who is above all gods.* If God is our home on this earth, we will live in confidence, sheltered by the Almighty. Christ says, *If you stay in me and obey my commands, you may ask any request you like, and it will be granted!* (John 15:7). The secret of a godly life is living in the Almighty. When the devil attacked him, the Lord quoted from Psalm 91. But Christ was victorious because he lived in the place described by this same psalm. We are told that there is a point of perfect calm at the center of a cyclone. There may be raging storms, snares, diseases, terror by night, darkness, and destruction, but when the soul is living within the shadow of the Almighty, it is safe.

If you wish to praise the Lord for his goodness, read Psalm 103. It is full of worship, adoration, praise, and thanksgiving. This is great exercise for the soul.

THE WORD OF GOD
PSALMS 107–150

All the teaching in the Psalms is grouped around the Word of God. This section opens with Psalm 107, which gives the key: *He spoke, and they were healed.*

Psalm 119 is the great psalm of the whole book. It extols the Word of God, which is the great revelation of the heart and mind of the Lord. This book is *sweeter than honey dripping from a honeycomb* and *more desirable than gold* (19:10). Almost every verse speaks of God's Word or law or precepts or statutes.

Value God's Word:

1. It blesses little children (Matthew 19:14)
2. It strengthens young men (1 John 2:14)
3. It makes holy and clean all who read it (Ephesians 5:26)
4. It protects the widows (Exodus 22:22-23)
5. It honors the aged (Leviticus 19:32)
6. It offers eternal life to everyone (John 3:36)

Praise is the highest duty that any creature can discharge. Man's chief end is to glorify God. There is no heaven either here or in the world to come for people who do not praise God. If you do not enter into the spirit and worship of heaven, the spirit and joy of heaven cannot enter you!

How can you make the Psalms your own in experience?

Why do you like the Psalms?

What psalms can you quote?

Probably no other book has so largely influenced the turning points in people's lives, given expression to their deepest experiences, and woven itself into every fiber of their character as has the book of Psalms.

THE POSITION OF THE BOOK

Hold your Bible in your hand and turn to the middle of the book. Most often you'll open to the Psalms. Not merely is this true physically. There is a deeper truth. The Psalms are central also in human experience.

This book is used by both Jews and Christians even in our day. The Psalms were for use in the Temple, for which many psalms were specifically prepared. They were written for the heart to worship God out under the open heavens or in the pit of despair or in a cave of hiding. When you find yourself in deep need you can always find a psalm that expresses your inmost feeling. Or, if you have an abounding joy, the words are there for you too.

It is the book for all who are in need, the sick and suffering, the poor and needy, the prisoner and exile, the man in danger, the persecuted. It is a book for the child of God, leading him into new experiences with the Lord. It tells of God's law in its perfection and pronounces blessings upon the one who will keep it.

SELECTED BIBLE READING

Sunday: Psalms of Law (Psalms 1; 19)
Monday: Psalms of Creation (Psalms 29; 104)
Tuesday: Psalms of Judgment (Psalms 52; 53)
Wednesday: Psalms of Christ (Psalms 22; 40; 41)
Thursday: Psalms of Life (Psalms 3; 31)
Friday: Psalms of the Heart (Psalms 37; 42)
Saturday: Psalms of God (Psalms 90; 139)

CHAPTER 17

UNDERSTANDING PROVERBS, ECCLESIASTES, SONG OF SOLOMON

Jesus Christ, Our Wisdom; the End of All Living; the Lover of Our Souls

UNDERSTANDING PROVERBS

The books classed as poetical are Job, Psalms, Proverbs, Ecclesiastes, and Song of Solomon. These are not "poetical" in the sense that they are fanciful or unreal, but in form only. There is no meter or rhyme, but rather a thought-rhyme expressed in parallelism—repeating the same thought in different words.

In Psalms we find the Christian on his knees. In Proverbs we find the Christian on his feet.

The Psalms are for the Christian's devotions. The Proverbs are for the Christian's activities.

The Psalms are for the closet of prayer. The Proverbs are for the business place, home, and playground.

We find in Proverbs that godliness is practical. Every relationship in life is mentioned. We find our duty to God and to our neighbors, the duty of parents and children, our obligations as citizens.

The Jews likened Proverbs to the outer court of the Temple; Ecclesiastes to the Holy Place; the Song of Solomon to the Most Holy Place. Remember that the altar of burnt offering and the basin of cleansing were in the outer court. If we come to the book of Proverbs with a cleansed and surrendered heart and mind, we will get most out of the book.

The book of Proverbs takes us out into the court of the congregation where the people are. Here they live their daily lives and jostle each other in the highways of life. This is a book for every-day instruction. It deals with the practical affairs of life. The author, Solomon, wrote more wisely than he lived. Solomon wrote four hundred years before the seven wise men of Greece. This book divides men into two classes—wise and foolish. The wise give heed to the commands of God and obey them. The foolish ignore God's will.

Notice how the book opens: *These are the proverbs of King Solomon.* Solomon was a great king, famous for his wisdom and riches. He wrote 3,000 proverbs and 1,005 songs (1 Kings 4:31-32). Solomon was especially qualified to write this book. God had given him *great wisdom and understanding, and a mind with broad interests* (1 Kings 4:29). Solomon was a philosopher, a scientist of no mean ability, an architect of a Temple that was one of the wonders of the world, and then, too, he was a king.

That Solomon was the author of this book implies no more than that he took the lead in gathering these sayings already current among the people, given by the Holy Spirit through the centuries, and put them into the orderly arrangement that we have today. See what Solomon said about this in Ecclesiastes 12:9, where it is recorded that *he collected proverbs and classified them.*

Someone has said that they were a collection of maxims, woven into a didactic poem around a general topic, wisdom.

Several names are given in Proverbs regarding its authorship.

Solomon (1:1; 25:1)
The wise (22:17)
Aides of Hezekiah (25:1)
Agur (30:1)
King Lemuel and his mother (31:1)

This book is filled with words of wisdom. There is one terse saying after another. Men have tried to add to them and failed. A brilliant lawyer tried it once. He thought he could write a few before breakfast. He came away from his task humbled and baffled and glorifying in the marvelous wisdom of God.

Proverbs is divided into three sections:

1. Counsel for young men (ch. 1–10)
2. Counsel for all men (ch. 11–20)
3. Counsel for kings and rulers (ch. 21–31)

The book closes with one of the most beautiful chapters in the Word (ch. 31). This is a chapter on women's rights. Wherever Christ goes, womanhood is lifted up.

This book presents a system of conduct and life. You cannot find any agnosticism here. God is taken for granted! Be wise and find God's way for your life! This book is to provide rules for the righteous life.

The real power and beauty in this book lie hidden in the true meaning of the word *wisdom*. It is evident that this word is more than an excellent tribute. It is found that the wisdom of Proverbs is the Incarnate Word of the New Testament. Christ himself is in this book (see Luke 24:27).

Wisdom is represented as dwelling with God from all eternity. *From ages past, I am. I existed before the earth began. . . . I was there when [God] established the heavens . . . when he set the limits of the seas . . . when he made the blueprint for the earth and oceans. I was the craftsman at his side* (8:23-31). Compare these with John 1:1-2; Hebrews 1:2; Colossians 2:3.

When you read the book of Proverbs, put *Christ* instead of *wisdom* in the verse. (See 1 Corinthians 1:30.) You will see a wonderful power in this book. *And we know that Christ, God's Son, has come to help us understand and find the true God* (1 John 5:20).

COUNSEL FOR YOUNG MEN
PROVERBS 1-10

The purpose of the book of Proverbs is stated clearly at the beginning. See Proverbs 1:2-4. We find that the first of all duties is the fear of God (1:7). God wants to give us of his wisdom—the wisdom that created heavens and earth, that we might use it in all of life (James 1:5). This would put an end to all the confusion and evil in this world, wouldn't it? Human wisdom can never solve life's problems. Only God knows the ways of men. *How can men be wise? The only way to begin is by reverence for God* (Psalm 111:10).

"Wise Up!"—worship is the first step to wisdom (1:7).

"Walk Straight!"—the straight and narrow has the lowest accident rate (2:20).

"Directions"—ask God about everything; he knows every road (3:6).

"Watch Your Step!"—every step helps mold character, so step well (4:26).

"God's Blacklist"—pride, lies, murder, deceit, mischief, betrayal, discord (6:17-19).

"A Bad Woman"—read carefully Proverbs 7:15-27.

"Riches"—rubies of wisdom command highest prices on the market of character values (8:11).

"More Fun"—nothing you ought not to do is ever more fun. Wait till you see what results (9:17-18).

"Wanted: Silence!"—wordy men seldom are wise men (10:19).

This whole book is extremely practical. It would be well for us all to give it closer study for our guidance in daily life. *In everything you do, put God first, and he will direct you and crown your efforts with success* (3:6). The way of evil—*turn away, go somewhere else* (4:15). This is God's "Stop! Look! Listen!"

The duty of parents to chastise their children is enforced and is based upon God's chastening of his children (3:11-12). One of the signs of the last wicked days on the earth is given by Paul as "disobedient to their parents" (2 Timothy 3:2). What happened to Eli and his sons because he allowed them to sin? (1 Samuel 2).

The young are warned against the influence of bad companions, against impurity and intemperance, against anger, strife, and quarrels. (See 1:10-19; 4:14-19; 19; also chapters 3; 10; 13; 15; 16; 18.)

There are many sins of the tongue. We use it too freely. We lie and are deceitful in dealings with others. Much is said about guarding the tongue, for in the tongue is the power of life and death. (See 12:22; 18:21.)

As we read this book, we find the author pleading with us to shun evil companions, pride, envy, intemperance, sins of the tongue, and idleness. This would be impossible to do unless we had Christ, the Wisdom of God, within us.

Read about pride and its consequences in Proverbs 8; 11; 16; 19. See Proverbs 16:18. The Lord wants us always to be humble before him and not to consider ourselves better than others. Every truly great person is humble.

COUNSEL FOR EVERYONE
PROVERBS 11–20

"False Economy"—a gift is never lost; only what is selfishly kept impoverishes (11:24).

"Fools"—you cannot convince a fool of his folly; only a wise man will accept a rebuke for foolhardiness (12:15).

"Lying"—goodness and lying are enemies; to a wicked man they are synonymous (13:5).

"Answers That Heal"—two people ought not to get angry at the same time (15:1).

"Clean Sin"—a man deep in wickedness will invent "pretty names for sin" (Spurgeon) (16:2).

"To Win Friends"—a friendly man will have friends; being a relative does not insure being a friend (18:24).

"Drink Up!"—When you decide for strong drink, don't be surprised when it decides against you (20:1).

People curse the man who holds his grain for higher prices (11:26). This reveals the sin of the grain speculator. It is a warning to the speculators of our day.

It is a wonderful heritage to have an honest father (20:7). This is a good man's legacy to the world. Godly parents are a blessing to children and should teach them to choose the right path (22:6).

There has never been a time when men did as well as they knew how. However imperfect their instructions, they have never lived up to them. The last thing a man could complain of is a lack of good advice.

Who has heart trouble? Who has woe? Sorrow? Contentions? (Read 20; 23; 31.)

The words in Proverbs are *gold apples in a silver basket* (25:11). Study the basket, but do not miss the gold apples in it.

Proverbs is an intensely practical book, exposing a series of traps that would ensnare us. *No one, regardless of how shrewd or well-advised he is, can stand against the Lord* (21:30). At last we see God's will and God's way! Hasten it, O Lord!

COUNSEL FOR KINGS AND RULERS
PROVERBS 21–31

"Self-Control"—a guarded mouth makes for a serene soul (21:23).

"Reputation"—choose a good name rather than great riches. Your name goes on; your wealth stops at death (22:1).

"Soberness"—wine sparkles but stings (23:31).

"Counsel"—the sober judgment of a sane thinking group is more reliable than your own opinion (24:6).

"Women"—better to be lonely in the attic than living in the house with a nagging woman (25:24).

"Gossip"—fire goes out when fuel gives out; scandal stops when mouths are stopped (26:20).

"Tomorrow"—there is never a tomorrow, only today. Get it done now, for now soon becomes then (27:1).

"Understanding"—rank does not guarantee an understanding heart (28:16).

"Bribes"—seek justice and our land shall stand; accept bribes and it will fall (29:4).

"Security"—a trust in God is the only safe soul armor (30:5).

UNDERSTANDING ECCLESIASTES

Jesus is the beginning of all in Proverbs. He is the end of all in Ecclesiastes, the *summum bonum* of life.

Wisdom in Proverbs is piety. Wisdom in Ecclesiastes is prudence and sagacity.

Ecclesiastes is the soul's autobiography, or the book of experience.

Futile is the key word. See Ecclesiastes 2:11.

We do not have to go outside the Bible to find the merely human philosophy of life. God has given us in the book of Ecclesiastes the record of all that human thinking and natural religion has ever been able to discover concerning the meaning and goal of life. The arguments in the book, therefore, are not God's arguments, but God's record of man's arguments. This explains why such passages as 1:15; 2:24; 3:3-4, 8, 11, 19-20; 8:15 are at positive variance with the rest of the Bible.

The writer is Solomon, and the book is a dramatic autobiography of his experience and reflections while he was out of fellowship with God. Solomon may have been wise, but he did not follow his own wisdom. Ecclesiastes has its origin in his tragic sin of forsaking God and seeking satisfaction based only upon speculation and thought. The inference of the book that *there is nothing really worthwhile anywhere* is, therefore, inevitable, and the message of Ecclesiastes is that, apart from God, life is full of weariness and disappointment.

The problem Solomon faced was how to find happiness and satisfaction apart from God (1:1-3). He sought satisfaction in science (1:4-11) but could get no answer. He sought it in philosophy (1:12-18) but in vain. He found pleasures—merriment, drinking, building, possession, wealth, and music—all empty (2:1-11).

He tried materialism (2:12-26), fatalism (3:1-15), and deism

(3:1–4:16), but these likewise were vain. Natural religion (5:1-8), wealth (5:9–6:12), and even morality (7:1–12:12) proved equally fruitless.

The conclusion is in Ecclesiastes 12:13 and is the best thing possible to man under the law. It is interesting to notice the place of youth in the argument (11:9–12:1). We must begin young to know God if we are to find life worth living.

Remember, Ecclesiastes only shows us the best that man can do apart from God's gospel of grace.

The name *Ecclesiastes* means "preacher." This is so named because it contains the meditations and sermons of the wise man, Solomon.

CONFESSION
ECCLESIASTES 1–7

The great question "Is life worth living?" is presented. Solomon had tested it to the full. No man could better do it or better tell it—and the answer he gave is not reassuring for the life that now is.

Try wisdom (ch. 1)! What better thing is there in all the world? Solomon declared, *I worked hard to be wise.* Yet he was forced to cry out, *Everything is futile . . . for the more my wisdom, the more my grief; to increase knowledge only increases distress* (vv. 2, 17-18). This is always true of mere earthly wisdom. *How can men be wise? The only way to begin is by reverence for God* (Psalm 111:10).

Try pleasure (ch. 2)! *I said to myself, "Come now, be merry; enjoy yourself to the full." But I found that this, too, was futile* (v. 1). This was his deliberate conclusion. God made us all to be joyful. He has given us a thousand avenues of enjoyment. Let us not sacrifice true happiness for questionable pleasure. Always make recreation a re-creation.

Philosophy has failed, said the preacher, so let merriment be tried. Music, dance, wine (not to excess), the funny story, the clever repartee; these were now cultivated. Clowns were now welcomed to the court where only grave philosophy had been. The halls of the palace resounded with laughter and gaiety. Yet after a while all this palled on the king's taste. He even went so far as to say that laughter all the time can be silly (vv. 1-2). Cheerfulness is admirable. A hearty laugh in its place is delightful, but the person who is always giggling is a bore.

Try architecture (ch. 2–4)! Now he became practical. He attended to great works of state. Aqueducts, pools, palaces, and other public buildings occupied his thoughts. Now the court fools were frowned upon and great architects were welcomed to the palace. But the excitement incident to building soon faded away.

Try gardening (2:5-6)! Vineyards, gardens, orchards, rare flowers, tropical plants were all the rage. Jerusalem and the vicinity bloomed like the Garden of Eden. Soon it was like a new toy for a child that pleases for a while but is soon tossed away.

Try cattle breeding and art collecting (2:7-8)! Then the king tried cattle breeding and art collecting, and he even became an amateur musician (v. 8). Choruses and orchestras gathered in the royal palace. But even though "music hath charms," it is powerless to charm with permanent happiness.

Try just living the weary round of life—with discretion (ch. 3)! But again, "What does a man get?" Everything is futile!

Try the stoic's philosophy (ch. 4)! Surely this also is futile. He wailed, *All is foolishness!* (v. 16).

Try ritualism—formal religion (ch. 5)! Be sure to *honor your vow* (v. 4). This, too, is futile.

Try wealth (ch. 6)! Solomon had it. He was a man to whom God gave great wealth and honor. What is the good of it? The rich *can have everything they want but he doesen't give them the health to enjoy it, and they die and others get it all!* (v. 2). Many agree with Solomon in the emptiness of pleasures, but they think that money is the supreme goal in life. Jesus told us to give God *first place in your life and live as he wants you to* and all these things would be added.

Try reputation (ch. 7)! *A good reputation is more valuable than the most expensive perfume. The day one dies is better than the day he is born* (v. 1). It doesn't last long in this world. Men are soon forgotten when they die. Futility still!

ADMONITION
ECCLESIASTES 8–12

Now comes a turning point. Ecclesiastes 8:12 says, *I know very well that those who fear God will be better off.* The full meaning of this is in the last chapter—*Fear God and obey his commandments, for this is the entire duty of man* (12:13).

The fear of the Lord spoken of here is not a fear of fright but a fear of a son who is afraid he might grieve his father's love. It is the fear coming from love, the fear of displeasing the Lord, that is *the entire duty of man.*

The "Preacher," as he is called, had been looking out and back and around. Now he looked up and he saw God and was satisfied.

We find in Ecclesiastes that we can never find satisfaction and happiness in this world. True happiness apart from Christ is impossible. We find dissatisfaction among the poor and rich alike, among the ignorant and learned, among people and kings.

Ecclesiastes closes with a call to the young! Lay the foundations early. *Don't let the excitement of being young cause you to forget about your Creator* (12:1). This book is given as a warning sign, so that we can be spared having to learn the bitterness of life by finding that the cisterns we have looked for were empty. The greatest proportion of men and women who are living to serve God have chosen him in childhood.

UNDERSTANDING SONG OF SOLOMON

The Song of Solomon has been called the Christian's love song. The key text is Song of Solomon 6:3.

This is a song of love in marriage in Oriental language and imagery. The persons are Solomon and the Shulamite woman and the daughters of Jerusalem. The idea of the love of husband and wife sets forth the love between God and his people. This is seen in many passages in the Bible. Moreover, Solomon as a lover was a type of Christ. See Ephesians 5. Personal love to Christ is the greatest need of the church today. The knowledge of sin forgiven and of Christ's redeeming work has drawn us to him.

SELECTED BIBLE READING

Sunday: Get Wisdom (Proverbs 1–4)
Monday: To Sons (Proverbs 5–7)
Tuesday: Good and Bad (Proverbs 15–17)
Wednesday: Wise Words (Proverbs 20; 22; 31)
Thursday: All Is Futile (Ecclesiastes 1–3)
Friday: Only God Satisfies (Ecclesiastes 11–12)
Saturday: Joyful Communion (Song of Solomon 1:1-7; 2:1-7)

UNDERSTANDING
ISAIAH

Isaiah Portrays Jesus Christ, the Messiah

INTRODUCTION TO THE PROPHETICAL BOOKS

The poetical books belong to the golden age of the nation. The prophetical books belong to the dark ages of God's chosen people.

The prophets were men whom God raised up during the dark days of Israel's history. They were the evangelists of the day, the religious patriots of the hour. Read what God says about them in 2 Kings 17:13: *Again and again the Lord had sent prophets to warn both Israel and Judah to turn from their evil ways; he had warned them to obey his commandments which he had given to their ancestors through these prophets.*

We read everywhere in the New Testament that God spoke through the prophets. The period of the prophets in Israel covered five hundred years from the tenth to the fifth century B.C. Then the voices of the prophets were silenced until John the Baptist. These prophets spoke fearlessly to kings and people alike of their sins and failures.

The office of prophet was instituted in Samuel's time. When the kingdom was divided, and Judah and Israel were established as separate monarchies, the great prophets appeared.

There are seventeen prophetical books in the Old Testament (including Lamentations). They are subdivided into four major and twelve minor prophets. This distinction is made not because of their importance but because of their length.

The captivities of Israel (the northern kingdom) and of Judah (the southern kingdom) are largely the theme of the Old Testament prophets. The record of them is found in 2 Kings 17:1-23;

24:11–25:21. They are called the Assyrian and Babylonian captivities. Some of the prophets served before the exile, some during, and some afterwards. They are known as pre-exilic, exilic, and post-exilic prophets.

The prophets to Israel before the exile were Jonah, Amos, and Hosea. The prophets to Judah before the exile were Obadiah, Joel, Isaiah, Micah, Nahum, Habakkuk, Zephaniah, and Jeremiah. The prophets during the exile (or captivity in Babylon) were Ezekiel and Daniel, who prophesied to all the Israelis. Jeremiah extended for a while into this period. Those who prophesied after the exile were Haggai, Zechariah, and Malachi.

Prophets according to special messages:

Three to Israel—Amos, Hosea, Ezekiel
Two to Nineveh—Jonah, Nahum
One to Babylon—Daniel
One to Edom—Obadiah
Nine to Judah—Joel, Isaiah, Micah, Jeremiah, Habakkuk, Zephaniah, Haggai, Zechariah, Malachi

THE PROPHETS—THEIR MESSAGE

The prophet's chief duty was to deal with the moral and religious life of his own people during his day. The prophet was never sent while the nation was walking in obedience to God. All of the writings are rebukes because of the bad condition that existed at that very time. There was nothing general about the prophet's denunciations.

The prophet was always an Israeli. He not only spoke of judgment that would happen to the people because of their sin, he was also a foreteller of future events. The events of which he spoke mainly concerned the nation of Israel. Other peoples were mentioned only as they came in contact with Israel.

Let us note some of the prophecies of the future that are recounted. Hold these in mind as you study their writings:

1. The dispersion and captivity of God's chosen people: Everywhere the prophet tells that the Jews are to be scattered among the nations of the world.
2. The coming of the Messiah: The Jew is still looking for his Messiah.

3. The restoration of the chosen people to their own land under the coming Messiah, David's greater Son: Jews have returned from the four corners of the earth to dwell in their own Promised Land—the nation of Israel.
4. The reign of the Messiah over the whole earth: Even though we see the collapse of God's people—at first Israel, then Judah being led into captivity—nevertheless God revealed that the ending of his nation did not end his plans. There is yet to be a glorious future when the Prince of Peace will reign over his people and sway his scepter *from sea to sea, and from the Euphrates river to the ends of the earth* (Psalm 72:8).

When you read the Gospels, you constantly find this phrase: *in fulfillment of the Scriptures.* We find in examining these passages that God fulfills prophecy literally. Learn to interpret the meaning of the words of the prophets in a literal, natural way. Do not force a spiritual interpretation and read out all the real meaning. There are figurative passages, of course. But you will find that as soon as you determine the meaning of the figure, it too will have its literal fulfillment. This method makes the study of the prophets a simple one.

Remember that the prophets speak only of the earthly ministry of Christ and say nothing of the church—his *called out ones (ecclesia).* This was announced by Jesus himself. This is the "mystery" that God kept until he wished it to be revealed (see Matthew 16:18; Ephesians 3:3-12).

THE PROPHETS—THEIR CHARACTER

The prophets were fearless men. They denounced the sins of their day. They called people away from idols back to God. It is true that the prophets were concerned about the moral and political corruption of the nation, but the fact that the people were worshiping idols was their greatest concern. The nation had a wrong attitude toward God. Christ gave us a succinct statement of what our attitude should be: *Love the Lord your God with all your heart* (Luke 10:27). A person's attitude toward God will affect his whole moral life. Creed always determines conduct. This is true not only of individuals but of nations. The adage "it makes no difference what a man believes" is completely refuted in the prophets.

The prophets exposed the cold formalism of their religion. They constantly reminded the people that Jehovah was the only true God. They pointed men to the law. They were statesmen of the highest order. They were prophets in that they came to tell forth what God said. They were not only forth-tellers but also fore-tellers.

So important is prophecy in God's Word that it occupies about one third of the whole Bible. Prophecy is God's revelation of his plans to his children.

G. Campbell Morgan says that there were three elements in the message of the prophets:

1. A message to their own age—directly from God
2. A message of predicted future events—(a) the failure of God's chosen people and God's judgment upon them and the nations around them (b) the coming of the Messiah and his rejection and final glory (c) the Messianic Kingdom ultimately to be established on the earth
3. A living message to our own age—eternal principles of right and wrong

The Spirit of God spoke by the prophets: *Just as he promised through his holy prophets long ago* (Luke 1:70). Read 2 Peter 1:21; Jeremiah 1:9; Ezekiel 2:7 to find how the message was given. Read what Christ said of the prophets (Luke 24:25-27).

The prophecies concerning Christ himself are so definite that it gives great assurance to us that the Bible is the Word of God.

UNDERSTANDING ISAIAH

The keynote of Isaiah is *salvation*. Isaiah's name means "Jehovah saves."

God put a telescope before the eyes of the prophets and let them look far into the future. Especially do we find this spirit of expectation in Isaiah. We hear the prophet cry, "He is coming!" Isaiah was a man of vision. Read the opening words: *These are the messages that came to Isaiah, son of Amoz, in the visions he saw . . . [concerning] Judah and Jerusalem* (1:1).

Isaiah was a man who certainly spoke boldly to his own time, but as a prophet he spoke of the future as well; hence he is the prophet for all times. We sit at his feet today, and following his index finger as it points into the future we hear him say, "Behold, your King!"

This great statesman was the prophet of the southern kingdom of Judah. He lived at the time that the northern kingdom of Israel was destroyed by Assyria. Isaiah was the one whose voice saved the kingdom of Judah during these trying hours.

It is interesting to note that this is also the time of Romulus and Remus and the founding of Rome. The traditional date of the building of Rome is 753 B.C., just a few years after the birth of the prophet Isaiah. About this time Sparta and Athens in Greece were founded.

The prophets were the most unpopular men in their day, for they dealt with the moral and religious conditions of the hour, which were generally bad. Prophets were sent when the nation was out of step with God—when they were walking in disobedience. The words the prophets used to rebuke or exhort the people were very pointed. They were for the very people to whom they addressed themselves. Truth is seldom popular with the sinner.

Let us find the scriptural definition of a prophet. Look in Deuteronomy 18:18: *I will raise up from among them a Prophet [like Moses]. . . . I will tell him what to say, and he shall be my spokesman to the people.* Also verse 19: *I will personally deal with anyone who will not listen to him and heed his messages from me.*

Although the prophets spoke to their own age, as we have already noted, they were ever looking forward to future events. Besides this, we find abiding principles stated for all times. They foretold the failure of the chosen people and the coming of the Messiah. Each showed how God was to bring to pass his purposes through the Messiah.

Isaiah told of the judgment that had to fall on Judah because she would not fulfill her mission in the world. But through the whole book we find the ultimate triumph of God's plan through his appointed Servant, the Lord Jesus Christ, who would bring in final victory through suffering and death (ch. 53).

TWO EMPHASES

This book of Isaiah is written with two distinct emphases. Because of this some Bible scholars believe that there was more than one author. This need not be the case. It is the work of one man with two messages. In the first part of the book Isaiah pictured Israel. In the last part of the book, the prophet saw Jesus bearing our load of sin, and he told the story. Then he saw Christ exalted and glorified and shouted of his vision from the housetop. It is the same prophet all the time but suiting his language to the theme at hand.

The only way to understand Isaiah is to understand the prophet's Christ. It is far more important that we be familiar with the truths of the book than the theories of its authorship. Don't let anyone interpret the book for you who does not know its Author.

The divisions of Isaiah are an interesting coincidence. Isaiah is a miniature Bible in structure. This book has sixty-six chapters, just as the Bible has sixty-six books. There are two great divisions, just as there are in the Bible, with thirty-nine chapters in the first (like the Old Testament) and twenty-seven chapters in the second (like the New Testament). (Of course, since chapters and verses were not written into the original text but were added many years later, this is just coincidence.)

The Old Testament opens with God's case against man because of his sin. Isaiah opens the same way (1:18). The first section closes with the prophecy of the coming King of Righteousness and the redemption of Israel (ch. 34–35), just as the prophets close the Old Testament with the prediction of his coming kingdom. Chapter 40 opens the second part of Isaiah with the voice of one shouting in the wilderness (John the Baptist), and is concerned with the person and work of Jesus Christ. The New Testament opens in exact accord with this. John the Baptist, the forerunner of Jesus, is announced (John 1:6, 23). Isaiah ends with the vision of new heavens and a new earth in which righteousness dwells. The New Testament closes with this same view in Revelation. This striking similarity between Isaiah and the whole Bible is unforgettable when once mastered.

Isaiah is like a jewel case, and chapter 53 is the jewel. This has a central position in the group of the chapters to which it belongs. As you see, it is located in the second division of the book. In the very middle of this group of twenty-seven chapters lies chapter 53. Store the whole chapter in your memory. Each verse is a nugget of golden truth. This is the chapter that pictures Christ, our suffering Redeemer.

TWO COMINGS OF CHRIST

In Isaiah we see Christ and hear the prophet crying, "He is coming!" and "He is coming again!" He is coming as Savior, pictured in chapter 53, in humiliation as our sin-bearer. He is coming again in power and great glory, pictured in chapter 34.

As we look through the telescope we see two mountain peaks with a valley between. One is called Calvary; on its hilltop is a cross. But as we look farther we see another peak. It is radiant with the light of a crown! This hill is Olivet. The eye of the ancient seer went farther than the sufferings of Calvary. His eye caught the kingdom and the glory that would follow!

Isaiah speaks of Christ's death when he says, *No matter how deep the stain of your sins, I can take it out and make you as clean as freshly fallen snow* (1:18). Again, *We despised him and rejected him* (53:3). This speaks of the first time when *the world didn't recognize him. . . . Only a few would welcome and receive him* (John 1:12). When he will come again we will hear, *Arise my people! Let your light shine for all the nations to see! For the glory of the Lord is streaming from you* (60:1). Then he tells us of his coming kingdom. *In the last days . . .* (2:2-5).

The life of Christ is portrayed in Isaiah:

Birth (7:14; 9:6)
Family (11:1)
Anointing (11:2)
Character (11:3-4)
Gentleness (42:1-4)
Death (53)
Resurrection (25:8)
Glorious reign (11:3-16; 32)

Isaiah was a man of royal blood. He was a young aristocrat from a princely line. He was brought up in the court and had high standing with the people of Jerusalem. He not only was a prophet, but he married a prophetess. His training was of the best. After his labor of sixty years, tradition tells us that he died a martyr during the reign of Manasseh at the age of 120.

Isaiah was a special messenger to Judah. Look over 2 Kings 15–20 and note the moral and political rottenness of Judah and Israel, and the danger from the surrounding Gentile nations.

Assyria was strong and aggressive, striving for world power. Egypt was on the south, and Palestine was the road between these two enemies. Both Assyria and Egypt aimed at world empire. Therefore Palestine became the battleground of the ages.

Isaiah did not fail in his ministry. He laid bare the sins of his people and called them to repent and turn to God. "Come back to God," he cried. But his chief theme was the coming One, Jesus. He saw Christ's near first coming and his faraway second coming, but in all he saw Christ.

Johannes Kepler, in failing to bring the heavenly bodies into satisfactory adjustment with one center, at last conceived of the ellipse with two foci, and everything fell into harmony. So when in our reverent study of God's Word we catch the dual center of Christ on the cross and Christ on the throne, then the Word shines clear and we begin to see what the prophet saw, the world's Redeemer, coming first in humiliation, then again in power and great glory.

Four words to Judah:

Rebellion—*Oh what a sinful nation!* (1:2-4, 10-15, 21-23)
Retribution—*You will be killed* (1:5-8, 15, 20, 28)
Repentance—*If you will only obey* (1:16-19, 27)
Restoration—*Those who return . . . shall be redeemed* (1:9, 18, 24-31)

The people of Judah thought that all would be well if they kept up all outward observances in their religious service. Isaiah denounced their hypocrisy (1:15). He told them of forgiveness if they would repent, but promised them death if they continued in their rebellion against God.

Because of their sin and their forsaking God, Judah was facing judgment (1:1-31; 2:6–3:26). Yet there is a glorious future for Judah when Christ comes again. Jerusalem is to be the capital of the coming kingdom (2:1–5:4).

God's truths of redemption go beyond our reason, but they do not insult our reason; they rather appeal to it. To worship rightly in the presence of God we must be right in the presence of men.

UNDER UZZIAH AND JOTHAM
ISAIAH 1–6

Read Isaiah 1:1 and you will discover that Isaiah was prophet during the reigns of Uzziah, Jotham, Ahaz, and Hezekiah. During this time the statesman-prophet preached in Jerusalem.

Now turn to Isaiah 6:1-13 and you see that Isaiah received his real commission in the year that King Uzziah died. No doubt he had written chapters 1–5 before this time. Uzziah's long and glorious reign of fifty-two years ended in gloom. For the last four years of his life Uzziah was a leper. He was shut off from all the business of state, and the kingdom was under the regency of his son Jotham. The early chapters of Isaiah fit the situation perfectly.

Jotham, Uzziah's successor, is only mentioned twice in the book (1:1; 7:1). It does not seem that Isaiah was active during his reign. It is with the reign of the next two kings, Ahaz and Hezekiah, that Isaiah's prophecy deals.

Ahaz reigned sixteen years and Hezekiah reigned twenty-nine years. Ahaz was a wicked king, and furthermore, he was an idolater. Hezekiah was for the most part a good king, and he did much to remove idolatry from the people.

Isaiah's Message
Isaiah warned Judah of her folly and rebellion (1:2-9). The people of Judah separated themselves from God by the sins of greed, heathen alliances, and idolatry (2:6-9). God had tried patience, then punishment; now they had to be destroyed by heathen kings.

God called Isaiah just as he called Moses, Joshua, Gideon, and Paul. His call was a never-to-be-forgotten experience. It taught Isaiah his own unworthiness and gave him his commission to a shining, needy world calling out for help. It came to him in the form of a "vision." For years Isaiah preached and told of doom and deliverance. Hardship and peril awaited him, but God gave him a victorious strength. He was the man of the hour. Let us look at the steps leading from the opening of the vision to his final commission.

Secret of Isaiah's life
The secret of all of Isaiah's power lay in this vision in the Temple: *I saw the Lord!* The experience of Isaiah, recorded in chapter 6, should be every disciple's experience:

1. Conviction—*My doom is sealed* was the cry brought on by the sense of sinfulness before God's holiness (6:5).

2. Confession—*I am a foul-mouthed sinner.* A broken and contrite heart is precious to the Lord (6:5).
3. Cleansing—*Your sins are all forgiven.* After confession, a mighty angel cleansed his lips with a hot coal from off the altar (6:7).
4. Consecration—*Lord, I'll go! Send me* (6:8).
5. Commission—*Go.* This was God's command (6:9).

UNDER AHAZ
ISAIAH 7-14

King Ahaz was utterly bad. He was an open idolater. For this sin God allowed Rezin, king of Syria, and Pekah, king of Israel, to invade his kingdom. Isaiah had been silent under Jotham, but this invasion brought him to the front in his ministry. *Then the Lord said to Isaiah, "go out to meet King Ahaz"* (7:3). Isaiah appealed to Ahaz to put his trust in God for help rather than call in Tiglath-Pileser from Nineveh.

God sent the prophet to encourage Ahaz. Besides predicting the Assyrian invasion in Isaiah 8, the prophet saw an end to all of Israel's troubles through the birth of Christ, who will rule over the kingdom of David in righteousness forever. He gave Ahaz a "sign" that Judah was not to perish—the prophecy of Immanuel, the virgin's Son, Jesus Christ. *The Lord himself will choose the sign—a child shall be born to a virgin! And she shall call him Immanuel* (7:14). Read these important words in Isaiah 7:10-16. Ahaz refused the evidence upon which his faith might have been established. He pursued his own plans with Assyria, and that nation on which they now leaned was to become the means of their punishment (7:17-20).

Then followed the sentence of doom upon king and land (8:6-22). With nations, this is God's policy: doom for idolatry.

In Isaiah 9:6-7 we find another great prophecy concerning Christ. *For unto us a Child is born; unto us a Son is given; and the government shall be upon his shoulder. These will be his royal titles: "Wonderful," "Counselor," "The Mighty God," "The Everlasting Father," "The Prince of Peace"* (9:6-7). The Son to be given, the child to be born, was to sit on David's throne. Remember the "throne of his father David" is as definite as the "throne of the Caesars." Yes, Christ will sit on the throne of David. Hear the angel's words to Mary: *He shall be very great and shall be called the Son of God. And the Lord God shall give him the throne of his ancestor David. And he shall reign over Israel forever; his Kingdom shall never end* (Luke 1:32-33).

We find present woe and future glory strangely mixed in Isaiah 10. But in Isaiah 11 we see the picture of the glory of the future kingdom that Christ is coming to establish on this earth. Some day he is coming to Jerusalem to sit upon the throne of David, and peace shall cover the earth.

In this kingdom the people will worship the Lord Jehovah. The prophet said, *Sing to the Lord, for he has done wonderful things* (12:5).

In Isaiah 13 we see great Babylon's doom. She was to carry Judah away captive, but the prophet saw her destruction. God was keeping his promise to Abraham. *I will bless those who bless you and curse those who curse you; and the entire world will be blessed because of you* (Genesis 12:3). God always brings a curse on any nation that afflicts Israel. You can follow this truth through history. God often allows nations to punish Israel for her national sins, but retribution is inevitable (Deuteronomy 30;5-7; Isaiah 14:1-2; Joel 3:1-8).

Read every word of Isaiah 11–12, which gives a picture of this coming King and kingdom:

The King himself (11:1)
His anointing (11:2)
His righteous reign (11:3-5)
His glorious kingdom (11:6-9)
His gathering together of his people from the
    four corners of the earth (11:10-16)
His kingdom worship (12:1-6)

When it was my privilege to drive out to old Babylon and look over the ruins of that once magnificent city and see the absolute devastation, I thought of Isaiah's prophecy concerning this city found in Isaiah 13:19-22. God said that *Babylon, the most glorious of kingdoms, the flower of Chaldean culture . . . will never rise again. . . . The nomads will not even camp there. . . . The wild animals of the desert will make it their home* (13:19-22).

This is true today. There is not even a tent pitched there. Only bats and owls make their home in its ruins. Not a shepherd is seen on the plains. There is only desolation. Yes, God's Word is true!

In Isaiah 14:28 we read that King Ahaz died. But Isaiah warned the people that his death must not be hailed as the end of their burdens. Even worse oppressors than Ahaz were yet to come (14:28-32).

UNDER HEZEKIAH
ISAIAH 15-39

The reign of Hezekiah occupied one of the most important periods in all of Israel's history. Hezekiah was a godly king. The Assyrian armies, like a dark storm cloud, were threatening the northern frontiers. Before Hezekiah had completed his sixth year, Samaria had fallen beneath this invader. This success only whetted the Assyrian appetite for further conquest. Eight years later Judah was invaded. Assyrian history tells us that the first invasion was by Sargon and the second by his son, Sennacherib. The critical year in Hezekiah's reign was the fourteenth (36:1). It was then we have the Assyrian invasion, the king's mortal sickness and recovery, and the final withdrawal of Assyrians from the land. (This covered a period of about four years.)

These stony-hearted Assyrian warriors came year after year, blazing with steel and banners. The watchmen on the walls of Jerusalem could see them advance by the smoke of the burning towns and cities.

King Hezekiah stripped the Temple of its gold and treasures and sent these to the Assyrians in order to buy them off (2 Kings 18:13-16). In desperation, help from Egypt was sought. But nothing availed in face of the fury of these Assyrians. Finally the Assyrians built their campfires around the city of Jerusalem and demanded its surrender. Read the intensely dramatic account of the parleyings between the Assyrian general and the officials of Jerusalem.

See the account of the swift and terrible disaster that fell on the Assyrians as they were slain by a mysterious visitation in their camp (37:36-38).

Isaiah denounced the alliance with Egypt and said it was *trusting their mighty cavalry and chariots instead of looking to the Holy One of Israel and consulting him* (31:1).

Is it not true that we today have put our trust in the "cavalry and chariots" of war's machinery? Have we not multiplied our "cavalry and chariots" beyond the wildest dreams of Egypt and Babylon? We have hitched all the forces of nature to our weapons.

War has been turned into a hideous prospect of devastation and death.

We need to hear the prophet say today, *Woe to those who run to Egypt for help. . . .* God wants us to recognize him in national affairs. He calls his people to *come, return to God* (31:6). As a people we must get right with God before we can get right with other nations.

The kingdoms of Judah and Israel had become so weakened by idolatry and corruption that the enemies swept down on them from the north like a wolf on sheep. First, Israel rolled in the dust under the tramp of the terrible Assyrian hosts (722 B.C.), and then Judah fell with the Babylonians thundering at her gate and breaking down her walls (586 B.C.). Both kingdoms ended and their people were carried into captivity.

Isaiah spent his life trying to get Judah to become acquainted with God and his Word. He wanted them to trust wholly in God's guidance. Isn't this a worthy aim for any minister today?

GLORIOUS FUTURE—RESTORATION!
ISAIAH 40-66

This last part of the book is called the *Book of Consolation* because Isaiah tells in glowing terms not only of the restoration of Judah but the coming of Jehovah's "Servant" to be the Messiah King.

The restoration is assured, for the people had to return to their own land to prepare the way for the coming Messiah, the Servant of Jehovah, who would redeem his people.

Isaiah 53 gives us a perfect picture of our suffering Redeemer. *It was our grief he bore, our sorrows that weighed him down* (v. 4). *We—every one of us—have strayed away like sheep. . . . Yet God laid on him the guilt and sins of every one of us* (v. 6). He was the substitute for the sinner.

Can you repeat verse 5 and say, *He was wounded and bruised for [my] sins. He was beaten that [I] might have peace; he was lashed—and [I was] healed?* It is accepting this great fact that makes you a child of God. He was wounded, bruised, pierced—not for his own sins, but for ours. He bore on his own body the sins of the world.

Isaiah 60–66 tells of the coming kingdom—the future glory of Israel. God's goodness to redeemed Israel is seen in chapters 61–62. He promises an era of prosperity in chapters 63–65.

SELECTED BIBLE READING

Sunday: God's Case against Judah (Isaiah 1)
Monday: Isaiah's Commission (Isaiah 6)
Tuesday: Christ—Israel's Hope (Isaiah 7:10-16; 9)
Wednesday: The Coming Kingdom (Isaiah 11)
Thursday: A Great God (Isaiah 40)
Friday: Christ Our Substitute (Isaiah 53)
Saturday: A Glorious Salvation (Isaiah 55)

CHAPTER 19

UNDERSTANDING JEREMIAH AND LAMENTATIONS

Jeremiah and Lamentations Portray Jesus Christ, the Righteous Branch

UNDERSTANDING JEREMIAH

Here is the story of a diffident, sensitive man who was called from the obscurity of his native town to assume, at a critical hour in the nation's life, the overwhelming responsibilities of a prophet. Jeremiah came from the village of Anathoth some three miles from Jerusalem. This gave him the advantages of the Holy City. His father, Hilkiah, was a priest. (Some think that this was "Hilkiah the priest" in 2 Kings 22 who brought the book of the Law to the notice of King Josiah, which started the great revival in the kingdom.) He inherited the traditions of an illustrious ancestry. His early life was, no doubt, molded by strong religious influences. God had something better for Jeremiah than to spend his life as a priest serving at the altars. God appointed this young man to be a prophet of the Lord in this most trying hour in the history of the chosen people.

God often chooses unlikely instruments to do his work. He chose the sensitive, shrinking Jeremiah for what seemed a hopeless mission with the words: *You will go wherever I send you and speak whatever I tell you to. And don't be afraid of the people, for I, the Lord, will be with you and see you through* (1:7-8). This is what a prophet is—one who speaks whatever God tells him to. Al-

197

though many prophets told of future events, it is not necessary that they do so to be a prophet.

Jeremiah, unlike many of the prophets, had much to say concerning himself. He tells us that he was a priest by birth (1:1). He was called by the Lord to be a prophet at an early age (1:6). As reasons for not accepting the call, he pleaded, first, his youth (only twenty-one); second, his inexperience; and third, his lack of eloquence (1:6). Are these not just the excuses that young people make today for not obeying Christ?

Jeremiah was assured that God had ordained him to this work before his birth (1:4-8). God tells us in Ephesians 2:10 that we were created to do good works before God even laid the foundation of the world. God has a plan for each one of our lives. Jeremiah was not allowed to marry, for God had a special mission for him in life (16:1-2). He prophesied during the time when Israel had been taken into captivity and Judah was in her declining days.

Soon after Josiah's death the kingdom of Judah hurried to its end. Judah was reduced to practical vassalage to Egypt at the battle of Carchemish. About twelve years later Nebuchadnezzar, king of Babylon, took Jerusalem and began the deportation of all the princes and officials, which ended in the complete captivity of Judah eleven years after. A few of the poorest people were left in the land. Jeremiah kept on with his ministry among them until they went into Egypt. He followed them into Egypt, and the last we hear of him he was still rebuking his people. There are conflicting traditions about his death. Tertullian says that the Jews in Egypt stoned him to death. According to the Jews, he escaped to Babylon and died there.

He was called to be a prophet in the thirteenth year of the reign of King Josiah (1:2). No doubt his early ministry, and that of the prophet Zephaniah, were among the influences that led to the reforms under the young King Josiah. Jeremiah prophesied for more than forty years. He began his ministry sixty years after the death of Isaiah, the great evangelical prophet.

Jeremiah was contemporary with the prophetess Huldah, and with Habakkuk, Zephaniah, Ezekiel, Daniel, and perhaps even Nahum.

Jeremiah's message was never a popular one. At one time he barely escaped with his life (26:7-16). At another time his enemies beat him and put him in prison. Men have always treated God's witnesses this way.

It is almost impossible to outline this book chronologically. Some of the first messages are found later in the book and some of the last messages are first. They were written on a great scroll. No doubt he had given his messages many times to the people and had repeated them often before he began to dictate. His faithful scribe, Baruch, wrote them down. After one of his discourses was written, some other message given years before might come to his mind and he would record it, possibly without dating it. He would fill up the parchment as it was unrolled. Later on, when he wished to record another incident message, he would have to begin on the scroll where he left off, whether it fitted in chronologically or not. This is important to remember when reading Jeremiah.

ANALYSIS OF JEREMIAH

Because the book of Jeremiah is not arranged chronologically, a division of the book is difficult. The analysis is more moral than structural.

Jeremiah prophesied concerning:

1. Judah—captivity, restoration
2. Cities—Jerusalem, Babylon, Damascus
3. Gentile nations—Egypt, Philistia, Moab, Ammon, Edom, Elam, Babylon
4. Messiah

Jeremiah used many symbols given him by God in teaching the people. On one occasion he wore a rotting loincloth; another time he put a yoke on his neck, like an ox; once he broke a jar in the presence of the ruler; he bought a field and buried the deed. The interpretation is given in the text.

Here is a list of object lessons found in the book:

The almond branch (1:1-12)
The pot of boiling water (1:13-14)
The rotting loincloth (13:1-11)
The full jug (13:12-14)
The drought (14:1-12)
The potter's jar (18:1-6)
The broken jar (19:1-2)

Two baskets of figs (24:1-10)
The yoke (27:1-12)
Buying a field (32:6-15)
The hidden stones (43:9-13)
Book sunk in the Euphrates (51:59-64)

Christ is pictured in Jeremiah as:

Fountain of Life-Giving Water (2:13)
Great Physician (8:22)
Good Shepherd (31:10)
The Righteous Branch (23:5)
David the King (30:9)
The Redeemer (50:34)
The Lord Our Righteousness (23:6)

Jeremiah was the ninth of the prophets. He prophesied to the southern kingdom of Judah before the exile and during the trying days of the captivity. He saw five kings on the throne of Judah: Josiah, Jehoahaz, Jehoiakim, Jehoiachin, and Zedekiah. He was to Josiah what Isaiah had been to Hezekiah. (Read 2 Kings 21:1-25 to find the history of Jeremiah's time.)

There were three great events in Jeremiah's life:

1. Battle of Megiddo, between Judah and Pharaoh Neco of Egypt, in which good King Josiah was killed.
2. Battle of Carchemish near the same spot about four years later, during Jehoiakim's reign. He had become a vassal of Egypt. In this battle the Egyptians were defeated by Babylon under Nebuchadnezzar, and the first deportation of Jews followed.
3. Capture of Jerusalem by Nebuchadnezzar, destruction of city and temple, and exile to Babylon of the greater part of those who were left.

There was a great contest for world supremacy in the day of Jeremiah. Assyria had been in the place of leadership for three hundred years. Now she was growing weak, and Babylon was ascending in power. Egypt too was striving for supremacy. In 607 B.C. Assyria was defeated by Babylon. In 605 B.C. Egypt was crushed in the battle of Carchemish, and Babylon became the world's master. In the few years that followed she invaded Jerusalem and took the Jews captive. False prophets swarmed the city of Jerusalem in those days. They flattered the king and prophesied to him whatever they thought he wanted to hear.

CALL AND COMMISSION OF JEREMIAH
JEREMIAH 1

This unique tragedy opens in the little village of Anathoth. At twenty-one, Jeremiah was becoming aware that God had ordained him before his birth to be a prophet (1:5). God has a plan for the life of every person. Some see clearly how their lives are to be used. Many learn to wait upon God and trust him for the outcome. These latter cannot understand the ways of the Lord, but they believe his promises. Jeremiah must have been one of these. He must have wondered what God had planned for him. But because he let the Lord have his way, his life affected all of Israel.

We hear Jeremiah speak: *"O Lord God,"* I said, *"I can't do that! I'm far too young! I'm only a youth!"* (1:6). He protested and shrunk from the task God gave him and begged to be excused.

A prophet is simply God's messenger, delivering not his own ideas but conveying to the last detail God's thoughts. (Compare Jeremiah's call with Moses', Exodus 4:10-12.) God had called Jeremiah to be a prophet, and he entered bravely upon the task, but now he was overwhelmed at the thought of hurting anyone. He would rather live at peace with them.

Jeremiah was saying, in effect, "I have not yet reached the years of maturity," for in Oriental society a young man has no role to play until he is of age. (Read Matthew 11:25.) His prophetic message would not be received. Wouldn't his career be cut short by those he provoked? Wouldn't they try to kill him?

The young man was only too conscious of his inexperience, and he almost made the great refusal. But God knew how to overcome his hesitancy. He made the young Jeremiah conscious of a divine call. He made him see that the work to which he was commissioned was not his own.

The path of duty is the path of safety! While Jeremiah was pondering, a hand touched his mouth and we hear a voice saying, *See, I have put my words in your mouth* (1:9). No longer could he complain of inability to speak. God promises to put the message into the mouth of his prophets. (See what Christ said to his disciples in Matthew 10:20.) Then Jeremiah heard the voice add, *Today your work begins, to warn the nations and the kingdoms of the world. . . . I will tear down some and destroy them, and plant others and nurture them and make them strong and great* (1:10).

Secret of National Power

What God asks us to do he fits us for, and what he fits us for he asks us to do. That was quite a position for just a poor country preacher.

The church and the minister who have answered God's call today are still in a place of power. They need no other weapons than the promises of God, and they really control the building and the breaking, the planting and the plucking of the community.

Jeremiah's commission was worldwide, including not only his own country but all the nations and kingdoms of Egypt, Ammon, Moab, Tyre, and Sidon. His commission was to tear down and to destroy. He had to tear out the idolatry and pride, but he had to finally "plant and nurture." Jeremiah was to go only to those persons or peoples to whom the Lord sent him. And he was to say only what the Lord commanded him to say. This must be true of us also if we are to be true workers together with God.

Jeremiah's Reluctance

Jeremiah, like people today, was engaged in the Lord's work because God said he must. He had heard the "You must" of heaven. Although at first the cost may be great, the gain in later years cannot be estimated. Jeremiah was shrinking and offering every excuse for his unfitness, but the task was forced upon him. *You will go* (1:7). He hated the limelight. He loved the simple life. He wanted to live in the country, but the Lord had work for him in the cities. Jeremiah had to choose between his desires and God's will.

Because he was forced into the task that was so distasteful to him, in later years he cried, *What sadness is mine, my mother; oh, that I had died at birth. For I am hated everywhere I go* (15:10). God told Jeremiah, *Don't be afraid of the people, for I, the Lord, will be with you and see you through* (1:8). He was not a public speaker, and he shrank from bearing such an unwelcome message to so undisciplined a people. How often he must have thought of that promise of God when he was hailed before princes and rulers. We like to carry good news, but to bear bad is always hard. We are afraid of people. When their faces register pleasure, we feel safe. When they show disgust, we melt before them.

The Touch of God's Hand

Then he touched my mouth . . . (1:9). Compare this story of Jeremiah's call with that of Isaiah's (Isaiah 6:7). Paul says that prophecy is a spiritual gift (1 Corinthians 14:1). The touch of God's hand was a tangible pledge for Jeremiah that God was with him. He could not get away from it.

The Word of the Lord is a power that carries out his will and accomplishes what he wishes (Isaiah 55:11; Hebrews 4:12). Against this power nothing can stand. It is a hammer that smashes rocks to pieces (23:29). God's Word shows its power in two ways—in destruction and in construction. We see this in God's words to Jeremiah. If people accept God's Word, it will give life; if they reject God's Word, it will bring condemnation (John 3:36).

BEFORE THE FALL OF JERUSALEM
JEREMIAH 2-38

The prophecies of Jeremiah before the fall of Jerusalem were made in this order (long silences divide these):

Prophecies in the reign of Josiah (2:1–12:17)
Prophecies in the reign of Jehoiakim (13:1–20:18; 25:1–27:11)
Prophecies in the reign of Zedekiah (21:1–24:10; 27:12–39:18)

Reign of Josiah

This message from the Lord came to me during the reign of King Josiah . . . (3:6). The first twelve chapters cover the prophecy of this period.

Jeremiah 2–6: These chapters tell of Judah's sin and give God's call to repentance. Judgments are predicted.

Jeremiah 7–9: Again we read of threatenings. We see the prophet's grief.

Jeremiah 10–12: Here we see idolatry and disobedience continued. The Lord's disappointment in his people is shown.

In the early years of his ministry, during the reign of Josiah, Jeremiah's message was for the most part a warning to Judah and a call to her to repent (3:6, 12-13, 22-23). He spared nothing in exposing the moral rottenness of the people (7:1-26). He warned them of coming judgments if they would not return to

God. He especially told them of the danger from the north (4:6). He said that the avengers would come like a raging lion from his lair (4:7). They would sweep over the land with chariots like the whirlwind and with horses swifter than eagles, spread terror before them, and leave ruin in their train (4:13).

In chapter 26 we see Jeremiah taking a stand on the same spot as in Jeremiah 7. On this occasion he nearly lost his life. The address in chapter 7 was probably given during the reign of Josiah.

It is probable that for some time after his call Jeremiah continued to reside in Anathoth, but before long he was compelled to leave the home of his birth and go to live in Jerusalem. The men of his hometown had made a conspiracy to put him to death (11:18-23). The disloyalty of his neighbors, and especially his own relatives, came as a painful shock to the unsuspecting prophet. But God told him that this was only the beginning of his troubles, and it was a time of preparation for still greater trials in the days to come (12:5-6).

Jeremiah's chief enemies were the priests and the prophets (26:7-8). They had a large following among the people. It is sad to notice that the principal opposition to the message of God came from the professedly religious people. It was the same in our Lord's case, and it is often the same today. You remember that the Pharisees and Sadducees always were plotting how they might kill Jesus. Jesus tells us that today if we live godly lives we will suffer persecution. Men hate God and they will hate his children.

We do not know much of Jeremiah's work during the later years of Josiah's reign. No doubt Jeremiah was in great sympathy with this young reformer, but he realized that the king's work did not go deep enough. In the death of the good King Josiah, at the battle of Megiddo, Judah suffered a calamity from which she never recovered. It was in this battle that Judah made a noble attempt to withstand the Egyptian army advancing against Assyria under Pharaoh Neco.

King Josiah was succeeded by his younger brother Jehoahaz whom the people placed on the throne instead of the older brother Eliakim. But Jehoahaz was allowed to reign for only three months. He was deposed by Neco and carried off in chains to Egypt, where he died. Neco now virtually was overlord of Judah. He appointed Jehoiakim to be ruler.

Reign of Jehoiakim

In substance Jeremiah predicted the judgment of the nations and Judah. He reproved the false prophets. He foretold the Babylonian captivity. He suffered for his message.

It was a sad day for Judah when Jehoiakim ascended to power. It was a bad day for Jeremiah, too. Read what God said to Jeremiah at the beginning of Jehoiakim's reign (26:1-7). Jehoiakim was a bad ruler. He was proud, selfish, covetous, and vindictive. He burdened the land with taxes to meet the demands of his Egyptian conqueror (2 Kings 23:35). He was indifferent to the suffering of his people. He devoted most of his time to enlarging and adorning his palace and carried out his costly schemes with incredible meanness.

Jehoiakim reigned eleven years, and after his death his son, a youth of eighteen, came to the throne. But Jehoiachin's reign was short (about three months and ten days) because Nebuchadnezzar's army soon appeared at the gates of Jerusalem, and after a three-month siege the city was captured. He took with him many of the princes and the flower of the people to Babylon. Among them was Jehoiachin and the queen-mother. *Only the poorest and least skilled people were left in the land* (2 Kings 24:14).

It was then that Jeremiah first mentioned the seventy years' captivity (25:1-14). God told them exactly how long they would remain in exile (Daniel 9:2).

Jeremiah did not hesitate to denounce even the king for his shameless wrongdoing. In Jeremiah 22:13-19 we see him verbally putting Jehoiakim in stocks and then releasing the lash of a righteous scorn, predicting that he would die without being mourned and would be buried with the burial of a donkey.

The reformation under Josiah only touched the surface. The work was abandoned after his death and the nation, in Jehoiakim's reign, fell back into the worst form of idolatry.

Jeremiah's mission was to endeavor to turn his people back to God. During the reign of Josiah he began to prophesy the dreadful calamity threatening them from the north if they would not return to God (4:6). Jeremiah told Judah that her salvation was still possible, but each year her sin grew worse and her doom more certain.

Standing in the Temple, Jeremiah told the people that the Temple would be destroyed and Jerusalem itself would become a desolation. Jeremiah's hearers were shocked (26:7-9). They called his words blasphemy. They said, *This man should die. . . . You have heard with your own ears what a traitor he is, for he has prophesied against this city* (26:11).

The Jewish people always remembered that they were the chosen people of God. God had given them privileges. Hence they concluded that God would not proceed to do such things as Jeremiah had said he would do against the people whom he had chosen (Amos 3:2). God had consecrated the Temple as a home for his name; therefore the people thought he would not let it be destroyed by enemies. This was quite false. Let us not entertain this spirit ourselves. We think: We are God's children; therefore he must forgive us and make us win in battle and put our enemies to rout.

Being confined in the court of the guard attached to the royal palace, Jeremiah had opportunities to talk to the soldiers on duty as well as to the citizens who came along (37:21). To everyone he declared the Word of the Lord (37:6-10). His message was that it was foolish to resist the Chaldeans. It would only result in destruction. This was so galling to national pride that the princes named in Jeremiah 38:1 resolved to kill Jeremiah. Yet King Zedekiah was convinced that Jeremiah was right.

Of course Jeremiah "undermined the morale" of the people (38:4). The people were convinced that resistance was useless, since God had said that Jerusalem would be captured and burned by the Chaldeans. People and soldiers were unwilling to sacrifice their lives any longer in defending the city.

Jeremiah was charged with being unpatriotic. For his opponents it was, "My country, right or wrong." For Jeremiah it was, "God's will in my country" (26:12-15). It is not so much a question of what we think is right as it is that we learn what God considers to be the best for us and our country. God said to Jeremiah, *Don't be afraid . . . for I . . . will be with you and see you through* (1:8). We may have to endure ostracism and ridicule for Christ's sake, but his promise is sufficient.

The priests and prophets, aided by the people, laid hold on Jeremiah and threatened him with death. But Jeremiah was delivered from the hand of his enemies (26:15-24).

The fourth year of Jehoiakim was one to be remembered because it was in this year that Jeremiah first put his prophecies in writing on a scroll (36:1-2). Baruch, his intimate friend who was such a comfort to him through his trials, took down the prophet's words.

We next see the prophet in a dimly lighted dungeon. What happened? The rulers had bound him so they would no longer be troubled by the word of the Lord. But the Lord told Jeremiah to write the words down. There he was, with his loyal friend Baruch at his side busily writing the words on the scroll as the prophet spoke them. *As Jeremiah dictated, Baruch wrote down all the prophecies. When all was finished, Jeremiah said to Baruch, "Since I am a prisoner here, you read the scroll in the Temple on the next Day of Fasting, for on that day people will be there from all over Judah"* (36:4-6). And Baruch read the scroll in the Temple (36:8).

Investigating Committee
The Royal Investigating Committee immediately sent for Baruch and commanded him to read the scroll again (36:14-15). They decided the scroll should be taken to the king. *We must tell the king* (36:16). Knowing full well the character of this ruler, they advised Jeremiah and Baruch to go into hiding before the scroll was read in the royal presence (36:19).

They asked Baruch, *"Did Jeremiah himself dictate [these messages] to you?"* So Baruch explained that Jeremiah had dictated them to him *word by word, and he had written them down in ink upon the scroll* (36:17-18). Then the princes wanted the king to see it.

The scene changes. We are no longer in the dark dungeon but in the winter palace of Jehoiakim, surrounded by all the luxury of an Eastern court. The king is sitting before his hearth. A fire is burning. Jehudi is reading the scroll of Jeremiah. All are listening intently. When three or four columns had been read Jehoiakim could stand no more. With penknife and angry hands he cut the scroll to pieces and threw it into the fire. The very act of Jehoiakim seemed to symbolize the doom of the city, the Temple, and all the people of Judah. They had heard God's Word and rejected it (36:20-26).

Of course, Jehoiakim gave the order to seize Jeremiah and Baruch, but God "hid them" (36:26). How often God does this for his children. He hides us under his wings and in the hollow of his hand far from harm.

Now the Lord commanded Jeremiah to take another scroll, *"and write everything again just as you did before"* . . . *only this time the Lord added a lot more* (36:28, 32).

Jeremiah stood in the Temple gate and spoke boldly for righteousness and God. He uttered a series of accusations against Judah and warnings of God's inevitable judgment of sin. But he always made an appeal to turn back to God and receive forgiveness. We see him standing in the gate, hurling thunderbolts into the faces of the false worshipers, but always holding up the pardon of God.

Jeremiah's was a moral battle, and a moral battle is harder to fight and keep fighting.

Hudson Taylor, one of God's great missionaries, wrote that "God delights to trust a trustworthy child with a trial." How God must have trusted Jeremiah!

AFTER THE FALL OF JERUSALEM
JEREMIAH 39-52

In the fourth year of Jehoiakim's reign Nebuchadnezzar invaded Judah, and it was then that Daniel and his companions were carried away to Babylon and Jehoiakim himself was put into chains.

Nebuchadnezzar placed Zedekiah, Jehoiakim's brother, on the throne in place of Jehoiachin. Only Zedekiah and his officials and others like them were left in Jerusalem now. Jeremiah likened them to bad, worthless figs, in contrast to the good ones who had gone (ch. 24). The picked men of the nation were carried away. You remember that Daniel afterwards became prime minister of Babylon. The men who were left were so weak and degenerate that the prophet could see nothing but doom for Jerusalem.

Zedekiah was disposed to be friendly to Jeremiah, but he was a weak man and had no courage to make decisions of his own. He was like clay in the hands of the princes who surrounded the throne. The remnant of men who were left were not qualified to govern. They had taken the places of the real nobility of the nation, but they were in great contrast to those who had been carried into captivity.

Jeremiah incurred the displeasure of the prophets who had gone to Babylon because, in a letter to the exiles, he directly opposed their prediction of an early return from captivity (29:1-14). Neither did the prophets in Jerusalem like it because they thought that soon they could throw off the yoke of Nebuchadnezzar. Zedekiah's advisers were in favor of throwing off the Babylonian yoke and looking to Egypt for help, but Jeremiah kept insisting that the Chaldeans would certainly capture the city (37:3-10). Finally, Zedekiah broke his covenant with the king of

Babylon. Nebuchadnezzar swiftly marched against Jerusalem and the final siege began.

As the siege proceeded, the hostility of Jeremiah's enemies became more intense. They charged him with desertion and threw him into prison. They even petitioned the king to put him to death (38:4). Weakling that he was, Zedekiah gave Jeremiah over into the hands of the princes. Then for some reason they shrank from killing him. But they chose a worse thing for Jeremiah; they lowered him with ropes into a miry cistern and left him to die of starvation and exposure.

But God was with Jeremiah and raised up a friend to deliver him. An Ethiopian, Ebed-melech, heard of Jeremiah's plight and made his way to the king. Gaining permission, he rushed to the cistern and lowered some "old rags" for the prophet to put under his armpits beneath the ropes, for Jeremiah had sunk in the mire, and the work of getting him out would mean a great strain (38:6-13).

After Jeremiah's deliverance, Zedekiah, driven by fear, visited Jeremiah to find out what was in store for him. Jeremiah could only promise him doom for the city. Jeremiah still insisted that the king should surrender to Nebuchadnezzar, but Zedekiah was afraid of the princes (38:14-28). We find in chapter 24 one of the first discourses of Jeremiah in Zedekiah's reign. Jeremiah urged Judah to submit to Babylon in accordance with God's will, but without effect (21:1-10). Jeremiah never ceased urging this submission to Babylon, so much so that his enemies accused him of being a traitor.

After eighteen months of siege, Jerusalem was taken, Zedekiah's sons were put to death before his eyes, and afterwards he himself was blinded and carried in chains to Babylon (39:1-7). King Nebuchadnezzar of Babylon protected Jeremiah and made him an offer of freedom and honor in Babylon. But Jeremiah chose to cast his lot with the remnant left in the land (39:11-12; 40:1-16).

We can see how close Jeremiah was to the affairs of Judah during her captivity. He had seen the condition of Judah's decline after Josiah's good reign till the day of Zedekiah. He saw the people carried away captive and witnessed the destruction of Jerusalem and the Temple.

At the same time Jeremiah was crying out against Babylon for her heinous crime in destroying God's children. He told them that Babylon would be demolished and would be in ruins forever.

This is literally true of this wonder city of the ancient world. Read again Isaiah 13:17-22 along with Jeremiah 51:37-43.

In 606 B.C. the first deportation of the Jews to Babylon occurred. It was this year that Jeremiah was ordered to write the predictions he had made and to have them read to the people.

These predictions are scattered throughout chapters 24–49 and concern the future of the Jews, the Babylonian captivity, and the coming Messiah.

Predictions
1. Concerning God's future dealings with Judah (ch. 23; 31)
2. Conquest of land by Nebuchadnezzar, king of Babylon (20:4)
3. Judah's exile or captivity in Babylon and return after seventy years (ch. 25–26)
4. Concerning the Messiah (23:6; 30:4-11; 33:14-26)
5. Israel will be scattered among all the kingdoms of the earth (ch. 24)
6. Final recovery of Israel (23:1-40; 32:37-41; Ezekiel 37:21-22)

In the days when David's throne was tottering and Judah was going into captivity the prophet announced the coming Christ, King of the house of David, a righteous Branch. *And this is his name: "The Lord Our Righteousness." At that time Judah will be saved and Israel will live in peace* (23:6).

Jeremiah 23 is dear to the Jews, God's chosen people, and dear to the heart of God. It tells of the future of Judah, redeemed through the work of their Messiah. Jesus, the Good Shepherd, is promised (23:1, 3). He will gather his sheep from every corner of the earth and they will return to their own country, the Promised Land. This will take place when the King shall come and sit on the throne of David (23:5).

Judah's History in a Word
"Chosen"—Jeremiah prophesied to God's chosen people Judah before their exile into Babylon.

"Captured"—He warned them of their captivity if they would not listen to Jehovah.

"Carried Away"—They sinned until God allowed them to be carried away by Nebuchadnezzar into Babylon. God told them they had to remain captive seventy years (25:1-14; Daniel 9:2).

"Coming Messiah"—But God would not allow his children to remain scattered through the nations of the world forever. Someday the Jews would be gathered to their own land and the good Shepherd would appear (33:14-17).

Finally those left in Jerusalem all fled to Egypt in spite of God's warning against it (ch. 43). They asked Jeremiah to pray for guidance, but when it was given they refused to obey it. The prophet and Baruch were compelled to accompany them. Even in Egypt we find the prophet carrying out his commission. He prophesied the conquest of Egypt by Nebuchadnezzar (43:8-13). The Jews who lived in the Nile valley were practicing idolatry, and Jeremiah warned them against this wickedness. When they refused to listen to his warning and went on worshiping these other gods, Jeremiah told them that the judgment of God would fall (44:26-28).

This is the last we hear of Jeremiah. How long he lived in Egypt afterwards we don't know. Other prophets had at least occasional successes to cheer their hearts in the midst of difficulties, but Jeremiah seemed to be fighting a losing battle to the very end. Disaster, failure, and hostility were rewards for his work. He preached to deaf ears and seemed to reap only hate in return for his love for his people. In life he seemed to accomplish little. He was brokenhearted. But God has given us a record that makes him one of the greatest of all prophets.

Jeremiah's life was one of deepening gloom. He had to watch the people and city that he loved fall from sin to sin. And all the time he had no hope that things might change. How deeply he felt all this can be seen in his Lamentations.

JEREMIAH AND HIS TIMES

The prophecy of Jeremiah comes out of the turmoil in Judah preceding and during the Babylonian captivity like the song of a lark on the battlefield of Flanders. It is like a beautiful symphony of sorrow, God's oratorio of tears and consolation as his great heart of love weeps over the people he is chastening. The message of the book deals with the certainty of God's judgment because of sin, yet the tenderness and eternity of his boundless love. Jeremiah is concerned with backsliding. Judah had forsaken the Lord, and through Jeremiah God sent warnings of impending judgments, beseeching his people to return to his commandments.

Christ appears in Jeremiah. He is wonderfully pictured in 23:5-6. His future kingdom is lavishly described in chapters 31 and 33. The whole book is a series of messages, each of which was spoken to fit the need of the moment. Therefore these messages are like *gold apples in a silver basket* (Proverbs 25:11), and when we apply them to ourselves we discover that they meet our needs just as they met the needs of God's wandering people.

UNDERSTANDING LAMENTATIONS

Here is another of the Bible's exquisite books of poetry. It is commonly attributed to Jeremiah. Five beautiful, distinct poems are bound together in the book. It is not all sorrow. Above the clouds of the poet's weeping over the sins of his people, God's sun is shining. In Lamentations 3:22-27 the light breaks through to throw a shining rainbow across the murky sky. God's grace always shines above the clouds of sin (see Romans 5:20), and it will always shine in the heart that is trusting in God through faith in the Lord Jesus Christ, who gives *beauty for ashes; joy instead of mourning; praise instead of heaviness* (Isaiah 61:3).

SELECTED BIBLE READING

Sunday: Jeremiah Warns Judah (Jeremiah 1:1-10; 2:1-13; 3:12, 22-23; 4:14-19; 6:1-30)
Monday: A Rebuke (Jeremiah 7:1-15; 9:1-16; 17:5-18)
Tuesday: The Potter (Jeremiah 18:1-17)
Wednesday: The Faithless Shepherds (Jeremiah 23)
Thursday: Repentance and Restoration (Jeremiah 24–25)
Friday: Israel's Last Days (Jeremiah 30:18–31:40)
Saturday: The Overthrow of Judah (Jeremiah 52)
Comfort to the Sorrowing (Lamentations 1–5)

CHAPTER 20

UNDERSTANDING EZEKIEL

Ezekiel Portrays Jesus Christ, the Son of Man

Ezekiel, the faithful preacher to the exiles in Babylon, is the author of this book.

Jeremiah, the great prophet whom we have just finished studying, was the last of the prophets in Jerusalem before the exile. His ministry was still going on when the end came. Meanwhile the young prophet Ezekiel was already at work among the exiles in Babylon. God had prepared a witness to the people in their captivity. God needed a voice to warn the people and to remind them of the reason why all these calamities had befallen them. For twenty-two years Ezekiel dealt with the discouraged captives to whom God had sent him.

God's greatest communications can only be made by his servants whose own hearts have been broken. The instrument in God's hands must himself be ready to share in suffering with others. Jesus' body was broken for us.

Ezekiel is for the Jew today. It tells God's chosen people that God will fulfill his sure promises. Their land, their city, their Temple will be restored to them. It reveals God's plan for them.

Ezekiel is for the Christian today. It is a book of the times, for God's time is always revealed by his dealing with the Jews. Israel is returning to her land, and divine history is being made. The nation now exists officially. When the Jews move we know God is getting ready to act.

You find little of Ezekiel in the Gospels or Letters. But look in Revelation. Ezekiel and John seem to lock arms across the cen-

213

turies, and looking into the future they see the unfolding of a new heaven and a new earth. Ezekiel, the prophet, peering forward with rapt gaze, half whispering, says, *For high in the sky above them was what looked like a throne made of beautiful blue sapphire stones, and upon it sat someone who appeared to be a Man* (1:26). And John, a little nearer, revealing God's vision to him, says in clearer tones these thrilling words, *And instantly I was, in spirit, there in heaven and saw—oh, the glory of it!—a throne and someone sitting on it! Great bursts of light flashed forth from him as from a glittering diamond, or from a shining ruby* (Revelation 4:2-3).

Soon after Ezekiel was born a great reformation of popular worship and social life was aroused. This was caused by the inspiration of the book of Deuteronomy, which had just been published in 621 B.C. But the reformation was only superficial. The religious decline was crowned by political disaster, and Jerusalem was taken after an eighteen-month siege amid horrors untold. The Temple, on which such a passion of love had been lavished, was reduced to ashes and the people deported to Babylon.

Like Jeremiah, Ezekiel was not only a prophet but a priest as well. When he was twenty-five years old he was carried captive to Babylon in 597 B.C. with the upper class of people, eleven years before the destruction of Jerusalem. This means that for eleven years there were ten thousand exiles living in a concentration camp in Babylon while Jeremiah and the folks at home tried to carry on at Jerusalem. For five years the captives had no preacher. Then Ezekiel began to serve them. He immediately tried to remove their false hopes of an early return to Palestine. He tried to prepare them for the news of the tragic destruction of their beloved Jerusalem. He lived at the same time as Daniel and Jeremiah. Jeremiah remained among the Jews in Jerusalem. Ezekiel lived with the exiles in Babylon, and Daniel lived in the court of the rulers in Babylon.

Daniel and a few other Jewish boys had been brought to Babylon in 606 B.C. Ezekiel came nine years later. Ezekiel found that Daniel had attained a high position in the palace of Nebuchadnezzar, although he was only a youth. No doubt Daniel helped ease the lot of the captives because of his position. Ezekiel and Daniel were both young men about the same age. Jeremiah was older. He had been prophesying for about thirty years in Jerusalem when Ezekiel was taken away. Most likely Ezekiel had been Jeremiah's pupil while he was in the Holy City, and we find him preaching to the captives in Babylon the same things that Jeremiah had preached. He told them of their sin and their certain judgment. He reiterated their folly in relying on Egypt.

EZEKIEL'S DAY

The kingdom of Israel had been taken captive 120 years before by the king of Assyria. Then God brought judgment upon the southern kingdom of Judah. Nebuchadnezzar had come to Jerusalem and carried away ten thousand of the chief men of the southern kingdom and some of the royalty, including Daniel and Ezekiel (2 Chronicles 36:6-7; Daniel 1:1-3; 2 Kings 24:14-16). It took Nebuchadnezzar twenty years to completely destroy Jerusalem. He could have done it sooner but he wanted tribute money. Then, too, Daniel was his court favorite, and he may have been influenced by his young prime minister. He was finally forced to devastate Jerusalem because the city persisted in allying herself with Egypt. It was a tragic hour for Jerusalem when her walls were laid flat, her houses burned, the Temple destroyed, and her people dragged away as captives.

God had told of Judah's captivity by Babylon more than one hundred years before it happened (Isaiah 39:6; Micah 4:10). Its duration of seventy years was foretold by Jeremiah (Jeremiah 25:11-12). It is interesting to notice that God told them the exact time of their exile. But the captivity did not bring the people of Judah back to God. This judgment of God only seemed to drive the people into greater wickedness. They worshiped idols and set up shrines in the hills and defiled the sanctuary of Jehovah (5:11).

Ezekiel's Babylonian home was by the Chebar River. It was probably one of the ship canals, which we know were dug by the Babylonian monarchs and which branched off from the Euphrates above Babylon. At that time Babylon was the most beautiful city of the world, filled with palaces, gardens, temples and bridges, making it an outstanding showplace of the East. Ezekiel was among the captives who dug the canal. Tradition tells us that the little village of Kifil was the town where Ezekiel lived, died, and was buried. Tel Abib, where a colony of Jewish captives lived, was nearby. Ezekiel lived with these captives. He was fifty miles from Babylon, and no doubt he often visited Daniel in the palace. The Jews presented a pitiable picture—no Temple, interrupted national life, little opportunity for business. To such an audience Ezekiel devoted the best years of his life.

Ezekiel had a style and method of preaching all his own. He used symbols, as in the mimic siege of Jerusalem (ch. 4), visions (ch. 8), parables (ch. 17), poems (ch. 19), proverbs (12:22-23; 18:2), and prophecies (ch. 6; 20; 40–48).

Ezekiel was an artist. He painted strange pictures for his readers. They are mystifying and full of terror and sometimes hard to decipher. They glowed with life and action. He talked of sin and punishment, of repentance and blessing.

God told Ezekiel to go to the people in captivity. He was a captive ministering to captives. We must get alongside people to help them. This was our Lord's way. God told Ezekiel to speak *whether or not they will listen* (3:11). Ezekiel's responsibility was to deliver God's message. The results were not in his hands.

THE GLORY OF GOD

"The glory of God" seems to be the key phrase to Ezekiel. It occurs many times in the first eleven chapters. Then it does not occur again until chapter 43. *The glory of the Lord* was grieved away from the Temple at Jerusalem by the idolatry of the people. God said, *You have defiled my Temple,* therefore *I will make a public example of . . . the ruins of your land.* In Ezekiel 8 we see Ezekiel transported to Jerusalem in a vision. He saw four kinds of idolatry that were practiced in the courts of the Lord's Temple, even to the worshiping of the sun, with the people's backs t the sanctuary and their faces to the east. We see *the glory of th I rd* gradually grieved away from the inner sanctuary by the ڊin of idolatry, and the brightness filled the court. Then it departed to the threshold and rested over the guardian angels. As they rose from the earth, *the glory of the Lord* abode above their pinions and mounted with them, forsaking the city and removing to the mountains (ch. 10).

Christians, this is just what can happen to us. We can grieve the Holy Spirit and resist him until he is quenched and our heart becomes like a ruined temple bereft of its glory. There are so many blighted Christian lives from which the radiance has gone through disobedience.

We grieve the Spirit when we do not allow ourselves time to read the Bible or pray. We limit the Spirit when we refuse to be clean channels through which he can work. We resist him by allowing idols to be in our hearts. Remember, your body is the temple of the Holy Spirit. Does his presence glow in your life?

In the Old Testament the glory of God refers to the light that shone between the guardian angels in the Most Holy Place as the evidence of the presence of God. Ezekiel opens with this heavenly glory in the vision (ch. 1). The book ends with earthly glory (ch. 40–48). Ezekiel's visions given in between tell of the departing of this glory (9:3). First, it left the cherubim for the threshold of God's house (10:4), from there to the east gate (10:18-19), and finally clear away from the Temple and city to the Mount of Olives (11:22-23). Thus gradually, reluctantly, majestically, the glory of the Lord left the Temple and Holy City. Then captivity came.

This was Ezekiel's message to the nation. Their captivity was a result of their sin, and before they could hope for return to their land they had to return to their Lord. This message reached its climax in the impassioned cry of Ezekiel 18:30-32.

God's judgment on sin is certain and severe. His redemption is equally certain when it is welcomed by the human heart. Ezekiel's message closes with the promise of future glory. Ezekiel 37 is the great classic of Israel's hope. The closing vision of the Temple is equally significant. *The glory of the Lord* returned and filled the Temple of the Lord (43:2-6).

Ezekiel's prophecy is intensely practical for nation and church. As Israel's captivity was the result of sin, so we must remember that sin is a reproach to any people. A nation's troubles are the result of national apostasy from God.

The same is true of the church of Christ. The glory of the Lord left the Temple of the Lord because of the sins of God's people. It is also true of individual Christian experience. God's blessing returns to his people when his people return to him.

EZEKIEL AND THE CAPTIVITY

It seems that God called Ezekiel so he could explain and justify his action in allowing his children to be taken into captivity. They had been wicked and stiff-necked; they were guilty of unspeakable sin and abomination. When other nations did what Israel had done, God wiped them out. But all of God's dealings with Israel were for correction. They should have said, *I know, O Lord, that your decisions are right and that your punishment was right and did me good* (Psalm 119:75). He was punishing his children for their sin and was teaching them great lessons. He said a remnant would survive. *They shall know that I am God* was his purpose. And it is true that, with all their sins, the Jews have never been idolaters since the captivity! They insisted upon it before, in spite of the warnings of God, but never after they came out of Babylon.

God set Jeremiah to be a tower of strength in the land of Judah. In the same way he set Ezekiel to be a tower among his own captive people by the Chebar River in the land of the Chaldeans. He told Ezekiel that he made his forehead *as hard as rock* (3:9). Strength characterized the ministry of Ezekiel, whose name means "God will strengthen."

Ezekiel—A Home Missionary
Ezekiel was sent to his own people. It is sometimes easier to go as a missionary to another culture like China or India than to speak to the members of your own household or your own friends.

Perhaps God is speaking to us as he spoke to Ezekiel: *I am not sending you to some far-off foreign land where you can't understand the language . . . go to your people in exile* (3:5, 11). It was difficult to speak to false prophets, elders, shepherds, and princes, but God commanded it.

Ezekiel—A Watchman
God told Ezekiel to be a watchman. He told the prophet not to fear the people but to give them warning, and that if he did not do it he would be charged with their deaths (ch. 3 and 33). These chapters state plainly our personal responsibility in giving out the gospel message. Paul was so faithful in doing this that he could say, *No man's blood can be laid at my door, for I didn't shrink from declaring all God's message to you* (Acts 20:26-27).

Ezekiel—The Sign
To be God's sign to the people, Ezekiel underwent the loss of all personal interests. He stood ready to do anything God asked of him in order to demonstrate the plan of God for his people, and God asked some extraordinary things of him. He shut himself up in his house (3:24). He was placed in weird positions (4:4-8). He ate his food by weight (4:10). He sacrificed personal appearance (5:1) and even moved personal and domestic goods

out of his house to show the removal of Israel into captivity (12:2-7). God may never ask these things of us, but he may ask us to do things that cross our wills and desires. Will he find us as obedient as Ezekiel? Christ seeks for such—*I looked in vain for anyone who would build again the wall of righteousness that guards the land, who could stand in the gap and defend you from my just attacks, but I found not one* (22:30).

In Ezekiel 25–32 we hear pronouncements of doom on surrounding nations. We remember that Isaiah gave warnings in Isaiah 13–23, and Jeremiah gave warnings in Jeremiah 46–51. Each mentioned different nations. Ezekiel warned Ammon, Moab, Edom, Philistia, Tyre, Sidon, Egypt.

The remarkable thing about these prophecies is that they were given at a time when these cities and nations were strong and powerful. Each one has passed into a state of utter desolation, as Babylon, or has been put into a place of insignificance among world powers. Many of the specific prophecies have already been fulfilled to the most minute detail. *Godliness exalts a nation, but sin is a reproach to any people* (Proverbs 14:34).

VISIONS OF EZEKIEL

Ezekiel is a prophet of visions. The key text of the book shows this: *One day . . . the heavens were suddenly opened to me and I saw visions from God* (1:1). It is urgent that you scan all these visions before you enter into further detailed study.

Vision of the Guardian Angels (1:1–3:13)
In this vision "four living beings" appear, having unusual faces, but each with the general appearance of a man. The main purpose of the vision is twofold—to commission Ezekiel for service, and to impress upon him the need for assimilating the words God spoke to him and giving them to the people. Note the scroll that he ate in his vision (3:1). The living beings' unswerving obedience to God's will symbolized the obedience expected of Ezekiel. Their movement as a single unit is the picture of God's will perfectly executed. Ezekiel and Revelation are often alike in symbolism. The "Man" upon the throne (1:26) is the Son of God. The "rainbow" spoke of the covenant God made with Noah (1:28). The "fire" (1:4, 13, 27) spoke of God's Spirit. In Revelation, all these appear. Christ figures prominently in all the symbolism.

Vision of Glory and Godlessness (ch. 8–11)

Before the siege of Jerusalem, Ezekiel was given an extended vision that showed the people's abominations in defiling the Temple, and the contrasting glory of God. "Great sins" occur all the way through this section. "Glory" stands in sharp contrast. God was trying to show why Israel would be led into captivity (8:17-18).

Vision of the Burning Vine (15:1-8)

The vine becomes the symbol of Judah, and the burning of a useless vine that bears no fruit is the destruction of the people of God. The great sins and abominations of Jerusalem warranted the most severe punishment. This vision of doom is followed by the parable of the unfaithful wife. Israel was Jehovah's "bride" who had forsaken God to be a prostitute with other gods. Love of idols, rather than the love of God, caused Israel's downfall (ch. 16).

Vision of Dry Bones (31:1-18)

In this vision Ezekiel saw a great valley filled with dry bones, said to represent the "all the people of Israel" (37:11). The main lesson of the vision is the restoration of God's people. He takes them from among the heathen and gathers them out of all countries through which, as bones without flesh, they have been scattered. It is a picture also of the power of God to raise those who have been not only scattered but dead in sins. This "new birth" was explained to Nicodemus (John 3). God promises it here to Israel. They are to be brought forth, filled with God's Spirit, and brought to their land.

PARABLES AND SIGNS IN EZEKIEL

Parables and signs, as well as visions, abound in Ezekiel. The more outstanding ones command great interest:

1. The riddle (parable) of the two eagles (ch. 17) revealed the king of Babylon (v. 12) and the king of Egypt. The "shoot at the top of the tallest cedar tree" (v. 3) corresponded to Jehoiachin carried captive to Babylon. The "tender sprout" (v. 22) Jehovah would plant was the Messiah, the future King of David's line through whom all nations would learn to know

God. (See also Jeremiah 23:5-6; Isaiah 11:1; Zechariah 3:8; Isaiah 53.) For the "mountain," see 17:22; 20:40; Micah 4:1-2; Isaiah 2:2-3.

2. Chapters 20–23 include several parables, prominent among which is that of the two sisters, Oholah and Oholibah. They represented Israel's and Judah's deterioration into idolatry.
3. The parable of the boiling pot (ch. 24) symbolized the holocaust in Jerusalem at the hands of the invading Babylonians. Much fuel, hot fire, boiled flesh, and burnt bones showed the intensity of the siege (vv. 5, 10).
4. Two sticks—one Judah, the other Israel—are shown as ultimately reunited under the Shepherd King of God's people— Christ (37:24). This was one of the important "signs."

PREDICTIONS BEFORE THE SIEGE OF JERUSALEM—AGAINST JUDAH
EZEKIEL 1–24

As the book opens we see Ezekiel, a young man of about thirty, captive yet being commissioned by God for a great service.

Like the prophets generally, Ezekiel began his ministry only after he had a vision and a call from God. (Read of Jeremiah's call in Jeremiah 1:4-10, and review the facts of Isaiah's commission in Isaiah 6.) Ezekiel opens with the description of the experiences of the prophet when he was called.

The pivot of the book is the destruction of Jerusalem:

1. Pre-siege (ch. 1–24)—Ezekiel began with his prophecies six years before the destruction of Jerusalem and kept predicting its certainty until it occurred.
2. Siege (ch. 25–32)—After that his prophecies dealt with Judah's enemies and the overthrow of these nations.
3. Post-siege (ch. 33–48)—Finally the restoration and reestablishment of Judah was pictured.

Ezekiel gives us a very dramatic picture of his vision and call to service. The Holy Being who appeared to him could go everywhere. He was all-powerful, could see everything, and could rule the entire universe by his mighty hand.

The vision he saw was unusually complicated and elaborate. Notice how Ezekiel uses words such as "like," "seemed," "as if." He knew he was trying to describe things impossible to picture.

The prophet saw a fiery cloud approaching. From out of the glow were four living beings, suggested by the angels of the Temple. (See 1 Kings 6:23-28; Genesis 3:24; Psalm 18:10.) Each had four wings and four faces: that of a man, a lion, an ox, and an eagle, symbolizing intelligence, dignity, strength, and speed. They faced east, west, north, and south, suggesting that all parts of the universe are open to the gaze of God. The wings showed that there was no spot inaccessible to divine power. There were eyes in the wheels—wheels so equipped cannot miss their way. We see a symbol of the omnipotence (all-power), omnipresence (all-presence), and omniscience (all-knowledge) of God.

The mysterious whir of the mighty wings was followed by an equally mysterious silence. The wings dropped. The beings stopped. Above their heads was a crystal sky, above which was what looked like a sapphire throne, and on the throne was Almighty God himself, a figure of supernatural brilliance and glory. The terror of divine majesty was softened by the sight of a rainbow around the throne. Little wonder that when Ezekiel saw this vision he fell prostrate. The vision was to destroy all self-confidence that the prophet might have.

THE CALL
EZEKIEL 2-3

Following the vision, the awful silence was broken by the Almighty upon the throne. The prophet was receiving his call. God told the prostrate prophet to rise and accept his commission for service. God wants more than inactive submission. He wants loving service. God called Ezekiel "son of dust." Over and over this phrase is used. Ezekiel was called to declare the message of God—a message of doom to the people. This doom was justified by their rebellion. Ezekiel had every temptation to "rebel," but he went without flinching to speak the word.

The prophet's authority is suggested by the symbolic swallowing of a scroll. He had to make the message his own. He had to eat it (3:3). Bitter as its contents were to his mouth, they were sweet as honey, for it is sweet to do the will of God and to be trusted with tasks for him.

Then Ezekiel heard the whir of the wings and the roar of the wheels when the glory of the Lord rose from the place and the beings departed, leaving the prophet in a state of bitterness and anger. In this mood he found his way to Tel Abib, a colony of his fellow exiles, and remained overwhelmed for a week.

The Watchman

At the end of the week he received another message from God. This time it was more explicit. He was called to be a watchman. *I have appointed you as a watchman. . . . If you refuse to warn the wicked . . . I will demand your blood for theirs. But if you warn them . . . you are blameless* (3:16-21).

God places a great responsibility on his watchmen. How can we be so careless in the light of such words as these? How can we go to sleep and fail to warn others of their sins? Let us answer this challenge and heed this warning.

Ezekiel 33:7 says, *I have appointed you as a watchman.* As a watchman Ezekiel had to warn individuals of the coming catastrophe that he so clearly saw. It is not enough to warn the crowd. He had to deal with individuals, good or bad, who composed the crowd and tell them to turn from their evil ways.

God impressed Ezekiel with individual responsibility. Each one must repent. Each one must hear the Word. How true this is today of every person. Each one must accept Christ for himself. No one can do it for another. *But to all who received him, he gave the right to become children of God. All they needed to do was trust Christ to save them* (John 1:12; see also John 3:16; 5:24; 3:36).

Four Symbols of the Coming Doom of Jerusalem

1. The siege of Jerusalem (4:1-3). Ezekiel couldn't speak, but he was still a prophet and could preach, if not by word, then by symbol (3:22-27).
2. The duration of the exile (4:4-8). This section is curious. Remember, Ezekiel was a sign. He lay on his side to symbolize the years of punishment the Jews were to suffer in exile—a day for a year.
3. The hardships of the exiles (4:9-17). The horrors of famine due to siege are symbolized here by the prophet's food and drink, carefully measured out—about one-half pound of food and a pint of water each day.
4. The fate of the besieged (5:1-17). This last symbol, the knife and razor, is the most terrible of them all. It suggests the completeness of the destruction.

All of these visions and symbols reveal the method of Ezekiel's prophecy. This is the method used in Daniel and Revelation.

The prophet was shown the way the people profaned the Temple of the Lord God. This justified to the new generation the national punishment (8:1–11:12).

The prophet pled that the Lord God would spare a remnant, and God promised to be a "sanctuary" to them in the land of their exile. He promised to restore them finally (11:13-21).

The next chapters reveal the past sins of both Samaria and Jerusalem, and the punishment and instructions in righteousness for the elders of Israel (11:22–24:27). God said, *I will give you one heart and a new spirit . . . so that you can . . . be my people, and I will be your God* (11:19-20). God wants a religious experience of the heart. God will give his people a new spirit (18:31; 36:26).

PREDICTIONS DURING THE SIEGE OF
JERUSALEM—JUDGMENT AGAINST JUDAH'S ENEMIES
EZEKIEL 25–32

Ezekiel's gloomy predictions were completed (ch. 1–24). With the news of the fall of Jerusalem he immediately began to prophesy about the future restoration of Israel. God often revealed a bright picture of Israel's future against the backdrop of divine judgment (ch. 33–48). But before Israel was restored to her land, those who were her enemies had to be put out of the way. So at this point we hear of the future doom of these foreign powers.

First, we hear of her near neighbors who have insulted and harassed her, and then of the more distant and more powerful ones. God pronounced his judgment on Ammon, Moab, Tyre, Sidon, and Egypt for their sins against Israel. All of these powers were ancient enemies of Israel. They dated back before the days of the monarchy. From Israel's petty neighbors with their petty spite, Ezekiel turned to the great empires of Tyre and Egypt. They, too, must go. In a passage of great power, Ezekiel described the brilliance of Tyre, the extent of her commerce, and the pity and terror inspired by her fall.

Ezekiel 29–32 tells of the collapse of Egypt. The mighty Nebuchadnezzar with his terrible army would deal a crushing blow and Egypt would be devastated.

PREDICTIONS AFTER THE SIEGE OF
JERUSALEM—JUDAH'S RESTORATION
EZEKIEL 33-48

We can now look into the future and see the final restoration and glory of Israel. God will gather together his scattered people. God says over and over, "I will, I will."

The shepherds of Israel had proven faithless to the people and the flock had been scattered, but now Jehovah will set up a Shepherd, "my Servant, David" (34:23-24). This, no doubt, refers to the Davidic covenant and to the offspring of David, the Messiah. Look up this series of passages: 2 Samuel 7:16; Psalm 89:20-36; Isaiah 7:13-14; 9:6-7; 11:1-12; Jeremiah 23:2-7; Ezekiel 37:21-28; Hosea 3:4-5; Luke 1:30-33; Acts 2:29-31; 15:14-17. All these reveal that the future blessing of Israel would come with the Messiah, David's Son. When the Jews rejected Jesus they did not thwart God's plan or defeat his purpose, for in Acts we read that he was raised from the dead to sit on David's throne, and he will return for that purpose (Acts 2:30).

The restoration Ezekiel tells about does not refer to the feeble remnant that returned to Jerusalem after the seventy years of captivity (see Ezra and Nehemiah), for it is a restoration from all nations (36:24).

Ezekiel saw a vision of all this. There was a valley of dry bones (37:1-14). The "bones" were the Jews who would be alive at the restoration of the nation. The "graves" were the nations where they were dwelling but "buried." God would first bring them into their own land. Then they would be converted—a nation would be born in a day. The Spirit would give them life.

The revival of national life is possible! It is not beyond the power of God. Even dry bones, without sinew and flesh, are made to live. The Holy Spirit can bring life. This truth is seen everywhere when the Spirit comes with his quickening power (see Genesis 2:7; Revelation 11:11). The Israelis will multiply as they return to their own land. This restoration of Israel will be a national one. *They will look on him they pierced and mourn for him* (Zechariah 12:10; see also John 19:37; Romans 11:26).

Ezekiel 38 opens with the doom of Gog, the king of Meshech and Tubal. (Read these passages in connection with Zechariah 14:1-9; 12:1-4; Matthew 24:14-30; Revelation 14:14-20; 19:17-21.) Before the curtain falls we read the description of the kingdom during the coming millennial age. This is what the thousand-year reign of Christ on earth is called when he will sit upon the throne of David in Jerusalem (Revelation 20:6). All the prophets tell us what a glorious day this will be for both Jews and Gentiles. We read of the Temple, the worship, and the final possession of the land given to Abraham and to his offspring according to the covenant God gave to him (see Genesis 12:1-3; 13:14-15; 15:18; 17:3-8).

GOLDEN TRUTH ABOUT THE GOLDEN AGE

Back here in the Old Testament, while the Jews were in what seemed to be hopeless captivity, God declared constantly that he would restore them to their own land and set up the throne and the kingdom of David through David's greater Son. With his reign will come such earthly and spiritual blessings as have not been known since the world began. This is the golden truth about the golden age that is coming here on this earth (34:22-31).

Gabriel's prophecy at Jesus' birth in Luke 1:30-33 will be literally fulfilled through David's Son, the Lord Jesus Christ. This promise of a Messianic King and kingdom must be carefully distinguished from our Lord's spiritual rule over hearts and lives. The words of Gabriel to Mary still wait complete, literal fulfillment (see Ezekiel 34:23-24; 37:24; 1 Kings 14:8; Jeremiah 30:9).

The appearance of the Messiah will usher in a glorious future. God will make a covenant of peace (Leviticus 26:6; Jeremiah 31:31; Ezekiel 37:26). Wonderful blessings are promised to his people. They will be assured of absolute protection from heathen nations ("dangerous animals") because they are possessed by none other than God himself (34:31).

SELECTED BIBLE READING

Sunday: The Prophet's Call (Ezekiel 2:1–3:9)
Monday: The Prophet, a Watchman (Ezekiel 3:10-27)
Tuesday: Israel Will Be Saved (Ezekiel 11:14-21; 28:25-26)
Wednesday: Israel's Sins (Ezekiel 22)
Thursday: Israel's Future (Ezekiel 34)
Friday: Israel's Restoration (Ezekiel 36)
Saturday: Vision of the Dry Bones (Ezekiel 37:1-14)

CHAPTER 21

UNDERSTANDING
DANIEL

Daniel Portrays Jesus Christ, the Crushing Rock

Strong, healthy, good-looking lads . . . who have read widely in many fields, are well informed, alert and sensible (1:4)—these are some of the men with whom this book deals. They were skilled in God's wisdom as opposed to man's. They had an understanding of God's revelation that unlocks the mysteries of human science. They had ability in them such as God gives to live the overcoming life!

Chief among these princely young men was the incomparable Daniel. He stands in God's Word as the man who dared to keep a clean heart and body (1:8), and the man therefore whom God chose as a channel for his message to the Gentile nations of the world. A large part of this book is concerned with the thrilling personal life of this peerless captive prince of Judah.

Daniel was in the palace at Babylon the same time that Ezekiel was toiling in a slave gang. If Daniel's was the easier life in many of its material aspects, it may also be considered by far the more perilous.

Ezekiel's work during these dreary exile years was to proclaim to his people God's truth and to explain the real meaning of the miseries that had befallen them. Daniel's task was to share in the actual government of Babylon.

Daniel has been called the prophet of dreams. God revealed to him his secrets. *That night in a vision God told Daniel what the king had dreamed* (2:19). Daniel, like Ezekiel, looked far into the future. He is quoted most in Revelation. One cannot understand the great signs of Revelation without looking at their meaning in Daniel.

Daniel belonged to a family of high rank. He was taken captive to Babylon during the first invasion by Nebuchadnezzar at about the age of sixteen. Ezekiel was taken captive eight years later during the second invasion. Daniel lived to be over ninety years of age. He saw the Babylonian kingdom fall and the Medo-Persian empire established. He held high positions under kings Nebuchadnezzar, Belshazzar, Darius, and Cyrus.

Daniel's whole life from the time of his captivity was spent in the great and glamorous city of Babylon. He spent sixty-nine years in a vile court. There he lived a life without blame and was well favored. Ezekiel 14:14-20 and 28:3 refer to him as a model of righteousness.

Although Daniel was a captive, he rose to be prime minister of Babylon. The wonderful thing is that he always remained true to God.

DANIEL—BOOK OF DEVOTIONS

This book is packed with heart-touching devotional passages for the personal Christian life:

The surrendered life (1:1-21)
Light amidst darkness (2:20-22)
Triumph through trial (3:17-25)
The reward of service (5:17)
Prayer and confidence in God (6:10-24)
Confession of sin (9:3-19)
The wisdom of soul-winning (12:3)

Daniel was among the great on this earth. The historical portions of his own book hint this. Ezekiel, nearest to him in his own day and therefore knowing him best, ranks him as one of the world's triumvirate of virtue—Noah, Daniel, and Job (Ezekiel 14:14).

Daniel was also great in heaven. God broke the silence of the skies twice over to cry out, *O Daniel, greatly beloved of God . . . God loves you very much* (10:11, 19). Furthermore, no position, no matter how difficult, found him without trust in God. God is able, in all temptations, to keep us from falling (Jude 24), unless we have deliberately placed ourselves, with Peter, at the fire of the enemy.

God honored Daniel in his prayers. Marvelous in power that they were, God sent a special embassy of angels from the throne with the thrilling words, *Your request has been heard in heaven* (10:12). God exhibited his power in a remarkable way in Daniel's life, and Daniel never introduced himself or his own actions except as illustrations of that power.

Daniel was the companion of kings. He was a leader of men. He was a pioneer in reform. He started the first Society of Total Abstinence (1:12). Daniel was, like Joseph, God's candle shining in darkness. He was chief statesman in the first empire of the world, chief adviser of a great monarch, and a great protector of his own people. God gave him favor and love in the sight of the court official, Ashpenaz. Even proud Nebuchadnezzar seemed to have had real affection for Daniel.

The feelings of Darius toward Daniel were revealed when Darius found that a trap had been set for Daniel. *The king was very angry with himself for signing the law, and determined to save Daniel* (6:14).

No doubt Cyrus was greatly influenced by the aged statesman. Daniel may have shown him the prophecy that Isaiah had written concerning him a hundred years before he was born. This may have made Cyrus issue the decree for the rebuilding of the Temple at Jerusalem (2 Chronicles 36:22-23; Ezra 1).

In the book that Daniel wrote we see him preeminently as a prophet of God. He drew back the curtain and unveiled, as no one had ever done before, the hidden things of the future. Indeed, we are seeing more and more that his great prophecies are only history written before it occurred. It was the world's great annals in anticipation.

This book reveals the power of God and his universal sovereignty. God's power is contrasted with world power.

God the Keeper (ch. 1): God's power in keeping Daniel and his companions. They were given understanding and wisdom above all the wise men of Babylon.

God the Revealer of Secrets (ch. 2): God's power in revealing the dream of Nebuchadnezzar to Daniel. None of the wise men of Babylon could do this.

God the Deliverer (ch. 3): God's power in delivering Daniel's three companions from the fiery furnace. These young men stood up alone, against a nation, with the calm assurance that God would deliver them, yet adding, *But if he doesn't, please understand, sir, that even then we will never under any circumstance serve your gods or worship the gold statue you have erected* (3:18). This occurred after they had been in Babylon about twenty years, and God was demonstrating in this most dramatic way his power over all of the gods of this country.

God the Potentate (ch. 4): God's power in dealing with a mighty monarch, Nebuchadnezzar. God struck him while the proud king was boasting of his power as he was strolling on the roof of his magnificent palace. He was driven from his kingdom to dwell among beasts—victim of a strange form of insanity.

God the Judge (ch. 5): God's power is shown in the awful judgment revealed to Belshazzar, son of Nabonidus, by the handwriting on the wall. That night the king was slain by the Persian army and his city was taken.

God the All-Powerful (ch. 6): God's power revealed in the deliverance of Daniel from the lions' den. Remember, Daniel was an old man. When he was a young man of about twenty he was honored by the highest office in the whole empire. Now more than eighty years old, he was thrown into the den of lions. It seems that even the lions honored him.

God used the times of captivity to reveal his power among the nations of the world. When the chosen people were captives in Egypt, he worked miracles and wonders by the hand of Moses and showed, not only to the Israelis but to the Egyptians, that the Lord God is almighty.

Now during the Babylonian captivity, God used this as a special occasion to manifest his power. We find these great world monarchs confessing that he is the living God, the Most High, the King of heaven. He visited his children even in exile and showed them again that he is mighty to save.

Unlike the other prophets, Daniel dealt more fully with the Gentile nations than with his own Jewish nation. The other prophets only mentioned the Gentiles as incidental to something concerning Israel. But Daniel gives us the history of the Gentile powers from Babylon to the end. The prophecies are considered among the most remarkable in the whole Bible.

The book of Daniel is divided into two great sections:

1. Historical—narration (ch. 1–6)
2. Prophetic—revelation (ch. 7–12)

REIGN OF NEBUCHADNEZZAR
DANIEL 1-4

This scene opens upon a little group of four young men, Daniel, Hananiah, Misha-el, and Azariah (their Babylonian names were Belteshazzar, Shadrach, Meshach, and Abednego). They had been taken captive from Jerusalem by Nebuchadnezzar and carried away to his palace in Babylon. Daniel was only about sixteen years old; Nebuchadnezzar was a little older. He came to the throne about the time that Daniel was taken captive into Babylon and was the most powerful and distinguished king of the Babylonian Empire. Daniel's career was marked by Nebuchadnezzar's long rule and great accomplishments.

Daniel was carried to Babylon during the first deportation of the captives. He gained a high position in the kingdom and was influential through the seventy years of his captivity. He saw his captive countrymen return to Jerusalem under the decree of Cyrus. He saw world-ruling Babylon pass away and a new empire arise. Even at the age of ninety he received a position of high distinction in the court of Persia.

Daniel and his friends lived in an atmosphere of loose morals and low standards, even though they were in a palace. Yet we read that they kept themselves apart from the evil of that court—true to God in a day when everything was against them. Evils much like those of today were rampant everywhere in the courts of royalty.

Listen to what these brave youths said when they faced their first temptation in the court of the Babylonian king: "We will not defile ourselves with the king's food." And they didn't. It was to young men like these that God could tell his secrets and demonstrate his power. Remember, *friendship with God is reserved for those that reverence him. With them alone he share the secrets of his promises* (Psalm 25:14). These youths met every emergency and were victors. We will find them in three difficult positions:

1. In the court of a powerful emperor
2. In the fiery furnace
3. In the den of lions

In this first scene we find them in the luxurious heathen court. The youths were brought very quickly face to face with a serious practical difficulty. As favored ones they had been given many of the delicacies of the king's table. They were to be trained in state affairs and equipped for high positions. It was hard indeed to refuse the king's food and ask for a simpler fare. It looked as if they had no choice in the matter. Many of us would have argued that way. They asked to be able to prove that their health would be satisfactory. And God gave them favor in the eyes of their companions. Remember, we should always obey God rather than men. The king's food had probably been offered to idols (see Exodus 34:15; 1 Corinthians 10:20), and the meat would have been cooked with the blood left in it, which was unclean (see Leviticus 3:17; 7:26).

There was nothing priggish about Daniel. It was something to make a man like Ashpenaz love him. Notice how loyal his companions were to him. This is a fine trait. Success did not turn Daniel's head. He was a man to whom, early in his career, men turned.

We are told that God gave these young men knowledge and skill in all learning and wisdom, and Daniel had special understanding in the meanings of visions and dreams. This was God's reward. God's power was shown through his dealing with Daniel and his three companions in all the wisdom and understanding that he gave them.

One day there was a stir in the palace. Nebuchadnezzar had dreamed a dream and not one of the astrologers of the kingdom could tell him what it was. A decree had been sent forth for all the wise men to be killed, and Daniel and his friends were rounded up with all the others. But Daniel was not afraid. God would tell him the dream and give him the meaning of it.

Daniel called his prayer partners (2:17) and they presented their problem before God. *And that night in a vision God told Daniel what the king had dreamed* (2:19). God never disappoints faith.

The Dream of World Empires
Nebuchadnezzar's dream and the interpretation teach us some very interesting things about the history of the world from that time till the end of this age. The Bible calls this period "the times of the Gentiles" because God has put aside his own people, the Jews, for a time and has passed over the government of the world to the Gentiles.

Daniel 2 has been called the ABC of prophecy. It stretches out before us the most complete picture in all the Bible of what will happen in the future.

God revealed his plan of the future to a heathen monarch in a dream (2:29). After Nebuchadnezzar had dreamed, he forgot! But it worried him. No one could tell him his dream except one who knew the "God in heaven."

Picture a huge statue. The head was of gold, its chest and arms of silver, the belly and thighs of brass, and its legs of iron, with its feet and toes of iron and clay. Then a Rock cut out without hands struck the statue and broke it to pieces, and the Rock became a great mountain and filled the whole earth. (This Rock was none other than Jesus Christ.)

Daniel's Historical Summary

God first revealed the Gentile powers. Four great empires were to succeed one another in the government of the world from Nebuchadnezzar to the end. Daniel tells us what each metal represents. The head of gold was Babylon (2:38). The chest and arms of silver represented the Medo-Persian Empire that over- threw Babylon and became its successor (8:20). Its power began with Cyrus under whom the Jews returned to Jerusalem (see Ezra 1:1-2). The belly and thighs of brass represented Greece, which overturned the Medo-Persians. It pictured the Grecian rule under Alexander the Great (8:21).

Daniel 9:26 indicates a fourth world power. More is said of the fourth Gentile government than of the others. Maybe it is because it is the last. There will be a division into many kingdoms, as the toes. There is deterioration represented by the feet and toes being part iron and part clay that cannot hold together. This last government will be the weakest. It will not be completely unified and will finally end in chaos.

Kingdom of Christ

In the "Rock" cut out by supernatural means we see the kingdom of Christ, whose kingdom will never be destroyed, bringing to an end all the other kingdoms. Christ will come and set up a kingdom that will last forever (2:44-45). If you want an interesting study, see what the Bible says about the "Rock" (Psalm 118:22; Isaiah 8:14; 28:16; Zechariah 3:9).

Remember, at the time Nebuchadnezzar dreamed his dream, the Persian kingdom did not exist. It was merely a Babylonian province. It would have seemed impossible that a strong Grecian empire would rise. Only wandering tribes inhabited the Hellenic states. The future city of Rome was only a little town on the banks of the Tiber. Yet God told Daniel what would happen.

Notice that the metals in the image deteriorated in value— gold, silver, brass, and iron. This revealed the weakening in the power of each succeeding empire. Finally we find a condition of iron mixed with brittle clay. Name the forms of government that exist today. Do these resemble the toes of clay, "brittle" and not holding together?

Many ask, "When will this Rock fall?" We don't know the day nor hour, but the King is coming with power and great glory with all his holy angels to establish his kingdom.

The great King Nebuchadnezzar fell on his face and worshiped Daniel and declared that his God was the God of all gods. But we find as we go on in the story that this wonderful revelation of God had little real effect upon Nebuchadnezzar. It did not bring him to his knees before God.

The Fiery Furnace
As the curtain is pulled back again we face a very tense moment (ch. 3). Nebuchadnezzar had set up a golden image on the plain of Dura and had commanded all the people to fall down and worship it. If anybody refused, he would be cast into a fiery furnace.

But there were three in the throng that refused to obey the king. Yes, here they were again after twenty years, Shadrach, Meshach, and Abednego. Spies reported their disobedience. These three knew what God had said: *You must not make yourselves any idols. . . . You must never bow or worship it in any way* (Exodus 20:4-5). They were fearless in the presence of this Eastern despot.

The story of the fiery furnace is a familiar one. What was the wonderful thing about that scene? Yes, the Son of God was with them. What effect did this have on Nebuchadnezzar? He was filled with great admiration for the miraculous power of the God of these men. But still he did not bow to worship God in humility. He called him, "their" God.

Remember, God wants us to say, "My Lord and my God." Christ said, "When you pray, say, our Father." This scene demonstrated in a most dramatic way, before the dignitaries of the far-flung empire, the power of the Most High God. The erecting of an image will be repeated by the beast, the Antichrist, last head of Gentile world dominion (Revelation 13:11-15; 19:20).

The King Dreams Again

This time the king had another dream (4:4-27). Job 33:14-17 says, *For God speaks again and again, in dreams, in visions of the night when deep sleep falls on men . . . and gives them wisdom and instruction . . . , keeping them from pride.*

God has spoken often to men in dreams to reveal his will when the Bible was not open to them. God spoke to Nebuchadnezzar once and gave him the statue representing the Gentile kingdoms and showed him his doom. But the king did not repent. Then God revealed his power to him again from the fiery furnace. But still Nebuchadnezzar's proud heart felt no repentance.

Now we find God speaking to Nebuchadnezzar for the third time in the dream of the great tree that was cut down (4:4-27). This was a warning to Nebuchadnezzar of his coming madness. God was trying to bring this proud king to the end of himself. But a year later we see him a madman, his mind gone. He fancied himself an animal (4:28-34). All this because he had set himself up as a rival against Almighty God. Hear him say, *I, by my own mighty power, have built this beautiful city as my royal residence, and as the capital of my empire* (4:30).

Through his insanity, Nebuchadnezzar's eyes were opened and his conscience was touched. He confessed to the greatness of God and bore testimony to the goodness of God (4:34). He learned that man is not the architect of his own fortune.

REIGN OF BELSHAZZAR
DANIEL 5; 7–8

The following outline may help you to know who Belshazzar was and where his reign fits in the Babylonian Empire:

1. Nebuchadnezzar—reigned to 605–562 B.C.
2. Merodach—dissolute son of Nebuchadnezzar, reigned two years.
3. Neriglissar—brother-in-law and murderer of Merodach, followed with a four-year reign. No successor.

4. Nabonidus—son of Nebuchadnezzar's second wife, ascended throne in 556 B.C. Other name, Labyretus.
5. Belshazzar—son of Nabonidus, co-regent with him. Medes, imprisoning Nabonidus, pressed on to capture revelling Belshazzar and Babylon.

During the first year of Belshazzar's reign, Daniel had a vision of four huge animals, which symbolized the four kingdoms pictured in Nebuchadnezzar's dream (ch. 7). Picturing them as vicious animals gives us a hint of the moral character of these empires. How history's wars reveal the true heart of nations!

In Nebuchadnezzar's dream-statue we have man's view of the magnificence of these kingdoms. In Daniel's dream we have God's view of the same. See who Daniel said these four beasts are in Daniel 7:17-23. The first—Babylon—was like a lion with eagle's wings. Jeremiah likened Nebuchadnezzar both to the lion and eagle (Jeremiah 49:19-22). Persia was the bear, the cruel animal who delighted to kill for the sake of killing. The third was a leopard or panther, a beast of prey. His four wings portrayed swiftness. Here we see the rapid marches of Alexander's army and his insatiable love of conquest. In thirteen short years he had conquered the world. The fourth beast was different from all the rest. *Too dreadful to describe and incredibly strong. It devoured some of its victims by tearing them apart with its huge iron teeth* (7:7).

This vision of the four beasts covers the same ground as the great image of Daniel 2. Compare them carefully.

The "small horn" coming up among the ten is the Antichrist yet to come. We see him represented in Revelation as the beast coming up out of the sea (see Daniel 7:15-25). The saints will be oppressed by Antichrist, the last world ruler before Christ comes (Revelation 13:1). Rule of the dictators is beginning to hint at the extent of the power and authority possible to this last great dictator, the Antichrist. This period terminates the Great Tribulation (see Revelation 5-18). This is the period during which the judgments of God are to come upon the earth for the rejection of Jesus Christ.

Two years later, in Daniel 8, we have another vision of the ram and the goat. Belshazzar was still on the throne. This vision includes only two of the four kingdoms, Persia and Greece (8:20-21).

The kingdom of Medo-Persia is overthrown by the king of Greece. It contains the prophecy of the division of the latter kingdom between the four generals of Alexander after his death. Daniel had this vision at Shushan, the capital of Persia, where seventy years later the events recorded in Esther took place.

As chapter 5 opens we see a great banquet hall with a thousand lords sitting around the tables. It was "ladies' night." All the king's sweethearts were there besides the thousand lords. Often the presence of ladies seems to inspire a man to do something spectacular. So, as an extra feature, Belshazzar sent for the sacred golden and silver vessels that his grandfather Nebuchadnezzar had stripped from the Temple in Jerusalem. He showed them just how little he regarded the God of Israel. As the people looked, behold, golden and silver vessels adorned the tables! The last prince of Babylon, Belshazzar, drank wine to the idols in these sacred vessels.

God showed his power in the awful handwriting on the wall. Daniel was called in to explain the meaning. The prophet fearlessly condemned this foolish and sensual young king. Read the details of the divine interruption in Daniel 5. A bad reign came to a sudden end. *That very night Belshazzar, the Chaldean king, was killed.*

REIGN OF DARIUS
DANIEL 6; 9

A difficult question in Old Testament study is the identity of Darius the Mede (5:31). He could have been someone appointed by Cyrus. Some think that he was the father or grandfather of Cyrus, known otherwise as Astyages, and thus allowed to act as king until his death. Others think that he was a commander in the army of Cyrus, named Gobryas (the difference between this name and Darius in the original would be slight).

Twenty-three years after the death of Nebuchadnezzar, his great city, Babylon, fell into the hands of the Medes. The Bible does not tell us how, but we learn from historians Xenophon and Herodotus and Berosus the strange story of the fall of the great city. Many of the tablets from Babylon tell us that the Persian army took Babylon without a battle. Four months later Cyrus entered the city. Darius probably received the kingdom from Cyrus as his vice-regent over some part of it.

Even under these new rulers Daniel was in a place of power. The jealousy of the other officials was aroused by the preference given to Daniel, and a plot to destroy him was quickly formed. *They began searching for some fault in the way Daniel was handling his affairs* (6:4). Of course they did. He okayed all their tax receipts, and they soon found that Daniel would not allow any graft. They had always "knocked down taxes." If Daniel didn't let them get by, how were they going to get along with the high cost of living in Babylon? So Daniel had trouble because he would not stand in with the political crowd.

They used his religion to set their trap, with the very same result as always when men are foolish enough to try to trip the Lord's faithful children (see 1 Peter 3:12-13; Deuteronomy 9:3). Remember, there is always access to God through prayer in Christ. We may speak not just three times a day but whenever the need arises. The Lord Jesus invites us to pray. (Read again John 14:13-15.)

Unaware of what was happening, the king was induced to pass a decree designed solely for Daniel's destruction. Just imagine, if you can, a David, an Alexander, a Caesar, a Peter the Great, a Napoleon, a Queen Victoria, or any other strong ruler letting a cabal of his court trick him into sacrificing a favorite if he did not want to! Signing that law without finding out what was back of it was inexcusable. When he discovered the trap he had walked into, he should have broken the promise. "A bad promise is better broken than kept."

Daniel's conduct in face of danger was quite deliberate. He knew he had to deny his religion or be prepared to die for it. There was nothing different in his actions. He prayed as was his custom. His example would influence the other Jews. By drawing attention to himself he might reduce the danger for others. Daniel's faith during this ordeal was glorious and just what we would expect from a man ripened in years with God.

The officials knew that the king would not lift a finger against Daniel, so they had to trap the king. What was their bait? Notice the subtle appeal to the king's pride.

The law of Medes and Persians was unchangeable (see Esther 1:19; 8:8). The king saw that he had been deceived, and realizing the injustice of putting Daniel to death, he did his best to avoid carrying out the law.

Contrast the edict of Darius before and after Daniel's deliverance from the den of lions (6:26-27). Over the vast realm a proclamation went out, declaring the power and greatness of Daniel's

God. This scene closes with Daniel's prospering during the reign of Darius and moves on to the reign of Cyrus.

Daniel was thrown into the den of lions, but he fell into the hands of the living God. The world cannot breed a lion that God cannot tame. Shutting lions' mouths of difficulty and temptation is God's specialty.

Notice that Daniel prayed with thanksgiving (6:10; see also Philippians 4:6-7). When Daniel found out that the writing was signed he did not fall down in terror and agony, but he praised God. *Commit everything you do to the Lord. Trust him to help you do it and he will* (Psalm 37:5).

REIGN OF CYRUS
DANIEL 10–12

It was during the reign of Cyrus that the decree was sent out for the captives to return and rebuild the walls of Jerusalem (Ezra 1:2-4). Daniel, now nearly ninety years old, was too aged to return. No doubt he was needed among the exiles in Babylon. Daniel had outlived all the friends and companions of his youth. Now he saw the Jews gathering in the streets of Babylon, and the aged man watched the last caravan leave the west gate of the city to return to Jerusalem. Daniel was concerned about his people. We will see how he was comforted in his perplexity. In Daniel 10 we see the vision of the glory of God.

The Last Days
In Daniel 11 we find the vision that concerns the near future of the kingdom in which Daniel was so great a personage. Three kings were yet to come in the Medo-Persian Empire. Then Alexander, the mighty king of Greece, would appear (11:2-3). His empire would be divided among his four generals as had already been predicted. The course of affairs is followed down to Antiochus Epiphanes, the "small horn" of Daniel 8. His desecration of the sanctuary is again mentioned (12:11). Beginning with Daniel 11:36 we see the description of the final "small horn."

The Great Tribulation follows. How is it described in Daniel 12:1? This is a time of unparalleled trouble, spoken of by Jesus in Matthew 24:21. Mention is made of two resurrections (12:2). These two will be one thousand years apart. (See Revelation

20:1-6.) The first is the resurrection of the saints at Christ's coming to life everlasting. This is followed by one thousand years, called the Millennium. The second is the resurrection of the wicked to shame everlasting. *And many of those whose bodies lie dead and buried will rise up, some to everlasting life and some to shame and everlasting contempt* (12:2). Those new *who turn many to righteousness* are given significant rewards, showing us the necessity of diligence in soul-winning during our wait for Christ's return (12:3).

DANIEL'S CALENDAR OF EVENTS

The Lord has commanded 490 years of further punishment upon Jerusalem and your people. Then at last they will learn to stay away from sin, and their guilt will be cleansed; then the kingdom of everlasting righteousness will begin (9:24).

Scripture divides these 490 years into three divisions (9:24-27), with a parenthetic time lapse for the present "Gentile rule."

"Forty-nine years" began at the command to build and restore Jerusalem under Ezra and Nehemiah.

"Four hundred thirty-four years" began at the building of the wall of Jerusalem and continued to the Crucifixion. *The Anointed One will be killed* (9:25-26). At this point, after 483 years, the clock of Israel's national life stopped.

("Gentile rule"—an unknown number of years, intervenes. We are in this period now, awaiting the coming of Christ.)

"Seven years" have not yet begun, during which God deals with Israel exclusively. Beginning after the coming of Christ, Antichrist takes power, covenants with the Jews, and breaks it after half the seven years is up. This ushers in the time of trouble of Daniel 12:1—the Great Tribulation of Revelation. When will the final seven years begin?

SELECTED BIBLE READING

Sunday: Daniel, the Captive (Daniel 1–2)
Monday: Nebuchadnezzar, the Proud King (Daniel 3–4)
Tuesday: Belshazzar's Reign (Daniel 5; 7–8)
Wednesday: Darius' Reign (Daniel 6; 9)
Thursday: God's Glory (Daniel 10)
Friday: The Conflict of Kings (Daniel 11)
Saturday: Daniel's Last Message (Daniel 12)

CHAPTER 22

UNDERSTANDING HOSEA, JOEL, AMOS

Jesus Christ, Healer of the Rebellious;
Restorer; Heavenly Husbandman

UNDERSTANDING HOSEA

With the study of Hosea's prophecy we enter upon twelve books known as the minor prophets. Remember the difference between the major and minor prophets is not a matter of importance but the amount of material written.

Hosea was sent to the ten northern tribes called Israel. He prophesied in the reign of Jeroboam II of Israel. He lived in this northern kingdom when the splendors of Jeroboam's brilliant reign of forty-one years were beginning to fade into the black midnight of Israel's captivity. He prophesied during the eighth century B.C. This was a stirring time in the world's history. Rome and Carthage were both founded around this period. Phoenician sea traffic founded the latter great city. The big Phoenician westbound ships made their terminus Tarshish, a Phoenician colony in southern Spain. But during the time of Hosea they ran northward to the tin mines of Cornwall.

Another important fact in this period was the religious reformation that Gautama introduced in India that has issued in Buddhism. It was a time of stir and change. It presented many things akin to those of the sixteenth century after Christ.

Hosea's contemporaries were Amos, Isaiah, and Micah. He has been called the Jeremiah of the northern kingdom. You remember Jeremiah prophesied to Judah. In Hosea, Israel means the ten tribes that formed the northern kingdom. Judah means the tribes of Judah and Benjamin that formed the southern kingdom. Hosea was not trained in a seminary (school of the prophets), but he was a layman called by God to give the distinct message to Israel that God loved them.

ISRAEL'S UNFAITHFULNESS
HOSEA 1-3

The hero of this book, Hosea, is one of the greatest lovers in all literature. We find his love so strong that even the worst actions of an unfaithful wife could not kill it. Read Hosea 1:1 for a bit of the personal history of the prophet. We hear God speaking his first words to Hosea himself (1:2). The people had given no heed to Amos. Hosea knew that the country was due for a downfall, but they were not disposed to listen to him.

Turn to 2 Kings 15–17 and read the page of history that covers the period of this prophet. As we have already stated, it was a very unsettled time. Sin was rampant. The golden age of Jeroboam II was passing and a dark cloud hung over Israel. On the death of Jeroboam, six kings followed in quick succession. Within twenty years, four were assassinated. About the middle of Hosea's ministry a great part of the nation was carried away by the Assyrians. At the end of Hosea's life the kingdom of Israel came to an end with the fall of Samaria. The prophet lived to see his prophecies fulfilled.

We know little about Hosea other than that he had a very sad home life. The book pictures this man as gentle, frank, and affectionate. He had a deep loving nature that made him attached to his home.

A Strange Love Story

As chapter 1 opens we see a young man marrying a girl unworthy of him. He loved her truly. God told him to do something that would have been very repulsive to him (1:2-3). It was a severe test. But as in the case of Isaiah, he was to be a sign for Israel.

Hosea was told to marry a woman worthless in character, in fact, a prostitute. God was using this for a sign to his people of how they remained the object of his love in spite of their sinfulness. This all seems very strange to us. But God was making this picture of his redeeming grace. Grace is unmerited favor. Here we see Israel so undeserving of God's love, yet still he was lavishing it upon them. *But God showed his great love for us by sending Christ to die for us while we were still sinners* (Romans 5:8). God's dealings with Israel picture his dealings with us now. *All these things happened to them as examples—as object lessons to us* (1 Corinthians 10:11).

Hosea obeyed God and married Gomer (1:3). His name was hers. Home, reputation, God's favor, comfort were Gomer's. All that he had he gave her. In return, Hosea's name, domestic reputation, love, were all sacrificed on the altar of a shameful and worthless woman. How like our Lord Jesus this is! He not only came to us while we were still in sin, but he died the death of shame on Calvary for us so that all he had might be ours. (See Titus 2:14.)

Gomer ran away from home and left her young husband, Hosea, with two little sons and a daughter to care for. Lured away by the sin about her, she fell into the moral cesspool of the day and finally was carried off a slave. Through it all Hosea was true to her. Still loving her, he tried everything to win her back to a happy family life. But she would not. What a sad picture of man's stubbornness! What a wonderful picture of God's love!

Just as Hosea was married to an unfaithful bride, Gomer, so God was married to unfaithful Israel. This experience of Hosea helped him to understand God's heart of love as he yearned over wayward Israel to come home to him. No doubt there were tears in Hosea's eyes and sadness in his voice, for there was tragedy in his life. He had thrown himself wholly into his mission. "Who best can suffer, best can do" (Milton).

God's Bride

God frequently used marriage to symbolize his relation to Israel. *God will rejoice over you as a bridegroom with his bride* (Isaiah 62:5). God said of Israel, *I will betroth you to me in faithfulness and love* (2:20). God had been true to his bride, the Jews. He had loved them and protected them and lavished every gift upon them. But they left God and went after other gods. They disobeyed his laws. Like Hosea's wife, they had broken their marriage vows and had fallen into slavery, sin, and shame. Israel, like Gomer, had forgotten who had given her past blessings in abundance. (See 2:8.)

There are differing interpretations of this part of the book of Hosea. Some believe that Hosea was told by God to marry a sinful woman, which he did; others, that God told Hosea to marry a woman who did not go into sin until after the marriage; still others, that this experience of Hosea's was only a vision, not an actual experience. In any case, the undefeatable love of a true husband, to whom God likens himself, is shown, and Israel's strange, sad, persistent backsliding is revealed.

Backsliding a Historical Fact

But why should Israel's backsliding seem strange to us? Isn't it exactly what we all know about by personal experience? The history of man has been a history of backsliding and will continue to be so.

Creation of man (Genesis 1:28): Man was started at the top, but soon he was moving toward the bottom.

Fall of man (Genesis 3:23): Man went steadily downhill from the expulsion from Eden to the time of the flood.

Human government (Genesis 11:4): Man went downhill until he tried to ignore God in exalting himself, and the judgment of the confusion of languages fell upon him.

Promise to Abraham (Genesis 12:1): Israel, God's chosen people, went down until they found themselves at the bottom of the hill in bondage in Egypt.

Mosaic Law given (Exodus 19:8): Israel, during its entire national history, had its ups and downs. Hosea's day was a picture of it.

The Word shows us that until the end, men will sin and break God's heart of love, but a wonderful and patient God has endured this through the centuries.

In Hosea 3:4 the present state of the Jews is described. Read it! Read it! Ever since the destruction of Jerusalem by Titus (A.D. 70) the Jews have answered the description given here by Hosea. They have been a nation of wanderers over the face of the earth, going from nation to nation and from city to city. They are scattered, despised, and often hated people. (See Deuteronomy 28:63-65.) But notice what is happening to them today. Hosea 3:5 describes the Jews' glorious future.

ISRAEL'S NATIONAL SIN AND CHASTISEMENT
HOSEA 4-10

Here we hear a voice from the north where Israel lived (4:1) Two hundred years before, the ten tribes had seceded from Judal and had set up an independent kingdom called Israel. They immediately began worshiping idols. God had sent Elijah, then Elisha, to warn them, but in vain. They refused to return to God. Now we hear a new voice. It is Hosea: *Return to the Lord!* (6:1) is the much needed cry of the prophet. Return to God and he will return to you, was his message.

Hosea, whose name means "salvation," was poet laureate to the king. But he was more than that. He was God's voice to the people. They did not care to hear his message, for his appeal was to a blackslidden nation in behalf of a God grieved by his children's sins. It is well to remember that a name of Israel was always connected with sin or backsliding. It is used over and over in this book: Ephraim. *O Ephraim! Stay away from idols* (14:8). *O Israel, return to the Lord, your God, for you have been crushed by your sins* (14:1).

It is not more liberty we need today, but more loyalty. Do not give God ready-made plans for him to bless. Do not make your plans and then come to him for approval. Let him make the plans. The Israelis had foolishly made their own decisions. They had become stiff-necked. God will not do anything with a rebellious spirit and a defiant will.

God's Word is a mirror. What is a mirror really for? Is it to see how well you look? No! I believe it is to see the flaws—to see what is wrong so you can correct it. *Hear the word of the Lord, O people of Israel. The Lord has filed a lawsuit against you* (4:1).

Israel's blacklist of sin:

"Faithlessness" (4:1)
"Licentiousness" (4:11)
"Robbery" (7:1)
"Cheating" (12:7)

God's figures for sin:

An adulterous wife (3:1)
A wine-inflamed drunkard (4:11)
A stubborn heifer (4:16)
Gangs of robbers (6:9)
Adulterers (7:4)
A half-baked cake (7:8)

A silly, witless dove (7:11)
A crooked bow (7:16)
A broken pot (8:8)
A wild ass (8:9)

ISRAEL'S HOPE
HOSEA 11–14

Light breaks over these last chapters. They give us a picture of Israel's ultimate blessings in the future kingdom. We get a glimpse into God's heart of love when he, as a father, says, *When Israel was a child I loved him as a son and brought him out of Egypt* (11:1).

God's Choice
God did not choose Israel as his people because they were the greatest or richest of the nations of the world (Deuteronomy 7:6-8).

As God looked over the vast and glittering expanse of empires, there lay Babylon in all her glory. She was then a strong and mighty nation and gave great promise of a powerful future. To the south was the glory of Egypt, wrapped in the rich and jewelled web of centuries that we are just now unwrapping. Even today our eyes are dazzled as we look on their splendors. The Hittites, to the north, had culture and power, and the ships of the Phoenicians were plowing the seas. But God did not choose these. He chose a slave child in Egypt who was making bricks without straw in awful bondage upon whom he could lavish his love and blessing (Exodus 3).

We can never understand God's choices. He chooses what the world considers to be of little worth in order to shame what the world considers to be great (see 1 Corinthians 1:27.) Whenever anyone loves God, it is because he loved him first (1 John 4:19).

Israel's Sin
But Israel, the child who had been outwardly adopted in history at the time of the Exodus from Egypt, began to grow persistently disobedient and rebellious. The more the prophets warned them, the farther they went away from God. They showed no gratitude to God for all the blessings of their land. But in their freedom they forgot God and fell into sin and idolatry and were plunging

into captivity (4:6-7; 11:2). Israel finished her training in the slave markets of Assyria and Babylon.

God has been good to us and set his love upon us and has sent us prophets and teachers and put us in the midst of resources and luxury. But the more they warn us, the more we are prone to turn away, and the greater our education and learning, the more sufficient we become unto ourselves. Nations today are educating themselves away from God. So did Israel. God taught Israel that when people refuse light, the light is withdrawn. (See 5:6.)

We must understand God's attitude toward sin. He says, *The wages of sin is death* (Romans 6:23). *Don't be misled; remember that you can't ignore God and get away with it: a man will always reap just the kind of crop he sows!* (Galatians 6:7).

God reveals to his children through Hosea that knowledge always creates responsibility. This truth is taught also by the Apostle Peter. He says, *It would be better if he had never known about Christ at all than to learn of him and then afterwards turn his back on the holy commandments* (2 Peter 2:21). It is a dangerous thing to play with God's grace.

The Grace of God

We find grace abounding in the Old Testament as well as in the New. God had agonized over his rebellious people and would not give them up. His mercy was kindled and he said, *Then I will cure you of idolatry and faithlessness, and my love will know no bounds* (14:4). *But the more we see our sinfulness, the more we see God's abounding grace forgiving us* (Romans 5:20).

God had threatened Israel with his wrath, but now God offered them grace. God appealed to Israel to return and repent (14:1-3). Then he gave them a promised blessing (14:4-8).

In Hosea 1:11 God told Israel that one day Judah and Israel would be gathered together and have one leader. They are looking for this Messiah to come who will be their ruler. God again promised this in Hosea 3.

God's great heart is bursting with love, but our sins keep him from telling us all that is there for us. As with Israel, you may know the joy of barriers broken down and love poured out. *I will refresh Israel like the dew from heaven; she will blossom as the lily* (14:5). The dew speaks of the presence of the Holy Spirit. See how God pictures his abiding joy in his people after they are healed.

UNDERSTANDING JOEL

Joel is considered by some to be one of the earliest of all the prophets whose writings have come down to us. He possibly would have known both Elijah and Elisha in his youth.

His personal history is stated in one verse: *This message came from the Lord to Joel, son of Pethuel* (1:1). His name means "Jehovah is my God."

Joel has been called the prophet of "religious revival." He knew that revival must follow repentance. "A rent heart is followed by a rent veil and heaven." He tried to bring his people to this place. We will find access to the throne of grace and know the presence of the Holy Spirit when we truly repent.

The land of Israel had just suffered a terrible plague of locusts that had devoured every green thing, leaving only desolation. Joel believed that this had been a judgment sent by God because of the sin of his people. He was the first to prophesy the outpouring of the Holy Spirit upon all people (2:28). Joel appeared just a little before Hosea, only he spoke to the southern kingdom of Judah, while Hosea spoke to the northern tribes. His message is to us all today.

THE PLAGUE—THE WARNING
JOEL 1

Appalling famine, caused by an awful plague of locusts followed by a prolonged drought, devasted the land. People and flocks were dying for lack of food and water.

Using the judgment of a plague of locusts, Joel called his people of Judah to repentance. He wanted to spare them from greater judgments at the hands of hostile armies. The locust was a symbol and forerunner of the devastation they would bring.

Graphically he described the plague, calling the old men to confirm the fact that there had never been one like it before (1:2). Drunkards felt the effect of it, for the vines had been destroyed (1:5). Priests had no grain nor grapes nor olive oil to offer (1:9). Cattle and sheep cried in the fields (1:20). Joel urged the people to call a fast (1:14). Then he continued to describe the plague.

Joel called the people to consider the cause of the calamity. They must mourn with true penitence if they wished to be spared further judgment (2:12-17). Desperate, they were ready to listen to anyone who could explain their plight. It was a great hour for the preacher, for now, in their extremity, men would turn to God.

THE FAST—THE PROMISE
JOEL 2

The blast of the trumpet calling an assembly for a great fast opens this chapter (2:1). Everyone was there—old and young alike. Even brides and bridegrooms on their wedding day attended (2:16). The priests came in black sackcloth and bowed to the ground and cried to God within the sanctuary. *Spare your people, O our God,* and to the people, *Let your remorse tear at your hearts and not your garments* (2:17, 13). It was an event to bring the people back to God.

The locusts had made an Eden into a desolate wilderness (2:3). For one who has not seen it, an army of locusts is an incredible thing. They fill the air and darken the sun like an eclipse (2:2). They spread for miles over the land. Armies of "soldiers" advance with leaders in front, destroying everything that is green. In a few minutes every leaf and blade is destroyed. Others following strip the bark from the trees (1:6-7). The people dig trenches and kindle fires and beat and burn to death heaps of insects, but the effort is utterly useless. A land that has been devastated by locusts takes years to recover (1:17-20). Their flight is heard for miles much like a roaring fire (2:5). The land over which they pass looks as if it had been fireswept (2:3). After the country is stripped, they go into cities and, like mailed horsemen, they march into houses and consume everything that can be consumed (2:4, 7-9). God's promise, *I will give you back the crops the locusts ate!* (2:25), becomes more graphic in the mind when one sees the desolation wrought by the consuming insects.

The Promise of Pentecost

The prophet assured the people that God would indeed send both temporal mercies (2:18-27) and spiritual blessings (2:28-32). Yes, and God would send deliverance from the sky! *I will pour out my Spirit upon all of you! Your sons and daughters will prophesy, your old men will dream dreams, and your young men see visions. And I will pour out my Spirit even on your slaves, men and women alike* (2:28-29). Here is the prophecy of Pentecost.

Spiritual deliverance is the great central promise of the book of Joel. Other prophets foretold details concerning the Lord's life on earth, and even his future reign. To Joel was committed the privilege of telling that he would pour out his Spirit upon all people. He tells us that the blessing will flow forth from Jerusalem (2:32; 3:18). This prophecy, we are definitely told, was fulfilled at Pentecost. Peter said, *What you see this morning was predicted centuries ago by the prophet Joel* (Acts 2:16). Read all of Acts 2.

There is a lesson for us today. The church is in a desolate condition. It has been laid waste by many spiritual foes, well described in Joel 1:4. There is famine and drought on all sides. The call goes to Christians today to go into the dust before the Lord in the true repentance of heart. This repentance must begin with ministers and elders. If we will return to the Lord, he will fulfill his promise to us by his outpouring of the Holy Spirit. This great outpouring on Israel is future (Ezekiel 36:23-33). The great need in pulpit and pew today is the power of the Holy Spirit.

The Day of the Lord
The Day of the Lord refers to judgment. It tells of a series of judgments—the present locusts, the armies of invasion that were about to come as a scourge of God upon the land, and the final Day of the Lord described in the third chapter of Joel. *The Day of the Lord* is the period of time from the return of the Lord in glory until the new heavens and the new earth. (See Isaiah 2:17-20; 3:7-18; 4:1-2; 13:6-9; Jeremiah 46:10; Malachi 4:5; 1 Corinthians 5:5; 1 Thessalonians 5:2; 2 Thessalonians 2:2; 2 Peter 3:10.) *The Day of the Lord* is at least one thousand years in length. (Read Revelation 20:4.)

THE BLESSING—THE FUTURE
JOEL 3

Enemies—Overthrown (3:1-15)
Jerusalem—Delivered (3:16-17)
Land—Blessed (3:18)
Judah—Restored (3:19-21)

Only God could have told Joel of the return of the Jews from captivity. Joel not only saw the return from Babylon but the last regathering of the Jews from among the Gentile nations. He also told of the judgment of the nations after the battle of Armageddon (3:27). (Read Matthew 25:32 and Revelation 19:17-21.) Man's day of decision is over. God's hour of destiny has arrived.

After Israel is restored and the nations of the earth are judged (3:1-2), then the everlasting kingdom will be set up (3:20). Once again Israel, the land of promise, will be the center of power and the gathering place of the nations for judgment. Christ will return to establish his rule as sovereign. God will dwell in Zion (3:17).

UNDERSTANDING AMOS

Amos was from Tekoa, a small town about twelve miles south of Jerusalem. He was not a prophet nor from a family of prophets (7:14). He was not a priest nor a member of the prophets' school. He was a herdsman and fruitpicker. He must have been educated, for his book shows literary skill. Perhaps he traveled extensively selling his wool. The places he mentions may have been scenes of his visits.

In Amos we find one of many instances in the Bible of God calling a man when he was occupied in his daily work (1:1). God called him, shepherd's crook in hand, and sent him forth to gather his straying people. Remember, David was caring for his sheep and Gideon was at the threshing floor when they received their commissions.

On the wild uplands of Judah, beyond Tekoa, Amos received his training as a prophet straight from the hand of God. His beautiful writing abounds with illustrations from his mountain home. Like David, he had gazed on the stars and looked beyond to their Creator. He was not a courtier like Isaiah, nor a priest like Jeremiah, but just an ordinary working man. Though a native of Judah, he prophesied in and about Israel.

Amos was not the only prophet of his day. God had sent a great galaxy of messengers to save his people from the destruction they were inevitably facing. As a boy he had probably known Jonah and possibly Elisha. Hosea was his co-worker. These men surely knew each other well. When Amos's work was coming to a close, Isaiah and Micah appeared. These men, when boys, might have heard Amos preach on one of his tours. These younger prophets would have received much from this champion of God.

Amos prophesied while Uzziah was on the throne of Judah and Jeroboam II was king of Israel. This was a time of great prosperity. The old boundaries of the kingdom of David were gained back. Money poured in and the armies were victorious. Amos and Hosea were prophets to the northern kingdom of Israel, and Isaiah and Micah to the southern kingdom of Judah.

Under these two kings mentioned above, the two kingdoms reached the summit of their prosperity (2 Chronicles 26; 2 Kings 14:25). Assyria had not yet risen as a conquering world power. The idea of the approaching doom of their kingdoms seemed utterly improbable to Israel. They were enjoying a period of peace. The surrounding nations were not strong enough to give them trouble (see 6:1-13). All they thought of was pleasure and having a good time (2:6-8; 5:11-12; 6:4-6). God tried to arouse his people to a sense of their danger; hence he sent two witnesses, Hosea and Amos.

Amos feared God so much that he feared no one else at all. "Amos proclaimed a message so far ahead of his time that most of the human race, and a large part of all Christendom, have not yet caught up with it." So says a modern student of Amos.

Such courage was no more heeded in Israel's time than it is today. Of course you will find among the evils that Amos denounced some of the very same that prevail in our day. Here you find his voice raised against intemperance, in a far larger sense than merely excessive use of wine. Were he speaking primarily to our day, he would raise his voice in thundering tones against this abuse, which has increased practices of intemperance unknown and undreamed of by the luxurious lives of Israel. But the secret of all such sin is revealed in Amos's words: The children of Israel have rejected the law of God and have not kept his statutes.

Amos was humble—in not hiding his station in life.

Amos was wise—in not preaching over the heads of the people.

Amos was clever—in catching people's fancy by judging their enemies first.

Amos was fearless—in not tickling the ear but telling the truth.

Amos was faithful—"The Lord says" was his message.

This raw young herdsman, Amos, had a certain rugged frankness about him that was refreshing. He always hit straight from the shoulder (1:2). He didn't fail to tell even King Jeroboam II what he should do. God wanted someone to bear his message courageously, and Amos did not fail him. Israel needed a prophet who would tear the scales from their eyes and let them know the sure consequences of their idolatry, and Amos fearlessly set them forth. God abhors sin. Sin must be punished.

Jeroboam had brought Israel to the zenith of her power. The kingdom was flourishing and was at peace with her enemies. About the most unpopular man would be a "calamity howler," and Amos knew that is what they would call him if he delivered God's message. David before Goliath could not have been more courageous than Amos before Jeroboam, the idolater "who made Israel sin." Hear Amos in some of his unique figures of speech:

The archer's aim will fail, Amos prophesied (2:15). Jeroboam's stalwart archers were accustomed to pressing forward upon the enemy. They never gave in. What foolishness to talk of the un-erring archers of Israel failing anywhere at anytime!

The swiftest runners won't be fast enough to flee, Amos went on. What? Will Israel's fleet-footed runners be using their speed to run away from battle? Has this insolent prophet gone crazy?

Even the best of horsemen can't outrun the danger, thundered the messenger. There were no horsemen in all the world like Jeroboam's invincible cavalry.

But the climax was reached in these words of Amos: *The Lord says, "A shepherd tried to rescue his sheep from a lion, but it was too late; he snatched from the lion's mouth two legs and a piece of ear. So it will be when the Israelites in Samaria are finally rescued"* (3:12). This sounded like mockery! The idea of powerful Israel being likened to a poor sheep—or rather the fragments of a poor eaten sheep!

Yet this is what happened! In less than fifty years Israel was utterly destroyed, and the pitiful remnant of her people was not even as the leg of a sheep taken from the jaw of the devourer. Such is the picture of God's abhorrence of sin.

To every question about why great empires have fallen, the answer is sin. The secret of a great man's undoing is sin. Let Amos help you see sin in its true light.

If a ship at sea follows a wrong course, what happens? Yes, some sort of trouble, and wreckage in the end. But what of a captain that follows a wrong course knowingly? Something is wrong with his mind. No wonder prophets like Amos spoke plainly in warning people about the wrong course of sin.

JUDGMENT AGAINST NATIONS
AMOS 1-2

This simple country preacher left his home in Judah and traveled twenty-two miles to Bethel in the northern kingdom to preach to the kingdom of Israel. Why did God send him to Bethel? Surely Jerusalem needed his ministry. But God wanted the kingdom of Israel to have a strong word of warning. Bethel was the religious capital of the northern kingdom. Idolatry was there. They had substituted calf-worship for God. The people felt no need of preaching. (See 1 Kings 12:25-33.)

Amos started his preaching to the assembled crowds at Bethel, for it was a sacred feast day, by proclaiming the Lord's judgment upon six neighboring nations—Damascus (Syria), Gaza (Philistia), Tyre (Phoenicia), Edom, Ammon, and Moab. Then he came nearer home and pronounced judgment against Judah (2:4), against Israel itself (2:6), and finally against the whole nation (3:12). Amos's approach was clever. We are always willing to hear of our enemy's doom. Our own is harder to swallow, but we are forced to take it with our enemy's.

When the people doubted his authority, Amos gave a series of seven questions to show that the Lord revealed his secret to him. Therefore he had to prophesy (3:3-8).

Amos denounced the sin of Israel more graphically than Hosea (ch. 2). He spoke of their careless ease and luxury, their oppression of the poor, their lying and cheating, and worse than all, their hypocrisy in worship. The Lord grieved over his people not heeding his warnings. *You still would not return to me* (4:6). Then the invitation, *Seek me and live* (5:4).

The book opens with judgments on the nations surrounding Israel:

Damascus was threatened because it had invaded Israel (Amos 1:3; 2 Kings 10:32-33); Gaza and Tyre for conspiracy with Edom in its invasion of Judah (Amos 1:6, 9; 2 Chronicles 21:16-17; 28:18); Edom for continuing hostility (Amos 1:11; compare Obadiah 10–12); Ammon for attacking Gilead (Amos 1:13); Moab for heathen practices (Amos 2:1; 2 Kings 3:27); Judah for neglect of God's law (Amos 2:4; 2 Chronicles 3–19; 2 Kings 25:9); Israel for her unrighteousness (Amos 2:6; 2 Kings 17:17-23).

The nations of the world, no matter how powerful they may be, cannot withstand the judgments of God. God sets up kingdoms and brings them down. The mighty power of the pharaohs has come to nothing. Napoleon thought he could rule the world, but he languished in Saint Helena. In World War I the Kaiser thought he could act independently of God, and he was soon brought low. In World War II there were tyrants who thought they could stamp out God's chosen people and set themselves up as rulers of the earth, but hinderers of God's ultimate plan are always brought low (Psalm 2).

JUDGMENT AGAINST ISRAEL
AMOS 3-6

Amos was called to tell of certain punishment (ch. 3). If men reject the repeated warning of God, they must be punished (ch. 5).

Amos told Israel they were greedy, unjust, corrupt, profane (2:6-12), and that they defended and excused themselves on the ground that they were God's chosen people (3:2). He reminded them that this made their sin the greater. The Israelis looked at their relationship to God differently. They saw it as merely an outward and formal thing. They boasted that they were the chosen nation and no real evil could befall them. We see many professing Christians today in the same danger. They imagine their salvation is secured by their being members of a church. They think they are conferring a favor upon God and he cannot condemn them. (Read Amos 5:21-24.)

The first of God's punishments concerned the sins of six of the heathen nations that surrounded Israel. Then the prophet passed on to Judah and Israel. The sin of Judah had been her contempt of God's law, expressed in her idolatry. Only during the exile was Judah freed of this sin. The punishment of Judah was fulfilled in the destruction of Jerusalem by Nebuchadnezzar (2:5).

Amos condemned Israel. Israel was a chosen nation. They knew God's law. Therefore their sin was the greater. Amos told them about their injustice in the administration of the law. They *perverted justice by accepting bribes.* He enumerated their evil oppression. They had forgotten righteousness. The rich were cruel and they longed to see the poor oppressed. Even among Christians today we find wealth often counts more than character. Nothing is more dangerous in the church than influence and power given to those who have wealth but no Christian scruples.

Amos called the women of his day "fat cows of Bashan" because they only cared for luxury and worldly pleasures (4:1). This was the prophet's picture of the cruel, heartless, brainless women—a herd of cattle, heavy, heedless animals treading on all in their way as they seek to gratify their appetites.

Even the religious sacrifices and feasts of the people became an abomination. God said, *I hate . . . your religious feasts* (5:21). When they made their pilgrimages from Gilgal to Bethel, they only sinned the more, for it was merely an outward form mixed with idolatry (5:4-6). God demands conduct worthy of himself, not just empty sacrifices. Amos called attention to how God sent drought, plagues, and earthquakes. Still they did not repent.

God always warns before a punishment, yes, and offers a way of escape. God denounces sin, but he offers a remedy for sin. Israel's rejection of repeated warnings should have led them to prepare for God's judgment (ch. 5). If Israel had sought the Lord, the Day of the Lord spoken of in Amos 5:20 would not have overtaken them. But they did not seek him, and Assyrian fighters ushered in that day.

Amos told of Israel's coming judgment in five visions:

1. The devouring locusts (7:1-3). In the first vision, the prophet saw green fields and grasshoppers that destroyed the grass. Amos prayed: *What hope is there?* God answered: *I won't do it [the famine]*.
2. The consuming fire (7:4-6). In this vision, fire so terrible as to consume the waters and the land was seen. Amos prayed: *What hope is there?* God answered: *I won't do that [the fire] either*.
3. The searching plumbline (7:7-11). In this vision, Amos saw God measuring the city for destruction. The measuring revealed how far out of line Israel was. This time Amos didn't have the heart even to pray. Israel's judgment was certain—*I will no longer turn away from punishing*.
4. The ripe fruit basket (8:1-14). "Ripe fruit" of the fourth vision was fruit that was "soon to spoil." The basket revealed the sad truth that Israel, like a basket of overripe fruit, looked fine outwardly but was rotting at the heart. The guilty nation was "ripe" for judgment.
5. The Lord at the altar (9:1-10). The last vision showed God standing upon the altar, bidding Amos to *smash the tops of the pillars* and shower the fragments over the people's heads.

All the worshipers were to be scattered and killed by the sword. This spoke of final dispersion. The visions ended with judgment, but God closed the book with a bright outlook.

VISIONS REGARDING THE FUTURE
AMOS 7–9

We do not know how long Amos preached in Bethel, but we know that throngs heard his fearless message. When he spoke of the doom of the surrounding nations, the people were drawn to him and they cheered him to the last echo.

Then Amaziah, the priest of Bethel, could not stand up against Amos's preaching. So, backed by the king, the priest rebuked Amos. Listen to the report he sent to the king: *Amos is a traitor to our nation and is plotting your death. This is intolerable. It will lead to rebellion all across the land* (7:10-11). Amaziah told Amos to go back and mind his own business.

Amos was silenced by the false prophet. He was driven from Israel. Freedom of speech was not given the true prophet of God. Neither Elijah nor Amos was safe in Israel. When Amos found that Israel would not hear him, he returned to Judah and put his writings in a book so all the people could read and understand them.

Amos tells us of a bright future for God's chosen people, as do most of the prophets. The whole land will once more be a kingdom under the house of David (9:11-12). The City of David, now torn down, will be rebuilt (Acts 15:16-17). Israel will be restored to her land and prosper. A happy people will dwell in a happy land.

Always keep in mind that the Jews, today scattered over the face of the world, are being gathered back to their land of promise. National prosperity will again flourish. Jerusalem will be the capital of a mighty kingdom. Converted Israel will be God's witnesses (9:13-15).

People need such dealing as Amos gives at times when sin abounds. We get to be too tender and gentle with the common sins of the people. We forget how to denounce; we lose the power of righteous indignation.

Not so with Amos, plumbline prophet that he was. The crooked wall always hates the straight line. So men hated Amos. They will hate us if we speak out. Nevertheless, learn to speak, no matter what it costs. Recall here the Man with the whip purging the Temple (John 2:13-16).

Repentance is not just an easy or jaunty turning to God and saying, "I'm sorry." Not even the truest repentance can remit sin. Redemption is costly. Christ has paid the price. Salvation is the establishment of a personal relationship between the individual person and God. Nothing can take the place of that (see John 1:12).

SELECTED BIBLE READING

Sunday: Israel's Willful Ignorance (Hosea 4)
Monday: Israel's Glorious Future (Hosea 3; 14)
Tuesday: Punishment and Blessing (Joel 2)
Wednesday: The Restoration of Israel (Joel 3)
Thursday: Personal Admonitions (Amos 3–4)
Friday: The Prophet's Intercession (Amos 7–8)
Saturday: Future Kingdom Blessings (Amos 9)

CHAPTER 23

UNDERSTANDING
OBADIAH, JONAH, MICAH

*Jesus Christ Our Savior; Our Resurrection
and Life; Witness against Rebellious Nations*

UNDERSTANDING OBADIAH

Petra is one of the wonders of the world. It was a city unique of
its kind among the works of men. It perched like an "eagle's
nest" (ch. 4) amid inaccessible mountain fastnesses. Its only approach was through a deep rock cleft more than a mile long with
massive cliffs more than seven hundred feet high rising on either
side. The city was able to withstand any invasion. We are told
that its temples numbered a thousand. They were cut out of the
pink rock on the side of the massive cliffs. The dwellings were
mostly caves hewn out of the soft red sandstone (ch. 3, 6) and
placed where you would hardly believe it possible for a human
foot to climb.

South of the Dead Sea and on the western border of the Arabian
plateau lies a range of precipitous red sandstone heights known
as Mount Seir. It was here that Esau settled after he sold his
birthright to his brother Jacob. Having driven out the Horites
(see Genesis 14:5-6), he occupied the whole of the mountain.
Read Deuteronomy 2:12. These Horites are first spoken of in the
time of Abraham (Genesis 14:5-6). Sela, or Petra ("Rock"), was
their capital. Today it is called "the silent city of the forgotten
past."

The descendants of Esau were called Edomites. They would
go out on raiding expeditions and then retreat to their impregnable fortress where they kept alive in their hearts a bitter enmity

toward the Jews that had begun with Jacob and Esau. They never failed in helping any army who attacked the Jews. During the period of the Maccabees they became bitter enemies of the Jews. And in the time of Christ, through Herod they obtained control of Judea. They disappear from the pages of history after the destruction of Jerusalem by Titus in A.D. 70.

This book is the shortest in the Old Testament. It contains only twenty-one verses, but it includes two important themes—the doom of the proud and rebellious, and the deliverance of the meek and humble.

It was directly spoken to Edom and Zion and represented Esau and Jacob, the two sons of Isaac. But it appeals to us all with our two natures—the earthly represented by Esau on one side, so proud and bold, and the spiritual by Jacob, chosen and set apart by God. The story of the bitter family feud unfolds before us, taking us back to the days of the two brothers, Jacob and Esau.

THE DOOM OF EDOM
OBADIAH 1-16

Of the prophet who wrote this book we know nothing. His contemporary was Jeremiah. The name *Obadiah* means "a worshiper of Jehovah." We find the occasion of this prophecy as we read it in Obadiah 11: *You deserted Israel in his time of need. You stood aloof, refusing to lift a finger to help him when invaders carried off his wealth and divided Jerusalem among them by lot; you were as one of his enemies.* No doubt, it was the awful day when Nebuchadnezzar took Jerusalem and reduced it to a desolate heap. The Edomites had helped the marauders by catching the fleeing Israelis, treating them with cruelty and selling them as slaves.

This prophecy was written because of this confederacy against Jerusalem in which Edom took the part of the enemy (vv. 7-14). Against this people the prophecy of the unknown prophet, Obadiah, was directed. Edom looked on while Jerusalem was being plundered. They seemed to manifest fiendish delights in the calamity that overtook its inhabitants.

We read the denunciation of the selfish, indifferent, and presently hostile spirit of nearby Edom! She, holding the attitude of Esau, remained aloof and allowed Jerusalem to be despoiled. She even became party in the destruction and went in for her part of the spoils.

God had commanded Israel, *Don't look down on the Edom-ites . . . the Edomites are your brothers* (Deuteronomy 23:7). But Edom had shown an implacable hatred to Israel from the time that Israel was refused a passage through Edom on the way to Canaan (Numbers 20:14-21) to the day of the destruction of Jerusalem by the Chaldeans, when Edom cried, *Raze her to the ground* (Psalm 137:7).

Because of the pride and cruel hatred of Edom, her utter destruction was decreed (vv. 3-4, 10). Nothing could save the guilty nation. The people were driven from their rocky home five years after the destruction of Jerusalem when Nebuchadnezzar, passing down the valley of Arabah that formed the military road to Egypt, crushed the Edomites. They lost their existence as a nation about 150 B.C., and their name perished with the capture of Jerusalem by the Romans. *As you have done to Israel, so will it be done to you* (v. 15).

ZION'S DELIVERANCE
OBADIAH 17-21

The book closes with the promises of deliverance for Zion. *Israel will reoccupy the land* (v. 17). The first step in the reestablishment of the Jews is the recovery of what was previously theirs.

God's chosen people had just been carried into captivity by Nebuchadnezzar, the Holy Land was deserted, and God had told Edom of her doom. Jeremiah gave this same prophecy in chapter 49. Both Jeremiah and Obadiah had probably said these things many times. Five years later Edom fell before the same Babylon she had helped. She would be as though she had never been, swallowed up forever. This was the prophecy against Edom. But Israel would rise again from her present fall. She would possess not only her own land but also Philistia and Edom. She would finally rejoice in the holy reign of the promised Messiah. God's chosen people, the Jews, would repossess the Holy Land.

Obadiah, as the other prophets, predicted the coming of the Day of the Lord and the establishment of Messiah's kingdom. Remember, a Christian, too, is an heir of promises to be fulfilled when Christ comes. The believer enjoys all things in Christ. (Read 2 Corinthians 6:10.)

God's judgment on Edom as Israel's notable enemy should

warn nations today that God has not cast off his people and that nations that oppress them will surely bring down his judgments (Genesis 12:3).

UNDERSTANDING JONAH

Jonah was a native of Gath-hepher, a town about an hour's distance from Nazareth. Jewish legend tells us that he was the son of the widow of Zarephath whom Elijah brought to life (see 1 Kings 17:8-9). Whether this is true or not we do not know, but he probably was a disciple of the great Elisha and succeeded him as a prophet.

Jonah lived during the reign of Jeroboam II and aided him in making the northern kingdom of Israel very powerful and prosperous (see 2 Kings 14:25). Jonah was a famous statesman.

For the past half century or so we have been living in an age that has created a certain attitude toward the book of Jonah. It is impossible to open the book and take a reading from it anywhere without people's thoughts centering upon a fish! People have been so busy with tape lines trying to find the dimensions of the fish's belly that they seem to have had no time to plumb the depths of the teaching of the book. Be sure to read this short book through. Many stumble over this book. Few know it.

God is in this book. He is taking care of his prophet. God is working. Find the statement four times concerning him. God prepared:

A great fish (1:17)
A vine (4:6)
A worm (4:7)
A scorching east wind (4:8)

Jonah is the test book of the Bible. It challenges our faith. Our attitude toward Jonah reveals our attitude toward God and his Word. Is the story of Jonah mere naturalism or supernaturalism? Right here we stand or fall.

Jesus Christ himself made the book of Jonah important. When he was asked for a sign to prove his claims, he gave the people only the sign of the prophet Jonah (Matthew 12:38-40).

There are two events of great importance in Jonah. One is the great fish swallowing Jonah, and the other is the possibility of such a large heathen city as Nineveh being converted by an obscure foreign missionary in just a few days. See what Jesus said in Matthew 12:41.

AN OBSTINATE PROPHET
J O N A H 1 – 2

As the book opens God was speaking to Jonah, giving him his commission. *Go to the great city of Nineveh, and give them this announcement from the Lord: "I am going to destroy you, for your wickedness rises before me; it smells to highest heaven"* (1:2).

God was very definite with his orders. He told Jonah to go. *But Jonah was afraid to go and ran away from the Lord. He went down . . . to Joppa* (1:3). He said no to God. Why did he run? Read Jonah 4:2. Jonah knew that Assyria was Israel's dreaded enemy. Just at this period in history Assyria seems to have been somewhat weakened in power. It was then that God told him to go to the capital of that hostile country and pronounce judgment against it for its great wickedness. Jonah feared that Nineveh would repent and be spared impending doom. If Assyria fell, Jonah's own beloved Israel might escape judgment at Assyria's hands. Jonah had the spirit of a national hero. He decided to sacrifice himself in order to save his people, but his heroism was sadly misguided.

Nineveh was one of the greatest cities of the world, situated on the east bank of the Tigris River, four hundred miles from the Mediterranean Sea. It was the capital of Assyria (Genesis 10:11-12). The stronghold of the city was about thirty miles long and ten miles wide. It was marvelous in appearance. There were five walls and three moats (canals) surrounding it. The walls were one hundred feet high and and were so thick that four chariots could be driven abreast on top of them. There were great and beautiful palaces with the finest of gardens. Fifteen gates guarded by colossal lions and bulls opened into the city. There were seventy halls decorated magnificently with alabaster and sculpture. The temple in the city was in the form of a great pyramid that glittered in the sun. The city was as great in wickedness as it was in wealth and power. Intellectual attainments were almost incredible.

As soon as Jonah ran, God began to act. *He flung a terrific wind over the sea, causing a great storm* (1:4). God loved Jonah too much to let him prosper. Failure never relieves us of responsibility to serve.

Read about the events that took place before the throwing of Jonah into the sea (1:3-15). Jonah was thrown into the sea, but he was gripped by the hand of God (1:17). God's way is best. If we don't accept it, he forces strange things upon us.

The story of Jonah 2 tells us how Jonah came to the end of himself. After much praying he confessed that he could do nothing by himself. *Deliverance comes from the Lord alone* (2:9). Then God could afford to set him at liberty (2:10).

AN OBEDIENT PEOPLE
JONAH 3-4

Then the Lord spoke to Jonah again. God gave Jonah another chance to be of service. How foolish he was to make the Lord repeat his call! How much better to obey at once!

God said again, *Go to that great city, Nineveh, . . . and warn them of their doom, as I told you to before!* (3:2).

It was not easy for Jonah to go through the streets and cry, *Forty days from now Nineveh will be destroyed!* (3:4). There was no mercy in his message. There was no tear in the prophet's voice. He was obeying God, but his heart was unchanged (4:1-3). The common people of Nineveh repented first. Then the nobles followed. This is always true. Revival starts among the people. Think of a city like Los Angeles repenting and turning to God in one day because of the preaching of a modern prophet. It would be a miracle of the ages. But this is what happened when Jonah preached in his day.

Obedient but Perplexed

Look at Jonah sulking as he sat out on the hill on the east side of the city under a vine that God "arranged" for a shadow over his head, waiting to see what God would do (4:6).

The book ends abruptly! But there are two things we must notice in this book. First, Jonah is a symbol of Christ in his death, burial, and resurrection. *For as Jonah was in the great fish for three days and three nights, so I, the Messiah, shall be in the heart of the earth three days and three nights* (Matthew 12:40). Second, Jonah is also a symbol of Israel—disobedient to God, swallowed by the nations of the world, who will yet give her up when Christ comes. Then will Israel be witnesses of God everywhere.

No doubt, two things hindered Jonah when God told him to go to Nineveh—his pride of self and his scorn of the rest of the world. God took this out of him in the fish's belly.

Jonah, Type of Israel

Jonah was called to a world mission. So was Israel.

Jonah refused to fulfill his mission by obeying God. So did Israel.

Jonah was punished by being thrown into the sea. Israel was punished by being scattered among the nations.

Jonah was preserved. So was Israel.

Jonah repented and was thrown out of the fish and restored to life. Israel will be thrown out by all the nations and restored to her former position.

Jonah, obedient to God, goes on his mission. Israel, in obedience, will become a witness to all the earth.

Jonah was blessed in that Nineveh was brought to salvation. Israel will be blessed in the conversion of the whole world.

UNDERSTANDING MICAH

Micah was a country preacher who lived in the days of Isaiah and Hosea. His home was about twenty miles south of Jerusalem in the town of Moresheth on the Philistine border. He was preaching there at the same time Isaiah was preaching in Jerusalem and Hosea in Israel. Micah was a prophet of the common people and country life; Isaiah preached to the court in the city of Jerusalem.

Micah knew his fellow countrymen well. Read what he said his real equipment was. *But as for me, I am filled with power, with the Spirit of the Lord, fearlessly announcing God's punishment on Israel for her sins* (3:8). Micah prophesied concerning Samaria, the capital of Israel, and Jerusalem, the capital of Judah, but the burden of his prophecy was for Judah. The times in which he lived were difficult. Oppression was within the walls and foes were coming from without. The condition was the same both in the kingdom of Judah and in the kingdom of Israel. Jotham, Ahaz, and Hezekiah were the kings who reigned during Micah's preaching.

The prophet denounced the social sins of his day (2:2). Micah felt keenly these social evils. He saw the unfair treatment of the poor by the rich. He felt that these sins cried up to heaven. No class was free from corrupting influences; leaders, priests, and people alike were all affected (2:2, 8-9, 11; 3:1-3, 5, 11). Micah made them all smart under the lash. Micah wanted the people to know that every cruel act to one's fellowman was an insult to God. God was offended by the conduct of the people and the rulers. In spite of the state of things, the people tried to carry on their religious observances. Micah showed the uselessness of all this (6:7-8).

The northern kingdom of Israel was taken into captivity during Micah's lifetime. Israel would not heed the warning of the prophets. Judah did and was spared for 150 years. Micah knew that national sins would lead to national downfall.

The book of Micah seems to be divided into three parts, each beginning with a command to listen (1:2; 3:1; 6:1). And each closes with a promise:

1. A promise of deliverance (2:12-13)
2. A promise to overthrow the enemies in the land (5:10, 15)
3. A fulfillment of promise to Abraham (7:20)

Catalogue of national sins:

Idolatry (1:7; 6:16)
Covetousness (2:2)
Oppression (2:2)
Violence (2:2; 3:10; 6:12; 7:2)
Encouraging false prophets (2:6, 11)
Corruption of leaders (3:1-3)
Corruption of prophets (3:5-7)
Corruption of priests (3:11)
Bribery (3:9, 11; 7:3)
Dishonesty (6:10-11)

Passages concerning Christ:

Birthplace named (5:2)
Christ as King (2:12-13)
Christ reigning in righteousness over the whole earth (4:1, 7)

Micah is quoted on three occasions:

1. By the elders of Judah (Jeremiah 26:18 quoting Micah 3:12)
2. By magi coming to Jerusalem (Matthew 2:5-6 quoting Micah 5:2)
3. By Jesus when sending out the twelve (Matthew 10:35-36 quoting Micah 7:6). See also Isaiah 2:2-4; 41:15; Ezekiel 22:27; Zephaniah 3:19.

God's government:

Jerusalem, capital of Christ's kingdom (4:1-2)
Universal, extent of Christ's kingdom (4:2)
Peace, keynote of Christ's kingdom (4:3)
Prosperity, blessing of Christ's kingdom (4:4)
Righteousness, basis of Christ's kingdom (4:5; 4:2)

A MESSAGE TO THE PEOPLE
CONCERNING ISRAEL'S SIN
MICAH 1–2

As the book opens we hear the cry, *Attention! Let all the peoples of the world listen. For the Lord in his holy Temple has made accusations against you!* (1:2).

God is not asleep. He knows the sad condition of his people. He will sit in judgment upon his people. Yes, the Lord was coming to call Israel to judgment because of her wrongs. Samaria and Jerusalem were pronounced guilty before the great Judge of the universe. Captivity and exile were their fate. God rebuked them for social injustice, unfaithfulness, dishonesty, and idolatry.

Micah told them that Samaria, the capital of Israel, would fall (1:6-7). A similar judgment would come upon Judah. Judah's sin was described as an incurable wound. Some kinds of disease are cured only by destruction. All Judah's people would be taken captive, for God found incurable oppression, violence, and injustice. Notice the towns of Judah mentioned in the last verses of Micah. Look at the map and you will see that they all surrounded the prophet's hometown.

The idolatry of Israel spread rapidly to Jerusalem and the strong city of Lachish (1:13). It was this awful spread of idolatry, and all its terrible evils, to Judah under King Ahaz that Micah especially denounced. The oppression of the poor (2:2), and women and little children being driven from their homes (2:9), were also rebuked by the prophet. The sins of the people are stated in blunt frankness in Micah 2:1-11. God would bring suffering and shame upon them for their unscrupulous use of power.

More and more we are realizing the social value of the gospel of the Lord Jesus Christ. Wherever this gospel goes we find conditions bettered and a brotherhood that is based on sonship. Heart worship of God always issues in practical demonstrations of changed lives. Missionaries all bear witness of this in a most wonderful way.

A MESSAGE TO THE RULERS CONCERNING THE COMING CHRIST
MICAH 3-5

Listen, you leaders of Israel (3:1). What did God say of them? Read Micah 3:1-4. God likened their covetousness and self-aggrandizement, even at the price of blood, to cannibalism. The leaders were devouring the poor, defenseless people (3:2-3).

The nation was ready to collapse, and the leaders and priests were responsible for it. God denounced the sin of the rulers (3:9), the bribery among the leaders (3:11), false weights and balances. God described these men in Micah 3:5: *You who lead his people astray! You who cry "Peace" to those who give you food, and threaten those who will not pay!*

Micah, brokenhearted, told of God's judgment upon Judah for their sins. Jerusalem and its Temple would be destroyed (3:12; 7:13). The people of Judah would be taken captive to Babylon (4:10). But he seemed to hasten over words of judgment and to linger over the message of God's love and mercy. God would bring his people back from captivity (4:1-8; 7:11; 14-17). Micah was a prophet of hope. He always looked beyond doom and punishment to the day of glory when Christ himself will reign, when peace will cover the earth. God gave the promise. The Messiah would come. He would be born in Bethlehem (4:8; 5:2-4).

Then Israel would be gathered from the nations into which she has been scattered (4:6). Oh, that the Prince of Peace would come soon and make all these things happen! We pray with John on the isle of Patmos, *Amen. Come, Lord Jesus* (Revelation 22:20).

Little Bethlehem, smallest among the towns of Judah, would be signally honored by the birth of God's Messiah, Jesus Christ, our Lord. His victories would not be won by might nor by power but by his Spirit. He comes as a little baby to bring salvation to a world so in need of a Redeemer. This seven hundred-year-old prophecy from Micah 5:2-5, together with the star, led the wise men to Jerusalem to seek the new King.

A MESSAGE TO THE CHOSEN PEOPLE
CONCERNING GOD'S ARGUMENT
MICAH 6–7

And now, O mountains, listen to the Lord's complaint! For he has a case against his people Israel! He will prosecute them to the full (6:2). God is pictured as one bringing a lawsuit against his people. They had ignored God. He told them to remember how good he had been to them and how he had kept his covenant with them (6:3).

The people, conscience-smitten, asked how they could please God. Frantically they asked if burnt offerings would do (6:6-7).

Man is always trying to get back in the good graces of God with some outward religious service or some material goods. But remember, *It is a broken spirit you want—remorse and penitence. A broken and contrite heart, O God, you will not ignore* (Psalm 51:17). God wants righteous conduct and a real personal experience of him in each life. Because of unrighteous conduct the people had to suffer unbelievable consequences. God is a righteous Judge (1:3, 5; 3:12). What does the Apostle Paul tell us to do in return for God's mercies? (Read Romans 12:1-2.) The best way to get back in God's graces is to accept God's grace.

SIMPLE ESSENTIALS OF REAL RELIGION

The Old Testament gives us a definition of religion. What does God require of you? (Read Micah 6:8.)

How does this compare with man's present-day definitions of religion?

Be fair and just—good ethics in all of life.

Merciful—consideration for others when justice has not been done.

Walk humbly with your God—personal experience with God.

Paul would call this the *mind of Christ. Your attitude should be the kind that was shown us by Jesus Christ* (Philippians 2:5). If our religion is only a great creed, grand cathedrals, and elaborate rituals, then we have nothing. All must be filled with the mind of Christ. Christ wants us to have more than a beautiful creed, even if it is spiritual and true. He wants the Spirit of Christ to be lived out through our daily lives and to be exhibited in all our conduct, in our homes, and in our business. Can our religion stand this test?

It is interesting that when Christ summed up the same matter (Matthew 23:23), he used the words *justice, mercy,* and *faith.* He thus equated faith with *walking humbly with your God,* an apt comparison.

SELECTED BIBLE READING

Sunday: Doom and Deliverance (Obadiah 1-21)
Monday: A Fish Story (Jonah 1–2)
Tuesday: An Obedient Prophet (Jonah 3–4)
Wednesday: A Message to the People (Micah 1–2)
Thursday: A Message to the Rulers (Micah 3–4)
Friday: The Birth and Rejection of the King (Micah 5)
Saturday: A Message to the Chosen People (Micah 6–7)

CHAPTER 24

UNDERSTANDING NAHUM, HABAKKUK, ZEPHANIAH

Jesus Christ, a Stronghold in the Day of Trouble;
the God of My Salvation; a Jealous Lord

UNDERSTANDING NAHUM

In name and in message, *Nahum* means "comfort" for Judah. *The Lord is good. When trouble comes, he is the place to go! And he knows everyone who trusts in him* (1:7). Deliverance for Judah and destruction for their enemy Assyria was God's great theme for his people. It is noteworthy that Capernaum, where Christ the Comforter did so many works, means "village of Nahum [comfort]." Nearby is the town where he was born, Elkosh.

Nahum was probably a native of Galilee and lived at the time of good King Hezekiah and the great prophet Isaiah. No doubt, when the cruel Assyrians invaded his country and carried away the ten tribes of Israel, he escaped into the southern kingdom of Judah. He probably took up his residence in Jerusalem where he later witnessed the siege of that city by Sennacherib that ended with the miraculous destruction of the Assyrian host. You remember 185,000 perished in one night, as 2 Kings 19:35 records. Nahum 1:2 may refer to this. Shortly after this event Nahum wrote his book.

The theme of this book is the destruction of Nineveh, the city that Jonah warned. Nineveh was a culprit, and God sent Nahum to declare his righteous judgment upon her. In the judgment of Nineveh, God is judging a sinning world. Nahum was written about one hundred fifty years after the revival of Jonah's day when the city of Nineveh was brought to repentence in "dust and ashes." Mercy unheeded finally brings judgment.

No doubt the Ninevites were sincere then, but it did not last. They were again guilty of the very sins of which they had repented. Nineveh, the glory of the Assyrians, had come to a complete and deliberate defiance of the living God. They purposely rejected the God they had accepted (2 Kings 18:25, 30, 35; 19:10-13).

God sent Nahum to predict the final doom and complete overthrow of Nineveh and her empire. This empire had been built up by violence. The Assyrians were great warriors, continually out on raiding expeditions. They built their state on the loot of other people. They did everything to inspire terror. They said they did this in obedience to their god, Asshur. God was going to doom Nineveh to perish in a violent and extraordinary way. Read of her beast-like violence and cruelty (2:11-12).

Assyria had enjoyed a brilliant epoch of three hundred years in which she was a world empire. Nineveh was the capital of this mighty empire. It was in 721 B.C. that she destroyed Israel and threatened Judah, but God was going to see that Assyria's doom was final. The message of Nahum shows what God can do with a wicked and rebellious people. He will utterly destroy them.

The doom of the city was delayed some one hundred fifty years after Jonah preached, but it fell at last. Nahum's prophecy was not a call to repentance but the statement of certain and final doom. Read Nahum 1:9; also 3:18-19. Nineveh would be utterly cut off (1:14). God would dig her grave.

THE JUDGE
NAHUM 1:1-7

In Nahum 1 we see God the holy Judge on the bench of the court of heaven, judging the wicked city of Nineveh. The case is presented. This God is a just God; therefore he must avenge all crimes.

There is a twofold revelation of the character of this Judge of all the world. We find a sublime and powerful statement of those attributes of God that constitute the basis of all his actions toward men. This lesson gives us an excellent opportunity of presenting the attributes of God. Study the prophet's vision of God in Nahum 1:2-3, 7.

As Judge, God:

1. Is jealous over those he loves
2. Takes vengeance on those who hurt them
3. Furiously destroys their enemies
4. Has incredible power

As Father, God:

1. Is slow in getting angry
2. Is good
3. Is a place to go when trouble comes
4. Knows everyone who trusts in him

The first words of the vision are awe-inspiring: *God is jealous . . . he takes vengeance* (1:2). To think of a God like this makes us examine ourselves. We will find that there is no righteousness in us. How this thought drives us into the loving arms of a Savior who is our "covering for sin" and clothes us with the robes of his righteousness.

Notice that God did not bring judgment on Assyria in hot haste. He had been patient for a long time. God is *slow in getting angry*, but he sent ruin. He is a God of absolute justice. He is the Lord, the Lord God, merciful and gracious, long-suffering and forgiving iniquity, yet he will by no means clear the guilty. Jonah dwelt on the first side of God's character, love (Jonah 4:2). Nahum brought out the second, the holiness of God that must deal with sin in judgment (1:2, 6). This holy Judge is just, the one *who in his kindness freely takes away our sins* (Romans 3:26) because his holy law has been vindicated in the cross of Christ.

THE VERDICT
NAHUM 1:8-14

These verses state the battle-and-destruction sentence upon corrupt Nineveh. She has been weighed in God's balances and failed the test.

Look at the verdict of Nineveh:

1. Condemned to utter destruction (1:8-9)
2. An end to her dynasty (1:14)
3. God to dig her grave (1:14)

We cannot read this without being struck by the solemnity of it all. Nahum told of this destruction as prophecy. We look at it today as history. Yes, the Judge has brought everything to pass. Today the traveler finds this great city of the past, Nineveh, still lying in ruins.

This book gives us the picture of the wrath of God. Read the second verse again: *God is jealous over those he loves; that is why he takes vengeance on those who hurt them. He furiously destroys their enemies* (1:2). This is a picture of God and of God acting in wrath. It is not pleasant to be reminded that God is a God of anger as well as a God of love. But remember both attributes are his. He is a holy God. He hates sin. He will bring judgment upon it.

THE EXECUTION
NAHUM 2–3

Read what God says in these short chapters. We find a picture of Nineveh's siege, fall, and desolation. All God can do with a rebellious and defiant nation is to destroy it.

The picture of the siege and fall of Nineveh and the desolation that followed are described graphically in Nahum 2–3. God would make an end of her with an overrunning flood, her name would be utterly cut off, and he would dig her grave. The mustering of the armies around Nineveh and the marshalling of the forces within the city are pictured in such a way that the prophet makes his hearers see all the horrid sights of the tragic scene.

Outside the walls the Medes have gathered. Shields are brilliantly painted. Robes are of purple. Terrible spears glitter in the sun. Knives on their chariot wheels flash in the light. Inside the city pandemonium reigns! The king tries to rally his officers to defend the beloved city, but it's too late! The Tigris River has caused a flood that has washed away most of the wall that had seemed to them an impregnable bulwark. This aids their enemies. The queen is taken captive, and her maidens, like a flock of doves, moan around her.

The cries of the Medes are heard as they shout to one another. *Loot the silver! Loot the gold! There seems to be no end of treasures.* The city is looted while the people stand with their knees quaking in fear. Nineveh will no longer terrify the nations, because God has made an end of her. This will happen to all wicked nations of the earth.

The Medes and Babylonians completely destroyed Nineveh in 612 B.C. at the zenith of her power. It came true as Nahum had prophesied—a sudden rise of the Tigris, carrying away a great part of the wall, assisted the attacking army of the Medes and Babylonians in its overthrow (2:6). The city was partly destroyed by fire (3:13, 15).

So deep and effectively did God dig Nineveh's grave that every trace of its existence disappeared for ages and its site was not known. When Alexander the Great fought the battle of Arbela nearby in 331 B.C., he didn't even know there had ever been a city there. When Xenophon and his army of ten thousand passed by two hundred years later, he thought the mounds were the ruins of some Parthian city. When Napoleon encamped near its site, he too was not aware of it.

This city had one denunciation more, given a few years later by Zephaniah (Zephaniah 2:13). In 612 B.C. the whole was fulfilled. So complete was the destruction that all traces of the Assyrian Empire disappeared. Many scholars thought the references to Nineveh in the Bible were only mythical. It seemed that no such city ever existed. But in 1845 the ruins of the magnificent palaces of the Assyrian kings and thousands of inscriptions were unearthed. These give us the story of Assyria as the Assyrians themselves wrote it. And so the magnificent capital of the wealthiest and most splendid empire in the world of its day has been discovered and the Bible account has been confirmed.

SOWING AND REAPING

As Nineveh sowed, so she had to reap. This is God's law. Nineveh had fortified herself so that nothing could harm her. She sat complacently with walls one hundred feet high and wide enough for four chariots to go abreast, a circumference of eighty miles, and adorned by hundreds of towers. A moat 140 feet wide and 60 feet deep surrounded the vast walls. But Nineveh reckoned without God. What are bricks and mortar to God! The mighty empire that Shalmaneser, Sargon, and Sennacherib had built up, the Lord threw down with a stroke. The inventions of civilization are powerless against heaven's weapons.

Nineveh is a symbol of all nations that turn their backs on God. In our day, proud civilizations are staking everything upon the strength of military power, and there is a terrible disregard of God. We find that Nineveh was overthrown because of her sin (3:1-7), and that her great wealth and strength were not sufficient to save her (3:8-19). Oftentimes nations depend on might and power to survive. They forget that it is *not by might, nor by power, but by my Spirit, says the Lord Almighty* (Zechariah 4:6). The person or nation that deliberately and finally rejects God, deliberately and finally and fatally elects doom.

UNDERSTANDING HABAKKUK

Watch and see (ch. 1)
Stand and see (ch. 2)
Kneel and see (ch. 3)

We know little about this prophet of faith except that he asked questions and received answers. He, like many people today, could not reconcile his belief in a good and righteous God with the facts of life as he saw them. He was troubled with an eternal "Why?" Even today people of faith find themselves bewildered at many things that are going on around them. We ask, "Why does God allow such awful crimes to go unchecked? Why doesn't God stop men in their mad rush if he is all-powerful?"

The question, "Why do the wicked prosper?" is discussed. It seems to contain a complaint to God that he would destroy his own nation for their wickedness by a much more wicked nation (1:13). We even see the prophet complaining of the lack of justice in God's management of the world. Why is God silent in times of disaster (1:13)?

Habakkuk, in all his difficuties, went to God in prayer and waited patiently for his answer (2:1). He went on the watchtower and listened to God. G. Campbell Morgan says that when Habakkuk looked at his circumstances he was perplexed (1:3), but when he waited for God and listened to him, he sang (3:18-19).

Habakkuk was a prophet (1:1), but we find something else of interest about him. He was one of the Levitical choristers in the temple (3:19) and helped in the arranging of the services.

We learn much about him as a thinker and a man of faith from his own words. He was a contemporary with Jeremiah at home and with Daniel in Babylon.

The world empire of Assyria had fallen just as Nahum had prophesied. Egypt and Babylon had then contended for the place of power. At the battle of Carchemish in 605 B.C., in which King Josiah was killed, the Babylonians were conquerors, and the great kingdoms of the Babylonians and Chaldeans were united under Nebuchadnezzar. Habakkuk knew only too well that Judah would fall before this great rising power. But one question arose in his mind and troubled him greatly. Why should any nation as wicked as Babylon conquer a nation like Judah that was less evil? It seemed to him that it was just a matter of evil triumphing over evil. What good could come of this? God had to show him his ultimate plan. Judah needed punishment. God was using Babylon to correct Judah, but Babylon's turn would come. Babylon would be utterly blotted out. As for God's people, there was yet to be a glorious future and a kingdom where God himself would prevail.

This book seems to be a dialogue between God and the prophet. Two conversations are recorded, and the book closes with a hymn and doxology that reveal that all the questions have been answered and there is a new confidence in God.

HABAKKUK'S COMPLAINT
HABAKKUK 1

This scene opens with the cry of a man who had a problem he couldn't solve. *O Lord, how long must I call for help before you will listen?* (1:2).

Habakkuk was confused and bewildered. It seemed to him that God was doing nothing to straighten out the conditions in the world. He had lived during the days of the great reformation under good King Josiah. He had seen Assyria fading in power and Babylon, under Nebuchadnezzar, rising to a place of supremacy. The world about him was in upheaval. Violence abounded, and God was doing nothing about it.

But worse, he saw his own land, Judah, full of lawlessness and tyranny. The righteous were oppressed (1:4, 13). The people were living in open sin. They were worshiping idols (2:18-19).

They were oppressing the poor. Habakkuk knew that the day was dark. He knew that this sin was leading to an invasion of Jerusalem by a strong enemy.

Habakkuk asked his question of God. He didn't call a committee or form a society to solve the problem of the day. He went straight to God and stated his problem. Then God answered, *I am going to do something in your own lifetime that you will have to see to believe* (1:5). God told Habakkuk that he was not indifferent to his people. He wanted Habakkuk to look beyond the present. He was already working. God called the Chaldeans to the work of punishing Judah. They were a cruel scourge that swept over the land to destroy it (1:5-11). The nations have always been God's object lessons, illustrating his moral laws (1:12).

God's answer horrified Habakkuk. He could not understand how God could allow such awful means to bring about the punishing of his people, Judah. How could he use such a cruel scourge? How was it possible for God to use such an enemy to punish his own people when he himself is so pure and holy? Listen to Habakkuk's challenge to God to defend his actions (1:13).

GOD'S REPLY
HABAKKUK 2

As this scene opens we see Habakkuk facing the great moment of his life. Watch him as he climbed up on the watchtower to wait for God. He expected God to answer him (2:1).

Everything lay in ruins around the prophet. Chaldea was coming up to destroy what was left. There was only One to whom he could turn, so he waited expectantly for God. God gave an answer. Read God's answer in Habakkuk 2:2-20. God admitted the wickedness of the Chaldeans but declared that they would destroy themselves finally by their own evil. Pride and cruelty always bring destruction. People sometimes have to wait to know what the final outcome will be. God sometimes takes ages to show his plans. *A day or a thousand years from now is like tomorrow to the Lord* (2 Peter 3:8). God's testing always reveals what people are. He burns out the dross. It may seem that the Chaldeans are prospering for a time, but they are doomed. *The righteous man trusts in me, and lives!* Habakkuk 2:4 is the heart of the book.

There are four "woes" in Habakkuk 2. Find what they are. Remember, evil will perish. Only righteousness will remain before God.

HABAKKUK'S SONG
HABAKKUK 3

Habakkuk is the prophet who sang in the night. Listen to the magnificent melody with which his prophecy closes: *Even though the fig trees are all destroyed, and there is neither blossom left nor fruit, and though the olive crops all fail, and the fields lie barren; even if the flocks die in the fields and the cattle barns are empty, yet I will rejoice in the Lord; I will be happy in the God of my salvation* (3:17-18). This ode was set to music and sung at the public worship by the Jews.

After a sincere prayer (3:1-16) God's glory appears. God always responds to the cry for help from his people. Habakkuk realized that God is in control of this universe and that he is working out his own purpose in his own time. Habakkuk learned that he could trust implicitly in God. He realized that he could see only a small part of God's plan at one time. One must wait for God to reveal his entire program. One must know that God's way is best.

God cannot always give us a satisfactory answer because our finite minds cannot grasp the thoughts of the infinite. His thoughts are high above our thoughts, and his ways above our ways (Isaiah 55:9), but we can trust God, always! *And we know that all that happens to us is working for our good if we love God and are fitting into his plans* (Romans 8:28).

Remember, God does not promise that he will unravel every problem, but he does assure us that we can put our trust absolutely in him. (Read Psalm 37:5 and 2 Timothy 1:12.)

One of the texts in Habakkuk has great significance in the history of the Reformation. Do you know the story of the young monk Martin Luther who rose to his feet as he was crawling up the steps of the Scala Sancta in Rome? He remembered these words, *The righteous man trusts in me and lives* (2:4). Not in works! This started him out on his great crusade that brought about the Reformation.

Find where Habakkuk 2:4 is quoted in the New Testament: Romans 1:17; Galatians 3:11; Hebrews 10:38. Mark them.

UNDERSTANDING ZEPHANIAH

Little is known of Zephaniah, the writer of this book. Two facts of his personal history appear in the first verse of the prophecy. We learn that very likely he was a prince of the royal house of Judah, being a descendant of Hezekiah. He was in a position to denounce the sins of the princes, for he himself was an aristocrat. He lived in the reign of good King Josiah. His name means "hidden of Jehovah."

Zephaniah began his ministry as a prophet in the early days of the reign of Josiah (641–610 B.C.). Fifty years had elapsed since the prophecy of Nahum. Three of Hezekiah's descendants had succeeded him (2 Kings 20–21). Two wicked and idol-worshiping kings had preceded Josiah on the throne, and the land was overrun with evil practices of every kind. Social injustice and moral corruption were on every hand. The rich had amassed great fortunes by oppressing the poor. The condition was as bad as it could be when King Josiah, only sixteen years of age, undertook to promote a religious revival. He became one of the most beloved of the kings of Judah. He took a hatchet and hewed down the altars and images. How the words of Zephaniah must have encouraged the reformers!

Zephaniah depicts God as both loving and severe. Zephaniah 1:2 and 3:17 give us these two characteristics.

Zephaniah foretold the doom of Nineveh (2:13). Who else had prophesied her doom? This came to pass in 612 B.C.

We hear Zephaniah denouncing the various forms of idolatry— Baal and Molech both being condemned (1:1–2:3). This idol worship was destroyed during Josiah's reign. No doubt Zephaniah was mainly responsible for the revival under Josiah. He was the pioneer in this reform movement. Tradition tells us that Jeremiah was his colleague.

As you start reading this book, you are appalled at its contents. There is nothing but denunciations, dire threats, and wrath. The English poet Cowper says that punishment and chastisement is "the graver countenance of love," *for when [the Lord] punishes you, it proves that he loves you . . . it proves you are really his child* (Hebrews 12:6). We see in all of this a proof of God's love. The book begins with sorrow but ends with singing. The beginning of the book is full of sadness and gloom, but the end contains one of the sweetest songs of love in the Old Testament.

Zephaniah showed that:

1. Faithful survivors would be delivered from captivity.
2. The heathen will be converted.
3. One day man could worship God anywhere, not only in Jerusalem (2:11; see John 4:21).

God is searching out the people. *I will search with lanterns in Jerusalem's darkest corners to find and punish those who sit contented in their sins* (1:12).

JUDAH SEARCHED
ZEPHANIAH 1

The Lord is in the midst of the land for judgment (3:5; 1:17). He first searches Judah and pronounces doom on all those who are worshiping idols. The land must be freed from idolatry. The Lord cannot allow such abomination to remain. We see the rulers are denounced as is every class of sinner (1:7-13):

1. The idol worshipers (1:4-5)
2. Those who swear by God one time and by Molech at another time (1:5)
3. Those who formerly worshiped the Lord (1:6)

Upon all these God will bring a blast of fire. It will strike the whole earth but especially the inhabitants of Jerusalem. The Day of the Lord is a day of dread. He calls the people to tremble at God's presence. He is in the midst of the land to judge her.

The Day of the Lord is mentioned five times in the prophecy. Almost without exception when *day* is used in Scripture it means a period of time. If a number is used before it—such as forty days, three days—then it is a day of twenty-four hours. But when you use *day* alone, such as "the day of the Puritan" or "Lincoln's day," you mean the time in which they lived. So when the Bible says "the Day of the Lord," it means a time of the Lord's special working. To the Jews of Zephaniah's day it meant the time when God would deal with his people in punishment and captivity. The future Day of the Lord is the period of the Great Tribulation and the Millennium. (See Revelation 6:1-17.)

Judah was taught that the Day of the Lord was coming when there would be a special reckoning.

THE NATIONS SEARCHED
ZEPHANIAH 2

After the prophet called the people to seek God (2:1-3) so that they could be protected *from his wrath in that day of doom*, he declared that nothing could save the nation but real repentance. *Beg him to save you . . . walk humbly and do what is right* was his admonition. Then he turned to the five heathen nations, Philistia, Moab, Ammon, Ethiopia, and Assyria. They would be visited with the wrath of God because of their pride and scorn toward the Lord's people (2:10). The desolation of Nineveh was described in wonderfully accurate terms (2:13-15). These began to be accomplished in the conquests of Nebuchadnezzar.

The judgment on Israel's local enemies was literally fulfilled (2:4-15). The judgment on Israel's enemies over this wide world is yet to be fulfilled. Read God's Word in Zephaniah 3:8; 2:10-11. God says the idols of their enemies will be broken up, and the heathen will worship God, every one in his own country (2:11). Instead of all having to make a pilgrimage to Jerusalem, they may worship God anywhere.

Men have always tried to establish sacred places and shrines. Rome and Mecca have long been "holy" spots, among hundreds of other places. People have undergone every hardship to worship at these shrines. In India, thousands make the pilgrimage to Benares, the Hindus' most sacred spot, to worship and to bathe in the Ganges, and to carry back with them its sacred water. The Jews taught that Jerusalem was the place of worship. The Samaritans declared that Mount Gerizim ought to be the religious center, but Zephaniah taught that spiritual worship did not depend on a place but on the presence of God.

ISRAEL RESTORED
ZEPHANIAH 3

The prophet concluded with the most wonderful promises of Israel's future restoration and of the happy state of the purified people of God in the latter days (ch. 3). The redeemed remnant would return cleansed, humbled, trusting, and rejoicing with their offerings to Zion. They would be established in their land with God, who would live among them (3:15, 17). Zion would then be a delight among nations and a blessing to the whole earth, as was foretold in the promise God made originally with Abraham (Genesis 12:1-3).

The rejoicing of Zephaniah 3:14-20 must refer to something besides the day when the Jews would return after the captivity of Babylon. Judah's worst judgment followed that return. She has seen little but misery ever since. Neither did anything like this occur at Christ's first coming. It must refer to the day when the Lord himself will sit on the throne of David, when his people will be gathered from the four corners of the earth (3:19). This prophecy will be blessedly fulfilled in the kingdom age when Christ comes to this earth to reign in power and great glory.

SELECTED BIBLE READING

Sunday: The Judge and the Verdict (Nahum 1)
Monday: The Execution (Nahum 2–3)
Tuesday: Habakkuk's Complaint (Habakkuk 1)
Wednesday: God's Reply (Habakkuk 2)
Thursday: Habakkuk's Song (Habakkuk 3)
Friday: Coming Judgments (Zephaniah 1–2)
Saturday: The Kingdom Blessings (Zephaniah 3)

CHAPTER 25

UNDERSTANDING HAGGAI, ZECHARIAH, MALACHI

Jesus Christ, the Desire of All Nations;
the Righteous Branch; the Sun of Righteousness

The greater number of Old Testament prophets spoke before the captivity. During the captivity Ezekiel and Daniel prophesied. After the return Haggai, Zechariah, and Malachi prophesied. This makes it easy to remember. Of the sixteen prophets, just two prophesied during the exile, three after, eleven before.

Haggai, Zechariah, and Malachi are the last of the prophetic books. They prophesied to the Jews after they returned to Jerusalem. Nebuchadnezzar had captured Jerusalem and completely destroyed the Temple. This, however, did not bring the Jews to national repentance. In reading Ezra we find that when Cyrus, king of Persia, issued a decree permitting all the captives to return to Jerusalem and to rebuild their Temple, only about fifty thousand returned. Most of these were priests and Levites and the poorer among the people. Although the Jews increased in power and in numbers, they never established their political independence. They were a subject people under Gentile rulers from this time on.

Before Haggai's time the Jews had returned to their own land under Zerubbabel and began to build the Temple (Nehemiah 12). But their enthusiasm soon waned. They made no progress beyond laying the foundation. The Samaritans and their enemy neighbors were determined that Jerusalem not be rebuilt. This meant that the work lay unfinished for fifteen years. During these years each person became interested in building his own private house. It was then that Haggai arose and gave his message. He encouraged the people to build the Temple again. This time it was finished in four years. It seemed incredible that God's people waited so long to do the very thing they came back to do.

UNDERSTANDING HAGGAI

We know little of Haggai except that he worked with Zechariah during the days following the exile. He prophesied two months before Zechariah. Zechariah prophesied for three years and Haggai prophesied for four months.

Haggai is the first voice to be heard after the exile. His name means "my feast." His book is a collection of four brief messages written between August and December.

Each message is specifically dated. These dates, rather than places and characters, dominate the scenes. These were given in "the second year of the reign of King Darius," 520 B.C. Confucius, the Chinese philosopher, was flourishing in China at this time. The book is domi ated by one central purpose: Haggai was determined to persuade the people to rebuild the Temple. It was no easy task to move a discouraged nation to rise up and build a temple. But he did it.

A MESSAGE OF REBUKE
HAGGAI 1

A poor handful of people returned to Jerusalem from Babylon where they had lived in captivity. With a colossal task before them of rebuilding the Temple and restoring the worship of the Lord, the Jews labored under the same old sins. They were few in number, poor, harassed by enemies, and worse, they had lost the inner strength that comes from a joy in the Lord. (Read Nehemiah 8:10.)

Because of all this the work dragged and the people lost heart and became selfish. Neglecting the Lord's house, they had become more interested in building homes for themselves than for

God (1:4). God would not allow this to go on, and so he sent punishment as a result. Poor crops, droughts, scanty trade, misery, and turmoil made their spirits fall. They were working and slaving but finding no real joy (1:6, 9-11).

We see the effect of Haggai's challenge. His stern call to duty proved to be a good tonic. Zerubbabel, the governor of Jerusalem, Joshua, the high priest, and the people arose and began the work of rebuilding the Temple (1:12-15). How did God respond to their repentance (1:13)?

God sometimes allows hardships because of our indifference to him. Crops failed and business was depressed because of the sin of the Jews. But God wants us to keep up the church. Without churches, sin and vice will grow. When men forget to love God they forget to love their fellowmen, too. We should beautify God's house. (See 2 Samuel 7:2.) We are not to live in fine homes and allow the church building to be in ruins.

A MESSAGE OF COURAGE
HAGGAI 2:1-9

How long after the first message was this one given (1:1; 2:1)? For the history of this period read Ezra 3:8-13.

As the people were building, a new discouragement seized them. The older ones, remembering the splendor of the Temple of Solomon, were greatly disappointed in this new Temple. It did not measure up in any way, they thought. How inferior in size and costliness of the stones! How much smaller in extent was the foundation itself! How limited were their means! And besides, this second Temple would not have the things that made the first one so glorious—the Ark, the Shekinah, and all that went with the service of the High Priest. These pessimists dampened the enthusiasm of the builders.

But Haggai came with a word of cheer that God would pour his resources into that new building. The living God was to be in the midst of this new Temple. *"I will shake all nations, and the Desire of All Nations shall come to this Temple, and I will fill this place with my glory," says the Lord Almighty. "The future splendor of this Temple will be greater than the splendor of the first one! For I have plenty of silver and gold to do it! And here I will give peace," says the Lord* (2:7-9). What a comfort this must have been to the Jews!

A MESSAGE OF ASSURANCE
HAGGAI 2:10-23

This message of cleansing and blessing was delivered three months after the Temple was started. By the use of questions and answers, Haggai showed the people their impurity. He made them realize their sinfulness. He showed them that the reason their prayers were not answered was because they had put off so long the completion of the Temple. They had spoiled all that they had done because of their guilt. If they would renew their zeal, they would find God would bless them. Haggai heard their complaints of seeing no visible signs of blessings although they had been working for three full months. Haggai showed them that the land had been rendered useless by their neglect, but God was working and it would be different now. *From this day I will bless you* (2:19). God begins when we begin.

UNDERSTANDING ZECHARIAH

Zechariah is a book of the future. It is a book of revelation of the Old Testament.

THE CHOSEN PEOPLE AND THE TEMPLE
ZECHARIAH 1-8

We now find Judah still a remnant, Jerusalem far from restored, and the Gentile nations at ease around her (1:14-16). Zechariah, a young prophet who had stood alongside the aged Haggai, strengthened the Jews as they built the Temple and warned them not to disappoint God as their fathers had done. He pictured God's love and care for his people. He quickened their hopes by painting in glowing colors the time of perpetual blessing that was coming to Israel in the far-off ages.

Zechariah, like Haggai, was a prophet to the Jews who returned from Babylon after the seventy years of captivity. The Jews, once a powerful nation as God had planned them to be, were now dwelling in their Promised Land only because of the courtesy of a foreign ruler. Both Haggai and Zechariah tried to tell the people that it would not always be so. One day the Messiah would come and God's chosen people would rise into power.

Zechariah was the prophet of restoration and glory. Born in

Babylon, he was priest as well as prophet. Zechariah, whose name means "Jehovah remembers," prophesied for three years. The glorious future, rather than the sad present, was his message. Whereas Haggai was a plain, practical preacher, Zechariah was a poet.

Zechariah's keen enthusiasm for the rebuilding of the Temple kept the people at the task of finishing the work. Serious crop failures and business depression among the Jewish people had made them so discouraged that only Haggai's blunt and consistent hammering kept them at the work. They needed a new voice. Zechariah's was that one. He threw himself into the work of helping his great friend Haggai.

Zechariah did not condemn the people but presented in glowing pictures the presence of God to strengthen and help. He especially encouraged the governor, Zerubbabel, who was conscious of his own weakness. Hear what Zechariah says, *Not by might nor by power, but by my Spirit, says the Lord Almighty* (read 4:6-10). He promised that the mountains of difficulty would be removed. How marvelously this truth was fulfilled at Pentecost when God filled people with his power.

Zechariah foretold the Savior more than any other prophet except Isaiah:

Christ the Branch (3:8)
Christ my Servant (3:8)
Christ's entry into Jerusalem on a colt (9:9)
Christ the good Shepherd (9:16; 11:11)
Christ the stricken Shepherd (13:7)
Christ betrayed for thirty pieces of silver (11:12-13)
Christ's hands pierced (12:10)
Christ's people saved (12:10; 13:1)
Christ wounded in the house of his friends (13:6)
Christ's coming on the Mount of Olives (14:3-8). (He who ascended from the Mount of Olives will come again just as he went. Read Acts 1:11.)
Christ's coming and coronation (ch. 14)

Two Searchlights

Someone has said to read the visions of this book in the right way you must get two lights upon them—the light of the cross and of the crown. Otherwise you will find these pictures of Zechariah to be without perspective or background. The prophet, looking far into the future, saw the Messiah of the days to come as one Person, but in two aspects. First, he saw him in humiliation and suffering, and again, in majesty and great glory.

The Jew ignores the Christ of the cross. The Christian too often ignores the Christ of the crown. Both are wrong!

Zechariah seems to let the glory of Christ glow in all his teaching and preaching.

Of the minor prophets, Zechariah alone majors in visions. *Another message from the Lord . . . in a vision in the night* (1:7).

The angelic horsemen (1:7-17). Here is a picture of Israel today, outcast but not forgotten by God.

The horns and blacksmiths (1:18-21). The overthrow of Israel by her enemies is foreseen.

The yardstick (2:1-13). The coming prosperity of Jerusalem is seen. The city, walled in by the presence of God, is great in extent and blessed by his favor.

Joshua, the High Priest (3:1-10). Filthy garments clothing the priest and representing Israel's sin are removed, replaced, and the Branch, Christ, is introduced.

The golden lampstand (4:1-14). Israel is shown as God's future light bearer. Olive trees, anointed of God, speak of Zerubbabel the ruler and Joshua the priest.

The flying scroll (5:1-4). Wicked governments receive God's curse in this unique picture.

The basket (5:5-11). Borne away on divine wings, wickedness is removed.

The four chariots (6:1-8). These represent "administrative forces of righteousness" (G. Campbell Morgan).

The Coronation Scene
The visions were followed by a symbolic act of crowning the High Priest (6:9-11). Gold and silver brought from Babylon were made into a crown and placed on the head of Joshua the High Priest. By this act the two great offices of priest and king were united. This is a symbol of Christ the King who will sit on his throne of glory as a priest when he returns to earth to set up his millennial kingdom.

Two years later we find a committee from Bethel waiting on Zechariah to ask him if the national fasts should be kept (ch. 7–8). The Jews themselves had instituted these fasts. They had been accustomed to fasting on their great anniversary days. Zechariah warned them against cold formalism in their religious observances. He urged them to change their fasts into feasts of joy and be practical in their righteousness. God says, *Obedience is far better than sacrifice. He is much more interested in your listening to him than in your offering the fat of rams to him* (1 Samuel 15:22).

Fasting is only profitable as an outward sign of an inward confession of sin. Merely refraining from eating will never bring a blessing. God wants a humble and contrite heart.

THE MESSIAH AND THE KINGDOM
ZECHARIAH 9–14

These chapters are full of promises of the coming Messiah and a worldwide kingdom. The prophet no longer pictures a city rebuilt on its old foundations but a glorious city whose wall is the Lord. It is not armed for war, but is a city filled with peace, for the Prince of Peace reigns. He will come the first time as the lowly One, riding on a donkey's colt (9:9).

But we see this lowly One becoming a mighty Sovereign (14:8-11). The Messiah in all his glory and might will put all the enemies under his feet and will establish his kingdom in Jerusalem and sit on the throne of David. *His realm shall stretch from sea to sea, from the river to the ends of the earth* (9:10).

If one would follow these chapters more closely, he would discover victory over all the enemies of Israel. Chapter 11 reveals the Shepherd who would seek to save Israel but is rejected. He is sold for thirty pieces of silver, the price of a slave. This all foreshadowed Christ and his betrayal by Judas. Chapter 12 gives us the prophecy of the siege of Jerusalem by the Antichrist and his armies in the last days. Then we see the repentance of the Jews (v. 12) when they shall see him whom they pierced. The fountain will be opened to the house of David for sin and defilement (13:1). Then the return of the Messiah upon the Mount of Olives, which will be split apart by an earthquake (14:4), reminds us of the day when he left the earth at that same spot with the promise of his return (Acts 1:11). Finally, he will be King over the whole earth and all people will be holy to him (14:9-20).

The blessings of the kingdom of Christ:

1. The extent of his kingdom (14:9)
2. Abundant rain (10:1)
3. Outpouring of the Spirit on Israel (12:10)

4. Revelation of the "pierced" Messiah (12:10)
5. Changes in Israel (14:4-5, 10-11)
6. Kingdom set up on earth (14:9-15)
7. Jerusalem center of worship (14:16-17)

UNDERSTANDING MALACHI

We have now come to the last book in the Old Testament. It sums up much of the history of the Old Testament. Martin Luther called John 3:16 "the little gospel." In the same way we might speak of Malachi as the "little Old Testament." Malachi is the bridge between the Old and New Testaments. To see this, read Malachi 3:1. Who is "my messenger"? Read John 1:23 and Luke 3:3-4. A silence of four hundred years lies between the voice of Malachi and the voice of one crying in the wilderness, *Prepare a road for the Lord.*

The Old Testament closes with a curse: *I will come and utterly destroy their land.* The New Testament closes with a blessing: *The grace of our Lord Jesus Christ be with you all. Amen.*

By this time, a hundred years or more had passed since the Jews had returned to Jerusalem after the captivity in Babylon. Malachi was the last prophet to speak to Israel in her own land. *Israel* here means all those of Israel and Judah that returned after the exile. The first enthusiasm after the return from Babylon had spent itself. Following a period of revival (Nehemiah 10:28-39), the people had become cold religiously and lax morally.

The prophet Malachi came as a reformer, but he encouraged while he rebuked. He dealt with a people perplexed, with spirits failing, whose faith in God seemed to be in danger of collapse. If they had not already become hostile to the Lord, they were in real danger of becoming skeptical.

Malachi means "my messenger" (that is, of the Lord). As a forerunner of John the Baptist, of whom he prophesied, he was but a voice.

THE SINS OF THE PRIESTS
MALACHI 1:1-2:9

The skeptical attitude aroused among the people showed itself in religious coldness and social laxity. This is always true. The priests became irreverent and neglectful. Read Malachi 1:6, 11-12. God said, *You don't honor me, O priests, but you despise my name.* The prophet rebuked these careless priests for offering worthless animals in sacrifice to God that they would not offer to the governor. They stood in marked contrast to God's ideal for the priesthood. They had completely lost sight of their high calling and deserved the ignominy heaped upon them. They refused to work except for money. God's condemnation began with the leaders (2:1-9). As long as the priests were openly unfit, what could be expected from the people at large? This resulted in a carelessness among God's people in keeping themselves separate from the heathen nations. Mixed marriages with women of out-side tribes became common. Some men had not hesitated to divorce their Jewish wives to make this possible (2:10-16).

THE SINS OF THE PEOPLE
MALACHI 2:10–3:18

What would you think of a person who deliberately held some-thing in front of his eyes and then complained that he couldn't see anything? What would you suggest might quickly solve the difficulty? Well, this is just what Malachi had to do. The Jews declared that the Lord did not love them as he said (1:2). They could not see that his love had been of any special advantage to them.

Another result of the people's laxity of loyalty to God was in the growing prevalence of social sin (3:5). Malachi 3:7 reveals the religious indifference and skepticism of the people.

Sins that Malachi rebuked:

Spiritless, routine worship (1:6-8)
Evil associations (2:10-12)
Questioning the Lord's justice (2:17–3:6)
Robbing God (3:7-12)
Impatience in waiting (3:17–4:3)

Are any of these your sins, too? Suppose we do find some of these sins in our daily lives, what are we to do? Confess them to the Lord. Israel was troubled about the result of her confession. Malachi had to encourage the people by assuring them of God's wonderful love and giving the beautiful promise of Malachi 3:7:

"Though you have scorned my laws from earliest time, yet you may still return to me," says the Lord Almighty. *"Come and I will forgive you."*

The Jews could depend on the Lord to forgive. It was this same picture of the Father that Jesus gave when he told of the prodigal's return. The father, seeing the boy while he was still a long distance away, ran out to meet him. This is ever God's attitude.

The Jews had been cured of idolatry, but they had grown careless and indifferent about many things. They had neglected the house of God. The priests had become lax. They were bringing inferior sacrifices to the Temple. They had robbed God of their tithes and offerings. They fell into social sins. They had become so selfish and covetous that Malachi dared boldly to challenge them with these words: *Will a man rob God?*(3:8).

The key that opens God's big windows of blessing is your recognition of his ownership by giving back to him a proper share of the money or the property that he permits you to acquire. *Bring all the tithes into the storehouse.* The tenth (or tithe) is the outward recognition that everything belongs to God. We are to bring him our whole selves—body, soul, and spirit. Then he will accept us and open the windows of heaven to pour out his blessings.

COMING THINGS
MALACHI 3-4

Why does God permit such things? This attitude of the people was probably due to the feeling that the glowing promises of Haggai and Zechariah and of the other prophets had not been realized. They said that the Lord did not seem to distinguish between good and bad men (2:17). He blesses all alike, and evil men often flourish at the expense of their fellows (3:14-15). What's the use of being good? Is this not one of the standing complaints of those who think they are good men? They say, "What is God doing that he permits such things?" The answer to such a complaint is that the Lord does care. He showed this to them by saying that one day he would send his messenger (John the Baptist) to prepare his way, then he will come in person "suddenly" and sit in judgment and separate the evil from the good (3:1). His judgment will be searching and effective *like a blazing fire refining precious metal* (3:2). When God really gets ready to act, what will he do? The action will be final (3:1-3).

We find the burden of God's message by Malachi to his people stated in the second verse of the book: *I have loved you very deeply, says the Lord.* What a message to a people who had sinned as Israel had and had spurned the love of the Lord Almighty. God is always sending his messenger before him to prepare his way (3:1). He wants all his children to honor and adore him. He longs to have us obey and worship him. But who can stand the day of his appearing? And who can endure his purifying fire (3:2)? God's messenger will be a witness revealing our cruelty, our lies, our injustices, our double-dealing. This can be said of us today just as much as of the Jews of old. The Lord's representative comes and finds us robbing him of his due (3:2-5). Yet the Lord Almighty is unchanging. He never forgets his promises of undying love and everlasting mercy.

Oh, how we need God's Malachi today to be sent before him to prepare his way so that God's people may honor and adore him! Malachi cries, "Back to God's house! Back to God's Word! Back to God's work! Back to God's grace!"

Each one may be like Malachi, a herald of the Christ whose coming we now await. Each one who loves and looks for him may help prepare his way by his very manner of living and work.

Think of the needs of this day, the needs of the church and the world. Is not formalism a just charge today against our churches—an outward observance without a wholehearted love? Are not we, too, offering gifts that cost nothing? Are we not robbing God in the matter of tithes?

Amid all the hypocrisy of the day there were those in the Jewish community (a remnant) who still feared God and remained faithful (3:16). Malachi longed to develop a strong body of enthusiastic believers who could influence his people's future.

Close by reading aloud Malachi's solemn declaration concerning the second advent of Christ for which we wait, Malachi 3:16–4:3. Yes, the Sun of Righteousness will come with healing in his wings.

SELECTED BIBLE READING

Sunday: Haggai's Message (Haggai 1–2)
Monday: Visions (Zechariah 1–6)

Tuesday: Fasts (Zechariah 7–8)
Wednesday: Restoration of Judah and Israel (Zechariah 9–11)
Thursday: The Messiah (Zechariah 12–14)
Friday: Sins of Priests and People (Malachi 1–2)
Saturday: Message of Hope (Malachi 3–4)

CHAPTER 26

A QUICK LOOK AT ESTHER—MALACHI

THEMES AND LESSONS

Esther
Theme: Jesus Christ is portrayed as our Advocate.
Outstanding Lesson: God will deliver his children!

Job
Theme: Jesus Christ is portrayed as our Redeemer.
Outstanding Lesson: Why do the righteous suffer?

Psalms
Theme: Jesus Christ is portrayed as our All in All.
Outstanding Lesson: Praise God!

Proverbs
Theme: Jesus Christ is portrayed as our Wisdom.
Outstanding Lesson: Get wisdom!

Ecclesiastes
Theme: Jesus Christ is portrayed as the End of All Living.
Outstanding Lesson: Try wisdom!

Song of Solomon
Theme: Jesus Christ is portrayed as the Lover of Our Souls.
Outstanding Lesson: Love God!

Isaiah
Theme: Jesus Christ is portrayed as the Messiah.
Outstanding Lesson: Salvation is of God!

Jeremiah
Theme: Jesus Christ is portrayed as the Righteous Branch.
Outstanding Lesson: Go and tell!

Lamentations
Theme: Jesus Christ is portrayed as the Righteous Branch.
Outstanding Lesson: God's grace always shines!

Ezekiel
Theme: Jesus Christ is portrayed as the Son of Man.
Outstanding Lesson: Judgment and restoration!

Daniel
Theme: Jesus Christ is portrayed as the Crushing Rock.
Outstanding Lesson: God is sovereign!

Hosea
Theme: Jesus Christ is portrayed as the Healer of the Rebellious.
Outstanding Lesson: Return to God!

Joel
Theme: Jesus Christ is portrayed as the Restorer.
Outstanding Lesson: Repent, for the Day of the Lord is coming.

Amos
Theme: Jesus Christ is portrayed as the Heavenly Husbandman.
Outstanding Lesson: Prepare to meet your God!

Obadiah
Theme: Jesus Christ is portrayed as our Savior.
Outstanding Lesson: Possess your possessions!

Jonah
Theme: Jesus Christ is portrayed as our Resurrection and Life.
Outstanding Lesson: Go!

Micah
Theme: Jesus Christ is portrayed as a Witness against Rebellious Nations.
Outstanding Lesson: Hear him!

Nahum
Theme: Jesus Christ is portrayed as a Stronghold in the Day of Trouble.
Outstanding Lesson: Beware, the Lord avenges!

Habakkuk
Theme: Jesus Christ is portrayed as the God of Our Salvation.
Outstanding Lesson: Live by faith!

Zephaniah
Theme: Jesus Christ is portrayed as a jealous Lord.
Outstanding Lesson: God is mighty to save!

Haggai
Theme: Jesus Christ is portrayed as the Desire of All Nations.
Outstanding Lesson: Build for God!

Zechariah
Theme: Jesus Christ is portrayed as the Righteous Branch.
Outstanding Lesson: Turn to him!

Malachi
Theme: Jesus Christ is portrayed as the Sun of Righteousness.
Outstanding Lesson: Repent and return!

FOUR HUNDRED YEARS OF SILENCE

By the time Old Testament history ended, a few of the Jews, chiefly of the tribe of Judah, had returned to Palestine under Zerubbabel, and about eighty years later another company had returned with Ezra. They were living peaceably in their own land with the Temple rebuilt and religious ceremonies established.

The last three books of history in the Old Testament—Ezra, Nehemiah, and Esther—give us the story of this time. They cover one hundred years (536–432 B.C.) following the decree of King Cyrus allowing the Jews to return to their land (read Ezra 1:1-4).

From Nehemiah to the beginning of New Testament times, four hundred years passed. During this period no biblical prophet spoke or wrote. In fact, it is called the "period of silence." As we come to the year when Jesus was born, it is important that we know some of the things that happened from the days of Nehemiah and Malachi to that time.

The Septuagint

Before Alexander the Great died he divided his empire among his four generals, for he had no heirs to his throne. Egypt, and later Palestine, went to his general Ptolemy. Great numbers of Jews at this time settled in Egypt, as well as other centers of culture, spreading everywhere the knowledge of their God and their hope of a Messiah.

It was during this time, about 285 B.C., that the Old Testament began to be translated into Greek. This version of the Scriptures is called the Septuagint, meaning "seventy," because seventy noted Hebrew scholars did this great work. You will find it referred to by Roman numerals LXX.

The Jews Persecuted

Now the Syrian kingdom arose. In the conflicts between Syria and Egypt, Antiochus Epiphanes, king of Syria, seized Palestine. He began a bitter persecution of the Jews. The Jews were forbidden by Antiochus Epiphanes to worship in the Temple and were compelled to eat the flesh of swine, which God through Moses had forbidden (Leviticus 11:1-8). Many Jews refused, and a period of martyrdom began.

The cruelties of this terrible king, Antiochus Epiphanes, brought about the revolt of the Maccabees under the leadership of Mattathias. Aroused by the patriotism and religious ardor of Mattathias, a group of patriotic Jews gathered about him and began an insurrection that spread rapidly. When he died, his son Judas took his place. In an attempt to crush this rebellion under the Maccabees, Antiochus was defeated in three deadly conflicts. The cause of Judas had seemed hopeless because his followers were untrained and without equipment, and they were opposed by the trained soldiers of a powerful king. But this band of ragged but loyal Jews, inspired by an undying faith in God, came out victorious!

THE ROMAN TRIBUTE

In 63 B.C. Rome gained possession of Palestine, preparing the way and the time for Jesus to be born. The Jews had some political liberty but were required to pay a yearly tax to the Roman government.

PART TWO
THE NEW TESTAMENT

CHAPTER 27

UNDERSTANDING THE GOSPEL

The Gospel Portrays Jesus Christ, Our Savior and Lord

Henry Van Dyke said, "If four witnesses should appear before a judge to give an account of a certain event, and each should tell exactly the same story in the same words, the judge would probably conclude, not that their testimony was exceptionally valuable, but that the only event which was certain beyond a doubt was that they had agreed to tell the same story. But if each man had told what he had seen, as he had seen it, then the evidence would be credible. And when we read the four Gospels, is not that exactly what we find? The four men tell the same story each in his own way."

The word *gospel* is derived from two Anglo-Saxon words: *god*, meaning "good," and *spell*, meaning "tidings" or "news." The four writers of the Gospels are called *evangelists*, from a Greek word meaning "bringer of good news." The first three Gospels, Matthew, Mark, and Luke, are called the Synoptic Gospels because, unlike John, they give a synopsis of Christ's life. The word *synopsis* is from the two Greek words meaning "a view together, a collective view." So these three Gospels may be viewed together.

The Synoptic Gospels are striking in their similarities. They are equally striking in their differences. The Synoptics narrate Christ's ministry chiefly in Galilee, but John's Gospel stands in a class by itself. He tells of Christ's ministry in Judea. The Synop-

tics narrate his miracles, parables, and addresses to the multitudes; John presents his deeper and more abstract discourses,
his conversations, and prayers. The three portray Christ in action;
John portrays him in meditation and communion.

He is here! The promised One has come! The One whom all
the prophets have foretold, Jesus Christ, the Lord.

Every prophet in the Old Testament assured God's chosen
people again and again that a Messiah would come who would
be the King of the Jews. They therefore looked forward with
passionate longing and patriotism to the coming of that King in
pomp and power.

Expect to find in the Gospels *the very person Moses and the
prophets told about* (John 1:45). But know that you will find him
infinitely more beautiful in person than any prophet's vision of
him.

We read in Isaiah 7:14: *The Lord himself will choose the sign—a
child shall be born to a virgin! And she shall call him Immanuel (meaning, "God is with us")*. This is just the One that the evangelists
tell us about. The Gospels present Jesus in our midst. John says,
Christ became a human being and lived here on earth among us (John
1:14). Think of God coming down to live with men!

It seems that the Gospels are the center of the whole Bible.
Notice where the four Gospels are placed. They stand after the
Old Testament and before the Letters. All that the prophets have
said leads us to our Lord's earthly life and work, and all that
follows in the Letters proceeds from them. The Gospels are the
source.

The Gospels tell us *when* and *how* Christ came. The Letters tell
us *why* and *for what* Christ came.

William H. G. Thomas suggests that we remember four words
to help us link together the whole of God's revelation:

1. *Preparation*—In the Old Testament God makes ready for the
   coming of the Messiah.
2. *Manifestation*—In the four Gospels Christ enters the world,
   dies for the world, and founds his church.
3. *Appropriation*—In the Acts and Letters, the ways are revealed
   in which the Lord Jesus was received, appropriated, and
   applied in individual lives.
4. *Consummation*—In the book of Revelation, the outcome of
   God's perfect plan is revealed.

WHAT IS THE GOSPEL?

Gospel means "good news." The good news concerning Jesus, the Son of God, is given us by four writers—Matthew, Mark, Luke, and John—although there is but one gospel, the glad story of salvation through Jesus Christ our Lord. The word *gospel* is never used in the New Testament to refer to a book. It always means "good news." When we speak of the Gospel of Luke we ought to understand that it means the Good News of Jesus Christ as recorded by Luke. Nevertheless, from the earliest times the term *Gospel* has been applied to each of the four narratives that record the life of Christ.

No doubt originally the Good News was oral. People went from one place to another telling the glad story by word of mouth. After a while a written record was necessary. More than one attempted this, with no success. See what Luke says in Luke 1:1-4: *Several biographies of Christ have already been written using as their source material the reports circulating among us from the early disciples and other eyewitnesses. However, it occurred to me that it would be well to recheck all these accounts from first to last and after thorough investigation to pass this summary on to you, to reassure you of the truth of all you were taught.*

There is but one gospel with four presentations. Four pictures of one Christ are given. The combined Gospel records set forth a Personality rather than present a connected story of a life.

WHY FOUR GOSPELS?

As everyone knows, there are four Gospels, but the question at once arises, Why four? Wouldn't one straightforward, continuous narrative have been enough? Would not this have been simpler and clearer? Might this not have saved us from some of the difficulties that have arisen in what some have said are conflicting accounts?

The answer seems plain: Because one or two would not have given us a portrayal of the life of Christ. There are four distinct offices of Christ portrayed in the Gospels. He is presented as King in Matthew, Servant in Mark, Son of Man in Luke, and Son of God in John.

It is true that each of the four Gospels has much in common

with the others. Each deals with Christ's earthly ministry, his death and resurrection, his teachings and miracles, but each Gospel has its differences. At once we see that each of the writers is trying to present a different picture of our one Lord.

Matthew deliberately adds to his account what Mark omits. There is a lack of completeness about his life history in any one of the four Gospels. Hear what John says in 21:25: *I suppose that if all the other events in Jesus' life were written, the whole world could hardly contain the books!*

There are deliberate gaps that none of the evangelists professes to fill in. For instance, all omit any account of the eighteen years of Christ's life between the ages of twelve and thirty. Although each Gospel is complete in itself, each is very selective. Only a few of his miracles are described and only a portion of his teachings are given. Each evangelist has recorded what is relevant and pertinent to his particular theme.

In the National Gallery in London there are three representations on a single canvas of Charles I. In one his head is turned to the right; in another, to the left; and in the center we find the full-face view. This is the story of this production: Van Dyck painted them for Bernini, the Roman sculptor, so that with their help he could make a bust of the king. By combining the impressions so received, Bernini would be better able to produce a "speaking" likeness. One view would not have been enough.

It may be true that the Gospels were intended to serve the very purpose of these portraits. Each presents a different aspect of our Lord's life on earth. Together we have the complete picture. He was a King, but he was the perfect Servant, too. He was the Son of Man, but we must not forget he was the Son of God.

There are four Gospels with one Christ, four accounts with one purpose, four sketches of one Person.

JESUS IN THE FOUR GOSPELS

Master this outline and you will be familiar for life with the contents of the Gospels:

King—Matthew presents Jesus as King. It was written primarily for the Jews, for he is the Son of David. His royal genealogy is given in chapter 1. In chapters 5–7, in the Sermon on the Mount, we have the manifesto of the King, containing the laws of his kingdom.

Servant—Mark depicts Jesus as Servant, written to the Romans. There is no genealogy. Why? People are not interested in the genealogy of a servant. More miracles are found here than in any other Gospel. Romans cared little for words; far more for deeds.

Man—Luke sets forth Jesus as the perfect Man. It was written to the Greeks; his genealogy goes back to Adam, the first man, instead of to Abraham. As a perfect Man he is seen much in prayer and with angels ministering to him.

God—John portrays Jesus as the Son of God. Written to all who will believe, with the purpose of leading people to Christ (John 20:31), everything in this Gospel illustrates and demonstrates his divine relationship.

William H. G. Thomas gives the pictures of the Gospels in this way: Matthew is concerned with the coming of a *promised Savior*. Mark is concerned with the life of a *powerful Savior*. Luke is concerned with the grace of a *perfect Savior*. John is concerned with the possession of a *personal Savior*.

Let us present another answer to the question, Why four Gospels? Many feel that the Bible uses numbers with precision, accuracy, and real meaning: seven is the perfect number; three is the number of the Godhead; forty is the number of testing. Four is the number of the earth. Look at a few illustrations. There are four points of the compass: north, east, south, and west. There are four seasons of the year: spring, summer, autumn, and winter. In the parable of the Sower, our Lord divided the field into four kinds of soil. Later he said, *The field is the world*. If four is the earth number, how fitting that the Holy Spirit gave us four Gospels in which to depict the earthly ministry of the heavenly One.

When we draw nearer we see then good reason for four Gospels. Christ is the one glorious theme of them all, but each of the writers is absorbed with some special feature in Christ's character and office. Each evangelist takes some office and develops it with convincing power. It is the unfolding of this particular view of the work of Christ that stamps the design on each book.

Let us pause to say this: All the Gospels are bound up with the promises of the Messiah in the Old Testament. We cannot explain the Gospels apart from the great Messianic prophecies in the Old Testament.

The prophets have portrayed a magnificent picture of the Messiah. They have told of his offices, mission, birth, suffering, death, resurrection, and glory. Let us consider the names and titles that the prophets have bestowed upon him.

He is called the *King:* Psalm 72; Isaiah 9:6-7; 32:1; Jeremiah 23:5; Zechariah 9:9; 14:9. These passages, among many others, tell of the kingly office of the Messiah. The prophets tell much of his kingdom and its extent, and of Christ's ultimate triumph.

He is called the *Servant of the Lord God:* Isaiah 42:1-7; 52:13-15; 53.

He is called the *Man, the Son of Man:* Genesis 3:15; 22:18; Isaiah 7:14-16; 9:6.

He is called *God:* Isaiah 9:6; 47:4; Jeremiah 23:6. It is as these four that Jesus is set forth in the Gospels.

TYPES OF PEOPLE THEN AND NOW

Christ was going to be presented to widely different types of people who made up the world. Each type was capable of appreciating one particular kind of presentation more than another.

The Jews—There were four classes of people in Jesus' day that represent four types of people today. Take the Jews first. They had special training in Old Testament Scripture and the prophets. Matthew writes the story of Jesus' life on earth especially for them. If the Jews were to be impressed, it would have to be by one of their own race. Their teacher had to be a man versed in the Old Testament and in the customs of the Jews. They had to know that this Jesus came to fulfill the prophecies of the Old Testament.

We have the same type of people today. They revel in prophecies fulfilled and unfulfilled. They seek to know what the prophets have spoken and how it has been fulfilled.

The Romans—Next came the Romans, the masters of the world at that time. Mark writes especially for them. The Romans knew nothing about Old Testament Scripture. They were not interested in prophecy being fulfilled. But they were vitally concerned over a remarkable Leader who had appeared in Palestine. He had claimed more than ordinary authority and had possessed extraordinary powers. They wanted to hear more about this Jesus—what sort of a person he really was, what he had said, and what he had done.

The Romans liked the straightforward message of one like Mark. Mark's Gospel is filled with deeds, not words. Clearly it is the Gospel of the ministry of Christ.

The Romans of Jesus' day were like the average businessmen of today. They are not concerned at first about the genealogy of a king but with a God who can meet man's every need. Mark is the businessman's Gospel.

The Greeks—Then there is Luke. This Gospel was written by a Greek doctor to his own countrymen who were lovers of beauty, poetry, and culture. The Greeks lived in a world of large ideas. Their tastes were fastidious. The Gospel of Luke tells of the birth and childhood of Jesus. It gives the inspired songs connected with the life of Christ. We find the salutation of Elizabeth when Mary visited her (Luke 1:42-45). We hear the song of the virgin mother (Luke 1:46-55). Even Zacharias burst into praise when speech was restored to him (Luke 1:68-79). At the Savior's birth a chorus of angel voices ring out (Luke 2:13-14), and then the shepherd's song of praise to God in Luke 2:20 is heard.

The Greeks of Jesus' day were like the students and idealists today who are seeking after truth, for they believe that truth is the means to happiness.

Everyone—John is written to everyone so that they will believe that Jesus is the Christ. Christ is portrayed as the Son of God. This Gospel is filled with extraordinary claims that attest his divine character and mission.

The "everyone" of John's day were like the masses today who need Christ. They include the "anyone" who will believe on the Lord Jesus because he has a sense of need and wants to receive the gift of eternal life through Jesus Christ the Lord.

KEYS TO THE GOSPELS

Front Door Keys

God has hung the key to the Gospel of Matthew right over the entrance. This is how the book opens: *These are the ancestors of Jesus Christ, a descendant of King David and of Abraham* (Matthew 1:1). This shows his covenant position as the Son of Abraham (see Genesis 12:1-3) and his royal position as Son of David. Matthew is presenting Christ as King; he gives the royal genealogy in the first seventeen verses. A king is not chosen by popular ballot but by birth.

Turn now to Mark. See how this book opens. No genealogy is given. The reason is that Jesus is portrayed as a servant, and no one is interested in the pedigree of a servant.

Turn to Luke. Is there a genealogy given? See Luke 3:23. Whereas Matthew traces Christ's line back to Abraham and David to show he was a Jew and of the royal line, Luke traces his line back to Adam. Christ is presented as the ideal Man. He was of the line of Adam.

Turn to John. How does this book open? No genealogy, but *Before anything else existed, there was Christ, with God. He has always been alive and is himself God* (John 1:1). Christ is portrayed as God in John.

Back Door Keys

Now let us see how the Gospels close. Turn to Matthew 28:18-20. Hear the King commanding and commissioning his disciples. The Messiah is still on earth, for it is on earth and not in heaven that the Son of David will reign in glory. *I have been given all authority in heaven and earth. Therefore go and make disciples in all the nations . . . and then teach these new disciples to obey all the commands I have given you; and be sure of this—that I am with you always, even to the end of the world.*

Now look at the close of Mark. It is very significant and appropriate. *And the disciples went everywhere preaching, and the Lord was with them* (Mark 16:20). Jesus, the Servant, is pictured as still working with his disciples.

Luke ends in a different way. Jesus, the perfect Man, is ascending to the Father. Notice Luke 24:51: *He blessed them, and then began rising into the sky, and went on to heaven.*

The closing verse of John is significant: *And I suppose that if all the other events in Jesus' life were written, the whole world could hardly contain the books!* (John 21:25). For he was the very Son of God.

SELECTED BIBLE READING

Sunday: The King, Christ Jesus (Matthew 2:1-12; 21:1-11)
Monday: The Servant, Christ Jesus (Mark 10:35-45; 2:1-22)
Tuesday: The Man, Christ Jesus (Luke 4:1-13; John 19:4-13)
Wednesday: The God-Man, Christ Jesus (John 1:1-18; 3:1-17)
Thursday: Our Redeemer, Jesus Christ (John 19:16-42)
Friday: The Master, Jesus Christ (Matthew 4:18-25)
Saturday: Our Master, Jesus Christ (John 21:1-19)

CHAPTER 28

UNDERSTANDING MATTHEW

Matthew Portrays Jesus Christ, the Promised Messiah

Matthew has a special object in his Gospel to show the Jews that Jesus is the long-expected Messiah, the Son of David, and that his life fulfilled the Old Testament prophecies. The purpose is given in the first verse. Matthew is the book of *the ancestors of Jesus Christ, a descendant of King David and of Abraham.* This statement links Christ with two of the great covenants that God made with David and Abraham. God's covenant with David consisted of the promise of a King to sit upon his throne forever (2 Samuel 7:8-13). God's covenant with Abraham promised that through him the entire world would be blessed (Genesis 12:3). David's son was a King. Abraham's son was a Sacrifice. Matthew opens with the birth of a King and closes with the offering of a Sacrifice.

From the beginning, Jesus is associated with the Jewish nation. Matthew used wisdom in not alienating the Jews who might read the story. He was convincing them that this One fulfilled every prophecy spoken concerning their promised Messiah. He quotes freely from the Old Testament more than any of the other evangelists. Twenty-nine such quotations are given.

Matthew links us up with the Old Testament. On every page he is trying to connect the Gospel with the prophets and showing that all of their teaching is being fulfilled in the person and kingdom of Jesus Christ.

It is difficult for us to appreciate how great the transition is from the old to the new. It seemed to the Jew that he had to give up his tradition and orthodoxy and accept another creed. Matthew, in his Gospel, and Paul, especially in Galatians, showed the Jewish Christians that they were not giving up their old faith, but rather were only giving up symbols and shadows for the real substance.

Matthew was well acquainted with Jewish history and customs. He speaks of farming and fishing and the housekeeping of his people in the seven parables in chapter 13. He knew this intimate record would strike responsive chords in the hearts of the Jewish people.

As you read Matthew, get a clear and comprehensive view of the entire Gospel. Keep in mind the Messianic character of this Gospel. Note the balance between Jesus' ministry and teaching. We find the genealogy of the King; his birth in Bethlehem, the city of David, according to Micah's prophecy (Micah 5:2); the coming of the forerunner, John the Baptist, as Malachi predicted (Malachi 3:1); the ministry of the King; his rejection by Israel; and the promise of his coming again in power and glory.

The author was no doubt a Christian Jew (9:9; 10:3). Matthew, "gift of the Lord," was a tax collector at Capernaum under the Roman law when Jesus chose him as one of the twelve disciples. His name is found in all the lists of the twelve, though Mark and Luke give his other name, Levi. The only word the author speaks about himself is that he was a "tax gatherer," which was then a term of reproach. The other evangelists tell about the great feast he gave Jesus and record the significant fact that he left all and followed him. No doubt he was a man of means.

Matthew breaks the silence of four hundred years between Malachi's prophecy and the announcement of the birth of Jesus. Israel was under the domination of the Roman Empire. No man of "the house of David" had been allowed to sit on the throne for six hundred years.

Herod was not the king of Israel but a governor of Judea, appointed by the emperor of Rome. The man who really had the throne-rights of the house of David was Joseph, the carpenter, who became the husband of Mary. See the genealogy of Joseph in Matthew 1, and notice especially one name, Jechoniah, in verse 11. If Joseph had been Jesus' father according to the flesh he could never have occupied the throne, for God's word barred the way. There had been a curse on this royal line since the days of Jechoniah. In Jeremiah 22:30 we read, *The Lord says: Record this man Coniah as childless, for none of his children shall ever sit upon the throne of David or rule in Judah.* Joseph was in the line of this curse. Hence, if Christ had been Joseph's son he could not have sat on David's throne.

But we find another genealogy in Luke 3. This is Mary's line back to David through Nathan, not Jechoniah (Luke 3:31). There was no curse on this line. To Mary, God's angel said, *Don't be frightened, Mary, . . . for God has decided to wonderfully bless you! Very soon now, you will become pregnant and have a baby boy, and you are to name him "Jesus." He shall be very great and shall be called the Son of God. And the Lord God shall give him the throne of his ancestor David. And he shall reign over Israel forever; his Kingdom shall never end!* (Luke 1:30-33).

Now the silence is broken and the coming of the Messiah declared.

The book of Matthew follows after the Old Testament and is the beginning of the New. It is the connecting link between the two. It is written for the Jews and it is fittingly placed. It takes for granted that the course of events is known to its readers. The Old Testament had closed with the chosen nation looking for their long-promised King, their Messiah. Matthew's Gospel shows that Jesus was that King. It is the Gospel of fulfillment.

Matthew presents the Lord Jesus in a distinctly Jewish relationship. Only in this one of the four Gospels do we find a record of the Messiah's declaration, *I was sent to help the Jews—the lost sheep of Israel—not the Gentiles* (15:24). What did his own people do with him? (See John 1:11.)

In numerical position, the book of Matthew is the fortieth in the canon. Thirty-nine books in the Old Testament, then Matthew. Forty is always a number of testing or probation in Scripture. Jesus was tempted by the devil forty days. Israel was in the wilderness forty years. David was king forty years. Moses was in a palace forty years, then on the back side of a desert for forty years. What other instances of this number forty do you remember in Scripture? Look it up in your concordance.

In this fortieth book of the Bible Israel is in the place of probation and testing by the presence of the Messiah in their midst. Christ is presented as King to the Jews, and they reject him not only as their Messiah but as their Savior (16:21).

COMING OF THE KING
MATTHEW 1-2

Matthew is the Gospel of the Messiah, God's anointed One. The main purpose of the Spirit in this book is to show that Jesus of Nazareth is the predicted Messiah, the Deliverer of whom Moses and the prophets wrote. He *is alive from everlasting ages past!* (Micah 5:2). He is the child that was to be born, the Son given, of whom Isaiah speaks who shall be called *"Wonderful," "Counselor," "The Mighty God," "The Everlasting Father," "The Prince of Peace"* (Isaiah 9:6).

Our maps and calendars tell of Christ's birthplace and birthday. Jesus was born in Bethlehem of Judea (2:1; Micah 5:2) *during the reign of King Herod.* We know this place and this king. We don't have to build the story out of the imagination. We are given names and dates. Christianity is a historical religion. The Gospel does not begin with "Once upon a time," but starts with Bethlehem in Judea. The town is there, so we can know the very place where Jesus was born.

The time is definite: *during the reign of King Herod.* History knows Herod. There is nothing mythical about this monster of iniquity.

These statements are facts, and no critic or unbeliever can doubt them. The Gospel narrative sets its records in the solid foundation of history. We are not building our faith on a myth but on substantial fact. This thing was not "done in a corner" but in the broad day, and it is not afraid of the geographer's map and the historian's pen.

The story of the birth of Jesus in Matthew differs from the record in Luke. They complement each other. While there is much untold, God has told us all we need to know. Jesus' earthly life began in a stable. His cradle was a manger. His family and associates were humble folk. He came as a helpless baby. How human was our Lord! But Jesus was heralded by an archangel, welcomed by an angel choir, and worshiped by earth's wisest philosophers! How divine was our Lord!

Most people, when they begin reading Matthew with its "was the father of's," wonder what these names are all about. We ought to realize that since these two genealogies were included in Scripture, they were put there for a purpose.

A genealogy is "the history of an individual or family from an ancestor" (Webster). There are two genealogies of Christ:

Matthew 1:1-17 and Luke 3:23-38. They are not alike, and the reason is that each traces the descent of Christ back for different purposes.

Matthew traces Jesus' line back to Abraham and David to show that he was a Jew (coming from David). Luke traces Jesus' line back to Adam to show that he belonged to the human race.

Matthew shows Jesus as of royal descent, the King, the Messiah, the Lion of the tribe of Judah, the promised Ruler of Israel. Luke shows Jesus as of human lineage, the ideal Man, born of woman.

Why are we concerned about these genealogies? Because they give us the key to the whole life of Christ. They show us from the very start that he was not just another man but that he was descended from a royal family, and there was a king's blood in his veins. If he were not a king, he could not claim the rulership of our lives. If he were not a man, he could not know "our sorrows" and bear "our grief."

Go through Matthew and follow this trail of the King:

1. A King's name—*He shall be called "Emmanuel"* (1:23).
2. A King's position—*A Governor shall rise from you to rule my people Israel* (2:6).
3. A King's announcement—*Prepare a road for the Lord—straighten out the path where he will walk* (3:3).
4. A King's coronation—*This is my beloved Son, and I am wonderfully pleased with him* (3:17).
5. A King's due respect—*Worship only the Lord God. Obey only him* (4:10).
6. A King's proclamation—*He taught as one who had great authority* (7:29).
7. A King's loyalty—*Anyone who isn't helping me is harming me* (12:30).
8. A King's enemies—*From then on Jesus began to speak plainly to his disciples about going to Jerusalem, and what would happen to him there—that he would suffer at the hands of the Jewish leaders* (16:21).
9. A King's love—*I, the Messiah, did not come to be served, but to serve, and to give my life as a ransom for many* (20:28).
10. A King's glory—*When I, the Messiah, shall come in my glory, and all the angels with me, then I shall sit upon my throne of glory. Then I, the King, shall say to those at my right, "Come, blessed of my Father, into the Kingdom"* (25:31, 34).

11. A King's sacrifice—*After the crucifixion . . . they put a sign above his head, "This is Jesus, the King of the Jews"* (27:35-37).
12. A King's victory—*He isn't here! For he has come back to life again, just as he said he would* (28:6).

Matthew alone tells of the visitors from the East. These were Persian magi, scholars, students of the stars. They came to worship and honor a king. They did not come inquiring, "Where is the newborn Savior of the world?" but, "Where is the newborn King of the Jews?"

Mark, Luke, and John are silent about the magi because they are not recording the birth of a king. The holy, sacred star had halted over a house in Bethlehem to tell of Christ's birth. The whole world at this time was expecting the advent of some great One. "Where is the newborn King of the Jews?" was the question on every lip. With all the prophecies that had been made to Israel, neither the world nor Israel could be criticized for expecting a king who would rule the earth from David's throne (Jeremiah 23:3-6; 30:8-10; 33:14-16, 25-26; Ezekiel 37:21; Isaiah 9:7; Hosea 3:4-5).

The priests knew where Christ was to be born, but they did not know Christ when he was born.

The magi were led to a person, not a creed.

The adoration of the magi foreshadowed Christ's universal dominion. Some day *every knee shall bow . . . and every tongue shall confess that Jesus Christ is Lord, to the glory of God the Father* (Philippians 2:10-11). *Let him reign from sea to sea, and from the Euphrates River to the ends of the earth* (Psalm 72:8).

The birth of Jesus was followed by twelve years of silence until his visit with the teachers of the Law in Jerusalem. Then silence shut him in again, with only the word *carpenter* to throw any light upon the next eighteen years and let us know what he was doing. Jesus took thirty years of preparation for three years of ministry.

PROCLAMATION OF THE KINGDOM
MATTHEW 3:1–16:20

John the Baptist had another name. As the prophet Isaiah began to unfold the real message of his book—the coming of the Messiah, Servant of the Lord—he introduced a character known simply as a voice. *I hear the voice of someone shouting, "Make a road for the Lord through the wilderness; make him a straight, smooth road through the desert"* (Isaiah 40:3). It is this "voice" that, although unnamed here, is to be the herald of Jesus Christ. His two functions—that of voice and that of messenger (Malachi 3:1)—are all that the Old Testament tells us of John the Baptist. But it is much. It is indeed wonderful not only that Christ should have been foretold all through the Scriptures but that his forerunner, John the Baptist, also is described.

In Matthew we hear the "voice": *"Turn from your sins . . . turn to God . . . for the Kingdom of Heaven is coming soon." Isaiah the prophet had told about John's ministry centuries before! He had written, "I hear a shout from the wilderness, 'Prepare a road for the Lord—straighten out the path where he will walk' "* (3:2-3).

The King must be announced! It was the duty of this herald to go before the King, as a Roman officer before his ruler, and command that the roads be repaired over which his Master would travel. John the Baptist did this. He showed that the spiritual roads of the lives of men and nations were full of the potholes of sin and sharp turns of iniquity, and they needed rebuilding and straightening.

We see the King stepping from his personal and private life into his public ministry (ch. 4). He was facing a crisis. Satan met him. After the benediction the Father had put upon him at his baptism when he said, *This is my beloved Son, and I am wonderfully pleased with him,* Jesus came forth to carry out the plans for which he came into the world. He was led into the wilderness to face the first major conflict of his public ministry.

Notice that Satan offered Jesus a shortcut to the universal Kingdom that he had come to gain through the long and painful way of the cross. But Christ came to be a Savior first, then a King. How strong is the temptation to take a shortcut to our ambitions! Jesus stood victor, his shield undented and untarnished. He went forth to conquer all other temptations until his final victory and ascension to heaven as Lord of all. (See 1 Corinthians 10:13.)

The Kingdom Laws
Every kingdom must have its laws and standards to control its subjects. The kingdom of heaven is no exception. Jesus declared

that he did not come *to cancel the laws of Moses . . . but to fulfill them.* The old law was good in its day. Moses and the prophets were far in advance of their time. They were pioneers. Jesus did not cancel this old law, but he treated it as rudimentary and not as perfect and final.

Jesus said that any reform that starts on the outside and works in is beginning at the wrong end. Christ starts on the inside and works out. The only way of getting a good life is first getting a good heart.

From the lofty pulpit of a mountain, Jesus preached the sermon that contains the laws of his kingdom (ch. 5–7). Read through these chapters and refresh your memory about this most wonderful of Jesus' discourses. It is filled with teaching. After over nineteen hundred years this Sermon on the Mount has lost none of its majesty or power. The teachings of this sermon surpass all human teachings. The world has not yet caught up with its simplest ideals and requirements. Many a person who is not a Christian claims that the Sermon on the Mount is his religion. How little he understands the depth of its meaning. It is important that we do not simply praise this rule as a wonderful theory but that we actually practice it in our own lives. If we let this rule operate in our lives, it will change all of our personal relations, heal our social wounds, solve every dispute between nations, yes, set the whole world in order. The root of this law is kindness. It is true, if human society would have its standards as theirs, the world would be set in order. One day filled with kindness would be a bit of heaven. Love would reign instead of lawlessness. Christ shows us that sin lies not just in committing the act but in the motive behind it as well. (See Matthew 5:21-22, 27-28.) No one can expect forgiveness who does not forgive (6:12, 14-15). Has anyone yet ever fathomed the depth of Matthew 7:12? It is easy to read; it is hard to do.

Jesus defined the nature and limit of the kingdom, the condition for entrance, its laws, its privileges and rewards. The Sermon on the Mount sets forth the constitution of the kingdom. Count the times the King says, "But I say." Mark them in your Bible. This will reveal Jesus' authority as he deals with the law of Moses. People must not only keep the law outwardly but in spirit as well. Notice the effect upon the people. *The crowds were amazed at Jesus' sermons, for he taught as one who had great authority, and not as their Jewish leaders* (7:28-29).

The King's Power

We find the King met human needs with the special miracles that he performed (ch. 8–9). There are twelve astonishing miracles in these two chapters. What are they? After Jesus had performed the miracles in chapter 12, *the crowd was amazed. "Maybe Jesus is the Messiah!" they exclaimed* (12:23).

The critical scribes now thrust themselves into the scene and passed their hostile judgment on the actions of Jesus (9:3).

The kingdom was proclaimed "near" because the King himself was there.

The King's Cabinet

Jesus not only preached himself, but he gathered others around him. It was necessary to organize his kingdom, to put it on a wider and more permanent basis. A king must have subjects. He would reflect his light through human instruments. He says, *You are the world's light* (5:14). Jesus still has a great message for the world, and he needs us to carry it. Spiritual ideas cannot stalk alone through the world and be of any value. They must be clothed with people and institutions who will serve as hearts and brains, hands and feet to carry them out. This is what Jesus was doing. He was calling people into his companionship to train them to carry on his work.

Where did Jesus find his helpers? Not in the Temple among the teachers or priests, nor in the colleges of Jerusalem. He found them on the seashore mending their nets. Jesus did not call many with power or wealth but rather chose the foolish things of the world to shame the wise (1 Corinthians 1:27).

A list of the disciples is given in Matthew 10:2-4. This is probably the most important catalogue of names in the world. These men were given a work to do that would make winning battles and founding empires seem of small consequence. We find their great message was the kingdom of heaven. *Go and announce to them that the Kingdom of Heaven is near* (10:17). Their tremendous mission was to start it.

Note some of the warnings and instructions for the disciples that Jesus stated in Matthew 10. What were they? If these requirements of discipleship hold true today, could you call yourself a disciple? Thoughtfully consider Christ's words in Matthew 10:32-33.

The Kingdom of Heaven

The word *kingdom* occurs some fifty times in Matthew, for this is the Gospel of the King. The expression "kingdom of heaven" is found thirty-five times here and nowhere else in the Gospels.

The Jews well understood the term *kingdom of heaven*. Neither Jesus nor John defined it. At Sinai, God had said to Israel, *And you shall be a kingdom of priests to God, a holy nation* (Exodus 19:6). Israel at first was a theocracy. God was their King; they formed his kingdom. The prophets had referred to the Messianic kingdom again and again.

In Matthew 13 Jesus likened the kingdom of heaven to:

The farmer
The yeast in the dough
The thistles
A hidden treasure
A mustard seed
A pearl of great value
A dragnet

These parables describe what the result of the presence of the gospel of Christ in the world will be during this present age until the time of his return when he will gather the harvest (13:40-43). We see no bright picture of a converted world. There will be thistles mixed with the wheat, good fish and bad, yeast in the loaf. (Yeast is often a symbol of sin. The Spirit never uses yeast as a symbol of anything good.) Then there is an abnormal growth of the mustard seed that allows "birds of the air" to lodge in its branches. This is Christendom. Only Christ can determine what is good and what is bad, and at the harvest he will divide. If we are to have a kingdom on this earth, with the laws that Christ set down, then we must have the King. Some day Christ will come in power and great glory and establish his throne on this earth. We will have peace when the Prince of Peace reigns!

REJECTION OF THE KING
MATTHEW 16:21–20:34

The kingdom was first presented to the rightful heirs, the Jews, but they refused the offer, rejected the King, and finally crucified him. From Matthew 12 on we see much controversy among the leaders concerning Jesus.

Jesus announced that the kingdom would be taken away from the Jews and given to another nation. *The Kingdom of God shall be taken away from you and given to a nation that will give God his share of the crop* (21:43). The announcement offended the rulers, and *they wanted to get rid of him* (21:46).

Our Lord told Nicodemus the requirement for entrance into the kingdom of heaven (John 3:3-7, 16). "Anyone" who believes may enjoy its privileges and blessings. The kingdom is for the Gentiles as well as the Jews.

Why did the Jews refuse the kingdom? The world today is longing intensely for the golden age. A millennium of peace and rest is the great desire of diplomats and rulers. But they want it in their own way and on their own terms. They desire to bring it about by their own efforts. They have no longing for a millennium brought about by the personal return of the Lord Jesus Christ. It was just so with the Jews in the days of John the Baptist.

Have you put Christ on the throne of your life? Have you the peace you long for? Have you accepted Christ's terms for your life?

The Church Promised
We find Jesus with his disciples up north in Caesarea Philippi, apparently with the object of having a private interview with them in which he would disclose a great truth (ch. 16).

Only in Matthew's Gospel is the church named. When the kingdom was rejected we find a change in the teachings of Jesus. He began to talk about the church instead of the kingdom (16:18). *Church* comes from the word *ecclesia*, which means "called out ones." Because all would not believe on him, Christ said he was calling out anyone, Jew or Gentile, to belong to his church, which is his body. He began to build a new edifice, a new body of people, which would include both Jews and Gentiles (Ephesians 2:14-18).

Life's Most Important Question
When they were far away from the busy scene in which they lived, Jesus asked his disciples the question: *Who are the people saying I am?* (16:13).

This is the important question today! First asked by an obscure Galilean in that far-off solitude, it has come thundering down through the centuries and has become the mightiest question in the world today. What do you think of Christ? What people think determines what they do and are. The ideas people hold about industry, wealth, government, morals, and religion mold society and alter lives. So what people think of Christ is the master force in the world today and more than anything else influences their life and thought.

The disciples gave the answers people were giving. The answers then were as varied as they are now. All agreed that Jesus was an extraordinary person, at least a prophet or a person with an element of the supernatural.

Jesus now turned the general question into a sharp personal inquiry. *Who do you think I am?* (16:15). Ask yourself this question. Important as the general question is, far more important to each one of us is this personal question. No one can escape it. A neutral answer is impossible. He is either God or an impostor.

Life's Most Important Answer

The Christ, the Messiah, the Son of the living God, exclaimed the impulsive, fervent Peter (16:16). This confession is great because it exalts Christ as the Son of God and lifts him above humanity and crowns him with deity. From then on he revealed to this handful of disciples new truths about his teachings. He said to Peter and the disciples after this answer concerning who he was, *Upon this rock I will build my church.* This is what Christ was going to do—build a church of which he himself was to be the chief cornerstone. This church was born on Pentecost (Acts 2).

For the first time the fateful shadow of the cross fell across the path of the disciples. From this time on Jesus began to draw back the curtain that veiled the future and to show his disciples the things that would happen. He saw his path running to Jerusalem into the awful hatred of the priests and Pharisees and then on to the terrible cross, but he also saw the glory of the resurrection morning (16:21).

Jesus did not reveal these things until his disciples were ready to bear them. God often in his mercy hides the future from us.

TRIUMPH OF THE KING
MATTHEW 21–28

On the morning of Palm Sunday there was a stir in Bethany and along the road leading to Jerusalem. It was understood that Jesus was to enter the city that day. The people were gathering in crowds. A colt was procured and the disciples, having thrown their robes over it, placed Jesus upon it, and the procession started. This little parade could not have been compared in magnificence with many a procession that has attended the coronation of a king or the inauguration of a president, but it meant much more for the world. Jesus for the first time permitted a public recognition and celebration of his rights as Messiah-King. The end was approaching with awful swiftness, and he had to offer himself as Messiah, even if only to be rejected.

In their enthusiasm the people tore off branches from the palm and olive trees and carpeted the highway, while shouts rang through the air. They believed in Jesus, and with all their warm enthusiasm were not ashamed of their King. In answer to the crowds who asked, "Who is this?" they boldly answered, "This is the prophet, Jesus, from Nazareth of Galilee." It took courage to say that in Jerusalem. Jesus was not entering the city as a triumphant conqueror as the Romans had done. No sword was in his hand. Over him floated no blood-stained banner. His mission was salvation!

In the evening the crowds dispersed, and Jesus quietly returned to Bethany. Apparently nothing in the way of making Jesus King had been accomplished. His kingdom came not with observation or pageantry. His hour had not yet come. Christ must be Savior first, then come again as King of kings and Lord of lords.

Christ's authority was brought into question as he went into the Temple and ordered the merchants out, overturning their tables and telling them that they had made the house of God a den of thieves. A bitter controversy followed. *Then the Pharisees met together to try to think of some way to trap Jesus into saying something for which they could arrest him* (22:15). He bade farewell to Jerusalem until he would come again to sit on David's throne.

The Future of the Kingdom

He delivered his Mount Olivet discourse. He foretold the condition of the world after his ascension until he comes back in glory to judge the nations as to their treatment of his brothers, the Jews (ch. 25). This is not the judgment of the Great White Throne, which is the judgment of the wicked dead. Neither is it the judgment seat of Christ (2 Corinthians 5:10), which is the judgment of saints according to their works. It is the judgment of

Gentile nations concerning their attitude toward God's people.

Much of Jesus' discourse in Matthew 24–25 is devoted to his Second Coming. He exhorts men to be ready in the parables of the faithful servant, the ten bridesmaids, and the money.

The Death and Resurrection of the King

We have been passing through some of the highlights in the life of Jesus; now we step into the shadows as we enter Gethsemane. We see the Son of Abraham, the Sacrifice, dying so that all the nations of the earth might be blessed by him. Jesus was slain because he claimed to be the King of Israel. He was raised from the dead because he was the King (Acts 2:30-36). Although a large number of disciples believed in Jesus and followed him, the opposition of the Jews was bitter, and they determined to put him to death. On the grounds of blasphemy, and of claiming to be the King of the Jews, thus making himself the enemy of the Roman emperor, Jesus was delivered up by Pilate to be crucified.

Matthew is not alone in his record of the terrible circumstances of the Savior's passion, but he makes us feel that in the mock array—the crown of thorns, the scepter, the title over the cross—we have a witness, though it be only scorn, to the kingly claim.

After hanging on the cruel tree for six hours, the Savior died, not from physical suffering alone but of a broken heart, for he bore the sins of the whole world. We hear his triumphant cry. "It is finished!" He paid the debt of sin and became the world's Redeemer!

Redemption Cost a Great Price!

The mode of the Messiah's death had been foreshadowed by various symbols in the Old Testament. The bronze snake in the wilderness signified that he was to be lifted up; the lamb upon the Jewish altar signified that his blood must be shed. His hands and his feet were to be pierced, he was to be wounded and tormented, his ears were to be filled with revilings, upon his clothes dice were to be tossed, and vinegar was to be given him to drink. All of these incidents at the Messiah's death had been foretold in Jewish prophecy. But this is not all of the redemption story. Jesus was put in Joseph's tomb, and on the third day he arose, as he had said. This is the supreme test of his kingship. Men thought that he was dead and his kingdom had failed. By his resurrection Christ assured his disciples that the King still lived and that one day he will come back to establish his kingdom on earth.

The ascension of Jesus is not recorded in Matthew. The curtain falls with the Messiah still on earth, for it is on earth and not in heaven that the Son of David is yet to reign in glory. The last time the Jews saw Christ he was on the Mount of Olives. The next time they see him he will be on the Mount of Olives! (See Zechariah 14:4; Acts 1:11.)

A Worldwide Commission

Jesus announced his program, and a crisis hour was struck in the history of Christianity. The climax is found in his great commission: *I have been given all authority in heaven and earth. Therefore go and make disciples in all the nations, baptizing them into the name of the Father and of the Son and of the Holy Spirit, and then teach these new disciples to obey all the commands I have given you; and be sure of this—that I am with you always, even to the end of the world* (28:18-20).

On what mission were they sent? To overrun the world with armies and make men submit under the sword? No, but to "make disciples in all the nations."

From the mountaintop of his ascension his disciples started forth on this mission, radiating from that center, and they have gone on until they have reached the rim of the world. Christianity is no national or racial religion. It knows no bounds of mountain or sea, but it envelopes the globe.

SELECTED BIBLE READING

Sunday: The King Born (Matthew 1:18–2:23)
Monday: The King Begins Work (Matthew 4)
Tuesday: The King States Kingdom Laws (Matthew 5:1-17, 41-48; 6:19-34)
Wednesday: The King and His Followers (Matthew 10)
Thursday: The Kingdom Parables (Matthew 13)
Friday: The King Offers Himself as King (Matthew 21:1-11)
Saturday: The King Will Return (Matthew 25:14-16)

CHAPTER 29

UNDERSTANDING
MARK

Mark Portrays Jesus Christ, the Servant of God

John, whose surname was Mark, was the writer of the Gospel of Mark (Acts 12:12, 25). He was the son of Mary, a relative of Barnabas (Colossians 4:10), and likely a native of Jerusalem. He accompanied Paul and Barnabas to Antioch and was the cause of some trouble between them (Acts 12:25; 13:5). Then he left them, probably on account of hardships (Acts 13:13). Finally he became a great help to Paul (Colossians 4:10-11; 2 Timothy 4:11). It is believed that the disciples met in the upper room of Mark's mother's house in Jerusalem. Peter was the means of Mark's conversion and affectionately speaks of him as "my son" (1 Peter 5:13). We see the influence of the teaching of Peter in this Gospel.

If we turn to Mark 10:45 we can quite easily determine Mark's object in writing his Gospel. *For even I, the Messiah, am not here to be served, but to help others, and to give my life as a ransom for many.* Unlike Matthew, Mark was not trying to prove certain statements and prophecies concerning Jesus. His only object in writing was to tell clearly certain facts about Jesus, his deeds more especially than his words. That Jesus is the Son of God he proves, not by declaring how he came to earth but by showing what he accomplished during his brief career on this earth, how his coming changed the world.

There is a general agreement that Mark's Gospel was written

for Roman readers. The Roman was different from the Jew. His genius was his strong common sense. His religion had to be practical. He would have no interest in tracing beliefs back into the past. Legal genealogies and fulfillments of prophecy would leave him cold. Jewish dogmas were not in his line. He might say, "I know nothing of your Scriptures and care nothing for your peculiar notions, but I would be glad to hear a plain story of the life this man Jesus lived. Tell me what he did. Let me see him just as he was."

Mark differs widely from Matthew in both character and scope. Mark's Gospel is the shortest of them all.

Matthew has twenty-eight chapters, abounds in parables, and portrays Christ as the Son of David with kingly dignity and authority (Matthew 28:18).

Mark has sixteen chapters and gives four parables. Mark portrays Christ as the humble but perfect Servant of God. We find the angels ministering to him.

GENERAL CHARACTERISTICS OF THIS GOSPEL

The skill of an artist may lie in what he leaves out. An amateur crowds everything in. Mark's omissions are in strict harmony with his central purpose of emphasizing Jesus as the Servant.

There is nothing about the virgin birth. No reference to Jesus' birth is made in the whole Gospel. This is significant. No one is interested in the pedigree of a servant.

There is no visit of magi. A servant does not receive homage.

No account of Jesus as the boy in the Temple is given. In this practical age, as in the age of Jesus, men demand a Christ who can do things. They are not interested in Jesus the boy but in Christ the man who is able and willing to accomplish today what he did of old.

There is no Sermon on the Mount. Matthew devotes three whole chapters to this sermon, which sets forth the laws of the kingdom and describes the character of its subjects. Mark presents Christ as a perfect "Workman"; a servant has no kingdom and frames no laws.

No quotations from the prophets are imparted. Mark's one direct quotation from the prophets is found in Mark 1:2. Matthew quotes on every page.

No divine titles are used. Jesus is never owned as King in Mark, except in derision. Matthew says, "He shall be called 'Emmanuel' (meaning 'God is with us')." Not so in Mark.

Matthew says, "Lord, save us! We're sinking!" Mark says, "Teacher, don't you even care that we are all about to drown?"

There is no statement that his work was finished at his death. In John 19:30 he said, "It is finished." This is not found in Mark. It is not for a servant to say when his work is done.

One of the first things that impresses us as we look at Mark's Gospel is its brevity. It is much shorter than any of the other Gospels. Very little is found here that is not found in the others. It moves off with precision.

Matthew records fourteen parables. Mark only four—the farmer, the seed growing secretly (found only in Mark), the mustard seed, and the wicked tenant farmers. Miracles have a leading place in Mark, as parables have in Matthew. Twenty miracles are given in Mark in detail. A servant works; a king speaks.

THE SERVANT PREPARED
MARK 1:1-13

The book of Mark skips over the first thirty years of Jesus' life, but these years were all needed for his human preparation for his life's work. He grew in sympathy with daily toil. He wrestled, like Jacob, with life's problems. He fought many battles in the arena of his heart. He meditated upon the needs of his nation till his heart burned within him.

Preparation in life is needed. Jesus' life illustrated this. The foundations of the lighthouse are so necessary though unseen beneath the surface. The coral colony builds the foundations for an island and its tropical growth. The plant sends its roots into the dark soil before it can bring forth the flower and leaf. Look at the forty years that Moses spent in the desert before he began his great work; the long period of Elijah's youth before he appeared before King Ahab; the youth of Amos spent on a farm; John the Baptist's thirty years of training. So with Jesus! He spent thirty years in obscurity in Nazareth before he appeared for the three years of public ministry. Getting ready for our life's work is of tremendous importance. Don't chafe if Christ uses time in preparing you for life.

Preparation by John the Forerunner

This Gospel begins with John the Baptist making ready for the coming of the Messiah. John's coming was in fulfillment of a Messianic prophecy: *I hear the voice of someone shouting, "Make a road for the Lord through the wilderness"* (Isaiah 40:3). It is this "voice" that is to be the herald of Jesus Christ.

We see this strange man who appears on the scene in an almost sensational way. *His clothes were woven from camel's hair and he wore a leather belt.* His food, too, was strange, for *locusts and wild honey* were his diet.

There is a lesson here for us. God does not always choose the kind of men we would select. He often picks *what the world considers foolish and of little worth . . . so that no one anywhere can ever brag in the presence of God* (1 Corinthians 1:27-28). No doubt, if we were to select a herald for Christ, we would choose one of high birth, university trained, a man of wide reputation. He would have to be eloquent and a fearless champion of great causes. Not so with God. Graduated from no outstanding school, of humble birth, little known, dressed like a desert hermit, John the Baptist was approved of God (Matthew 11:11).

John's message was as startling as his appearance. He went before his Monarch as any Roman officer would go before his, demanding that the road be repaired and the highway reconstructed. *Everyone must straighten out his life to be ready for the Lord's arrival* (1:3). A true revival is always a revival of righteousness.

Preparation by Baptism

John and Jesus met one day. John recognized immediately that this Man was not a subject for the baptism of repentance that he was preaching. There was in this face a purity and majesty that struck John's heart with a sense of his own unworthiness. He was the Son of God. John hesitated and said, *This isn't proper. . . . I am the one who needs to be baptized by you* (Matthew 3:14).

Jesus was baptized with John's baptism in obedience to an appointed ordinance. *Please do it, for I must do all that is right* (Matthew 3:15). He set a seal of approval on John's message and work, and acknowledged him as the true forerunner of Christ. The baptism by John was ordained of God and therefore was binding on all those who acknowledged God and meant to keep his commandments.

Christ was the standard and example of what is right. He

would fulfill every duty he required of others (1 Corinthians 10:13).

Preparation by Receiving the Holy Spirit

The moment Jesus came up out of the water, he saw the heavens open and the Holy Spirit in the form of a dove descending on him (1:10). The Spirit descended in the bodily shape of a dove (Luke 3:22). This was a symbol. The coming of the Spirit himself was a reality. Every event in Jesus' life had significance. In any service for God, the Spirit always prepares the life by giving power and equipment. He is God's great agent for spiritual warfare.

Because Jesus went down into the baptismal water of obedience to God, he could come up under an opened sky with the Holy Spirit descending upon him and hear the voice of his Father declaring him to be his beloved Son.

Jesus came up out of that water a new Man into a new world. His relationship to his Father and his mission were proclaimed.

Preparation by a Divine Call

A voice from heaven said . . . (1:11). God endorsed Jesus and his mission and showed to the Jewish nation that he was the Messiah. *Jesus of Nazareth was anointed by God with the Holy Spirit and with power, and he went around doing good and healing all who were possessed of demons, for God was with him* (Acts 10:38). This has been called "Mark's Gospel in a nutshell." Later we hear this same voice at his transfiguration. *This is my beloved Son. Listen to him* (9:7).

Preparation by Testing

Baptism and temptation are here crowded together. Hardly had the voice from heaven died away than we hear a whisper from hell. Out of the baptismal benediction of the Father, Jesus stepped into a desperate struggle with the devil.

Mark says, *Immediately the Holy Spirit urged Jesus into the desert,* which shows how quickly the Spirit moves (1:12). "Immediately" also indicated continuity, showing that temptaion was as much a part of the preparation of the Servant for his work as his baptism. Suffering and trial are as much God's plan as thrills and triumphs. It was no accident or evil fate but a divine appointment.

Temptation has its place in this world. We could never develop without it. There is nothing wrong in being tempted. The wrong begins when we begin to consent to it. We are not to run into temptation of our own accord. Jesus did not go of himself but was "urged" by the Spirit. We will find that the path of duty often takes us through temptations, but *you can trust God to keep the temptation from becoming so strong that you can't stand up against it. . . . He will show you how to escape temptation's power so that you can bear up patiently against it* (1 Corinthians 10:13). He always shows a way of escape!

THE SERVANT WORKING
MARK 1:14–8:30

There is continuous, unbroken service of the Servant recorded in this Gospel. He had to teach men; they were in darkness. He had to cheer men; they were without hope. He had to heal men; they were sick and suffering. He had to free men because they were under the power of Satan. He had to pardon and cleanse men because they were sinful.

We see Jesus preaching by the seashore and selecting four of the fishermen to become his first disciples to learn under his guidance how to become "fishermen for the souls of men." Who were they? (See Mark 1:16-20.) They were to turn all the practical knowledge and skill they exercised in the art of catching fish into the work of catching the souls of men. What disciple was called in Mark 2?

It is interesting to note that Jesus never called anyone from idleness. He called busy and successful people to follow him. Everyone can turn their business into a channel of service for Christ. How was Christ's call received? *At once they left their nets and went along with him* (1:18). Too often there is lost time between our call and our coming; our doing lags far behind our duty.

Jesus is introduced at once as "anointed with power" and as fully engaged in his work. You will find no long discourses in these next chapters, but many mighty deeds. Demons were cast out (1:21-28); fever put down (1:29-31); different diseases healed (1:32-34); lepers made whole (1:40-45); paralyzed men made to walk (2:1-12); withered hand cured (3:1-5); multitudes healed (3:6-12); storm at sea quelled (4:35-41); maniac's mind restored (5:1-15); woman's hemorrhage of blood stopped (5:21-34); Jairus's daughter brought back to life (5:35-43); five thousand fed (6:32-44); the sea made his sidewalk (6:45-51); all that touched him made whole (6:53-56); deaf and dumb hearing and speaking (7:31-37); four thousand fed (8:1-9); blind man healed (8:22-26).

The action is rapid, and events appear to be happening before our very eyes. Mark's descriptions are abrupt and outspoken, but he preserves many things for us that would otherwise have been lost. It is only in the Gospel of Mark that we are told that Jesus was a carpenter.

Mark tells us that Jesus *took one by the hand*, and took little children *in his arms*. Mark tells us that Jesus sighed, that he loved, that he was angry.

Let us spend with Jesus the Sabbath that is recorded in Mark 1:21-34, going with him to church, listening to his preaching, watching him when interrupted by a maniac, casting out the demon, and making the healing a powerful aid to his teaching. Then after service let us go with him to Peter's house and see him heal Peter's mother-in-law of a severe fever, and then let us spend the Sabbath afternoon in quiet rest and friendly conversation. Toward evening we will look out in the beautiful twilight and see men coming toward the house, bringing great numbers of people who are sick with every kind of disease, and watch them as Jesus lays his tender hands upon them and heals them. The lame jump from their stretchers and leap for joy; the blind open their eyes and see their healer; lines of suffering are turned to an expression of unbelieveable happiness as others are delivered from their painful diseases.

Mark records a wonderful statement concerning the Sabbath: *The Sabbath was made to benefit man and not man to benefit the Sabbath* (2:27). This great saying of Jesus is the central principle of Sabbath observance. The Sabbath is not made to annoy people, to confine them and impoverish them, but to enrich and bless them!

Christ answers the question of Sabbath-keeping with a practical illustration (3:1-5). His conclusion is that whatever deed is really helpful to man is proper for the Sabbath and is in perfect harmony with God's design of the day. He illustrated this truth with this miracle of healing. Seven of Jesus' recorded miracles were performed on the Sabbath. The Sabbath was "made." It is God's gift to man.

The Servant at Work
The miracles of Jesus were proofs of his mission from God. They showed that he was the promised Redeemer and King, the One

who we all need. Because Jesus was God, miracles were as natural to him as acts of will are to us! Through his miracles Jesus inspired faith in many of those who saw and heard him.

The Servant is always found "working." *All of us must quickly carry out the tasks assigned us by the one who sent me, for there is little time left before the night falls and all work comes to an end* are his words. Read this memorandum of the full days of our Lord's ministry. How empty our own lives will seem in comparison!

The Servant at Prayer

The morning following the great Sabbath day of preaching and healing, in which we followed Jesus, he got up very early and went out of the city to a lonely place and prayed (1:35). His work was growing rapidly, and Jesus needed heavenly communion. The seeming answer was a larger work, the entrance upon his first Galilean tour of healing and preaching (1:37-39). Only one healing event of this tour, which lasted several days, is recorded—that of a leper whose disease was incurable (1:40-45).

If the Son of God needed to pray before he undertook his work, how much more should we pray. Perhaps our lack of success in life is because we fail at this point. We do not have because we do not ask.

The Servant Forgives Sin

Several days later . . . the news of his arrival spread quickly through the city (2:1). It is remarkable how rapidly news spread in the East, without newspapers, television, telephones, or radios. But in another part of the city a paralyzed man had heard of this new Prophet and his gospel of healing. His four friends brought him to Jesus and let him down into the presence of the Teacher. We find in this healing the test and proof of Jesus' power not only as a physician of the body but as a healer of the soul. *For only God can forgive sins* (2:7). Sins are against God and, therefore, he only can forgive. Jesus said, *I, the Messiah, have authority on earth to forgive sin. . . . I'll prove it to you. . . . Pick up your stretcher and go on home* (2:9-11).

God endorsed Jesus' claim to be the Messiah in this miracle. The man jumped up, took his stretcher, and left, a living witness to Jesus' power over sin, a visible illustration of the work that Jesus came to do. Jesus came to give his life a ransom for many that he might forgive men their sins. *All have sinned,* and all need a Savior (Romans 3:23).

We find the account of the choosing of the twelve apostles in Mark 3:13-21. Notice the fourteenth verse. It tells why Jesus chose these men, *to be his regular companions.* This is what Jesus wants of his disciples today—that they will take time to be in his presence and commune with him. In John 15:15, he says, *I no longer call you slaves . . . now you are my friends.*

As you turn to Mark 4, notice that *once again an immense crowd gathered around him on the beach as he was teaching* (4:1; 2:13). What a wonderful teacher is Jesus!

The parable of the farmer sets forth the hindrances to the gospel that dwell in the hearts of the hearers (4:3-20).

Everyone should master these parables of the kingdom in chapter 4. They were a special teaching instrument of Christ. The interpretation of the farmer is given in Mark 4:13-20. Jesus used this method of instruction because of the growing hostility to him and his message. He was surrounded by enemies who tried to catch him in his words, but no one could object to a simple story. Besides, stories are remembered by the dullest of hearers.

A parable is an analogy. It assumes a likeness between higher and lower things. *Parable* comes from the Greek word meaning "beside" and "to throw." A parable, then, is a form of teaching in which one thing is thrown beside another.

Beside the parable of the farmer, our Lord spoke other parables as recorded by Mark:

1. The parable of the lamp (4:21-25)
2. The parable of the seed springing secretly (4:26-29)
3. The parable of the mustard seed (4:30-33)

After interpreting the parables, Jesus took a ship to escape the crowd. On the way, as the weary Teacher fell asleep, a violent storm arose on the Sea of Galilee. About to drown, the frantic disciples awoke Jesus. At a word from his lips the sea became calm. He had power over nature (4:35-41).

In Mark 5 Jesus is still working. What does he do now? Read parallel accounts in Matthew 8:28-34 and Luke 8:26-39. Compare this miracle with other recorded cures of demoniacs in Matthew 9:32-33; Mark 1:23-26; Matthew 17:14-18; Luke 9:38-42.

The miracle recorded in Mark 5, like all others, tested the

people's character. It took them off their guard and disclosed their true natures. Notice the contrast in the way people receive the work of Christ.

Some shun the Savior. *The herdsmen fled.* Others *were frightened* and *began pleading with Jesus to go away and leave them alone!* (5:14-17). Doubtless there were other herds of hogs, and they feared the loss of them. What a true picture of the attitude of many toward Christ! There is some gainful business they do not want to give up. There is some sin that lies close to the heart. It is for these reasons that men thrust away Christ.

Some seek the Savior. The healed man begged him *to let him go along.* It is this way with people today. They either ask Jesus to "go away" because they want to keep their sin, or they ask to "go along" with him because they want to lose their sin. Do you want to keep or lose your sin?

After healing the demoniac, Jesus returned to Capernaum. He healed a woman who had been sick for many years, and *while he was still talking to her* he was called to raise a child already lying in death, Jairus's daughter (5:35).

Jesus started out on a third preaching tour of Galilee (ch. 6). He sent out the twelve disciples, two by two, on independent missions (6:7-13). Matthew 10 records the instructions they received. As they preached, Herod heard them, and we read of his uneasy conscience, thinking that the man he had murdered was back to haunt him (6:14-29).

How much people recklessly give away for passing pleasures. For a glass of wine, a moment of passion, a little more money, a position of empty honor, they give away half—yes, all the kingdom of their souls, their health, home, friendships, peace, happiness, and eternal life. Like Esau, they sell their birthright for a serving of stew. Like Judas, they sell their Savior for thirty bits of metal.

After the apostles were trained, Jesus sent them out on an extensive missionary tour among the villages of Galilee (6:12-13). When they came back they *returned to Jesus* (6:30), probably at their regular rendezvous, Capernaum. They reported their sermons, the number of conversions, and the miracles that took place. No Christian work can be carried on long without frequent talks with Christ. We need his sympathy, approval, guidance, and strength.

We must hasten if we would follow this mighty Servant, this

Workman of God. Jesus had gone apart in a desert to rest awhile, but the crowds followed him (6:31). The feeding of the five thousand follows without an interval (6:32-44). This is one of the most important miracles. Evidently it made a special impression upon the writers of the Gospels, as it is the only one of the thirty-five miracles that is recorded by all four. Review it carefully. Notice Jesus served in an orderly way.

What miracles are next (6:45-52 and 53-56)? Follow Jesus in what he does and says (7:1-23; 7:24-30; 7:31-37; 8:1-9; 8:22-26).

Peter's confession of faith should be mastered by everyone—Mark 8:29. Jesus did not tell his disciples who he was. He waited until they told him. When he asked, *Who do you think I am?* the climax of his ministry was reached. He was testing the aim of all his training of the chosen twelve. Peter's answer gave him the assurance that his goal had been attained.

What did the Pharisees think of Jesus? Already they had agreed to put him to death.

What did the crowds think of him? Already they were deserting him.

What did the disciples think of him? Peter gives the answer.

What do you think of Christ?

THE SERVANT REJECTED
MARK 8:31–15:47

Even before Mark sets forth Christ's direct claim to be King of the kingdom, he reveals the way the King is to be received. His is a pathway of suffering and rejection. Jesus told them *about the terrible things he would suffer* (8:31). The evangelists wrote it down in plain language.

Jesus told his disciples that he would be rejected by the elders, chief priests, and scribes (8:31). He would be delivered by treachery (9:31). He would be put to death by the Romans (10:32-45). He would rise again the third day (9:31). Jesus, nevertheless, claimed the kingdom by presenting himself at Jerusalem as the Heir of David, according to the prophecy of Zechariah 9:9 (11:1-11).

How did the people accept this King? At first they welcomed him because they hoped that he would deliver them from the yoke of Rome and free them from the poverty they were enduring. But when he entered the Temple and showed that his mission was a spiritual one, he was hated by the religious leaders with a satanic hatred that led to the plot to put him to death (14:1).

The World's Greatest Sin

The greatest sin of this age, as of every age, is the rejection of Jesus Christ. Yet remember, everyone who has heard the Gospel must either accept the Lord as Savior or trample him underfoot. The people of Jesus' day made their choice, and the people of our day must make theirs.

This wonderful Presence that shines forth in the Gospels, this vision of God as a human being—will you look at him and then pass on as though you had seen a work of art? This voice that sounds throughout the centuries—will you listen as though it were just the voice of a gifted orator? What is Jesus to you? A name? or your Master? If you cannot answer the question as Peter did, will you sign this covenant, worded by Dr. R. A. Torrey?

I promise to examine carefully the evidence that the Bible is God's book, and Jesus Christ is God's Son and man's Savior; and if I find reason to believe that this book is true and he is man's Savior, I will accept him and confess him before men, and undertake to follow him.

(Signed)_____

After Christ's public ministry, described in Mark 10:46–11:26, we read of his last conflict with the Jewish authorities and of his triumph over the leaders (11:27–12:44).

Jesus sought to persuade the Jews to receive him as the Messiah (11:15–12:44). It was a busy Tuesday, occupied from morning till night in one great and powerful effort to induce the Jewish nation to acknowledge him, and thus become that glorious nation, blessing the world, for which it had been set apart.

In the beautiful Temple courts the simple Galilean met the Jewish authorities, arrayed in all the pomp of their official regalia. There was a sharp and prolonged controversy on puzzling questions.

The scribes and chief priests asked him, *Who gave you the authority to drive out the merchants?* (11:28).

The Pharisees and Herodians tried to catch him in his words: *Is it right to pay taxes to Rome, or not?* (12:14).

The Sadduccees, who didn't believe in the resurrection, asked him, *In the resurrection, whose wife will she be, for she had been the wife of each of them?* (12:23).

The scribes asked him, *Of all the commandments, which is the most important?* (12:28).

After Jesus answered them all, *No one dared ask him any more questions* (12:34).

It would seem that he could not escape treason to the Roman government in answering them, but he came out unscathed. Hour by hour Jesus met the attack.

All the way through, the perfect Servant of God was dogged by his enemies. The Enemy is not dead! God's servants today are called to tread a similar path. Jesus silenced his enemies, but their hearts would not yield. Then he exposed all their hypocritical practices in words that fell like bombs. He tried to break through their walls of prejudice and cause them to repent before it was too late, but all seemed to be in vain.

Before he went to the cross, Jesus revealed the future to his troubled disciples in the Olivet discourse (Mark 13). He told them of the end of this age and of the great tribulation, and he climaxed it with the promise of his return in power and glory.

The plotting of the chief priests, how they could arrest him secretly and put him to death, and the anointing of his body for burial by his friends, opens chapter 14. Then comes the ever-sad story of his betrayal at the hand of his own disciple (14:10-11). The betrayal, the celebration of the Passover, and the institution of the Lord's Supper all are crowded into twenty-five short verses. Adding insult to injury, we read of Peter's denial of his Lord (14:26-31, 66-71).

Isaiah's great message was that the Son of God would become the Servant of God in order to die to redeem the world. Mark records how the sufferings of Jesus in Gethsemane and on Calvary fulfilled the prophecies of Isaiah 53.

Jesus was sold for thirty pieces of silver, the price of a slave. He was executed as only slaves were! Yes, Christ was the suffering Servant and died for me! He bore my sins in his own body on the tree.

No reference is made by Mark that in the garden he had the right to summon twelve legions of angels if he so willed. No promise of the kingdom is given to the dying thief on the cross. These claims are made by a King (in Matthew), but they are not mentioned by a Servant.

THE SERVANT EXALTED
MARK 16

After the Servant had given his life *as a ransom for many,* he arose
from the dead. We read again the great commission (16:15), also
recorded in Matthew 28:19-20. Compare the two. In Mark we do
not hear a King say, *I have been given all authority in heaven and in
earth,* as in Matthew. In Mark we see in Jesus' words that his
disciples are to take his place, and he will serve in and through
them. He is yet the Worker, though risen (16:20). The command
rings with urgency of service. Not a corner of the world is to be
left unvisited; not a soul to be left out!

Finally he was received into heaven to sit on the right hand
of God (16:19). He who had taken upon himself the *disguise of a
slave* is now *raised to the heights of heaven* (Philippians 2:7-9). He
is in the place of power, ever making intercession for us. He is
our Advocate.

But Christ is with us. The Servant is always working in and
through us. We are co-workers with him (1 Corinthians 3:9). He
is still working "with us" (16:20). Let us, being redeemed, follow
our Pattern and go forth to serve!

*So, my dear brothers, since future victory is sure, be strong and
steady, always abounding in the Lord's work, for you know that nothing
you do for the Lord is ever wasted* (1 Corinthians 15:58).

SELECTED BIBLE READING

Sunday: The Servant's Coming and Testing (Mark 1:1-20)
Monday: The Servant Working (Mark 1:21–3:35)
Tuesday: The Servant Speaking (Mark 4:1–6:13)
Wednesday: The Servant's Miracles (Mark 6:32–8:26)
Thursday: The Servant's Revelation (Mark 8:27–10:34)
Friday: The Servant's Rejection (Mark 11–12)
Saturday: The Servant's Death and Triumph (Mark 14–16)

CHAPTER 30

UNDERSTANDING LUKE

Luke Portrays Jesus Christ, the Son of Man

The writer of this third Gospel was Luke, Paul's companion (Acts 16:10-24; 2 Timothy 4:11; Colossians 4:14). He was a native of Syria and apparently was not a Jew, for Colossians 4:14 places him with the other Gentile Christians. If this is true, he was the only Gentile writer of the New Testament books.

It is easily seen that Luke was an educated man, a physician, in fact, and a keen observer. We learn from Acts 1:1 that Acts was written by the author of this third Gospel.

Luke's Gospel was written for the Greeks. Beside the Jew and the Roman, the Greek was another who had been preparing for Christ's coming. He differed from the other two in many particulars. He possessed a wider culture and loved beauty, rhetoric, and philosophy. Luke, an educated Greek himself, was well fitted for this task. Luke presents Jesus as the ideal of perfect manliness.

Notice that inspiration does not destroy individuality. In the introduction, verses 1-4, the human element is seen in connection with God's revelation. Luke addressed his Gospel to a man named Theophilus, who is thought to be an influential Christian layman in Greece.

Matthew presents Christ as King, to the Jews.

Mark presents him as the Servant of God, to the Romans.

Luke presents him as the perfect Man, to the Greeks.

This is the Gospel for the sinner. It brings out Christ's compassionate love in becoming man to save man. In Luke we see God manifest as a human being. Luke reveals the Savior as a man with all his sympathies, feelings, and powers—a Savior suited to all. In this Gospel we see the God of glory coming down to our level, entering into our conditions and being subject to our circumstances.

Luke's Gospel is the Gospel of Christ's manhood. This we must know, however: although he mingles with men, he is in sharp contrast to them. He was the solitary God-Man. There was a great difference between Christ as the Son of Man and us as the sons of men, between Christ as Son of God and us as the sons of God. The difference is not merely relative but absolute. Read the words of the angel to Mary: *So the baby born to you will be utterly holy* (1:35). This refers to our Lord's humanity. It is in contrast to ours. Our human nature is impure (Isaiah 64:6), but the Son of God, when he became a man, was "holy." Adam in his unfallen condition was innocent, but Christ was "holy."

In keeping with the theme of his Gospel, Luke gives us the fullest details concerning the miraculous birth of Jesus. We are grateful that our chief testimony concerning this fact should come from a physician. Christ, the Creator of this universe, entered this world like any other man. It is a mystery of mysteries, but enough facts are given to let us see that the predictions were fulfilled.

Luke alone tells the story of the visit of the shepherds (2:8-20).

We learn from this Gospel that as a boy Jesus developed naturally (2:40, 52). As a child he was obedient to Joseph and Mary (2:51). There was no record of unhealthy or supernatural growth. Only Luke tells of Jesus' visit to the Temple when he was twelve years old.

As a man he toiled with his hands, wept over the city, "knelt down and prayed," and was in "agony of spirit." All is strikingly human. Five out of six of the miracles were miracles of healing. Luke alone tells of healing Malchus's ear (22:51).

Luke is the Gospel for the outcast on earth. It is Luke who tells of the good Samaritan (10:33), the tax collector (18:13), the prodigal (15:11-24), Zacchaeus (19:2), and the thief on the cross (23:43). He is the writer who has the most to say for womanhood (ch. 1–2). Luke records Jesus' compassion for the woman of Nain, and the depths of his mercy to the woman who was a sinner. His regard for women and children is shown in 7:46; 8:3; 8:42; 9:38; 10:38-42; 11:27; 23:27.

Luke alone tells us of our Lord seeing the city of Jerusalem and weeping over it, of the bloody sweat in Gethsemane, of the

Lord showing mercy to the dying thief on the cross. Luke alone mentions the walk with the two to Emmaus. He also tells of Jesus leading his disciples out as far as Bethany, and that as he lifted up his hands and blessed them, he was parted from them.

Luke is a poetic book. It opens with a song, "Glory to God!" It closes with a song, "Praising God." The world has been singing ever since. Thank God for such a Gospel! It preserves the precious gems of Christian hymnology:

The Magnificat—Mary's hymn of rejoicing (1:46-55)
Song of Zacharias (1:68-79)
Song of the angels (2:8-14)

Luke speaks more of the prayers of our Lord than any other Gospel writer. Prayer is the expression of human dependence on God. Why is there so much working and activity in the church and yet so little result in positive conversions to God? Why so much running hither and thither and so few brought to Christ? The answer is simple: There is not enough private prayer. The cause of Christ does not need less working but more praying.

The hardest thing the Jews and the early Christians had to learn was that the Gentiles would have full and free admission into the kingdom and into the Church. Simeon taught this (read Luke 2:32). Christ sent the seventy disciples not to the lost sheep of the house of Israel alone, as Matthew says, who wrote especially for the Jews, but "to all the towns and villages" (10:1). All of Jesus' ministry over the eastern side of Jordan was to the Gentiles.

THE PREPARATION OF THE SON OF MAN
LUKE 1:1-4:13

The opening of this beautiful book is significant. A man is to be described, and the writer, Luke, will draw his good friend Theophilus into it. He tells him of his own personal knowledge of his subject and seems to bring something warmly human into his task of presenting the man Christ Jesus.

The opening chapter is characteristic, too. John, as befits his theme, begins, *Before anything else existed, there was Christ with God*. His tone throughout is not of this world. But Luke, so different, begins like a simple story touching men with, *My story begins with a Jewish priest, Zacharias.* As the story progresses we are introduced to human sympathies and relationships that none of the other Gospels tells us. We learn all about the circumstances that accompanied the birth and childhood of the holy baby, and about the one who was sent as his forerunner. The birth of John the Baptist (1:57-80), the angels' song to the shepherds (2:8-20), the circumcision (2:21), the presentation in the Temple (2:22-38), and then the story of the boy Jesus, twelve years of age (2:41-52), are all recorded here.

In chapter 2 Luke notices that *about this time Caesar Augustus, the Roman Emperor, decreed that a census should be taken* (2:1-3). Then comes a fact that we would never find in Matthew, that Joseph (with Mary) *was required to return to his ancestral home* with the rest, who went each to his own city. Luke is not showing here One who is coming down to take the place man then occupied.

God brings to pass what the prophets had spoken. Micah said that Bethlehem was to be the birthplace of Jesus (Micah 5:2-5), for he was of the family of David. But Mary lived in Nazareth, a town one hundred miles away. God saw to it that Imperial Rome sent forth a decree to compel Mary and Joseph to go to Bethlehem just as the child was to be born. Isn't it wonderful how God uses the decree of a pagan monarch to bring to pass his prophecies! God still moves the hand of rulers to do his bidding.

Now look on! We hear the message of the angels to the watching shepherds, but we do not find the kings of the East asking for One "who is the newborn King." The angels tell the poor shepherds, *Don't be afraid. . . . I bring you the most joyful news ever announced, and it is for everyone! The Savior* (not a King) *. . . has been born tonight* (2:10-11).

Why did the Father allow his blessed Son, now a human being, to be born in this lowly place? Luke is the only one of the four evangelists who touches this point concerning his humanity.

Boyhood Days

The child became a strong, robust lad . . . and God poured out his blessings on him (2:40). When he was twelve years old he went up with his parents to Jerusalem to the feast, as every Jewish boy did at that age (2:41-50). *But Jesus stayed behind in Jerusalem. His parents . . . assumed he was with friends.* How characteristic of a boy this is! He was found *sitting among the teachers of Law, discussing deep questions with them.* How intensely human this is!

Yet we read, *he was amazing everyone with his understanding and answers.* Luke says that he was *known for wisdom beyond his years.* Side by side with the human he was always more than a man. We find Jesus' first words here: *Didn't you realize that I would be here at the Temple, in my Father's house?* It is the first self-witness to his deity.

Again we read, *Then he returned to Nazareth with them and was obedient to them*—these earthly parents. *So Jesus grew both tall and wise, and was loved by God and man* (2:51-52). All of these things are peculiar to Jesus as man, and Luke alone records them. It is important that we notice Jesus was a "favorite" in Nazareth. It is not a sign that we are in the grace of God when we are out of favor with man.

Eighteen years of silence followed. We read of John the Baptist, preaching *that people should be baptized to show that they had turned to God and away from their sins, in order to be forgiven* (3:3). Then Jesus came to be baptized. Only Luke tells us that *after the crowds had been baptized, Jesus himself was baptized* (3:21). He is linked with "the crowds." He came down to the level of man. Matthew and Luke record the baptism of Jesus, but John omits it, for Christ is viewed in John as God's only Son. Here only do we read of the age at which our Lord entered his public ministry (3:23).

Genealogy

The genealogy of Jesus in Luke is given at the time of his baptism, and not at his birth (3:23). There are noticeable differences between the genealogies in Luke 3 and Matthew 1. In Matthew we have the royal genealogy of the Son of David through Joseph; here in Luke it is his strictly personal genealogy through Mary. There it is his legal line of descent through Joseph; here it is his lineal descent through Mary. There his genealogy is traced forward from Abraham; here it is followed backward to Adam. Each is significant! Matthew is showing Jesus' relation to the Jew; hence he goes back no further than to Abraham, father of the Jewish nation. But Luke shows his connection with the human race; hence his genealogy is traced back to Adam, the father of the human family.

In Luke our Lord's line is traced back to Adam, and is, no doubt, his mother's line. Notice in Luke 3:23 it does not say Jesus was the son of Joseph. What are the words? *Was known as.* In Matthew 1:16, where Joseph's genealogy is given, we find Joseph was the son of Jacob. Here it says he was of Heli. He could not be the son of two men by natural generation. But notice this carefully—the original Greek record does not state that Heli "was the father of" Joseph, but that Joseph was "of Heli," so it is supposed that Joseph was the son-in-law of Heli. Heli is believed to have been the father of Mary.

The Davidic genealogy goes through Nathan, not Solomon. This, too, is important. The Messiah had to be David's son and heir (2 Samuel 7:12-13; Romans 1:3; Acts 2:30-31), and his offspring. He had to be a literal flesh and blood descendant. Hence Mary had to be a member of David's house as well as Joseph (1:32).

Then Jesus, full of the Holy Spirit, left the Jordan River, being urged by the Spirit out into the barren wastelands of Judea, where Satan tempted him for forty days (4:1-2). Only here do we learn that the Savior was *full of the Holy Spirit* as he returned from his baptism. Then follows the account of his temptation. We may also notice that Luke is the only one to tell us that *Jesus returned to Galilee, full of the Holy Spirit's power* (4:14), showing that the old Serpent had utterly failed to break the fellowship of the Son of Man on earth with his Father in heaven.

As Jesus came forth from the fire of testing in the unabated power of the Holy Spirit, so can we. It is only as we are filled with his Spirit that we can overcome temptation with the power of the Spirit.

The purpose of the temptation was not to discover whether or not Jesus would yield to Satan but to demonstrate that he could not, to show forth the fact that there was nothing in him to which Satan could appeal. Christ could be tried and proven. The more you crush a rose, the more its fragrance is recognized. So the more the devil assaults Christ, the more his perfections will be revealed.

THE MINISTRY OF THE SON OF MAN
LUKE 4:14–19:48

Scan through Luke from 4:14 on and find the events in Jesus' life as they are recorded in succession:

Jesus' ministry in Galilee (4:14–9:50):
Ministry in Nazareth, his hometown (4:16-30)
Preaching in Capernaum (4:31-44)

Tried before Pilate (23:1-26)
Crucifixion (23:27-49)
Burial (23:50-56)
Resurrection (24:1-48)
Ascension (24:49-53)

This list is not complete, of course, but it gives a bird's-eye view of the busy life of the Son of Man on earth. The key word of his ministry is *compassion*.

Following the temptation, when Jesus *came to the village of Nazareth, his boyhood home, he went as usual to the synagogue on Saturday, and stood up to read the Scriptures* (4:16). He went to the place where he had been brought up. Bringing up is an important thing in life. We find that Jesus was accustomed to going to the synagogue on the Sabbath. He had been reared in a godly home.

Jesus here stated that God had appointed him to announce release to the captives and to bring Good News to the poor and brokenhearted (4:18-19). He selected a text from Isaiah 61:2, which announced the object of his whole mission on earth. He was commissioned and sent of God, and divinely qualified for his work. He became man so that he could bring man close to God.

Early in Jesus' ministry we see those of his own hometown determining to kill him (4:28-30). They said, *Isn't this Joseph's son?* This is the first hint of his coming rejection. He proclaimed himself to be the Messiah (4:21). They were angered that he should hint that their Jewish Messiah would also be sent to the Gentiles (4:24-30). They believed God's grace was to be confined to the Jews, and so they were ready to kill him. He refused to work miracles for them because of their unbelief. They attempted to push him over the edge of the hill, but he escaped and went to Capernaum (4:29-31). (By comparing Luke 4:16 with Matthew 13:54, it would seem that he made another visit to Nazareth some months later, but with no success.)

A World Gospel
The Jews hated the Gentiles for their treatment of them when they were captives in Babylon. They regarded them with contempt. They considered them impure and enemies of God. Luke pictures Jesus as tearing down these barriers between Jews and Gentiles, making repentance and faith the only condition of admission to the kingdom. *This message of salvation should be taken*

from Jerusalem to all the nations: There is forgiveness of sins for all who turn to me (24:47). The gospel of Jesus Christ is not just one of the religions of the world. It is the living truth of God, adapted to all nations and to all classes. Read Romans 1:16.

As the Son of Man, Christ is looking at the needs of the Gentiles as he is looking at the needs of all people. In Luke 6, which in substance is the same as the Sermon on the Mount in Matthew 5–7, we find simple, broad moral teachings suited to the needs and wants of all people. What Matthew puts into three chapters, Luke condenses into a few verses, Luke 6:20-49.

Jesus spoke choice words here to his disciples. The beatitudes are a picture of the Christian. "What happiness it is . . . ," each one of them begins. It is not what you are striving to be, but what you are in Christ that brings you joy. The beatitudes are a picture of Christ. They are the picture of the face of Jesus himself, not boastingly but truly describing the perfect Christian.

Disciples Commissioned

When the twelve are commissioned (ch. 9), a broader field of ministry begins. In Matthew we hear the Lord saying, *Don't go to the Gentiles or the Samaritans, but only to the people of Israel—God's lost sheep* (Matthew 10:6). Luke omits this and says, *He sent them away to tell everyone about the coming of the Kingdom of God* (9:2).

Wherever this man Christ Jesus went, a whole multitude followed him and *everyone was trying to touch him, for when they did healing power went out from him and they were cured* (6:19). He gave of himself. Our service must be of this kind.

Jesus Christ, the Teacher

The school—Jesus was a teacher. His disciples were taught and trained to carry on his message (6:12-16).

Entrance requirement—Matriculation in this school is guarded. Requisites are demanded. Yet, on the other hand, entrance is easy. There is no barrier of age, sex, race, or color. Read Luke 14:25-33: *No one can be my disciple who does not carry his own cross and follow me. . . . No one can become my disciple unless he first sits down and counts his blessings—and then renounces them all for me.*

Examinations—Jesus knows the ability and weakness of each student in his school. His examinations are not the same for everyone. He gives individual tests. It is easy to follow Jesus' tests with Peter. In Luke 5 he is testing Peter on obedience (5:5). In Luke 9:18 Jesus sprang an examination upon this impetuous fellow, and Peter gave a startling answer (9:18-20).

Rules to be observed—Right relationship with the Teacher must be maintained at all times. Many think that just because they have at one time entered into a relationship with the great Teacher, this is all that is necessary. But this is false. There must be a constant study of his Word, a laboratory time of prayer (11:1-4), a gymnasium of spiritual exercise (9:59; 5:27).

A practice school—Jesus not only taught them, he made them try out the great facts that he presented (10:1-12, 28, 36-37; 11:35; 12:8-9; 14:25-33; 18:18-26).

The course—The curriculum included a study of the kingdom and the King (7:28; 8:1; 9:2, 11, 62; 13:20-21; 12:32; 19:12, 15; 22:29; 13:28-29; 17:20; 18:29).

THE SUFFERING OF THE SON OF MAN
LUKE 20–23

Jesus was sitting with his disciples around the table, celebrating the feast of the Passover. At this time he instituted what we call the Lord's Supper. Listen to his words: *This is my body, given for you. . . . This wine is . . . the blood I shall pour out to purchase back your souls* (22:19-20). This is different from the account in Mark, which says, *This is my blood, poured out for many.* His love is expressed in such a personal way in Luke.

See the sad record of events in connection with his death. The disciples were arguing over which one of them would have the highest rank in the kingdom (22:24-27). We follow Peter from that moment and we read a lamentable story—one that ends in denial of his Lord (22:54-62).

Look into the Garden of Gethsemane. Jesus was praying, and sweat, like great drops of blood, was on that holy brow. Luke tells us that the angels came to minister to him, the Son of Man. Matthew and Mark omit the mention of the ministering angels.

In the shadow of the garden a band of soldiers was approaching; leading them was Judas. He stepped up to kiss Jesus. Why, yes, he was a disciple. But the Scriptures had said that Jesus would be betrayed by a friend and sold for thirty silver coins (22:47-62; Psalm 41:9; Zechariah 11:12).

Worst of all, his friends deserted him. Peter denied him, and all forsook him and fled except John the beloved. Luke alone tells us that Jesus looked on Peter, the denier, and broke his heart with that look of love.

We follow Jesus into Pilate's hall, then before Herod (23:1-12). We follow along the Via Dolorosa to the cross (23:27-38). Luke omits much that Matthew and Mark record, but he alone gives the prayer (23:13-46).

There were three crosses on Calvary's hill. On one of them was a thief, dying for his crimes. Luke tells us this story, too (23:39-45). The way this thief was saved is the way every sinner must be saved. He believed on the Lamb of God who died on the cross that day to pay the penalty of sin.

The scene closes with the Son of Man crying with a loud voice, *Father, I commit my spirit to you.* The centurion, in keeping with this Gospel, bears this witness: *Certainly this man was innocent.*

THE VICTORY OF THE SON OF MAN
LUKE 24

We turn with great relief from the sorrow and death of the cross, the darkness and gloom of the tomb, to the brightness and glory of the resurrection morning.

Luke gives us a part of the scene that the others leave untold. It is the story of the walk to Emmaus. Jesus showed these disciples that he, as their resurrected Lord, was the same loving, understanding friend he had been before his death.

After Jesus' walk and conversation with them, these disciples urged him to come in and spend the night with them. He revealed who he was when he lifted up those hands that had been pierced on the cross and broke the bread. Then they knew him, but he disappeared. On returning to Jerusalem they found abundant proof of his resurrection. He proved to them that he was a real man with flesh and bones. All these details belong to the Gospel of Luke.

No less than eleven appearances of Jesus are recorded following his resurrection—not only to individuals but to companies and crowds. First, to the women, to Mary, and then to the others (Mark 16; John 20:14); then to Peter alone (24:34); then to two walking to Emmaus (24:13); to ten apostles in Jerusalem (Thomas being absent; John 20:19); and subsequently to the eleven remaining disciples (John 20:26, 29); yet later to seven men at the sea of Tiberias (John 21:1). Yet again Jesus appeared to the whole number of the apostles on a mountain in Galilee (Matthew 28:16); afterward to five hundred Christian brothers at once (1 Corinthians 15:6); then to James (1 Corinthians 15:7).

We are told three times that his disciples touched him after he arose (Matthew 28:9; Luke 24:39; John 20:27). He ate with them, too (24:42; John 21:12-13).

Finally, Jesus appeared to the little group on the Mount of Olives at his ascension. As Jesus put out his hand to bless them, he *began rising into the sky, and went on to heaven* (24:51).

He is no longer a local Christ, confined to Jerusalem, but he is a universal Christ. He could say to his disciples who mourned for him, thinking when gone he could be no more with them, *I am with you always.* How different was the hope and joy of those chosen followers from their despair and shame at the crucifixion! They returned to Jerusalem with great joy.

SELECTED BIBLE READING

Sunday: The Man Who Was "Like Us, His Brothers" (Luke 1–3)

Monday: The Man Who Has "Been through Temptations" (Luke 4–7)

Tuesday: The Man Who "Knows What It Is Like When We Suffer" (Luke 8–12)

Wednesday: The Man Who Was "Sent to Preach" (Luke 13–16)

Thursday: The Man Who "Spoke as One Who Knew the Truth" (Luke 17:1–19:27)

Friday: The Man Who Has "Been through Suffering" (Luke 19:28–23:56)

Saturday: The Man in Resurrection Glory (Luke 24)

CHAPTER 31

UNDERSTANDING JOHN

John Portrays Jesus Christ, the Son of God

The author indicates the purpose of this book in the opening eighteen verses, the prologue, and states it very plainly in John 20:31. John wrote to prove that Jesus was the Christ, the promised Messiah (for the Jews), and the Son of God (for the Gentiles), and to lead believers into a life of divine friendship with him. The key word is *believe*.

The theme of John's Gospel is the deity of Jesus Christ. More here than anywhere else his divine Sonship is set forth. In this Gospel we are shown that the baby of Bethlehem was none other than the "only Son of the heavenly Father." There are numerous evidences and proofs given. Although *he created everything* and *eternal life is in him,* yet he *became a human being and lived here on earth among us.* No man could see God; therefore, Christ came to declare him.

John omits details that the other Gospels record:

No genealogy
No account of his birth—because he was *before anything else existed*
Nothing about his boyhood
Nothing about his temptation. Jesus rather is presented as Christ
   the Lord, not as the One *who had the same temptations we do.*
No transfiguration
No appointing of his disciples

No parables
No account of the ascension
No Great Commission

Yet only in John is Jesus called:

The Creator
The only Son of the Father
The Lamb of God
He is revealed as the great "I AM" (Exodus 3:14).

The author was John, "son of thunder," "the disciple Jesus loved." His father was Zebedee, a well-to-do fisherman; his mother was Salome, a devout follower of the Lord who may have been a sister of Mary, the mother of Jesus (19:25). His brother was James. His position was probably somewhat better than that of the ordinary fisherman.

John may have been about twenty-five years of age when Jesus called him. He had been a follower of John the Baptist. Later, in the reign of Domitian, John the Disciple was banished to Patmos, but afterward he returned to Ephesus and became the pastor of that wonderful church. He lived in that city to an extreme old age, the last of the twelve apostles. During this time he wrote his Gospel concerning the deity of the Christ, coeternal with the Father.

John wrote nearly a generation after the other evangelists, somewhere between A.D. 80 and 100, when all the New Testament was complete except for his own writings. The life and work of Jesus were well known at this time. The gospel had been preached, Paul and Peter had suffered martyrdom, and all the other apostles had died. Jerusalem had been destroyed by the Roman legions under Titus in A.D. 70.

All the Synoptic Gospels—Matthew, Mark, and Luke—were written before A.D. 70, the fateful year of the overthrow of Jerusalem. Already false teachers had arisen, denying that Jesus Christ was the Son of God, come as a human being. John, therefore, wrote emphasizing those facts, gave the witnesses, and recorded the words and works of Jesus that reveal his divine power and glory.

John is more elevated in tone and more exalted in view than the other Gospels. In each of the first three Gospels, Christ is viewed in human relationship with an earthly people, but in

John we find spiritual relationships with a heavenly people.

In Matthew and Luke, "Son of David" and "Son of Man" link Christ to the earth. In John, "Son of God" connects him with the Father in heaven.

As in Luke divine care was taken to guard our Lord's perfection in his humanity, so in John his deity is guarded. In these days of widespread departure from the truth, the deity of Christ Jesus must be emphasized.

In John, Jesus is shown dwelling with God before ever a creature was formed (1:1-2). He is denominated as the only Son of the heavenly Father (1:14). *He is the Son of God* (1:34; etc).

Thirty-five times he speaks of God as "my Father." Besides his own affirmation, six different witnesses avow his deity.

JESUS' DEITY REVEALED

In every chapter we see Jesus' deity:

Nathanael confessed, *You are the Son of God* (1:49)

In the miracle of Cana he demonstrated *his heaven-sent power* (2:11)

In his talk with Nicodemus he said he was the *only Son* (3:16)

In his conversation with the woman of Samaria he stated, *I am the Messiah* (4:26)

To the Jewish leaders he disclosed that *the voice of the Son of God* would give life (5:25)

In the "bread chapter" he stated that he was *the true Bread from heaven* (6:32)

In the "water of life chapter" he proclaimed, *Let him come to me and drink* (7:37)

To the Jewish leaders he disclosed, *I was in existence before Abraham was ever born* (8:58)

At the temple Jesus stated, *I and the Father are one* (10:30)

Martha declared, *You are the Messiah, the Son of God* (11:27)

To the Greeks Jesus stated, *And when I am lifted up [on the cross], I will draw everyone to me* (12:32)

At the supper he said, *You call me "Master" and "Lord,"and you do well to say it, for it is true* (13:13)

To his disciples he stated, *You are trusting God, now trust in me* (14:1)

Likening us to branches on a vine he said, *Apart from me you can't do a thing* (15:5)

In promising the Holy Spirit he said, *I will send him to you* (16:7)
In the "prayer chapter" he said, *Reveal the glory of your Son* (17:1)
In his atonement he had the right to say, *It is finished* (19:30)
In his confession Thomas the doubter exclaimed, *My Lord and my God!* (20:28)
Jesus demanded obedience: *Follow me* (21:22)

Seven Witnesses

The book of John was written so that we would believe that Jesus Christ is God. John brought seven witnesses to the stand to prove this fact. Here they are. Turn to the Scripture and hear each one making his own statement:

What do you say, John the Baptist? *He is the Son of God* (1:34)
What is your conclusion, Nathanael? *You are the Son of God* (1:49)
What do you know, Peter? *You are the holy Son of God* (6:69)
What do you think, Martha? *You are the Messiah, the Son of God* (11:27)
What is your verdict, Thomas? He is *my Lord and my God* (20:28)
What is your statement, John? *He is the Messiah, the Son of God* (20:31)
What do you say of yourself, Christ? *I am the Son of God* (10:36)

Seven Miracles

Besides the seven witnesses in John, we find seven signs or miracles that prove he is God. *We all know that God has sent you to teach us. Your miracles are proof enough of this* were Nicodemus's words (3:2).

Look over these signs that occur throughout the book:

Turning water into wine (2:1-11)
Healing the government official's son (4:46-54)
Healing the man at Bethsaida (5:1-47)
Feeding the five thousand (6:1-14)
Walking on the water (6:15-21)
Healing the blind man (9:1-41)
Raising Lazarus (11:1-57)

The "I AM'S"

There is another proof of his deity running through John. He reveals his God-nature in the "I AMs" of this book. He says:

I AM the Bread of life (6:35)
I AM the Light of the world (8:12)
I AM the Good Shepherd (10:11)
I AM the One who raises the dead (11:25)
I AM the Way—yes, and the Truth and the Life (14:6)
I AM the true Vine (15:1)

Only John records the triumphant shout, "It is finished!" The finished work of salvation was accomplished only by the Son of God (19:30).

John said that he wrote his Gospel so that men would believe that Jesus was the Christ. This part is especially for the Jews, to lead them into a personal belief in the historical Jesus, who came in fulfillment of all the Old Testament prophecies.

In John, Christ the Messiah is revealed. Messiah means "God's anointed One, to come as King."

Nathanael said, *Sir, you are the Son of God—the King of Israel* (1:49).

To the woman at the well, Jesus declared himself to be the long-expected Messiah (4:26).

To Pilate, Jesus testified that he was King.

Three Keys
There are various ways of remembering the contents of the book of John. Someone suggested the following three-part division:

1. What individuals thought about Christ (ch. 1–5)
2. What Christ said about himself (ch. 6–10)
3. What the crowds thought of Christ (ch. 11–20)

Someone else suggested, "There are three keys that unlock John's Gospel":

Back door key (20:31): This key unlocks the whole book. It states the purpose of the Gospel.

Side door key (16:28): At the side, a bit toward the back, we find a second key. At the last supper with his disciples, Jesus revealed this truth to them: *Yes, I came from the Father into the world and will leave the world and return to the Father.* His constant thought was that he used to be with the Father. He came down to earth on an errand and stayed for thirty-three years. He would go back again to his Father.

Front door key (1:11-12): This key hangs right at the very front, outside, down low, within every child's reach. *But to all who received him, he gave the right to become children of God.* This is the great key, the master key to the whole house. Its use permits the front door to be flung wide open. Anyone who believes may enter.

THE GREAT PROLOGUE
JOHN 1:1-18

We open the book of John with this question in mind: "What do you think of Christ?" (See Matthew 22:42). Is he only the world's greatest teacher, or is he actually God? Was he just one of the prophets, or is he the world's Savior whose coming was foretold by the prophets?

All that John will discuss in his book he crowds into these first eighteen verses.

Let us study this Gospel with John's purpose clearly in mind. Read John 20:31 over again. Let us see how the plan is developed and how the purpose is shown as we read the book.

The Son of God
John begins his wonderful record with Jesus the Christ before his incarnation. God did not send his Son into the world so that he could become his Son, for he *is* the eternal Son.

Comparing the first verses of John with the other three Gospels, we see how differently it opens, how exalted is its theme. Omitting the birth of Jesus, the Son of Man, John begins, "Before anything else existed." Read John 1:1-18 carefully. This opening is similar to the book of Genesis. Jesus is portrayed as the Son of God.

Our Lord had no beginning. He was *before anything else existed.* He is eternal. Christ was before all things; therefore Jesus is no part of creation—he *is* the Creator (Colossians 1:16; Hebrews 1:2).

He was with God. He is a Person of the Godhead. He came to tell us about God. As words utter thoughts, so Christ utters God. Words reveal the heart and mind; Christ expresses and shows God. Jesus said to Philip, *If you had known who I am, then you would have known who my Father is* (14:7).

Then comes the wonderful announcement that *he created every-*

thing there is and *eternal life is in him.* Yes, he *became a human being and lived on earth among us.*

The Son of Man

Christ became what he was not previously—a man. But Christ did not cease to be God. He was God-Man. Incarnation comes from two Latin words, *in* and *caro,* meaning "flesh." So Christ was God in the flesh, a human being.

Man had sinned and lost the image of God, so Christ, *the exact likeness of the unseen God* (Colossians 1:15), came to dwell in man. No man could see God; therefore the only Son, who was *the companion of the Father,* came to tell us about him.

Even the witness of John the Baptist is different in John's Gospel. In Matthew he tells of the coming kingdom. In Luke he preaches repentance. In John, the Baptist is a witness to the Light so that all men might believe (1:7). He points to "the Lamb of God" (1:32-36). These are all characteristics of this Gospel.

Jesus was God himself in human form, coming to earth. Jesus was the Witness of the Father to men. Jesus knew the Father. He had lived with him from the beginning. He came down to tell what he knew. He wanted people to know the Father as he knew him.

He told about God by his words, his deeds, his character, his love, and most of all by dying on the cross and rising the third day. All this was a witnessing, a telling.

How was Christ received? Read John 1:11. He presented himself as King to his people, but he was rejected. All through the book we see Jesus dividing the crowds. As he came out and spoke the truth, the crowds listened. Some believed and some rejected. Tragedy indeed! But not all rejected him. John presents the results of faith.

The Way of Salvation

What we must do for salvation (1:12): Believe and receive. Result: you become a child of God.

What not to count on for salvation: Sometimes the way to better understand what a thing is, is to find out what it is not. John tells us what salvation is not: *Not a physical rebirth resulting from human passion or plan—but from the will of God* (1:13). These things are what people are counting on today for eternal life. The "new birth" makes us "sons of God" by the power of the Holy Spirit. God comes down and redeems us, if we will only believe and receive him as Savior and Lord.

PUBLIC MINISTRY
JOHN 1:19–12:50

When John the Baptist stepped into the scene, the great drama of John's Gospel began. *Truly, of all men ever born, none shines more brightly than John the Baptist,* Jesus declared. He was the forerunner of the Messiah. In this Gospel, the Baptist is not described. He merely bears his witness that Jesus is the Messiah (1:18-34).

A delegation of Jews and priests were sent to ask John who he claimed to be. He told them he was not the Messiah, not even Elijah or any other prophet Moses spoke of, but merely *a voice from the barren wilderness, shouting as Isaiah prophesied, "Get ready for the coming of the Lord."*

The next day, on seeing Jesus, John pointed to him and said, *Look, there is the Lamb of God.*

Then John the Baptist indicated that he knew that Jesus was the Messiah because he saw the Holy Spirit descending. John adds, *I saw it happen to this man, and I therefore testify that he is the Son of God.*

Jesus Gives Signs
Jesus' disciples were convinced of his deity by his first miracle, turning water into wine. He spoke and it was so. This was one of the big factors that brought faith into the hearts of the disciples. This was the first "sign" to prove that he was the Messiah (2:1-11).

There was only one place where Jesus could start his ministry—in Jerusalem, the capital city. Just before the Passover the Lord entered the Temple, and taking a whip made of ropes as a badge of his authority, he cleansed the sanctuary, which he declared was his Father's House. By this act he claimed to be the very Son of God.

When the rulers asked for a sign to prove Jesus' authority after he had cleansed the Temple and ordered out the moneychangers, Jesus said, *Destroy this sanctuary, and in three days I will raise it up.* The rulers were shocked, for it had taken forty-six years to build this edifice. *But by this sanctuary he meant his body,* John explains. The supreme proof of Christ's deity is the resurrection (2:12-22).

Jesus gave to Nicodemus the wonderful teachings about eternal life, his love, and the new birth (3:1-21). Nicodemus was a moral, upright man; yet Christ said to him, *Unless you are born again, you can never get into the Kingdom of God.* If Jesus had said this to the woman of Samaria, Nicodemus would have agreed with him. She was not a Jew and could not expect anything on the ground of her birth as a Samaritan. But Nicodemus was a Jew by birth and he had a right to expect something on this basis. But it was to him that Jesus said, *Unless you are born again, you can never get into the Kingdom of God.* Have you been born again?

Like the Jews of his day, Nicodemus knew God's law but knew nothing of God's love. He was a moral man. He recognized Jesus as a Teacher, but he did not know him as a Savior. This is just what people do today. They put Jesus at the head of the list of the teachers of the world, but they do not worship him as God.

Jesus revealed to one woman the truth of his Messiahship. This story gives us Christ's estimate of a single soul. He brought this immoral woman face-to-face with himself and showed her what kind of a life she was leading. Her loose view of marriage is not unlike the view taken today by many people. Christ did not condemn her or pass judgment upon her, but he did reveal to her that he was the only One who could meet her needs.

Christ revealed the wonderful truth to her that he is the water of life. He alone can satisfy. The wells of the world bring no satisfaction. Men are trying everything, but they still are unhappy and restless. Did the woman believe Christ? What did she do? Her actions spoke louder than any words could have. She went back and by her simple testimony brought a whole town to Christ (4:1-42).

In healing the son of the government official, Jesus gave another sign of his deity. During his interview with the official, Jesus brought him to an open confession of Jesus as Messiah—yes, and his entire household believed, too (4:46-54).

The miracle of the feeding of five thousand was an acted parable. Jesus himself was the Bread from heaven. He wanted to tell them that he will give satisfaction and joy to all who put their trust in him (6:35).

The people wanted to make Christ their King because he could feed them. How like people today! They long for someone who can give them food and clothing. But Christ would not be King on their grounds. He dismissed the excited crowd and went up into the mountains. People were disappointed that he would not be a political leader, and so *many of his disciples turned away and deserted him* (6:66).

The people were divided because of Jesus (7:40-44). We find that unbelief was developing into actual hostility, but in his true followers faith was growing. Some people said, "He is a good man." Others said, "Not so." People must say one or the other today when facing Christ's claims. Either he is God or an imposter. There is no middle ground.

The healing of the blind man led Jesus to reveal to this fellow who he was. When "they threw him out" because of his confession of Christ, Jesus gave a great discourse on the Good Shepherd (ch. 10). Notice the accusations of blasphemy they made of Christ when he said, *I and the Father are one.* They *picked up stones to kill him* (10:31). But in the face of all this criticism and opposition, his words produced the opposite result as well: *Many came to the decision that he was the Messiah* (10:42)!

The raising of Lazarus is the final "sign" of John's Gospel. The other Gospels give the raising of Jairus's daughter and the son of the widow of Nain. But in this case Lazarus had been dead four days. In reality, would it be any harder for God to raise one than the other? Nevertheless, it had a profound effect on the leaders (11:47-48). The great claim that Jesus made for himself to Martha is recorded here: *I am the one who raises the dead and gives them life again. Anyone who believes in me, even though he dies like anyone else, shall live again. He is given eternal life for believing in me and shall never perish. Do you believe this, Martha?* (11:25-26).

This scene closes with Jesus' triumphant entry into Jerusalem. His public ministry had come to an end. It is recorded that many of the Jewish leaders believed on him without making an open confession.

Jesus' Startling Claims
Claims to be equal with God: Jesus called God *my Father* (5:17). The Jews knew what he meant. He made *himself equal with God*, they said. They knew that he claimed God as his Father in a sense in which God is not the Father of any other man.

Claims to be light of the world: *I am the Light of the world. So if you follow me, you won't be stumbling through the darkness, for living light will flood your path* (8:12).

Claims to be eternal with God: *The absolute truth is that I was in existence before Abraham was ever born* (8:58). This claim of eternity with God was unmistakable. He was either the Son of God or a deceiver. No wonder the Jews "picked up stones to kill him."

PRIVATE MINISTRY
JOHN 13–17

Here we leave the crowds behind and follow Jesus as he lived the last week of his life on earth before his crucifixion. We call it Passion Week.

Sunday—the triumphant entry into Jerusalem
Monday—the cleansing of the Temple
Tuesday—the conflicts in the Temple
Evening—the discourse on the Mount of Olives
Thursday—preparation for the Passover
Evening—the Last Supper with his disciples

The Last Evening Together
Last words are always important. Jesus was leaving his disciples and was giving them his last instructions. This passage, John 13–17, is called the Most Holy Place of the Scriptures. Prayerfully read it all at one sitting.

The Jews had rejected Jesus completely. Now he gathered his own around him in an upper room and talked with them before he departed from them. He wanted to comfort his disciples, for he knew how hard it would be for them when he was gone. They would be like sheep without a shepherd.

It is wonderful that Jesus selected and loved men like these. They seem to be a collection of nobodies, with the exception of Peter and John. But he loved them. One of Jesus' specialties is to make somebodies out of nobodies. This is what he did with his first group of followers, and this is what he has continued to do down through the centuries.

What a picture we have in John 13:1-17! Jesus, the Son of God, wrapped with a towel, a basin of water in his hands, was washing his disciples' feet! He wants us to serve in the same spirit. He teaches us that greatness is always measured by service. There is no loving others without living for others. Christ said, *To be the greatest, be a servant.* The biggest merchant in the city is the one who serves the greatest public.

Jesus foretold his betrayal by Judas (13:18-30), and Judas went out into the night. It was night in Judas's heart, too. Fellowship brings light; sin brings darkness. What a pitiable picture Judas is. His opportunities of knowing Jesus were unsurpassed, but he rejected the Lord. This is what unbelief can do. Belief means life; unbelief means death.

After announcing his going, the Lord gave his disciples "a new commandment" that they love one another. *Your strong love for each other will prove to the world that you are my disciples.* Discipleship is tested not by the creed you recite, not by the hymns you sing, not by the ritual you observe, but by the fact that you love one another. The measure in which Christians love one another is the measure in which the world believes in them and their Christ. It is the final test of discipleship. He mentions this "new commandment" again in John 15:12.

Christ's Answer for a Life Beyond

I am going to prepare . . . then I will come again and get you (14:2-3). This is Jesus' cure for heart trouble—faith in God. We see there is no break between chapters 13 and 14. Jesus went right on with his discourse. How many hearts have been put at ease and how many eyes have been dried by these words in John 14!

Jesus had spoken of his Father, but now he spoke of the other Person of the Godhead, the Holy Spirit. Since Christ was to go away, he would send the Comforter to live with them. This is a wonderful promise for the child of God! Jesus repeated the promise in 15:26 and 16:7. Look them up. Few know of this Presence in their lives. It is by his power that we live. Never call the Holy Spirit "it." He is a Person, One of the Godhead.

I am leaving you with a gift—peace of mind and heart! This is Christ's legacy to us. The only peace we can enjoy in this world is his peace.

Jesus revealed the real secret of the Christian life to his disciples in John 15. Live in Christ. He is the source of life. Live in Christ as the branch lives in the vine. The branch cannot sever itself from the trunk and join itself to the trunk whenever it wants to. It must remain on the vine to bear fruit. This is the picture of our lives in Christ. Live and walk in Christ and you will bear fruit. If you are not living in Christ, the fruit will soon disappear.

After he ended his talk with the eleven disciples, Jesus spoke to the Father (ch. 17). The disciples listened to his loving and solemn words. How thrilled they must have been as he told the Father how much he loved them and how he cared for them! He mentioned everything about himself that he had taught them. He would keep them, he would make them pure and holy, he would make them one, and he would let all his children share in his glory some day.

If you want to know the beauty and depth of these wonderful words, kneel and let the Son of God lead in prayer as you read John 17 aloud.

Let us look at the teaching about the Holy Spirit as given by John:

1. *The Incoming Spirit* (3:5): This is the beginning of the Christian life, the new birth by the Spirit. We are born by the Spirit into the family of God.
2. *The Indwelling Spirit* (4:14): He fills us with his presence and brings us joy.
3. *The Overflowing Spirit* (7:38-39): *Rivers of living water shall flow from the inmost being of anyone who believes in me*—not just little streams of blessing, but rivers—Mississippis and Amazons—if the Holy Spirit dwells within us.
4. *The Witnessing Spirit* (ch. 14–16): He speaks through us. This is the particular task of the Christian through the Holy Spirit —to testify of Christ.

SUFFERING AND DEATH
JOHN 18–19

Immediately following his prayer Jesus went into the Garden of Gethsemane, *fully realizing all that was going to happen to him.* The change from the scene in the upper room is like going from warmth to cold, from light to darkness. Only two hours had passed since Judas left the supper table. Now we see him betraying his best Friend. Remember, Judas did not have to betray his Lord to fulfill prophecy or carry out God's plan. Nothing happens because it was prophesied to happen. It was prophesied because it was going to happen. No man ever had to sin to carry out any of God's plan.

The time had come! The mission of our Lord on earth was ended. The greatest work of Christ remained to be done. He was to die that he might glorify the Father and save the sinful world. He came to give his life as "a ransom for many." Christ came into the world by a manger and left it by the door of the cross.

Jesus was now ready to give the real sign of his authority in answer to the challenge in 2:18-19: *If you have this authority from God, show us a miracle to prove it.* He answered, *Destroy this sanctuary and in three days I will raise it up!*

We see Jesus always poised, always gentle. He knew his time had come. He was not surprised when he heard the soldiers approach. He stepped forward to meet them. The men retreated and fell before the majesty of his look.

Follow him, bound as a captive, to the hall of the High Priest. Jesus was the One in command of the situation all through this terrible drama. He "stepped forward" (18:4), a voluntary sacrifice. He deliberately tasted death for every man.

Almost as sad as Judas was Peter, the deserter in the hour of need, denying three times that he had any connection with his best Friend! This is a lesson for us—overconfidence. Poor Peter is to be pitied, for he really loved the Master.

Peter did not know that the supreme trial of his life would come in the question of a servant girl. It is so often this way. We lock and bolt the main door, but the thief breaks into a tiny window we hadn't thought of. We would die at the stake but deny Christ in our speech.

All the disciples but John deserted Jesus in the hour of his greatest need. (Peter denied Jesus but he stayed close by.) In that fleeing nine is James of the "inner circle," Nathanael the honest one, and Andrew the personal worker. Yet here they were, running pell-mell down the road together, away from their Friend. A sorry sight! But wait! Don't start blaming them. Suppose you look up and see where you are. Are you following Jesus closely? Remember, majorities aren't always right. Be sure you are right! Can Christ count on you?

Jesus has come to the supreme, crowning act of his life on earth. It was not a crisis but a climax. He came to earth, he had said, *to give my life a ransom for many.*

Finally the make-believe trials are over. It is morning at last, and yet it seems like night. It is the world's blackest hour. The courtyard is deserted. The fire at which Peter warmed himself is only gray ashes. The soldiers' jeers and Herod's sneers and Pilate's vacillation are over.

The brief interval between Peter's denial and Jesus' climbing the hill to Golgotha was crowded with incidents. The night trial before Caiaphas and the Sanhedrin probably preceded the last denial of Peter. Then came the awful treatment up to the morning session of the Sanhedrin.

Often the cruel scourging of the Romans was so severe that prisoners died under the torturing blows. The crown of thorns that was placed on his head was only another act of cruel torture. When he comes again he will wear many crowns (Revelation 19:12).

Finally Pilate led him forth and said, *Behold the man!* What a sight! To see the Creator of this universe, the Light and Life of the world, the Holy One treated so! But Satan energized the rulers of the Jews, and they cried, *Crucify! Crucify! . . . He called himself the Son of God!*

At the cross we have hate's record at its worst and love's record at its best. People hated so much that they put Christ to death. God loved so much that he gave people life.

Our religion is one of four letters instead of two. Other religions say, "Do." Christianity says, "Done." Our Savior has done all on the cross. He bore our sins and when he gave up his life he said, *It is finished!* This was the shout of a conqueror. He had finished man's redemption. Nothing was left for man to do. Has the work been done in your heart?

Jesus was crucified on Golgotha, the place known as "The Skull." He is crucified there today—in men's minds. They crucify him afresh and put him to an open shame. Salvation is costly. *Christ died for our sins* (1 Corinthians 15:3). It cost him his life.

VICTORY OVER DEATH
JOHN 20–21

On the third day the tomb was empty! The grave clothes were all in order. Jesus had risen from the dead, but not as others had done. When Lazarus came forth he was bound in his grave clothes. He came out in his natural body. But when Jesus came forth, his natural body was changed to a spiritual body. The changed body came right out of its linen wrappings and left them, as the butterfly leaves the chrysalis shell. Read John 20:6-8.

Jesus' appearances, eleven in all after his resurrection, helped his disciples to believe that he was God. Read the confession of the sixth witness, Thomas the doubter (20:28). Jesus wanted every doubt to be removed from each one of his disciples. They had to carry out his Great Commission and bear the gospel into all the world (20:21).

Jesus gave Peter, the disciple who denied him three times, an opportunity to confess him three times. He restored him to full privileges of service again. Christ only wants those who love him to serve him. If you love him you must serve him. No one who loves Christ can help but serve.

What are Jesus' last words in this Gospel? *Follow me.* This is his word to each one of us. May we all follow him in loving obedience "until he returns!"

SELECTED BIBLE READING

Sunday: Christ Became a Human Being (John 1)
Monday: Christ Loved So Much (John 3)
Tuesday: Christ Satisfies (John 4)
Wednesday: Christ, the Bread of Life (John 6)
Thursday: Christ, the Light of the World (John 9)
Friday: Christ, Our Shepherd (John 10)
Saturday: Christ Promises the Comforter (John 14)

CHAPTER 32

UNDERSTANDING ACTS

Acts Portrays Jesus Christ, the Living Lord

Luke, in his Gospel, shows what Christ began to do on earth; Acts shows what he continued to do by the Holy Spirit through his disciples.

The ascension of our Lord is the closing scene in Luke. It is the opening fact in Acts (Luke 24:49-51; Acts 1:10-11).

GOSPELS AND ACTS

The Gospels set forth the Son of Man, who came to die for our sins. Acts shows the coming of the Son of God in the power of the Holy Spirit.

The Gospels tell of the crucified and risen Savior. Acts portrays him as the ascended and exalted Lord and Leader.

In the Gospels we hear Christ's teachings. In Acts we see the effect of his teachings on the apostles.

Acts is not a record of the acts of the apostles, as no extensive accounts are given of any apostles except Peter and Paul. It records the acts of the Holy Spirit through the apostles. His name is mentioned about seventy times. Look for some work of the Holy Spirit in every chapter of this book.

You will receive power to testify about me is the heart of the book of Acts. Salvation comes to this world through Christ alone (4:12); hence people must know him. Christ's plan includes us. Are you testifying for Christ? If not, why not? It is true that Christ alone can save the world, but Christ cannot save this world alone. If you have no testimony for Christ, look into your heart. "For a man's heart determines his speech" (Matthew 13:34).

Christ told his disciples that he would send the Spirit, and he *will tell you all about me. And you also must tell everyone about me, because you have been with me from the beginning* (John 15:26-27). Christ's promise was fulfilled on the Day of Pentecost when he poured forth the Holy Spirit upon the disciples (2:16-17, 33). From that moment, as they told everyone about the Savior, the Holy Spirit bore witness at the same time, and multitudes were brought to the Lord.

It is a wonderful thing to know that when the Spirit prompts you to speak to someone about Christ he has been working in that heart and making it ready to receive what you say. There is a perfect example of this in Acts 8 where Philip was sent to speak to the Ethiopian. Read this ever-thrilling story!

What was the result of the first sermon on the Day of Pentecost (ch. 2)?

In each widening circle of influence we find a marked outpouring of the Holy Spirit. Isn't it amazing that in one generation the apostles moved out in every direction and preached in every nation of the then known world (Colossians 1:23)?

The infant church was slow to realize the extent of their commission. They confined their preaching to Jerusalem until persecution drove them out. The blood of Stephen, the first Christian martyr, proved to be the seed of the growing church.

The book of Acts opens with the preaching of the gospel in Jerusalem, the metropolis of the Jewish nation. It closes with the gospel in Rome, the true metropolis of world power.

The book tells of the extension of the gospel to the Gentiles. All through the Old Testament we find God dealing with the Jews. In the New Testament we find him working among all nations.

No doubt Acts is the best guidebook to missions that has ever been written. We find in it the motive for missions. The believers' one aim was to bring people to a saving knowledge of Jesus Christ. He was their one theme, and the Word of God their one weapon.

We find the first church pursuing a definite program in carrying out its plans. They chose some great radiating population center for a base from which the influence of their work might spread to the surrounding area.

The disciples were simple, straightforward, and successful. They depended entirely upon the power of God, through his Spirit. They moved with a zeal that could not be quenched and a courage that was unflinching.

POWER FOR WITNESSING
A C T S 1 – 2

What a wonderful forty days after the resurrection of Jesus the disciples spent with the Lord before his ascension! How anxious they were to hear his last words of instruction! He *talked to them about the Kingdom of God.* It was then that *he told them not to leave Jerusalem until the Holy Spirit came upon them in fulfillment of the Father's promise* (1:3-4).

Acts 1:1-26 is an introduction to the rest of the book. It tells of:

The Great Commission (1:6-8)
The ascension (1:2, 9)
The promise of Christ's return (1:10-11)

The disciples still were not satisfied as to the time when Christ would set up his kingdom on earth. They still expected a kingdom that would give them political independence and establish them in a place of leadership in the world (1:6). What was Jesus' answer (1:7)?

One day *Jesus led them out along the road to Bethany, and lifting his hands to heaven, he blessed them* (Luke 24:50). He told them their power was not to be political but spiritual.

After he had spoken his last words to his disciples (1:8), he was taken up *and disappeared into a cloud.* Think of so great an event told in such a few words! The Father took his Son back to glory.

Christ Will Return
Jesus has gone away to heaven, and some day, just as he went, he will return! (1:11). How will his "return" be, as spoken of here? Will

it be merely at death? Is it merely as he comes to dwell in our hearts? No. The promise is that he will come "just as he went." If this is so, we should examine how he went. Then we will know how he will come back. See the Scriptures. It will be:

Personal (1 Thessalonians 4:16)
Visible (Revelation 1:7)
Bodily (Matthew 24:30)
Local (Luke 24:50)

Picture the disciples as they returned from the Mount of Olives to Jerusalem. They went into "an upstairs room." It might have been the very same room where Jesus had eaten the Last Supper with them (Luke 22:12). They *held a prayer meeting* that *went on for several days.* Jesus had told them to stay in Jerusalem until they received power from heaven (Luke 24:49). Even though they had been three years in training with the Lord, they needed the presence of the Holy Spirit, whom Jesus said he would send to empower them. They had proved to be a weak lot in themselves.

Christ had told them not to leave Jerusalem but to wait there. It would have been natural for them to flee from that place where their Lord had been crucified and to go back to Galilee. But Christ had said, "Stay at Jerusalem," because it was the center of widest influence. We cannot always choose our place of service.

Next in importance to the coming of the Lord Jesus Christ to this earth is the coming of the Holy Spirit. The church was born on that Day of Pentecost. Become familiar with this account given in Acts 2:1-13. Pentecost was one of the most popular of the feasts, and Jerusalem would be crowded with pilgrims from everywhere. It was fifty days after the crucifixion. From this time Pentecost was not to be a Jewish feast but the dawn of a new day, the birthday of the church of Christ.

The scene opens with the disciples assembled together, with their hearts fixed on Christ, waiting for his promise to be fulfilled. The Holy Spirit himself descended that day. Luke does not say there was a wind, but sound was a symbol, as were the "tongues of fire." The mighty wind represented heavenly power. The luminous tongues conveyed the symbol of fire, and tongues expressed power to testify. See the results of this advent in Acts 2:6, 12. Fire is a symbol of divine presence. It illumines; it purifies.

The Holy Spirit at Pentecost

The Spirit fell on them (2:1-3). The Spirit came in them (2:4). The Spirit worked through them (2:41-47).

They were filled with the Holy Spirit and thus endowed for special service. They not only were enabled to preach in power but to speak in the different languages represented that day at Jerusalem (2:2-4). Was the speaking in new languages a jargon not understood by anyone, or were those present able to understand and benefit (2:6)?

The wonderful thing about Pentecost was not the roaring of the mighty windstorm or the tongues of fire, but the disciples being filled with the Holy Spirit so they could testify to others. If we do not have the desire to tell others of Christ, it is evident that we do not know the fullness of the Holy Spirit.

Do not think that at this Pentecost the Holy Spirit came for the first time to the world. All through the Old Testament we see accounts of how he had been guiding people and giving them strength. Now the Spirit was to use a new instrument, the church, which was born on that very day.

They stood there amazed and perplexed (2:12). People by nature are unbelieving. Is it not a great exhibition of God's grace when people truly come to believe God and accept his Word?

Some mocked. *They're drunk, that's all!* (2:13-15). People always try to explain away the miracles of God on natural grounds. But rationalism can never give a reasonable explanation of anything that is divine. Also, it was only nine in the morning, and no Jew could touch wine till then. Read Peter's defense against this false charge in Acts 2:15-21.

Peter's Sermon

The theme of this first Christian sermon was that Jesus is the Messiah, as shown by his resurrection.

Peter is the outstanding figure in the first twelve chapters of Acts. The real power of the Holy Spirit was shown when Peter, the humble fisherman, rose to speak and three thousand souls were saved! How can we account for cowardly Peter's boldness as he stood that day to preach before a crowd on the streets of Jerusalem? What was the secret of Peter's ministry?

It is a serious thing to charge men with murder; yet Peter did just this (2:36). Will he get away with it? Will he be stoned? The last verses in chapter 2 answer the question (2:37-47).

What a church was this First Church of Jerusalem, organized with a membership of three thousand on the Day of Pentecost! *Each day God added to them all who were being saved* (2:47). This is the real objective of the church. Are we seeing it today in our churches?

Just as marvelous as the gift of tongues was the daily life of this first church. It is not surprising that *the whole city was favorable to them* and that additions were made *each day*.

These first Christians were "regular Christians" (2:44-47):

Regular in churchgoing—*They worshiped together*
Regular in church giving
Regular in the church's mission

WITNESSING IN JERUSALEM
ACTS 3-7

Chapter 3 opens at The Beautiful Gate of the Temple. Peter healed an incurable cripple, lame from birth, who had been carried daily to this place to beg for his living. The miracle attracted the notice of the Jewish leaders and resulted in the first real opposition to the church.

When a great crowd had gathered around the lame man who had been so miraculously healed, Peter took advantage of the circumstances to preach his second recorded sermon. He did not spare the Jews. Again he told them that Christ, whom they had crucified, was the long-promised Messiah. So powerful were the words of Peter and John that a total of five thousand men now turned to this Christ!

The leaders were aroused because the apostles taught the people that this Jesus, whom they had crucified, had risen from the dead, and would appear again (4:2). They commanded the apostles not to preach, but opposition made the church thrive. Opposition should never be a matter of amazement, not even a matter of surprise to any Christian. The work of the Spirit is always a signal for Satan to work. Whenever the Spirit comes to bless, the Adversary comes to curse. But martyrdom is an aid to the church, and whenever the truth is faithfully preached, fruit will be brought forth (see 4:3-4).

As soon as Peter and John were released by the rulers they sought their friends, reported their experiences, and united in prayer and praise. The church must expect opposition, but in all circumstances we can find courage and help in God. *After this prayer, the building where they were meeting shook and they were all filled with the Holy Spirit and boldly preached God's message* (4:31).

We find that this kind of preaching brought unity in the church. *All the believers were of one heart and mind* (4:32). They went out to tell that "Jesus is risen" (4:33). Let us tell it out! Dying men need it; the day demands it!

No one was compelled to part with his personal possessions. It was not expected of him. If he brought what he had it was a purely voluntary act. The sharing of property was voluntary, not obligatory; individual, not general; confined to Jerusalem; temporary; limited to believers.

The church became so unselfish that many sold all they had and gave it to the apostles to distribute "to others in need." But even this act of love and generosity was open to abuse and deception. Barnabas's liberality was an illustration of the spirit of love. Ananias and Sapphira were an illustration of deception in that they deceived themselves and the apostles as well. But the Holy Spirit revealed the truth about it all. Ananias and Sapphira wanted glory without paying the price. They wanted honor without honesty. They were punished with instant death, for while claiming to give all to God, they had kept back part (5:4-5).

As Christians, we claim to give all to Christ. Complete surrender is the condition he sets down for discipleship. "Forsake all and follow me" is his condition (see Luke 14:33). Do we hold anything back from Christ? Are we hypocrites in our testimony?

The power in the apostles' story was in the fact that their lives fitted in with the life of their risen Christ. "You've got to show me" is the attitude of the world today. Those early Christians did show the world. Do you show by your life and conduct that you are a Christian?

When miracles were performed for the people, the crowds came to see. When the Holy Spirit was in the midst, the people saw the power of God. The same is true today. When churches present Christ in his winsomeness and the Holy Spirit in his power, the people will come. Christ draws all people to himself.

Miracles commonly result in converts. Look in this book of Acts. When the miracle of tongues appeared, the people thronged to the place (ch. 2). When Peter healed the man at The Beautiful Gate, *they all rushed out to Solomon's Hall* (3:11). When the miracle of judgment came upon Ananias and Sapphira, *more and more believers were added to the Lord, crowds both of men and women* (5:14). We find instances of this all through the book.

Thousands of articles have been written as to how to put people to work in the churches. There will be plenty of service in the church when we give place to the Holy Spirit. The Spirit-filled church will be a serving church.

The High Priest and his relatives and friends . . . arrested the apostles and put them in the public jail (5:17-18). Again we see that the wonderful work of the apostles aroused the opposition of the Sanhedrin (a court of seventy religious rulers). A few unlearned fishermen had risen up to teach, and crowds were listening and following after them; hence the religious leaders were disturbed. Even though the apostles were beaten and prohibited to preach, we find them rejoicing that they were counted *worthy to suffer dishonor for his name!* We find their boldest words in this statement: *We must obey God rather than men* (5:29). Is this the conviction of your life?

Let us have the spirit of these apostles! Let us not be discouraged when opponents multiply.

A meeting of the church was called, and seven members were elected as deacons. There were two offices in the church now. One was to "administer a feeding program," to care for the needy. The other was to spend time "in prayer, preaching, and teaching."

The first two deacons named were Stephen and Philip (6:5). These two men were mighty in their influence over the church, perhaps more than any others besides Peter and Paul.

The opposition was centered around Stephen. Read the experiences as recorded in Acts 6–7. Stephen was just a layman. Like thousands of other laymen since his time he *did spectacular miracles* because he was *full of faith and the Holy Spirit's power* (6:8). We have a record of only one day of his life—the last. What an account it is! It is not the length of time we live that counts, but how we live. Someone has said, "A Christian is always on duty." This means that every minute of his life is important and under God's direction.

The layman Stephen's life and death had an incalculable effect on the history of the world through his influence on Saul of Tarsus. Who can tell what your life may do through your influence on some friend?

The leaders in the synagogue were not *able to stand against*

Stephen's wisdom and spirit (6:10). Their anger flared into murderous hatred. Stephen was the first martyr of the Christian church.

WITNESSING IN JUDEA AND SAMARIA
ACTS 8–12

The disciples had been witnesses in Jerusalem, but Jesus had told them they must go into Judea and Samaria.

If you were quite sure that you would lose your life by remaining in your own hometown but would be safe in some nearby village, do you think you would go to that village? This is the very problem that faced the early church in Jerusalem. There were religious leaders there who thought they were doing God's will when they tried to wipe out Christianity by killing the Christians. Paul said: *I used to believe that I ought to do many horrible things to the followers of Jesus of Nazareth* (26:9).

Paul really began his work of spreading the gospel then but he didn't know it. Read Acts 8:3. He thought he was stamping out Christianity. Instead, he was spreading it. Just laugh when you see anyone opposing Christianity. Persecution always has spread Christianity like wind spreads fire. This has been true all down through the centuries since our Lord lived on the earth.

See what kind of a church this early church was. *But the believers who had fled Jerusalem went everywhere preaching the Good News about Jesus* (8:4).

This is the reason the gospel spread at first. What commission did the disciples have? *Go into all the world and preach the Good News.* How many did Jesus train for his work? Just twelve, and one of them forsook him.

Well, here were the rest of the Twelve, sitting down at Jerusalem and "all the world" needing the Good News. Saul's persecution, like the confusion of languages at the tower of Babel, scattered the Christians throughout the world. Cowardice did not prompt them to flee, for everyplace we find them preaching the Good News.

Philip, the Evangelist
Philip (not the apostle), one of the seven who had been chosen as a deacon (6:5), was an evangelist. He had settled in Samaria as a result of the persecution. Jesus had said, *You will receive*

power to testify about me . . . in Samaria. Philip preached Christ.
Crowds were following him in his evangelistic campaign. But
God called him to leave his successful work and *go over to the
road that runs from Jerusalem through the Gaza desert* (8:26). Philip
obeyed and left, and on the way he met an Ethiopian. "By
chance," you say? When you are in the will of God, things do
not just happen. No friend crosses your path by accident. No
joy or sorrow comes into your life except by God's permission.

This story brings up the question as to which brings the larger
results—preaching to great crowds or telling people individually
about the Lord. Some people think that winning just one person
at a time to Christ would be a slow process, but listen to this!

There are over 230 million people in the United States. Suppose
you were the only Christian among these 230 million today. You
win one soul of the 230 million today. Then tomorrow the two
of you win one soul each, for Christ. On the following day each
one of you four do the same; next day the eight of you win one
apiece. If each of these Christians and the newly won Christians
were to win one soul a day to Christ, how long would it take to
win 230 million? Here is a startling fact. Just less than one month
from the day the first one began!

Philip's convert no doubt preached the gospel in Africa. There
is nothing to show that Africa previously had any knowledge of
the Son of God. The Good News was on its way to the ends of
the earth.

Saul

The first mention of Saul is at Stephen's death. Stephen's martyrdom seemed to have inflamed this persecutor of the church.
Saul was struggling with an aroused conscience. He knew he
was in the wrong, but he wouldn't give up. This is why Jesus
told him in his vision, *You are only hurting yourself* (26:14).

Saul made havoc of the church! The more moral and intelligent
a man is, the more harm he can do when controlled by Satan.

The story of Saul's conversion is one of the most thrilling
accounts in history. Become familiar with this great story. He
was a man *threatening with every breath and eager to destroy every
Christian* (9:1-2). Then we find that he *went at once to the synagogue
to tell everyone there the Good News about Jesus—that he is indeed the
Son of God* (9:20).

At every step of his three great missionary journeys, Paul made

known Christ's will with unmistakable clarity. There is no doubt
that Paul holds the most important place of any follower of Christ
in the New Testament. He was converted and made an apostle
by Christ himself. It was to him Christ committed the doctrine
of the church. To what people was Paul especially sent? He was
the apostle to the Gentiles, as Peter had been to the Jews.

Peter
What had Peter done since Pentecost? It is not only what a person
believes but what he is doing about it that counts. Christ had
told Peter that he was to testify. Peter helped start the first church,
worked miracles, and baptized thousands. His work had been
among the Jews.

We find Peter now in the house of Simon the tanner (10:5-6).
God was going to show Peter that the gospel was for the Gentiles
as well as the Jews (10:9-16). The high wall of religious difference
between Jews and Gentiles must be broken down. Peter was the
man God used to start leveling it. Christ was building a church
and he wanted both Jews and Gentiles to be part of it (Ephesians
2:20-22).

At Pentecost, Peter had used the "keys of the kingdom" entrusted to him to open the door of the gospel to the Jews. While
Paul was in Tarsus, Peter in the house of Cornelius put the key
into the lock of the door that had barred the Gentiles and opened
it (10:14-16).

WITNESSING TO THE ENDS OF THE EARTH
ACTS 13-28

The death of Stephen was only the beginning of great persecution
of the Christians. How did they ever get to Antioch? (See 11:19-
21.) Someone has called Christianity in the early days "A Tale of
Two Cities"—Jerusalem and Antioch.

Up through Acts 12 we have seen the beginning of the church,
with Peter as its leader, in Jerusalem. In Acts 13-28 we see Paul
and the church at Antioch. Antioch was the new base of opera-
tions. All the wonderful missionary journeys of Paul started from
there, not from Jerusalem. It became the new center of the church
for carrying out Jesus' commission.

The Jewish Christians who had been compelled to leave
Jerusalem because of persecution were naturally thrown with all

the Gentiles. These early Christians could not help but talk about what interested them most. The power of the Lord was so evident that a great crowd joined the church (11:21).

It was here in this church that a new name was given to Christ's disciples. They were first called "Christians" at Antioch (11:26).

It is interesting to note here that the church had lost track of Paul. They did not care what had become of him, but Barnabas looked him up (11:25). He had kept track of him all these years. If it had not been for Barnabas, Paul might have remained in obscurity all his life! Think of what the world would have missed had Paul not been discovered! Many a person is waiting to be discovered for God.

Beginning of Foreign Missions
Do we realize that we might have been pagans living in darkness and superstition, while people to the east of Antioch would have been Christians, if the first missionaries had gone east instead of west? Wouldn't you think that we in the West, above every people, ought to believe in missions? Think of what our condition might have been today if missionaries had not brought Christ to us.

We see Paul and Barnabas, the first foreign missionaries, starting westward from Antioch (13:2-3). The greatest enterprise in the world is foreign missions, and this is the very start of this great movement. The whole idea began just the way it should, at a prayer meeting.

While Paul and Barnabas were preaching the gospel and suffering all kinds of persecution and hardship, there were many at home at Jerusalem stirring up the most troublesome question the church had ever faced. It was this: "Must a Gentile become a Jew, and accept his laws and ceremonies, before he can become a Christian?" (15:1). Paul and Barnabas had said nothing about the law of Moses. They had stated: *Believe on the Lord Jesus, and you will be saved* (16:31). The law doesn't save anyone.

Luke now joined the missionary party (16:10). The first convert in Europe was not a famous scholar or some mighty ruler, but a businesswoman, Lydia, a merchant who sold purple cloth.

In Philippi we find Paul and Silas in prison. Why do we find men like these locked behind iron bars? Read Acts 16:16-24. The second Christian in Europe was very different from the first. Lydia was converted in a prayer meeting, but it took an earthquake to arouse the next convert—a jailer. The jailer's question is one of the most important questions in all the world: *What must I do to be saved?* (16:30).

Paul's experiences in the greatest cities of his day are crowded with interest. He founded a church at Thessalonica (17:4).

In famous Athens, Paul preached his immortal sermon on Mars Hill. This is one of the great scenes in history. What effect did it have on those listeners (17:32)?

Paul was not only giving a wonderful message to the Athenians when he preached that day, but he was speaking to you and to me. Paul tells us that God is near. He seems so far away to some that they do not even try to reach him, yet God hears our faintest whisper if we speak to him.

Paul left Athens and arrived at Corinth very much discouraged. We do not know whether he was successful in starting a church in Athens, but in Corinth, one of the most wicked cities of the ancient world, he founded a church and remained there eighteen months to establish the people in the faith (18:8). It was here Paul found Aquila and his wife, Priscilla, who afterward became his loyal friends.

After an absence of three or four years, Paul returned to Antioch by way of Ephesus. In Antioch he reported his entrance into Europe.

Paul's Third Missionary Tour

Now we find Paul spending three years in one of the greatest cities of his day. Next to Rome, Ephesus was perhaps the world's largest and most cosmopolitan city. Crowds of Jews and Gentiles of Asia heard the Good News preached. Ephesus was notorious for its luxury and licentiousness, and for the worship of the goddess Diana.

The years Paul spent here are crowded with interesting events (ch. 19). At one point there was a great bonfire in Ephesus as enthusiastic converts burned their books on "the black art," magic, and threw away their silver idols. It almost seems as though we can see the flames burning to this day. It represented the burning of their old lives. Paul has taught us that every idol must be torn down from its place in our hearts and the Lord alone must occupy the throne. Is there anything in our lives that calls for a bonfire? Don't be afraid of bringing yourself face-to-face with your inner self.

Such blessings as these could not last long without opposition. The end of chapter 19 records the results of Paul's work. The silversmiths stirred up a riot, and the apostles were rescued from danger only by the help of the city officials.

As Paul traveled, he kept writing his wonderful letters. We read them today with great profit and interest. From Ephesus Paul sent his first letter to the church at Corinth (1 Corinthians 16:8). During this third journey Paul wrote 2 Corinthians, Galatians, and Romans.

Paul's Farewell

Paul's last missionary journey must have been a heart-breaking experience. He had to say farewell at every place. He knew it was a final farewell. Read Acts 20:37-38. They all wept and "embraced him," knowing they would never see him again. Think of this sad experience repeated a dozen times over. Probably no man except David has ever inspired such intense personal love to so many hearts.

Sailing out of the harbor of Ephesus, Paul bid his friends a last farewell. He was headed for Jerusalem, and from then on he was seen as "the prisoner of the Lord." Paul made his last visit to Jerusalem, and here one of those swiftly formed mobs, which gather so quickly in the excitable East, rushed against the apostle and bound him, declaring he was teaching the Jews to forsake Moses. No doubt he recalled the fact that outside that city he himself, twenty-six years before, had assisted in the murder of Stephen. Finding that Paul was a Roman citizen, the commander of the Roman garrison promised to give him a fair trial. Paul made his defense before the Roman governor Felix at Caesarea. After two years' imprisonment, Paul was tried a second time before the new governor, Festus, and appealed from him to Caesar himself, the emperor (21:27–26:32).

After a most exciting voyage, in which his ship was wrecked in a terrific storm off the coast of Malta, Paul arrived in Rome. Here he was kept a prisoner in his own rented house for two years. Even in prison the great preacher and evangelist led the servants in Nero's own palace to Christ. Service for the Master can brighten life's darkest hours. When we seek to lift others' burdens, we lighten our own (ch. 27–28).

During his imprisonment, Paul wrote many of his letters— Philemon, Colossians, Ephesians, and Philippians. It was while he was in a dungeon in Rome, expecting at any hour to be beheaded, that he wrote his second letter to Timothy.

Finally (according to tradition) the beloved apostle was condemned and beheaded. His heroic soul was released and the feeble body buried in the catacombs.

Paul changed Christianity from its Jewish tribal confines to a worldwide influence. He tried to break down the barriers between Jew and Gentile and between slave and freeman.

Acts is the only unfinished book in the Bible. Notice how abruptly it closes! How else could it close? How could there be a complete account of a Person's lifework as long as he lives? Our risen and ascended Lord still lives. From the center, Christ, the lines are seen proceeding in every direction, but the ends of the earth are not yet reached. The book is evidently a fragment. The Good News of Christ moves on! You are still living the Acts.

SELECTED BIBLE READING

Sunday: First Church in Jerusalem (Acts 1–4)
Monday: Testifying in Jerusalem (Acts 5–7)
Tuesday: Testifying in Judea and Samaria (Acts 8–12)
Wednesday: Paul Establishes the Churches—First Tour
(Acts 13:1–15:35)
Thursday: Paul Revisits the Churches—Second Tour
(Acts 15:36–18:21)
Friday: Paul Encourages the Churches—Third Tour
(Acts 18:22–25:9)
Saturday: Paul Sent to Rome (Acts 25:10–28:31)

CHAPTER 33

UNDERSTANDING ROMANS

Romans Portrays Jesus Christ, Our Righteousness

We now begin a study of the letters, often called *epistles*, in the New Testament. Thirteen of the twenty-one were written by Paul, hence they are called "the Pauline epistles." He wrote his letters to the churches at Thessalonica, Galatia, Corinth, and Rome during his missionary journeys. It was while he was a prisoner in Rome that he wrote his letters to the church at Ephesus, one to the Colossians, one to Philemon, and one to the Philippians. After his imprisonment he wrote two letters to Timothy and one to Titus.

Paul, whose Jewish name was Saul, was born at Tarsus, of pure Jewish stock. His teacher was Gamaliel, the great teacher of the Pharisees. Like all Hebrew boys, he learned a trade—he was a tentmaker. At Jerusalem he was present at the stoning of Stephen, the first Christian martyr. No doubt this scene made a tremendous impression upon the young Saul. On the way to Damascus, on a mission of persecution of the Christians, the young Pharisee had a head-on collision with Jesus Christ! After his miraculous conversion he was baptized and received his commission to preach the gospel. He retired to Arabia and spent three years there in study and preparation.

After laboring for three years in Tarsus and one year in Antioch, directed by the Holy Spirit, Paul became the great missionary to the Gentiles. On his three missionary journeys he founded many churches and wrote his letters. The combination of Roman citizenship, Greek education, and Hebrew religion wonderfully qualified him for his great work, but you will find that he trusted alone in God's kindness and the call to preach, which he received directly from Jesus Christ (1:5).

After a life filled with sacrifice and suffering, he sealed his testimony with his own life's blood. Tradition says he was beheaded at Rome and his body buried in the catacombs.

THE CHURCH AT ROME

Who founded the church at Rome we do not know. Most likely, visitors from Rome, in Jerusalem for the Passover and converted at Pentecost, carried the seed of the gospel back to the capital and established this new center in Rome. During the twenty-eight intervening years many Christians from all parts of the East had migrated to Rome, some of them Paul's own converts.

Paul was eager to visit this church and sent them this letter from Corinth, from the home of Gaius, a wealthy Corinthian Christian, while he was on his third missionary journey. It was written in the fourth year of Nero, then emperor of Rome. In this letter he sets forth his gospel, "God's Good News" (1:16-17).

Paul the servant, "Jesus Christ's slave" (1:1), writes to the saints, "God's holy people," at Rome (1:7) concerning the Savior, the "mighty Son of God" (1:3-4).

After Paul greeted the church, he thanked God for their faith (1:8). Notice Paul's expression of obligation to this church (1:14-16):

I owe a great debt to you.
I am ready to fulfill my obligation.
I am not ashamed of the message.

Why was Paul not ashamed of the Good News about Christ? Because it reveals what the sinner needs to make him "ready for heaven." He must be made "right in God's sight"—righteous. This righteousness, that only God himself can give, comes from faith in Jesus Christ.

Paul was not ashamed of the Good News about Christ even in Rome. The terrible sinfulness of man, as pictured in 1:18-32, had reached its climax in Rome.

Paul spoke from the white-hot conviction that is born of experience. On the road to Damascus, at one blow, he had all the props of works, of race, and of character knocked out from under him. He caught a full glimpse of the glorified Christ. From then on he had but one message—faith in the crucified and risen Lord. He would hear nothing else; he spoke nothing else; he lived nothing less. He proclaimed that *the man who finds life will find it through trusting God.* One must simply believe. Salvation is not of works—works are damning; not of race—the race is under the curse of death; not of character—because our character is as filthy rags! There is only one salvation, and that is by the acceptance of the Good News about Christ.

The book of Romans tells us of God's method of making guilty men "not guilty." The key of this great thesis is found in Romans 1:16-17:

The Person of the Good News—Christ
The power of the Good News—God's power
The purpose of the Good News—salvation
The people to whom sent—everyone
The plan of acceptance—all who believe it
The particular result—life, through trusting God

Paul was proud of the Good News because he had proved its power in his own life and in the lives of all who would believe.

Good news! These words will command the attention of anyone. Say, "I have good news for you!" and one can always secure a listener. The real value of good news depends on the source—who said it. That is why the Good News Paul presents is so welcome. The news comes from God. Romans is Paul's shout of joy to a lost world.

After Paul states the subject of the book of Romans, in 1:16-17, he then reveals man's need of God's righteousness. *Yes, all have sinned,* and *all the world stands hushed and guilty before Almighty God.* From his elevated pulpit, Paul looks around and sees zealous Jews, proud Greeks, boastful Romans, and a multitude of ordinary, common sinners like ourselves. What a terrible picture he presents in 1:18-32! First the unrighteousness of the Gentiles is portrayed; then that of the Jews.

The first three chapters describe the hell of sin. The last five chapters describe the heaven of holiness. The intervening chapters describe Christ, the Way.

WHAT WE ARE BY NATURE
ROMANS 1:1-3:20

Why does man need salvation? Because he is a sinner. God has x-rayed the human heart and has given us the picture. He shows us what he finds in us all. But remember, this is the picture of us that God sees. I know your picture is there because it says, *No one anywhere has kept on doing what is right, no, not one.* Paul proves this fact conclusively in the first three chapters of this book. This is the picture of man without God. Read every word of Romans 3. You will believe then that the natural heart is desperately wicked. Have you ever asked the Holy Spirit to throw a searchlight on your own heart? If you have, you know today that you need a Savior.

The book of Romans presents a courtroom scene. God, the Judge of all the earth, summons Jews and Gentiles before the bar of justice. Prisoner after prisoner is brought up.

The general charge is stated—"all under sin" (3:19). Both the Gentiles (2:1-16) and the Jews (2:17–3:8) are given the opportunity for a hearing. Their special pleas of "not guilty" are carefully considered and answered, clearing the way for the final verdict from the Judge.

Finally the Judge pronounces the verdict. *All the world . . . guilty before Almighty God* (3:19). If this were today, newspapers everywhere would blaze this headline: ALL THE WORLD FOUND GUILTY! All the television newsmen would be announcing it. Can't you hear them?

Against all this there is no defense. The Judge says, "Is there anyone to plead the cause of the prisoners?" And there is no answering voice. Every mouth is hushed (3:19). There is no room for excuse.

The condemnation of the world is settled. The next step in order will be to reveal the plan of God to save a lost world. Remember, the book of Romans tells us God's method of making people "not guilty."

Do not say, "God is love. He will not condemn me." Listen to God's words here: *God shows his anger from heaven against all sinful, evil men who push away the truth from them* (1:18). He has already passed sentence on everyone. "All . . . guilty." There is no chance of appeal. It is the decision of the Supreme Court of the universe. Sin is universal—*All have sinned!* Hence we need a world's Savior. Because God is a God of love he has provided just this One! Read aloud John 3:16. The Judge on the bench says, "Is there anyone to appear for the prisoners?" Then the Son of God says, "Yes, I am here to represent these. It is true that they committed these sins. It is true that they are guilty, but I bore their guilt on the cross. I died in their place so they could go free. In me they are made right." And the Judge sets them free.

We get an awful picture of sin in these first three chapters of Romans. Remember, *sin* is a marksman's word. It means "missing the mark"—the standard that God has set for us. God's Word says, *All have sinned; all fall short.* In our good deeds? No—of God's glory. Do not measure your life by any other standard but this. Do not compare yourself with others. Of course you may not have fallen as short as some others you know, but you are "short" as far as God is concerned.

We are all sinners because we were born into a sinful race. We are all "sons of Adam." But we were not only born into sin; we have sinned ourselves, for "all have sinned." Remember this—we sin because we are sinners. This is our nature. A plum tree bears plums because it is a plum tree. The fruit is the result of its nature. Sin is the fruit of a sinful heart. *The heart is the most deceitful thing there is, and desperately wicked* (Jeremiah 17:9).

Christ not only saves us from the penalty of sin. He is also able to free us from the consciousness of guilt and the power of sin. The result of sin is a sense of guilt. When one has broken the law he feels guilty and seeks to hide. This is what the first man, Adam, did. A guilty conscience brings a fear of punishment. The sinner is always trying to flee from the consequences of the broken law. He fears the judge. This is why a man's sins and his consciousness of guilt banish him from the presence of God. God does not need to banish the sinner. He flees of his own accord. This is what will happen in the day when "God shows his anger from heaven" (see Revelation 6:15-16).

The first thing necessary for the freedom of a sinner is that the dreadful consequences of his guilt be taken away. He needs more than pardon, for that would leave him with his guilt. Any president or governor or king can pardon a criminal, but no one has the power to remove his guilt. Proper punishment for the deed must be given. This is what Christ has done. *The wages of sin is death* and since all of us *have sinned,* Christ came to die and bear the penalty for the sins committed against a holy God.

HOW TO BECOME A CHRISTIAN
ROMANS 3:21–5:21

God's plan of salvation runs through the entire Bible. It is like the cordage of the British Navy with a scarlet line interwoven through it that you cannot take out without destroying the cord. There is a scarlet line of salvation running through Scripture. You can see it very plainly in certain portions of the Bible. Romans 3 is one of them.

When God looks at us he sees no righteousness (3:10). When God looks at us "in Christ," he sees not only improvement but perfection, for God sees only his own Righteousness, Jesus Christ.

You have become acquainted with one great word of Scripture, *salvation.* Here is another—*justification,* "just-as-if-I'd. . . ."

When Christ's righteousness is delared as ours, this is called *justification*—a man justified before God. Everything that Christ has done has been credited to my account—"just-as-if-I'd" done it. His righteousness is mine! A man is not made just by his works but by believing on Christ (3:28). This great truth gave birth to the great Reformation. It freed believers from the idea that people were saved by good deeds, and it freed them to live a life of faith and liberty in Christ. Not only are we saved by faith, we must live by faith, trusting in Christ.

Paul gives us illustrations of justification by faith from the Old Testament. Especially he tells us that because of Abraham's faith, God declared him "not guilty" (ch. 4). Abraham received three things by faith: righteousness, inheritance, posterity (4:3, 13, 17).

We, too, have great benefits when we are justified by his grace. Grace is unmerited favor, God's undeserved kindness. In this life we find that faith is followed by peace, pardon, and promise (5:1-5), and more than all, an assurance of salvation (5:6-11).

How can a person be justified by God? Read Romans 3:24-28. God gives his righteousness to us in the following ways:

1. By grace—the source of it (3:24)
2. By God—the giver of it (3:25; 8:33)
3. By blood—the reason for it (3:25; 5:9)
4. By faith—the means by which it is received (3:22)
5. By works—the way it is shown (James 2:21-23)
6. By experience—the blessings we enjoy from it (5:1-4)

When I look into heaven and remember that God who sits on his throne has condemned me, I am in despair. But I see One sitting at his right, holding up a wounded hand and presenting his pierced feet and side. With these wounds Christ pleads for me, and I have his own assurance that they are sufficient to meet my needs.

Salvation

You will find the stream of sin and the river of salvation running along together from the beginning of Romans 1 to the end. *The more we see our sinfulness, the more we see God's abounding grace forgiving us.* Paul shows sin in all its squalor and salvation in all its splendor. Some simple steps in these next paragraphs will show you how to become a Christian!

One does not have to be a sinner in the sight of men to be lost. Of course there is a difference in the degree of sin, but not in the fact of sin and its results, *for the wages of sin is death.* A person drowned in seven feet of water is as dead as if he had been submerged in seventy feet of water. In our inability to save ourselves, we are all on the same level—*no matter who we are or what we have been like* (3:22).

We are saved by Christ's righteousness. He has made it available for us by his death. *God declares us "not guilty" of offending him if we trust in Jesus Christ, who in his kindness freely takes away our sins. For God sent Christ Jesus to take the punishment for our sins and to end all God's anger against us* (3:24-25).

I am a person condemned to die because of my sin, *for the wages of sin is death.* But I can look at the cross and see that Christ has already died for me. I believe that he died for my sin. And so in exchange for my poor, sinful, condemned life I can accept his righteousness and his life (see 1 Peter 2:24). *And all who trust him—God's Son—to save them have eternal life* (John 3:36). *Now God has shown us a different way to heaven—not by "being good enough" and trying to keep his laws, but by a new way . . . if we trust Jesus Christ to take away our sins* (3:21-22). *Our righteousness is as filthy rags* (Isaiah 64:6). Apart from man's effort to be good, God has provided his righteousness, the Lord Jesus Christ. Your sin is on Christ. He has borne it for you. Have you accepted him as your Savior and *passed out of death into life* (John 5:24)? If you have decided to let Christ be your sin bearer, you now have his salvation (3:24).

Justified by Faith

A murderer may stand at the bottom of a mine and you on the highest peak of the highest mountain, but you are as little able to touch the stars as he. You cannot attain the righteousness that God demands no matter how far you climb.

Forgiveness is the removal of our unrighteousness, a shedding or putting away of sin.

Justification is the act of being clothed with the righteousness that God provides. It is perfect.

The person who put his faith in Christ an hour ago is just as much justified as the oldest Christian living. We never become any more justified than the minute we receive Christ. Justification depends on something done outside of us, something done on the cross of Calvary.

Justification takes care of all the sin and guilt upon us, buries all this sin and guilt in the grave of Jesus Christ, and then sets us in heavenly places with Christ our Savior.

There is a question that many ask. "How could one man die for the whole world?" One man could take one other man's place and be his substitute. That would be all right, you say, but for one to die for the whole world—that is nonsense! Let us see if this is true!

None of us likes the idea of being called a "sinner," but we must face what we are. Listen to what Paul says in Romans 5:12-21. We were born sinners. We were not asked if we wished to come into this world. We woke up to the fact one day that we were subject to a sinful nature. Adam, the head of our race, was not created that way (Genesis 1:26). He deliberately sinned, and his sinful nature was passed on to us all. We sin because we are sinners.

But over against Adam, the head of the natural race, we find Christ, the Head of a spiritual race—"a new creation." When I was born in this body, I was born a descendant of Adam. I have his nature, which is sinful. When I am born into the family of God, by Christ Jesus, I have Christ's nature, which is holy. In the words of Scripture, *Everyone dies because all of us are related to Adam, being members of his sinful race, and wherever there is sin, death results. But all who are related to Christ will rise again* (1 Corinthians 15:22). I did not choose to be a descendant of Adam. I may choose to be a child of God. If one man's sin made it possible for all the race to die, one Man's righteousness made it possible for all the race to get out of this condition (5:15).

Have you received "eternal life through Jesus Christ our Lord"? Are you a sinner "in Adam," or are you a son "in Christ"?

HOW TO LIVE A CHRISTIAN LIFE
ROMANS 6–8

We have learned how to become Christians. Now we must find out how to live like Christians. It is one thing to accept what Christ has done for us. It is another thing to experience it as personal and real.

In Romans 6 there are three important ideas:

Know this: Christ died for you (6:3-5, 10), and you died with Christ (6:8).

Consider this: *Look upon your old sin nature as dead and unresponsive to sin, and instead be alive to God, alert to him, through Jesus Christ our Lord* (6:11). If a relative told you that he had put $500 in the bank for you for a trip and you could withdraw it anytime you needed it, you would count on it, I am sure, without ever seeing the money. If you were to question it, and not draw it out, the money would never be yours. If you look upon it as yours by signing a check and giving it to the bank teller, that which you have never seen becomes a reality. Since we are dead to sin and alive unto God, how shall we live?

Give yourself to this: *Do not let any part of your bodies become tools of wickedness, to be used for sinning; but give yourself completely to God* (6:13).

This means "let go" of your life and "let God" live through you. This is the surrendered life. This is the right way to live a life of victory and blessing. Let him work his will in you and through you.

The Christian soon finds a new standard for his life. He does not try to live up to the Law, for he is no longer under it. He strives to please the One who lives within him. *For me to live is Christ*, and I *do all to the glory of God.*

Romans 6 reveals the secret of a life of victory. I am living in Christ! Dead to sin but alive to God! It tells me how to lead a Christian life. Self, we have learned, was a condemned thing, unable to be good, never righteous (ch. 3). Now when self becomes a Christian and tries to live a Christian life, it finds this to be impossible. We are saved by faith, and we cannot live by our own efforts.

The sad truth is revealed in Romans 7. It tells us how we cannot live a victorious life. Mark the little word *I* and you will find it is used thirty-nine times in the twenty-five verses of this chapter. The Holy Spirit is never mentioned. Although *I* tries, it finds only defeat.

Dr. Griffith Thomas said, "It is not hard to live a Christian life; it is impossible."

Paul said, *I myself no longer live, but Christ lives in me.*

Listen to the words of the man who tries to live by his own effort. *My new life tells me to do right, but the old nature that is still inside me loves to sin. Oh, what a terrible predicament I'm in! Who will free me from my slavery to this deadly lower nature? Thank God! It has been done by Jesus Christ our Lord. He has set me free* (7:24-25).

Finally, *I* finds that there is One who is sufficient. Struggling gives in to power; defeat is changed to victory; misery is transformed into joy. When *I* goes out, Christ comes in.

The life "in Christ" is a wonderful thing. Paul says, *The power of the life-giving Spirit—and this power is mine through Christ Jesus—has freed me from the vicious circle of sin and death.* In this physical world I am subject to the law of gravity. But when I get in an airplane, the lift of the plane overcomes the force of gravity and lifts the plane off the ground. The force of gravity is not destroyed, but the plane soars above the clouds. This is what happens in my life when I am "in Christ." The law that operates by the Spirit in my life lifts me above the world and sin, and sin no longer has dominion over me. I am free. I am without condemnation. Have you stepped into Christ? Are you living on a plane far above evil principalities and powers?

Have you come to the end of "self"? Remember, *I* never brings anything but failure. It is the *I* in "SIN" that must be removed. Put *O* in its place and you have "SON." He will give you victory!

Step out of the self life into the Spirit-filled life. In Romans 8 instead of the word *I* we find the word *Spirit* used fifteen times. We must yield our lives to him. This is our part. Then he will fill us with his Spirit. That is Christ's part.

This glorious chapter opens with "no condemnation," and ends with "no separation." This is a picture of our life "in Christ." The Christian is safe: Christ is around him, the Spirit is within him, and God is for him.

WHY ISRAEL IS SET ASIDE
ROMANS 9–11

The story of the Jews being set aside and scattered throughout the world without a homeland, without a king, is a warning for us. God is a sovereign God, and he will do what he will. He has a perfect right to turn to the Gentiles, because the Jews *were trying to be saved by keeping the law and being good instead of by depending on faith* (9:32). If God will put aside his chosen people, will he not put us aside if we are disobedient?

Let us be careful lest we become self-willed and disobedient, too, not heeding God's commandments.

Ask Christ to take control of your life and guide you in his path. There are wrecks outside his divine course. The Jews are a solemn lesson to us. Read the wonderful description of God's mercy in Romans 11:32-36.

HOW TO SERVE GOD
ROMANS 12–16

And so, dear brothers, I plead with you to give your bodies to God. Let them be a living sacrifice, holy—the kind he can accept. When you think of what he has done for you, is this too much to ask? (12:1).

In this appeal, Paul urges us to have our life measure up to our belief. He shows that believing that we are justified by faith does not allow laxity in life or conduct. We are saved to serve. The Christian life must be lived in right relation to God, self, and others.

It may surprise you to find out that up to this point we have not had to do a thing but believe on Christ and give ourselves to him to use as he will. Now we are to serve!

Until we have been saved by his undeserved kindness and transformed by his love, we can do little for God. Read about God's love in 1 Corinthians 13. But when we present ourselves to Christ and become filled with his love we can find much to be done. Christ wants a "living sacrifice," not a dead one (12:1). Many will die for Christ; few will live for him. There are many who would rather be burned at a stake than stand the ridicule of their associates. One definition of a modern Christian is "a person who will die for the church he will not attend." How many of us say nothing when Christ's name is brought into question or is used in vain!

Let others see Jesus in you! Live for him, then you will be ready to die for him.

The first part of Romans is what God did for us. The last part of Romans is what we can do for God.

We find our Christian service in:

Church (12:3-8)
Government (13:1-14)
Questionable things (14:1–15:3)
The whole world (15:4-13)

SELECTED BIBLE READING

Sunday: What We Are by Nature (Romans 1:1–3:20)
Monday: How to Become a Christian (Romans 3:21–5:21)
Tuesday: How to Live a Christian Life (Romans 6)
Wednesday: A Struggle (Romans 7)
Thursday: The Life of Victory (Romans 8)
Friday: The Jews Set Aside (Romans 9–11)
Saturday: The Christian's Service (Romans 12)

CHAPTER 34

UNDERSTANDING
FIRST CORINTHIANS

First Corinthians Portrays Jesus Christ, Our Lord

Corinth was the most important city of all Greece in Paul's day. Its wealth was fabulous. Men spent their days in tournaments and speeches. Luxury, drunkenness, and public immorality were rampant among this great industrial and seafaring population. Corinth attracted great crowds of foreigners from the East and West. Their gods were gods of pleasure and lust. There was, besides, much culture and art. The city abounded in studios of language and schools of philosophy.

As in most cities, there was a large colony of Jews who had kept a strong moral standard and held to their religious beliefs. But the city itself was the center of a debased form of the worship of Venus.

If we read Acts 18 we find how the gospel reached this wicked city. The Apostle Paul, then about fifty years of age, dressed as a working man, entered the busy metropolis and went through its streets in search of a workshop where he could earn his own living. There were no billboards advertising the coming of a world-renowned evangelist. This tradesman came into town and began his tentmaking, which was a leading industry in that day like building is today. He went into business with the well-to-do tentmakers Aquila and Priscilla. He was always able to support himself, making enough to carry on his missionary work. A wonderful work was done in Corinth during the year and a half that Paul was there. He began by speaking in the synagogues to mixed congregations of Jews and Greeks.

First Corinthians is a difficult book to outline, for it takes up many wonderful subjects. In Romans, Paul told us that Christ *brought us to this place of highest privilege where we now stand* (Romans 5:2). So enter this privileged place in Christ Jesus, our All in all. First Corinthians deals with Christian conduct.

CORRECTIONS IN CHRISTIAN CONDUCT
1 CORINTHIANS 1–11

The name *Lord* is very prominent in this book (1:31; 2:8, 16; 3:20; 4:4; 5:4-5; 6:13, etc.). This is full of meaning, because much of the confusion that had crept into the church at Corinth had come because the believers failed to recognize Jesus Christ as Lord.

The wonderful church at Corinth, the brilliant jewel in the crown of Paul's labor, was failing. It was all because the worldliness of the city had gotten within the church. It was all right for the church to be in Corinth, but it was fatal when Corinth got into the church. It is a glorious sight to see a ship launched into the sea, but it is a tragic sight to see when the sea gets into the ship. The church of Christ should be set as a light in a dark place, but woe to the church when the wickedness of the world invades.

Practices common to this wicked city soon crept into the church. There were divisions among them; Christians were suing Christians before heathen judges; behavior at the communion table was disgraceful; the women of the church no longer observed standards of modesty; the church membership was arguing over marriage and even spiritual gifts. Finally, the church wrote Paul about these things and asked his advice. These two letters to the Corinthians were written in answer to their requests.

After the usual greeting (1:1-3), Paul refered to the return of our Lord Jesus Christ (1:7-8). Then he plunged right into the question of the failure of the church about which he had been told. He gives the source of his information (1:11).

The people had lost sight of God. Three kinds of selfishness had blinded them:

1. *Self-admiration*—their intellect had been perverted.
2. *Self-will*—their conscience had been darkened.
3. *Self-indulgence*—their passions had been given full rein.

The greatest danger to the Corinthian church was from within.

Paul spoke first of the divisions and cliques about which he had learned from friends and travelers. Nothing eats out the heart and life of the church like party politics.

The Greek spirit of party politics had entered into the church, dividing it into four parties, each trying to get the mastery (1:12). Paul, Apollos, and Peter were parties named for their favorite teachers. The Christ Party held to that name as if it did not belong to everyone in the church.

The dissension about religious leaders meant that the Christians at Corinth had slipped off center. There is only one Leader in every church. That Leader and center is Christ. If the church gets off center here, it goes off all down the line. A great flywheel on center moves quietly; off center it shakes the machine to pieces. Christianity must be Christ-centered. If it is Christ-centered it is powerful. Christ himself is the "Good News." He not only brought God's message, he was God's message. The Corinthians had slipped off center. Paul, Peter, and Apollos were all good men, but not God-men. How many are following religious leaders today rather than Christ himself!

Jesus Christ is the only cure for division (1:13). Every eye, every heart, every spirit must be turned to one object—Jesus Christ, our personal Savior. Paul said, in effect, "Your party spirit is a sin. Can you follow a mere man, hoping that he can give you life? Was that man crucified for you? Trusting in what man has to say is foolish. Men see nothing in the cross of Christ. Christ alone has all the power and wisdom of God."

Young and old alike follow Christ to the cross and then stumble at the blood of the sacrifice. This is what the Jews and Greeks of Paul's day did. Shall we remove the cross from the gospel because people do not like it? If we do, we remove the world's only way of salvation. We must preach "Christ crucified."

The Cross
The Jews are offended (1:23). They could not understand how such a display of weakness could be a source of power. A man dying on a cross did not look much like a world Savior to them. The scribes and Pharisees scornfully turned from the cross. To them, the cross meant failure. The Jews demanded signs of power, something they could see and grasp. The Messiah had to be a world prince, a miracle worker. A multitude of Christians are

like this today. They worship success as much as did the Jews. They despise weakness and admire force. These people tell us that scientists are apt to stumble at the cross because they cannot explain how the blood of one Man could wash away the stain of sin.

The Gentiles say it's all nonsense. The Greeks regarded with contempt the unscientific religion first taught in an unschooled corner of the world like Nazareth, by the son of a carpenter who never studied in Athens or Rome. The Greeks idolized brains. But God has never despised the humble things.

Either the cross is the "power of God" or it is "nonsense." If "nonsense," then you think it is unfit to do any good in your life. But listen! That condemns you, not the cross.

No man ever leaves the cross in exactly the same condition as he came to it. He must receive it or reject it. If he receives it he becomes a son of God (John 1:12); if he rejects it he is lost (John 3:36). If he neglects it he is in effect rejecting it.

Paul did not preach Christ the conqueror or Christ the philosopher, but Christ crucified, Christ the humble. Read his words in 1 Corinthians 2:2. Paul remembered that his words would be "put through the fire" (3:13). To know Christ crucified is the maximum of knowledge.

The Minister

One objection to Paul was that his preaching was too simple. He answered that he could not preach any differently because the Corinthians were mere babies in Christ. They could not stand anything but a milk diet. The proof of their childish state was this division among them (3:1-4).

Paul pointed out that the Christian minister is not the head of a school or a rival sect, as were the Greek philosophers. He is the servant of God, not a master of men. Paul always called himself a servant of the Lord Jesus Christ. Christian service is only acceptable to God when done in the spirit of Christ, for his glory.

Everyone of us is four people—one the world knows, one our friends know, one we ourselves know, one God knows. Paul describes this in 1 Corinthians 4:3-4. There are three courts before which we stand: man, our own conscience, and Jesus Christ.

Do not depend on man's judgment. The world judges our character by a single act. The voices of criticism may be loud, but if you go high up on the hilltop with God, you will see the bustle of the crowd but you won't hear it.

Beware of your friend's judgment, because he may be too favorable in his opinion of you. We like to believe all the good things said about us and resent unfavorable criticism.

Paul says, *I don't even trust my own judgment on this point* (4:3). Beware when you stand at the bar of your own conscience. When your conscience says to you, "You may do it," it is always well to go to Jesus Christ and say, "May I?" It is hard to be fair with ourselves. No man, no matter how honest he is, is permitted to judge in his own cause.

Paul says there is one judgment to which he will submit—one that is always right. *It is the Lord himself who must examine me and decide* (4:4). I am Christ's steward and to him am I ultimately responsible. From his judgment there is no escape. His calm eyes are upon me.

Seek praise from him that is praise indeed. If he says, "Well done, good and faithful servant," what else matters?

Vice in the Church
In Paul's letter to the Romans we find his theme to be the righteousness of God. In Corinthians he enlarges it to the Christian's life of righteousness. We, as Christians, must act out in our lives what we believe in our hearts. It is a serious thing to profess to live the life of a Christian. If we lower the standard Christ has set, we give the wrong testimony to the world. You are a letter from Christ. What kind of a gospel is "The Gospel According to You"?

Do not let your life be so near the edge of questionable things that some day you will slide off. If you fall, others will fall with you. Watch your testimony.

Righteousness comes from God, but it must be shown in our daily lives. The Corinthians needed admonition just as we do. Righteousness is from Christ and for Christ. "What would Jesus do?" should be the query to every questionable thing of life. "Christ in you" is the secret and the way of life.

In the church at Corinth, a member actually married his own stepmother, which was socially immoral among the pagans, to say nothing of Christians. Paul reproved them for being puffed up with pride while this scandal existed in the church. He urged them not to tolerate evil among them while calling themselves

Christians. Just as yeast spreads through all the dough, so a bad man's spirit spreads through all the church. The church should exclude the wrongdoer to prove that it does not condone sin (5:13). Discipline in the church should always commence with mourning and sympathy, not anger or pride or revenge (5:2).

Paul then makes a personal application, useful in our own lives. *Let us feast . . . upon the pure bread of honor and sincerity and truth.* Self-examination is often the most difficult thing we do, but it is one of the most important.

In chapter 6 Paul states that although it might be necessary at times for Christians to go to law, Christians never should quarrel with each other and then drag this quarrel before a worldly court. What a terrible impression of Christianity this gives to the world! When we do this we say, "We, as Christians, are just as bad as other folks. We want our way. We are covetous and just as ambitious for our own rights as you are." Paul asks, "How dare you do such a thing?"

In 6:9 Paul gives us a picture of the Corinthians as he had found them. When we finish verse 11 we find what grace has done!

Christ has paid a great price to purchase us, and it is his purpose to make us like himself (6:19-20).

If our bodies have been redeemed by the Lord Jesus Christ, then they no longer belong to us but to the One who purchased us with his precious blood. *God has bought you with a great price.*

God used to have a temple for his people; now he has a people for a temple. We are taught as boys and girls not to be noisy or boisterous in the church, for it is the house in which we meet God. How much more important it is that we remember that our body is his dwelling place and that we should do nothing to grieve him.

Liberty, Not Recklessness

The Bible does not lay down little rules for our conduct and tell us just the things we ought to do or not to do, but rather it states principles that should guide the Christian's actions. Someone has well said that Christian liberty does not mean the right to do as we like but rather to do as we ought. Paul put it, *I can do anything I want to if Christ has not said no, but some of these things aren't good for me. Even if I am allowed to do them, I'll refuse to if I think they might get such a grip on me that I can't easily stop when I want to* (6:12).

A man was walking down the street swinging his arms and, by mistake, struck a passerby in the face. The man struck was furious and started to strike the man back. "Hey, isn't this a free country? Can't a fellow do his exercises on the street if he wishes?" "Yes," was the answer, "but remember, where my nose begins, your liberty ends."

If your liberty harms another, then your liberty has gone too far. Let this be in your mind constantly as far as your conduct is concerned.

Yes, I can do anything I want to, but I must be sure my desires are to please Christ. What I do is an example to others and may harm or bless them. I should not only answer the question, "Does my action harm weaker Christians?" but also, "Does it glorify God?"

Marriage

Paul discusses the subject of marriage for the Christian. Controversy had arisen between the Jewish and Greek philosophers about the importance of marriage. Paul wanted to keep sin out of the church; hence his words in 7:2. Society is pure and virtuous in proportion as marriage is regarded as honorable. Some of the church had tried to discourage marriage, and others thought that when one became a Christian he should divorce an unbelieving mate. But Paul was wise. He knew the evil condition in Corinth and advised every man to have his own wife and every woman to have her own husband. He did not believe in a Christian divorcing a pagan partner. He told them that it would be very likely that the Christian would lead his unbelieving mate to Christ (7:16).

The Lord's Supper

Paul gave a careful account of the beginning of the Lord's Supper, told of its value, and gave specific instructions about its observance (11:17-34):

1. It was established on the night Christ was betrayed.
2. It is celebrated in remembrance of his undying love for his followers.

3. It was a symbol of his body that was broken for them (10:16).
4. It was a new agreement in his blood.
5. It was a pledge of his coming again.

We should be careful not to eat or drink in an unworthy manner. "A man ought to examine himself" carefully and never eat without self-judgment and thankful love.

Do this in remembrance of me whenever you drink it. Christ wants us to remember him! Think on Christ when you go to his table. He longs for your love!

It was the custom of the Corinthian church to eat a meal in connection with the Lord's Supper. Each person brought his own food. Often this led to excesses among the rich, while the poor had nothing. What an unworthy observance of the supper itself this led to! Paul reminded them of the deep spiritual significance of this supper, and of the scandal of their behavior.

Paul closed this scene with these words: *I'll talk to you about other matters after I arrive.* There were other things to be straightened out, but he would leave his corrections and go on with his instructions.

INSTRUCTIONS IN CHRISTIAN CONDUCT
1 CORINTHIANS 12–16

In 1 Corinthians 12 we see the gifts the Spirit gives to believers. In verses 1-3, he tells of the change that had come into the lives of these Corinthian Christians when they turned from worshiping dead idols to the living Christ. For them to develop in their Christian life, Christ gave them the gifts of the Spirit (12:4-7). The Holy Spirit is the Giver of spiritual gifts (12:8-11). One cannot teach the Scriptures unless the Spirit gives him wisdom. One must pray "in the Spirit" and sing acceptably to God "in the Spirit." Sometimes we say when we look at a successful Christian, "My, he is a man of natural abilities," when really he has received many gifts from the Spirit.

Many people in Paul's day were making much of the spiritual gifts that Paul mentioned. They were coveting the more showy gifts, such as speaking "in tongues"—in languages they never learned.

The Corinthian Christians were using these gifts as ends in themselves. Many people today, like the Corinthians of old, pray constantly for the power of the Spirit. They forget that all the gifts God gives are given so that Christ will be exalted and others blessed. If God gives me any little gift at all, he gives it not so that I can gather people around myself, but so that it can through me be a blessing for others. God gave the gifts mentioned in 1 Corinthians 12 to assist in the founding of the new church, but they were being used by people to gratify their pride. Paul showed that the purpose of the gifts is for the building of the church, that they should be used in love (ch. 13), and that their value is to be measured by their usefulness to the church.

God gave gifts such as healing, miracles, and "tongues," we believe, for "sign" gifts, to prove to the world that Jesus was the true Messiah and that the apostles were divinely appointed. These miracles, tongues, visions, and signs were given to put the stamp of authority upon the apostles and their preaching. Today we are to believe and walk by faith. We are to covet the best gifts of wisdom, knowledge, and faith. If it is God's will for us to have any of these gifts, he will give them to us; otherwise he will not. The Holy Spirit *gives all of these wonderful gifts. He decides which gifts each of us should have* (12:11).

The way to use these gifts that the Spirit gives is beautifully told in 1 Corinthians 13. This chapter is called the Hymn of Love. Gifts without love are poor things. People talk of love, but they do not live it. Until the love of Christ is in a heart it is impossible for people to love one another with any degree of permanency. People seem to worship force. But history shows us that the victories of force do not last.

THE PILLARS OF THE GOSPEL

No doubt there was a group in the Corinthian church who did not believe in the resurrection of the dead. Paul in answering this started out by giving a wonderful statement of what the gospel is (15:1-11). Paul did not give a new gospel. It was the old gospel, given in Genesis, Exodus, Leviticus:

1. *Christ died for our sins just as the Scriptures said he would* (15:3).
2. *He was buried* (15:4).
3. *He arose from the grave on the third day just as the prophets foretold* (15:4).
4. He was seen by many witnesses (15:5-8).

If we deny the resurrection we deny one of the greatest truths of the gospel. Without the resurrection, preaching is vain; faith and hope are all vain. But more than that, no resurrection would mean no gospel at all, for we would be worshiping a dead Christ. There would be no "Good News," for there would be no proof that God had accepted Christ's death as an atonement for our sins. If a sailor jumped overboard to rescue a drowning man and drowned himself, we would know that he did not save the man he went after. If Christ did not come out from the grave, then he could not bring anyone with him from the grave. Christ's body died, and it was his body that was raised again. His soul was committed into the hands of the Father.

Because Christ lives, we will live also. *O death, where then your victory? Where then your sting?*

Paul gives the many proofs of Christ's resurrection in chapter 15:

1. Christ's resurrection
2. His coming again
3. Resurrection of believers
4. Overthrow of Christ's enemies
5. His glorious reign
6. Our earthly bodies will be changed to heavenly bodies

SELECTED BIBLE READING

Sunday: Divisions in the Church (1 Corinthians 1:10-31)
Monday: Human Wisdom (1 Corinthians 2)
Tuesday: Worldliness in the Church (1 Corinthians 3)
Wednesday: Immorality in the Church (1 Corinthians 5)
Thursday: The Lord's Supper (1 Corinthians 11)
Friday: Hymn of Love (1 Corinthians 13)
Saturday: The Resurrection (1 Corinthians 15)

CHAPTER 35

UNDERSTANDING
SECOND CORINTHIANS

Second Corinthians Portrays Jesus Christ, All We Need

Paul was somewhat worried about how the church at Corinth would receive his first letter. He wondered how they had accepted his rebukes, so he sent Titus, and perhaps Timothy, to Corinth to find out the effect of his letter. During Paul's third missionary journey, while he was in Philippi, Titus reported that the majority of the church had received the letter in the proper spirit. But there were those who doubted his motives and even denied his apostleship, saying that he did not have the proper credentials for an apostle. Perhaps they questioned this because he was not one of the original Twelve.

Under these circumstances he wrote his second letter, to express his joy over the encouraging news of how his first letter had been received and to defend his apostleship.

Paul gave more of his personal history in this letter than in any of his others. He revealed his courage and his self-sacrificing love. He spoke of "boasting" because he was compelled to. Read 2 Corinthians 12:11.

Paul tells us of some things that happened in his life that are revealed only in this letter:

His escape from Damascus in a basket (11:32-33)
His experience of being "taken up to heaven" (12:1-4)
His thorn in the flesh (12:7)
His unusual suffering (11:23-27)

He told none of these until he was compelled to, to prove that if he wanted to boast, he had good reason.

The letter begins with comforting words: *What a wonderful God we have—he is the Father of our Lord Jesus Christ, the source of every mercy, and the one who so wonderfully comforts and strengthens us in our hardships and trials* (1:3).

It closes with comforting words: *May the God of love and peace be with you* (13:11).

In the middle we find the Source of comfort: *I am with you; that is all you need* (12:9).

PAUL'S MINISTRY
2 CORINTHIANS 1–7

Paul opened this second letter with his usual greeting and thanksgiving (1:1-3). Everyone loves a true story. Paul told so many personal experiences of his life in this letter that it makes everyone love to read it. He began by telling of the great trouble he had been going through. In all of his trials he had learned to know God better. God is always made more real to us in times of sorrow. We find that God never fails.

Paul's sufferings in Asia were of a very serious nature. Very likely he went through a dangerous sickness in which they despaired of his life (1:4-11). He appreciated their prayers, and now he was appealing to their love and sympathy. He wanted them to be ready for much that he was to write about concerning the defense of his apostleship.

Paul had a clear conscience about his sincerity and faithfulness while he had labored among them. He explained that he sent his first letter instead of coming himself so that when he did come he would be able to praise and not scold them (1:23–2:4). He calls God to witness this statement.

The Judaizing teachers (or law teachers) of Paul's day always carried letters of introduction with them. They were Paul's chief troublemakers. They tried in every way to fight him. We hear them asking, "Who is this Paul? What letters of recommendation from Jerusalem does he have?" How foolish this question was to Paul! Did he need a letter of recommendation to a church that he himself had established? He answered, *The only letter I need is you yourselves! By looking at the good change in your hearts, everyone can see that we have done a good work among you* (3:2).

The lives of true Christians at Corinth served as letters to recommend both Paul the servant and Christ the Lord. People read people. Living letters are read when Bible letters are not. Remember, your life is an open letter. Christian lives are about the only religious books the world reads. They do not study God's Word, but they do study God's people. This gives us a great opportunity for good, for we may lead people to Christ.

Paul's gospel was triumphant and transforming (3:18). Paul's ministry was a triumphant one, but it was filled with suffering. Warfare always is full of illustrations of triumph through suffering. Victory costs! Paul tells us much about his tribulations (ch. 4; 6; 11). When Paul was so gloriously converted, the Lord said, *I will show him how much he must suffer for me* (Acts 9:16). It seems as though the trials began immediately and followed his pathway for thirty years. But Paul was always optimistic because he knew that sufferings here would increase joy beyond (4:17-18).

The pessimist sees a difficulty in every opportunity.
The optimist sees an opportunity in every difficulty.

Paul could sing as he suffered, for he knew the wonderful grace of God. He was always conscious of the presence of the Lord Jesus Christ. He knew that the greater the suffering in this present world, the greater the glory of eternity (4:8-18). Paul lived with his eye on the future!

Christ nowhere promises that a Christian will be free from suffering or sorrow. Rather, we hear that *here on earth you will have many trials and sorrows* (John 16:33). Christ allows us to get into trouble so that he can deliver us. He allowed Daniel to be put into the den of lions so that he could pull him out. He allowed Shadrach, Meshach, and Abednego to go into the fiery furnace so that he could deliver them. He allowed Paul to be shipwrecked so that he could save him. Our God is able to deliver!

Paul found comfort through all his troubles in the fact of the resurrection that Christ promised. He lived under the inspiration of the promise that one day he would have a changed, glorified body. Our suffering bodies will soon be exchanged for painless glorified bodies. Whether we live or die, we must keep this reward in view (5:20).

The aim of Paul's ministry was for people to be reconciled to God (5:20). People are God's greatest concern. As Christ's ambassador, Paul made his appeal to people of the world.

He followed this with an appeal to holy living (6:11–7:16). Holy living means living wholly unto God. Read these verses, every one! He appeals to his fellow-workers not to receive God's loving-kindness in vain, but to open their hearts to him. God demands a clean and separated life. He wants Christians to separate themselves from unbelievers.

LIBERAL GIVING
2 CORINTHIANS 8–9

Paul told the church at Corinth of the generosity of the churches of Macedonia to the Palestine Famine Fund. Although poor themselves, they begged for an opportunity to give, and they gave liberally because they had given themselves first to the Lord. The fund was gathered from all the churches of Asia Minor and Greece. It had been started a year before (1 Corinthians 8:10). Paul was in Macedonia at the time he wrote this. He had accepted no pay for his work from any of the churches except Philippi. Christ was the example for these early Christians (8:9). The Lord knows that if he gets us he will get our gifts and our service.

How should we give?

Give out of poverty (8:2)
Give generously (8:3)
Give willingly (9:7)
Give proportionately (8:12-14)
Give cheerfully (9:7)
Give bountifully (9:6)

God promises to reward the generous giver (9:6). He enriches us with spiritual graces as well as with material things. These gifts strengthened the ties of brotherhood between the Jewish and Gentile Christians. *Thank God for his Son—his Gift too wonderful for words* (9:15).

This is the reason for our giving, *for God loved the world so much that he gave his only Son.* God himself delights to give.

PAUL'S APOSTLESHIP
2 CORINTHIANS 10–13

The charge against Paul by some in the church was that he was a coward. They said he was bold in his writings but was weak in personality. The New Testament gives us no suggestion about what Paul looked like. To imagine that this man, who turned city after city upside down, was weak is absurd. He was a powerful and dominating person. He was a man of outstanding gifts and had a keen and inquiring mind. Beside this, Christ lived in him and worked through him.

His enemies said that no apostle would work with his own hands and support himself; they pointed to the other apostles. But Paul explained that he had the right to receive pay but refused it lest his example be abused by these false teachers who would commercialize the ministry. He declared that at least he founded his own churches and did not go around troubling churches founded by others, as they were doing.

Paul stated also that if these false teachers could boast of their power and authority, then he would boast, too. In a dramatic manner he challenged these critics to compare themselves with him in every way. He was a loyal Hebrew; he had worked more than all the rest of them put together; as a martyr he had suffered more than them all, on land and sea. He realized the poor taste of boasting about oneself, and he disliked to do it, but they had forced him to it.

When Paul boasted, it was for the glory of God. *Their trouble is that they are only comparing themselves with each other, and measuring themselves against their own little ideas. What stupidity!* (10:12). We all have a tendency to take a wrong standard for measuring character. We compare ourselves among ourselves. We conclude we are as good as the average. But average Christians are not what the Bible requires. Let us pray Wesley's prayer, "Lord make me an extraordinary Christian."

Paul had been caught up into "paradise." You recall that Jesus went into paradise at his death (Luke 23:43). There Paul had been given marvelous visions and revelations, hearing things that could not be put into speech (12:4). No doubt no human language could describe the glory. It would have been like trying to describe a sunset to a man born blind. Paul had nothing to compare it with that we could understand.

It seemed as though because of these heavenly experiences God allowed Paul to suffer a "thorn in the flesh." The Lord knows the danger of pride of heart after such an experience, and so he permitted *a messenger from Satan to hurt and bother him.* Paul himself called his affliction a *thorn in my flesh* (12:7). There have been many speculations as to what this "thorn" really was.

It would appear that God has not told us what it was so that we all can know that the grace that was sufficient for Paul in his trouble is enough for any thorn given to us.

Purpose of Testing

Many wonder why God does not remove "thorns" from the flesh when we pray to him. We must learn that God always answers prayer, but sometimes the answer is no. He knows it will be better for us to bear the thorn than be without it. Thorns in the flesh have made many people lean on Christ.

Sometimes a "thorn" is a warning to keep us from sin and failure. God proved to Paul that no matter what his weakness was, God's strength was all he needed.

A minister one day buried his only child. He went into the study the next day to prepare his message for Sunday, but he could not. His grief was too great. Through his tears, which would insist upon coursing down his cheeks, his eyes fell on these words in his King James Version: "My grace is sufficient." It seemed to read this way: "My grace IS sufficient." He wrote it that way on a card and hung it in front of his desk. He learned to know a God who is always present. Every word is important.

My—means God's.

Grace—unmerited favor. I bring Christ what I have—my sin. He brings me what he has—his righteousness. The exchange is made. He takes my sin and gives me his righteousness. This is grace, wonderful grace!

Is—the present, always.

Sufficient—enough and to spare. *Our only power and success comes from God* (3:5). Here is where that minister, Charles Haddon Spurgeon, laughed out loud. "To think," he said, "that our little cups could exhaust the ocean of his grace."

We are satisfied with Jesus. Is he your personal comfort? God gives us unusual strength for unusual tasks. Paul says, *When I am weak, then I am strong* (12:10). There is strength and courage in the heart in which Christ is living.

The Duty of Self-Testing

Check up on yourselves. Are you really Christians? Do you pass the test? Do you feel Christ's presence and power more and more within you? (13:5). In this second letter, Paul emphasized that the Corinthians had to know themselves—test themselves to make sure of their faith. He was anxious that none of them be deceived.

Use every means to know where you really stand spiritually.

Do not depend on a mere profession of religion. Do not rely on church membership. Joining the church saves no one. Joining Christ saves us. Check up on your standing.

Do not trust a past experience. Live only for today. Trust only in a present love, a present faith, and a present service. This gives you the test of your spiritual life in Christ.

Do not rest on mere approved methods of conduct. One can go through the forms of religious worship and not be religious. Wax museum figures wink and blink and seem to breathe, but there is no particle of life in them. Some people go through the motions of religion. Check your motives that move your life. Are they to please God or man? What do you love? The Adversary always tells us we are "good enough," but Christ says we must be perfect. Here are some tests to use:

Do I love to think of Christ?
Do I love to pray?
Do I love to study God's Word?
Do I love Christian friends?
Do I love the church?
Do I love to serve Christ?

Second Corinthians closes with the benediction that today brings to a close many church services: *May the grace of our Lord Jesus Christ be with you all. May God's love and the Holy Spirit's friendship be yours.*

SELECTED BIBLE READING
Sunday: Christ Our Comfort (2 Corinthians 1–2)
Monday: Living Letters (2 Corinthians 3–4)
Tuesday: Ambassadors for Christ (2 Corinthians 5–6)
Wednesday: The Heart of Paul (2 Corinthians 7:1–8:15)
Thursday: Christian Giving (2 Corinthians 8:16–9:15)
Friday: Paul's Apostleship (2 Corinthians 10–11)
Saturday: God's Strength (2 Corinthians 12–13)

CHAPTER 36

UNDERSTANDING GALATIANS

Galatians Portrays Jesus Christ, Our Liberty

Galatians shows that the believer is no longer under the "Jewish law and ceremonies" but is saved by faith alone. *Christ has made us free. Now make sure that you stay free* (5:1). The "laws" are that portion of God's Word found in the first five books of Moses (Genesis–Deuteronomy) by which every phase of Israel's life was to be guided.

During Paul's second missionary journey (Acts 16:6) he was delayed in Galatia by sickness (4:13). Though ill, this tireless servant of the Lord could not remain silent but kept on preaching the gospel. The theme of his sermon was Christ dying on the cross (3:1). It was at this time that he succeeded in founding the Christian churches in Galatia (1:6). They were scattered over a rural district, and the people were country folk. Teachers of the law had followed Paul, teaching salvation by works, claiming that even if Christianity was true, Christians had to be circumcised and obey all the laws. These teachers explained that the reason Paul had not taught the Galatians this was because he was not a true apostle and had learned his doctrines from others. This had upset the new converts.

Circumcision was the initial rite of the Jewish religion. If a person born a Gentile wished to become a Jew, he had to observe this ceremonial law. It was much like a foreigner in our country taking out citizenship papers. If he actually takes out papers, although he was born on foreign soil, he is just as much a citizen as one born here.

False teachers had begun to "cast an evil spell" on the people by telling them they had to keep all kinds of ceremonies. Paul wanted them to know that nothing, no fetishes or works or ceremonies, could bring them to Christ. Salvation comes by believing on Christ—nothing else.

It has been said that Judaism was the cradle of Christianity and very nearly its grave. God raised up Paul as the Moses of the Christian church to deliver it from this bondage. This letter has done more than any other book in the New Testament to free our Christian faith from Judaism (law), and from the burden of salvation by works, taught by so many false cults, which has threatened the simple gospel of the Lord Jesus Christ. So many people want to do something to be saved. The question of the Philippian jailer is the question multitudes ask: *What must I do to be saved?* The answer is always the same: *Believe on the Lord Jesus Christ and you will be saved* (Acts 16:31).

A religion without the cross is not Christ's religion. Christ did not come merely to blaze a trail through a tangled forest or to set us an example of true living. He came to be a Savior. The power of the cross is:

To deliver from sin (1:4; 2:21; 3:22)
To deliver from the curse of the law (3:13)
To deliver from the self-life (2:20; 5:24)
To deliver from the world (6:14)
In the new birth (4:4-7)
In receiving the Holy Spirit (3:14)
In bringing forth the Spirit's fruit (5:22-25)

This letter to the Galatians is the Christian's Declaration of Independence. Our battle hymn is "Christus Liberator." *If the Son sets you free, you will indeed be free* (John 8:36). Folks imagine that restrictions destroy liberty. The opposite is true. On entering a free public park the first thing we see is, DON'T WALK ON THE GRASS; NO DOGS ALLOWED; DON'T PICK THE FLOWERS. And yet this is a free park! We do not complain. These laws preserve the park. If they weren't enacted it would be no more a park than any vacant lot in the neighborhood. Thus it is with society at large. If we revolt against God and his order, civilization will lapse into barbarism. This is what is happening in the world today. Liberty is not freedom from law; that is recklessness. Liberty is freedom in law. Paul speaks of the liberty we have "in Christ" (2:4), for *the Lord is the Spirit who gives them life, and where he is there is freedom* (2 Corinthians 3:16). This is the one great secret of liberty.

This is the liberty that is told of in this book, so get hold of Galatians and let Galatians get hold of you. In Galatians we are not servants working for a living, but sons working in our living. Learn what it is to be free in Christ! Christ said, *I no longer call you slaves . . . now you are my friends* (John 15:15).

Galatians contrasts law and grace: In Romans we find our standing. In Galatians we take our stand.

Paul tells us:

In Romans to use our *heads* to grasp the great facts of Christianity.

In 1 Corinthians to put out the *hand* to grasp our privileges in Christ.

In 2 Corinthians to lift our *hearts* to receive the comforts that are ours.

In Galatians to stand on our *feet* in the liberty that Christ gives.

INTRODUCTION
GALATIANS 1:1-11

This is the only time in all of Paul's writings in which he does not express his thankfulness. Rather he says, "I am amazed." This is the only church of whom he does not ask prayers. How could he, seeing they were bringing dishonor upon the Lord (1:1-5)?

Paul was amazed that these new Christians could give up the gospel of liberty so quickly and accept a Jewish message that was not good news at all. Twice he pronounced a curse upon those causing the trouble. He said if an angel from heaven were to preach any other gospel than the one he preached, *let God's curse fall upon him* (1:8-9).

What is this gospel Paul preached? Paul's gospel shuts out all works. *We cannot become right with God by obeying . . . laws, but only by faith in Jesus Christ. . . . For no one will ever be saved by obeying them* (2:16). The difficulty about salvation is not that we should be good enough to be saved but that we should see that we are bad enough to need salvation. Christ can save only sinners. Grace cannot begin until the law has proven that we are guilty, as the book of Romans shows each of us to be. Then Christ offers us his righteousness.

A gospel of mixed law and grace has no power. The false teachers of this kind of gospel were "cursed" because they perverted (not denied) the gospel. They admitted that Christ had to die upon the cross but denied that faith alone in his sacrifice was sufficient for salvation. They taught that to be saved one had to keep at least some part of the law. They thought that simple faith according to the gospel that Paul preached was not sufficient for salvation. People still like this kind of preaching because they feel they can do something to obtain merit before God.

Paul shows us the seriousness of our condition outside Christ. When a medical specialist says, "Your only hope is this or that," you know what a critical and serious condition you must be in. Here are the words of a great gospel expert. Paul declares that our position is so serious that the gospel of the grace of God is our only hope. There is no other.

Paul introduced the atonement (1:4), a truth once so dear to the Galatians but now practically rejected. Christ *died for our sins.*

PAUL DEFENDS HIS APOSTLESHIP
GALATIANS 1:12–2:21

Paul's teaching was authorized by God himself (1:11-24). He proved that he received his gospel directly from the Lord. Only God could have changed him from a murderer to a preacher.

There are many things we can learn by experience, but that is not so with the things of God. To know them they must be revealed to us. *For my message comes from no less a person than Jesus Christ himself, who told me what to say. No one else has taught me* (1:12).

Paul did not consult with anyone about what he should preach, but he retired to the wilds of Arabia for three years and there listened to God. He was taught by the Spirit. He had been with Peter and James only fifteen days after the three years in Arabia, so he couldn't have learned much from them.

The authority behind Paul's gospel is shown by his rebuke of Peter (2:11-21). To prove that Peter was not a greater apostle than he, he points out in Galatians 2:11-21 how he had openly rebuked Peter for being two-faced about Jewish customs when he was in

Antioch. He made no secret attempt to undermine Peter's authority. Paul was not dominated by this strong apostle to the Jews. It is good to know that the friendship between Peter and Paul was so real that it withstood this severe test. (See 2 Peter 3:15.)

Recall that *justified* means that God credits to my account what Christ has done—"just-as-if-I'd" done it. A criminal is pardoned though he cannot be regarded as righteous. But justification is the act of God whereby he not only forgives us but puts Christ's righteousness to our account. God justifies the sinner without justifying his sin. He gives us a righteousness that is not our own but Christ's.

There are no degrees of justification. The moment we believe on Christ we are made just. Justification is:

By God (Romans 3:26; 8:33)
By grace (3:24)
By faith (3:21-28)

Paul ended his great defense with a personal testimony that gives us a complete picture of the Christian life both positively and negatively. *I have been crucified with Christ: and I myself no longer live, but Christ lives in me. And the real life I now have within this body is a result of my trusting in the Son of God, who loved me and gave himself for me* (2:20). It is a paradox.

This verse is true of every believer. We do not need to *be* crucified with Christ. We *have been* crucified with him. He died in our place. Now we live not by law but by faith. Christ was our sacrifice for sin, and now he is our sufficiency for the new life. The Christian life is a dying life—dying daily to self and sin. It is the crucified Savior who lives in those who have shared his crucifixion.

PAUL DEFENDS THE GOSPEL
GALATIANS 3–4

"I've tried religion for the past five years and it hasn't worked. I gave it up," were the words of a young man when a preacher asked him to accept Christ. "Why, I tried religion for fifteen years and it did nothing for me. I gave it up too," the preacher said. A pause followed. "Then why are you a minister?" the youth asked. "Then I tried Christ, and he fully met my needs. It is not religion I am recommending to you but a living, loving Savior."

Religion, a word once so commonly used among Christians, is fast becoming out of vogue because it has been twisted and misapplied. A religious person now means one who has accepted a creed or observes certain ceremonies or attends certain places of public worship. But all this is not sufficient. There must be a living faith in a living Savior. It is possible to have a religion without the gospel. This was the peril that faced the Galatian Christians. So many people count on their sincerity in believing some creed they have worked out to save themselves. They say, "The golden rule is my religion." But there is no salvation in that, for *without the shedding of blood there is no forgiveness of sin* (Hebrews 9:22).

People who do not believe in foreign missions say that the heathen have their own religion and why disturb them? Yes, they have so much religion that they are bowed down under the weight of the load, but they have no good news of the gospel. It is the gospel we are commanded to preach to every creature.

Religion is the best man can do. Christianity is the best God can do. See the results of man's best. *We cannot become right with God by obeying . . . laws* (2:16). How can a man be made right with God? *By faith in Jesus Christ.* Christianity is God's best. Christ is no sheriff. He is *the Lamb of God who takes away the world's sin!* (John 1:29). We are pronounced righteous not by works of the law but by faith in him.

Paul is defending the gospel of Christ. He describes his own preaching as having so fully set forth the cross that it was as if the Galatians had seen Christ dying on the cross in their midst (3:1). He shows what the law could not do and what grace had done.

Paul put a challenging question to these "foolish Galatians." He cried, "Oh, foolish Galatians, I brought you the true gospel, and you received it with eagerness and gratitude. Now suddenly you drop the gospel. What's gotten into you?

"Come on now, my smart Galatians, you who all of a sudden have become professors while I seem to be your pupil, did you receive the Holy Spirit by the works of the law or by the preaching of the gospel?" Paul asked. This question was a challenge to them because their own experience proved the truth of Paul's preaching to them.

"You cannot say you received the Holy Spirit because you kept the law. Nobody ever heard of such a thing. But as soon as the gospel came, you receive the Holy Spirit by the simple hearing of faith," Paul added.

It is hard for us to believe that the priceless gift of forgiveness of sins and the gift of the Holy Spirit are not gained by real effort, but God offers them to us free of charge. Why not take them? Why worry about our own unworthiness? Why not accept them with thankfulness?

Immediately foolish reason says, "If people don't have to do a thing for their salvation or for an atonement for their wrongdoings then they will become shiftless and will not even try to do good." But we have found that when we have accepted the gospel with a thankful heart then we get busy on good works. We want to please God. Those who think we ought to be saved by our works think faith is an easy thing, but we know from personal experience how hard it is to simply believe.

Luther told us that a Christian is not sinless, but God no longer chalks sin against him because of his faith in Christ. *God declared [Abraham] fit for heaven only because he believed God's promises* (3:6). Abraham may have had good standing with men for his upright life, but not with God. In God's sight, Abraham was a condemned sinner. You see, righteousness had been given to Abraham on the ground of his faith, not his works. If faith without works was sufficient for Abraham, why should we turn from faith to law? Abraham "believed." That is faith. Faith says to God, "I believe what you say."

It must have startled the proud and troublesome Jews when Paul told them that the true descendants of Abraham are not those born of Abraham's flesh and blood but those who believe in Christ Jesus (3:26-29). Though born in obscurity, through the new birth, all can sit down with Abraham as a child of the father of the faithful (3:14, 29). Abraham believed God, and *God declared him fit for heaven* (3:6-7).

The Curse of the Law

The curse of God is like a flood that swallows everything that is not of faith. Remember, the law Paul is talking about is not civil law. Civil law has its place, but civil righteousness will never deliver a person from the condemnation of God's Law. Just because I am a law-abiding citizen does not mean that I am a Christian. Governmental laws are blessings for this life only, but not for the life hereafter. A guilty man would never come before a court and plead innocent because he is a good church member, a fine giver, a member of a Sunday school class. Neither can a sinner come before the court of heaven and plead that because he is in public office or a good citizen or a moral man that God should accept him. The civil courts require that you keep the law. The court of heaven requires that you have faith in Jesus Christ.

The law cannot give righteousness, but it does bring death upon all those who do not keep it (3:10). Law demands perfect obedience. Many think that they should get something for keeping the law. Really they should get nothing. You live in a city all your life, and during your lifetime you keep the laws of that city. Will the city council present you with a gift because you have not broken the laws? Of course not. You ought to keep the law. But suppose after twenty years of law-keeping you then commit a crime. The authorities will then give you something—a jail sentence for breaking the law. The Bible tells us that a curse (a sentence) is upon all who break the law, while a blessing is upon all those who live by faith.

Christ has bought us out from under the doom of that impossible system by taking the curse for our wrongdoing upon himself (3:13). As all had broken the law, all had come under its curse. But Christ has redeemed us. "Don't turn back to the law from which Christ redeemed us. Oh, foolish Galatians, who has hypnotized you so that you turn from the blessing of faith to the curse of the law?"

The law deals with what we are and do, while grace deals with what Christ is and does. What good is the law? We find the answer in Galatians 3:19-20. Everything has its purpose. Let us see the purpose of the law. The law is given to restrain the wicked by giving punishment for crime, just as civil laws are given to keep people from murder and theft because of the fear of jail or the electric chair. These restraints do not make people righteous, but they do restrain them from crime.

Another purpose of the law is spiritual. The law reveals to a person his sin, blindness, and contempt of God. As long as a person is not a murderer or thief, he would swear that he is righteous. How does God show such a man what he really is? By the hammer of the law. As long as a person thinks he is right, he is proud and despises God's grace. This monster of self-righteousness needs a big axe, and the law is just that. When anyone sees by the law that he is under God's wrath he begins to rebel and complain against God. The law inspires hatred of God. What does this beating by the hand of the law accomplish? It helps him to find the way of grace. When the conscience has been thoroughly frightened by the law, it welcomes the gospel.

Law reveals sin but does not remove it. The law proves that every person is a sinner by nature and directs him to Christ! We so often think that we become sinners when we commit some sinful acts. But it is because we are already sinners that we commit the act. A man lies because he is a liar. He steals because he is a thief. He does not become a liar when he utters the lie. It only proves he is a liar.

The law was given also to drive us to Christ by showing us our need. The gospel tells us that Christ is the only One who can meet that need (3:23–4:11). Paul says that the law was our "teacher" to shock us into a sense of our need of Christ so that we could be given "right standing with God through our faith" (3:24). God's law is not like the cruel schoolmaster of former times, a regular tyrant. His law is not to torment us always. God's law is like the good teacher who trains children to find pleasure in doing the things they formerly detested.

The law really has a place in leading us into a Christian experience. Did you ever see anyone trying to sew without a needle? That person would make poor speed if she sewed with only a thread. This is like God's dealing with us. He puts the needle of the law first, for we sleep so soundly in our own sins that we need to be aroused by something sharp. Then when he has the needle of the law fairly in our hearts, he draws a lifelong thread of gospel love and peace and joy.

Children of God
Paul tells us that all are not the children of God. We find that it is faith in Christ, not works of the law or the Fatherhood of God or the brotherhood of man, that makes us children of God. *For we are all the children of God by faith in Christ Jesus* (3:26). It is faith, not works, that puts us into the family of God.

Adoption is a Roman legal word and means "the placing of a son" in a son's legal position. It might be receiving into a family one who does not belong to it by birth, or the legal act of acknowledging his coming of age. Christ came to ransom us so that we would be no longer slaves under the law but would possess all the privileges of full-grown sons and heirs.

As another illustration of their state as free people in Christ,

Paul reminded them that Abraham had two sons—Ishmael, the child of Hagar the slavewife, and Isaac, the child of Sarai the freeborn woman. Ishmael did not enjoy the blessings of a son in Abraham's house but was left out in the cold although he was the firstborn; Isaac was called. This is what happens to those who seek to be saved by keeping the law. But Isaac, the child of promise and faith, was the heir of all things. So we are heirs of a spiritual promise.

PAUL DESIRES THE GOSPEL BE APPLIED
GALATIANS 5–6

The first application of the gospel pertains to one's own personal freedom from the law. Paul wanted the Galatians to hold fast to their personal liberty. It is the gospel of God's grace that gives true liberty (5:1-12). *Christ has made us free. Now make sure that you stay free* (5:1). If the Galatians sought to be saved by keeping the law, they were bound by the law. Their liberty should be prized because it cost so much, the blood of Christ.

The gospel of grace guards against recklessness (5:13-15). Many people are afraid to live under grace instead of law for fear it will lead people to "live as they please and do as they like." Grace will always lead a person to live as God pleases and like what he likes.

We abuse our liberty:

By lack of love (5:13-15). *The whole Law can be summed up in this one command: "Love others as you love yourself."* Use love!

By unclean living (5:16-26). See how the flesh "acts up." Read this list of evil works (5:19-21). These are sins of the mind as well as of the body. This is what we are by nature, and these are the things we do. Christ has given the Holy Spirit to make us free from these. *Obey only the Holy Spirit's instructions . . . and then you won't always be doing the things your evil nature wants you to.* Let the Holy Spirit rule your life.

When the Holy Spirit controls your life, he will produce this kind of fruit in your life:

Toward God: (1) love, (2) joy, (3) peace
Toward others: (4) patience, (5) kindness, (6) goodness
Toward myself: (7) faith, (8) gentleness, (9) self-control

If we live in Christ (John 15) we will be free to bear fruit with God. Are we showing this cluster of fruit in our lives?

SOWING AND REAPING
GALATIANS 6:7-9

A man will always reap just the kind of crop he sows (6:7). If we sow to the Spirit, we will reap a spiritual harvest. If we sow to the flesh (our own wrong desires), we will reap moral weakness (6:7-8).

The harvest will not be according to how much we know but how much we sow. We may have a large supply of seed in the barn of the mind, but unless it is planted in suitable soil it will bear no harvest. Sow the seed of thoughts in word and deeds. God's Word always brings forth seed after its kind.

Sow the seeds of your life in the soil of the Spirit, not the soil of the flesh. In the Spirit it will honor God, but in the flesh the seed will rot and bring forth corruption. The Spirit brings forth only good fruit; the flesh only evil.

So many deceive themselves by saying, "It doesn't matter what I sow if I am sincere." Would that be good advice for a farmer? Self-life will never produce the fruit of the Spirit. Sowing and reaping are agricultural terms. The Christian worker is not likened to a salesman or mechanic but to a farmer. Christian work is not buying and selling but sowing and reaping. When dealing with souls we are not mechanics. We are not just to fix over "run-down" lives, but we are to plant the living Word.

Paul bore in his body the slave marks of Jesus. These were marks of:

Ownership—"I belong to another." The Greek word *stigma* means a brand, a mark, sometimes burnt into the face, body, or arm of a slave or criminal. What were Paul's stigmata? They were scars he had received by persecution and hardship he had endured for Christ (2 Corinthians 6:4; 11:23). The rough hands of a laborer tell that he is the slave of hard toil; the weatherbeaten face of a sea captain, the wounds of a soldier, the lines in a mother's brow are all honorable. The slave marks of Christ speak, first, of a changed character and, second, of a labor of love for him.

Devotion—What scars had the false teachers received for

Christ? None. They saved themselves. "But look at me!"

Commission—The false teachers came armed with letters of authority. "I am without letters of recommendation. But look at my scars! They constitute my commission."

In Christ we are free to know the boundless life that is in him. In him we are "new and different people" (6:15). We are a new creation; we have a new life in Christ. No wonder Paul cries out, *God forbid that I should boast about anything except the cross of our Lord Jesus Christ. Because of that cross my interest in all the attractive things of the world was killed long ago, and the world's interest in me is also long dead* (6:14). "Let the world go by! I have Christ, and having him, I have all things," Paul is saying. Oh, the joy of a free, full life in Christ Jesus!

CONTRASTS IN THE BOOK OF GALATIANS

Grace and Law
The one thing that distinguishes our Christian faith from all others is the grace of God. Grace is God's undeserved kindness to us.

Law shows us our need. Grace shows God's provision to meet that need.

Law says we must work for our salvation—"Do." Grace says salvation is free, a gift—"Done."

Faith and Works
Faith makes us receive salvation by believing.
Works keep us striving to earn it.

Fruit of the Spirit and Works of the Flesh
The Spirit gives us daily victory over sin.
The flesh makes us prone to sin.

The Cross and the World
The cross means love and sacrifice.
The world suggests force and selfishness.

SELECTED BIBLE READING

Sunday: Only One Gospel (Galatians 1)
Monday: Justified by Faith (Galatians 2)

Tuesday: The Law Points to Christ (Galatians 3)
Wednesday: Law and Grace (Galatians 4)
Thursday: Christian Liberty (Galatians 5:1-16)
Friday: Flesh versus Spirit (Galatians 5:17-26)
Saturday: Sowing and Reaping (Galatians 6)

CHAPTER 37

UNDERSTANDING EPHESIANS

Ephesians Portrays Jesus Christ, Our All in All

In this letter we enter the Most Holy Place in Paul's writings. Paul speaks in 2 Corinthians 12:2 of being "taken up to heaven." Here, as it were, he gives his report. He seems to be carried away as he tells of it. It is the greatest revelation of truth that God has given to man. It is the mystery that has been hidden from before God made the world.

This book shows us the great mystery of the church. The real church is the body of Christ, and believers are members of that sacred body of which Christ is the head. The Father not only prepared a body for Jesus Christ to suffer in but he prepared a body for him in which he would be glorified. The Greek word for church is *ecclesia*, which means an assembly of called-out ones. Christ is taking out a people for his name (Acts 15:14). The church is an organism. It is the body of Christ. Every believer is a member of Christ's body, and he is the Head of the church.

Imagine for a moment that the body is like a great building. The "stones" are redeemed human beings. Christ, the Head, occupies the great throne room. All the parts are like "rooms" in the building. With this picture in mind, it is easy to see the whole story of the mystery of the church. The suffering of Christ in an earthly body is now to be made up for by erecting a spiritual body or "building." Come with Paul through this glorious structure as he outlines it in Ephesians.

The believer's position (ch. 1–3):

1. In Christ
2. In "heaven"

The believer's life (ch. 4–6):

1. Ecclesiastically (ch. 4)
2. Morally (ch. 5)
3. Socially (5:21–6:9)
4. Martially (6:10-24)

Paul seems to present a picture of "Christ's Temple of Ephesus," which the Christian may enter. It is a *beautiful, constantly growing temple for God* (2:21). We approach in these chapters, one after another, six magnificent rooms in this great temple. They are all "in Christ." Let the scenes of this book be laid in each of these rooms successively.

THE ANTEROOM
EPHESIANS 1

Let us enter this sacred temple with hushed voices. Christ is going to allow us to go into his holy presence. The door opens into the spacious anteroom, where we read upon the walls our standing with God through Jesus Christ. *Blessed . . . with every blessing in heaven.* Chosen *by God to be his very own. Holy in his eyes, without a fault. Covered with his love.* These are some great wall mottoes for Christians. It will tax every spiritual energy to live up to them.

Our Blessings
Go through this first chapter and mark all the blessings that are ours through Christ:

We are Christians (1:1)
Blessed because we belong to Christ (1:3)
Chosen through him (1:4)
Adopted by God (1:5)
God's wonderful kindness (1:6)
Redeemed and forgiven (1:7)
Everything will be gathered together in Christ (1:10)
We have become gifts to God (1:11)
Faith in the Lord Jesus (1:15)
Wisdom (1:17)

Hope (1:18)
Power (1:19-20)
Given back our lives (2:5-6)
Made near to God (2:13)
Part of a growing temple (2:21)
Joined with Christ and each other (2:22)
Sharers of his promise in Christ (3:6)
Boldness and access through Christ (3:12)

Was this always our position (2:11-13)?
We learn on entering this temple that our calling and position have been planned and worked out by God the Father, the Son, and the Holy Spirit before the world was made (1:4). Every Christian should know *the future he has called you to share* (1:18). The true knowledge of it will govern your life.

Our Redemption

To *redeem* means to buy back, to pay the ransom price, to purchase in order to bring back. Note these facts about our redemption by God:

The Father planned it (1:4-6)
The Son paid for it (1:7-12)
The Spirit applied it (1:13-14)

So overflowing is his kindness toward us that he took away all our sins through the blood of his Son, by whom we are saved; and he has showered down upon us the richness of his grace (1:7-8).
Redemption is the most glorious work of God. It is far greater than his work of creation. He spoke a word and worlds were formed, but it cost him the life of his beloved Son to redeem the world. Paul delighted to dwell on this theme. The reason was that he had experienced Christ's redeeming love. He had been redeemed from sin, from the curse and bondage of the law. He had been washed clean in the blood of Christ, and annointed by the Holy Spirit. He had good reason to glory in his Redeemer.
Redemption is what Christ did for us when we were captive under sin. Let us consider that the sinner is a captive:

1. To sin—*Jesus replied, "You are slaves of sin, every one of you"* (John 8:34). We feel that bondage. We know sin rules our lives.

2. To Satan—Paul speaks of sinners, escaping *from Satan's trap of slavery to sin* (2 Timothy 2:26).
3. Under law—We have broken the law and for this reason *the Scriptures insist we are all its prisoners* (Galatians 3:22). We have been put under arrest for violating the law.

The captive is in a miserable state and needs to be redeemed.

The provision for our redemption: Christ is our Redeemer! *By whom we are saved.*

The means of redemption: *He took away all of our sins through the blood of his Son* (1:7). *The ransom he paid was not mere gold or silver. . . . But he paid for you with the precious lifeblood of Christ* (1 Peter 1:18-19). Christ voluntarily took our place. He stood charged with our sins and paid the penalty with his blood.

The fruits of redemption: He took away all our sins. Forgiveness is the result of redeeming love, and this is according to *the richness of his grace.* His forgiveness is according to his abounding kindness, without limiting it by our demerit.

He casts our sins behind his back. He blots them out of his book of remembrance. He sinks them into the depths of the sea. He removes them as far as the east is from the west. Yes, he forgives according to *the richness of his grace.*

We hear a great prayer in this anteroom. Think of hearing Paul pray (1:15-23)! Paul wants every one of us who are believers to realize fully his privileges in Christ. He wants our *hearts to be flooded with light,* so we can *see something of the future he has called [us] to share.* There is no point in showing a gorgeous sunset to a blind man. So we cannot understand the greatness of God until he has flooded our hearts with light.

THE AUDIENCE CHAMBER OF THE KING
EPHESIANS 2

Next we are conducted into the glorious audience chamber of the King, right into God's presence. *Now all of us . . . may come to God the Father with the Holy Spirit's help* (2:18). We would tremble as we entered if we did not hear the gracious words sound out, *Even though we were spiritually dead and doomed by our sins, he . . . lifted us up from the grave into glory along with Christ, where we sit with him in the heavenly realms* (2:5-6). But best of all, there is a sweet voice sounding through the corridors, "Welcome here!" *Now you are no longer strangers to God and foreigners to heaven, but you are members of God's very own family, citizens of God's country, and you belong in God's household with every other Christian* (2:19). All of this in sharpest contrast to what we were "in those days" (2:11-13). We once were "far away." Now we are "very near."

In this audience chamber we find that God has made both Jews and Gentiles "one" in Christ. We can better understand this by an illustration. A missionary in pre-Communist China told of a barber who was marvelously converted. He had been an opium addict. In desperation he came to the missionaries, and prayer was answered for him. His appetite for opium left and he became a living witness for Christ.

During the barber's stay in the mission a young man of the "student class" came as an inquirer but, seeing the barber, he refused to go in. (A barber's occupation was at that time held in contempt in China.) One day, thinking the barber had gone, he entered the mission and met the barber. Being too polite not to speak to him, he engaged in conversation. The barber told of the wonderful change that had come into his life through Christ. Class barriers melted away. The barber soon was a guest in the student's home, surrounded with wealth and culture. Christ had made both "one family." This is what Christ can do with both Jews and Gentiles, slaves and free men. Christ makes each one a new person and gives access and approach into the very audience chamber of the King.

This new person has access to God through the blood of his Son (2:13). He is our Mediator, and he says, *No one can get to the Father except by means of me* (John 14:6). Then when we have been redeemed, the Holy Spirit introduces the new person at the court of heaven. He asks no one for the privilege and consults no one. There is only one Mediator and that is the Lord Jesus Christ. The Father rejoices in the new person and welcomes each one into his very presence.

The Masterpiece
God is producing a masterpiece, his church. Paul says, *It is God himself who has made us what we are* (2:10). "What we are" comes from the Greek word *poiema*—poem or masterpiece.

In Ephesians 1 we find how God planned and worked in the production of this masterpiece. We were chosen through Christ to be holy and without fault (1:4). In the ages of past eternity God was thinking about us, loving us, and planning to bless us. Know this: Before Satan ever appeared to spoil the happiness of man on this earth, God made plans to make all who would believe on him to be without fault.

Then in Ephesians 2:1-10 we find how the masterpiece was produced. Look at the material he used. Read these verses. How does God take us up and produce a masterpiece out of such material? We see:

What the nature of man is (2:1-3)
What the way of a natural man is (2:2)

"But God"—see God act! He changes all by his touch! This "But God" is the bridge that leads people out of their dark and hopeless condition (2:4). When all human strength is at an end— "But God." Remember, Christ comes to give life to the dead.

A quaint old legend tells of a piece of marble crying from a pile of material that was left as rubbish after a great building had been erected. It was saying, "Glory, glory!" A passerby, hearing the cry, stopped. He learned from the marble, half-covered with dust and rubbish, that Michelangelo had just passed by and said, "I see an angel in that stone." Now he had gone to get his mallet and chisel.

Humanity was like that stone in the heap, broken and useless, but the great Sculptor saw it and began his masterpiece. As Michelangelo saw the angel in the old stone, so God sees the image of his Son in wretched humanity.

Salvation is the gift of God. *Because of his kindness you have been saved through trusting Christ. And even trusting is not of yourselves; it too is a gift from God* (2:8). Faith is a gift! It is the channel of salvation, the hand that receives the gift. It connects man with God.

THE THRONE ROOM
EPHESIANS 3

Standing at the doors of the throne room are the stalwart guards of Law. They demand: "Who goes there? Why do you come? What are your credentials?" I answer feebly, "A sinner. I come to see the Lamb. I have nothing to recommend me for admittance." Then I hear the voice of the Lamb from within, the call of the Son of Grace. "It is one of my sheep. Invite him in. My blood covers all. He needs no credentials." And Grace brings me past the stern guards of Law to the throne of his mercy. *Now we can come fearlessly right into God's presence, assured of his glad welcome when we come* (3:12). What a mighty assurance to persuade us of our privilege and position as Christian believers! *We belong to his dearly loved Son* (1:6).

Here we behold the King! With Paul we *fall on [our] knees and pray to the Father of all the great family of God* (3:14-15). Is posture a small thing? Kneeling is the attitude of humility, confession, and entreaty. Remember, the holiest of all men have approached God this way. David, Solomon, and Daniel knelt. These men stooped to conquer, knelt to prevail.

Paul tells how God had held back from the Gentiles the secret that they would be heirs and shareholders of the gospel and have admission into the church (his Body) on the same terms as the Jews (3:8-10). *To gather us all together* in Christ was God's plan (1:10).

The word *secret*, which occurs three times here, does not mean something mysterious. It merely means it is hidden until the appropriate time comes for God to reveal it.

The secret of the church is that the Gentiles are to have an equal position with the Jews, God's chosen people (3:6). All this was "by faith" (Romans 15:9-10; Galatians 3:8-9). This is a radical thing that God would make the Gentiles with the Jews co-heirs of Christ and co-members of his church.

Paul prays again, and his prayer is steeped in the love of Christ (3:13-21). He prays:

That they would be strengthened by his Spirit.
That they will have Christ at home in their hearts.
That they might understand *how long, how wide, how deep, how high* is the love of Christ.
That they will *be filled up with God himself.*

Paul enjoys the riches of the gospel. It is so bountiful in its gifts and so inexhaustible in its resources.

If we are to enjoy this life in the Temple of God, we must be yielded in obedience to him. If we yield to his plan for our lives as willing subjects, we will find that in his hand our lives will be filled with joy and beauty.

THE JEWEL ROOM
EPHESIANS 4

Here amid the flash of the jewel room we will get our epaulets and our garments of holiness—humility and gentleness and patience. Here are our banners and escutcheons—*one Lord, one faith, one baptism.* Here are the brilliant gems of the gifts as we will take them—*Christ has given each of us special abilities—whatever he wants us to have out of his rich storehouse of gifts* (4:7). We must "throw off," or lay aside, the old life as we would lay aside a garment, and clothe ourselves with the new life as with a new garment (4:22-24).

We must be different, but how? In what respect? What are the things we should be very careful about? We must lay aside lying. Our speech shows our spirit. We must lay aside all bitterness and anger and harsh words. Be kind to each other. We must not have anything to do with deeds of darkness, for we are children of light. Read all of Ephesians 4:31-32.

We must go into God's robing room not to make the garments but to put them on. God is the Tailor and he makes our clothes to conform to our position and purpose in life. God wants his sons to wear suitable garments.

We have discovered as we have come into this temple what our riches are in heaven (1:18-21). Now we must *follow the example of Christ.* The way we live must correspond to our creed. A heavenly calling demands a heavenly conduct.

We are to live (4:1-3):

Humbly—*Be humble and gentle.*
Lovingly—*Be patient with each other, making allowance for each other's faults because of your love.*
Peacefully—*Be led along together by the Holy Spirit, and so be at peace with one another.*

We know that our spiritual lives affect our social lives. But so many turn it around and attempt to create a social life that will create a spiritual life. This cannot be. When man is in right relation to God he will be in proper relation to man.

When God puts on us his jewels of grace, he marks us by his Spirit (4:30). It is like a young man putting a diamond on the engagement finger of the one he has promised to marry. *The*

Lord knows those who are really his. We belong to him. Do you have the mark? Show it then!

THE CHOIR AND ORATORY ROOM
EPHESIANS 5

In the jewel room we were bedecked as children of God and enjoined to *follow the example of Christ.* We were marked with his mark. Now we are to go out and follow God as much loved children. A Christian is *I* following Christ—Christ-I-an.

Follow in love (5:1-2)
Follow in light (5:8)
Follow carefully (5:15-16)

Don't drink too much wine, for many evils lie along that path; be filled instead with the Holy Spirit, and controlled by him (5:18). The body, mind, and spirit cannot function without outside stimulants. No one will think clearly or feel deeply unless something excites him. But this is where the tragedy comes. The world has plenty of powerful stimulants that give quick and joyous reactions. But the results are devastating. Our bodies and minds are for God's altars. *Dear brothers, I plead with you to give your bodies to God . . . a living sacrifice* (Romans 12:1). The Holy Spirit fires our bodies and spirits and sets them aglow but never destroys. Therefore God commands, *Don't drink too much wine . . . be filled [set aflame] instead with the Holy Spirit.* We can burn and never be consumed. We can live dangerously for God and never be in danger.

It is just as great a sin not to be filled with the Spirit of God as it is to drink too much wine. Don't think that only ministers and missionaries need to be filled with his blessed presence. We all do! God's Spirit is waiting to fill his temples (5:19-20).

Talk with each other much about the Lord, quoting psalms and hymns and singing sacred songs, making music in your hearts to the Lord (5:19). Sing, Christian, sing! Christ wants it so. A singing heart guarantees a transformed life. When the Spirit fills the heart, the lips overflow with praise. We will live the Christian life as we sing and talk about Christ.

This joyful praise of Christian meetings is in contrast to the noisy drunken revellings of Ephesus. Singing is the most natural joyous expression of the Christian life. Have much of it in your church groups. There is music in God's house. God does not delight in sighing and groaning or weeping but in songs of praise and adoration, in rejoicing and thanksgiving. He is the One who inspires the poet, the hymn writer, the artist in the world. The devil is the author of distress and discord.

There is social life in this great music room of God's temple. We find it in relationship to everyone.

The Lord not only tells us to follow carefully in the spiritual sphere of our lives but in every other field. How is your life as a Christian before your family, your friends, and your acquaintances? God demands a life worthy of him everyplace and everywhere. How practical all of this is! How simple yet how spiritual! Only people who believe that "I myself no longer live but Christ" could fulfill such demands. Christ is the key to a life of victory in the Son of God. He teaches that a child of God can and must, under all circumstances, be a living witness to the power of Christ in his life.

THE ARMORY
EPHESIANS 6

Now we stand in a room hung with all God's armor. The armor is his, not ours! But he tells us to put it on. We must put on all of it to be safe. The armor is not for a museum where we can go and look over its strength, but it is for the battlefield. Polished armor hanging up in the hall of our creed will not save us in the day of battle. What a relief to know that we do not have to provide the armor! How ignorant we are of the strength and stratagem of the enemy. How inadequately we judge our own ability and weakness.

Paul says, *Last of all I want to remind you that your strength must come from the Lord's mighty power within you* (6:10). As soon as we are brought into communion with God, we need to be fitted for the fight of faith. All who belong to the kingdom of God's dear Son have the forces of the kingdom of Satan against them, so they need to be covered with all God's armor.

The Christian's life includes warfare. We should know the wiles of the forces marshalled against us! As good soldiers let us defend our interests. The crying need of our day is for strong people.

In Ephesians 5 we were asked to put on clothing suited to the new person moving in society. Here we are to put on armor necessary for the soldier.

We must come to Calvary for each piece of this wonderful armor. When we come and take it for ourselves, we can see that the armor covers our whole body. We are to "be able to stand safe against" the enemy. Stand, Christian, in the victory Christ wrought on Calvary. But notice, there is no armor for the back. The Christian is never supposed to run from his enemies but to fight the good fight of faith, praying always!

All of God's armor:

Belt of truth
Breastplate of God's approval
Shoes of readiness to preach the Good News
Shield of faith
Helmet of salvation
Sword of the Word
Prayer

SELECTED BIBLE READING

Sunday: The Believer's Position (Ephesians 1)
Monday: Saved by Grace (Ephesians 2)
Tuesday: A Secret Revealed (Ephesians 3)
Wednesday: A Christian's Life (Ephesians 4)
Thursday: Following Christ (Ephesians 5:1-20)
Friday: Living with Others (Ephesians 5:21–6:9)
Saturday: Christian Warfare (Ephesians 6:10-24)

CHAPTER 38

UNDERSTANDING PHILIPPIANS

Philippians Portrays Jesus Christ, Our Joy

The letter to the Philippians was written to the first church founded in Europe. Paul was called there by the vision of the man in Macedonia calling, *Come over here and help us* (Acts 16:9).

Paul urged the church to have Christian unity and joy. This letter shows how unity among Christians can be broken. Christ is the secret of joy. *Be glad in the Lord* (3:1).

Then there was a pause. Paul tried to think of some better last word to speak, but he couldn't find it. Presently he cried out, "And again I say . . . well . . . just rejoice, that's enough" (4:4). This is joy in the midst of trouble and problems.

Paul and Silas, you remember, sang in the jail there at Philippi at midnight when their backs were bleeding and sore! Paul rejoiced as he wrote this letter, chained to a Roman soldier, for he knew that his very chains were helping him to spread the Good News. He could reach some in Caesar's household that he never otherwise could have brought to Christ. He urged his Philippian converts to rejoice because they were allowed to suffer for Christ (1:29).

The joy of the Lord is your strength. Paul seemed to laugh out loud for sheer joy in this letter. He was the rejoicing apostle. *Joy* and *rejoice* and *be glad* are the words to underline. We are commanded to rejoice. We break a commandment if we do not rejoice, for joy drives out discord. It helps in the midst of trials. "Joy is a bird; let it fly in the open heavens, and let its music be heard of all men." Sinners, like Augustine, are attracted to Jesus by the joy of Christians.

It hardly seems possible that Paul wrote from prison with chains holding him. His words seem to come from a light heart. It is evident that the soul of this great apostle was free! There was an atmosphere of joy even from prison.

This letter has no definite outline, but it is the sweetest of all Paul's letters. There is no scolding. It is more of a love letter.

Paul mentioned the Savior's name forty times in this short letter. Some of the most wonderful things concerning Christ and the Christian life are here. In order that your life may be purified, dangers avoided, and progress made, Christ must be your joy, your trust, and your aim in life. Paul tells us of his joyful triumph over trying circumstances because of his trust in Christ.

JOY IN LIVING
PHILIPPIANS 1

Paul loved to call himself the slave (really "bond slave") of Jesus Christ. He had been made free by Christ and he wanted to serve him as long as he lived. That is the reason he said, *For to me, living means opportunities for Christ.*

You notice when Paul wrote his letters he put his name first. How sensible this is, for the first thing you do in opening a letter is to turn to the end and find out who wrote it.

Although in prison, Paul could pray for his friends. *All my prayers for you are full of praise to God! When I pray for you, my heart is full of joy . . .* (1:3-4).

Paul lived to intercede for others. So should every true Sunday school teacher, Christian friend, father, mother, brother, or sister remember others in their prayers without ceasing. Do you have a prayer list? Do you talk with the Lord about your friends? Is your heart full of joy? Why can we rejoice in prayer? What is your answer?

Although Paul was in prison, chained to a soldier, people came to hear him preach. The Roman guards were so interested in the gospel that they spread it around. This encouraged others to be bold in preaching, and many found Paul's Christ.

There is great power in the witness of a consistent life. You may be bound to unsympathetic companions, but by your life you may win them for God. Your obstacle may become your pulpit. The Christian who works for Christ when everything is against him stirs others up.

For to me, living means opportunities for Christ (1:21). Can you say this? Is Christ everything to you? Do you live for him? Is your one aim and purpose to glorify him?

Listen to the cries of this world. What are they? The successful person in business: "To me, living means wealth." The scholar: "To me, living means knowledge." The soldier: "To me, living means victory." The young person: "To me, living means pleasure." The one who wants recognition: "To me, living means fame." The high school student: "To me, living means recognition." So we could go on and listen to all the voices of the world, but one is heard over them all: "To me, living does not mean wealth or knowledge or fame or glory but Christ. Christ first, last, in everything, and always."

Christ is the *giver of life—My purpose is to give life in all its fullness* (John 10:10).

Christ is *life itself—I myself no longer live, but Christ lives in me* (Galatians 2:20).

Christ is the *model of my life—But you are to be perfect, even as your father in heaven is perfect* (Matthew 5:48).

Christ is the *reward of my life—Thank God for his Son—his Gift too wonderful for words* (2 Corinthians 9:15).

Paul says:

When I travel, it is on Christ's errands.
When I suffer, it is in Christ's service.
When I speak, the theme is Christ.
When I write, Christ fills my letters.

JOY IN SERVICE
PHILIPPIANS 2

Paul gives us the wonderful Example of the Christian life so we can follow in his steps. We must imitate Christ, for although he is Lord of all he became servant to all! Paul urged the church to complete his happiness by living together in love and unity. Is there anything more Christlike for Christians to do? *Then make me truly happy by loving each other and agreeing wholeheartedly with each other* (2:2). This is not an easy thing to do. It means love without compromise.

What is the most important social grace? Elegance of manners? The gift of saying agreeable things? No, it is courtesy of heart, not mere fashion. *Thinking of others as better than yourself* (2:3) is an astonishing phrase! In other words, "I am willing to be third."

We must always bear in our thoughts the example of Jesus Christ (2:5-11). Paul said, "Have the attitude of Christ," which is self-forgetting love. Although he was God, he humbled himself. Not only did Christ take on himself the form of man but the form of a slave. Then he humbled himself more. He who was the author of life became obedient unto death. But even more than this. He faced an ignominious death, *a criminal's death on a cross*. This must be our attitude. (See Matthew 16:25.)

Paul is practical as well as profound. He never leaves us in the clouds. He never separates knowledge from action. Christianity is both life and creed. The creed without the life amounts to little. After Paul has scaled the heights in Christ's exaltation, he has no intention of leaving us there. *Be . . . careful to do the good things that result from being saved* (2:12). God has a plan for each of our lives as he had for Jesus. We must live it out. It is an absolutely personal matter. No one can do it for you. God plants in our hearts salvation in Christ—great, divine, and wonderful to be lived out. Happy is the person who finds God's plan for his life and lives it out.

Christian experience is not something that is going on around you; it is in you. *Christ lives in me!*

Stay away from complaining and arguing (2:14). Paul is saying, "Don't be grouchy! You can't glow if you are!"

Having committed our lives to the control of the Lord, we are under orders. Don't argue or complain! "If God is supreme, why did he allow this thing to happen?" should never pass your lips. You cannot ask your Commander-in-Chief the "why" of anything he asks you to do.

Paul shows us too that there is a sacrificial side of the Christian life. That which costs nothing amounts to nothing. Paul was glad that his work was "so worthwhile." He had feared it might be in vain. So much in life is done in vain. Are we running in vain or working in vain? So many days are spent in vain! So many books are written in vain! So many sermons are printed in vain! So many gifts are given in vain! The Christian life should be a sacrifice if we are to follow Christ. Does your faith cost anything?

If Christ is our Example, then we see that there is no cross without a crown. If we suffer with him, we will also reign with him. We are God's luminaries in a dark age. No flame can shine brightly when it is filthy. The Christian who brings honor to the Lord must be faultless, innocent, and unblameable.

JOY IN FELLOWSHIP
PHILIPPIANS 3

Paul told the Philippians that the duty of every Christian is to be joyful. A long-faced Christian is the worst advertisement for Christianity. The world doesn't want a greater burden; it wants a light heart. How can a Christian be joyful in a world so full of sorrow? Paul tells us in the first verse: *Be glad in the Lord!*

Saul of Tarsus was a man rich in religious background, seeking for the best. He was an earnest searcher after truth and blameless as far as the law was concerned, but he had found nothing that satisfied him. One day Christ found him, and in this marvelous paragraph we see that he gladly sacrificed everything and counted the treasures of this world as nothing in comparison with Christ. He set a new standard of values. He had a new reason for life. Christ had stepped between Paul and his old ideals and made him change the headings at the top of his ledger. He erased "Worthwhile" (credits) and wrote "Worthless" (debits). This was his choice in life.

Paul weighed both the world and Christ and remembered the words of the Lord Jesus: *What profit is there if you gain the whole world—and lose eternal life?* (Matthew 16:26).

In Philippians 3:12-14, Paul tells us that every man's life is a plan of God! The one thing I should do is to carry out this plan. Neither the successes nor failures of the past should keep me from "straining to reach the end" today. *For I can do everything God asks me to with the help of Christ who gives me the strength and power* (4:13).

When Paul met the Lord on the way to Damascus, his whole being was changed (Acts 9). His eyes were opened. He discovered in Christ a store of spiritual wealth that made him count all that he had before as trash (3:7). He had boasted of lineage and pedigree, he was blameless in the law, he had every honor and privilege, but now he was willing to lose everything to gain Christ.

Here are some of the ambitions of Paul's heart. Mark these in your Bible:

To really know Christ (3:10). There are degrees of knowing him.

To become one with him (3:9). To be one with Christ means we are blameless and complete.

To experience the mighty power that brought him back to life again (3:10). The power of the gospel is in the risen Christ.

To find out what it means to suffer and to die with him (3:10). This means a life consecrated to him, willing even to die for him.

To be *all that Christ saved me for* (3:12). He wanted to know Christ's purpose for seizing him on that road to Damascus.

I strain to reach the end of the race and receive the prize for which God is calling us up to heaven (3:14). The higher the calling, the greater the prize.

Do you know that your citizenship (homeland) is in heaven, that you have been born from above (3:20-21)? Therefore, we should live as citizens of a better country, a heavenly kingdom. Don't love the world or the things of this world, but be loyal to him who rules in the "heavenly Jerusalem." When Christ comes, he will change these bodies of ours into bodies like his own, fit for his heavenly kingdom.

Christ's residence was for thirty-three years here on earth, but it did not naturalize him as a citizen of earth. Let us not forget where our citizenship is. Remember Paul's advice in Romans 12:2: *Don't copy the behavior and customs of this world, but be a new and different person with a fresh newness in all you do and think.*

JOY IN REWARDS
PHILIPPIANS 4

Always be full of joy in the Lord; I say it again, rejoice! Let everyone see that you are unselfish and considerate in all you do. Remember that the Lord is coming soon (4:4-5). This blessed hope of Christ's coming again casts its gracious influence over all of life. Paul prays that the Christian will have joy at all times and not be worried by cares.

Yes, the way to not worry about anything is to pray about everything. The prayer of faith must be a prayer of thanksgiving, because faith knows how much it owes to God. Put your prayers into God's hands and go off and leave them there. Do not worry about them. Give them completely as the farmer gives the wheat to the soil after the soil has been properly plowed. If you do this, then the peace of God will stand guard over your thoughts and heart.

Guard your thoughts! Paul tells us what to think about and remember. Thoughts determine your life! Therefore whatever things are true, good, right, pure, lovely . . . think about these things!

Paul expressed his gratitude for the loving thought that had promoted the church at Philippi to send him gifts. He was especially happy about their gifts, not because he was in need, for he had learned to be content in any circumstance with Christ (4:11). He could do all things with the help of Christ who gave him strength. But their gifts meant *the well-earned reward you will have because of your kindness.* He opened God's bank account to them. God *will supply all your needs from his riches in glory, because of what Christ Jesus has done for us.*

SELECTED BIBLE READING

Sunday: Joy Triumphs over Suffering (Philippians 1)
Monday: Joy in Christ (Philippians 2:1-11)
Tuesday: Joy in Salvation (Philippians 2:12-30)
Wednesday: Joy in Christ's Righteousness (Philippians 3:1-9)
Thursday: Joy in Christ's Will (Philippians 3:10-21)
Friday: Joy in Christ's Strength (Philippians 4:1-7)
Saturday: Joy in Christ's Provision (Philippians 4:8-23)

CHAPTER 39

A QUICK LOOK AT
MATTHEW—PHILIPPIANS

INFORMATION PLEASE

1. Which of the Gospels portrays the manhood of Jesus?
   a. Matthew
   b. Mark
   c. Luke
   d. John
2. In which Gospel is the plan of salvation best presented?
   a. Matthew
   b. Mark
   c. Luke
   d. John
3. The Sermon on the Mount is stated at greatest length in:
   a. Matthew
   b. Mark
   c. Luke
   d. John
4. The genealogy of Jesus is given in:
   a. Matthew
   b. Mark
   c. Luke
   d. John

WHAT'S THE ANSWER?

1. Name five outstanding miracles of Jesus.
2. Name three persons with whom Jesus had a personal interview.

3. In which one of Paul's letters is the "Love Chapter" found?
4. How is Jesus portrayed in each of the four Gospels?
5. How is Jesus portrayed in each of the six of Paul's letters we have studied so far?
   Romans:
   1 Corinthians:
   2 Corinthians:
   Galatians:
   Ephesians:
   Philippians:
6. Why did Paul call the Galatians "foolish"?
   a. Because they followed their leaders
   b. Because they turned back from their liberty in Christ to the bondage of the law
   c. Because they formed a new church
7. A Christian's "works" count before God:
   a. For his salvation
   b. For his rewards
   c. For escape of punishment
8. Trace the spread of Christianity from Jerusalem to Rome as given in the book of Acts.

COMPLETION TEST

1. Matthew was written especially for the
2. The only Gospel that tells the story of the wise men is
3. The two greatest preachers in the book of Acts whose names begin with *P* are   and
4. The greatest event in the book of Acts begins with *P* also. What is it?

CHAPTER 40

UNDERSTANDING COLOSSIANS

Colossians Portrays Jesus Christ, Our Life

Ephesians and Colossians were written about the same time, while Paul was a prisoner in Rome. They both contain great doctrines of the gospel and were to be read aloud in the churches. They are very similar in style, yet very different in emphasis.

Ephesians talks about all believers, calling them the "body of Christ." Colossians talks about the Head of the body, Jesus Christ.

In Ephesians, the church of Christ is the important item. In Colossians, the Christ of the church is emphasized.

Both are needed. There cannot be a body without a head, nor a head without a body. Notice this all the way through Colossians —"Christ," "Christ," "Christ."

Heresy had broken out in the church at Colossae, misleading the young believers, calling for the worship of angels (2:18) and a strict observance of Jewish ceremonies (2:16, 21). This heresy was a mixture of Jewish, Greek, and Oriental religions, and all this called forth this statement of the truth of the supreme lordship of Christ. This letter draws a faithful portrait of Christ in all his glory and dignity.

Christ Our Head

Christ is All in all. The failure of the Colossians was at this very point, not holding strongly to the Lord. The place that Christ holds in any religious teaching determines whether it is true or false. As now, some in Paul's day thought that Jesus was only a man, and that Christ was the divine Spirit who came at his baptism and left him at the cross. This meant that Christ did not die but simply that Jesus died. You can see that this is the root error of many cults today. They are based on the same old heresy and misrepresent the truth in regard to Christ and his person and work. It is good for us, in reading the Colossian letter, to examine our own belief and see that we always put the Head, Christ Jesus, in his rightful place in our thinking and glorify this wonderful One.

This letter begins, like twelve others, with the name of Paul, and is addressed to Gentile believers.

The church was likely founded by Epaphras (1:7) in the town of Colossae, about one hundred miles east of Ephesus. It consisted of Gentile Christians. Philemon was a member. Paul kept in close touch with the people and was greatly loved by them.

Epaphras went to Rome to tell Paul of the heresies that were creeping into the church. These false teachings took Christ off the throne and denied his headship of the church. To help answer them, Paul sent this letter back with Epaphras. He writes especially on the preeminence and deity of Christ, for Christ is very God.

The gospel, by this time, "was going out all over the world" (1:6). Thirty-two years after Christ's death, the Good News had reached the whole Roman world. Only one generation was needed to establish the church as a worldwide fact.

The church's position in Christ:

United in Christ (2:2)
Complete in Christ (2:10)
Dead with Christ (2:20)
Buried with Christ (Romans 6:4)
Alive again with Christ (3:1)

Christ Our Life

Your real life is in heaven with Christ and God (3:3). This letter tells us that Christ is our life and we have everything when we have him (2:10).

The Christian life is not a creed or a system of doctrine or a certain kind of worship but a life that is Christ's very own within you. Christ is all in all:

In his deity—The exact likeness of the unseen God (1:15)
In creation—Sovereign Creator of the universe (1:15-16)
In preeminence—First in everything (1:18)

In redemption—Reconciling the universe through his blood (1:20-22)
In headship—Over Satan's power (2:15)
In his church—The Head of the Body (1:18; 2:19)
In his indwelling presence—The Christian's hope (1:27)

God has given Christ first place in everything (1:18). We dare not give him a lower place!

In Romans we are justified in Christ. In 1 Corinthians we are enriched in Christ. In 2 Corinthians we are comforted in Christ. In Galatians we are free in Christ. In Ephesians we are made alive in Christ. In Philippians we are happy in Christ. In Colossians we have everything in Christ.

Colossians presents the glorious culmination of it all. We *have everything when we have Christ.* Our roots grow down into him and draw up nourishment from him; we are steadfast and firm. We discover the facts of this growing process in the four chapters of this book:

1. Growing "downward": Rooted in Jesus, *steadfast and firm* (1:23)
2. Growing "upward": *Go on growing in the Lord* (2:7)
3. Growing "inward": *Your real life is . . . with Christ* (3:3)
4. Growing "outward": *Tell others the Good News* (4:5)

The deeper life is rooted in eternity. It begins in him who *has always been alive.* God gives eternal life.

The higher life is the life Jesus is living for us at the right hand of God, and living in us, for *I myself no longer live, but Christ lives in me* (Galatians 2:20).

The inner life is all the life we have as Christians. It is the real and sufficient life, *for we have everything when we have Christ* (3:3; 2:10).

The outer life is that expression of life that makes Christ known to others. "What you are speaks so loudly, no one can hear what you say."

THE DEEPER LIFE
COLOSSIANS 1

Paul opens this letter as he opened so many. *We always begin by giving thanks to God* (1:3). He rejoiced in the good news from the brothers scattered abroad in the various churches that he had founded.

Notice Paul's favorite themes, "faith," "love," and "hope" about which he so often writes (vv. 4-5). He wants everyone to trust in Christ, love others, and look forward to heaven.

Paul tells us the secret of the deeper life that we as Christians should have in Christ. Dig downward first and become *steadfast and firm* in Christ (1:23). Send the taproot of your Christian faith down deep into his life, as the great oak sends its root into the heart of the earth. We find that although storms beat against the solid oak it stands fast, for it is rooted deep. In sharp contrast is the California redwood. It may have acres of roots, but they are spread close to the surface of the earth. The giant redwood lifts its head several hundred feet into the air, but it has no taproot. Its roots cannot hold. When the storm beats against it, it topples.

Send your roots down into Christ. The source of your life is in him. The Japanese have a way of cutting the taproot of the trees of the forest and confining them in miniature gardens and flower pots. The tree gains its life from the little surface roots and only grows to a few feet in height. Every soul is stunted until it puts its taproot into God and begins to draw up nourishment from him.

Next, Paul presents a glowing description of the mighty Christ, the Superior One.

We find in this first scene that not only are we in Christ but Christ is in us. *Christ in your hearts is your only hope of glory* (1:27). This is what it is to be a Christian: living in him—this glorious, wonderful person, the Creator of this universe, "who bought us our freedom with his blood"—and having him live in us.

In closing this scene, notice Paul's beautiful prayer for the church (1:9-14). He expresses his desire for all Christian believers:

1. That they will be *wise about spiritual things*. He wants us to know how to live a Christlike life, for the fullness of Christ's wisdom will keep us from error.
2. That the way they live *will always please the Lord and honor him*, that they *will always be doing good, kind things for others, while . . . learning to know God better and better.*
3. That they *will be filled with his mighty, glorious strength so that [they] can keep going no matter what happens.*
4. That they will be *always thankful to the Father.*

THE HIGHER LIFE
COLOSSIANS 2

And now just as you trusted Christ to save you, trust him, too, for each day's problems; live in vital union with him. Let your roots grow down into him and draw up nourishment from him (2:6-7). Paul is always practical. Again he says, "Act out what you believe. You began well; go on as you began! We have trusted Christ and have stood steadfast and firm in him" (1:23). Therefore, "live in vital union with him." Paul always wants our life to correspond with our belief. It is sad when a Christian believes in Christ and acts like the devil. No one will accept his profession as sincere. If we have trusted Christ, let us live as he wants us to. If we have been rooted in him, let us grow up in him. All of these are outward evidences of a changed heart.

We have to do a great deal more than just believe truths about Christ. We must *trust Christ* if we are to have life. We cannot earn it or purchase it. It is a free gift (2:6). We are rooted in Christ. That means we draw our nourishment from him. A plant cannot grow unless it is in touch with the lifegiving soil. The Christian life is starting in Christ and then growing in his grace and gifts. We must be as dependent on Christ for the steadfastness of our life as we are for our assurance of salvation.

We find in this chapter that Christ is all-sufficient, *For in Christ there is all of God in a human body.* This is a tremendous truth for us to grasp. In this Jesus, who walked on the earth, dwelt all of God. Neither angels nor prophets nor saints rank with him—for he is the very embodiment of God!

Our life must first grow downward, "rooted" in Christ. Next we must grow upward and *become strong and vigorous in the truth . . . overflow[ing] with joy and thanksgiving for all he has done* (2:7). This is the higher life.

The higher you go with the Lord, the steadier is your disposition, the less disturbing are temptations, and the smoother is your everyday life.

We see Paul's personal concern for the church at Colosse. He longed for the Christians to be established and kept firm in their convictions so that the shrewd philosophers and legalists of their day would not deceive them. The best way to be protected from the snares of the world and its philosophy is an understanding of the perfection of Christ, for he is All and in all. Be rooted in the Word lest you be swept away by false teachers.

Some of the popular street-corner philosophers of the day were teaching that man is unworthy to approach Christ directly. He needed to approach him by means of angels (2:18). Christ says he is the only mediator between God and man. He adds, *I am the Way. . . . No one can get to the Father except by means of me* (John 14:6). Paul rebuked the Colossians for their failure to recognize Christ as the supreme Head and the only Mediator between God and man.

Paul reminds the Christian that when Jesus died on the cross he freed us from the law. We need not keep fast days. There is nothing Christian in punishing the body or in fasting as ascetics have done through the centuries and are still doing. The sacrifice that God asks is a broken spirit, not a beaten body. A sinful heart can dwell in a fasting body. Self-imposed hardships are of no value in offsetting the thoughts of a sinful heart. They only make it proud.

THE INNER LIFE
COLOSSIANS 3

Our life cannot be growing only downward and upward, but also inward. We should know that Christ is the believer's life. Many believe that Christ gave us life as one would put a living seed into a flowerpot. The pot would hold a detached thing—life. But Christ is more than that. He himself is in the believer. The life that is in Christ is in the believer. Notice the illustration he gave: *I am the Vine; you are the branches* (John 15:5).

We find that our new life in Christ makes us less interested in the things the world offers. We become "dead to the world." We find that our real life is with Christ, and as we know him we discover, one by one, the beauties of the Lord Jesus—mercy, kindness, humility, gentleness, patience (3:12). *Remember what Christ taught and let his words enrich your lives and make you wise* (3:16). It will make the difference.

The Brown family lived in a house that was an eyesore in the neighborhood. Weeds grew over the porch; the shades were always torn; the curtains were sagging and soiled. One day in passing by the house we saw the grass cut and fresh white curtains hanging in the windows. The broken steps were mended. "When did the Brown's move?" we asked. "Why, they haven't moved," answered our neighbor. "Oh, yes, they have.

The Browns don't live in that house anymore. A new family has moved in. I haven't seen the people yet, but I know by the appearance that a new owner occupies the house." Yes, our outward life will be different. Others will see Christ living in us.

Since we are rooted in Christ and our life is in him, we are not only identified with him in his death, but we are in union with him in his resurrection. In Christ's death we died to sin, and in his resurrection we rose to live a new life. Since *we became alive again . . . when Christ arose from the dead, we should set our sights on the rich treasures and joys of heaven* and show to the best of our ability the goal of our lives.

For example, the submarine is made to travel under the water. Yet, every submarine is equipped with a periscope by which it seeks those things that are above. It travels in the water, but the well-being of those in it depends on a knowledge of what is above.

We live in the world, but we "let heaven fill our thoughts." Look at Christ, and he will draw you upward.

The Christian's Wardrobe
First, we must "have nothing to do with" the old nature. Paul tells us to deaden our evil desires (3:5-9). After we receive our new life in Christ Jesus, then we must do away with the old life and its deeds. It should not be necessary to tell Christians that they must do away with things that are more like the devil than the Savior!

Any self-denial or asceticism not built on our union with Christ—whether practiced by the priests of India or the Buddhists of Thailand or the monks of Catholicism or a Protestant layman—is condemned at the start.

Christianity is not a series of giving-ups; it is a new life. Women do not give up playing jacks; they outgrow it. As we come to know Christ better we find that some things no longer interest us. Christ adds so much to our lives that there is no room for the old things. The first thing we know we have lost interest in the old and are busy with the new life in Christ.

Paul admonishes us to destroy our old nature and do away with all its vices. Read over Paul's dark catalogue: immorality, impurity, passion, greed. Then there are passionate anger, wrath, and the many sins of speech. Let us forever give up these sins. It is possible in Christ.

Can you imagine how ridiculous you would look if you went to buy a new suit but refused to take off the old one you had on, insisting that the new one should be tried on without taking off the old one! This is what many Christians do. They try to put the garment of a new life on over their old nature. It just doesn't fit. We must lay aside sin first, then put on the new life.

A Christian's conduct is what people see you do. As clothes indicate much about you—whether you are careful or careless; whether you are a soldier or civilian, a king or a commoner—so outward expression will show "to whom you belong and whom you serve" (Acts 27:23).

Now Paul thinks of our new life in Christ. This new kind of life we receive from Christ is always being renewed as we grow in the knowledge of our Lord and Savior. But we must not become so absorbed in our great privileges in Christ that we neglect our duty to our fellowmen. Our knowing Christ should make us much more thoughtful of others. Let us continually learn more of this new life, such as tenderness, kindness, humility, patience, forgiveness, and love (3:12-14). Yes, these are the things with which we are to adorn ourselves. If we lived like this we would find perfection on earth. Paul says these virtues are like pieces of clothing all held in place by a belt of love. This fills our life with the peace of God.

Do you remember how Luther Burbank took the little wild daisy and developed it into a bloom of five to seven inches in diameter, and developed the little poppy into a blossom ten inches across? So our Christian graces must be cultivated and enlarged. Too often they perish for want of care. Too often the fruit of our lives looks only like the ordinary fruit of the world. We must grow into the full stature of the fullness of Christ. As long as we live there is something new for us to learn. We should never stop growing.

Write down all the commands given to you in this chapter.

Christ Is What Matters
No surer test can be given to any false teaching of today than this: Where does it put Jesus Christ? *Does it really agree that Jesus Christ, God's Son, actually became man with a human body? If so, then the message is from God* (1 John 4:2). This is the test of every creed. Does it proclaim that he *bought our freedom with his blood and forgave us all our sins* (1:14)? If so, it is true; if not, it is false (1 John 4:1-3).

A Christian heart is a singing heart (3:16). Christ wants us to be taught in his Word, and then he wants us to express our joy in him by singing hymns.

THE OUTWARD LIFE
COLOSSIANS 4

This chapter introduces another phase of our life in Christ, the outward life. We found we must grow within, cultivating the virtues of the new life in Christ. But there is something more. We want our new life to be seen and felt among others (4:5). This is the way we present Christ to the world. Remember, *Christians* means "little Christs." The life of Christ did not end when the Gospels were completed. Christ is living in us. His life is told today in living letters that are known and read by all people.

SELECTED BIBLE READING

Sunday: Paul's Greeting and Prayer (Colossians 1:1-14)
Monday: Seven Superiorities of Christ (Colossians 1:15-29)
Tuesday: Christ Exalted (Philippians 2:1-16)
Wednesday: Complete in Christ (Colossians 2:1-19)
Thursday: Old and New Life (Colossians 2:20–3:11)
Friday: Christian Living (Colossians 3:12-25)
Saturday: Christian Graces (Colossians 4)

UNDERSTANDING FIRST THESSALONIANS

First Thessalonians Portrays Jesus Christ, the Coming One

The second coming of the Lord Jesus Christ is the truth that Paul is presenting in these two letters to the Thessalonians, and it would be missing the mark not to recognize it. The two letters contain twenty different references to the coming of the Lord. This is the hope of the church. It is mentioned in the closing of every chapter: *Looking forward to the return of God's Son from heaven* (1:10). *We stand together before our Lord Jesus Christ when he comes back again* (2:19). *On that day when our Lord Jesus Christ returns* (3:13). *Caught up with them in the clouds to meet the Lord in the air* (4:17). And in the last chapter: *May your spirit and soul and body be kept strong and blameless until that day when our Lord Jesus Christ comes back again* (5:23). In view of all this, should anyone raise the question, "Will Christ come again?"

Christ's first coming was sudden and a surprise to the philosophers of his time. We learn that his Second Coming will be no less surprising.

Paul, accompanied by Timothy and Silas, had spent only three Sundays at Thessalonica on his second missionary journey, but during that time he not only founded a church, he also grounded it firmly in the faith. In the short time he was there Paul created a great stir. His enemies accused him of "turning the world upside down" (Acts 17:6). On account of this great stir, the brothers sent the apostle away. He went on to Berea and Athens and Corinth. From there he wrote this first letter to the Thessalonians and sent it by Timothy. We know he had only been gone a short time, for he said he *had been away from you but a very little while.*

It is an unprecedented thing even in the ministry of Paul, this establishment of a flourishing church in less than a month. He preached to them for three Sabbath days, although no doubt he continued his meetings during these weeks. Paul's success in Thessalonica has not been the usual experience of missionaries. Carey in India, Judson in Burma, Morrison in China, and Moffat in Africa each waited seven years for the first convert. But here the Holy Spirit allowed Paul to reap a sudden harvest.

During this short stay in Thessalonica a great number of Greeks and women believed (Acts 17:4). He began at once to feed this church with the meat of the Word. He talked of the Holy Spirit (1:6), of the Trinity (1:6) and of the second coming of Christ (1:10). The church was composed mostly of Gentiles rather than Jews. Being greatly concerned about the young converts, Paul sent Timothy from Athens to strengthen their faith and to bring him news of how they were getting along. Timothy brought back a favorable report that was a great comfort to the apostle-founder of the church. However, Timothy had discovered that there were some faults to be corrected. The church held some false views concerning the Lord's coming. They were worried about some who had died, fearing that they would not have any part in the rapture and glory of the Lord's return. Others were so overwhelmed by the truth of Christ's return that they were neglecting their daily tasks (4:10-12). Wishing to correct these wrong views and to inspire and comfort these new converts, Paul wrote this letter.

This is an intimate letter, a heart-to-heart talk. Paul gets very close to his "brothers." This word occurs fourteen times. It is a message of comfort and instruction to those who are in the midst of persecution.

There should be nothing doubtful or divisive about this "blessed hope" of our Lord's return. No one can read the Word without finding the teaching. Let us not quarrel with one another about so sweet a message as our Lord's "I will come again." This is the Christian's hope. Let us rather be prepared, for we do not know the date or the moment of the Son of Man's return.

CHRIST'S COMING
1 THESSALONIANS 1

If you wish to know how to get along with other folks in Christian work, just go over the things Paul said under the guidance of the Spirit. This is the kind of service the Lord Jesus would have us render in his name. Notice Paul's example:

Paul did not try to please men in ways that displeased God.
Paul did not try to capture men by flattery.
Paul was not covetous of what they had.
Paul was not seeking glory for himself out of his work.
Paul kept at his task day and night.
Paul always encouraged others.

In Paul's greeting he included his fellow-workers, Silas (Silvanus) and Timothy. Silas had been with him when he founded the church at Thessalonica, and Timothy had been his special messenger to them, carrying the good news of their progress and reporting their needs back at Corinth. We can learn much from Paul. He knew the secret of friendship that so many would like to possess. He loved people. He always acknowledged others in his service and expressed appreciation for their part in every work done.

Praying as Paul Prayed
We always thank God for you and pray for you constantly (1:2). Do we follow up our new converts as Paul did? Paul's converts were in more than a score of different cities, yet he carried all of them in his heart and kept in touch with them.

Do you have a prayer list? Do you pray for others by name? If you find it difficult to speak to others about Christ, try speaking to Christ about others, and soon you will be speaking to others about him. All of us can do this, even the most timid.

Are we realizing as Christians why we are in the world? How seriously are we taking our task? Paul set forth in this letter the intensity of his ministry, his willingness to die for his new converts, and his dealing with each one.

Paul thanked God for this church. The beauty of this church did not consist of a gorgeous building of mortar and stone but a people who *belong to the Father and the Lord Jesus Christ* (1:1). He was very pleased over the wonderful growth these young converts had made. He held them up as an example everywhere he went (1:7). Already their zeal had made a profound impression all over Macedonia and Greece, and everyone was talking about the wonderful way God was working in this young, vigorous church at Thessalonica.

You yourselves became an example to all the other Christians (1:7). This is what everyone in the world is looking for—Christians who live the Christian life, who act what they believe. This is just what the Thessalonians did. Nothing was mentioned of the financial condition of their "annual budget." But their faith in God was known everywhere (1:8). Their missionary enthusiasm in sounding forth the Word of God had been felt all through Greece. They were what every church should be.

Life in Three Tenses

Past tense—"turned from idols." The believers at Thessalonica turned from idols to God. There must be a personal turning to God from sin and unbelief if one is to become a child of God. The idols of our lives are numerous and varied. To turn to God is to forsake everything that would divide our affections or hinder us in following him with our whole heart.

Present tense—"the living and true God is your only Master." What a change! Serving a living God instead of going through a dead ritual that only mocked their needs by a dead silence!

Future tense—"looking forward to the return of God's Son from heaven." They were serving and waiting! These early Christians believed that Christ would come again as he had promised. This was called "that blessed hope." The prophets of old waited for the coming of the Messiah long ages before he came, but "when the right time came," Christ did come. The church may have to wait long for his promised Second Coming. Many have lost the vision and hope. But at the right time he will come as he said. Mark in your Bible these blessed promises: John 14:3; Acts 1:11; 1 Thessalonians 4:16; Revelation 1:7.

CHRIST'S COMING
1 THESSALONIANS 2

Paul gives us these descriptions of his services at Thessalonica:

"Worthwhile" (2:1)
"Bold," in spite of contentions (2:2)
No "false motive or evil purposes in mind" (2:3)
"Serving God alone" (2:4)
No flattery (2:5)
Not for anyone's praise but God's (2:6)

"Gentle" (2:7)
"Loved you dearly" (2:8)
"Night and day we toiled" (2:9)
Backed by holy living (2:10-12)
Successful in its results (2:13-18)

What a man was Paul! He preached to please God and lived to convince men of the truth of his preaching. His conduct commended his preaching. The Thessalonians became an eager missionary church. He was not a flatterer, nor did he seek wealth. He came as simple as a child and as gentle as a nurse caring for little children. He was never idle but toiled night and day. Giving them this example of his own life, he pleaded with them to make their daily lives worthy of the name *Christian*.

Paul urged *that your daily lives should not embarrass God, but bring joy to him* (2:12). An Indian pastor who was worried over the inconsistent lives among some of his flock said to a missionary, "There is much crooked walk by those who make good talk." Our walk and our talk should be twins going along on the same trail.

This life holds such strong interests, such demanding problems, such vital experiences, that even this most blessed hope for the future is not the only teaching we find in God's Word. Paul's letter to the Thessalonians proves how well Paul knew this, for it is full of encouragement to do right while we wait for that day of Christ's appearing. All the way through Paul enjoins us to "work" while we "hope."

Paul looked forward during these trying days to the Lord Jesus Christ at his coming. His greatest reward, after he has seen his wonderful Savior's face, would be to present to Christ the young converts of his ministry, letting them share in the glory of his advent. They will be his crown of rejoicing (2:19-20).

CHRIST'S COMING
1 THESSALONIANS 3:1–4:12

Paul was aware of the strain under which the members of the church at Thessalonica were living. He sent Timothy from Athens to encourage them under their bitter persecution.

Timothy had brought back the good news of their "strong faith" and "loving deeds." This report filled Paul with unbounded joy. How glad Paul was to hear of their firm stand in the faith and to know that they thought kindly of him and his fellow workers and longed to see them. In the midst of their persecution and suffering Paul flashed the light of that wonderful day when they would be made perfect and guiltless, when they will be changed in a moment and be holy before God (3:13).

The test of any hope a man holds is what it does for him now. Paul told them that the coming of the Lord should be an incentive to:

Right living (3:13)
Consistent daily living (4:1)
Purity (4:3-7)
Love (4:9-10)

Paul urged personal purity and a life that was consistent with their testimony (4:1). Let us strive to have our ideals beyond reproach. Our attitude toward each other should be one of love. You remember the two commandments Jesus gave. First, *Love the Lord your God*, and second, *love your neighbor as much as you love yourself*. Paul charges us to *make your love to grow and overflow to each other and to everyone else* (3:12; 4:9-10).

We discover that looking for his glorious appearing does not mean living a life of idleness (4:11-12). Looking for Christ never makes idle hands. If we were expecting a loved one to return home after a long absence, we would not just sit down as the day of his return approached. Rather, we would be busy getting everything ready, doing the things he wanted done. Can you imagine a mother waiting for her grown son to come home? She would be fixing up a room, making his favorite cake, and preparing his favorite food as she listened for his footsteps. This is the true Christian's attitude concerning our blessed Lord's return.

CHRIST'S COMING
1 THESSALONIANS 4:13-18

A little band of Indian converts in Canada came to a missionary with a strange request. "We are always hearing what God has done," they said. "Now tell us what he is going to do."

Where would you find an answer to that wise request? We

have it in our Bibles. He shall come again (4:16)! If one of your best friends said he was coming to see you, you would not rest until you found out when and how he was coming. But our wonderful Lord and Savior says he is coming, and he will transform the whole world and glorify all humanity. Can it be possible that we would be less curious about his coming than we would be about the fleeting visit of an earthly friend?

There is so much in these few verses that end with, *So comfort and encourage each other with this news* (4:18). There is comfort because of his sure return.

The Christians at Thessalonica were disturbed because of their mistaken ideas about Christ's coming. They were under the impression that Christ's coming was soon, and they were worried as to what would happen to those who had died. What part would they have in his glorious coming and kingdom?

When Christ returns to earth, he will not come alone. Our loved ones who have died in Christ *God will bring back with him.* What a meeting that will be! Death does not end all. Parents and children, husbands and wives, loved ones and friends will be united. How anxious we are to know that "ours" will be in that happy throng.

The Lord himself will come down from heaven (4:16). Christ does not say he is going to send the messenger of death to bring his bride (the church) home. He is coming for her himself! *Jesus has gone away to heaven, and some day, just as he went, he will return* (Acts 1:11). And they *will see me arrive in the clouds of heaven, with power and great glory* (Matthew 24:30). What a marvelous hope this is!

The Dead Shall Rise
Those who have Christian loved ones who have died should not give way to undue sorrow when they lay them in the grave, for they have a double assurance from Christ's Word. There is the hope that one day all the dead in Christ will rise and the additional assurance that he may come again at any time. When Christ comes he will greet the believers who are dead first and bring them with him (4:13-14). When the archangel sounds the trumpet call of God, announcing the Lord's coming, then *the believers who are dead will be the first to rise to meet the Lord* (4:16).

The second coming of Christ was the bright hope of the early church. The greatest fact of the past is that Christ came the first time, as a man, and died on the cross to free us from the penalty of sin. The greatest fact of the future is that he is coming again, as a King, to free us from the presence of sin (Matthew 24:42).

The Living Shall Meet Him

Then we who are still alive and remain on the earth will be caught up with them in the clouds to meet the Lord in the air (4:17). Paul assures us that all shall not die before he comes. *We shall not all die, but we shall all be given new bodies! It will all happen in a moment, in the twinkling of an eye, when the last trumpet is blown* (1 Corinthians 15:51-52).

And we will *remain with him forever* (4:17). Made like him, we will remain with him. He has gone to prepare a place for us. *I will come and get you* (John 14:3). Heaven is where Christ is now. There we will be. This is heaven's greatest honor conferred on mortals. This is the order of these great events:

The Lord's descent from heaven
The dead in Christ raised
The living believers changed
The whole company caught up to meet the Lord in the air

The truth of Christ's coming again thrills us. He went away in the clouds (Acts 1:9). He will come back in triumphal glory (Revelation 1:7). The angels will be with him (Matthew 25:31). The believers of the past ages will be raised, those that are alive will be changed, and as Enoch and Elijah were translated into heaven, so will the whole church be caught up, to give a joyful welcome to the returning Savior!

CHRIST'S COMING
1 THESSALONIANS 5

Christ's Second Coming will be like the coming of a thief in the night or like the flood in Noah's time. The world will know nothing of his return. They scoff at the idea. But Jesus said there would be "signs" before his coming so that watchful believers may know when the time is drawing near. Over and over again Jesus told his disciples that his coming would be as a thief in the night (Matthew 24:36, 42; 25:13; Mark 13:32-37; Luke 12:40; 21:25-35). He warned them to be always on the watch. This should be their duty and their attitude. Christians need have no fear of that glorious day.

Don't fix dates! We should live watchful lives. We should not live lives of sleepy indulgence but of wakeful watching (5:6). The hope of Christ's coming does not mean a life of idleness. Activity should be the theme of our lives as we find it in this chapter.

While you wait, Paul gives you a grand octave on which to play great melodies of hope. Strike every note on this wonderful octave. If you do, your life will be rich.

Always be joyful (5:16)
Always keep on praying (5:17)
Always be thankful (5:18)
Do not smother the Holy Spirit (5:19)
Do not scoff at those who prophesy (5:20)
Test everything (5:21)
If it is [true], then accept it (5:21)
Keep away from every kind of evil (5:22)

Have you ever thought of Paul as a human example of what it means to follow Christ? Paul was "as straight as an arrow" and "as clean as a hound's tooth." Paul could challenge a critical examination of his record as a Christian. Paul had a brilliant and highly cultured mind. We are apt to say, "How hard it is for a brainy man to remain loyal to his Maker!" But Paul humbly prostrated his wonderful intellect at the feet of his Master. The only explanation of such a life is that it was entirely yielded to Christ. You can't be perfect in this life, but there is one thing you can do 100 percent. It is what Paul did. You can give yourself totally and without reserve to the Master.

So be ready all the time. For I, the Messiah, will come when least expected (Luke 12:40). Every morning when we rise we should say to ourselves, "Be ready for your Lord's return, for he may come today." Every night our closing question should be, "Am I ready for my Lord if he comes before I wake?" (3:12-13). Don't live to be ready to die, but live so you're ready for Christ's coming (5:4-8)!

SELECTED BIBLE READING

Sunday: Christ's Coming an Inspiration to Young Christians (1 Thessalonians 1)

Monday: Christ's Coming an Encouragement to the Faithful Servant (1 Thessalonians 2)

Tuesday: Christ's Coming an Incentive to Love among Christians (1 Thessalonians 3:1–4:12)

Wednesday: Christ's Coming a Comfort to the Bereaved (1 Thessalonians 4:13-18)

Thursday: Christ's Coming a Challenge to Holy Living (1 Thessalonians 5)

Friday: Christ's Sudden Coming (Matthew 24:1-27)

Saturday: Tribulation Days (Matthew 24:29-51)

CHAPTER 42

UNDERSTANDING SECOND THESSALONIANS

Second Thessalonians Portrays Jesus Christ, Our Returning Lord

This is the second letter on the "blessed hope," or the coming again of our Lord Jesus Christ. These Thessalonians were forward-looking people. Paul talked to them about what was uppermost in their minds and thoughts. The first letter says "He is surely coming again." The second letter says, "But work and wait till he comes."

The second coming of Christ is mentioned 318 times in 260 chapters of the New Testament. From this we see how important this subject is. With deepest interest we read the prophecies of the Old Testament to find out about our Lord's first advent upon this earth. We should be just as interested to discover what the New Testament teaches regarding his Second Coming "in power and great glory." He said he was coming again. Here are his words: *When everything is ready, then I will come and get you* (John 14:3). He intended that his disciples should understand that his Second Coming would be in as literal a sense as his going away.

First Thessalonians tells about Christ coming for his church. The coming of Christ should be cleared up a bit in our minds. One day Christ will come to take away his bride, the church. He will not be seen by the world at that time, but those who are his, including the dead in Christ, will be "caught up" to meet him. This is the teaching of 1 Thessalonians. After a period of seven years of tribulation for those left on the earth, Christ will appear to the world with his church to establish his throne on the earth. Then he will be seen by all people. His "coming," then, includes both of these two events, seven years apart. We as Christians are looking for the first event. The world will not see him until the end of the seven years.

Second Thessalonians tells about Christ coming with his mighty angels. The two events, Christ coming for his church and his coming with his mighty angels, are really two aspects of but one occurrence. Between these two aspects, the Jews occupy their own land of Palestine; the gathering of the Gentile nations against them takes place; the Antichrist becomes the world ruler; he makes a covenant with the Jews and breaks it. Following this is the Great Tribulation (see Matthew 24:21-22). Then Christ will come with his saints and set up his kingdom on earth with Jerusalem as the center. Christ will come first and receive his own unto himself before that great and terrible day "of his revelation" in judgment upon his enemies.

This second letter was written almost immediately after 1 Thessalonians. In addition to their trials and persecutions, the Thessalonian Christians were "upset" and "excited" by deceivers who made some believe that they were already passing through the Great Tribulation and that "the day of the Lord was already here." Paul tried to clear up the difficulty. Always, when war is threatening and sorrow seems to cover the earth, people wonder if they are in the end "tribulation" time. This second letter to the Thessalonians is good for all to read so that these errors in our thinking will be cleared up.

The church at Thessalonica was carried away with the expectation of Christ's glorious return. Who can help but be thrilled when he thinks about his triumphant coming? But we must keep our feet on the ground. We must work while we wait and pray as we watch, for there is much to do while Christ tarries.

The message here is something like our Lord's word to his disciples in Acts 1. You remember their eager question: *Lord, are you going to free Israel [from Rome] now and restore us as an independent nation?* "Leave that with the Father," Jesus in effect replied. "Do your day's work and wait. The kingdom is coming."

CHRIST'S COMING
2 THESSALONIANS 1

We find that Silas and Timothy are mentioned again in the salutation of this letter. From this we judge that this letter followed the first rather quickly. These two aides were still with Paul. Paul commended the young Christians at Thessalonica warmly before he rebuked them. Let us always look and see if we can find something to commend in those we would criticize. Paul did this so often. He noticed that the promise of the Lord's coming again had inspired them to a "growth in faith" and "patience" (1 Thessalonians 1:3-4). They knew that when Christ came, wrongs would be righted and the Lord would deal with those who had oppressed them, for this was a much persecuted church (1:5-7).

How did Paul describe this event of the coming of Christ? It will be sudden and startling. *The Lord Jesus appears suddenly from heaven in flaming fire with his mighty angels, bringing judgment.* This is no mild appearing for "those who refuse to accept his plan to save them." It will be very different for his own. We read about *the glory of his power, when he comes to receive praise and admiration because of all he has done for his people, his saints* (1:9-10). What a wonderful day this will be for them! Yes, he is coming. Remember the promise of the two white-robed men as Jesus went into heaven (Acts 1:11). What a sharp contrast is shown between the glorious destiny of believers when Christ comes and the punishment of the wicked (1:7-12).

Many believe that Christ will not come to set up his kingdom till all the world is converted, but 1:7-12 seems to destroy this view. Read carefully and you will find that the thing emphasized is that the coming of the Lord will be a terror for the disobedient, and Christ says, *When I, the Messiah, return, how many will I find who have faith?*

The world has never seen our Lord Jesus since it crucified him. He has been hidden from its view. But one day he will appear to the whole world. In 1 Thessalonians 4 Paul says that at first Christ will descend from heaven and, with the shout of the archangel, the church will be caught away to be forever with the Lord. At that time he will be seen only by his own. He is coming for his church. Paul says, *For the Lord himself will come down from heaven. . . . And the believers who are dead will be the first to rise. . . . Then we who are still alive . . . will be caught up with them in the clouds* (1 Thessalonians 4:16-17).

Here in 2 Thessalonians Paul says Jesus will appear to the world with the angels of his power, *bringing judgment on those who do not wish to know God* (1:8). First he will come to take his own out of this world. They will be caught up to meet him in the air. Then he will appear for judgment (Jude 15). Later he will come to the earth with his saints to set up his kingdom. *When I, the Messiah, shall come in my glory, and all the angels with me, then I shall sit upon my throne of glory* (Matthew 25:31).

CHRIST'S COMING
2 THESSALONIANS 2

The Thessalonian Christians were suffering great persecution, and some of them had begun to think that they were passing through the Great Tribulation Christ spoke of as the terrible time that would precede his coming. They thought that the Day of the Lord was already present. They were disturbed about the time of the Lord's coming and were entertaining wrong views as to the nearness of his return. The reason for this was that a forged letter and report, both supposed to have come from the Apostle Paul, had confused the church and added fuel to the fire (2:2). Jesus had told the disciples, *Don't let anyone fool you* (Matthew 24:4).

The coming again of Christ to the earth is the great future event that the church has looked forward to since Christ ascended from the Mount of Olives. Because of its greatness it has overshadowed all other events.

One day we traveled up the western highway to Mount Rainier. The morning air was clear. The vision was perfect. There ahead was the majestic snow-covered mountain. It seemed so near that we thought it would be a few minutes until we would be climbing up its side. We ate our breakfast and started off in anticipation. We rode on and there it was, but we hadn't reached it. Every once in a while a low hill and a turn in the road would cut it off from our vision, but though it would reappear in all its glory, we weren't there yet. For three hours we traveled. There it was, the greatest thing on our horizon. Other things fell into insignificance in proportion to its grandeur and importance. Lunch time came and still we had not arrived, but it kept beckoning us on. Finally it was upon us. We were there!

This is a picture of Christ's coming again in glory. It has loomed big on the horizon of every Christian's life since the early church. It is the "blessed hope" of the church. His coming is "at hand" because it is the greatest future event, but it may not be immediate because God must finish his plan before Christ comes. Do not be anxious. God will take care of his own program of the ages. But know this—the "man of sin" will come first, and the *work this man of rebellion and hell will do* will work itself out.

The *man of sin* is the same as the Antichrist spoken of by Daniel the prophet, by the Lord in Matthew 24:23-24, and by John in Revelation 13:1. The Antichrist is a counterfeit Christ. Satan in a last desperate effort will try to imitate Christ. The world would not have God's Man; now they must have Satan's man.

Before the Day of the Lord's Judgment

The Lord's coming will be "sudden," but sudden does not necessarily mean "immediate." They were to wait anxiously for this time when the Lord will gather his children to himself. Christ tells us to always be ready. The Day of the Lord will not come until certain things take place. God always follows his program. Paul warned the people against confusing the hope of Christ's coming for his church with the day of the Lord's judgment. Before this "day" the following things must happen:

A time of great rebellion against God (2:3). How true this is in the day in which we are living! People are leaving *the truth which God gave, once for all, to his people to keep without change through the years* (Jude 3). They are *turning against even their Master who bought them* with his own precious blood (2 Peter 2:1) and are nailing *the Son of God to the cross again by rejecting him, holding him up to mocking and to public shame* (Hebrews 6:6). The world acknowledges Christ to be a teacher but not the Savior. *Sin will be rampant everywhere and will cool the love of many* (Matthew 24:12). These are perilous times. Scoffers will arise and ridicule the idea of Christ's coming.

The "wicked one" will appear (2:4). He will be revealed before Christ appears to the world. But not until the Lord has caught up his own will the wicked one come into public view (2:8).

The "man of sin" will open his awful campaign against the Lord. When Christ comes, he will find him ruling with satanic power. It will be a time marked with strong delusions. This is Paul's prediction of the Antichrist. "The sin of man has its final outcome in the man of sin." Read Matthew 24:24. He will be destroyed by Christ.

The Antichrist—"Christ's counterfeit":

Will establish himself in Jerusalem (Matthew 24:15)
Will make war with the saints (Revelation 13:7)

Will be worshiped as God (2 Thessalonians 2:4)
Will do great miracles (2 Thessalonians 2:9)
Will work for only three and a half years (Revelation 13:5-6)
Will be cast into the lake of fire at Christ's coming (Revelation 19:20)

Is the World Getting Better?

Does Paul teach that the world is getting better? Is it true that the preaching of the gospel is going to win the whole world for Christ? If so, has the gospel failed? What is God's plan for this present age?

The gospel has not failed. It is accomplishing just what Christ intended it to accomplish—the gathering out from the world of a people for his name, the church. On the other hand, there is this mystery of rebelliousness working (2:7), a development of anarchy among all classes of society. Don't be disheartened. Paul gives us a picture of the state of the world at the close of this age when Christ will come again. There will be a great departure from the faith. In fact, Christ asks, *How many will I find who have faith?* This is the picture of the church preceding Christ's return—a great rebellion against God. Does Christ really mean this? We should judge so from his description of the end days in Matthew 24:1-14, 36-42.

When Christ returns, he will find the Antichrist (the man of sin) carrying out his satanic plans. From the description of the man of sin in the Scriptures and his diabolical use of strange demonstrations and great miracles, we do not see how that and the millennial glory could exist together. It is just as God said it would be. Indeed, the darkest clouds that are gathering are but harbingers of the golden day that is surely coming when our Lord himself will return to take up the reins of government.

CHRIST'S COMING
2 THESSALONIANS 3

The time of this glorious event is to be left with God. The delay in the Lord's coming gives us real opportunities for service. There are two wrong views of the Lord's coming that we might have. Either we become restless and troubled because of having to wait so long, or we grow idle because of knowing that when he comes he will right every wrong and overthrow iniquity. But both of these attitudes are wrong. We are not just to stand and wait, but rather to be ready to serve, preparing for the glorious day when he will come. Let us not abandon the work that Christ has given us to do.

First, Paul gave some instructions to the Thessalonians (2:15-17):

Stand firm—don't be influenced by false teaching.
Keep a strong grip on the truth that we taught you—don't lose any of your foundation truth.

Next, Paul prayed that "our Lord Jesus Christ himself and God our Father" would:

Comfort your hearts.
Help you in every good thing you say and do.

Then Paul asked for their prayers (3:1). His heart was burdened and he needed their fellowship. He had great confidence in their faith.

The hope of Christ's coming stimulates without exciting; sobers without depressing. It is a balancing doctrine. We find in this letter that our Lord's delay gives us opportunities to:

Be loyal to him (2:15)
Evangelize the world (3:1)
Pray for his servants (3:1-2)
Patiently wait for him (3:5)
Live a holy life (3:6-14)

Some thought that because Christ was coming they would just withdraw from business and not work, claiming the right to be supported by the brothers who had money. Paul was very drastic in his dealing with these lazy fellows. The attitude on the part of these men was absolutely wrong, and he asked them to look to him for an example. He never stopped working while he was preaching to them. He laid down a great principle of life: *He who does not work shall not eat.* Any view of Christianity that makes a man neglect working for his livelihood is not of God. Although Paul always advocated charity toward those in need and spent much time in taking up offerings for the poor, yet he was very severe in condemning the able-bodied person who could but would not work. He forbade the church to support these folks and even urged them to withdraw fellowship from them.

SELECTED BIBLE READING

Sunday: Paul's Greetings (Ephesians 1:1-2; Philippians 1:1-4; Colossians 1:1-3; 1 Thessalonians 1:1-3; 2 Thessalonians 1:1-4)

Monday: Christ's Coming, Our Comfort (2 Thessalonians 1:5-12)

Tuesday: Events Preceding Christ's Coming (2 Thessalonians 2:1-12)

Wednesday: An Appeal to Sound Doctrine (2 Thessalonians 2:13-17)

Thursday: The Close of the Age (Matthew 24:13-31)

Friday: Warnings to the Wicked Concerning His Coming (Matthew 24:30-31; Mark 8:38; 2 Thessalonians 1:7-8; Jude 14-15; Revelation 1:7)

Saturday: Consistent Christian Conduct (2 Thessalonians 3)

CHAPTER 43

UNDERSTANDING
FIRST TIMOTHY

First Timothy Portrays Jesus Christ, Our Teacher

First and Second Timothy and Titus are the three pastoral letters, written to ministers in charge of important churches instead of to the churches themselves. Both Timothy and Titus were given explicit directions for shepherding the sheep, for guarding the churches after Paul would be called "home," as he knew he soon would be (2 Timothy 4:7-8). Timothy had been entrusted with the government and supervision of the church at Ephesus and Titus of the church at Crete. How inadequate both of these young men felt!

Because Timothy was a young man, we may expect to find in Paul's writings to him valuable suggestions for other young people who are living the Christian life. We are not disappointed in this expectation, but we also find helpful suggestions for those who are older.

In this day of modern education it is well to offer to young people a commendation of the faith of their fathers, and to warn them against *those who boast of their "knowledge" and thus prove their lack of it*. It is well to enjoin them to *fight on for God [and] be earnest, wholehearted followers of Christ*. And when athletic contests threaten to consume the major portion of interest and time in scholastic circles, it is good for a young Christian to remind himself that *bodily exercise is all right, but spiritual exercise is much more important*, both here and hereafter. And who can hear Paul's words to his young associate without hearing him say across the years to our own young people, "And whatever it costs, keep yourself pure."

It was a real honor for the young Timothy to enjoy the friendship of the Apostle Paul. He was one of Paul's own converts, and Paul calls him *a beloved and trustworthy child in the Lord* (1 Corinthians 4:17). It was during the impressionable days of Timothy's boyhood, while Paul was visiting Lystra, that the people first tried to worship the apostle and then sought to take his life. How Timothy had listened to the gospel preached by Paul! He saw him heal the cripple, heard him as he appealed to the multitude, and then saw him stoned and left for dead. But the next day Paul got up and came again into the city. Among the most enthusiastic converts of that city were Eunice and her son Timothy.

When Paul came back to Lystra on his second missionary journey, he took Timothy as his companion. What a wonderful thing for so young a man! After long years of training under this mighty man of God, Timothy was left in charge of the important church at Ephesus. This brought the timid young man face-to-face with serious problems. Think of this inexperienced young fellow being left in that big church to take the place of a man like its founder Paul! How unworthy he must have felt! How he leaned on the apostle for advice and direction!

It was while Timothy was acting as pastor in Ephesus that Paul wrote his two letters to Timothy. They were indeed letters of instruction and guidance to Timothy, but they have also served as a handbook for Christian pastors through the centuries. Paul instructed Timothy to deal severely with false teachers, to direct public worship, to choose church officers, and to work with all classes of people found in the church. But most important of all, he was to lead a life that would be an example to all. Timothy had a hard task.

Paul had won a vast multitude to Christ during his stay in Ephesus. In the succeeding years the number of converts increased tremendously. Within the next fifty years so many of the non-Christians turned to Christ that their temples were almost forsaken.

One of the things to remember about this time of the early church is that there were no church buildings. Groups of Christians met in homes. No church buildings were built until about two hundred years after Paul's day, and not until Constantine put an end to the persecution of Christians. This meant that there were hundreds of small congregations, each with its own leader. Timothy's work was with these various pastors. Remember, there were no seminaries to prepare leaders. Paul had to train his own men. But in spite of no buildings and no theological seminaries, and also in spite of continued persecution, the church grew by leaps and bounds.

WARNING AGAINST FALSE TEACHING
1 TIMOTHY 1

Paul calls Timothy *a son to me in the things of the Lord*. It is clear that the boy was led to Christ by Paul. He was an example of one accepting Christ as a child because he had been brought up in a home where the Scriptures were taught. This is the kind of Christian experience that we need to emphasize today as not only possible but as the normal experience.

There has never been a day when the church has been free from false teachers who present new and strange doctrines. They are hard to combat since they base their teachings on parts of God's Word but do not correctly understand and interpret it as a whole. What the church needs today is instruction in the vital truths. Over against the teacher of the Law and myths and fables, Paul puts *the glorious Good News of our blessed God.* Therefore Timothy had to safeguard against any other doctrine. Don't mix fables and legends with the gospel!

Paul warned Timothy to *cling tightly to your faith in Christ and always keep your conscience clear,* because this saves people from spiritual shipwreck. It is a thrilling sight to see a ship loosened from her moorings and plunging into the ocean. But it is a solemn sight, too, considering the many storms she is likely to meet. If this is true of a ship, how much more so of a Christian starting out on the voyage of life.

Paul speaks plainly of some who, having lost their faith and their good conscience, have caused spiritual shipwreck and are wrecked for two worlds. Let us pay heed to his warnings.

Even in that first century church, Paul was called upon to warn his young co-worker Timothy against the false teaching that is much like the false doctrine of the twentieth century. Paul had warned them when he left Ephesus seven years before that vicious wolves would not spare the flock (Acts 20:29-30). Now they were there in full force and presented young Timothy with his worst problem.

Paul's charge to Timothy included more than soundness in

doctrine. He wanted soundness in life. Paul realized that a person can believe the Word of God completely and yet live a life far from its truth. It is sad when one's life and one's belief are poles apart!

In this letter Paul says that the best way of fighting error is with a life that measures up to the standards set down in God's Word. Remember, many of us are the only Bibles others ever read. Christians have to live better than other people in this world if their testimony is to count. We either commend Christ to others by our lives or we drive them away from him. How often have we heard, "Well, if that's what Christianity does for a person, I don't want any of it!"

Paul wanted Timothy to live a life that would vindicate the truth he preached. He challenged him to be a good soldier of Jesus Christ. Let us remember that we will not fight very hard for a truth that we do not live. As with Timothy, so with us. "What Timothy will preach will be empowered and made mighty by what Timothy is." Timothy was charged to fight the Lord's battles (1:18). This presents the thought of a campaign and all the responsibilities of the officer in command.

Paul humbly declared: *Christ Jesus came into the world to save sinners—and I was the greatest of them all* (1:15).

Here we catch a glimpse of the man, who probably did more for Christ than any other throughout the ages since the world began, bowed to his knees with the feeling of his own unworthiness. Although Paul was once a blasphemer, God in his grace had appointed him an apostle. Although Paul had persecuted him, now he could proclaim his love. The closer we get to the heart of Christ, the more we realize our own unworthiness. The reason many people today do not have a sense of sin is because they are not near to Christ. Just to stand in Christ's presence is enough to make us feel condemned. Paul did not realize how sinful he was until he was brought face-to-face with his Lord and Savior. He felt that his miraculous conversion was intended to be an example of how God can save and use the chief of sinners. Read 1:2-15.

DIRECTIONS FOR THE CHURCH
1 TIMOTHY 2–3

The church has a great calling. We are not only called upon to plead with people to turn to God, but to plead with God the cause of people. Read what Paul says: *Pray much for others; plead for God's mercy upon them; give thanks for all he is going to do for them. Pray in this way for kings and all others who are in authority* (2:1-2). Yes, he tells us to pray for those who govern. It is well to remember that Nero was the emperor of Rome at this time! It was under this wicked despot that Paul was imprisoned and soon would be beheaded. This proves to us that we must pray for bad rulers as well as good, *so that we can live in peace and quietness, spending our time in godly living and thinking much about the Lord* (2:2).

Remember when we pray that God *longs for all to be saved* (2:4). And our blessed Lord himself stands in God's presence pleading for them.

Do you remember the legend of Aeschylus who was condemned by the Athenians and was just about to be executed? His brother Amyntas, the brave warrior who had just gained a victory for Athens, came into the court. Without a word he held up the bleeding stub of the arm that had been severed in the battle. As the judges looked upon the wound, they said, "For the sake of Amyntas, Aeschylus is counted innocent and set free!"

When we look to heaven and remember that God has condemned us because of our sin, we would despair. But we see Jesus sitting at the right hand of the throne on high, holding up his nail-printed hands and presenting his pierced feet and wounded side, pleading for you and me.

Finally, let all who pray be clean in conduct and pure in character (2:8-10). Let us lift up "holy hands" when we pray. That means that we should not fill our lives with worthless pleasures or needless things that absorb, but come to the Lord with a heart that is cleansed (1 John 1:9).

Church Officers
When we think of church officers we immediately think of the "official board." Paul tells us the kind of people that really ought to be on the church board. If the church is to fulfill her mission of proclaiming the Good News and praying for all, then she must be governed properly and know the real reason for her existence. There are two officers described who are to direct the church, pastors and deacons. Paul outlines the requirement for both groups.

We find as we look this over that the pastor must be a man of blameless character, "have only one wife," not quarrelsome, not greedy for money. He must be a skillful teacher, and one who makes his own children obey. He must not be a new convert lest his head be turned with pride. He must have a good reputation in the community. It is important that the church have the right leadership. Good pastors lead a church forward. How we need good and faithful shepherds today!

Deacons must have the same moral qualifications as elders or pastors. This office is not inferior, but different. The two offices were to be complementary to each other. A deacon or deaconess must be as carefully chosen.

Paul shows us the need of Christian conduct. Church manners are a lost art in most places today. It makes a great deal of difference how we behave, for behavior reveals character. It is not "do-havior" but "be-havior" that counts. It is what we are that speaks so loudly that people cannot hear what we say.

The Church

Paul gives us a beautiful description of the church and states her purpose. She is *the church of the living God, which contains and holds high the truth of God* (3:15). The church upholds all truth in the sight of men. She is the only earthly institution to which Christ committed the preaching of the Good News.

DIRECTIONS FOR THE PASTOR
1 TIMOTHY 4–6

Picture the young pastor Timothy awed by his instructor, the fifty-year-old Apostle Paul, as he says, "Now in these last days some will depart from the faith, giving themselves up to spiritualism and all of its teachings. They will tell you if you want to be holy you mustn't marry or eat certain kinds of food. But let's not put a ban on what God has given for our good. Turn a deaf ear to foolish 'isms' filled with 'do this' and 'don't do that.' People are always trying to find what they can 'do' to inherit eternal life. But," Paul goes on to say, "as a good minister of Jesus Christ, remind your church of these things."

Lead a godly life. *Spiritual exercise is much more important* (4:8). Religion is an appeal to common sense. God says it pays. In one way, Christianity is a business. It asks us to get out our account books, to study the current prices, to consider the possibilities of profit and loss, and decide this question: *How does a man benefit if he gains the whole world and loses his own soul in the process?* Paul, after taking account, found that what he had counted as "gain" was "loss."

Does it pay to invest in the Christian life? Does it pay from the standpoint of life right now? God says it does. Christ said, *Don't worry at all about having enough food and clothing. . . . Your heavenly Father . . . will give them to you if you give him first place in your life and live as he wants you to* (Matthew 6:31-33).

Paul said to Timothy, and to each of us, "Don't think entirely in terms of the physical, how you can please your body." Everyone is thinking in terms of "having fun," of "doing things." The body must be fed, clothed, entertained, and pleased! "Bodily exercise is important for some things," says Paul, "but spiritual exercise is important both for this life and the life to come." Start living for eternity!

Be an example—in both word and deed, in your love, faith, and purity. Carry conviction and command respect. In order to do this, give much attention to your reading and preaching and teaching. The best way to combat any error is by reiterating the simple gospel truth. The Bible itself will do the job, if only you give it a chance. If anyone is to succeed in the ministry, he must pour all his strength into it. It demands the whole man, the whole time. Godliness does not starve real living.

The way a minister treats his flock is of vital importance. He must deal wisely and fairly with each one. The widows must be cared for. Elders must be honored and supported, but they must also be reproved even in public, if they are found guilty, that others may be warned. In other words, sin can never get by in the church, no matter who is guilty of that sin.

Paul even remembers the Christian slaves. They must be taught. Those who serve unbelieving masters are to let their service be a testimony to these unbelievers. Those who serve Christians should not take advantage because of their spiritual relationships. Love should make us serve the better.

Fight on for God (6:12). Christ makes his appeal to the heroic in a man or woman. The Christian life is not a thing to be entered into lightly. We will not be carried into heaven "on flowery beds of ease." We must fight if we would be conquerors. But it is a good fight.

SELECTED BIBLE READING

Sunday: Put Up a Good Fight (1 Timothy 1)
Monday: Pray for All People (1 Timothy 2)
Tuesday: The Official Board (1 Timothy 3)
Wednesday: The Good Minister of Jesus Christ (1 Timothy 4)
Thursday: A Minister's Task (1 Timothy 5)
Friday: Briefing the Christian Minister (1 Timothy 6)
Saturday: The Whole Book (1 Timothy)

CHAPTER 44

UNDERSTANDING SECOND TIMOTHY

Second Timothy Portrays Jesus Christ, Our Example

Take your share of suffering as a good soldier of Jesus Christ (2:3). Be loyal to Christ and his Word!

In 1 Timothy, Paul says, "Guard the true teaching that is our message from God." In 2 Timothy, Paul says, "Guard the testimony that is our life from God."

First Timothy seems to say, "Shoulder arms! Polish the metal! Ammunition ready!" Second Timothy says, "Attention! Forward march! Face front, shoulders square, keep step with our Leader, who is Christ!"

The life is as necessary as the weapon. The sons of William Wilberforce said of their father, who campaigned against the slave trade in Britain, "After a while father gave up preparing his discourses and simply prepared himself." Guard the witness diligently.

We are reading a letter of Paul's, written from his last imprisonment in Rome, in which he himself said, *And now the time has come for me to stop fighting and rest.* What battles had he fought? Note every city or province and island in answering this question. To how many thousands had he preached his Christ, do you suppose, in those at least thirty different localities? In how many languages had he testified for Christ?

After writing his first letter to Timothy, Paul was arrested again, in Greece or Asia Minor, and hurried back to Rome, this time as a criminal (2:9). While waiting in the Roman dungeon for "his time to run out," he wrote this last letter to his beloved son in the gospel, Timothy. His arrest had been so sudden and unexpected that he had had no time to collect his valuable books or even to take his warm coat with him (4:13). This second imprisonment was very different from the first. Then he had his own rented house; now he was kept in close confinement. Before he was the center of a large circle of friends, accessible to all; now he was alone (4:10-12). Before he had hoped for freedom; now he was expecting to die (4:6). Paul had already appeared before Nero, but his case had been postponed (4:16-17). He expected to appear again in the winter and wrote urging Timothy to come immediately and bring Mark with him. He asked him to bring the things he had left behind. Being uncertain whether Timothy could get there before his death (and he did not, for his trial probably took place in June rather than the next winter), he wanted to give him his last words of warning and encouragement.

It is well to remember that this is Paul's last writing! His pen was to be dried forever. This letter was very personal. He mentioned twenty-three individuals. Although alone and facing death, he forgot himself in thinking of others. The Bishop of Durham said, "I have often found it difficult to read these short chapters through, without finding something like a mist gathering in my eyes. The writer's heart beats in the writing."

ENDURE IN THE CAMP—THE HOME
2 TIMOTHY 1

Parental example is the greatest answer to the problem of juvenile delinquency. We must first guard our testimony in the home, which is the training center of the Christian life. This is the hardest place to begin. So many young people today do not have a strong Christian influence in their homes. The problem of youth today is so often the problem of parents. Parents are never found in church, they never hear the Word preached or taught, and the "family altar" is unheard of. This kind of a home produces spiritual and social illiterates.

Timothy had been reared in a Christian home with his mother, Eunice, and his grandmother, Lois. Paul mentioned these wonderful Christian women and commended Timothy for having had early training at a consecrated hearth (3:15).

Paul remembered Timothy's pure faith: *I know how much you trust the Lord, just as your mother Eunice and your grandmother Lois do* (1:5). Someone said, "When you want to make a great person, start with his grandmother." Whatever may be the value of that observation, one thing is sure—when you want to build a Timothy you must begin in the Primary Department of your Sunday school.

Paul called Timothy his "dear son" (1 Timothy 1:2). It seems clear that the youth was led to confess Christ by Paul during his first missionary journey. He was a Christian from childhood. It is no surprise that Paul saw in Timothy a lad of promise as a minister in the early church. He became Paul's understudy, and at the end of the apostle's life he was the best man to whom Paul could turn over his work.

Timothy possessed fine qualities, but he had excellent training as well. He was a thoroughly Christian young man. He had a splendid reputation in his own church. He was the constant companion of the great Apostle Paul. He knew the Word of God and made use of it in his life and teachings (3:14-16). He demonstrated a splendid spirit of unselfishness in his service. He was given great responsibilities by Paul. All this was instrumental in a large degree in his training (1:3; 3:15; 4:6-12).

Man of God
Timothy was addressed as "God's man" (1 Timothy 6:11). What does that mean? Godliness comes from the Word and prayer, God speaking to us and us speaking to God. Manliness includes truth in the mind, love in the heart, and righteousness in the life. Manliness is due to godliness. The grace of God makes a man godly and then proceeds to make him manly.

No man ever lived a life of such constant abiding in Christ as Paul. Now that he was about to leave the church that he had established, he was concerned about its future. He warned the youthful and timid Timothy that from now on he had to stand alone in comforting and directing the church. Paul's son in the gospel, now perhaps thirty-five years of age, had to emphasize above all things teachings that were true and sound, for "vicious wolves" had already begun to play havoc with the church.

The key verse is 2 Timothy 1:13: *Hold tightly to the pattern of truth I taught you, especially concerning the faith and love Christ Jesus offers you.* Paul's life was characterized by an unceasing effort to guard in its purity the priceless treasure of the Christian faith. He wanted it kept untarnished. It is easy to say that it is deeds, not doctrine, that count, but Paul's teaching was that conduct must be based on creed. Wrong thinking makes for wrong acting. For instance, World War II was brought about by men possessed with wrong creeds. These creeds soon became conduct, and millions died to correct it.

Stir the Gift

How easy it is for us not to make use of our gifts and natural endowments. How many lose all initiative. How few people think! Timothy had one of the gifts of the Spirit (1 Corinthians 12). He seems to have been neglecting to use it. In the first letter (4:14) Paul had said, *Be sure to use the abilities God has given you*, and in this second letter Paul wrote, *Stir into flame the strength and boldness that is in you, that entered into you when I laid my hands upon your head and blessed you* (1:6). How about our gift? Have we ever let God tell us what it is? Cultivate whatever God has given. Remember, everyone has some talent. To be sure, some have more than others. But stir into flame the gift you have.

Two men had been discussing the possibility of permanently destroying weeds in the garden, and failed to agree. A third person who had been listening said, "You differ, my friends, concerning the possibility of utterly destroying the weeds in the garden plot. One thinks fire will permanently destroy the weeds, while the other is sure fire will only increase their next growth. But in one thing you will agree with me: No weeds will spring up in the garden as long as the fire is kept burning." Stir up the fire in your heart. It is easy to let it die down. This will keep down the weeds in your life. Keep your love constantly burning for Christ by serving him.

We find in this first chapter one of the apostle's "I know's." It is a verse that gives us great assurance. *I know the one in whom I trust, and I am sure that he is able to safely guard all that I have given him until the day of his return* (1:12).

What are you sure of? Will your answer come swift and strong as Paul's: *I am sure that he is able to safely guard all that I have given him until the day of his return?*

I know the One who is able to safely guard. Put your life in his hands. He will hold you firmly. The psalmist said, *Commit everything you do to the Lord. Trust him to help you do it and he will* (Psalm 37:5). Second Timothy 1:12 is the sequel.

ENDURE IN THE FIELD
2 TIMOTHY 2

We must take our *share of suffering as a good soldier* (2:3) away from home, in the school, in the office, in the place of business. This is our field of service and discipline. Here we are to stand the test as one who "does not need to be ashamed."

Paul was saying to Timothy, "As a faithful steward, teach the truths you have learned from me to trustworthy men who in turn will teach others. As a brave soldier, take your share of suffering. A soldier does not become tied up with ordinary affairs but is under the authority of his superior officer. He leaves his business and friends to serve in the army. Avoid business entanglements that will keep you from rendering the best service. Don't make comfort and 'the good life' your goal. As an athlete must follow the rules to win the prize, you must follow the Lord's rules. And as a farmer gets paid well for raising a large crop, you should work hard, too. Think about how these illustrations apply to your life."

Take your share of suffering with the spirit of a hero. Don't just take it!

For one who was a good man, Paul was enduring the cruelest of suffering. He had been charged as a criminal and put in chains. But he was glad to suffer anything, just so the gospel would not be chained. He reminded Timothy that he worshiped a living Christ. *Don't ever forget the wonderful fact that Jesus Christ . . . rose again from the dead* (2:8). Even though his body was bound, his mind was on "eternal glory."

Paul urged the people to keep away from foolish discussions, for these only breed quarrels, and a Christian should not quarrel (2:24). Do not argue about the Christian life. Live it! Outlive the world—live better than they do—and they will soon listen to what you have to say. The best argument for Christ is a victorious life.

God gives us a sure foundation on which to build our lives— the foundation of God's truth (2:19). It "stands firm like a great rock," for that Rock is Christ. All who build on it are sealed for him. This is the inscription: *The Lord knows those who are really his.* It is wonderful to know that we are known personally by him. This is not true of any other religion under heaven. In Christianity we are God's children and he knows every one of us. *The very hairs of your head are all numbered* (Matthew 10:30). He calls us by name.

God's work needs real gentleness. It was said of the Messiah, *Your gentleness has made me great* (Psalm 18:35). Gentleness and conviction in the ministry will break down hatred for the church and give the church its rightful place. Study to be gentle. Don't send people away by your cruel criticism, but draw them to Christ by love.

ENDURE IN THE FIGHT
2 TIMOTHY 3

When the battle is on and our faith is attacked, stand firm and strong. Fight effectively by pleasing *Christ Jesus by living godly lives.* During every battle let us wield the Word, which is the sword of the Spirit. Let us be soldiers, fully equipped to do good to everyone.

There is only one way to be strengthened against all of the vices today. We find it in 3:14-17. The Scriptures will make us wise to accept salvation. Jesus met his temptations with the Word of God. We can do no better.

Have you ever heard anyone say, "I was a drunkard, a disgrace to my family, a nuisance to the world, until I began to study mathematics and learned the multiplication table, but since then I have been as happy as the day is long. I feel like singing all the time, for my heart is at peace!" Have you ever heard a person ascribing his salvation to the multiplication table or to science? Of course not! But thousands have said, "I was unhappy and heartbroken. I had no reason for living until I heard God speak to me through his Word, and now I know the living Savior."

The Word of God is the only thing that will guard the church in this terrible day. The church of Rome put aside the Word and the Dark Ages was the result. The Protestants brought it back into circulation, but Christians everywhere are neglecting it. The ignorance of the Word today is appalling.

Paul's catalog of first-century vices sounds like a list of twentieth-century vices (3:1-5):

People will love only themselves.
Greedy—they will do anything to make money.
Proud and boastful—pride fills the natural heart.
Sneering at God—taking God's name in vain.
Disobedient to parents—no respect in the home.

Ungrateful—taking everything for granted.

Thoroughly bad—caring neither for God nor man.

Think nothing of immorality—divorce, pornography, and homosexuality rampant.

Constant liars—promises mean nothing.

Prefer good times to worshiping God.

ENDURE TO THE DEATH
2 TIMOTHY 4

To endure to the end and look back over a hard and bitter fight and say, "I have won!"—that is enduring as a good soldier. Life's last hours for Paul were full of glory. He forgot that the lions in the arena or the flames at the stake or a cruel cross might end his earthly life at any moment. His fight was ended and now only the memories of a noble life gave him great peace.

He closed this letter with a solemn farewell charge to Timothy before God and Christ, who will judge him and who soon will appear to spread the gospel everywhere. *Preach the Word of God . . . in season and out*, for a time is coming when people will not listen to sound teaching.

Paul's Valedictory

Where can we match the words Paul wrote from his dungeon to Timothy, his own dear son in the faith? Let us picture the old battle-scarred hero of the cross, standing in the gloomy dungeon, bound with chains, and looking up through the one opening in the roof of his cell through which only a tiny shaft of light could enter, revealing his face with an expression of perfect peace. His lips are moving, and we hear him say, *I have fought long and hard for my Lord, and through it all I have kept true to him. And now the time has come for me to stop fighting and rest. In heaven a crown is waiting for me which the Lord, the righteous Judge, will give me on that great day of his return. And not just to me, but to all those whose lives show that they are eagerly looking forward to his coming back again* (4:7-8).

Ever since Jesus had laid his hand on him, Paul seemed to have been contending in the arena. There had been scarcely a moment of rest. It was an intense training and a strenuous wrestling all the way through. But within, peace reigned. His questions were answered. His sins were forgiven. His needs were supplied. Peace within but the athlete's contest without. This is the true Christian life.

Coming with Crowns

The crown was for Paul but it is also for us—*all those whose lives show that they are eagerly looking forward to his coming back.* You and I, whose achievements are so much less than Paul's, may yet be partakers of Paul's heaven.

Surely the "crown" that gleams before us should spur us on to a new diligence in service. Do we eagerly look forward to his return?

The last verses of this letter give us a glimpse of the loneliness of this great soldier of Jesus Christ. Many were leaving him under the stress of persecution. *But the Lord stood with me and gave me the opportunity to boldly preach a whole sermon for all the world to hear* (4:17). This was the secret of Paul's success. This was why he could fight a good fight. His greatest opportunity seemed to be reserved for the end. He stood in Nero's courthouse. He was alone as far as human help was concerned. The great hall was crowded and every eye was fastened on the forsaken old man at the bar. Did he quail? Was he afraid? No, indeed! He leaped to the height of the momentous occasion. He was not content in defending himself. That he did, but much more. To the curious and hostile crowd, he clearly preached the gospel of Christ, and all the Gentiles heard.

SELECTED BIBLE READING

Sunday: Stir into Flame (2 Timothy 1:1-9)
Monday: Hold Tightly to the Truth (2 Timothy 1:10-18)
Tuesday: Take Your Suffering as a Soldier (2 Timothy 2:1-15)
Wednesday: Follow Righteousness (2 Timothy 2:16-26)
Thursday: Know the Scriptures (2 Timothy 3)
Friday: Be Faithful to the End (2 Timothy 4)
Saturday: Receive a Crown (1 Corinthians 9:25; 2 Timothy 4:8; James 1:12; 1 Peter 5:4; Revelation 2:10; 3:11)

CHAPTER 45

UNDERSTANDING
TITUS AND PHILEMON

Titus and Philemon Portray Jesus Christ,
Our Pattern; Our Lord and Master

UNDERSTANDING TITUS

The importance of good works is stressed in this letter. Not that
we are saved by good works, but we are saved for the purpose
of doing good. God presents his ideal for the church and its
officers and members.

The letter to Titus was written by Paul. Titus was bishop of
Crete, a hard post (1:12-13). Paul had given Titus the difficult
task before of settling the differences at Corinth and tactfully
persuading the church to do the right thing in the matter of
divisions. Paul's second letter to the Corinthians shows how
successful Titus was in this mission. Titus was a Gentile. No
doubt he was one of Paul's converts during the early years of
the apostle's ministry. He accompanied Paul and Barnabas to
Jerusalem seventeen years after Paul's conversion.

When Paul heard that Apollos was about to go to Crete, he
took the opportunity to send this letter to Titus (3:13). It was full
of practical advice to the young pastor. It directed him in his
administration and warned him against the heretics of his day.
Paul asked Titus to come to him and to report on the condition
of the church on the island. Although this was a personal letter,
it undoubtedly was to be read to the church also.

The letter is very much like Paul's first letter to Timothy, being
written about the same time and dealing with the same subjects.

WORKS FOR CHURCH OFFICERS
TITUS 1

Paul introduces himself as the "slave" of the Lord Jesus Christ, then as his messenger, or apostle. Paul loved to call himself a bondslave of Christ. It is terrible to be a slave to most anyone or anything, but to be a slave of Jesus Christ—to be bought by him—that is wonderful! It is a slavery of love.

"In grace," Charles Haddon Spurgeon once said, "you can be under bonds yet not in bondage. I am in bonds of wedlock but I feel no bondage. On the contrary it is joy to be so bound."

Paul kept his eyes steadfastly on heaven as he neared the end of his earthly life. Read what he says of his apostleship: *I have been sent to bring faith to those God has chosen . . . so that they can have eternal life.*

Paul left Titus in Crete to superintend the work of the church organization there. It was a hard situation, but Paul had given him a difficult task before at Corinth and he had worked out the problem. In Crete he was to set things in order and ordain pastors in every city (1:5).

The qualifications of church officers are stated carefully (1:6-9). Only a man of character should even be considered. He must be blameless in his home life, blameless in his personal life, and true to the Word.

How do you act at home? What kind of a Christian are you there? This is so often the test of your Christianity. It is the home life that counts. The Christian household is the main evangelizing agency everywhere. When the home is Christian, the community is Christian. For this reason, the pastor is enjoined to set a good example before the people. He must have but one living wife, but he is not compelled to be married. On the other hand, he is not to refrain from marriage. Because a minister is judged by his family life, he must rule his own children well, for he who cannot rule his own household well cannot rule the church of God (1 Timothy 3:5). He must be a man of moral courage and sympathy. He must be a good teacher and encourage others by his teaching.

The Cretan churches were being upset by outside teachers who, for the sake of making money, were working havoc in "whole families" (1:11). This probably meant whole congregations, for the early church met in private homes. Paul called these fellows "rotten and disobedient" (1:16) and said they must be stopped in their teaching. He demanded severity in dealing with them. How much false teaching there is today everywhere! There are more cults and sects that men and women are starting, by which they make themselves rich.

During the great San Francisco earthquake an old saint remained in her room, joyously rocking back and forth in her chair, singing, while all around her people were running in dread of death. After all was over someone asked her how she could have had such a feeling of joy. "Oh," she replied, "I was so happy in the thought that my God was mighty enough to rock the world like that, while he held me securely in his hand, I did not have time to be frightened."

So it is in this day in which we are living, when all is being shaken in confusion about us and there are *many who refuse to obey. . . . Whole families have been turned away from the grace of God. Such teachers are only after your money* (1:10-11) and *claim they know God, but from seeing the way they act, one knows they don't* (1:16). So let us, I say, rest our faith not on the reasonings and opinions of men but on the infallible Word of God. By this Word alone judge new and strange doctrines, and stop the mouths of those who handle the Word of God deceitfully (1:9-11).

WORKS FOR CHURCH MEMBERS
T I T U S   2 – 3

Paul believed that doctrine must be expressed in life, and so he had a word to Titus about the older people (2:2-3), the young people (2:4-6), and the slaves (2:9-10).

Men—be serious, sensible, believing the truth, doing everything with love and patience.

Women—be respectful, avoid drink and scandal, teach good things, become good wives and mothers.

Young people—exercise self-control, be examples of a noble life.

Slaves—obey masters, be diligent and faithful, give satisfaction, don't contradict, don't steal.

Life with a Capital L
Leave the old life.
Live the new life.
Look for the glorious appearing of Christ (2:11-13).

How essential that this be our foundation! Then we can *make people want to believe in our Savior and God* (2:10). To think that we in any way can make people want to believe the wonderful gospel by our lives! As we put a frame on a beautiful picture to enhance its beauty and make it more conspicuous, so we must make more beautiful the Good News of Christ. A king in his royal robes is more easily recognized as such than one in ordinary clothing. How we can either make or mar the gospel! What is the "gospel according to you"? In all things be an example of good deeds of every kind. The test of fellowship is not warmth of devotion but holiness of life. One cannot live on strong "feelings." Some mistake religious feeling for holiness and good thoughts for good conduct. There is use and abuse in religious emotion.

Be so faithful in your attitudes and obligations of life that critics of your religion will be silenced (2:8). Make others say, "If this is what Christ can do for you, there must be something to your religion."

Not that we are saved by good works, but we are saved for the purpose of doing good works. Paul says we are saved by God's mercy (3:5) and justified by his grace (3:7). But because we have been saved at such a cost, we should show it by "good works."

Good Works
"Our Savior and God" did not save us as a result of our good works, but through his kindness and according to his mercy. He cleansed us by his blood and gave us a new life by his Holy Spirit. But we are to do good works:

An example of good deeds (2:7)
Enthusiasm for doing kind things (2:14)
Ready for any honest work (3:1)
Careful to do good deeds (3:8)
Learn to help all who need assistance (3:14)

Paul urged citizens of the heavenly kingdom to be good citizens of the country under whose flag they live. Every Christian should be submissive to rulers and authority (3:1-2; Romans 13:1-7; 1 Peter 2:13-17).

"Don't say anything of a person if you can't say something good" is a wonderful admonition to follow. Paul said it long ago. *You must not speak evil of anyone.* Don't be quarrelsome. Show a gentle spirit in your dealing with others. It is well for us to remember that *once we, too, were foolish.* Yes, we had all the faults we hate in others. It is well to remember that the things we criticize in others are very likely to be our own weaknesses. We like to call attention to these faults in others to take eyes off of ourselves. Try this test on yourself.

Avoid controversies and foolish discussions. They are always useless and futile. So often an argument only strengthens a person in what he believed before. Do all you can to correct a person, but if he persists in causing divisions among you, after warning him once or twice, have nothing more to say to him. Reject him (3:10). Devote your time to doing good.

UNDERSTANDING PHILEMON

Christian love and forgiveness are given prominence in this book. It shows the power of the gospel in winning a runaway thief and slave, and in changing a master's mind. This is a book of applied Christianity, a textbook of social service.

The Reverend Sir W. Robertson Nicoll once said, "If I were to covet any honor of authorship, it would be this: That some letters of mine might be found in the desks of my friends when their life struggle is ended."

We don't know whether Paul coveted this honor or not, but tucked away in your New Testament, between Titus and Hebrews, you will find a model letter written by a master of letter writing. It is a personal letter from Paul to Philemon. Only one chapter of twenty-five verses, Philemon contains such strong, beautiful, and well-expressed statements that it stands out as a gem, even in the Book of books.

Notice the courtesy and tactfulness of Paul's letter. Our letter writing can be a ministry for God if we make it so. Some who find it hard to speak to anyone about Christ can write about him. Then too, a letter is good for the one who receives it, for he has a chance to read and reread and think it over. Use the pen in witnessing to your friends. Remember all that has been preserved to us of Paul's ministry has come mainly through his letters. What a heritage they are for all Christians today! In order to appreciate what God thought of correspondence, see how many letters he kept for us in Holy Scripture.

In this letter Paul interceded with Philemon (who was an outstanding member of the church at Colossae) for a runaway slave by the name of Onesimus, who had stolen from his master and made his way to Rome. There he had been providentially brought face to face with Paul and had found Christ as his Savior. He became endeared to the apostle by his devoted service. But Paul knew he was Philemon's lawful slave and so he could not think of keeping him permanently. So Paul sent him home and pleaded with Philemon to take him back. He made himself personally responsible for the debts that Onesimus owed, asking that they be charged to his (Paul's) account. He wished to save the runaway slave from the severe and cruel punishment he deserved according to Roman law. Paul didn't want the slave to encounter his outraged master alone.

This letter deals with the question of slavery. Paul did not demand the abolition of slavery, but he showed that slavery can never be the fruit of Christianity. This beautiful letter from God's aged servant, in jail for the gospel, foreshadowed the time when the bonds of Christ's love would break the bands of slavery.

Onesimus was merely one of a world of slaves belonging to a handful of masters. In 300 B.C., twenty-one thousand citizens of Athens owned four hundred thousand slaves. It was not so different proportionately throughout the Roman Empire at the time of the writing of this letter. Roman masters owned from ten to two hundred, even a thousand or more slaves, who had no rights of life or liberty!

PAUL'S PLEA FOR ONESIMUS
PHILEMON 1-25

Here is a letter from Paul, now an old man (v. 9). It is not always the passing of years that brings old age. The apostle had become prematurely old through work, anxiety, and eagerness of spirit. He was only about sixty, but he was a prisoner, and as such he appealed to his friend Philemon.

Paul spoke of himself as a prisoner, not, as in the letter to the Colossians, with the authority of an apostle. He wrote as a friend to a friend. He said, *Our much loved fellow worker.* He did not say these kind things just to flatter his friend, but because he always looked for the good in others.

The letter was addressed to a man and his wife, and presumably a son, in Colossae. A little meeting of Christians was held at their home. Paul gives us a beautiful picture of a Christian home in the time of the early church. This family was the nucleus of that home church, and doubtless other believers in Colossae gathered there for worship. One of the causes for the spiritual decline today is the lack of *the church that meets in your house.* Is there one in your house? It begins around the family altar.

Paul always began his letters with commendations unless there was a reason for not doing so, as in Galatians. To Philemon he spoke of love and faith, and told of the joy he found in fellowship. Even though he was separated by a great distance from his friend Philemon, nevertheless this man's loving helpfulness to others had done Paul good in that far-off prison in Rome. He prayed that Philemon would be successful in sharing his faith.

Paul was a wonderful student of human nature. The picture he portrayed of himself as the bent and battered prisoner in jail for the sake of Jesus Christ (v. 9) opened a well of sympathy in the heart of Philemon as he read his friend's letter. Onesimus, whose name means "useful," had robbed his master and run away to the big city of Rome. Somehow he fell in with the little band of Christians surrounding Paul and was converted. Paul sent the boy back to his master with this friendly personal note. He took pleasure in playing with the fellow's name. The "useless" servant now will be "useful." Christ makes a person useful to others.

In approaching the main purpose of the letter, Paul did not blurt it out at once. He anticipated anger, and so he used the finest tact. He admitted that Onesimus had been good for nothing in the past, but playfully alluded to his name, hoping to put the reader into a favorable mood.

While Philemon's voice trembles, Apphia is wiping her eyes on her apron, and son Archippus is clearing his throat. All three read on into the letter. Paul has his little joke and pun, and the faces of the trio break into smiles. Onesimus, meanwhile, nervously fumbles with his cap in back of the door, then breaks into a broad grin, and the tension is over.

Paul's action with regard to Onesimus is an illustration of the Lord's work on behalf of the sinner. Paul did not minimize the sin but pleaded for forgiveness for the sinner on the ground of his own merit in the eyes of Philemon, his friend. More than that, he made himself personally responsible for the debts of Onesimus. *Charge me for it.* This is the message of the gospel. For Christ bore our sins in his own body on the tree. This is what Christ does—takes the sinner's place.

SOCIAL MANAGEMENT

The secret of the solution of the capital-labor problem lies in the love of Christ, such as undoubtedly existed between Philemon and Onesimus after the slave returned home.

This letter gives a clear idea of the attitude of Christianity to the social organization of the world. The subject of the letter is slavery, which was widespread in that day. If slavery is wrong, why did not Paul say so instead of apparently condoning it in this letter to the owner of a runaway slave? If Paul had made slavery an issue he would have torn society to shreds. Instead he presented principles that would surely undermine slavery and in time actually did so. Brotherhood in Christ is more than emancipation. Christianity does not merely free the slaves but teaches them that they and their masters are one in Christ.

Has Christianity yet driven slavery from the world? Here in this letter began the abolition of slavery. This terrible menace has been vanquished wherever brotherly love of Christ has been expressed. But there are still portions of the world in which slavery is practiced. Sometimes it is disguised by other names, but wherever human life is sold, wherever forced labor is carried on, it exists. It takes changes in people's thinking to destroy slavery. Christ came to change people; he frees us from sin's slavery and sends us forth to abolish slavery of every kind.

SELECTED BIBLE READING

Sunday: Church Officers (Titus 1:1-9)
Monday: Church Enemies (Titus 1:10-16)
Tuesday: Church Influence (Titus 2:1-8)
Wednesday: Church Rule (Titus 2:9-15)
Thursday: Church Works (Titus 3)
Friday: A Christian Gentleman (Philemon 1-7)
Saturday: A Prisoner's Plea (Philemon 8-25)

CHAPTER 46

UNDERSTANDING
HEBREWS

Hebrews Portrays Jesus Christ,
Our Intercessor at the Throne

The author of the letter to the Hebrews is unknown. Many have speculated, but there is no certainty. Hebrews is attributed to Paul, and although many question his authorship, there is abundance of evidence in his favor.

This book has been called the fifth Gospel. The four describe Christ's ministry on earth; this one describes his ministry in heaven at God's right hand.

The glories of our Savior are exhibited in this letter. Our eye is fixed on Jesus, *our leader and instructor* (12:2). He is set before us *crowned now by God with glory and honor* (2:9).

This book was written, first of all, to Jewish Christians, probably of Jerusalem, who were wavering in their faith. Because of the taunts and jeers of their persecutors, the Jewish Christians were beginning to think they had lost everything—altar, priests, sacrifices—by accepting Christianity. The writer proved that they had only lost the shadow to be given the substance (Jesus Christ). They were undervaluing their privileges in Christ and engaging in self-pity and discouragement. They were in danger of even giving up their faith (5:11-12). They had started well but had not made progress (6:10-11). The Christian life is like riding a bicycle—if you do not go on, you go off. The writer was trying to lead them from an elementary knowledge to a mature grasp. He exhorted them to be loyal to Christianity. He showed them the superiority of Christianity over Judaism. The writer wanted to

keep them from drifting back into their Jewish rites and ceremonies. They were urged to let go of everything else in order
to hold fast the faith and hope of the gospel.

The book is also a timely warning and a word of comfort to
all, especially in this day when many have so little instruction
in the things of Christ and are inclined to be led astray by so
many fads and cults.

How often when you take a trip for the first time over a new
road you drive straight along anticipating where it will lead and
what difficulties you may encounter. It seems to be the thing to
do. Coming back over the same road, you look around and notice
things. Do this in studying the book of Hebrews. Read it through,
and do not be over-anxious about the things you can't understand. Then you can go back over the road in your reading and
take notice of the many things along the way. You could spend
months in Hebrews. It presents so many wonderful truths. At
the first reading you will be impressed by one fact above all
others: that Jesus Christ is prominent on every page. This is not
true in all the other books of the New Testament. In Acts, the
apostles, disciples, the Jews, and pagans are predominant. In
Romans, great doctrine attracts our attention. In the other letters
the church and its problems are considered. But here it is our
Lord himself. He is:

Greater than prophets (1:1-3)
Greater than angels (1:4–2:18)
Greater than Moses (3:1-19)
Greater than Joshua (4:1-16)
Greater than Aaron (5:1–10:18)

The reason the writer used these comparisons is because each
of these held a great importance in the Jewish religion. They
were the framework of their worship, and it had to be proved
that something or Someone better had come to take their place
if their followers were to transfer allegiance.

This book was written to strengthen the faith of wavering
Christians. Paul's great argument is the superiority of Christ over
all others.

Do we know the real difference between having Christ as a
Savior and as a Priest? Well, this book answers the question.

The book of Hebrews proves that we can never understand
the Old Testament without the New, or the New without the Old.

THE SUPERIORITY OF THE PERSON OF CHRIST
HEBREWS 1:1–4:13

Nowhere is our Lord's deity and humanity so emphasized as in Hebrews 1–2. As our great High Priest, Christ is able to understand all our needs because he is perfect Man. He *understands our weaknesses, since he had the same temptations we do.* He is able to meet all our needs because he is perfect God. He is able.

The opening sentences of the book of Hebrews (1:1-4) rank with the opening words of Genesis and of John. We find Jesus there: his deity, his glory, a Creator, heir of all things, superior to all things, and Savior.

Write down all that you find about Christ in Hebrews 1–2. If you knew nothing more about him than you found in these two chapters, you would know much.

Two great truths are taken for granted—the existence of God, and that he reveals himself to people. He revealed himself before, *long ago . . . through the prophets; . . . in these days . . . through his Son.* The Bible records a series of stories of how God speaks to people and reveals his will and his plan to them. How marvelous to hear his only Son speak!

Remember, this letter was written to correct the erroneous idea, to remove this misconception, that the Christian Jews had lost some things because they had taken up Christianity. Christianity is not "giving up" but "receiving," receiving the greatest gifts of life—in fact, Life itself, for Christ is Life.

Superiority of the Person of Christ
The Lord Jesus Christ is greater than any human leader (prophets) (1:1-3):

He is God's Son.
He has been given everything.
He made the world.
He is himself God.
He regulates the universe.
He cleansed us from sin.
He sat down at the right hand of God.

The Lord Jesus Christ is greater than angels (1:4–2:18):

He has a far greater name of Son (1:4-5).
Angels worship him (1:6).

He is the eternal God (1:7-12).
His kingdom is forever (1:8).
He is the ruler of the coming age (1:11-13).

The Lord Jesus Christ is greater than Moses (3:1-19):

Moses was a faithful servant.
Christ is the Son over his own house.

The Lord Jesus Christ is greater than Joshua (4:1-16): Joshua was a great leader. He led the Israelis into the Promised Land, but he did not lead the people into rest. What he failed to do, the Son accomplished. Jesus is greater, for he alone gives real rest.

It is well to notice that angels and human spirits (of those who die) are not the same. Human life is a different order of creation than angels. We do not become angels when we die. Angels are a separate creation of God. They are now, and will be in heaven, our servants (1:14). Angels worship Christ just as we do.

When God wanted to save man from his sin, he did not send an angel but his Son. God did not come in the form of an angel but in the form of a man. He became man to redeem man. He suffered as a man and died as a man so that he could be our Redeemer (2:10). Jesus tasted the bitterness of death for us in order to render the devil, who had the power of death, powerless. He came up from the grave with the keys of hell and of death; no longer can the devil lock any of us in death.

Think about Jesus
This is our weakness. We look at ourselves and our own weakness. Think about him (3:1). Like an astronomer, set your telescope to the heavens and gaze upon him.

Many Christian Jews were confused about Christ's ministry on earth. They thought that he came to enforce the laws that Moses had given. Moses was the law-giver and Christ had to enforce them. This was their interpretation. But Christ is his own Lawgiver. The old Mosaic system was imperfect and weak (7:11, 18). It had served its purpose. Now Christ has a better way. Christ is over Moses. Moses was only a servant; Christ is a Son, the Master in his own house. He is the Heir (3:6).

Canaan, the land that flowed with milk and honey, was the Promised Land into which Joshua led the Israelis. But this is only a picture of the rest of faith in God himself, that every

Christian should enjoy. Saint Augustine said that no soul found rest until it found its rest in God. Joshua could not lead the Israelis into this perfect rest and trust in God, but Jesus did. Rest from self-effort and yield yourself to Christ (4:10). Trust Jesus as your Joshua and "go in" to his land of promise. Stop struggling and place all in his hand. (Read Psalm 37:5.)

Two Great Warnings
Warning 1: Listen carefully so you do not become indifferent to the salvation announced, not by angels, but by the Lord himself (2:1-4).
Warning 2: Beware not to be led away from the living God (3:12).

Hebrews 4:12 shows the living power of God's Word. Let the Word search and test you! Let God's Word have its proper place in your life. It searches out every motive and desire and purpose of your life and helps you in evaluating them. Christ is the living Word of God. He is alive and powerful and all-wise and all-knowing.

THE SUPERIORITY OF THE PRIESTHOOD OF CHRIST
HEBREWS 4:14–10:18

Here begins the main theme. *What we are saying is this: Christ . . . is our High Priest* (8:1). Christ has been compared with all others, the prophets, angels, Moses, and Joshua, but the most important comparison is with Aaron, the High Priest. The writer shows that the priesthood of Christ is greater than the priesthood of the Levitical law.

The central point in the book is Christ's eternal priesthood and his sacrifice, which availed for the sin of the world. The letter dwells upon the supreme importance and power of the blood of Christ in obtaining redemption for us. He has purged us from our sins and opened the way into the heavenly sanctuary and to the very throne of God.

Christ is himself a priest. Listen to the Word: *Jesus the Son of God is our great High Priest who has gone to heaven itself to help us; therefore let us never stop trusting him* (4:14).

Jesus Christ not only had the qualifications of a priest like Aaron, the earthly High Priest, but he is a High Priest forever after the order of the eternal Melchizedek priesthood, because this priesthood is continuous and will never end. The Aaronic priests could not make people perfect because they themselves were sinful, but Christ is eternal and sinless.

Christ Is Like Melchizedek (Genesis 14)
A royal priesthood—Both were kings of peace and justice.
Universal—Not just for the Jews.
No human ancestry—"No father or mother."
No successor—When Melchizedek passed away no one stepped into his place. So Christ is a priest forever.

Let us find an important fact here. Christian ministers are nowhere called priests in the New Testament except as all Christians are called priests (1 Peter 2:9). We have learned from Paul's letters that Christian ministers are called teachers and pastors.

The glories of our Savior are exhibited in this letter. There are three great "betters" connected with our High Priest.

Christ—A Better Priest
Of a better agreement (8:13): A better agreement because it is based on better promises. These promises are written on the heart, not on tablets of stone (8:10).

Of a better sacred tent (9:1-12): Christ officiates in heaven. The sacred tent was of this world. The High Priest entered into the Most Holy Place once a year, but Christ has entered into the heavenly sanctuary "once for all."

Of a better sacrifice (10:18): He himself is the sacrifice. He offered himself as a lamb without blemish to cleanse us. The sacrifices of the Old Testament were calves and goats. They could not take away sin. They were but the shadow. This Sacrifice needed to be offered only once.

Christ is called our High Priest. What does that mean? We are taught very plainly in the Word that sin has cut people off from God. No sinner can approach God. The way has been closed. In the Old Testament a representative, the High Priest whom God appointed, could come into God's presence only once a year after sacrifice for the sins of the people had been made. He had to offer the blood of calves and goats not only for the sins of the people but for his own sins, for he too was a sinner. He then would go into the Holy Place, then on beyond the veil into the Most Holy Place where the Ark of the Covenant rested. Here was the mercy seat, and here God met man through the mediator, the High Priest.

How can we approach God today? Christ has made that possible. He is our High Priest, our representative before the Father. He entered into the heavenly sanctuary, God's presence, bearing the blood of his own sacrifice to cleanse us from our sins and to give to us eternal salvation. His blood had to be shed, for *without the shedding of blood there is no forgiveness of sins* (9:22). *But Christ gave himself to God for our sins as one sacrifice for all time, and then sat down in the place of highest honor at God's right hand* (10:12). *It is finished*, he said on the cross. All his work of redemption had been completed; hence we see him sitting. We find this picture of Christ often in Hebrews.

Our High Priest is at the right hand of the Father at this minute, making intercession for you and for me (7:25; 8:1; 10:12). He has gone *to appear now before God as our Friend* (9:24). This is why we can boldly enter God's presence through the blood of Jesus, by a new and living way (10:19-20). Avail yourself of this glorious privilege.

In Hebrews 9, our Lord's three great appearings stand out:

1. *Past*—On the cross: *He came once for all, at the end of the age, to put away the power of sin forever by dying for us* (9:26).
2. *Present*—At the right hand of the throne: *To appear now before God as our Friend* (9:24).
3. *Future*—In the clouds of glory: *He will come again, but not to deal with our sins. This time he will come bringing salvation to all those who are eagerly and patiently waiting for him* (9:28).

Christ, a Better Sacrifice
Christ offered himself as the sacrifice, a Lamb without blemish or spot. The priest offered the lives of calves and goats, but these sacrifices could not take away sin. This better Sacrifice had only to be offered "once for all" (10:10-18).

Since Christ has made this new and living way into the presence of the Father, let us come boldly to the throne of grace. The sin question is settled forever.

Let us not only approach the throne of grace, but *let us not neglect our church meetings* (10:25). There is nothing like Christian fellowship to make us grow. A pastor once visited a woman who had grown cold in her Christian life. She said she had not been able to come to church, but otherwise she could not understand what had happened to make her feel as she did about spiritual things. Without saying a word, the pastor got up and lifted out a live coal from the grate and placed it on the hearth. In a few moments the glow was gone and the coal was black. "I see it," she said. You can't continue to glow in your Christian life alone. You need the warmth of fellowship with other Christians. This is a command to us.

THE SUPERIORITY OF LIFE IN CHRIST
HEBREWS 10:19–13:25

From now on, the writer tells us the kind of life we should live because of Christ's work as High Priest for us. We know he is at the right hand of God and that he *intercedes for us*.

After one has accepted Christ, there are levels of Christian living. Some Christians live in the basement of Christian experience—inside the building, but where it is dark, dismal, and gloomy. Others live on the ground floor. They leave the first foundations and go on. Some sunlight enters, but their outlook is based on the circumstances around them. They live very close to the world. Still others live up higher. Sunlight and warmth flood the rooms. The noise and attractions of the worldly street do not disturb them. The air is pure. The outlook is toward the blue skies and distant mountains. These people live above the world, surrounded completely with Christ in God. It is in this high realm that God wishes us all to live continuously.

Let us look at a few men and women of God, whose names are given in Hebrews 11, who lived with a high look. The Holy Spirit tells us that the secret of each life is faith. Each one relied completely on our faithful God.

A Working Faith
The secret of Christian living is simply allowing Christ to meet our needs. Some say, "I have no faith; I can't believe." Yet we constantly place faith in our fellowmen. You want to go to New York from San Francisco. You buy your ticket and get on the airplane. In the course of your journey a pilot will guide your plane. Without seeing him or knowing a thing about his ability, you trust your life to him. Faith is just trusting God, believing him. There is nothing mysterious about faith. It is a simple act

of the will. Either we will believe God or we won't. We decide. It is as simple as turning an electric light switch. This is not a difficult or baffling or mysterious thing to do. But the result? Light and power. When we decide to believe God absolutely, then supernatural life and power enter our lives. A miracle is done within us. One of the practical results of faith is that it makes weak people strong (11:34).

To live in the Hall of Faith forever we need to do two things. First, like anyone entering a race, we must *strip off anything that slows us down or holds us back.* Yield everything to Christ. Second, we are really to believe that Jesus is trustworthy. When we do, we have given up the sin that so easily trips us up—the sin of unbelief. We give up that sin by keeping our eyes on Jesus.

There is only one kind of human being in the world who can please God. Who is it (11:6)? It is not what we do for God but what God does for us that makes a life of power and strength. Our great God, rather than our great faith, is the thing to think most about. It is fashionable to be doubtful rather than sure about the great facts of God and Christ and salvation. But this cannot please God. To please God:

Forsaking
All
I
Take
Him

Christ is the belief that brings salvation.

Because of the great crowd watching us from the bleachers of heaven, let us run the race of life God has set before us. As any athlete does when he is preparing for a race, we should:

Strip off anything that slows or trips us up (12:1)
Run with patience (12:1)
Endure correction (12:11)
Seek peace and live a holy life (12:14)
Always look to Jesus, our leader and instructor (12:2)

A life that is pleasing to God is made possible by the Lord himself.

And now may the God of peace, who brought again from the dead our Lord Jesus, equip you with all you need for doing his will. May he who became the great Shepherd of the sheep by an everlasting agreement between God and you, signed with his blood, produce in you through the power of Christ all that is pleasing to him. To him be glory forever and ever. Amen (13:20-21).

SELECTED BIBLE READING

Sunday: Christ Superior to Prophets and Angels (Hebrews 1)
Monday: Christ Superior to Moses (Hebrews 3)
Tuesday: Christ Superior to Aaron (Hebrews 5)
Wednesday: Christ's Superior Agreements (Hebrews 8)
Thursday: Christ's Superior Atonement (Hebrews 10)
Friday: Christ's Superior Faith Life (Hebrews 11)
Saturday: Christ's Superior Privileges (Hebrews 12–13)

CHAPTER 47

UNDERSTANDING JAMES

James Portrays Jesus Christ, Our Pattern

The author of the book is no doubt James, the brother of our Lord. He may well be called the practical apostle. He stands for efficiency and consistency in life and conduct.

There are three men by the name of James mentioned in the New Testament—the son of Zebedee, the son of Alphaeus, and James the Great, our Lord's brother. Although James refers to his own brother Jesus only twice, he does it in a most reverent manner. Though he knew him so well there was no familiarity, for he called him Lord and Christ. He associates his brother with God so as to imply an equality with the Almighty. If Jesus were not God, this would be blasphemous.

GUIDEBOOK FOR EVERYDAY RELIGION

The book of James is the most practical of all the letters and has been called "A Practical Guide to Christian Life and Conduct." This book is the Proverbs of the New Testament. It is filled with moral precepts. It states the ethics of Christianity. It is full of figures and metaphors. It is often quite dramatic in style. It compels real thought. Hebrews presents doctrine; James presents deeds. They go together in vital Christianity.

Neither is there conflict between Paul and James. Only superficial reading of both would bring that indictment. Paul says, "Take the gospel in." James says, "Take it out." Paul sees Christ in the heavens establishing our righteousness. James sees him on the earth telling us to be perfect even as our Father in heaven is perfect.

Paul dwells on the source of our faith. James tells of the fruit of our faith. One lays the foundations in Christ; the other builds the superstructure. But although Paul lays great stress upon justification by faith, we have noticed in his letters, especially in Titus, that he lays great stress on good works. It is an astounding fact that while Paul uses the expression *rich in good works* (1 Timothy 6:18), James uses *rich in faith* (2:5). It is well to notice too that when James seems to speak in a slighting way of faith, he means a mere intellectual belief and not a "saving faith" that is so essential. James exalts faith. His letter opens and closes with a strong encouragement to pray (1:6; 5:14-18). He only denounces the spurious faith that does not produce works.

James calls himself a "servant of Jesus Christ." He proudly accepts this title as a description of what his relationship was to Jesus. This speaks of real humility, because James nowhere refers to the fact of his earthly relationship to the Lord Jesus Christ, a brother.

James mentions the name of God seventeen times, but he repeats the name of Jesus only twice. James was bitterly opposed to Jesus and his claims up to the time of his death, but after the Resurrection he was converted by a special and private interview with the risen Lord (1 Corinthians 15:7). This adds value to James's testimony as to the deity of our Lord. Immediately he became a man of prayer and was made pastor of the church at Jerusalem (Acts 15:13-21). His life work was to win the Jews and to help them understand Christianity. At the end he was killed by the Jews in A.D. 62. Tradition says that he was probably forced to the roof of the Temple by the high priests and rulers and commanded to blaspheme the name of Christ. He, rather, boldly proclaimed the fact that Jesus is the Son of God. James was hurled from the roof to instant death.

James wrote his letter *to Jewish Christians scattered everywhere*, to those who lived outside the Holy Land. Then there were no lost tribes, for he addressed his letter to the twelve whose location was well known at the time. Like Hebrews, it was addressed to the Christian Jews. The Jews to whom he wrote had not ceased to be Jews, although they had embraced Christianity. Many of them had been converted on the Day of Pentecost and had carried home only a partial understanding of Christianity. In their enthusiasm at having found the true Messiah they neglected the graces and virtues that should accompany the Christian life. They taught that all that was necessary to have salvation was to believe that Jesus was the true Messiah and Savior. They were in great danger of being discouraged in their Christian life by the persecution of their own unbelieving countrymen.

FAITH VICTOR OVER TEMPTATION
JAMES 1:1-21

After the briefest of greetings, James plunged straight into his subject. Realizing that these Christian Jews scattered everywhere outside of Palestine were undergoing severe testing of their faith, he began by telling them how they must meet temptation and tried to encourage and comfort them.

We usually consider ourselves happy when we escape temptation and sorrow. Instead we should consider testing as a glorious opportunity of proving our faith, just as the automobile manufacturer knows that the best proof of a car's worth is the road test. Why we must "be happy" is not because of the trial itself but what it will work out. In other words, use your trials. What is the purpose of testing? God makes our trials the instrument of blessing (1:3). Too often our trials make us impatient, but God will give grace so that his real purpose will be accomplished. Patience is more necessary than anything else in our life of faith. We forget that time is nothing with God, for with him a thousand years is as one day, and one day as a thousand years. Christ's purpose in our lives is for us to be *ready for anything, strong in character, full and complete.*

Let us be careful where we lay the blame of temptation. Read James 1:13-15 carefully. Testings of character do come from God (see Genesis 22:1), but temptations to evil never come from him, but from the Adversary through our *own evil thoughts and wishes.* Instead of wrong things coming from God, we find that only *whatever is good and perfect comes to us from God, the Creator of all light,* who never changes (1:17). Our God is a God who loves to give. Alexander the Great said to someone overwhelmed with his generosity, "I give as a king!" Our Father in heaven gives to us as the infinite God.

It is hard to behave wisely, but God's wisdom will help you to do it. Put together the teaching on wisdom in this short letter. Pray for wisdom to behave wisely in times of difficulty. When you are wronged and insulted, ask God how you should act. *If you want to know what God wants you to do, ask him, and he will gladly tell you, for he is always ready to give a bountiful supply of wisdom to all who ask him* (1:5). Does James say, "If you want wisdom, sit down and think or study"? No, he says the wisdom we need is from God.

Did it ever occur to you to thank God for temptations? Do you think of your temptations as blessings? Yet James says, *Is your life full of difficulties and temptations? Then be happy* (1:2). *Happy is the man who doesn't give in and do wrong when he is tempted* (1:12). How spineless and weak you would become without temptation. Valueless is the character that knows no testing. There is a joy of overcoming. There is no greater satisfaction than to know we have resisted temptation victoriously.

James began and ended with prayer (1:5-8; 5:13-18). Prayer is one of the easiest subjects to talk about but one of the hardest to practice. Find all you can on this subject in this letter. What about James's practice? Tradition tells us that on his death they discovered that his knees were worn as hard as a camel's from the constant habit of kneeling to pray.

FAITH SHOWN IN OUR ACTIONS
JAMES 1:22–2:26

Don't be merely listeners to God's Word, but put the gospel into practice. What is the good of a man saying that he has faith if he does not prove it by actions? We must not be satisfied with only "listening." We must go on "obeying" (1:22). If anyone listens and does not obey, he is like a person looking at himself in a mirror and then going away and forgetting how he looked (1:23-24).

James says we must keep looking into the mirror of God's Word to remember how we look, to find out the sin in our life. He who looks carefully into the Bible and puts it into practice will be blessed in what he does. If anyone thinks he is a Christian and doesn't control his tongue, this man's religion "isn't worth much." The religion that does not influence the tongue is not a true or vital one. An uncontrolled tongue in a Christian is a terrible thing—guard it. Control your temper. It is dangerous. Under trial, speak little. Keep the draft closed and the fire will go out (1:26).

What shall we do with the Word?

Receive it (1:21)
Hear it (1:23)
Do it (1:22)
Examine it (1:25)

Works Are Results

Works do not save us, but they are a pretty good evidence that we are saved. *When you did it to these my brothers you were doing it to me* (Matthew 25:40) is not a "saving" text but a "sign" text. What Jesus did is our salvation; what "you did" is the proof of it. Keep faith and works in their proper place.

Because of all this, James says in effect, "The faith you have is the faith you show." *The Christian who is pure and without fault, from God the Father's point of view, is the one who takes care of orphans and widows, and who remains true to the Lord—not soiled and dirtied by his contacts with the world* (1:27).

Christianity is a brotherhood that shows no "favoritism" (2:1-4).

How the world today ignores James's command not to show favoritism of persons! The world worships the successful, strong, and wealthy, and despises the man who is poor. A Christian must not show partiality to the man of wealth and position, James tells us, but it seems that money and honor are the only things that people worship today. Showing favoritism is a breach of good manners and a discourtesy to the poor. Moreover, it is a sin to worship rank and insult the poor. By doing this we break the law of God. *You must love and help your neighbor just as much as you love and take care of yourself* (2:8). We are not only to admire and respect others; we are to love them as we love our own selves (2:1-13).

What Is Sin?

To disobey God's law is sin. It is human to gloss over sin. A little girl said when excusing herself for something she had done, "I haven't broken the commandment; I only cracked it." James says that whoever keeps the whole law of God and only makes a single slip is guilty of everything (2:10-11). He is a lawbreaker. We may have a fine chain, but of what use is it if all the links are good except one? That broken link renders the entire chain useless.

It is clear that the one sin thought of here is mentioned in 2:9—"favoritism."

Faith that does not express itself in good deeds is of no value. Faith is revealed by what we do. What is the use of anyone's saying that he has faith if he does not prove it by his actions? Faith is dead and useless without actions (2:17).

Has the phrase "friend of God" ever gripped you? God evidently needed a friend, and he found in Abraham the friendship he desired. What is essential to become a friend of God? See 2:23.

FAITH SHOWN IN OUR WORDS
JAMES 3

Our speech reveals what and whose we are. It expresses our personality more than anything else. Anyone who controls his tongue, James says, "has perfect control over himself" (3:2). If he has mastery over that difficult part of the body, the tongue, the rest is easy. He is able to keep his sinful inclinations under control. Just as we control a spirited horse by a bit in its mouth and a firm hand on the bridle, so the hand of Christ Jesus can grip and firmly use the bit and bridle on our tongues. Just as a great ship is controlled by a very small rudder and turned in any direction the captain determines, so the pierced hands of Jesus can firmly control and wisely use the helm of our lives—our tongue. The tongue, though small, is very powerful. It can determine the course of human life.

Remember, this same tongue can be used to testify for Christ and praise his holy name. It is the instrument that the Holy Spirit uses to magnify the Lord (3:9-10). We should not praise God and curse people who are made like God! Cruel words have wrecked homes, broken friendships, divided churches, and sent untold millions to ruin and despair. There are so many people who call themselves Christians who seem not to make the slightest effort to control their tongues.

FAITH SHOWN IN OUR PURITY OF CHARACTER
JAMES 4

The devil has organized this world system on principles opposed to God in every way. They are principles of force, greed, ambition, selfishness, and pleasure. The believer should have his *interest in all the attractive things of the world . . . killed long ago* (Galatians 6:14). We should count passing pleasures, honors, treasures as of little value and remain unmoved by the world's attractions. The world is that system of things about us or that spirit within us that is blind and deaf to the value of spiritual things and cares nothing about doing the will of God. Because we live in the world, surrounded by all its attractions and the things needed for daily living, we must be watchful to maintain our friendship with God and keep our affections off the evil pleasures of this world (4:4-6).

People keep asking, "How can we end war?" But James goes back further and tells us what causes war. A cause of most of the wars that have devastated the earth has been some nation's desire to get what does not belong to it. This has always been the cause of quarrels between individuals. Selfishness is the root of it all. Next, people fail to pray, or if they do it is with a wrong motive—to spend what they get on themselves instead of having their lives glorify God (4:1-3). God promises to answer prayer, but he will not give to those who want only what gives them pleasure.

It is common to see worldly-minded Christians praying for purely selfish reasons. So often you hear people say, "I don't believe in prayer. I prayed for a new car, but God didn't give it to me," or, "My husband was sick and I prayed that God would heal him, but he died." In either case, the answer might easily have led the person further away from God. The car might have been used to carry him to the beach and not to church. The family circle restored could make the wife find her joy in her husband rather than in her Lord.

Three times the words *evil desires* are found in the first five verses of James 4. These words can also be translated "pleasures." This helps give meaning to these verses and furnishes the clue to the teaching they contain.

Overindulgence in pleasure is sinful:

1. There are *quarrels and fights among you*. The newspapers are filled with horrible pictures of this every day.
2. *There is a whole army of evil desires within you*. If pleasure is allowed to have its own way in us, a war is on and we are mastered by it.
3. *Even when you do ask you don't get it because . . . you want only*

what will give you *pleasure.* Overindulgence in pleasure always affects the prayer life. We stagnate in our Christian life.

4. *You are like an unfaithful wife*—how a pleasure-lover degenerates in his Christian life! He becomes a friend of the world, an enemy of God.

What is the cure for all this? Examine 4:6-10:

1. *Give yourselves humbly to God* (4:7). We have made a mess of our lives because of lack of surrender to God.
2. *When you draw close to God, God will draw close to you* (4:8). Come with clean hands and a pure heart.
3. *Realize your worthlessness before the Lord* (4:10). Remember yourself as a sinner and take the lowly place. Then God will lift you up, encourage you, and help you.

To be friends with the world means to be an enemy of God (4:4). Jesus said, *You cannot serve two masters* (Matthew 6:24). Therefore surrender yourself to God and do not be subject to the devil. When the devil is resisted by those who have surrendered themselves to God, he flees.

How easy it is for us to plan without God, yet how futile! Let us submit all of our plans to the Lord and see what his will is in the matter. *If the Lord wants . . .* (4:15). One of the most amazing things in all of God's Word is that though he holds the whole universe in his hands he has a definite plan for each one of our lives. Life is a series of surprises. We live just one day at a time. We do not know what will happen tomorrow, but God takes care of us. What a wonderful God we have!

FAITH SHOWN BY OUR PRAYER LIFE
JAMES 5

Evidently many of the poor people in the church were being oppressed by the rich, and they were being *cheated of their pay* (5:4). James warns the rich! *You have stored up [gold and silver] for yourselves, to receive on that coming day of judgment* (5:3). How true that is today—stored up millions, yes, billions. The coffers of the rich are full indeed. They are charged with fraud and injustice. How much goes on today under the cloak of Christianity! It is true there are some great Christians among the rich, but for the most part, James's picture of wealth holds true. You remember that Jesus said it was *easier for a camel to go through the eye of a needle than for a rich man to enter the Kingdom of God* (Mark 10:24)

Here again the tongue is brought in. It is amazing how many Christians take the name of the Lord in vain in ordinary conversation (5:12). God says, *You shall not use the name of Jehovah your God irreverently, nor use it to swear to a falsehood. You will not escape punishment if you do* (Exodus 20:7). This is a serious indictment.

Prayer is a golden key that, kept bright by constant use, will unlock the treasures of earth and heaven.

James gives us a series of short phrases of advice. If anyone is suffering, he should pray. If anyone is thankful, he should sing. If anyone is sick, he should send for the elders of the church and let them pour a little oil on him and pray for him (5:13-14). The Bible says, *And their prayer, if offered in faith, will heal him, for the Lord will make him well; and if his sickness was caused by some sin, the Lord will forgive him* (5:15). The prayer of faith demands confession of sin and a will surrendered to God. Elijah's mighty prayer that stopped and started rains is an example to us, for *the earnest prayer of a righteous man has great power and wonderful results* (5:16).

The letter closes abruptly on a high plane. It talks of the gracious act of a Christian who finds someone slipping away from God and brings him back to the truth. Although only God can save a soul, he uses human instruments to accomplish it. That person *will have saved a wandering soul from death, bringing about the forgiveness of his many sins.*

SELECTED BIBLE READING

Sunday: Faith Tested (James 1:1-21)
Monday: Faith Lived Out (James 1:22-27)
Tuesday: Faith and Brotherhood (James 2:1-13)
Wednesday: Faith Dead without Works (James 2:14-26)
Thursday: Faith and Tongue Control (James 3)
Friday: Faith Rebukes Worldliness (James 4)
Saturday: Faith in Prayer (James 5)

CHAPTER 48

UNDERSTANDING
FIRST PETER

*First Peter Portrays Jesus Christ,
Precious Cornerstone of Our Faith*

Peter talks about seven precious things. Mark these in your Bible:

Precious trial of faith (1:7)
Precious blood (1:19)
Precious Cornerstone (2:4-6)
Precious Christ (2:7)
Precious spirit (3:4)
Precious faith (2 Peter 1:1)
Precious promises (2 Peter 1:4)

Peter has been called the "apostle of hope," as John was the "apostle of love" and Paul the "apostle of faith." Peter speaks of looking forward in hope.

Another word (or its equivalent) is used fifteen times in this short letter, and that is *suffering*, the suffering of Christ and of Christians in following him.

Try a complete reading at one sitting of this short letter. Mark in two colors, marking each mention of joy and blessing and glory (in red, perhaps), and of suffering (in black). At least twenty-two times Peter dwells on the joy and glory that are ours who have received God's grace, as against the fifteen times he mentions the suffering of Christ and the Christian following him.

Try to see that Peter was enlarging on the statement that *Jesus, our leader and instructor . . . was willing to die a shameful death on the cross because of the joy he knew would be his afterwards; and now he sits in the place of honor by the throne of God* (Hebrews 12:2). Peter knew the connection between suffering and joy and glory.

This book was written by Peter toward the close of his busy life (around A.D. 67) and was delivered by Silvanus (Silas), one of Paul's companions (5:12). Peter had become a leader of the apostles. He was the spokesman. He belonged to the inner circle of the three friends of Christ. He was the preacher at Pentecost. The first twelve chapters of Acts are centered around this apostle and his ministry to the Jews. At last he died a martyr's death, being crucified under the Roman emperor Nero. According to tradition, at his own request, he was crucified with his head downward, considering himself unworthy to even resemble his Master in death. Read 1:1-3, 6-9; 2:13-17; 4:12-19.

The picture of Peter in the Gospels is amazingly different from that found in his own writings. In the Gospels we see Peter, the impulsive, restless soul, sometimes fearless but again a coward, even going so far as to deny his Lord with a curse! In his own letters we see him patient, restful, and loving, with a courage purified and strengthened by the indwelling Holy Spirit. This is a wonderful illustration of the transforming work of God in a human life.

The Christians to whom Peter wrote were suffering "fiery trials" from the hostile Jews and fanatical Gentiles. The Christians would not join their pagan neighbors in idolatry and drinking and lust, so they were called haters of the human race and were classed with thieves and murderers. This letter was evidently written at a time when general dislike of Christians was threatening to become active persecution (2:15; 3:13-17; 4:12). Lives today are on the auction block, sold to the highest bidder. The world is bidding high. Let Christ have a chance (see 1:18-19).

A subject repeatedly mentioned is the return of our Lord and Savior. Mark this also as you read the letter. The influence of this "blessed hope" on the Christian's way of life cannot be escaped. This short letter is full of golden nuggets of truth that can be marked and memorized. Try it!

Let us discover what this letter has for our own lives as we read it. We are not enduring persecutions of heathen emperors, but we are meeting on every side the alluring temptations of that same Adversary, the devil, who is seeking those whom he may win away from Christ, who endured all for us. Although we are not witnesses of the suffering of Christ as was Peter, we may be taught by the same Holy Spirit. Ask the Holy Spirit to teach you today!

This book gives us good, plain advice from Peter on how we ought to live. Read it and take heed! We find here how Peter has been growing in his experience. This letter shows him some twelve or more years after the last record of him in Acts 15. He wanted to encourage the believers, and so he gave his own personal testimony. He added assurance because he could prove from his own experience all he was saying. There is power in personal testimony. This personal note sounds through all the letter. The Christians were experiencing a time of trial (1:6). They needed encouragement from one who knew what trial meant. Peter pointed away from the trials to the future glory that awaited them (1:7), to the example of Christ (2:21), and to the reward that would follow (4:13).

PRIVILEGES OF THE CHRISTIAN
1 PETER 1:1–2:10

Peter, who is an apostle of jubilant hope, addressed this letter to homesick Christians. He told these persecuted and discouraged people of a near and precious Savior. Let it lift you up and fill you with joy! This is the purpose of the book.

What are our privileges as Christians? First, we are redeemed by the precious blood of Christ. This is our position in Christ (1:18-19). Because of this relationship to Christ, we have everything in him that God desires us to possess. If God has given us his Son, *won't he also surely give us everything else?* (Romans 8:32).

The life of faith is described at the beginning. We are born of God (1:3). At the end there is a priceless gift for us (1:4), and to assure us of it we are protected and provided for by the power of God (1:5). What a life this is!

We are members of God's family with hope of eternal life (1:3).
We have in reserve an incorruptible gift (1:4-5, 10).
We are protected by the power of God (1:5).
We are being purified to fit us to stand with Christ (1:7).
We have salvation for our souls (1:9).
We have the Good News that even angels want to know more about (1:12).

We have a great hope (1:13).
We have redemption through his blood (1:18-19).
We will not be disappointed (2:6).
We have a new life (1:23).
We have become living building stones (2:5).
We are chosen (2:9).
We will be rewarded with glory (5:4).

Peter gives good plain advice on how we ought to live (1:13-16). Fashion your life after the Lord Jesus Christ. Don't live your life after the old pattern. *You must be holy, for I am holy.* Love one another (1:22). Seeing you "have a new life" (1:23), live like it. You are a new person in Christ Jesus.

How can anyone *put away all evil* as Peter commands (ch. 2)? Not by effort! Not by trying! Not by practice! Not by setting our willpower against sin! But by trusting that God by his grace can do it. The only person who can "put away" sin is the one who, having received Christ as Savior, knows that Christ has "put away" his sin.

First, we must "get rid of." Peter summons us to abandon some ugly things—hatred, deception, dishonesty, jealousy, talking about others behind their backs (2:1). From the root of wickedness all these noxious weeds spring. These must go from our hearts if we want to grow. Weeds always choke out the plant if we allow them to spread. All that challenges the supremacy of the Lord Jesus Christ must go, whether it's our sin or our righteousness. Sometimes even good things keep us from God's best. We must be careful of this. The choices you must make are not always between bad and good, right and wrong, but between the good and the best.

Christian Infants

Long to grow up into the fullness of your salvation; cry for this as a baby cries for his milk (2:3). Newborn babies have no treasury of supplies in themselves. They are helpless and dependent from morning till night. They need food, clothing, shelter, the tireless care of a mother and protection of a father. It is a parable of Christian men and women. A Christian has nothing in himself, but he has access to the endless treasures of Christ and he is filled with God himself. As new Christians we have a new longing in our hearts, a new hunger. We are not self-sustained; we are

God-sustained. We are newborn babies the whole way through. Peter describes what our attitude should be: desiring spiritual milk, which will make us grow into the fullness of our salvation.

A Study in Stones

Right here Peter turned to another figure and called Christ a "Foundation of Rock," rejected by men but precious in God's sight (2:4). Everyone in this world has to do something with this "Stone," Christ Jesus. He is in every person's path. We can lift him up and put him in as the chief Cornerstone of our lives, which is God's will. But if we do not, we must stumble headlong over him, tragically, to our death. To the Jews he was a stone to stumble over and a rock to fall upon. To many today he is just that. What have you done with this precious "Cornerstone"? Is he in his rightful place in your life?

And we are stones too, built on Christ, the foundation and cornerstone, to make a spiritual temple to God. This makes it very important for each one of us to find our right place in God's plan and stay in it. The "house" (2:5), built up of believers, is the corporate temple of the Holy Spirit, as the individual Christian is the individual temple of the Holy Spirit (1 Corinthians 6:19).

We are not only "living building stones" in a spiritual temple, but each of us is a priest in this temple. Priests represent God to men, and men to God. Christians are "his holy priests" (2:5). Are you representing God to men by your life, and men to God by your intercessory prayer? As priests we cannot offer lambs and goats today, but Paul tells us to offer ourselves a living sacrifice (Romans 12:1).

A Precious Savior

He is very precious to you who believe (2:7). Charles Spurgeon's wonderful preaching started here. When only a teenager, he was unexpectedly asked to preach to a few farmers gathered in a cottage. "I hope the Lord will bless you," said a companion. "Me!" exclaimed the young Spurgeon. "I've never preached." "Well, if you don't preach this time there will be no preaching." Right there the young man, appointed of God, unaware that he was to be the greatest preacher of the late nineteenth century, bowed his head. In a few minutes he rose and addressed the crowd in the words of this text in 1 Peter. God was there. It was his first text and the theme of all his gracious ministry. Christ was always precious to him, and his sermons were precious to the people.

DUTIES OF THE CHRISTIAN
1 PETER 2:11–4:11

Peter is giving us wise counsel by telling us how to behave in the game of life. Up to this point he had been exhorting the Christians to walk worthy of their new calling. Now he urged them to glorify God before an ungodly and persecuting world. A greenhouse religion is of very little value to others. It is good for us to be compelled to justify our faith before our fellows.

Peter offers a simple program. Anyone can follow it. Any earnest seeker can find the way that Peter commends. His first suggestion is that we remember that we are "visitors." We are not settled here, but we are pilgrims on our way to an eternal city. It is important that we keep this in mind; otherwise we will be tying our lives to stakes that will be shaken loose some day.

But for the Christian who has followed Peter's plan, all is different. He has invested time and thought and money in the pursuit of Christ's plan for his life. He finds life "sweeter as the years go by," and the end is the best of all!

The greatest satisfaction that can come to a Christian is to realize that he is pleasing his Lord and Savior. In the power of the Lord, live for Christ in all phases of your life. Do not shut him out of even the most insignificant parts. It will not be easy— the devil will see to that. He will use every weapon against you. But Christ has already won the victory over him, and that victory is yours for the asking. Read again 1 Corinthians 12:5-7.

Peter makes an earnest appeal in this scene. First there is a call to purity of life. Christians are warned against all of the "evil pleasures of this world," for they are like an infection in our blood. If we once let them have a place in our lives they will contaminate our souls and pollute our characters worse than any disease harms our bodies. There will be no health or strength left in us, and all on account of sin. The soul may be dragged down to hell or lifted up to heaven. The body is the main channel through which debasing influences affect the soul. A Christian's life is to be true in the presence of those who are not yet Christian. This will disarm opposition and glorify God. Peter says, *I beg you to keep away from the evil pleasures of this world; they are not for you, for they fight against your very souls* (2:11).

The Power of Influence

We are to influence others by what we say and do. *Be careful how you behave among your unsaved neighbors* (2:12). People are not reading much religious literature on paper, but they are doing a lot of reading in religious (or antireligious) works by those professing Christ. It seems trite to say, but it is true that more are won to Christ by the true Christian life of the believer than by any other means. If it is true that what you are speaks so loudly I cannot hear what you say, then it is equally true that your deeds speak so loudly that I cannot help but believe what you say.

This subject of the way a Christian lives is discussed from 2:12–4:11. It was the all-important topic in Peter's mind, for those Christians were the only "Bible" known or read by the world in their day.

If they are suspicious of you and talk against you . . . (2:12). The Christians were accused of horrible crimes. They were called atheists because they denied the heathen gods. They were regarded as unpatriotic because heathenism was the official religion. To reject the state religion was considered an outrage against the state itself. The Christians would often be obliged to depart from social customs and often bore the stigma of criminals. The answer to all this had to be in the superior moral life of every Christian. They had to live beyond reproach.

Today some of us are subjected to severe tests. There are many things our companions do, both in business and recreation, that we as Christians cannot do. Our actions sometimes will be misunderstood and misrepresented. We will be called "narrow" or a "killjoy" or a "wet blanket." The best way to meet all such criticism is not to assume an air of superiority or a holier-than-thou attitude. We shouldn't regard ourselves as martyrs but accept the position with a smile and try to be helpful to those who are finding fault. Nothing cools opposition like a gentle laugh of love.

Freedom Defined

You are free from the law, but that doesn't mean you are free to do wrong (2:16). There is an amusing story of the early days of the Russian Revolution. After the czar had abdicated, a stout old woman was seen walking leisurely down the middle of one of the busiest streets in Saint Petersburg, at no small peril to herself and to the great confusion of traffic. A policeman pointed out to her that there was a sidewalk for pedestrians and that the street was for wagons, automobiles, and horsemen. But she was not to be convinced. "I am going to walk just where I like," she said. "We've got liberty now." When we assert to do to as we like, we are as thoughtless and foolish as the old woman. Freedom is not a question of doing as we like. It is rather a question of doing as we should.

Peter tells his readers how to live their lives (2:17). *Show respect for everyone.* Honor all people. *Love Christians everywhere.* Every social problem could be solved. *Fear God.* The fear of the Lord is the beginning of wisdom. *Honor the government.* Show respect for your political leaders.

One of the most convincing and powerful demonstrations that a Christian can give that he has a newborn life is patiently enduring wrong and injustice (2:19-20). That is when we show forth the grace of God. That is what Christ did while he was on earth and in submitting to his crucifixion and death. This is what his followers are to do as we *follow in his steps* (2:21).

Patience in undeserved punishment is one way of testifying for Christ. A wicked crowd in his regiment took a violent dislike to one Christian soldier because he wouldn't swear or gamble or join them in their loose living. His days were made miserable. But he never lost his temper or gave in or tried to pay them back, and in the end he led one of the worst of the fellows to Christ.

Such suffering by Christians from injustice, without retaliation or defense, is a reflection of the vicarious atonement of Christ (2:24). We are to suffer and be "patient." Patience is noble because it is Christlike. Peter points to the example of his Master (3:17-18; 4:12-16). *When the way is rough, your patience has a chance to grow. So let it grow, and don't try to squirm out of your problems. For when your patience is finally in full bloom, then you will be ready for anything, strong in character, full and complete* (James 1:3-4).

The Man Who Suffered for Me
Christ also *suffered for you* (2:21). A lady was visiting in a hospital. She went up to a bed on which lay a wounded soldier and said gently, "Thank you for being wounded for me." The young man's face brightened. That was a new thought to him. It made the pain more bearable to look upon it in that light. Do you realize

that many years ago One was wounded for you? And that One was the Son of God himself? Yes, he was wounded and bruised for my sins; by his lash marks I am healed (2:24).

Spurgeon put it this way: "The remedy for your sins and mine is found in the substitutionary suffering of the Lord Jesus Christ, and in this only. But if I say of a certain ointment that it heals, I do not deny that you need a bandage with which to apply it to the wound. Faith is the linen which binds the plaster of Christ's reconciliation to the sore of my skin. The linen does not heal; that is the work of the ointment. So faith does not heal; that is the work of the atonement of Christ."

We find in 1 Peter 2–3 some instructions for the various relationships of our lives. First, there are some personal instructions (2:1-12). Next we find our social relationships. Servants should obey their masters with respect, not only those masters who are good and considerate, but also those who are arbitrary. In 3:1-7 our home relationships are mentioned. Naturally, the home begins with the marriage relationship. *Wives fit in with your husbands' plans.* This means unselfish devotion so as to win his love and admiration. This might sound unreasonable if we did not hear the injunction to husbands that they *must be careful of their wives, being thoughtful of their needs* (3:7). This makes a wife subject to love that acts thoughtfully and not according to the husband's selfish desires. It is sign of Christian masculinity for a man to be tender toward his wife. God's plan is that the love of husband and wife should be a mutual thing. Each one should consider the other. The result of all this will be a marriage relationship in which prayers "will get ready answers" (3:7). Prayer is the surest secret of success in any married life.

Peter says that the Christian is a:

Baby—desiring the milk of the fullness of salvation.
Living building stone—built into the temple of life.
Priest—offering spiritual sacrifices.
Visitor—keeping clean from the world's evil pleasures.
Citizen—rendering obedience to rulers.
Man—giving honor to everyone in the fear of God.
Servant—subject to Christ
Sufferer—patient, committing all to Christ.

Peter gives the way to be happy in a world that is wretched. *If you want a happy, good life, keep control of your tongue, and guard your lips from telling lies. Turn away from evil and do good. Try to live in peace even if you must run after it to catch and hold it! For the Lord is watching his children, listening to their prayers; but the Lord's face is hard against those who do evil* (3:10-12). He quotes Psalm 34:12-14. This is a remedy that works today as well as it worked in David's time. The best way of making this life happy and prosperous is to keep from speaking evil and slander and to be always ready to overcome evil with good.

A Ready Answer
Another important command is given in 1 Peter 3:15. This is for every one of us. *If anybody asks why you believe as you do, be ready to tell him.* Have you an intelligent answer to give to others of your trust in Christ? If not, stop right here and get one ready. What does Christ mean to you?

Christ's sufferings in the flesh were physical and literal. *He personally carried the load of our sins in his own body when he died on the cross* (2:24). The Christian's suffering, spoken of in 4:1, is spiritual. The Christian takes up his cross and follows Christ, denying himself. The phrase, *You must have the same attitude he did,* means the same as the words, *If anyone wants to be a follower of mine, let him deny himself and take up his cross and follow me* (Matthew 16:24). Such a high resolve will involve a measure of actual suffering, for God's will may cut across our desire to gratify some bodily craving. Very few in this world escape suffering, either mental, physical, or spiritual. We cannot choose the way we will suffer.

Often God allows us to go through life denied the one thing we wish more than anything else. But we should be comforted in this, that whom God loves, he disciplines. If he grinds down the surface of our lives, it is so the stone will shine all the more brilliantly. It is the many facets of the diamond that make it dazzling. Know that the greater the suffering in this world, the greater the glory in heaven.

The Christian sometimes has to forego the gratification of even right desires. The natural cravings of the body for food and drink, for example, are not to be considered merely as ends in themselves. They come to have a spiritual meaning that whatever we do, even eating and drinking, we do to the glory of God (1 Corinthians 10:31). *So if eating meat offered to idols is going to make my brother sin, I'll not eat any of it as long as I live* (1 Corinthians

8:13). Sometimes we must refuse for the sake of others. This is the "mind of Christ."

Be careful not to follow the world, *the evil things the godless enjoy* (4:3). What the heathen world wanted the Jewish Christians to do, Peter names here.

TRIALS OF THE CHRISTIAN
1 PETER 4:12–5:14

Nero was subjecting the church to awful persecutions. Trials resulting from loyalty to Christ are inevitable. Christ sits as a refiner before the fire. It is with the most precious metals that the assayer takes the most pains as he subjects them to the heat. Such fires melt the metal and only the molten mass releases the alloy or takes its new form in the mold. Christ allows us to be subjected to the heat until all the dross is burned out, and as the assayer sees his face in the molten mass and knows it is pure, so Christ can see his own face reflected in our lives.

Christians were burned every night in Nero's gardens. It looked as if the devil was about to devour the church (5:8). It was a "fiery trial," but God would use its very heat to burn out the dross and leave the pure gold (1:7). History is replete with the record of the many persecutions of Christians. Some have been even more brutal than Nero's. Millions of Christians through the centuries have been subjected to every conceivable kind of torture. These words of Peter's have been for them, too. How ashamed we should be even to mention our little troubles in light of these!

Don't be surprised when you are tried in the fire, as if something strange were happening to you (4:12). Don't think that Christ has promised that we, as Christians, will be spared from pain or misfortunes or death. In fact, Christ said, "Here on earth you will have many trials and sorrows." This means that the real Christian will be persecuted, because the world hates Christ and anything called by his name.

Peter exhorted the leaders of the church to care for the flock. He told them, *Don't be tyrants, but lead them by your good example* (5:3). Jesus had told Peter to "take care of my sheep" (John 21). Undershepherds will receive their rewards from the Chief Shepherd when he comes (5:4). His glory will never end.

The Christian life is like a jungle battle. Peter tells us who our enemy is—the devil. His work is opposed to all that is good in this world. He is pictured as a roaring lion, seeking his prey (5:8). This adversary is cagey, appearing sometimes as an angel of light, at another time as the serpent, coiled for the strike. He is always *looking for some victim*. He is watching for the vulnerable spot, for the unguarded door to our hearts. Paul tells us what armor we should wear in Ephesians 6. We need not be afraid, for *after you have suffered a little while, our God, who is full of kindness through Christ, will give you his eternal glory. He personally will come and pick you up, and set you firmly in place, and make you stronger than ever* (5:10).

SELECTED BIBLE READING

Sunday: Precious Faith (1 Peter 1:1-12)
Monday: Precious Blood (1 Peter 1:13-25)
Tuesday: Precious Cornerstone (1 Peter 2:1-10)
Wednesday: Precious Savior (1 Peter 2:11-25)
Thursday: Precious Is a Gentle and Quiet Spirit (1 Peter 3)
Friday: Precious Suffering of Christ (1 Peter 4)
Saturday: Precious Promises (1 Peter 5)

CHAPTER 49

UNDERSTANDING SECOND PETER

Second Peter Portrays Jesus Christ, Our Strength

Peter's first letter was to console; the second to warn. In his first letter, Peter was trying to encourage Christians who were suffering terrible persecutions from outside the church. In this second letter, he warned them of danger within the church.

Christians need moral courage even more than physical courage. It is our duty to do right under all circumstances, with no qualification and no hesitation. "A Christian is never off duty." To stand up for truth is often more difficult than to go into battle. Illustrations from the Bible are found in Joseph (Genesis 39:9), Nehemiah (5:7; 6:1-16), Daniel (1:8), Paul, and others. History is full of instances, too: Polycarp, Luther, Wesley, Joan of Arc. They were never ashamed of Christ because they knew him.

Peter, in warning against the dangers from within, urges us to "grow in spiritual strength and become better acquainted with our Lord and Savior Jesus Christ." Christian knowledge is the best way to overcome false teaching. We learn to know Christ through his Word. In 1 Peter we hear much about suffering. In 2 Peter we hear much about knowledge. Shallow knowledge makes superficial Christians. Paul said, "I know the one in whom I trust." It is not what you believe that gives you strength, but *whom* you believe. Peter knew that heresy often leads to immoral living. Christianity must have a creed if right conduct is to be assured. Church leaders were using the church for money-making schemes and permitting wrongdoing of every sort. The false teachers were laughing at the Lord's coming, and the church could easily have stopped looking for that "blessed hope."

Simon Peter, a servant and missionary of Jesus Christ, was the writer. The first name, Simon, suggests his old, unstable nature. The name Peter (meaning "rock") suggests the new nature that Christ had given him, strong and true.

Peter, the apostle of hope, spoke again to the younger Christians in the faith. He urged them to look toward heaven while dwelling only a while in a very bad world. He talked about the readers as those who have obtained *our kind of faith* (1:1). We remember how Peter's faith was kept through Christ's prayer for him: *But I have pleaded in prayer for you that your faith should not completely fail. So when you have repented and turned to me again, strengthen and build up the faith of your brothers* (Luke 22:32). This is how our faith can be preserved also.

CHRISTIAN VIRTUES
2 PETER 1

Do the days seem dark to you and does sin seem to abound everywhere? That is the way the world looked to the young Christians of Peter's day. So that they would not be discouraged by this outlook, he showed them how to escape *the lust and rottenness all around us* (1:4). Here it is. God will give you *everything you need for living a truly good life* (1:3).

Look at a criminal condemned to be hanged. Suppose a messenger comes to him and says, "The governor has taken your case into consideration, and I have brought you a purse of a thousand dollars." The criminal will say, "What good will it do me? I am to be hanged tomorrow." "Well, I have another message. He has considered your case and sent you the deed to a million-dollar estate." The condemned man despairingly shakes his head and says, "What can I do with that? I will be hanged tomorrow." But the messenger goes on. "Stop! I have another offer to make. I have brought you the governor's own inauguration robe for you to wear with special favor." The condemned man bursts into tears as he says, "Do you intend to mock me? How would I appear ascending the steps of the gallows, wearing the governor's own robe?" Then the messenger says, "Wait, I have one more message. The governor has sent you a pardon. What do you say to that?" The poor man looks at him and says he doesn't believe it. But the messenger hands him the pardon, signed by the governor, with the official stamp upon it. Then the man leaps for joy while tears of gratitude run down his face. Then the messenger says. "I am not through yet. I have brought you the pardon, but the purse of gold, the deed, and the royal robe are yours in addition." God has given us "everything" in Christ, his Son. With these, nothing can defeat the young Christian.

The way I can escape the awful sins in this world each day is by letting God live through me, since *he even shares his own glory and his own goodness with us!* (1:3). Lay hold of the *rich and wonderful blessings he promised, for instance . . . to give us his own character.* I share the very character of God (1:4). Everyone does not have the character of God. The divine is not in all men. His image remains in us, though marred (1 Corinthians 11:7), but not an atom of his life. We are dead and lifeless apart from Christ. The "character" of God becomes ours only when the Savior becomes ours. This is a wonderful truth. We ought to take courage when we remember that with Christ in us, "his own character" also is within us. The "rich and wonderful blessings he promised" are before us. We ought to go straight ahead, fearing nothing (1:4).

The "character" that God has given us should be shown in the everyday practices of the Christian life, which is no more or less than the practice of Christian virtues. In Galatians 5 we find that Christian virtues are the fruit of the Spirit.

Do others know that you are a Christian by the way you act? Remember that night by the fire, when a smart young girl recalled that Peter had been with Jesus, Peter gave her some of the choice language of the Galilee fishing trade to try to prove otherwise. The crowd picked him out by his accent (Mark 14:66-71). Later, the rulers picked him out as a companion of Jesus by his appearance and talk. The world recognizes us in exactly the same way. There is something about a person's whole bearing that proclaims him as a companion of Jesus Christ. As soon as we hear a man speak about Christ, we can tell what he is.

Although God gives us a changed character, he wants us to do our part in developing this priceless gift (1:5-11). We share the very life of God; therefore we should press on to possess more. God says, "Add one grace to another."

Steps to Heaven

There are seven steps going up from faith, and the last one is love. These steps are the Christian virtues that every Christian should have. Let's climb slowly and thoughtfully up this flight of stairs and see how far we have gone. To your faith add goodness, knowledge, self-control, patience, godliness, enjoyment of other people, love. This is the result of our precious faith.

The fuller the measure of these virtues, the greater will be our knowledge of Jesus Christ our Lord. Know Christ, for to know him is life eternal, and in no one else is there salvation (see Acts 4:12).

Someone has said that this is a seven-story-and-basement building. Add story to story, but be sure to put faith at the foundation. If you try to build without the proper base, the building will become top-heavy. To be sure, faith is the foundation. But a foundation is of little use if no building follows. During the days of the Great Depression it was a common sight to see the framework of a great building standing stark and gaunt, with weeds growing around it, abandoned by the men who had begun a good work but because of the depression had ceased before it was finished. The foundation was substantial and adequate but for years was entirely useless because nothing was added to make the building usable.

Peter, like Paul, warns Christians against standing still. Don't remain babies in Christ, tripping over every teaching, but grow strong.

But anyone who fails to go after these additions to faith is blind indeed, or at least very shortsighted (1:9). Nearsighted Christians we will be, unfit for enlistment in God's army, if we do not have these virtues. Be sure of your position in Christ. Don't ever doubt your calling in him. Spare no effort to put God's call and choice beyond all doubt. Spare no effort in prayer, in study, and in talking with older Christians. Life is full of so much uncertainty, but you do not have to be uncertain in spiritual things. A spiritual certainty produces a stability in life, and *you will never stumble or fall away* (1:10).

A Christian's ambition should be to have a full life. Peter wants you to have an abundant entrance into the haven of rest, Christ's eternal kingdom (1:11).

Numbered Days

Peter, like Paul, was conscious of his approaching death. Because he knew he was about to leave them, he wanted to remind them of what he so well knew. His memory pictured before him the great transfiguration scene. There he had witnessed the glory of Christ. Any doubt as to his reality or of his coming again in power was forever banished from his mind. God himself had borne testimony of his glory and honor, and a voice had said, *This is my beloved Son, and I am wonderfully pleased with him.* He had heard the voice from above, proving Jesus' deity. Now Peter knew. He was sure. He wanted them to know that he was not telling them fairy stories when he told them of the power and coming of the Lord Jesus Christ, but he was an eyewitness of his majesty.

Remember, Peter suffered and died for this truth he was telling. At one time he said, *We cannot stop telling about the wonderful things we saw Jesus do and heard him say* (Acts 4:20).

People depend too much on feeling instead of knowledge based on facts. Peter didn't want these Christians to rest on feelings. When the devil sees a poor soul in agony on the waves of sin getting close to the Rock of Ages, he just holds out the plank of feeling to him and says, "There, get on that. You feel more comfortable now, don't you?" And while the man stands there getting his breath again, out goes the plank from under him and he is worse off than ever.

Added to the evidence of the transfiguration was that Peter had *seen and proved that what the prophets said came true* (1:19). This does not put Christian experience (the vision on the mountain) over against prophecy, but it says that what the prophets said is confirmed by experience. They go together. Peter throws much light on the inspiration of the Scriptures. See 1 Peter 1:10-12; 2 Peter 1:4, 16-21; 3:15.

A native in India, writing to a friend about a great revival they were having, said, "We are having a great 'rebible' here." Not a bad idea. The church needs to be re-Bibled!

CHRISTLESS TEACHERS
2 PETER 2

Are the times in which we live hard, and temptations strong, and opposition powerful? Expect it and rise above it. We are warned that it will be so. The world always has been and always will be full of antagonism to the truth and to those who speak it. But God will bring the antagonism to naught. In the meantime, *the Lord can rescue you and me from the temptations that surround us* (2:9).

Peter tells of the coming, the influence, and the doom of the false teachers in this dark and appalling chapter. We need not be surprised at their coming, for Christ warned us of that in Matthew 7:15; 24:11, 24, and we have listened to Paul's words about them to Timothy (1 Timothy 4:1-3; 2 Timothy 3:1-9).

What an evil list is this account in Peter's second letter of the false teachers' deeds. It is a sad picture indeed. Read it! No wonder Peter warned the church of false prophets!

Tell clever lies (2:1)
Turn against their Master who bought them (2:1)
Scoff at Christ and his way (2:2)
Greediness (2:3)
Evil, lustful thoughts (2:10)
Scoff at angels (2:10)
Proud and willful (2:10)
No better than animals (2:12)
Laugh at what they know so little about (2:12)
Live in evil pleasure day after day (2:13)
A disgrace and stain among you (2:13)
Never have enough adultery (2:14)
Lure unstable women (2:14)
Doomed and cursed (2:14)
Become lost (2:15)
Dried up springs of water (2:17)
Like clouds before storm winds (2:17)
Boast about their sins (2:18)
Slaves to sin and destruction (2:19)

The false teachers of today do just what is told here. *They cleverly tell lies about God.* They do it subtly. They don't believe in the deity of Christ—that Jesus, who was born of a virgin, was actually God. Peter describes the "clever lie" they bring in. This is it—*Turning against their Master who bought them.* It does not say that they turned against the Master who *taught* them. Practically every false religion acknowledges Christ a great teacher but will not accept him as Savior, the One who *bought* us with his own precious blood. They deny the blood atonement.

Blood test—This is the mark by which to test and reject the false teacher. Ask for credentials of teachers who are around today. When any teacher does not put the cross at the center of his teaching, beware! Turn from him. Our redemption is in the blood. Jesus bought us with his blood.

Popularity Test—These teachers are popular. *Many will follow their evil teaching* (2:2). Don't think it strange that false religions, of which there are many varieties, are able to procure a large following. Peter told us they would. People do not want to be told that they need a Savior. That makes them admit that they are sinners. They only want to be *taught*, not *bought. Christ and his way will be scoffed at* (2:2). All of these false teachings talk about "truth," but they forget that Christ said, *I am the Way—yes, and the Truth and the Life. No one can get to the Father except by means of me* (John 14:6). He is not just a part of truth—he is *Truth.* He is not a way-shower—he is the *Way.* He does not come to show us how to live—he is *Life.*

Vocabulary test—*These teachers in their greed will tell you anything to get hold of your money* (2:3). Words mean so little in many of these false religions. There is a new meaning given to so many words. They say they believe in everything, but when asked what they mean, their beliefs are far from what the Scripture says. They keep the form of words, but the meaning is pumped out. It is like an egg with holes in either end and the inside blown out. The form of the egg is there, but the real substance is gone. Christ said that people would even say, "Lord, Lord," but he would say, "Go away, you have never been mine." Words mean nothing unless there is heart in their meaning. *To get hold of your money* is added. How these false religions prey upon the people for money! You cannot have healing unless you pay. A "practitioner" demands a price. God says you may come to him *even if you have no money* (Isaiah 55:1)!

There is only one thing God can do with these kinds of people, and that is to destroy them. "Light that is trifled with becomes lightning." Peter declares with no uncertainty that this will be the end of false teachers who cover themselves with the cloak of the church (2:3-9). They will certainly be punished. God did not even spare the angels who sinned! He sent a flood upon a godless world in Noah's day. Sodom and Gomorrah were reduced to ashes. All of these were as a warning to the godless of every generation of what God has in store for them. One thing we can be sure of: no matter how severe the judgment for false teachers may be, the deliverance of God's people is promised. Leave the punishment of the wicked with God.

As we read on we find much else that these wicked teachers will do. They will malign Christ's apostles. They will trap weak people, promising them freedom while actually enslaving them in corrupt habits (2:2-22).

CHRIST'S COMING
2 PETER 3

False teaching about Christ that denies his deity and power results in false thinking. The first question it raises is about the coming of Christ. To help the church in this, Peter reminded them of the things Jesus had said. People misunderstood him and thought his return would be in that generation. Peter told them that time is nothing with God—*that a day or a thousand years from now is like tomorrow to the Lord* (3:8). He will keep this promise as he has kept all of his promises, but according to his own time.

He isn't really being slow about his promised return . . . he is not willing that any should perish, and he is giving more time for sinners to repent (3:9). The last days are to be sad days, for scoffers will make fun and say, "Ha, ha, where is the promise of Christ's coming? As far as we can see, everything is going on just as it has from the beginning of creation. There have been no signs of any radical change. The promise of his coming has failed." These scoffers were evil men, but the sad truth today is that even good men scoff at the promise of his coming. They make sport of the great hope of the church. How illogical was their reasoning about Christ's not coming: He had not come; hence he was not coming. Nothing different had happened; hence nothing unusual was going to happen. Because our Lord has not come as yet, shall we give up hope? No, indeed. Rather, rejoice in the fact that his return comes nearer every day.

Floods and Fires
Peter reminded these skeptics that a mighty flood did drown the world once. Christ has likened his coming to the flood in Matthew 24:37-38, and no doubt Peter had heard him say it. But next time God will destroy the earth by fire. Will it be literal fire? Was the flood literal water? Stored within the earth are oils and gases and fire enough to burn it up. Volcanoes are the release of these elements. Scientists now tell us we are sitting on a crust of earth only thirty miles in depth. Beneath this is a mass of molten matter. At a word, God could release a spout that would bury the earth in literal fire. The devastation caused by the atomic bomb has proved the possibility of such catastrophe. Or our earth may collide with some other heavenly body.

We know that when God's clock strikes the hour the earth will melt with a fervent heat. The earth will be burned up, and in the great explosion the heavens will pass away. Then *new heavens and a new earth* will emerge (3:13).

Today people are heady and high-minded. They think they know everything. But all this is to be expected. Satan will not give up his hold on this earth without protest. But his days of liberty are numbered, and Jesus shall reign. Scorn and scoffing did not hold back the flood when it was unloosed. The angel's mighty trumpet will make short work of men's foolish "I don't believe it" and "I don't think it is true" and "I don't see it." Nevertheless, we, according to his promise, look for *new heavens and a new earth . . . where there will be only goodness.* It will not be entirely a destruction, but a new earth will be constructed. *But for you who fear my name, the Sun of Righteousness will rise with healing in his wings* (Malachi 4:2).

What effect should all this have on our lives? Peter answers in 3:14. We should *try hard to live without sinning; and be at peace with everyone.* Don't grow careless because he is delaying, for one day the Lord will come suddenly. Be patient while he delays, knowing that he does it because he is patient and would give the last man, woman, and child a chance to accept him.

What lives we ought to live while we wait for his coming! We can speed his return by our holy living. Faith in the return of our Lord must lead to this. Then we can speed it by a holy conversation. Watch your speech. Don't forget to look forward with an eager gaze. *Try hard . . . so that he will be pleased with you when he returns* (3:14). Are you looking forward to his coming? What effect has this hope had on your life and conversation?

Peter's last words are words of warning, a note of caution. Be careful, *so that you can watch out and not be carried away by the mistakes of these wicked men, lest you yourselves become mixed up too.*

Know and Grow
The remedy against becoming mixed up is to "grow"—make progress. *Grow in spiritual strength and become better acquainted with our Lord and Savior Jesus Christ.* Are you growing better acquainted with Christ? If you are not growing, be careful lest you become mixed up, for we are living in a wicked world where people are enemies of God and his truth. A living thing ought to grow. When there is no growth, there is no life. The foundation of growth is knowing Christ. As we grow in this, we grow in likeness to him.

SELECTED BIBLE READING

Sunday: Christian Virtues (2 Peter 1:1-14)
Monday: Christ's Word Exalted (2 Peter 1:15-21)
Tuesday: Christless Teachers (2 Peter 2:1-14)
Wednesday: Christ against the Backslider (2 Peter 2:15-22)
Thursday: Christ's Coming Scoffed (2 Peter 3:1-9)
Friday: Christ's Coming Assured (2 Peter 3:10-18)
Saturday: Christ Our Hope (2 Peter 1–3)

CHAPTER 50

UNDERSTANDING FIRST, SECOND, THIRD JOHN AND JUDE

Jesus Christ, Our Life; the Truth; the Way; Our Keeper

UNDERSTANDING FIRST JOHN

First John was written by the aged Apostle John in A.D. 90, probably in Ephesus. Unlike the other apostles, he did not address his letter to any church or any particular person. He wrote to all Christians, old and young (2:12-14). He called Christians by a tender word, *teknia*, which means "born ones" or "children." God is dealing with his very own born-again children.

John told us why he wrote his Gospel—*so that you will believe that [Jesus] is the Messiah, the Son of God, and that believing in him you will have life* (John 20:31).

He wrote his letter so that those who believe in Christ could *know* that they have eternal life (5:13).

The letter of 1 John appears to have been intended as a companion to the Gospel of John. Thus we find the word *believe* running all through the Gospel of John, and the word *know* running through the letter.

John wrote for four reasons:

1. That they might be happy (1:4)
2. That they might not sin (2:1)

3. That they might be on guard against error (2:26)
4. That they might *know* (5:13)

Someone has well named this the "Really and Truly Letter." It has a confident, exultant tone all the way through. John was the disciple whom Jesus loved. He stood close to him on the cross of Calvary. He looked into the empty tomb on that morning of the Resurrection. On Patmos he was lifted up by the Spirit and saw a door opened into heaven. This John, who had all these experiences, gives us his personal witness of these facts. "We know," he says. "There is no possibility of doubt about it." *I myself have seen him with my own eyes and listened to him speak. I have touched him with my own hands. He is God's message of life—* JESUS! John gives us evidence for his knowledge. He had heard and seen and handled the One who is eternal Life. He longed to bring his hearers into intimate fellowship with the Father and his Son so that they would be full of joy (1:3-4, 7; 2:13-14).

Christ, who was God, took on flesh and lived with men so they could hear his voice, see his face, and feel the touch of his loving hand. This brought God down to man so that we "may share the fellowship." To share the fellowship is to live in agreement.

God wants us to have fellowship with him, and in him to have fellowship with one another (1:3).

John says that we not only must believe like Christians, but we must act like Christians. In chapters 1–3, we find out whether we are living like Christians. In chapters 4–5 we discover whether we are believing like Christians. Striking lightning is accompanied by thunder. So "striking" faith is accompanied by life and testimony (2:3). Some people say they believe God but act more like the devil. This cannot be. We must be as orthodox in our behavior as we are in our belief. Believe the truth and do the truth. *If we say we are his friends, but go on living in spiritual darkness and sin, we are lying* (1:6).

John exalts God in his letters:

God is Light (1:5)
God is Love (4:8, 16)
God is Righteous (2:29)
God is Life (5:11-12)
God is Truth (2 John)
God is Good (3 John)

RIGHT BEHAVIOR
1 JOHN 1–3

John gives us seven tests of Christian behavior. Read these and find what your rating is as a Christian. The test is this—*if we say* one thing and do another, we are not living as Christ would want us to, in full fellowship with himself. How much easier it is to talk than it is to do. As Dwight L. Moody said, "We talk cream and live skim milk."

We are to walk together, talk together, and live together. We are to eat at the same table (Revelation 3:20). We are one family (Ephesians 3:15). God is my Father because Jesus Christ my older Brother has made me a child of the King. Therefore I must behave that way. Fellowship brings joy (1:4). There is no joy greater than fellowship with a friend.

I live in the presence of a God of light. *God is light, and in him is no darkness at all* (1:5). If I live in his presence, I will live in the light of his love and grace. There are seven tests of our life with God.

First Test—Live in the Light
If we say we are his friends, but go on living in spiritual darkness and sin, we are lying (1:6).

Is there known sin in your life? If there is, you are not living with Christ. His presence throws light on your conscience and heart and shows the presence of sin in your life (Ephesians 5:13). A Christian who is living in fellowship with God will enjoy fellowship with other Christians (1:7). Have you ever picked up a stone that had been lying on the ground for a long time? The minute you lift it, loathsome things move in every direction to flee from the light. Light reveals sin. Known sin will keep you from fellowship with Christ, but fellowship with Christ will keep you from sin. Do you ask him to throw his searchlight on your heart?

Second Test—Admit You Are a Sinner
If we say that we have no sin, we are only fooling ourselves, and refusing to accept the truth (1:8).

You cannot live with God and practice sin in your life at the same time. God keeps showing us the sin in our lives. On the cross he redeemed us from the penalty of sin once and for all.

But let us know too that if we confess our sins he keeps cleansing us from the sins that creep into our lives by our contact with this world.

When a farmer plows his field he throws out every stone that he finds. But the next year as the plow goes deep in the furrow, he finds other stones that had remained hidden the year before. He throws these aside as they turn up. Then the next year the same thing occurs. So in our lives! God will reveal by the plow of his Spirit the sins that are hidden in our lives that we did not know were there. Don't be discouraged, but use his remedy.

If we confess our sins to him, he can be depended on to forgive us and to cleanse us from every wrong (1:9). Don't pray in an indefinite way. Name your sin before God. Is it pride, lack of trust, anger, love of pleasure more than God? Well, whatever it is, lay it out before God and tell him what it is. Call it by name. Then claim God's promise. *He can be depended on* not only *to forgive us* but *to cleanse us from every wrong.* A human parent can forgive our misbehavings, but only God can cleanse us from sin.

Third Test—Obey God's Will

Someone may say, "I am a Christian. . . ." But if he doesn't do what Christ tells him to, he is a liar (2:4).

Obedience is a real test. God makes a very strong statement. If you say you are a Christian and do not obey him, you are a liar. The man that is a Christian keeps God's commandments.

What are Christ's commandments? Love the Lord your God with all your heart, soul, and mind, and your neighbor as yourself. Do you love God that way? Put yourself to a few tests. Do you spend more time watching television than you do with God? Are you ambitious to carry out some plan in your life that you hope will bring you fame or wealth or just enjoyment? Do you know his will for your life? Do you want to? This is a test of your Christian life. Are you obedient to his Word? To his still small voice? Many times we do not want to let God talk to us. We will not listen to him because we are afraid of his will for us. God has a plan for every step of our lives, for "the steps of good men are directed by the Lord."

Christ says, *If you love me, obey me,* and *you are my friends if you obey me.* What does he ask us to do? *I demand that you love each other* (John 14:15; 15:14, 17).

Fourth Test—Imitate Christ

Anyone who says he is a Christian should live as Christ did (2:6).

We should be Christlike in all our life. Christ says, *You are the salt of the earth.* Salt preserves food from spoiling. Are you the preservative of your crowd? Do you keep your language clean? Do you refrain from using God's name in vain? Does your presence keep them from doing questionable things?

A little Chinese girl once said, "I know why Christ said, *You are the salt of the earth.* Because salt makes folks thirsty and Christians should make others thirsty for Christ." Are you making folks thirsty?

In the famous Sistine Chapel in Rome, the beauty of the art is in the ceiling. As you enter you are given a mirror. It seems strange to see people walking around looking down when the paintings are above. But they see all the glory reflected in the mirrors before them, without breaking their necks. Be a reflector. Let the beauty of Jesus be seen in you.

Fifth Test—Love Others

Anyone who says he is walking in the light of Christ but dislikes his fellow man, is still in darkness (2:9).

Another acid test of the Christian life is love (2:7-11). Love changes a person. Love makes us have a concern for the welfare of others.

God speaks of loving others in our personal attitudes. There are three chief attitudes toward others: hatred, which is murder (3:15); indifference—no concern—which is akin to hate (4:20-21); love. Love shows itself in different ways (2:9-11; 3:14): physically—concern for another's needs (3:16-18); spiritually—concern for another's soul.

Sixth Test—Relationship to the World

Stop loving this evil world and all that it offers you, for when you love these things you show that you do not really love God (2:15).

We live in an evil world (Galatians 1:4). The scheme of things as they exist today is not the standard for the Christian. Whenever a Christian is loving the evil things of this world, he is walking on forbidden ground.

All sins may be put into three categories: lust of the flesh, lust of the eyes, pride of life.

1. *Lust of the flesh.* Temptations come through the body and its appetites and passions. The devil tempted Jesus in this way first. Jesus had been fasting forty days, and every atom of his being cried out for food. How plausible was Satan's temptation! It was the same appeal to the appetite that Satan had made to Eve. In thousands of years the devil has invented no new weapon of attack. *Get food by changing stones into loaves of bread.* The temptation for self-gratification is one of the strongest that can assail us. Appetite is still one of the most vulnerable points when Satan attacks us. The need for bread and pleasure is supposed by some to justify any means to get them. But it isn't necessary that we live at all! There is only one moral necessity—to trust God and obey his commandments.

2. *Lust of the eyes.* Foiled with one weapon, Satan quickly dropped it and tried another. Taking Jesus to the peak of a high mountain, he showed him all the kingdoms of the world in a moment of time. *I will give you all these splendid kingdoms and their glory . . . if you will only get down on your knees and worship me* (Luke 4:7).

   How people worship at the altar of riches and honor because they long for what their eyes see of this world!

   Your eyes can blacken your soul! Be careful what you see. If you throw a new tennis ball against a sooty wall, the ball will have a black mark on it. If your eye is thrown against impure objects, be sure a mark will be left on your mind and heart. Be careful what you see!

3. *Pride of life.* Everyone wants spectacular success. The devil took Jesus to the pinnacle of the Temple and told him to jump off, because if he was the Son of God he would be guarded by angels. It was a proposal to leap from the pinnacle of the Temple into immediate popularity. It is a temptation for any person to be popular. We all have human ambitions. How many people of genius have been led astray because the glittering prize of ambition has been held up before them! We want to win it at a single stroke. How strong is the temptation to take a shortcut to our ambition, whether of education or wealth or position and power. We are in danger of selling our very souls to gain our end! Even Jesus saw the world spread before him and saw how short and alluring was the step that was promised him, but to worship Satan would have ended his mission as the Savior of the world.

Seventh Test—Prove Christ Is Righteous by Your Life

Since we know that God is always good and does only right, we may rightly assume that all those who do right are his children (2:29).

Do we acknowledge Christ by our life? Others watch us to see if we "do right." He who lives in Christ will bear the same fruit in his life that Christ bears, and that is righteousness.

Those who keep on sinning are against God, for every sin is done against the will of God (3:4). If we know Christ as God dwells in our lives, we will not "keep on sinning." *But as for those who keep on sinning, they should realize this: They sin because they have never really known him or become his. . . . The person who has been born into God's family does not make a practice of sinning* (3:6, 9). It is possible for a Christian under strong temptation to fall into sin, but he will not keep practicing it. If a person continually practices sin, he may well doubt his conversion! We should consider sin as God does. Sin cost God his Son!

RIGHT BELIEF
1 JOHN 4:1–5:12

We need a creed by which to live. The word *creed* comes from the Latin word *credo*—"I believe." There are sins of the body that we all commit, but there are sins of the heart and disposition as well. God is as interested in what you believe as in how you act.

You cannot believe things that are not true about Christ and at the same time have fellowship with him. It is absurd to say that it doesn't make any difference what you believe as long as you are sincere. This statement is unsound. You can't believe that an eight o'clock train leaves at nine o'clock, show up at nine, and not miss the train. And you can't sincerely believe a bottle of poison contains a healing medicine, swallow some, and find anything but death. We cannot believe what is false, have it affect our life, and then go out and live a life that is true.

The unsound teachers of John's day were denying the fact that Christ truly suffered and truly rose again. They said he was only a mystery man who appeared and vanished but was not God.

You cannot deny the death of Christ on the cross and find a pardon for your sin. You cannot deny the resurrection of Christ and enjoy the privileges of Christianity that are found in a living Christ. You cannot deny that Christ is God and find any access to the Father.

Your sin can start in your intellect. What do you believe? Christ wants to be our only Teacher. What we believe determines how we act.

Is a creed necessary? Read John 3:16 and see if you think it is. It says, *Anyone who believes in him shall not perish but have eternal life.* Christianity is Christ-centered. Christ out of Christianity leaves nothing. This means death. If we do not believe, we will die, but if we believe, we will live (Romans 10:9-10).

So many Christians are spiritual babies in Christ. They are susceptible to every new doctrine around them. When doubt fills their minds they sink in despair. Hence everyone ought to be given a way whereby he can test every religion to see if it be true. This is especially true in this day of so many religious beliefs. John states the test very clearly in 4:1-3: *Dearly loved friends, don't always believe everything you hear just because someone says it is a message from God: test it first to see if it really is. For there are many false teachers around, and the way to find out if their message is from the Holy Spirit is to ask: Does it really agree that Jesus Christ, God's Son, actually became man with a human body? If so, then the message is from God. If not, the message is not from God but from one who is against Christ. . . .*

What Shall We Believe?

John makes some plain statements in 1 John 4:1-3:

First, *we must believe that Jesus Christ actually became man with a human body* (4:1-2; 5:20-21). He is the incarnate Lord. This is the first thing we must be sure of. We must believe that when Jesus walked this earth he was God clothed in human flesh. "Veiled in flesh the Godhead see, hail the incarnate deity," wrote Charles Wesley. Jesus took upon himself the form of a man so that he could die in man's place, bearing our sins in his own body on the tree.

John records, *And Christ became a human being and lived here on earth among us and was full of loving forgiveness and truth. And some of us have seen his glory—the glory of the only Son of the heavenly Father!* (John 1:14). Christ's earthly life lasted thirty-three years, but that was not his whole existence. Christ was with the Father from the beginning. Over nineteen hundred years ago this man of the ages came to this earth at his first advent. He did not begin life at the manger. That was merely the point at which he took upon himself the form of a man. Then he remained on this earth thirty-three years. He died and was buried and rose again. Then he went back to where he came from.

Second, *we must believe that Jesus is truly the Son of God* (4:15; 5:5). He is actually God. The liar is the one who denies that Jesus is the Christ, the promised Messiah (2:22). The Old Testament prophets told us the Messiah was coming. The angel chorus said that the baby born in Bethlehem was this Messiah who had been prophesied. Simeon recognized that the baby was the Messiah (Luke 2:25-35).

Third, *we must believe that God is love* (4:8). There is no force in the world to compare with Christian love. Its power is seen in the great fact that "God is love." All through this chapter it isn't our love that is the definition of love at its best; God's love is the measure. Listen! *Love comes from God. . . . God is love. . . . God showed how much he loved us by sending his only Son. . . . In this act we see what real love is . . . his love for us. . . . His love within us grows ever stronger. . . . Our loving him comes as a result of his loving us first* (4:7-19). Love turns our hearts away from ourselves. We cannot really love God without loving others. So we become channels of blessing to others around us because of what God is in us.

Nothing could influence our lives as much as the love of God. For *God lives in us* (4:12). A man went to a pastor and said, "Sir, I want to enter into your religion." "My friend," said the pastor, "our religion must enter into you." God's love was shown in the gift of his Son to be a sacrifice for our sins (John 3:16; 1 John 4:9-10). When we look at the cross we catch a glimpse into God's heart of love. The cross was the only way God had of showing us his heart. It is a picture of infinite love poured out in all of its fullness. Christ did not die to make God love man. He died because God had loved man always with an everlasting love. *For God loved the world so much. . . .* Our salvation does not depend on what we are but on what God is, and God is love!

God's love is first directed toward the individual. Then the individual must affect society. God is unseen, and there are many who need God's love. So we will show it to others when we love. And when we love, we are like God. *We surely ought to love each other too.*

Fourth, *we must believe that Christ is our Savior* (5:10-12). Christ was sent to provide forgiveness for our sins, because sin barred man from God's love: *The wages of sin is death* (Romans 6:23). So

Christ took the judgment of sin upon his own body on the cross and made it possible for God to show mercy righteously.

All who believe this know in their hearts that it is true. If anyone doesn't believe this, he is actually calling God a liar, because he doesn't believe what God has said about his Son. And what is it that God has said? That he has given us eternal life, and that this life is in his Son. So whoever has God's Son has life; whoever does not have his Son does not have life (5:10-12).

God and Love

Love is the supreme test of our Christian faith. *If we love other Christians it proves that we have been delivered from hell and given eternal life. But a person who doesn't have love for others is headed for eternal death* (3:14). We find out how love acts in 1 Corinthians 13.

But if a person isn't loving and kind, it shows that he doesn't know God—for God is love (4:8). Love is the first instinct of the renewed heart. Where do we get our love? From within? No, from above. *Our love for him comes as a result of his loving us first* (4:19). What if we do not love? God says that we don't know God.

We should show our love to him by loving one another (4:7). He who has love in his heart has fellowship with God (4:16). But where there is no love, there is no fellowship (4:19-21).

RICH REWARDS
1 JOHN 5:12-21

The rewards of life in Christ are stated in the last verses:

Assurance of eternal life (5:13)
Power of prayer (5:14-15)
Power of intercession (5:16)
Victory (5:18; 5:4-5)

Underline the word *know* in 5:13-20. We can have confidence when we know Christ. John uses the word *know* over forty times in his letters. True Christianity is more than a creed—it is something that can be known and felt. We *know* that Christ "became a man so that he could take away our sins." We *know* that "we have been delivered from hell and given eternal life." We *know* that "we can . . . get whatever we ask for." John assures us of these truths.

UNDERSTANDING SECOND JOHN

Second John is a good example of John's private correspondence to an individual. This letter was addressed to a Christian woman that we don't know anything else about.

The word *truth* is found four times in this short letter of thirteen verses. *Love* occurs five times. Truth and love are inseparable.

The truth that John speaks of is from above, the Truth as it is in Christ Jesus. We are to live in the truth, not just admire it. Then we will love one another (v. 5). This love is genuine and not subject to change. The truth of our love is in our life. *If we love God, we will do whatever he tells us to* (v. 6).

John speaks of the teaching of Christ: *If you wander beyond the teaching of Christ, you will leave God behind* (v. 9). This is the test of the gospel. Not what I think or what someone else has thought or said or done, but what has Christ said? What is he to you? Is he the Son of God?

Many false teachers were traveling among the churches who would not confess that Jesus Christ was here "with a human body like ours." These were "against the truth and against Christ" (v. 7). See also 1 John 4:1-2. They did not believe in the humanity of Christ. They denied his incarnation. If you call him "Lord" but deny that he is God, you are a liar and against Christ. John says this plainly.

UNDERSTANDING THIRD JOHN

Do you remember what Christ said of himself in John 14:6? *I am the Way—yes, and the Truth and the Life.* This is how John portrays Jesus in his letters:

First John—Jesus the Life
Second John—Jesus the Truth
Third John—Jesus the Way

Third John was written to a generous and warmhearted friend named Gaius. This man was the type of true Christian layman who dedicated his wealth and talent to the Lord. His financial resources were available and his home was open—all he had belonged to Christ. He is the picture of the man who had found Christ to be the "Way," and in his everyday life he tried to show that gracious Way to others. Such people, scattered here and there, have through the years kept not only the church alive in an unfriendly world but have kept Christ's love burning brightly in the midst of God's people when all seemed dark.

Gaius was noted for his loving hospitality. John urged him to continue entertaining the traveling preachers in spite of bitter opposition of an autocratic and blustering church official named Diotrephes. Hospitality demonstrates Christian love.

You can be either a Gaius, helping in the kingdom, or a Diotrephes, hindering the cause. What a splendid thing to be rich and powerful and to choose to lay all your gifts and talents at Jesus' feet, like Gaius and his friend Demetrius!

UNDERSTANDING JUDE

Jude was a brother of the Lord. He knew Peter. They walked with the Master and no doubt talked together after his departure. They evidently thought much alike on the great issues of the day. Second Peter and Jude are very similar in thought and language. Both men were dealing with the dangers confronting the doctrines of the church.

No doubt certain persons who denied *our only Master and Lord, Jesus Christ* had joined the church. They were not outside but inside the church. They had crept in unawares.

Alas! What church is without them today? They are with us but not of us. Christ will judge these evil men as he did the fallen angels.

These intruders had begun to teach error in the church (vv. 3-4). There was a yeast of evil at work among the readers. These intruders were:

Worldly—*godless teachers, saying that after we become Christians we can do just as we like*
Skeptical—*turned against our only Master*
Lawless—*laughing at those in authority over them*
Critical—*constant gripers, never satisfied*
Flatterers—*when they show respect for others, it is only to get something from them in return*
Aliens—*they love the evil things of the world; they do not have the Holy Spirit living in them*

In contrast to these evil fellows we find the true followers of the faith, who lift high the cross of Christ (vv. 20-23). They must build on the foundation of Christ:

Praying in the Holy Spirit (v. 20)
Staying in God's love (v. 21)
Waiting for God's mercy (v. 21)
Saving souls for him (vv. 22-23)
Resting on his keeping power (v. 24)

Thank God for this noble army of faithful ones! God says their reward will be that here he will *keep you from slipping and falling away* and up there *bring you, sinless and perfect, into his glorious presence* (vv. 24-25).

SELECTED BIBLE READING

Sunday Living in Fellowship (1 John 1:1–2:14)
Monday: Living as Children of God (1 John 2:15–3:24)
Tuesday: Living in Love (1 John 4)
Wednesday: Living in Knowledge (1 John 5)
Thursday: Living in Truth (2 John)
Friday: Living in the Way (3 John)
Saturday: Living without Falling (Jude)

CHAPTER 51

UNDERSTANDING REVELATION

Revelation Portrays Jesus Christ, Our Triumphant King

Revelation is the only book of prophecy in the New Testament. The content of the book seems to indicate that most of its events are yet to be fulfilled. It is the only book in the divine library that especially promises a blessing to those who read and hear. *Blessed* is a strong word, but after reading the first chapters about the churches and the last chapters about heaven, not many of us read much in this book.

Revelation presents a glorious, reigning Christ. The Gospels present him as a Savior, One who came to take the curse of sin, but in this last book we see no humiliation. In one way Revelation is the most remarkable book in the Bible. Revelation tells us about the reign of Christ on this earth that Satan wants to control. It tells of Christ's complete and eternal victory over Satan. It describes Satan's defeat and punishment, first for a thousand years, then eternally. It tells more about Satan's final doom than any other book. No wonder Satan doesn't want people to read it!

Does *revelation* mean "riddle"? Most people, when speaking of this book, seem to think so. No, it means just the opposite— "unveiling." It is written in symbols. It was sent and explained by an angel to John. The hard of hearing have a sign language. Each gesture is filled with meaning. So is every sign in Revelation. There are three hundred symbols in this book, and each has a definite meaning. Symbols are wonderful and speak great truths.

This book is the Revelation of Jesus Christ. It is not the revelation of the growth of the church and the gradual conversion of the world, but it is the revelation of Jesus Christ! It was given by Christ himself to John (1:1-2). The book deals with the return of the Lord to this earth. It describes the readiness or unreadiness of the church for this great happening (3:20). There are descriptions of the tremendous events on earth and in heaven just before, during, and after his coming.

What is meant by *the time is near* (1:3)? Almost two thousand years have passed since these words were spoken, but the idea is "the next on the program." No matter how much time may intervene, the next thing after the day of grace is the kingdom age to be ushered in by our Lord's coming.

Christ says that when he comes *those who pierced him* will see him (1:7). While this means especially the Jews, who at Christ's coming will turn to him as a united people and be saved (Romans 11:25-26), at the same time it means many others who have pierced Christ will see him. Have *you* pierced him? Remember, Jesus died on the cross for the sins of each of us.

Christ is the theme of this wonderful book, which gives an authentic portrait of the Lord Jesus as the triumphant One. No less than twenty-six times we find Christ's sacrificial title, "Lamb." In addition, we see a vision of the future of the church and the world in relation to him.

It has been said that the saving blood of Christ runs through the entire Bible like a red cord. It has also been said that the second coming of Christ runs through the Bible like a golden cord. We are saved and washed clean in his blood in order that we may be ready and eager for his return.

A TO Z

Revelation is a wonderful way to finish the story that began in Genesis. All that was begun in the book of beginnings (Genesis) is consummated in Revelation. In Genesis the heaven and earth were created; in Revelation we see a new heaven and new earth. In Genesis the sun and moon appear; in Revelation we read that there is no need of the sun or moon, for Christ is the light of the new heaven. In Genesis there is a garden; in Revelation there is a holy city. In Genesis there is the marriage of the first Adam; in Revelation the marriage supper of the second Adam, Jesus

Christ. In Genesis we see the beginning of sin; in Revelation sin is finished. In Genesis we see the appearance of the great Adversary, Satan, and sorrow and pain and tears; in Revelation we see their doom and destruction.

Things are very difficult and uncertain in the world today. But things were difficult and uncertain when the Apostle John, an old, old man, was exiled to the island of Patmos. He had been banished for his testimony about Jesus (1:9). While on the island, John was suffering, likely in forced labor in the mines and quarries. But his Commander in Chief appeared to him and delivered a ringing message of ultimate glory—the triumphant Christ. God had determined from the beginning that his Son would be the Ruler of this universe (Isaiah 9:6-7).

Revelation is the greatest drama of all time. The plot is tense throughout; the final scene is glorious, for Christ comes to get his people who have been faithful to him. The hero is our Lord himself; the villain is the devil. The actors are the seven churches. The characters unloosed by the seals of chapters 6–7 are introduced by the "four horsemen." Then those summoned by the trumpets in turn leave center stage, and we see the Antichrist, the world ruler, stalking into view (ch. 13). This incarnation of the devil himself is determined to set up his own kingdom and be worshiped by all people. But Christ brings it all to nothing. This majestic actor, Christ, bringing his hosts with him, comes forth—the long-looked-for King of kings and Lord of lords. He drives his enemies from the stage in utter defeat (ch. 19).

After all the struggle has ended and the beasts have been destroyed and the devil bound and all the old things have gone forever, then we hear these words, full of hope: *See, I am making all things new!* (21:5). This book brings to a climax the great story commenced in Genesis, and as all good stories should, it ends, "And they lived happily ever after."

Notice the sevens in this book:

Seven churches
Seven signs
Seven seals
Seven last plagues
Seven trumpets
Seven dooms
Seven new things

PAST—WHAT YOU HAVE JUST SEEN
REVELATION 1

Here is the last picture of Jesus Christ given in the New Testament. Many artists have tried to portray him, but they have failed. Here is an authentic portrait (1:13-16). He is standing in the midst of the seven golden candlesticks, representing the churches (v. 20). Candlesticks prove that the church is to be a light-bearer. *You are the light of the world.* How many churches today—electronic or otherwise—are for entertainment and to promote money-making schemes instead of lights shining in a dark place!

It is clear from the vision that the One whom John saw was more than human. He was the Son of Man. Everything symbolizes majesty and judgment, and this thought of judgment strikes the keynote of the book. Christ is presented to the whole world as Judge:

Wearing a long robe—a token of dignity and honor.
Hair . . . white as wool—he is the Ancient of Days.
Eyes . . . like flames of fire—intelligence; bringing hidden things to light.
Feet like burnished bronze—bronze symbolizes judgment.
Voice . . . like the waves against the shore—power and majesty.
Hands—in these are kept the ministers of Christ.
Mouth—out of it went judgment.
Face . . . the power of the sun in unclouded brilliance (1:12-18).

John's vision was not of this age in which we are living but of a future day when people will appear before Christ to be judged (John 5:27-29). Now, we may have all of God's grace, mercy, and forgiveness for the taking. Now, Christ is before us to be judged. We can reject him if we choose. In Revelation, John pictures Christ in judgment. The day of mercy is past; we stand before the Judge.

When John saw this glorious One he "fell at his feet as dead," so overpowering was the vision (1:17). But Christ's words were reassuring. He said he was the living One, and though he had been dead, he was alive forevermore, and he held the keys of death and hell. Then follows the command to write what is found in this book (1:19). We do not have the usual picture of Christ starting in Bethlehem and ending at the Mount of Olives; here we have his life in heaven, as the crown and culmination of all.

Have you ever seen the Lord? When Moses saw him his face shone. Job abhorred himself and repented in ashes. Isaiah saw himself unclean. Thomas said, "My Lord and my God." Paul fell down and worshiped him as Savior. What would happen to us if we really saw the Lord?

PRESENT—EVERYTHING YOU SEE
REVELATION 2–3

Here we find Christ's love letters to his churches. These letters are alike in pattern. Christ dictated them to the leaders of the seven churches to whom he addressed these letters. In each, look for the speaker, praise, reproof, exhortation, and promise.

The churches named were churches that actually existed in John's day. In dealing with them, Christ seems to give us a brief church history from the first century church to the church of today, in seven periods.

1. Ephesus—the church of the first-love: the apostolic church (2:1-7)
2. Smyrna—the persecuted church: Diocletian to Constantine (2:8-11)
3. Pergamos—the church under imperial favor: under Constantine (2:12-17)
4. Thyatira: the church of the Dark Ages (2:18-29)
5. Sardis—the reformed church: sixteenth and seventeenth centuries (3:1-6)
6. Philadelphia—the missionary church: period ushered in by the Puritan movement (3:7-13)
7. Laodicea—the rejected church: church of the final apostasy (3:14-19)

Discover where you find Christ at the end of this church age. *Look! I have been standing at the door and I am constantly knocking. If anyone hears me calling him and opens the door, I will come in and fellowship with him and he with me* (3:20). He is outside, knocking to get in. The church will not let him in, but he pleads with the individual: *If anyone . . . opens the door, I will come in.* Have you opened your heart's door to Christ?

Let us take heed to the words found in these letters to the

churches: *Yet there is one thing wrong. . . . And yet I have a few things against you. . . . Yet I have this against you* (2:4, 14, 20). These are the warnings of a faithful Savior.

Discover how Christ is set forth in these letters. Remember, this book is the Revelation of Jesus Christ. What are the promises to the overcomers? See if you can find seven.

FUTURE—WHAT WILL SOON BE SHOWN TO YOU
REVELATION 4–22

The great revelation proper unfolds with the sound of trumpets. A door is *standing open in heaven* and a voice says, *Come up here, and I will show you what must happen in the future.*

First, the throne of God comes into view (4:1-3). Revelation becomes the "book of the throne." This is the great central fact that pervades the book. This throne speaks of judgment. The throne of grace is no longer seen. The scene is a courtroom. The Judge of all the earth is on the bench; the twenty-four elders, representing the twelve patriarchs of the Old Testament and the twelve apostles of the New, are the jury (4:4). The sevenfold Spirit of God (4:5; 5:6) is the prosecutor, and the four living creatures are court attendants, ready to carry out the will of the Judge.

Next in importance to the Lamb himself is the sealed scroll (5:1). Who can possibly open the scroll? None, save One. He *has conquered, and proved himself worthy to open the scroll.* Christ conquered in the wilderness after forty days. He conquered in Gethsemane. He conquered on Calvary when he said, "It is finished." On the third day he arose from the dead and conquered death, sin, hell, and Satan. The same Christ now claims the kingdom of the world by right of conquest.

The day of tribulation begins with the opening of the seven seals (ch. 6). This describes the Great Tribulation period spoken of by the prophet Jeremiah in Jeremiah 30 as the *the time of trouble for my people.* Christ also referred to it as a *time of persecution* such as has never happened on the earth (Matthew 24:21). During the Great Tribulation God will allow sin to work out its tragic results. God's hand will be lifted from man and beast. The earth will be filled with war, hunger, famine, and disease. Judgment must come on those who have rejected and ridiculed the Son of

God. We as Christians can look for Christ, not for calamity, because our Savior is coming to receive us to himself and free us from this day.

Four Horsemen

In the sixth chapter we see the famous "four horsemen" (6:1-8). Restraint is removed as the seals are broken. The forces of evil have been held in check. When the seals are torn away, war and destruction are set loose. Man is reaping what he himself has sown. The anguish and horror of the period will be the result of human ambition, hatred, and cruelty.

We see first the white horse of religious witness come before the final catastrophe upon the earth. Then comes the red horse, and universal war breaks upon the world and peace is banished from the earth. The black horse of famine and scarcity follows upon universal war. Lastly, the pale horse of plagues and death comes forth with merciless tread.

The sixth seal (6:12-17) brings social chaos, the complete breakup of society and a boasted civilization. Darkness, falling stars, heavens rolled up like a scroll, and islands moving is the picture presented. Then comes the most tragic prayer meeting on earth, with kings and priests, rich and poor, fleeing from God in a general stampede, praying for death, *for the great day of his anger has come.*

There is a momentary pause while the saved of the tribulation period are presented (ch. 7). These are "a vast crowd" with their robes washed and whitened in the blood of the Lamb. The "sealed" are all Israelis—God is starting to gather his people to himself (Hosea 1:9-10). The "vast crowd" is from all nations. This proves that the gospel preached in the tribulation period will be most effective.

The Seven Trumpets

Silence in heaven for thirty minutes! Orchestras cease! Mighty angels fold their wings! All is still! It is as though all heaven was waiting in breathless expectation. This is the calm before the storm (ch. 8). War, famine, and plagues have devastated the earth. Now God's judgments have come upon the earth and Satan, knowing his time is short, is very angry. We find unprecedented activity of demons—200 million of them sweeping across the earth. Hell is let loose! Sin is allowed its full sway, and death is preferable to life (9:1-21). Satan does his last work upon the earth.

Finally we see Satan incarnating himself in the Antichrist. His portrait is given in Revelation 13. (See also Daniel 12:11; Matthew 24:15; 2 Thessalonians 2:3.) This Antichrist will be a world ruler. He demands the honors due to Christ himself. He will be the political ruler of this world. He is the embodiment of wickedness. He will be shrewd and clever and a real leader of men. *No one could get a job or even buy in any store without the permit of that mark.* The "mark of the beast" is like the brand mark of ownership or the token of allegiance like Hitler's swastika. Six is the number of evil, so three sixes, 666, express a trinity of wickedness.

The final doom of the Antichrist will be the lake of fire at Christ's coming (19:20). There will be plagues like those of Egypt—blood, hail, fire, locusts, darkness, famine, sores, earthquakes, war, and death. In these plagues is summed up the wrath of God upon a Christ-rejecting world.

The Seven Golden Bowls
In the trumpets, Satan is releasing his power to accomplish his objectives. The bowls are God's power released against Satan. The bowls are God's answer to the devil. Satan has dared to challenge God's power. God is now answering the challenge. Satan is forced into action. His kingdom is shaken to its foundations and he is undone. This event ends in the battle of Armageddon (16:13-16). This battle is described in chapter 19. In the closing scene of the war, Christ takes the leadership of his armies and brings his foes to their doom.

The Dooms
The seventh bowl announced the "dooms" that were to follow. Civilization has come to utter collapse. Even though God has revealed its utter evil, nevertheless people curse the name of God and refuse to repent (16:9, 11). Today, amid the luxuries of invention, people are dissatisfied and far from God. Hatred has turned into wars of worldwide impact. God pronounces seven "dooms." First, the doom of great systems—ecclesiastical (ch. 17), commercial (ch. 18), political (19:11-19); of the evil creature and the false prophet (19:20-21); of the nations (20:7-9); of the devil (20:10); and finally, the doom of the lost is pronounced (20:11-15).

The Marriage of the Lamb

The hallelujah chorus announces the coming of the long-promised King, our Lord Jesus Christ, the heir of David's throne, to catch away his bride (1 Thessalonians 4:17). Hell has been let loose on earth. Satan and his cohorts have done their worst and Christ has finally triumphed. Righteousness, long on the scaffold, is now to mount the throne. The marriage of the Lamb is come (19:7). The wedding banquet of Christ will take place in the air. The saints will be rewarded in the air according to their works. This time of rejoicing will continue until Christ returns to the earth with his bride to set up his millennial kingdom.

After the Battle of Armageddon (19:17-19), Christ, having subdued all his enemies, will take alive the evil creature and the false prophet and cast them into the lake of fire, where torment never ceases and from which none return (19:20). Christ will make an end of Satan's entire system.

The Millennium

This is the time when Christ, the Prince of Peace, will establish his kingdom on the earth for a thousand years. The devil is to be bound for a thousand years (20:3); the saints that Christ brings with him will reign with him for a thousand years (20:4, 6); the wicked dead will not rise until the end of the thousand years (20:5).

There will be a thousand years of peace and joy on the earth, *when all the earth is filled, as the waters fill the sea, with an awareness of the glory of the Lord* (Habakkuk 2:14). It will be a glorious time to live. No wars, no weeds, no wild animals, no taxes, no heartache of death! When this period has come to an end, then the devil will be released again. He will come to test the nations (20:7-9). We discover their real attitude and learn that they prefer Satan to Christ. We can hardly believe it, but read 20:7-8: *When the thousand years end, Satan will be let out of his prison. He will go out to deceive the nations of the world and gather them together, with Gog and Magog, for battle—a mighty host, numberless as sand along the shore.*

Satan is the author and instigator of war. After a thousand years of peace, Satan gathers them to "the battle." Not a few gather, but a countless number, like the *sand along the shore. But fire from God in heaven will flash down on the attacking armies and consume them* (20:9). People's rebellion against God seems almost unbelievable, but *the heart is the most deceitful thing there is, and desperately wicked. No one can really know how bad it is!* (Jeremiah 17:9).

Satan's Doom
Satan is treated too lightly by the average person. He is mighty! He is the deceiver of the whole world. He fell from the highest place, next to God himself, to the lowest depths—*the lake of fire.* Christ described it as *the eternal fire, prepared for the devil and his demons* (Matthew 25:41). The devil is given a life sentence (20:10).

The blazing white throne of the final judgment is set. The One sitting on it will judge all people. Read Revelation 20:11-15. The "dead" are brought before him. The oceans give up their dead. The earth gives up its dead. The underworld gives up the dead. The dead are judged according to their works (20:12-13). Final doom is pronounced. The Savior is now the Judge. *If anyone's name was not found recorded in the Book of Life, he was thrown into the Lake of Fire* (20:15). Judgment must come before the golden age of glory can be ushered in. Someone has called hell the penitentiary of the universe, and the universal cemetery of the spiritually dead.

John names seven new things:

A new heaven and earth (21:1)
A new people (21:2-8)
A new bride (21:9)
A new home (21:10-21)
A new temple (21:22)
A new light (21:23-27)
A new paradise (22:1-5)

Happily Ever After
Yes, God's story ends "and they lived happily ever after." Read the triumph of God in Revelation 21–22. Satan has not been victorious in his attempt to separate man from fellowship with God by sin ever since his meeting with the first man and woman in the Garden of Eden. He has utterly failed, and we will be with Christ forever and ever!

Don't try to analyze or interpret these chapters. Rather meditate upon them. This is heaven! How limited words are in explaining its glory! The fellowship between God and man is restored. *The home of God is now among men.* Every purpose is realized and every promise is fulfilled. Heaven is the opposite of what we experience here. All is beautiful!

The last words of Christ in his Revelation are, *Yes, I am coming soon!* Our response should always be, *Amen! Come, Lord Jesus!*

SELECTED BIBLE READING

Sunday: Christ and the Churches (Revelation 1–3)
Monday: Christ's Throne and the Seven-Sealed Scroll (Revelation 4–6)
Tuesday: Christ's Trumpets Sounded (Revelation 7–9)
Wednesday: Christ and the Woes (Revelation 10–12)
Thursday: Christ and Antichrist (Revelation 13–15)
Friday: Christ's Final Triumph (Revelation 16–18)
Saturday: Christ the Lord of All (Revelation 19–22)

CHAPTER 52

A QUICK LOOK AT
COLOSSIANS—REVELATION

OUTSTANDING TRUTHS

Christ's Second Coming
Twentieth-Century False Religions
Christ the Head of the Church
The Power of a Christian Life
The Word *Better* in Hebrews
The Power of the Tongue

WHAT'S THE ANSWER?

1. What was the occasion for each of the following statements, and in which book is it found?
   a. *I have fought long and hard for my Lord, and through it all I have kept true to him. And now the time has come for me to stop fighting and rest. In heaven a crown is waiting for me which the Lord, the righteous Judge, will give me.*
   b. *For the Lord himself will come down from heaven with a mighty shout and with the soul-stirring cry of the archangel. . . . And the believers who are dead will be the first to rise. . . .*
   c. *I am not ashamed of this Good News about Christ. It is God's powerful method of bringing all who believe it to heaven.*
   d. *We know that all that happens to us is working for our good if we love God and are fitting into his plans.*
   e. *Come boldly to the very throne of God.*
   f. *If you read this prophecy aloud to the church, you will receive a special blessing from the Lord. Those who listen to it being read and do what it says will also be blessed. For the time is near when these things will all come true.*

3. Here are some of the most notable sentences in the Letters. Pick out the ones that seem most important to you.

a. *The whole Bible was given to us by inspiration from God* (2 Timothy 3:16).

b. *What is faith? It is the confident assurance that something we want is going to happen. It is the certainty that what we hope for is waiting for us, even though we cannot see it up ahead* (Hebrews 11:1).

c. *Faith that does not result in good deeds is not real faith* (James 2:20).

d. *He is very precious to you who believe* (1 Peter 2:7).

e. *But if we confess our sins to him, he can be depended on to forgive us and to cleanse us from every wrong* (1 John 1:9).

3. What were the last words of:

Christ?	(Luke 24:46-53)
Paul?	(2 Timothy 4:1-9)
Peter?	(2 Peter 3:10-18)
James?	(James 5:10-20)
Jude?	(Jude 17-25)
The Bible?	(Revelation 22:8-21)

4. Check the correct answer:

a. Thessalonians tells:
   □ The sin of the tongue
   □ Of Christ's second coming
   □ Of Christ, the High Priest

b. The heroes of the faith are found in:
   □ Timothy
   □ Hebrews
   □ Revelation

c. Timothy was:
   □ Paul's son
   □ An early missionary
   □ Paul's convert

d. God's future plans are revealed in:
   □ Hebrews
   □ Titus
   □ Revelation

CHAPTER 53

TEACHING
SUGGESTIONS

The primary purpose of this book is to give the Bible student a panoramic view of the Bible so that he sees it as a cohesive whole instead of a series of unrelated stories. The Bible is the story of what God is doing in history. Like any good story, it has a beginning and an ending. It starts with the creation. Conflict is introduced with the workings of Satan and the fall of man, introducing the dilemma. The rest of the story is the solving of that great dilemma by God and the final triumph of his purpose at the second coming of Christ. All the events in between fit into that story and contribute to the unfolding of the "plot."

The Bible has one main theme—redemption—and many subthemes that run through the entire book. Redemption is hinted at in the beginning (Genesis 3:15) and developed as the main theme, coming to a climax with the advent of Christ. The subthemes, interwoven into the narrative and all dependent upon the main theme of redemption, are all defined and illustrated in the events of the Bible. For instance, the innate rebelliousness of sinful man is played up and becomes a major chord in the story of the wandering in the wilderness and in Judges, as well as in other minor episodes. The mercy of God is portrayed in Hosea; the victory he gives, in Joshua.

CLASS TEACHING METHODS

Fortunately, twentieth-century thirst for knowledge includes a wholesome curiosity about what the Bible teaches. In accompaniment to Sunday school, home Bible study groups are springing up, and churches are gladly responding to desires for weekday classes.

If you are teaching the Bible, there are two things to remember about your class or home study group:

1. Chances are they *do not* have any systematic knowledge of the Bible. Most of your students will not have attended Sunday school consistently enough to be really well informed. They see the Bible as a collection of unrelated stories with morals, interspersed with long, dull passages they have never bothered to read; some beautiful poetry; some outstanding verses. The pattern of the Bible will be new to them. The history will certainly be a hazy impression of dignified characters in flowing garments either wandering in the wilderness or tending sheep in Palestine.

2. You can get across one main idea each lesson—and only one.

Now, with those two facts firmly in mind each time you teach, you want to do these things: give your class a picture of the whole of God's pattern, emphasizing how the particular book you are teaching fits into that whole, and drive home the major lesson of that book.

There is ample material provided for you to use any of several different approaches, but there are a few very broad principles that apply, whatever method you pursue.

First, always keep the whole scope of the Bible in mind. To begin with, read through this book for main impressions and emphases—quickly, just picking out the main points. Details will come later as you work on each chapter.

Second, begin preparing each lesson a week in advance. You may have had some issues raised during the last class session that need to be clarified. Write those down. It's better to work on the lesson a little bit each day and then put the final touches on it at the end of the preparation period. You will find that preparing a lesson this way is a little bit like making a pot of stew—the longer it simmers, the better it gets.

Third, though by no means third in importance, do as much reading as you can in the book of the Bible you are teaching. This book has the most important passages emphasized. For instance, in the chapter on Genesis is a list of the beginnings that are noted in that book, along with the references. In each chapter the outline covers the major events of the book.

Fourth, constantly bring your thinking back to the central theme of each book. This is the thing you want to get across to your students! There may be other lessons drawn—other themes you'll mention—but keep referring back to this main theme. Cohesiveness ought to be the watchword of the teacher using this material.

Fifth, bear in mind the character and needs of the students you are teaching—they are not all alike. You may have a class of young adults, all wearing that brittle mask of self-sufficiency that cracks so easily to show the uncertainty underneath. They need firm principles, and they will respond to the firm principles of the Bible. They also need love and understanding, and they will open up like flowers to the understanding grace of God. Teach to those needs.

A middle-aged group is another thing entirely. They may still have many of the same needs as the young adults, but added to this is the new dimension of attainment and power. It's up to the teacher to present the Bible in a manner suited to its importance. This age group especially needs to be buttressed against the persuasively presented false philosophy that security is to be found in "things." We ought to stress that God's kingdom must always have priority.

Finally, do remember that you are primarily teaching, not giving a devotional. Because we are all aware, as we ought to be, of the need to know Christ better and to love him more, we tend to forget that one of the major means to achieve these ends is to teach what the Bible says. There is no substitute for real teaching. There are all kinds of inspirational meetings designed to impel Christians to action, to move them to decision, to help them with their devotional lives—but the Bible study is to give knowledge and directive to their faith.

Anything that makes your teaching clear and explicit, that clarifies and explains, is good. If you use stories and illustrations to bring out your point, be sure they do just that. If they have an emotional punch, well and good, but beware of mere sentimentality. You may move a class to the edge of tears with a touching little story of a dying child, but if there isn't a real solid Bible truth in that story the effect is not so lasting.

Now, there are three basic teaching methods that can be used with this material:

1. Student preparation method
2. Class discussion method
3. Lecture method

Each method has some advantages and certain disadvantages. Consider them and see which one will best suit your class and its needs.

Student Preparation

Preparing for the lesson requires real work by the students. For instance, on the week preceding the study of the chapter on Genesis you might assign sections to the students. Tell each one to read the section assigned, study the Scriptures, and then give in his or her own words at the next session the lesson to be drawn from that story. Give each one a specified time to speak, allowing yourself at least ten minutes to sum it all up and bring out the main theme of the book.

The advantages are obvious—this method encourages interest and Bible study on the part of the students. Most of them love to have a part, and unless you have an entire class of introverts you should be able to find enough each week to participate.

There are also some drawbacks to this method. Unless your people are dependable they may either prepare poorly or be absent from class when they are supposed to shine. This can be avoided by a telephone check during the week. Occasionally you'll get the original thinker who becomes so entranced with an obscure passage that he dwells on it to the exclusion of the main part of the story, sometimes drawing some very odd conclusions from the Scripture! Also, the time can get away from the speakers and you may be left with only one minute for summing up.

Experiment with this way of teaching—perhaps you will want to modify it a bit or use it once in a while. It requires just as much preparation on the part of the teacher, for you must be on your toes to see that the lesson is rightly presented.

Class Discussion

Class discussion can be done in one of several ways. You might hand out discussion topics for the following week. These topics should be worked out from the lesson material. For example, in the lesson on Genesis you might find the following topics: How did sin enter the world? What is God's answer to man's disobedience? How does the covenant with Abraham illustrate the grace of God?

It is amazing how many people are seriously concerned about an issue such as the origin of sin. They may ask some searching questions and want to go far beyond the pointing out of Satan as the tempter. They may well ask you, "Yes, but if Satan was originally created by God, how could he be evil? How can a good God create something evil?" Be prepared to treat such a question with respect. A quick answer is not always the best answer, and such a profound question demands more than a facile reply. Sometimes it may be a good thing to tell the class you will bring the answer next week rather than hurrying through.

In using this class discussion method, you as the teacher must be sure to keep the talk from wandering far afield. Remember, you have a point to get across, and you can't do justice to more than one major lesson. If the discussion dribbles off into pointlessness, keep pulling the class back to the main theme. One great secret in teaching is to know when an issue raised by the class is vital to their faith—something they've wondered about, puzzled over, and need an answer to—and when it is merely an oddity to quibble over. If, in the course of the lesson, your students seem concerned about a point you are making, don't be hesitant about taking more time to clarify that point. You may have to skim lightly over the rest of the lesson because of it, but you remember the fifth basic principle—that you are teaching to their needs. As you can see, this kind of classroom work requires a nice balance between adherence to the main purpose of your lesson and flexibility within that framework. Such a method is very demanding on the teacher, but the rewards are great.

Another way of using the discussion method is to ask the students to hand in the questions they would like to have answered and then guide the discussion. This assumes a great deal of interest and intelligence on the part of your students, and there is one caution: you may have two or three very precocious and uninhibited students who are all too willing to speak at length on their ideas about the lesson. They may be getting a great deal out of being so talkative, but the rest of the class is not. Regardless of the brilliance of the few vocal ones, the others don't want to listen to them; they want to hear from someone "in the know"—someone with more authority behind his statements than simply "Joe, who always talks too much anyway." Frequently these extroverted pupils are the ones who linger after class with special questions, or problems. They do need attention, but not to the exclusion of the rest of the class and some of the quieter students who need to be gently coaxed into sharing their ideas.

Lecture
Lecture does not mean a rigid, formal presentation. It can be as flexible as either of the other methods or used in combination with one of them. After you have established a good rapport with your class, they'll feel free to interrupt the lesson when they have questions.

Let's take the chapter on Genesis, again, as our example. Read over this chapter carefully. Read through the book of Genesis, not stopping for details but simply reading to get the broad outline of the book. This can be done, remember, at the first of the week. Let the lesson build slowly in your thinking.

Now you are ready to begin thinking about the emphasis you want to give the chapter. Genesis is so long that even if you merely read through it your class time would be consumed. But what you have been provided with here is the raw material of the lesson. It is up to you to shape it and give it emphasis.

First, think of the whole scope of the Bible as you want to present it. Beginnings are vitally important, and Genesis contains the plot, in seed form, of the whole story of the gospel. Read over the first portion of the chapter carefully until you understand it thoroughly.

Second, go over the rest of the material and decide where you want to stress a point, where you can cover lightly. Since all of the Old Testament stories are referred to again and again in the Bible as examples, they need to be well told. You may wish to dwell longer on one than on the others in order to make a point. These should be related not as different stories but as parts of the whole. You have a double purpose in each lesson—to present the book in its proper relation to the entire scope of the Bible and to bring out one grand truth, one practical lesson, from each book. Of course, you may cover several subthemes, but keep coming back to the main lesson.

Third, go over your lesson, tie up any loose ends, and decide how you are going to sum it all up. The closing portion of your lesson is of prime importance. Here is where many good speakers go wrong. There is, as you know, a sense of timing that is the one main source of effective speaking or teaching. Some fortunate people have a built-in sense of timing—they know just how to build interest, when to hesitate the merest fraction of a second before uttering the punch line of a funny story, just when to move in fast for a climax, and, most important of all, when to stop. There is a Spirit-chosen time to stop. When you have made your point, don't embellish it. After you have said, in the most effective way you can, what you want them to remember, that's all. Resist the temptation to add just one more effective little sentence; it will not be at all effective if it's said after the psychological stopping time. Your audience has already mentally left, so you might as well close.

Now, here are some reminders—little tips to tuck away in the back of your mind. It would be ideal if your students remembered everything you gave them each week, but be realistic—they won't. Review a little—not in detail, which would bore them terribly, but briefly summarize the material covered. Do this in a positive way so you won't make them conscious of their failure to remember. Say "Of course you recall . . ." and then tell them what they may not have recalled. Since none of us assimilates knowledge in wholesale gulps, the teaching process consists largely of telling and retelling the same truths in different ways, so that gradually—very, very gradually—those truths become a part of the lives of those who are learning them.

Because this is a discussion of methods, we have not mentioned the very obvious things that underlie successful teaching—your desire to present Christ in a winning way, your constant dependence on prayer, and your utter reliance on the guidance of the Holy Spirit.

Beyond and above all the timeworn and timeless truths about teaching—our duty to do it, the satisfaction it gives, and all the reasons for devoting the time and the work and the energy to it—lies the deep and abiding pleasure of handling the Word of God, to which we are all committed.

Guiding the Prayer Time
Begin each class session with prayer.

Prayer is the keynote of success. Neither a class nor an individual can succeed in Christ without it. We are commanded to *always keep on praying* (1 Thessalonians 5:17). Prayer is the breath of the Christian. As natural as breathing is to a natural man, so natural should prayer be to a spiritual man. Does all of this describe you? Does the time of prayer in class have meaning, or is it just a part of the normal procedure? It is a true statement that the class will go no further spiritually than you as teacher lead them.

What does prayer mean to *you?* To guide the time of prayer in class you must be completely sold on its necessity yourself. You might make it a standard practice to ask the Lord daily for his guidance as you lead your students. Ask him to give you a love and understanding of them that is like his love and understanding of you. Pray for the individuals by name if possible. Prepare your lesson with prayer receiving an important part in your consideration.

As you come to class, have an attitude that shows your complete dependence on the Holy Spirit to guide your thoughts and words. Before you teach, ask that God will lead you. Do not rush through the opening prayer time, but do not prolong it to the place of boredom. Give opportunity for the students to take part if they desire. Encourage, but do not force participation. Be careful that neither you nor any other more mature Christian monopolizes the prayer time. This is a time to talk to God, not the time to preach a sermon. When you pray, really *pray.*

VISUAL TEACHING AIDS

Visual aids for adults may be divided into four main types: chalkboard, projected, diagrams and charts, and maps. Use the aid (or combination of aids) that best illustrates a particular lesson.

Chalkboard

A chalkboard may be purchased, or you can make it yourself out of masonite painted with chalkboard paint. Or you can use a piece of white plastic and write with a grease pencil or marking pen. Suit the size of the board to the size of your class. Often a portable board is sufficient.

The chalkboard is an economical piece of teaching equipment because it can be reused repeatedly and doesn't require any electrical equipment. A chalkboard serves to center the student's interest on the point under discussion. But, needless to say, if the chalkboard is to be used successfully it must be wisely and efficiently used. All representations placed upon it should be definite and immediately purposeful; meaningless doodlings are confusing and distracting and are evidences of the teacher's lack of skill. In order to be easily readable, the material should be clearly and accurately reproduced with a minimum degree of artistry. Not too much material should be used at any one time because this clutters up the board and gives it a messy appearance. It also tends to reduce the space left for writing and makes it less intelligible. Generally speaking, it is a good idea to erase material that is not needed in order to avoid distraction.

When outlines, summaries, or similar materials are to be used by the group immediately, they should be placed on the board before the class convenes. If the teacher writes on the board while the class waits, valuable time is lost and interest wanes. Do not be afraid, however, to use the chalkboard as the lesson develops. Put certain points on the board. List ideas that discussion brings forth. Write the reference for some Scripture you are using. Let the students do some of the writing. Use the chalkboard often in your lesson presentation. It will assist in keeping the development clearly in mind.

Projected Aids
If you use a film, review the film before class. In this way you can prepare for the discussion that will follow the presentation and foresee any difficulties that the film may create. Films and slides should not be looked upon as "teaching crutches" but should be used either to introduce the lesson or to summarize what has been taught.

Set up the projector well in advance of the presentation. Be sure that all is in good working order. The projector should have an adequately strong bulb for the size of room you're using. The projector should be placed on a rigid stand at the back of the room, high enough to avoid head shadows on the screen.

Place the screen in line with the projector and high enough to allow clear view by the class. Where it is not feasible to use the screen and darken the room, the projector may be placed at the front of the room and a sheet of white paper suspended between projector and class. The film or slides should be reversed so the class can read the titles.

If you use an overhead projector, again make sure that the screen is clearly visible to all. A great advantage of the overhead projector is that you can carefully prepare your outlines, quotes, diagrams, and charts before class. This way you don't have to spend extra time and effort during class trying to write out your visual aids. Also, an overhead projector magnifies the image on the transparency so that even normal-size writing is big enough for all to read, unlike on a chalkboard. By putting your outlines on transparencies, you can easily refer back to them later in the lesson or in later sessions. Transparencies, as with the chalkboard, should be effectively used to reinforce the point you are teaching.

Diagrams and Charts

A good diagram must maintain two standards. First, it must be technically correct. It must be correctly and neatly drawn in proper proportions and completely labeled. The diagram must be adequately explained or interpreted and have a definite application made from it. Nothing should be left to the imagination. Second, it has to be artistic because it must command the students' respect and thus encourage their interest and understanding.

Various types of charts may be used. For example, a chronological chart that lists events in the proper sequence is often helpful in getting an overall view of the book or topic under study. The use of titles, labels, columns, lines, arrows, numerals, colors, variations in sizes of charts, light and heavy type, diagrams, illustrations, pictures, maps, appended explanatory notes, and other devices help to clarify the material and make it more readable and meaningful.

Charts may be shown to clarify genealogy or to trace historical sequences. A time-line chart will serve to keep specific events within the right general periods. Charts may be used effectively to show the relationship of one main thought to its several component parts.

Charts and diagrams may be prepared on poster board, on flannelboards, on chalkboards, or on overhead transparencies. Flip charts may be made in which each event or thought has its own specific representation.

Maps

Maps are indispensable. We are continually making and using maps—either mentally or graphically. When taking a long trip by car we use a road map until it is worn out.

As educational devices, maps help students to visualize and locate important places and events. For example, a map helps to follow the progress of the Israelis from Egypt to the Promised Land. A map of Paul's journeys is helpful to trace the spread of Christianity throughout the world, maybe by shading the area on the map. Areas of non-Christian influence can be indicated also, perhaps with overlays of plastic. A world map will show the mission work that is being done on the foreign and home fields. You may want to show the mission areas to which your own church has contributed.

Make sure that the students understand the purpose of the map—what is intended to be made clear with the use of the map. Is it the distance between two places? Is it the extent of territory covered? Or is it the type of terrain present in certain sections?

Use maps at the opportune moment. The map should be used when it is most needed to answer questions, solve problems, or supply information or data. Studying a map apart from an actual situation makes it a meaningless exercise that lacks purpose and life.

Visual teaching aids need not be elaborate to be effective. A simple statement of what is being taught is all that is required. Use a variety of methods to impress these great truths upon the minds of your students.